fourth
edition

Law of the European Union

Penelope Kent

PEARSON

Longman

Harlow, England • London • New York • Boston • San Francisco • Toronto
Sydney • Tokyo • Singapore • Hong Kong • Seoul • Taipei • New Delhi
Cape Town • Madrid • Mexico City • Amsterdam • Munich • Paris • Milan

Pearson Education Limited
Edinburgh Gate
Harlow
Essex CM20 2JE
England

and Associated Companies throughout the world

Visit us on the World Wide Web at:
www.pearsoned.co.uk

First published 1992   © Longman Group UK Limited
Second edition published 1996 © Pearson Professional Limited
Third edition published 2001   © Pearson Education Limited
Fourth edition published 2008 © Pearson Education Limited

© Pearson Education Limited 2008

ISBN: 978-1-4058-3526-8

British Library Cataloguing-in-Publication Data
A catalogue record for this book is available from the British Library

Library of Congress Cataloging-in-Publication Data
Kent, Penelope.
   Law of the European Union / Penny Kent. – 4th ed.
      p. cm.
   Includes bibliographical references and index.
   ISBN 978-1-4058-3526-8
   1. Law – European Union countries.   I. Title.
   KJE947.K46 2008
   341.242'2–dc22

                              2008026594

10 9 8 7 6 5 4 3 2 1
11 10 09 08

Typeset in 9.5/13 pt Stone Sans by 35
Printed in Great Britain by Henry Ling Ltd, at the Dorset Press, Dorchester, Dorset.

The publisher's policy is to use paper manufactured from sustainable forests.

Contents

Preface	xxiii
Abbreviations	xxiv
Guided tour	xxvi
Table of treaties	xxix
Table of UK statutes	xxxvi
Table of European Community secondary legislation	xxxvii
Table of cases in the Court of Justice and the Court of First Instance (alphabetical)	xliii
Table of cases in the Court of Justice and the Court of First Instance (numerical)	lxv
Table of cases before the national courts	lxxxv
Table of Commission decisions	lxxxvii

Part 1 THE CONSTITUTIONAL LAW OF THE EUROPEAN UNION — 1

1 The development of European Union law — 3

Introduction	**3**
Inspiration	3
The creation of the ECSC, EEC and EURATOM	3
Sovereignty and the Treaty of Rome 1957	4
Aims of the Community	5
Position of the UK	6
Widening the ties: enlargement	**6**
First three rounds of enlargement 1973–86	6
European Economic Area and enlargement	7
Enlargement 2004–07	7
Deepening the ties: further integration	**8**
The Single European Act 1986	8
European Union and the Maastricht Treaty 1992	9
The Three Pillar structure of the EU	11
Objectives of the Union	12
Other changes introduced by the Treaty on European Union	12
Titles and terminology	13
Ratification of the Treaty on European Union	13

The Treaty of Amsterdam 1997   14
Policies and tasks under the Treaty of Amsterdam   14
The Treaty of Nice 2001   15
The Charter of Fundamental Rights 2000   16
The Constitutional Treat (failed) 2004   16
The Treaty of Lisbon 2007: a summary of key changes   17
A new set of aims   17
Ratification of the Treaty of Lisbon   19

Questions   **19**
Further reading   **19**

2   **The institutions of the EU: the Parliament, the Council,**
    the Commission and the Court of Justice   **21**

Institutions   **21**
Five principal institutions   21
The European Parliament   **22**
The Treaty of Lisbon   22
Composition of the Parliament   23
Political groups   23
Functions of the Parliament   24
Parliament and the Budget   24
Supervision of the Commission   24
Parliament's role in the legislative process   25
Consultation procedure   26
The co-decision procedure   26
Assent procedure   31
Other bodies   31
National parliaments under the Treaty of Lisbon   32
The Council of the European Union   **33**
Composition and functions   33
Voting procedures   34
Qualified majority voting   35
Unanimity   36
The European Council   37
Committee of Permanent Representatives   37
The European Commission   **37**
Features   37
Composition   38
The President of the Commission   39
Functions   39
Comitology   40
The Courts   **43**
Main functions   44
Composition   44

Judicial style   45
Role of the Court of Justice   45
The Court of First Instance   46
Judicial Panels   47
Preliminary rulings   47
The Court of Auditors   48
Other bodies in the decision-making process   **48**
The Economic and Social Committee (ESC)   48
The Committee of the Regions   49
The European Central Bank   49

Questions   **50**
Further reading   **50**

3 The sources of EU law: competences of the EC and EU   52

Introduction   **52**
The study of EU law   52
Treaties   **53**
Treaties creating the institutions   53
Subsidiary treaties   55
Acts of the institutions   **55**
Legislative powers of the Council and the Commission   55
Regulations   56
Directives   57
Decisions   57
Binding nature of secondary legislation   58
Soft law   58
Classification   59
Changes under the Treaty of Lisbon   **59**
Legislative and non-legislative acts   59
The competence of the Community   **60**
Express and implied powers   60
The external competence of the Community   61
General powers under Article 308   62
Legal proceedings under Article 300   63
The principle of subsidiarity   63
Competence of the Union under the Treaty of Lisbon   **63**
The principles of conferral, subsidiarity and proportionality   63
Exclusive competences under the Treaty of Lisbon   64
Shared competences under the Treaty of Lisbon   65
Decisons of the Court of Justice   **65**
Where to find the law   65

Questions   **66**
Further reading   **66**

4 General principles of law 68

Introduction 68
Sources of general principles of law 68
General principles in the legal systems of the Member States 69
Role of general principles in EC law 69
Fundamental rights 70
The protection of fundamental rights in the ECJ 70
European Convention on Human Rights and Fundamental Freedoms 71
The values of the Union 72
Accession to the ECHR 72
The ECHR and ECJ 73
The Charter of Fundamental Rights 75
Protection of fundamental rights under the Charter 75
Current reliance on the Charter of Fundamental Rights 77
Proportionality 77
Principle of proportionality 77
Internal market 78
Freedom of commercial activity 78
Equality 79
A general principle of non-discrimination 79
Legal certainty 80
Principle of legal certainty 80
Retroactivity 80
Legitimate expectations 81
Procedural rights 82
Other general principles 84
Subsidiarity 84
Protocol on subsidiarity 84
Application of subsidiarity to legislation 84
Can subsidiarity be invoked before the ECJ? 85
Transparency 86

Questions 86
Further reading 86

5 The supremacy of Community law 88

Introduction 88
The EC Treaty and TEU as international treaties 89
Role of the Court of Justice 89
Need for a uniform approach 89
A new legal order 90
EC law may not be invalidated by national law 91
Conflicting national legislation should not be applied 91
National statutes may be set aside 91

State liability 92
Supremacy and the Second and Third Pillars 92
EC Law in the UK 92
Direct applicability, direct effect and indirect effect 93
Approach of the House of Lords 93
The *Factortame* series of decisions 94
EC Law in other Member States 95
Belgium 95
France 96
Germany 97
Italy 98
Poland 98
Academic commentary on supremacy 99
Questions 99
Further reading 100

6 **The principles of direct effect, indirect effect and
state liability** 101
Introduction 101
Direct applicability and direct effect 101
Treaty articles 102
Vertical and horizontal direct effect 102
Regulations 103
Directives and decisions 104
How far is it possible to rely on a directive? 105
Public bodies 106
International treaties 107
General principles of law 107
Indirect effect 107
The duty of consistent interpretation 108
Von Colson upheld 108
Incidental horizontal effect 109
UK decisions on indirect effect 110
State liability 111
Clarification of conditions for State liability 111
Breach must be sufficiently serious 112
Other aspects of the ruling 113
Clarifying 'sufficiently serious breach' 113
Breach where Member States have exercised discretion 113
Failure to implement a directive on time or correctly 114
Liability of national courts 114
Approach of the national courts to cases of State liability 115
Questions 115
Further reading 116

**7   Enforcement actions against Member States:
Articles 226 to 228, 88, 95 and 298**   **117**

Introduction   **117**
Direct action under Article 226   **117**
Power of the Commission under Article 226   117
Function of Article 226   117
Failure to implement an obligation   118
Procedure   118
Defences   119
Parallel proceedings   120
Action under Article 227   **121**
Action by Member States: Article 227   121
Action before the ECJ   121
Voluntary procedure: Article 239   121
Sanctions against Member States under Article 228   122
Specific enforcement procedures: Articles 88(2), 298 and 95(4)   **122**
State aids: Article 88(2)   122
Measures to prevent internal disturbances: Article 298   123
Improper use of powers under Article 95(4)   123

Questions   **123**
Further reading   **124**

**8   Judicial review: annulment under Article 230,
failure to act under Article 232, and indirect
review under Article 241**   **125**

Introduction   **125**
Action for annulment: Article 230   **125**
Scope of Article 230   125
Five essential questions   126
Acts which may be challenged   **126**
Reviewable acts   126
Right to challenge   **127**
Privileged applicants   128
Non-privileged applicants   128
Measure must be equivalent to a decision   128
Measure must be of direct and individual concern to the applicant   129
Back to the *Plaumann* formula   131
Treaty reform   132
Time limits   **133**
What are the relevant time limits?   133
Grounds for challenge   **133**
Grounds for annulment   133
Lack of competence   134

Infringement of an essential procedural requirement   134
Infringement of the Treaty or of any rule relating to its application   135
Misuse of powers   135
Effects of annulment   **136**
Action for inactivity under Article 232   **136**
Provision   136
Scope of Article 232   136
Right to complain (standing)   **137**
'Privileged applicants'   137
Individuals   137
Procedure   137
Effects of successful action   138
Indirect review under Article 241   **138**
Provision   138
Scope of the provision   138
Standing   138
Reviewable acts   139
Grounds of review   139
Effects of a successful action   139

Questions   **139**
Further reading   **139**

9   **Liability of the Community institutions**   **141**

Non-Contractual liability of the EC institutions   **141**
Standing and limitation   141
Elements of non-contractual liability   142
Requirements of the Schöppenstedt formula   142
Extending liability: The importance of discretion   **143**
Liability arising from a lawful act   144
Causation and damages   **145**
Causation   145
Contributory negligence   145
Damage   **145**
Recoverable damage   145
Role of the national courts   **146**
Concurrent liability   146

Questions   **146**
Further reading   **147**

10   **Preliminary rulings under Article 234**   **149**

Procedure   **149**
Article 234: the provision   149
What is a 'court or tribunal'?   150

Courts with a discretion to refer 151
When is a reference necessary? 151
There must be a genuine question of EC law 152
Notes for guidance on references by national courts for
    preliminary rulings 152
Acte clair and *acte éclairé* 153
Courts for which referral is mandatory 153
Abstract or concrete theory? 153
Rulings on validity 155
Effects of an Article 234 ruling 155
Third Pillar competence 156
Reforming the preliminary reference procedure 157

Questions **158**
Further reading **158**

Part 2 FREE MOVEMENT WITHIN THE SINGLE MARKET **161**

11 **Customs duties and discriminatory internal taxation;**
    State monopolies of a commercial nature **163**

Introduction **163**
Customs union 163
Prohibition of customs duties on imports and exports within
    the EC and of all charges of equivalent effect: Article 25 **164**
'Charges having equivalent effect' 165
Prohibition of discriminatory taxation: Article 90 **167**
A 'genuine tax' 167
'Similar' products 168
Indirect discrimination against imports 168
State monopolies under the EC treaty **169**
Adjustment of State monopolies: Article 31 169
State monopolies and other provisions of the treaty **170**

Questions **171**
Further reading **171**

12 **Quantitative restrictions and measures having**
    equivalent effect **172**

Introduction **172**
Non-tariff barriers and the need for elimination of quantitative
    restrictions and measures having equivalent effect 172
Principal Treaty provisions 172
'Measures taken by Member States' 173
Prohibition of quantitative restrictions on imports and of
    measures having equivalent effect: Article 28 **174**

Prohibition | 174
Distinctly and indistinctly applicable measures | 174
Dassonville Formula | 174
ECJ decisions after *Dassonville* | 175
Cassis de Dijon | 176
Decisions since *Cassis* | 178
Failure to establish 'necessity' | 179
Justification in the interests of consumers | 179
Principle of mutual recognition | 180
Article 28 as a defence | 180
Selling arrangements: Calling 'time' on Article 28 as a defence | 181
When is a selling arrangement outside Article 28? | 181
Product requirements | 182
Criticisms of the Court's approach to indistinctly applicable measures | 183
Prohibition between member states of quantitative restrictions on exports and of measures of equivalent effect: Article 29 | **184**
Approach of the House of Lords | 185
Derogation from articles 28 and 29 | **186**
Main principle for derogation: Article 30 | 186
Grounds of derogation | 186
Justification and arbitrary discrimination | 186
Public morality | 186
Public policy | 187
Public security | 188
Protection of the health and life of humans, animals and plants | 188
When may a restriction be justified on health grounds? | 189
Examples where restrictions were found to be justified under Article 30 | 189
The precautionary principle in relation to health | 191
Protection of national treasures possessing artistic, historic or archaeological value | 191
Protection of industrial and commercial property | 192
Internal market measures | 192
Derogation outside Article 28 | 192
Questions | **193**
Further reading | **193**

13 Union citizenship | **195**
Introduction | **195**
Who is a Union citizen? | 195
Martinez Sala: a blueprint for citizenship | 196
Citizenship as a 'fundamental status' | 197
A directly effective right | 197
The need for integration | 198

Jobseekers and the economically inactive	198
The rights of children and their parents	199
Political rights of Union citizens	199
Directive 2004/38	**200**
Three categories of residence rights	200
Definition of 'family members'	202
Who is a 'spouse'?	202
Marriages of convenience	203
Effect of divorce and separation	203
Cohabitees and registered partners	204
Equality of treatment	205
Rights of exit and entry	205
Limitations justified on grounds of public policy, public security or public health	**206**
Scope of the limitation	206
Personal conduct	207
Convictions	207
Supply of information	209
Protection against expulsion	209
Notification of decisions: procedural safeguards	209
Duration of exclusion orders: expulsion as a penalty of legal consequence	210
The public health exception	210
Nationals of third countries	210
The Schengen Agreement	211
Changes under the Treaty of Lisbon	212
Questions	**213**
Further reading	**213**
14 Free movement of workers	**215**
Introduction	**215**
Non-discrimination	215
Treaty provision	215
Secondary legislation	216
Scope of Article 39	**216**
'Workers'	216
Jobseekers and the unemployed	217
Workers from the Accession States	218
Employment in the public service	**219**
Exclusion of public service employment	219
Rights enjoyed by workers and their families	**220**
Regulation 1612/68 and Directive 2004/38	220
Internal situations	221

Regulation 1612/68	221
Equality of treatment	**222**
Eligibility for employment	222
Equality in employment	222
Rights relative to trade union activities, sport and housing	225
Children's access to educational training	225
Social security	**227**
Regulation 1408/71	227
Social assistance	228
Social advantages	228
Union citizenship and social advantages	228
Regulation 883/2004	229
Questions	**229**
Further reading	**229**

15	**The right of establishment and the freedom to provide services**	**231**
	Introduction	**231**
	Right of establishment	**231**
	The General programme	232
	Beneficiaries of the right of establishment	232
	Establishment or services?	234
	Freedom to provide services	**234**
	Services	234
	Limitation on establishments and the provision of services	234
	General programme on the abolition of restrictions on the freedom to provide services 1961	235
	Elimination of barriers to the free movement of professional persons	235
	Harmonisation of professional qualifications	235
	Beneficiaries of the right of establishment and the freedom to provide services	236
	Additional requirements	237
	Application of the principle of non-discrimination	237
	Human rights and the provision of services	239
	Professional rules of conduct	239
	Respect for the legitimate rules and standards of Member States	240
	'Insurance' cases	241
	The single market programme	**242**
	Financial services	242
	A fresh initiative on qualifications	242
	Directive 2005/36 on the mutual recognition of professional qualifications	242
	A 'regulated profession'	243

Routes to recognition under the Directive 244
Cases outside the legislation 244
The services directive: Directive 2006/123 245
Restrictions on the provision of services 245
Industrial property rights and the freedom to provide services 246
Freedom to receive services 246
Principle of non-discrimination 247
Medical treatment 248
Educational and vocational training: *Gravier* 249
Education and training after *Gravier* 250

Questions 251
Further reading 252

16 **Capital movements and economic and monetary union** 253

Introduction 253
Completion of the internal market 253
Treaty of Maastricht 254
What constitutes a restriction on the movement of capital? 254
Exceptions to the free movement of capital under the Treaty 255
Restrictions on capital from 'special' or 'golden' shares 256
Economic policy before the Treaty of Maastricht 257
European Monetary System 257
Exchange Rate Mechanism 258
European currency 258
Economic and monetary union 258
Treaty on European Union 259
Legal basis of EMU 259
European Central Bank 260
Management of EMU 261
A two-speed Europe 262

Questions 262
Further reading 263

Part 3 COMPETITION LAW AND POLICY 265

17 **Introduction to competition** 267

Understanding competition 267
Terminology 267
Theory of competition: perfect competition 268
An opposing view of competition: the Chicago school 269
A compromise approach: 'workable competition' 269
Theory of 'contestable competition' 269
Competition law and policy in the EC 270

Purpose of competition law in the EC   270
Legal framework of competition law in the EC   270
Criticism of EC competition policy   271
Modernisation   271
Competition law in the UK   272

Questions   **272**
Further reading   **272**

18 **Article 81**   **274**

Introduction   **274**
Article 81: the prohibition   274
Infringement   **275**
Infringement of Article 81(1)   275
Agreements   275
Undertakings   275
Decisions by associations of undertakings   277
Concerted practices   277
Effect on trade between Member States   279
Prevention, restriction or distortion of competition   279
Object or effect   281
Within the EC: the 'effects' doctrine   282
Minor agreements: the de *minimis* principle   282
Agreements likely to infringe Article 81(1)   283
Rule of reason   284
Distribution agreements   284
Invalidity under Article 81(2)   286
Guidance letters and Notices   286
Exemptions and exceptions   **287**
Individual exceptions   287
Article 81(3): the conditions   288
The relationship between Article 81(1) and 81(3)   289
Commission guidelines on the application of Article 81(3)   289
Block exemptions   **290**
Pattern of the Regulations   290
Block exemption Regulation on vertical agreements   291
Other restraints   291

Questions   **292**
Further reading   **293**

19 **Article 82**   **294**

Introduction   **294**
Article 82: the prohibition   294
'Undertakings' and the control of oligopoly   294

Commission discussion paper and reform of Article 82   295
Essential elements for a breach of Article 82   295
Dominance   **295**
Product market   296
Product substitution   296
Decisions on the product market   297
Other examples of the product market   298
Geographical market   299
Temporal market   300
Assessing dominance   300
Abuse of a dominant position   **301**
Comparison with Article 81   301
Categories of abuse   302
Examples of abuse   302
Effect on inter-member trade   **307**
Mergers and concentrations   **307**
Merger control under Article 82   307
Merger control under successive merger regulations   307
Procedures under the Regulation 139/2004   309
Collective dominance and the merger regulation   310
Further decisions under the merger regulation   311
Effect of decisions in Airtours, etc.   313
'One-stop shopping'   313

Questions   **315**
Further reading   **315**

20 **Articles 81 and 82: enforcement and procedure**   317

Introduction   **317**
Regulation 1/2003   317
Application by parties to a possible infringement   318
Investigative powers   **319**
Investigations   319
Inspections   319
Right to be heard   321
The decision   321
Interim measures   321
Confidential information   **322**
Professional secrecy and business secrets   322
Fines and penalties   **323**
Factors to be taken into account   323
Leniency programme   324
Periodic penalties   325
Enforcement in the Member States   325

Questions   327
Further reading   327

21 Intellectual property   328

Introduction   328
Scope of intellectual property rights   328
Intellectual property rights and the free movement of goods   329
Treaty provision   329
A compromise approach   330
Exhaustion of rights   331
Patents and trade marks   331
Trade marks and luxury goods   333
Copyright   333
Registered designs   334
Plant breeders' rights   335
Common origin principle   335
Goods from third countries   336
Intellectual property rights and competition law   337
Improper exploitation of intellectual property rights   337
Non-discrimination and intellectual property rights   337
Licences   337
Specific subject-matter of the property   338
Patent rights   339
Trade marks   339
Copyright   339
The group exemption for technology transfer under Regulation
    774/04   340
Relationship between Articles 28–30 and Articles 81 and 82   341
Harmonisation of intellectual property   341
Patents   341
Trade marks   342
Copyright   342

Questions   343
Further reading   343

22 Competition law and state regulation   345

Introduction   345
Public undertakings   345
The obligation under Article 86(1)   345
Categories of undertaking in Article 86(1)   345
Examples of public undertakings   346
Scope of the obligation under Article 86(1)   346
Application of Article 86(1)   347

Exception for entrusted undertakings and fiscal monopolies:
    Article 86(2)   347
Entrusted undertakings   348
Undertakings having the character of a revenue-producing monopoly   348
Exemption under Article 86(2)   348
Article 86(2) and the national courts   349
Application of Article 86(2)   349
Article 86(3): the powers of the Commission   350
Decisions under Article 86(3)   350
Article 86(3) as the basis of directives   351
State aids   **352**
Aid compatible with the common market: Article 87(2)   352
Aid which may be compatible with the common market: Article 92(3)   353
Procedure   354
Compliance   355
Scope of state aids   355
Commission policy on state aids   356
Modernisation   356
Exercise of discretion   357
Rights of individuals   357

Questions   **358**
Further reading   **358**

Part 4 THE SOCIAL DIMENSION   **359**

23 Social policy   **361**

Introduction   **361**
Legal basis for social policy under the EC Treaty   361
Social policy under Articles 136–149   362
The Social Charter and Supplementary Action Programme   364
The Social Charter and Social Action Programme   364
The Social Chapter   364
Policy areas introduced by the Maastricht Treaty   **365**
Other changes   365
Non-discrimination   366
Soft laws   367

Questions   **367**
Further reading   **368**

24 Equality of pay and treatment   **369**

Introduction   **369**
Direct effect of Article 141   369
Meaning of 'pay'   **370**

Treaty definition   370
The *Barber* decision   372
Impact of the *Barber* decision   373
Equal work   **373**
Equal pay for work of equal value: Directive 75/117   373
Equal work   374
Work of equal value   374
Direct and indirect discrimination   374
Assessment of equal value claims   377
Criteria in job evaluation schemes   377
Equal treatment in employment   **378**
Pregnancy and maternity   380
Parental leave   381
Retirement ages   381
Determination of pensionable age 'for other purposes'   382
Derogation under Articles 2(2), 2(3) and 2(4) of Directive 76/207   382
Remedies   386
Obligations on Member States under Article 3(2) of Directive 76/207   386
Non-discrimination, sexual orientation and fundamental rights   388
Equal treatment in relation to race or ethnic origin   388
The framework directive for equal treatment in employment and
    occupation   389
Equal treatment in matters of social security   **391**
Equal treatment in matters of social security: Directive 79/7   391
Personal scope   392
Risks covered   392
Meaning of the equal treatment principle   393
Exclusion from the equal treatment principle   394
Remedies   395
Equal treatment in occupational social security schemes   **395**
Equal treatment in self-employment   **396**
Conclusion   **397**

Questions   **397**
Further reading   **398**

Appendix 1 Bibliography   399
Appendix 2 Where to find the law   401
Appendix 3 Timeline   403
Index   405

mylawchamber

Visit the *Law of the European Union*, fourth edition, **mylawchamber** site at
http://www.mylawchamber.co.uk/kent to access valuable learning material.

For students

Companion Website support

- Use the answer guidance to questions in the book to test yourself on each topic throughout the course.
- Use the updates to major changes in the law to make sure you are ahead of the game by knowing the latest developments.
- Use the students' guide to using *Europa* to help you navigate through relevant and important issues of the European Union.

Case Navigator*

POWERED BY LexisNexis

This unique online support helps you to improve your case reading and analysis skills.

- **Direct deep links** to the core cases in Law.
- **Short introductions** provide guidance on what you should look out for while reading the case.
- **Questions** help you to test your understanding of the case, and provide feedback on what you should have grasped.
- **Summaries** contextualise the case and point you to further reading so that you are fully prepared for seminars and discussions.

Also: The Companion Website provides the following features:

- Search tool to help locate specific items of content.
- E-mail results and profile tools to send results of quizzes to instructors.
- Online help and support to assist with website usage and troubleshooting.

For more information please contact your local Pearson Education sales representative or visit http://www.mylawchamber.co.uk/kent

*Please note that access to Case Navigator is free with the purchase of this book, but you must register with us for access. Full registration instructions are available on the website. The LexisNexis element of Case Navigator is only available to those who currently subscribe to LexisNexis Butterworths online.

Preface

The pace of change in EU law has not slackened. Since the third edition of this book in 2001, the Treaty of Nice has been adopted and ratified, the Constitutional Treaty had been adopted but *not* ratified and the Treaty of Lisbon has been adopted, with a target date for ratification of 1 January 2009. The EU has enlarged from 15 to 27 Member States. The latest edition of *Law of the European Union* is intended to provide a student-friendly approach to a subject which many find very challenging. The student's attention is directed through the text to 'Key Points' and 'Key Cases', with definitions, where appropriate, of 'Key Terms'. There are questions at the end of each chapter, with guidance on answers provided on the accompanying website.

Thanks are due to my husband, David, for his support during the writing of the fourth edition and to the staff at Longmans, particularly Zoë Botterill, Commissioning Editor for Law, for her support and encouragement throughout the long gestation of this edition. I am also grateful to Cheryl Cheasely, Editorial Assistant, and, at the production stage, Christine Statham, Associate Editor for Law, Linda Dhondy, Freelance Editor, Jill Wallis, proof-reader, and Sarah Beauchamp-Gregory, tabler. The many students of EU law I have taught over the years at Middlesex University deserve recognition for their contribution to the development of my own ideas about the subject.

I should also like to thank the Getty Archive for supplying the photographs. Any errors or omissions, of course, remain my own responsibility.

The law is as stated on 31 March 2008, although brief reference is made to the negative referendum result in Ireland on the Lisbon Treaty in June 2008.

Penelope Kent
June 2008

Abbreviations

ASDL	Asynchronous Digital Subscriber Line
CAP	common agricultural policy
CAT	Competition Appeal Tribunal
CCT	common customs tariff
CEEP	European Centre of Enterprises with Public Participation and of Enterprises with General Economic Interest
CFI	Court of First Instance
CFSP	Common Foreign and Security Policy
CISA	Convention Implementing the Shengen Agreement
CMLR	Common Market Law Report
COR	Committee of the Regions
COREPER	Committee of Permanent Representatives
CT	Constitutional Treaty
DG	Directorate General
EAT	Employment Appeals Tribunal
EAW	European Arrest Warrant
EC	European Community/Communities
ECB	European Central Bank
ECHR	European Convention on Human Rights and Fundamental Freedoms
ECtHR	European Court of Human Rights
ECJ	European Court of Justice
ECOFIN	Economic and Financial Affairs
ECR	European Court Report
ECSC	European Coal and Steel Community
ECU	European currency unit
EEA	European Economic Area
EEC	European Economic Community
EFTA	European Free Trade Association
EMI	European Monetary Institute
EMS	European Monetary System
EMU	Economic and monetary union
EP	European Parliament
EPO	European Patent Office
EPU	Economic and political union
ERM	Exchange Rate Mechanism
ERTA	European Road Transport Agreement

ESC	Economic and Social Committee
ESCB	European System of Central Banks
ESF	European Social Fund
ETUC	European Trade Union Confederation
EU	European Union
EURATOM	European Atomic Energy Committee
GATT	General Agreement on Tariffs and Trade
GDP	gross domestic product
HL	House of Lords
IGC	intergovernmental conference
IIA	inter-institutional agreement
MAFF	Ministry of Agriculture, Fisheries and Food
MEP	Member of the European Parliament
MEQR	measures having equivalent effect
NCA	national competition authorities
PJCC	Police and Judicial Co-operation in Criminal Matters
PR	proportional representation
QBD	Queen's Bench Division
QMV	qualified majority voting
RAG	regional aid guidelines
SAAP	State Aid Action Plan
SAP	Social Action Programme
SEA	Single European Act
SGEIs	Services of general economic interest
SIS	Shengen Information System
SSNIP	small but significant non-transitory increase in price
TEC	Treaty establishing the European Union
TEU	Treaty on European Union
TFU	Treaty on the Functioning of the Union
TOA	Treaty of Amsterdam
TOL	Treaty of Lisbon
TON	Treaty of Nice
TRIPS	Trade-Related Aspects of International Property Rights
TTBER	Technology Transfer Block Exemption Regulation
UAPME	European Association of Craft, Small and Medium-Sized Enterprises
UNICE	Union of Industrial and Employers' Confederations of Europe
WTO	World Trade Organisation

Guided tour

Clear headings and sub headings keep you firmly focused and constantly aware of the context and structure of each chapter.

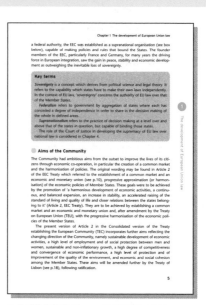

Key Terms boxes will help you to understand and remember technical, legal and constitutional terms.

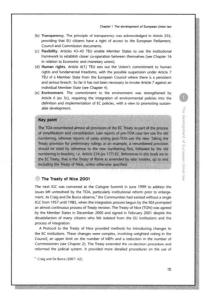

Key Points within each chapter provide instant clarification for the most important concepts you should know, highlighting essential information that you will need to remember for your studies.

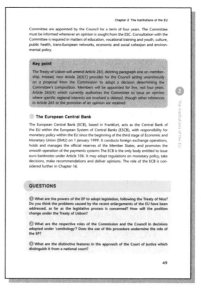

Questions located at the end of every chapter will aid you in your exam preparation, allowing you to test your knowledge, and explore your understanding of the subject.

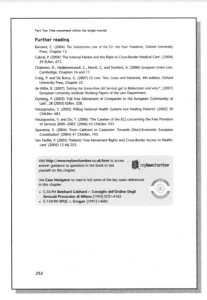

Further Reading sections at the end of each chapter present you with a thorough list of relevant resources for you to look at, giving you the opportunity to read those texts and articles that will assist you in your independent study of Law of the EU.

Key Cases clearly identify and outline details of vital cases you should know for your assessments.

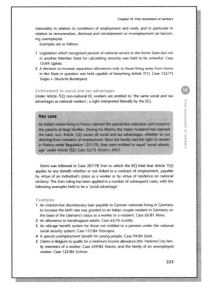

Examples are highlighted throughout to help you contextualise the theory you have been learning.

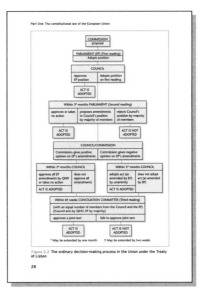

Diagrams are used to explain the legislative processes and changes under the Treaty of Lisbon.

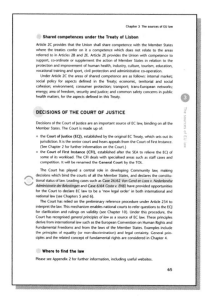

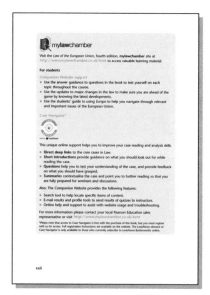

Case Navigator icons indicate cases which may be read in greater depth in full on the companion website.

Accompanied by a **Companion Website**, including answer guidance to questions in the book, you can test yourself on each topic throughout the course. You can also use the updates to major changes in the law to make sure you are ahead of the game by knowing the latest developments.

Table of treaties

Budgetary Treaty 1975 *24, 48*

Community Patent Convention 1976 *341, 342*

Constitutional Treaty (failed) 2004 *16, 17, 37, 52, 54, 70, 75, 88, 132*

Convention Implementing the Schengen Agreement (CISA) *211*

Convention on Jurisdiction and Enforcement of Judgments in Civil and Commercial Matters 1968 *55*

Convention on the Future of Europe *16, 17*

EC Act on Direct Elections 1976 *74*
    Annex 2 *74*

EC Treaty (Treaty establishing the European Community) (as amended by the Treaty of Amsterdam) *9, 11–13, 15–17, 19, 21, 24–26, 36, 38, 39, 43, 45, 46, 49, 52–55, 58, 60–63, 65, 66, 68, 69, 73–75, 78–80, 84, 88–90, 95, 96, 98, 101–103, 106, 107, 117, 118,* *121, 125, 133–136, 149, 156, 163, 165, 172, 196, 198, 205, 209, 212, 216, 225, 231, 234, 237, 240, 251, 254, 255, 258, 259, 261, 272, 274, 275, 285, 330, 345, 347–349, 352, 353, 361–363, 366, 367, 397, 401*

Article 1 (ex 1) *102*

Article 2 (ex 2) *5, 41, 42, 102, 260, 270, 361*

Article 2B *86*

Article 2B(1)–(4) *86*

Article 3 (ex 3) *102*

Article 3(1) (ex 3(1)) *259*

Article 3a *221*

Article 3b *85, 221*

Article 3c *215*

Article 3(g) *270, 274, 301*

Article 4 (ex 3a) *42, 102, 345*

Article 5 (ex 3b) *12, 42, 60, 77, 84, 85*

Article 5(1) *63, 84*

Article 5(2) *63, 84*

Article 5(3) *84*

Article 5a *42, 43*

Article 6 (ex 3c) *15*

Article 7 (ex 4) *21, 337*

Article 8 (ex 4a) *42, 43, 120*

Article 10 (ex 5) *39, 88, 91, 107, 108, 111, 119, 120, 173*

Article 12 (ex 6) *79, 170, 204, 215, 221, 232, 235–238, 247, 250, 251, 337, 345*

Article 13 (ex 6a) *14, 29, 79, 80, 366, 367, 388, 397*

Article 14 (ex 7a) *9, 163, 379*

Article 17 (ex 8) *12, 16, 74, 195, 196, 365, 387*

Article 17(1) *196*

Article 17(2) *196*

Article 18 (ex 8a) *45, 102, 195, 196, 199, 200, 365, 387*

Article 18(1) *196, 197, 228*

Article 18(3) *196*

Article 19 (ex 8b) *195, 199, 387*

Article 20 (ex 8c) *195, 199, 200, 387*

Article 21 (ex 8d) *195, 199, 200, 387*

Article 22 (ex 8e) *35, 195, 387*

Article 22(1) *200*

Article 23 (ex 9) *163, 166, 387*

Article 23(2) *164*

Article 24 (ex 10) *387*

Article 25 (ex 12) *90, 95, 102, 164–166, 387*

Article 26 (ex 28) *164, 387*

Article 27 (ex 29) *77*

Article 28 (ex 30) *46, 91, 102, 110, 121, 163, 165, 170–184, 186–188, 190–192, 270, 329, 330, 333, 336, 341, 352, 356, 387*

Article 29 (ex 34) *102, 121, 163, 165, 170, 172, 175, 184–186, 192, 270, 290, 329, 330, 336, 341, 387*

Article 30 (ex 36) *78, 102, 107, 121, 123, 163, 165, 170–172, 173, 177, 178, 185–187, 189–192, 270, 328–332, 334–336, 341*

Article 31 (ex 37) *163, 169–171, 348, 352*

Article 31(1) (ex 37(1)) *169*

Article 31(2) *169*

Article 34(3) (ex 40(3)) *79*

Article 37 (ex 43) *29*

Article 37(2) *26*

Article 39 (ex 48) *83, 102, 107, 114, 195, 207, 215–217, 219, 221, 224, 225, 229, 361*

Article 39(1) (ex 48(1)) *215*

Article 39(2) (ex 48(2)) *215, 221*

Article 39(3) (ex 48(3)) *78, 205, 207, 215, 216*

Article 39(4) (ex 48(4)) *215, 219, 220*

Article 40 (ex 49) *195, 215, 361*

Article 40(3) *79*

Article 41 (ex 50) *195, 215, 361*

Article 42 (ex 51) *195, 215, 227, 361*

Article 43 (ex 52) *95, 102, 195, 215, 217, 231, 232, 233, 236–238, 240, 241, 361*

Article 43(1) *231*

Article 43(2) *231, 235*

Article 44 (ex 54) *195, 215, 217, 231, 232, 238, 361*

Article 45 (ex 55) *195, 215, 217, 231, 232, 234, 238, 361*

Article 46 (ex 56) *195, 215, 217, 231, 232, 235, 238, 361*

Article 47 (ex 57) *195, 215, 217, 231, 232, 235, 238, 361*

Article 48 (ex 58) *195, 215, 217, 231, 232, 233, 238, 241, 361*

Article 48(2) *231*

Article 48(3) *383*

Article 49 (ex 59) *102, 170, 195, 215, 217, 231, 236–241, 245–247, 249, 251, 254, 361*

Article 49(1) *234*

Article 50 (ex 60) *170, 195, 215, 231, 237, 241, 246, 249, 361*

Article 50(1) *234*

Article 50(3) *234, 235*

Article 51 (ex 61) *170, 195, 215, 231, 361*

Article 52 (ex 62) *170, 195, 215, 231, 361*

Article 53 (ex 63) *170, 195, 215, 231, 361*

Article 54 (ex 64) *170, 195, 215, 231, 361*

Article 55 (ex 66) *170, 215, 231, 235, 361*

Article 56 (ex 73b) *231, 254*

Article 56(1) *254*

Article 56(2) *254*

Article 57 (ex 73c) *231, 254, 255*

Article 57(3) *256*

Article 58 (ex 73d) *231, 254, 255*

Article 58(1) *254*

Article 58(1)(b) *255*

Article 58(2) *255*

Article 58(3) *255*

Article 58(4) *256*

Article 59 (ex 73f) *254, 256*

Article 60 (ex 73g) *254, 256*

Article 61 *212*

Article 66 *215*

Article 68 *156*

Article 68(3) *156*

Article 71 (ex 75) *29*

Article 81 (ex 85) *82, 102, 267, 270–272, 274, 276, 282, 286, 294, 295, 301, 307, 308, 317, 318, 321, 323, 325, 326, 329, 337, 339–341, 345, 346, 349, 350*

Article 81(1) (ex 85(1)) *271, 274–287, 289, 317, 318, 320, 326, 329, 337–340*

Article 81(1)(a)–(e) *274, 280, 283*

Article 81(2) (ex 85(2)) *271, 274, 286, 346*

Article 81(3) (ex 85(3)) *271, 274, 284, 286–289, 292, 301, 317, 318, 340*

Article 82 (ex 86) *102, 169, 170, 267, 270–272, 274, 276, 286, 294–299, 301, 302, 305–308, 313, 317, 318, 321, 323, 325, 326, 329, 337, 339, 341, 345–351*

Article 82(d) *303*

Article 83 (ex 87) *345*

Article 84 (ex 88) *276, 345*

Article 85 (ex 89) *276, 345*

Article 85(1) *317*

Article 85(2) *317*

Article 86 (ex 90) *270, 339, 345, 346, 349, 350, 352*

Article 86(1) (ex 90(1)) *276, 345–347, 351*

Article 86(2) (ex 90(2)) *347–350, 353, 354*

Article 86(3) (ex 90(3)) *350–352*

Article 87 (ex 92) *166, 345, 346, 352, 354–357*

Article 87(1) *270*

Article 87(2) (ex 92(2)) *352, 356*

Article 87(3) (ex 92(3)) *352, 353, 356*

Article 87(3)(a) *356*

Article 87(3)(b) *356, 357*

Article 87(3)(c) *356*

Article 87(3)(a) *356*

Article 88 (ex 93) *117, 123, 345, 352, 354, 355, 357*

Article 88(1) (ex 93(1)) *354*

Article 88(2) (ex 93(2)) *122, 123, 354, 356*

Article 88(3) (ex 93(3)) *354, 357*

Article 88(4) *354*

Article 89 (ex 94) *117, 345, 352, 354, 355, 357*

Article 90 (ex 95) *96, 163, 165–171*

Article 90(1) *168*

Article 90(2) *168*

Article 92(3) (ex 98(3)) *353*

Article 94 (ex 100) *36, 361*

Article 95 (ex 100a) *135, 362*

Article 95(2) *168*

Article 95(4) *122, 123, 192*

Article 97 (ex 102) *355*

Article 97A *329, 341*

Article 98 (ex 102a) *259, 261*

Article 99 (ex 103) *192, 261, 262*

Article 99(2) *262*

Article 99(4) *262*

Article 100 (ex 103a) *259*

Article 101 (ex 104) *259, 261*

Article 102 (ex 104a) *261*

Article 103 (ex 104b) *261*

Article 104 (ex 104c) *261, 262*

Article 104(6) *262*

Article 105(2) (ex 105(2)) *260*

Article 106 (ex 105a) *50*

Article 107(1) (ex 106(1)) *260*

Article 107(2) *260*

Article 108 (ex 107) *192*

Article 109 (ex 108) *192*

Article 110 (ex 108a) *260*

Article 111 (ex 109) *192, 260*

Article 115A *262*

Article 116 (ex 109e) *259*

Article 121 (ex 109j) *34*

Article 121(4) (ex 109j(4)) *259*

Article 130 (ex 109s) *135*

Article 133 (ex 113) *55, 61, 63*

Article 134 (ex 115) *192*

Article 136 (ex 117) *362*

Article 137 (ex 118) *60, 362–365*

Article 137(2) *362*

Article 137(4) *363*
Article 138 (ex 118a) *362, 363*
Article 139 (ex 118b) *362, 363*
Article 140 *362*
Article 141 (ex 119) *74, 79, 81, 93, 102,*
  103, 106, 362, 363, 367, 369–379,
  382, 385, 395, 397
Article 141(4) *379, 385, 386*
Article 142 *362, 363*
Article 143 (ex 120) *362*
Article 144 (ex 121) *362*
Article 145 (ex 122) *362, 363*
Article 146 (ex 123) *361–363*
Article 147 (ex 124) *362, 363*
Article 148 (ex 125) *362, 363*
Article 149 (ex 126) *362, 363*
Article 150 (ex 127) *250, 362*
Article 151 (ex 128) *29*
Article 152 (ex 129) *29*
Article 152(4) *29*
Article 172a *365*
Article 175 (ex 130s) *29, 133*
Article 177 (ex 130u) *149*
Article 191 (ex 138a) *24*
Article 193 (ex 138c) *31*
Article 194 (ex 138d) *31*
Article 195 (ex 138e) *31*
Article 200 (ex 143) *25*
Article 201 (ex 144) *25*
Article 202 (ex 145) *33*
Article 203 (ex 146) *33*
Article 204 (ex 220) *55*
Article 205 (ex 148) *19, 34–36*
Article 207 (ex 151) *37*
Article 207(1) *37*
Article 208 (ex 152) *39*
Article 210 (ex 154) *25*
Article 211 (ex 155) *40*
Article 211a *38*
Article 213 (ex 157) *38*
Article 214 (ex 158) *25, 38, 39*
Article 215 (ex 159) *39*
Article 220 (ex 164) *47, 68*
Article 221 (ex 165) *35, 44, 45, 47*
Article 222 (ex 166) *44*
Article 223 (ex 167) *44, 45*
Article 224 (ex 168) *46*
Article 224(1) *47*
Article 224a *44, 47*

Article 225 (ex 168a) *44*
Article 225(3) *48*
Article 225a *47*
Article 226 (ex 169) *40, 46, 95, 117–124,*
  126, 236, 241, 256, 350, 383
Article 226(1) (ex 169(1)) *117*
Article 226(2) (ex 169(2)) *117*
Article 227 (ex 170) *117, 121, 122, 124*
Article 227(1) (ex 170(1)) *121*
Article 227(2) (ex 170(2)) *121*
Article 227(3) (ex 170(3)) *121*
Article 228 (ex 171) *9, 68, 117, 122,*
  124
Article 229 (ex 172) *310*
Article 230 (ex 173) *46, 47, 58, 59, 68,*
  78, 79, 122, 125–127, 132, 133,
  136–139, 141, 143, 260, 262, 310,
  321, 329, 338, 354, 357, 358
Article 230(1) (ex 173(1)) *125, 138*
Article 230(2) (ex 173(2)) *125–128*
Article 230(3) (ex 173(3)) *126, 128, 133,*
  138
Article 230(4) (ex 173(4)) *126, 128, 132*
Article 231 (ex 174) *136*
Article 232 (ex 175) *119, 125, 136–138,*
  141, 358
Article 232(1) (ex 175(1)) *47, 136, 137*
Article 232(3) (ex 175(3)) *137*
Article 233 (ex 176) *44, 136, 138*
Article 234 (ex 177) *15, 45–47, 65, 82,*
  89, 94, 102, 105, 120, 132, 138, 149,
  150, 152, 155–158, 173, 179, 180,
  185–187, 196, 197, 199, 203, 204,
  207, 226, 236, 238, 240, 246, 249,
  250, 281, 303–305, 326, 330, 333,
  336, 349, 350, 369, 383, 391
Article 234(1) (ex 177(1)) *149*
Article 234(2) (ex 177(2)) *149*
Article 234(3) (ex 177(3)) *150, 151,*
  153–155
Article 234(3)(b), (c) *150*
Article 234(4) *150*
Article 235 (ex 178) *47, 141*
Article 236 (ex 179) *47*
Article 238 (ex 181) *47*
Article 239 (ex 182) *121*
Article 241 (ex 184) *98, 105, 125, 133,*
  138, 139
Article 242 (ex 185) *155*

Article 243 (ex 186) *123*
Article 249 (ex 189) *55–59, 88, 92, 101, 103, 104, 108, 109, 367*
Article 249A *59, 60*
Article 249B *60*
Article 249B(2) *41*
Article 249C *60*
Article 249D *59*
Article 250 (ex 189c) *35*
Article 251 (ex 189b) *22, 25, 26, 30, 55, 60, 135*
Article 251(2) *29*
Article 252 (ex 189c) *55, 56*
Article 252a *26*
Article 253 (ex 190) *58, 134*
Article 254 (ex 191) *133*
Article 255 (ex 191a) *15*
Article 255(1) *86*
Article 255(2) *86*
Articles 257–262 (ex 193–198) *48*
Article 257 (ex 193) *49*
Article 258 (ex 194) *49*
Article 258(2) *49*
Article 259(1) (ex 195(1)) *49*
Article 261 (ex 197) *49*
Article 263 (ex 198a) *49*
Article 263(1) *49*
Article 264 (ex 198b) *49*
Article 265 (ex 198c) *49*
Article 265(4) *49*
Article 272 (ex 203) *24*
Article 288 (ex 215) *141, 323*
Article 288(2) (ex 215(2)) *141, 142, 146*
Article 292 (ex 219) *63*
Article 295 (ex 222) *328–330*
Article 296 (ex 223) *123, 192, 193*
Article 297 (ex 224) *123, 192, 193*
Article 298 (ex 225) *117, 122, 123, 192, 193*
Article 300 (ex 228) *40, 134*
Article 300(6) *63*
Article 308 (ex 235) *35, 39, 61, 62, 341, 362, 378*
Article 310 (ex 238) *31, 61*
EC Treaty (provisions repealed by Treaty of Amsterdam)
Articles 12–17 *164*
Articles 31, 32 *172*

European Atomic Energy Community Treaty (Euratom Treaty) 1957 *3, 4, 11, 13, 47, 52*
European Coal and Steel Community Treaty (ECSC) 1951 *3, 4, 11, 13, 47, 52, 71, 135*
Article 35 *138*
Article 60 *135*
European Convention on the Protection of Human Rights and Fundamental Freedoms (ECHR) *13, 16, 18, 56, 65, 68, 71–74, 89*
Article 6 *83, 131*
Article 7 *73*
Article 8 *73, 74, 207, 239*
Article 9 *73, 207*
Article 10 *73, 207*
Article 11 *73, 207*
Article 12 *73, 74*
Article 13 *73, 83, 131*
Article 53 *76*
European Convention on the Protection of Human Rights and Fundamental Freedoms, Protocol No 1
Article 1 *73, 74*
Article 3 *74*
European Economic Area Agreement (EEA) 1992 *7, 211*
European Economic Community Treaty (EEC Treaty) (Treaty of Rome) 1957 *3, 4, 6, 8, 9, 11, 13, 15, 19, 88, 92, 96–98, 137, 253, 257, 258, 361, 363, 367*
Article 2 *5, 361*
Articles 9–11 *165*
Articles 12, 13 *164, 165*
Article 14 *165*
Articles 15, 16 *164, 165*
Articles 30–34 *175*
Article 37 *170*
Articles 67–73 *253*
Article 95 *170*

Free Trade Agreement between Portugal and the EC
Article 1 *107*

General Agreement on Tariffs and Trade (GATT) 1947 *55*
Article XI *107*

Merger Treaty 1965 *4*

Protocol on enlargement of the EC 2003 *10, 12, 38*
   Article 4(3) *38*

Rules of Procedure of the European Court of Justice
   Article 104 *157*

Schengen Agreement 1985 *14, 211*
   Protocol *14*
Single European Act 1986 *8, 9, 15, 46, 54, 57, 65, 66, 258, 361, 362, 401*
   Preamble *361*
Statute of the Court of First Instance *157*
Statute of the Court of Justice
   Article 46 *141*

Treaty of Paris 1951 (France, Germany, Italy, Belgium, The Netherlands and Luxembourg) *3*
Treaty of Accession 1972 (UK, Ireland, Denmark) *6, 52, 54*
Treaty of Accession 1979 (Greece) *54*
Treaty of Accession 1985 (Spain and Portugal) *54*
Treaty of Accession 1994 (Austria, Finland and Sweden) *7, 54*
Treaty of Accession 2003 (Czech Republic, Estonia, Cyprus, Lativa, Lithuania, Hungary, Malta, Poland, Slovenia and Slovakia) *8, 17, 21, 35, 38, 54, 98, 218*
Treaty of Accession 2005 (Bulgaria and Romania) *8, 17, 21, 35, 45, 218, 219*
Treaty of Amsterdam 1997 *10–12, 14, 15, 19, 29, 31, 54, 57, 66, 79, 84, 86, 156–158, 172, 173, 211, 212, 254, 361, 364, 366, 378, 402*
   Article 2 *14*
Protocol on Subsidiarity and Proportionality *84, 85*
Treaty of Lisbon (Reform Treaty) *5, 13, 16–19, 21–23, 25, 26, 29–36, 38, 39, 41, 43, 44, 47, 49, 50, 52–56, 58, 59, 63–66, 70, 72, 73, 75, 77, 84–86, 88, 125, 128, 132, 139, 150, 196, 199, 200, 211, 212, 255, 256, 262, 329, 341, 354–366, 402*

Article 1a *18, 72*
Article 2 *18*
Article 2C *18*
Article 2F *18*
Article 7a *18*
Article 8C *32*
Article 18 *31*
Article 18b *22*
Article 28 *18*
Treaty of Nice *15, 16, 19, 21, 29, 35, 36, 47, 50, 53, 54, 66, 70, 73, 128*
Protocol *15*
Treaty on European Union 1992 *5, 9–14, 17–19, 22, 31, 48, 49, 52–54, 57, 63, 65, 68, 84, 86, 89, 97, 122, 127, 128, 135–137, 156, 195, 196, 247, 251, 254, 257–259, 361, 362, 365, 373*
   Article 1 (ex A) *17, 86*
   Article 1a *72*
   Article 2 (ex B) *12*
   Article 2B *64, 65*
   Article 2C *64, 65*
   Article 2E *65*
   Article 3 (ex C) *12, 63*
   Article 3a *63*
   Article 3b *64*
   Article 3b(1) *64*
   Article 3b(2) *64*
   Article 3b(3) *64*
   Article 4 (ex D.2) *12, 37*
   Article 5 *64*
   Article 6 (ex F) *17, 70*
   Article 6(1) *15, 68, 72, 73, 75*
   Article 6(2) *18, 72, 73*
   Article 6(3) *72*
   Article 6(4) *72*
   Article 7 (ex F.1) *15, 16, 31, 70, 72*
   Article 7a *212*
   Article 8B *32, 200*
   Title IV *156*
   Article 11–28 *11, 14*
   Article 23 *11*
   Article 26 *34*
   Title V *11*
   Articles 29–42 *11*
   Article 29 (ex K.1) *14*
   Article 34 (ex K.6) *58*
   Article 34(2)(b) *92*
   Article 35 (ex K.7) *58, 127, 156, 157*

Title VI *11, 156*
Articles 43–45 (ex K.15–K.17) *10, 15*
Article 43 (ex K.15) *16*
Article 48 (ex N) *32, 33, 63*
Article 49 (ex O) *31*
Article 49A *33*
Treaty on the Functioning of the Union
    (renaming of the EC Treaty) *17–19,*
    52–54, 213
    Part 3 *33*
    Title IV *19*
    Article 46A *18, 73*
    Article 61 *32*
    Article 61(1) *212, 213*
    Article 61(2) *212*
    Article 61(3) *212, 213*
    Article 61(4) *212*
    Article 61A *212*
    Article 61E *212*

Article 62(1) *213*
Article 62(2) *213*
Article 62(4) *213*
Article 63 *213*
Article 63A *213*

World Trade Organisation Agreement *89*
Annex on the Agreement on Trade-Related
    Aspects of International Property Rights
    (TRIPS)
    Article 50 *89*

UN Convention on the Rights of the Child
    1989 *209*

Yaoundé Convention between the EC and
    Developing Countries
    Article 2(1) *107*

Table of UK statutes

Airports Act 1986 *257*

Competition Act 1998 *272*
  s.60 *272*
Competition Act 1998 and
  other Enactments
  (Amendment)
  Regulations 2004
  (SI 2004/1261) *272*
Consumer Protection Act
  1987 *57*

Employment Protection
  (Consolidation) Act
  1978 *377*
Enterprise Act 2002 *272*

Equal Pay Act 1970 *93*
  s.6(1)(a) *370*
  s.6(4) *93*
European Communities
  Act 1972 *52,*
  92–94
  s.2(1) *93, 102*
  s.2(2) *93*
  s.2(4) *93*
  Schedule 2 *93*
European Parliament
  (Representation)
  Act 2003 *74*

Fair Trading Act 1973
  272

Merchant Shipping Act 1988
  94, 95, 120

Sex Discrimination Act 1975
  105, 110, 372, 382
  s.41 *383*
Sex Discrimination (Northern
  Ireland) Order 1976 (SI
  1976/1042) (NI 15)
  Article 53(2) *83*
Shops Act 1950
  s.47 *180*
Sunday Trading Act 1994 *180*

Weights and Measures Act
  1985 *93*

Table of European Community secondary legislation

Directives

Directive 64/221 [1964] OJ L 158/77 *96, 200, 206, 211, 216, 245*
  Article 3 *104*
  Annex *206, 210*

Directive 68/151 [1968] OJ L 65/18 *108*
Directive 68/360 [1968] OJ Spec. Ed. 485 *200, 216*

Directive 70/50 [1970] OJ L 13/29 *174*
  Article 2(1) *174*
  Article 3 *174*

Directive 73/148 [1973] OJ L 172/14 *231*

Directive 75/34 [1975] OJ L 14/10 *231*
Directive 75/117 [1975] OJ L 45/19 *373, 374*
  Article 1 *373, 374, 377*
  Article 1(2) *377*
  Article 6 *377*
Directive 75/362 [1975] OJ L 167 *237*

Directive 76/206 *366*
Directive 76/207 [1976] OJ L 39/40 *83, 105, 106, 108, 110, 369, 378–386, 388, 391, 396, 397*
  Article 1(1) *378, 384*
  Article 1(2) *378, 379*
  Article 2 *379*
  Article 2(1) *380, 381*
  Article 2(2) *379, 382, 383*
  Article 2(3) *382, 384, 393*
  Article 2(4) *382, 384, 386*
  Article 3(1) *380*
  Article 3(2) *386*
  Article 3(2)(a), (b) *386*
  Article 5 *105, 106, 381, 382, 386*
  Article 5(1) *381, 382*
  Article 6 *83, 108, 381, 386*

Directive 77/187 [1977] OJ L 61/26 *110*
Directive 77/249 [1977] OJ L 78/17 *236, 243*

Directive 79/7 [1979] OJ L 6/24 *105, 369, 378, 379, 381, 391–393, 395, 396*
  Article 2 *392*
  Article 3(1) *392, 393*
  Article 3(2) *393*
  Article 4(1) *393*
  Article 4(2) *393*
  Article 6 *395*
  Article 7 *382, 394*
  Article 7(1) *394*
  Article 7(1)(a) *394*

Directive 80/723 [1980] OJ L 195/35 *346, 350*
Directive 80/987 [1980] OJ L 283/23 *111*

Directive 83/189 [1983] OJ L 109/8 *110*

Directive 85/374 [1985] OJ L 210/29 *57*
  Article 1 *57*
Directive 85/577 [1985] OJ L 372/31 *109*

Directive 86/378 [1986] OJ L 225/40 *369, 373, 378, 379, 395*
Directive 86/613 [1986] OJ L 359/56 *369, 396, 397*
  Article 1 *396*
  Article 2 *396*
  Article 3 *396*
  Article 4 *397*
  Article 5 *397*
  Article 6 *397*
  Article 9 *397*

Directive 88/357 [1988] OJ L 172/1 *242*
Directive 88/361 [1988] OJ L 178/5 *253, 254*
  Article 4 *253*

Directive 89/48 [1989] OJ L 19 *242–244*
Directive 89/104 [1989] OJ L 40/1 *342*
  Article 7(1) *333*
Directive 89/646 [1989] OJ L 386 *242, 253*

Directive 90/354 *196*
Directive 90/364 [1990] OJ L 243 *200*
Directive 90/365 [1990] OJ L 243 *200*
Directive 90/366 [1990] OJ L 243 *136, 196*
Directive 90/619 *242*

Directive 91/250 [1991] OJ L 122 *342*

Directive 92/51 [1992] OJ L 209 *242, 243*
Directive 92/85 [1992] OJ L 348/1 *380, 381*
  Article 10 *380, 381*
  Article 10(1) *380*
Directive 92/100 [1992] OJ L 346/61 *343*
  Article 1(1) *334*

Directive 93/7 [1993] OJ L 74/74 *191*
Directive 93/83 [1993] OJ L 248 *343*
Directive 93/96 [1993] OJ L 317 *136, 196–198, 200*
Directive 93/98 [1993] OJ L 290 *342*
Directive 93/109 [1993] OJ L 329 *200*

Directive 94/46 [1994] OJ L 268 *351*
Directive 94/80 [1994] OJ L 368/38 *200*
Directive 94/95 [1994] OJ L 256/64 *57, 365*

Directive 95/51 [1995] OJ L 256/49 *351*
Directive 95/533 *200*

Directive 96/2 [1996] OJ L 20/50 *351*
Directive 96/9 [1996] OJ L 77/28 *342*
Directive 96/19 [1996] OJ L 74/13 *351*
Directive 96/34 [1996] OJ L 145/4 *365, 381*
Directive 96/97 [1996] OJ L 46/20 *395*
Directive 97/75 [1998] OJ L 10/24 *381*
Directive 97/80 [1997] OJ L 14/6 *365*
Directive 97/81 [1997] OJ L 14/9 *365*
Directive 98/5 [1998] OJ L 177/36 *236, 243*
Directive 98/44 [1998] OJ L 213/13 *31, 85, 342*
  Article 3 *342*
Directive 98/71 [1998] OJ L 289/28 *343*

Directive 99/42 [1999] OJ L 201/77 *242*

Directive 2000/43 [2000] OJ L 180/22 *79, 366, 388, 391*
  Article 2 *389*
  Article 3 *389*
  Article 4 *389*
  Article 5 *389*
Directive 2000/75 [2000] OJ L 327/74 *366*
Directive 2000/78 [2000] OJ L 303/16 *77, 79, 366, 367, 388–390*
  Article 1 *389, 390*
  Article 2 *389*
  Article 2(1) *390*
  Article 2(1)(a) *390*
  Article 2(1)(b) *390*
  Article 2(3) *390*
  Article 3 *390*
  Article 3(1) *390*
  Article 4(1) *390*
  Article 5 *390*
  Article 6 *391*
  Article 6(1) *391*
  Article 7 *391*
  Article 9 *391*
  Article 10 *391*
  Article 11 *391*
  Article 12 *391*
  Article 13 *391*
  Article 14 *391*
  Article 16 *391*
  Article 17 *391*

Directive 2003/54 [2003] OJ L 176/37 *351*
Directive 2003/55 [2003] OJ L 176/57 *351*
Directive 2003/86 [2003] OJ L 251/12 *59*
Directive 2003/88 [2003] OJ L 299/9 *85*

Directive 2004/38 [2004] OJ L 158/77 *56, 77, 136, 195, 196, 198, 200–206, 213, 215–217, 220, 221, 226, 229, 231, 235, 245*
  Article 2(2) *202, 204, 210, 220, 221*
  Article 3(2) *204, 221*
  Article 4 *205*
  Article 5 *205*
  Article 5(4) *204, 210*
  Article 6(1) *201*
  Article 7 *201, 205*

Article 7(1) *201, 220*
Article 7(3) *217*
Article 8 *205*
Article 9 *205*
Article 12(3) *225, 226*
Article 13(2) *203*
Article 14(2) *201*
Article 14(3) *201*
Article 16 *201, 216, 220*
Article 16(2) *201*
Article 17(1)(a) *202, 216*
Article 17(1)(b) *202*
Article 17(1)(c) *202*
Articles 19–21 *216*
Article 24(1) *205*
Article 24(2) *205*
Articles 27–33 *206*
Article 27 *200, 201, 210*
Article 27(1) *209*
Article 27(2) *206, 207*
Article 27(3) *209*
Article 27(4) *209*
Article 28 *209, 210*
Article 28(1) *209*
Article 28(2) *209*
Article 28(3) *209*
Article 29 *210*
Article 29(1) *210*
Article 29(2) *210*
Article 29(3) *210*
Article 30 *209*
Article 31 *209*
Article 32 *210*
Article 35 *203*

Directive 2004/109 [2004] OJ L 390/38 *354*
Directive 2004/113 [2004] OJ L 27/46 *367, 369, 378*

Directive 2005/36 [2005] OJ L 255/22 *242–244*
Article 1(a) *243*
Article 2 *243*
Article 4(1) *243*
Article 13(1) *244*
Article 14 *244*
Article 15 *243*
Article 16 *244*
Article 21 *244*

Directive 2006/1 [2006] OJ L 33/82 *123, 124*
Directive 2006/7 [2006] OJ L 64/37 *30*
Directive 2006/54 [2006] OJ L 204/23 *80, 367, 369, 373, 374, 378, 383, 385, 387, 389, 392, 395–397*
Article 2 *377*
Article 2(f) *396*
Article 3 *385*
Article 4 *374*
Article 4(1) *374*
Article 4(2) *377*
Article 5 *373, 395*
Article 6 *377, 396*
Article 7 *396*
Article 8 *396*
Article 9 *396*
Article 9(1)(f) *382*
Article 10 *396*
Article 11 *396*
Article 14 *374*
Article 14(1) *379*
Article 14(2) *383*
Directive 2006/123 [2006] OJ L 376/36 *245*
Article 1 *245*
Article 2 *245*
Article 3 *245*
Article 4 *245*
Article 5 *245*
Article 6 *245*
Article 7 *245*
Article 8 *245*
Article 9 *245*
Article 10 *245*
Article 11 *245*
Article 12 *245*
Article 13 *245*
Article 14 *245*
Article 15 *245*
Article 16 *245*
Article 17 *245*
Article 18 *245*
Article 19 *245*
Article 22 *245*
Article 23 *245*
Article 24 *245*
Article 25 *245*
Article 26 *245*
Article 27 *245*
Article 28 *245*

Article 29 *245*
Article 30 *245*
Article 31 *245*
Article 32 *245*
Article 33 *245*
Article 34 *245*
Article 35 *245*
Article 36 *245*

Regulations

Regulation 17/62 [1962] OJ L 13 *126, 270, 271, 274, 284, 286, 287, 295, 317, 318, 320, 321, 325*
Articles 1–9 *56*
Article 9 *56*
Article 11(2) *320*
Article 14 *320*
Article 14(3) *320, 321*
Article 17 *321*
Article 19 *321*
Article 19(2) *322*

Regulation 1612/68 [1968] OJ Spec. Ed. L 257/2 *56, 197, 200, 216, 220–222, 226, 228, 229, 231, 237, 250*
Part I *221*
Part II *221*
Part III *221*
Article 1 *221, 222*
Article 2 *221*
Article 3 *221*
Article 3(a) *222*
Article 3(1) *222*
Article 3(2) *222*
Article 4 *222, 225*
Article 5 *222*
Article 6 *221*
Article 6(1) *222*
Article 6(2) *222*
Article 7 *221*
Article 7(1) *222, 223*
Article 7(2) *223, 224*
Article 7(3) *224, 250*
Article 8 *221, 225*
Article 9 *221, 225*
Article 10 *202, 220, 221*
Article 10(1) *221*
Article 11 *220, 221*
Article 12 *225, 226, 250*

Regulation 1251/70 [1970] OJ L 142/24 *216, 223*

Regulation 1408/71 [1971] OJ L *227–229*
Article 1(1)(a) *227*
Article 2(1) *227*
Article 3(1) *227*
Article 4(1) *227*
Article 4(2)(a) *227*
Article 4(4) *228*
Article 10(1) *227*
Article 12(1) *227*
Article 13 *227*

Regulation 1983/83 [1983] OJ L 173/1 *290*
Regulation 1984/83 [1983] OJ L 173/5 *290*

Regulation 2349/84 [1984] OJ L 219 *290, 339*

Regulation 417/85 [1985] OJ L 53 *290*
Regulation 418/85 [1985] OJ L 53 *290*

Regulation 4056/86 [1986] OJ L 378 *276*

Regulation 3975/87 [1987] OJ L 374 *276*
Regulation 3976/87 [1987] OJ L 374 *276*

Regulation 2672/88 [1988] OJ L 239 *276*
Regulation 4078/88 [1988] OJ L 359 *290*
Regulation 4087/88 [1987] OJ L 359 *290*

Regulation 556/89 [1989] OJ L 61 *290, 339*
Regulation 4064/89 [1989] OJ L 395 *270, 302, 307, 310, 311*
Article 2(3) *311*
Article 21(3) *314*

Regulation 2410/92 [1992] OJ L 240 *276*
Regulation 3911/92 [1992] OJ L 395 *191*

Regulation 731/93 [1993] OJ L 75/7 *135*

Regulation 40/94 [1994] OJ L 11 *89, 342*
Regulation 240/96 [1996] OJ L 31/2 *290, 339*

Regulation 1310/97 [1997] OJ L 395 *307*

Regulation 994/98 [1998] OJ L 142 *356*

Regulation 1216/99 [1999] OJ L 148 *286*
Regulation 2790/99 [1999] OJ L 336 *271,*
  281, 284, 290–292
  Article 1 *291*
  Article 2 *291*
  Article 3 *291*
  Article 4 *291*
  Article 5 *291*

Regulation 2658/2000 [2000] OJ L 304/3
  290
Regulation 2659/2000 [2000] OJ L 304 *290*

Regulation 1049/2001 [2001] OJ L 145/43
  86

Regulation 1/2003 [2003] OJ L 1 *271, 274,*
  286, 290, 317, 318, 325, 327, 350
  Article 1 *317, 318*
  Article 3 *322, 325*
  Article 5 *318*
  Article 7 *321, 325*
  Article 8 *321, 325*
  Article 9 *321, 325*
  Article 10 *318, 321, 325*
  Article 11 *319, 325*
  Article 11(6) *325*
  Article 12 *325*
  Article 14 *325*
  Article 16 *287, 325*
  Article 17 *319, 323, 325*
  Article 18 *319*
  Article 18(1) *319*
  Article 18(3) *323, 325*
  Article 18(5) *319*
  Article 18(6) *319*
  Article 19 *319*
  Article 20 *319*
  Article 20(2) *320*
  Article 20(5) *320*
  Article 20(6) *320*
  Article 21 *319, 320*
  Article 22 *320*
  Article 23 *325*
  Article 23(1) *323*
  Article 23(1)(b) *319*
  Article 23(2) *323*

  Article 24 *319, 325*
  Article 24(d) *319*
  Article 24(2) *325*
  Article 27(1) *321*
  Article 27(2) *321*
  Article 27(4) *321, 322*
  Article 28 *320*
  Article 29(1) *325*
  Article 30 *321*
  Article 31 *321*
Regulation 990/2003 [2003] OJ L 143/16 *74*

Regulation 139/2004 [2004] OJ L 24/1 *270,*
  295, 301, 302, 307–309, 313, 315
  Article 1(2) *308*
  Article 1(3) *308*
  Article 2 *308*
  Article 2(1) *309*
  Article 2(2) *309*
  Article 2(3) *309, 311*
  Article 3(1) *308*
  Article 3(4) *308*
  Article 4 *309*
  Article 6(2) *309*
  Article 7(2) *309*
  Article 2(1) *309*
  Article 8 *309, 310*
  Article 9(2) *314*
  Article 11 *310*
  Article 12 *310*
  Article 13 *310*
  Article 14(2) *310*
  Article 21(1) *314*
  Article 22(1) *314*
Regulation 773/2004 [2004] OJ L 123 *318,*
  321
  Article 19 *320*
Regulation 774/2004 [2004] OJ L 123 *340*
  Article 1 *340*
  Article 1(1)(b) *340*
  Article 2 *340*
  Article 3 *340*
  Article 4 *340*
  Article 4(1) *340*
  Article 4(2) *340*
  Article 5 *340*
  Article 6 *340*
  Article 7 *340*
Regulation 883/2004 [2004] OJ L 166 *229*

Decisions

Decision 87/373 [1987] OJ L 197/33 *40*

Decision 93/350 [1993] OJ L 144/21 *47*

Decision 99/468 [1999] OJ L 184/23 *40, 41,*
43

Decision 2000/520 [2000] OJ L 215/7 *43*

Decision 2006/512 [2006] OJ L 200/13
40–42

   Article 3 *42*

Table of cases in the Court of Justice and the Court of First Instance (alphabetical)

Abrahamsson and Leif Anderson v. Elisabet Fogelqvist (Case C-407/98) [2000] ECR I-5539 *386*

Achterberg-te Riele and others v. Sociale Verzekeringsbank (Cases 48, 106, 107/88) [1989] ECR 1963, [1990] 3 CMLR 323 *392*

Adams v. Commission (No.1) (Case 145/83) [1985] ECR 3539, [1986] 1 CMLR 506 *145, 323*

Adoui and Cornaille v. Belgian State (Cases 115 & 116/81) [1982] ECR 1665, 1982 3 CMLR 631 *207–209*

AE Piraiki-Patriki v. Commission (Case 11/82) [1985] ECR 207, [1985] 2 CMLR 4 *131*

Ahlström Osakeyhtiö and others v. Commission (Cases C-89/85, C-104/85, C-114/85, C-116/85, C-117/85 and C-125/85 to C-129/85) [1993] ECR I-1307 *324*

Ahmed Saeed Flugreisen v. Zentrale Zur Bekämpfung Unlauteren Wettbewerbs (Case 66/86) [1989] ECR 803, [1988] 1 CMLR 879 *276, 349*

Airola v. Commission (Case 21/74) [1975] ECR 221 *80*

Airtours plc v. Commission (Case T-342/99) [2004] ECR II-1785 *311, 313, 315*

Aktien-Zuckerfabrik Schöppenstedt v. Council (Case 5/71) [1971] ECR 975 *142, 143*

Alfons Lütticke GmbH v. Commission (Case 48/65) [1966] ECR 19, [1966] CMLR 378 *118, 137, 145*

Al-Jubail Fertilizer v. Council (Case C-49/88) [1991] ECR I-3187, [1991] 3 CMLR 377 *83*

AKZO Chemie BV v. Commission (Case 53/85) [1986] ECR 1965, [1987] 1 CMLR 231 *322*

AKZO Chemie BV v. Commission (Case 62/86) [1991] ECR I-3359, [1993] 3 CMLR 601 *302*

ALBAKO v. BALM (Case 249/85) [1987] ECR 2354, *79*

Allué & Coonan v. Università degli Studi di Venezia (Case 33/88) [1989] ECR 1591, [1991] 1 CMLR 283 *220*

Alfons Lütticke GmbH v. Commission (Case 4/69) [1971] ECR 325 *141, 142*

Alpine Investments BV v. Minister van a Financien (Case C-384/93) [1995] ECR I-1141, [1995] 3 CMLR 209 *238*

Altmark Trans GmbH and Regierungspräsidium Magdeburg v. Nahverkehrsgesellschaft Altmark GmbH, and Oberbundesanwalt beim Bundesverwaltungsgericht (Case C-280/00) [2003] ECR I-7747 *353, 354*

Amministrazione della Finanze dello Stato v. San Giorgo (Case 199/82) [1983] ECR 3595, [1985] 2 CMLR 658 *166*

Amministrazione delle Finanze dello Stato v. Simmenthal SpA (Case 106/77) [1978] ECR 629; [1978] 3 CMLR 263 *91*

Amylum v. Council & Commission (Cases 116 & 124/77) [1979] ECR 3497, [1982] 2 CMLR 590 *143*

André Marchandise, Jean-Marie Chapuis and SA Trafitex (Case C-332/89) [1991] ECR I-1027, [1993] 3 CMLR 746 *177, 181*

Angestelltenbetriebsrat der Wiener Gebietskrankenkasse (Case C-309/97) [1999] ECR I-2865, [1999] 2 CMLR 1173 *375*

Apple and Pear Development Council (Case 222/82) [1983] ECR 4083 [1984] 3 CMLR 73 *173*

Arcaro (Case C-168/95) [1996] ECR I-4705, [1997] 1 CMLR 179 *109, 111*

Association des Centres Distributeurs
  Edouard Leclerc v. 'Au Blé Vert' Sarl
  (Case 229/83) [1985] ECR 1, [1985]
  2 CMLR 286 *186*
Association Eglise de Scientologie de Paris
  and Scientology International Reserves
  Trust v. the Prime Minister (Case C-53/99)
  [2000] ECR I-1335 *255*
Atkins v. Wrekin District Council (Case
  C-228/94) [1996] ECR I-3633, [1996]
  3 CMLR 863 *393*
Australian Mining & Smelting Europe Ltd v.
  Commission (Case 155/79) [1982]
  ECR 1575, [1982] 2 CMLR 264 *84, 321*
Automec v. Commission (Case T-64/89)
  [1990] ECR II-367, [1991] 4 CMLR 177
  126

Backman v. Belgium (Case C-204/90) [1992]
  ECR I-249, [1993] 1 CMLR 785 *224*
Badeck (Case C-158/97) [2000] ECR I-1875
  385
Bakker v. Hillegon (Case C-111/89) [1990]
  ECR I-1735; [1990] 3 CMLR 119 *166*
Baldinger v. Pensionsversicherungsanstalt
  der Arbeiter (Case C-386/02) [2004]
  ECR I-8411 *224*
Barber v. Guardian Royal Exchange
  Assurance Group (Case C-262/88)
  [1990] ECR I-1889; [1990] 2 CMLR 513
  81, 371–373, 378, 382, 395
Bauhuis v. Netherlands (Case 46/76) [1977]
  ECR 5 *166*
Baumbast and R v Secretary of State for the
  Home Department (Case C-413/99)
  [2002] ECR I-7091 *197, 198, 214, 226*
Baustahlgewebe v. Commission (Case
  C-185/95P) [1998] ECR I-8417, [1999]
  4 CMLR 1203 *324*
Bavarian Lager Co. Ltd v. Commission
  (Case T-194/04) [2007] ECR 000 *77*
Bayer & Hennecke v. Süllhöfer (Case 65/86)
  [1988] ECR 5249, [1990] 4 CMLR 182
  338
Bayerische HNL Vermehrungsbetriebe GmbH
  & Co KG v. Council & Commission
  (Cases 83 & 94/76, 4, 15 and 40/77)
  [1978] ECR 1209, [1978] 3 CMLR 566
  112, 142, 143

Becker v. Finansamt Munster Innenstadt
  (Case 8/81) [1982] ECR 53; [1982]
  1 CMLR 499 *106*
Beets-Proper v. F. Van Lanschot Bankiers NV
  (Case 262/84) [1986] ECR 773, [1987]
  2 CMLR 616 *394*
Béguelin Import Co. v. GL Export-Import SA
  (Case 22/71) [1971] ECR 949, [1972]
  CMLR 81 *277, 282*
Belasco v. Commission (Case 246/86)
  [1989] ECR 2117, [1991] 4 CMLR 96
  279
Belgapom v. ITM Belgium SA and Vocarex SA
  (Case C-63/94) [1995] ECRI-2467 *182*
Belgian State v. Humbel and Edel (Re Higher
  Education Funding) (Case 263/86) [1988]
  ECR 3565, [1989] 1 CMLR 393 *226, 250*
Belgian Telemarketing (Centre Belge d'Études
  de Marché-Télémarketing (CBEM) v. SA
  Compagnie Luxembourgeoise de
  Télédiffusion (CLT) and Information
  Publicité Benelux (IPB)) (Case 311/84)
  [1985] ECR 3261, [1986] 2 CMLR 588
  305, 349
Belgium v. Commission (Re. Tubemeuse)
  (Case C-142/87) [1990] 1 ECR 959;
  [1991] 3 CMLR 213 *355*
Belgium v. Spain (Case C-388/95) [2000]
  ECR I-3123 *121*
BENIM v. Commission (Case T-114/92)
  [1995] ECR II-147 *326*
Bestuur van het Algemeen Burgerlijk
  Pensioen-fonds v. Beaune (Case C-7/93)
  [1994] ECR I-4471 *371*
Bethell v. Commission (Case 246/81) [1982]
  ECR 2277, [1982] 3 CMLR 300, [1985]
  ECR 1, [1985] 2 CMLR 286 *137*
Bettray v. Staatsecretaris Van Justitie
  (Case 344/87) [1989] ECR 1621, [1991]
  1 CMLR 459 *217*
Bickel and Franz (Case C-274/96) [1998]
  ECR I-7637, [1999] 1 CMLR 348 *195,
  238*
Bilka-Kaufhaus v. Weber Von Hartz
  (Case 170/84) [1986] ECR 1607, [1986]
  2 CMLR 701 *370, 371, 373, 376*
Blaizot v. University of Liège (Case 24/86)
  [1988] ECR 379; [1989] 1 CMLR 57 *250,
  251*

Bleis v. Ministère de l'Education
(Case C-4/91) [1991] ECR I-5627, [1994]
1 CMLR 793 *220*

Bobie v. HZA Aachen-Nord (Case 127/75)
[1976] ECR 1079 *169*

Bodson v. Pompes Funèbres des Régions
Libérées SA (Case 30/87) [1988]
ECR 2479, [1989] 4 CMLR 984 *276*

Boehringer v. Council (Cases T-125 and
126/96) [1999] ECR II-3427 *188*

Bonsignore v. Oberstadtdirektor of the City of
Cologne (Case 67/74) [1975] ECR 297,
[1975] 1 CMLR 472 *207, 208*

Borker (Case 138/80) [1980] ECR 1975,
[1980] 3 CMLR 273 *150*

Bosman (see URBSFA v. Bosman)

Boyle and Others v. Commission
(Cases T-218 to 240/03) [2006]
ECR II-1699 *132*

BP v. Commission (Case 77/77) [1978]
ECR 1513, [1978] 3 CMLR 174 *300*

BPP Industries plc and British Gypsum Ltd
v. Commission (Case 50/89) [1990]
1 CMLR 34 *303*

Brasserie du Pêcheur v. Germany
(Case C-48/93) [1996] ECR I-1029, [1996]
1 CMLR 889, [1996] All ER (EC) 301,
[1996] 2 WLR 506 *94, 112, 113, 115,
116, 143, 317*

Bristol-Myers Squibb and Others v. Paranova
(Cases C-427, 429 and 436/93) [1996]
ECR I-3457, [1997] 1 CMLR 1151 *331,
332*

British Aerospace & Rover Group Holdings
plc v. Commission (Case C-294/90) [1992]
ECR I-493, [1992] 1 CMLR 853 *123*

British Airways v. Commission (Case
T-219/99) [2003] ECR II-5917 *300*

British American Tobacco (BAT) & Reynolds v.
Commission (The 'Philip Morris' case)
(Cases 142, 156/84) [1986] ECR 1899,
[1987] ECR 4487, [1987] 2 CMLR 551
307

British Leyland plc v. Commission
(Case 226/84) [1986] ECR 3263, [1987]
1 CMLR 184 *307*

British Plasterboard Industries plc v.
Commission (Case T-85/89) [1992]
ECR II-315, [1990] 4 CMLR 464 *298*

Broekmeulen v. Huisarts Registratie
Commissie (Case 246/80) [1981]
ECR 2311, [1982] 1 CMLR 91 *150, 236,
237*

Brown v. Rentokil (Case C-394/96) [1998]
ECR I-4185, [1998] 2 CMLR 1049 *381*

Brown v. Secretary of State for Scotland
(Case 197/86) [1988] ECR 3205, [1988]
3 CMLR 403 *198, 224, 251*

BRT v. SABAM (Case 127/73) [1974] ECR 51
& 313, [1974] 2 CMLR 238 *274, 303,
317, 325, 348*

Buchman v. Commission (Cartonboard)
(Cases T-295/94 etc.) [1998] ECR II-813
278, 324

Burbaud v. Ministère de l'Emploi et de la
Solidarité (Case C-285/01) [2003]
ECR I-8219 *243*

Burton v. British Railways Board (Case 19/81)
[1982] ECR 555, [1982] 2 CMLR 136,
[1982] 3 WLR 387, [1982] 3 All ER 537
381, 382, 394

Cadbury Schweppes plc and Cadbury
Schweppes Overseas Ltd v. Commissioners
of Inland Revenue (Case C-196/04) [2006]
ECR I-7995 *233*

Cadman v. Health & Safety Executive
(Case C-17/05) [2006] ECR I-9583 *376*

Calpack v. Commission (Cases 789 &
790/79) [1980] ECR 1949, [1981]
1 CMLR 26 *128*

Camera Care v. Commission (Case 792/79R)
[1980] ECR 119, [1980] 1 CMLR 334
321, 322

Campus Oil v. Minister of State for Industry
and Energy (Case 72/83) [1983]
ECR 2727, [1984] 3 CMLR 544 *188*

Capalonga v. Azienda Articola Maya
(Case 70/72) [1973] ECR 77, [1973]
CMLR *166*

Cartonboard (Cases T-295/94 etc.) (see
Buchman)

Carvel (John) and Guardian Newspapers
Ltd v. Council of the European Union
(Case T-194/94) [1995] ECR II-2765 *86*

Casagrande v. Landeshauptstadt München
(Case 9/74) [1970] ECR 773, [1974] 2
CMLR 423 *226*

Cassis de Dijon (see Rewe-Zentral
Case 120/78)
Castelli v. ONPTS (Case 261/83) [1984]
ECR 3199, [1987] 1 CMLR 465 *224*
Centrafarm BV v. American Home Products
Corporation (Case 3/78) [1978]
ECR 1823, [1979] 1 CMLR 326 *331, 332*
Centrafarm BV v. Sterling Drug Inc.
(Case 15/74) [1974] ECR 1147, [1974]
2 CMLR 480 *331, 332*
Centrafarm BV v. Winthrop BV (Case 16/74)
[1974] ECR 1183, [1974] 2 CMLR 480
331, 332, 339
Centros Ltd v. Erhvervs- og Selskabsstyrelsen
(Case C-212/97) [1999] ECR I-1459 *233*
Chasse (Case 15/57) [1957 & 1958] ECR 211
78
Chevalley v. Commission (Case 15/70)
[1970] ECR 975 *136*
CIA Security International SA v. Signalson SA
and Securitel SPRL (Case C-194/94)
[1996] ECR I-2201 *110*
CILFIT Srl (Case 283/81) [1982] ECR 3415,
[1983] 1 CMLR 472 *151–153, 155, 157*
Cinéthèque SA (Cases 60 & 61/84) [1985]
ECR 2605, [1986] 1 CMLR 365 *178*
CNTA SA v. Commission (Case 74/74) [1975]
ECR 533, [1977] 1 CMLR 171, [1976]
ECR 797 *82, 145*
Coditel v. Ciné Vog (Case 62/79) [1980]
ECR 881, [1981] 2 CMLR 362 *246*
Codorniu v. Council (Case C-309/89)
[1994] ECR I-1853, [1995] 2 CMLR 561
129
Colegio Oficial de Agentes de la Propriedad
Inmobiliaria v. José Luis Aguirre Borrell and
others (Case C-104/91) [1992] ECR I-3003
244
Collins v. Imtrat Handelsgesellschaft
(Cases C-92/92 and C-326/92) [1993]
ECR I-5145; [1993] 3 CMLR 773 *337*
Collins v. Secretary of State for Work and
Pensions (Case C-138/02) [2004]
ECR I-2703 *199, 217, 218*
Coloroll Pension Trustees v. Russell
(Case C-200/91) [1994] ECR I-4389 *370,
371*
Commercial Solvents (see Instituto
Chemicoterapico Italiano SpA and

Commercial Solvent Corporation v.
Commission)
Commission v. Austria (Case C-328/96)
[1999] ECR I-7479 *118*
Commission v. BASF AG (PVC) (Case
C-137/92P) [1994] ECR I-2555 *40, 82*
Commission v. Belgium (Case 156/77) [1978]
ECR 1881 *122, 133, 138*
Commission v. Belgium (Re Public
Employees) (Case 149/79) [1980]
ECR 3881, [1981] 2 CMLR 413 *219*
Commission v. Belgium (Case 132/82)
[1983] ECR 1649, [1983] 3 CMLR 600
166
Commission v. Belgium (Re Health Inspection
Services) (Case 314/82) [1984] ECR 1543,
[1985] 3 CMLR 134 *166*
Commission v. Belgium (Case 52/84) [1986]
ECR 89, [1987] 1 CMLR 710 *355*
Commission v. Belgium (Re University Fees)
(Case 293/85) [1988] ECR 305, [1989]
1 CMLR 57 *118, 119*
Commission v. Belgium (Re Higher Education
Funding) (Case 42/87) [1988] ECR 5445,
[1989] 1 CMLR 457 *226, 250*
Commission v. Belgium (Re Walloon Waste)
(Case C-2/90) [1992] ECR I-4431 *163*
Commission v. Belgium (Case C-323/97)
[1998] ECR I-4281 *200*
Commission v. Belgium (Case C-471/98)
[2002] ECR I-9681 *62*
Commission v. Belgium (Case C-503/99)
[2002/ ECR I-4809 *257*
Commission v. Council (Re European
Road Transport Agreement (ERTA))
(Case 22/70) [1971] ECR 263, [1971]
CMLR 335 *61, 62, 126, 134*
Commission v. Council (Case 81/72) [1973]
ECR 575, [1973] CMLR 639 *136*
Commission v. Council (Case 45/86) [1987]
ECR 1493; [1988] CMLR 131 *134*
Commission v. Council (The Titanium
Dioxide case) (Case 300/89) [1991]
ECR I-2867, [1993] 3 CMLR 359 *135*
Commission v. Council (Case C-27/04)
[2004] ECR I-6649 *262*
Commission v. Denmark (Re Disposable Beer
Cans) (Case 302/86) [1988] ECR 4607,
[1989] 1 CMLR 619 *178*

Commission v. European Parliament and
Council (Case C-122/04) [2006]
ECR I-2001 *42*

Commission v. France (Cases 6 & 11/69)
[1969] ECR 523, [1970] CMLR 43 *133*

Commission v. France (Re French Merchant
Seamen) (Case 167/73) [1974] ECR 359,
[1974] 2 CMLR 216 *120, 222*

Commission v. France (Re Lamb Wars)
(Case 232/78) [1979] ECR 2729; [1980]
1 CMLR 418 *120*

Commission v. France (Re Levy on
Reprographic Machines) (Case 90/79)
[1981] ECR 283, [1981] 3 CMLR 1 *167*

Commission v. France (Re Italian Table Wines)
(Case 42/82) [1983] ECR 1013, [1984]
1 CMLR 160 *190*

Commission v. France (Re French Nurses)
(Case 307/84) [1987] 3 CMLR 555 *220*

Commission v. France (Case 196/85) [1980]
ECR, [1988] 2 CMLR 851 *168*

Commission v. France (Case C-64/88) [1991]
ECR I-2727 *122*

Commission v. France (Case C-265/95)
[1997] ECR I-6959 *120, 173*

Commission v. France (Case C-483/99)
[2002] ECR I-4781 *257*

Commission v. France (Case C-304/02)
[2005] ECR I-6263 *122*

Commission v. France (Case C-232/05)
[2006] ECR I-10071 *355*

Commission v. Germany (Meat Preparations)
(Case 153/78) [1979] ECR 2555, [1980]
1 CMLR 198 *188*

Commission v. Germany (Re Beer Purity
Laws) (Case 178/84) [1987] ECR 1227,
[1988] 1 CMLR 780 *190, 191*

Commission v. Germany (Re Insurance
Services) (Case 205/84) [1986] ECR 3755,
[1987] 2 CMLR 69 *234, 241*

Commission v. Germany (Case C-5/89) [1990]
ECR I-3437, [1992] 1 CMLR 117 *355*

Commission v. Germany (Case C-191/95)
[1998] ECR I-0000 *118*

Commission v. Germany (Case C-503/04)
[2007] ECR I-6153 *122*

Commission v. Greece (The Greek Insurance
case) (Case 226/87) [1988] ECR 3611
350

Commission v. Greece (Case 305/87) [1989]
ECR 1461, [1991] 1 CMLR 611 *225, 238*

Commission v. Greece (Case C-45/91) [1992]
ECR I-2509 *122*

Commission v. Greece (Case C-120/94)
[1996] ECR I-1513 *192*

Commission v. Greece (Case C-120/94R)
[1994] ECR I-3037 *193*

Commission v. Greece (Case C-387/97)
[2000] ECR I-5047 *122*

Commission v. Ireland (Re Restrictions on
Importation of Souvenirs) (Case 113/80)
[1981] ECR 1625, [1982] 1 CMLR 706
186

Commission v. Ireland (Re 'Buy Irish'
Campaign) (Case 249/81) [1982] ECR
4005, [1983] 2 CMLR 104 *173, 174, 352*

Commission v. Ireland (Re Protection of
Animal Health) (Case 74/82) [1984]
ECR 317 *189*

Commission v. Ireland (Re Dundalk Water
Supply) (Case 45/87R) [1987] ECR 783,
[1987] ECR 1369, [1987] 2 CMLR 197
163

Commission v. Italy (Re Ban on Pork Imports,
'Pigmeat' case) (Case 7/61) [1961]
ECR 317, [1962] CMLR 39 *126, 174*

Commission v. Italy (Re Export Tax on Art
Treasures) (Case 7/68) [1968] ECR 423,
[1969] CMLR 1 *163, 165, 171, 191, 194*

Commission v. Italy (Re Statistical Levy)
(Case 24/68) [1969] ECR 193, [1971]
CMLR 611 *165*

Commission v. Italy (Re Reimbursement of
Sugar Storage Costs) (Case 73/79) [1979]
ECR 3837, [1980] 2 CMLR 647 *166*

Commission v. Italy (Case 28/81) [1981]
ECR 2577 *118, 119*

Commission v. Italy (Case 95/81) [1982]
ECR 2187 *186*

Commission v. Italy (Case 101/84) [1985]
ECR 2629, [1986] 2 CMLR 352 *119,
124*

Commission v. Italy (Re Import of Foreign
Motor Vehicles) (Case 154/85R) [1985]
ECR 1853, [1986] 2 CMLR 159 *119*

Commission v. Italy (Re Housing Aid)
(Case 63/86) [1988] ECR 29, [1989]
2 CMLR 601 *238*

Commission v. Italy (Case 104/86) [1988] ECR 1799, [1989] 3 CMLR 25 *120*

Commission v. Italy (Case 58/99) [2000] ECR I-3811 *256*

Commission v. Jégo-Quéré & Cie SA (Case C-263/02P) [2004] ECR I-3425 *132*

Commission v. Luxembourg and Belgium (Cases 90 & 91/63) [1965] ECR 625; [1965] CMLR 58 *164*

Commission v. Luxembourg (Case 58/81) [1982] ECR 2175; [1982] 3 CMLR 482 *377*

Commission v. Luxembourg (Case C-473/93) [1996] ECR I-3207, [1996] 3 CMLR 981 *219, 220*

Commission v. Luxembourg (Case C-193/05) [2006] ECR I-8673 *236, 237*

Commission v. Portugal (Golden Share) (Case C-367/98) [2002] ECR I-4731 *255, 257*

Commission v. Spain (Case C-463/00) [2003] ECR I-4581 *254*

Commission v. Spain (Case C-503/03) [2006] ECR I-1097 *211*

Commission v. Tetra Laval (Case C-12/03) [2005] ECR I-987 *312, 313, 315*

Commission v. United Kingdom (Cases 31/77 & 53/77) [1977] ECR 921; [1977] 2 CMLR 359 *122*

Commission v. United Kingdom (Re Tachographs) (Case 128/78) [1979] ECR 419, [1979] 2 CMLR 45 *119*

Commission v. United Kingdom (Re Excise Duties on Wine) (Case 170/78) [1980] ECR 417, [1980] 1 CMLR 716, [1983] CMLR 512 *168*

Commission v. United Kingdom (Re Equal Pay for Equal Work) (Case 61/81) [1982] ECR 2601 *377*

Commission v. United Kingdom (UHT Milk) (Case 124/81) [1983] ECR 203, [1983] 2 CMLR 1 *189*

Commission v. United Kingdom (French Turkeys) (Case 40/82) [1982] ECR 2793, [1982] 3 CMLR 497, [1984] ECR 283 *189*

Commission v. United Kingdom (Re Equal Treatment for Men and Women) (Case 165/82) [1983] ECR 3431, [1984] 1 CMLR 108 *382, 386*

Commission v. United Kingdom (Case 207/83) [1985] ECR 1201, [1985] 2 CMLR 259 *178*

Commission v. United Kingdom (Re Merchant Shipping Rules) (Case C-246/89R) [1989] ECR 3125, [1989] 3 CMLR 601 *95, 120*

Commission v. United Kingdom (Case C-98/01) [2003] ECR I-4641 *257*

Compagnie Continentale v. Council (Case 169/73) [1975] ECR 177, [1975] 1 CMLR 578 *145*

Conegate Ltd v. Customs and Excise Commissioners (Case 121/85) [1986] ECR 1007, [1986] 1 CMLR 739, [1987] 2 WLR 39, [1986] 2 All ER 68 *186, 187, 194*

Confédération Nationale des Producteurs de Fruits et Légumes v. Council (Cases 16 & 17/62) [1962] ECR 471, [1963] CMLR 160 *59, 128*

Consorzio Industrie Fiammiferi (CIF) v. Autorità Garante della Concorrenza e del Mercato (Case C-198/01) [2003] ECR I-8055 *317*

Consorzio Italiano della Componentistica de Ricambio per Autoveicoli v. Régie Nationale des Usines Renault (Case 53/87) [1988] ECR 6039, [1988] 3 CMLR 686 *335, 338*

Consten and Grundig v. Commission (Cases 56 & 58/64) [1966] ECR 299, [1966] CMLR 418 *128, 136, 280, 281, 288, 329, 337*

Continental Can (see Europemballage and Continental Can)

Corsica Ferries Italia Ltd v. Corpo dei Piloti del Porto di Genoa (Case C-18/93) [1994] ECR I-1783 *300, 350*

Costa v. Ente Nazionale per l'Energia Elettrica (ENEL) (Case 6/64) [1964] ECR 585, [1964] CMLR 425 *65, 88, 90, 92, 100, 154, 169, 171*

Council v. Heidi Hautala (Case 353/99P) [2001] ECR I-9565 *135*

Courage Ltd v. Bernard Crehan and Bernard Crehan v. Courage Ltd and Others (Case C-453/99) [2001] ECR I-6297 *326*

Cowan v. French Treasury (Case 186/87)
[1989] ECR 195, [1990] 2 CMLR 613 *247*

Criminal proceedings against André
Marchandise, Jean-Marie Chapuis and SA
Trafitex (see André Marchandise)

Criminal proceedings against Harry Franzén
(see Harry Franzén)

Criminal Proceedings against Keck &
Mithouard (see Keck & Mithouard)

Criminal proceedings against Kenny Roland
Lyckeskog (see Kenny Roland Lyckeskog)

Criminal proceedings against Maria Pupino
(see Maria Pupino)

Criminal Proceedings against Sanz de Lera
(see Sanz de Lera)

Cullet v. Centre Leclerc (Case 231/83) [1985]
ECR 306, [1985] 2 CMLR 524 *188*

D. v. Council (Case T-264/97) [1999]
ECR IA-1, [1999] ECR II-1 *388*

Da Costa en Schaake NV v. Nederlandse
Belastingadministratie (Cases 28–30/62)
[1963] ECR 1, [1963] CMLR 10 *153, 155*

Danfoss (Handels-og Kontorfunktionaernes
Forbund v. Dansk Arbejdsgiverforening for
Danfoss) (Case 109/88) [1989] ECR 3199,
[1991] 1 CMLR 8 *373, 378*

Dany Bidar (see R (on the application of
Dany Bidar) v. London Borough of Ealing
and Secretary of State for Education and
Skills)

Dassonville (see 'Procurement du Roi')

Deak (Case 94/84) [1985] ECR 1873 *223*

Decker v. Caisse de Maladie des Employés
Privés (Case C-120/95) [1998] ECR I-
1831, [1998] 2 CMLR 879 *190, 191*

Defrenne v. Belgian State (No.1) (Case
80/70) [1971] ECR 445, [1974]
CMLR 494 *372*

Defrenne v. SA Belge de Navigation Aérienne
(SABENA) (No.2) (Case 43/75) [1976]
ECR 455, [1976] 2 CMLR 98 *81, 103,
369, 370*

Defrenne v. Société Anonyme Belge
de Navigation Aérienne Sabena
(Case 149/77) [1978] ECR 1365 *378*

Dekker v. Stichting Vormingscentrum Voor
Jong Volwassenen (Case C-177/88) [1990]
ECR I-3941 *375, 380*

Delimitis v. Henninger Bräu (Case C-234/89)
[1991] ECR I-935, [1992] 5 CMLR 210
284, 286

Dem 'Yanenko' (Case C-45/03) *156*

Demont v. Commission (Case 115/80)
[1981] ECR 3147 *84*

Denkavit Futtermittel v. Land Nordrhein-
Westfalen (Case 73/84) [1985] ECR 1013,
[1986] 2 CMLR 482 *190*

Denkavit International v. Bundesamt für
Finanzen (Cases C-283, 291 & 292/94)
[1996] ECR I-5063 *114*

Deuka v. EVGE (Case 78/74) [1975] ECR 421,
[1975] 2 CMLR 28 *81*

Deutsche Grammophon Gesellschaft GmbH
v. Metro-SB-Grossmärkte GmbH & Co. KG
(Case 78/70) [1971] ECR 487, [1971]
CMLR 631 *330*

Deutsche Paracelsus Schulen für
Naturheilverfahren GmbH v. Kurt
Gräbner (Case C-294/00) [2002]
ECR I-6515 *243*

Deutsche Post AG v. Sievers and Schrage
(Cases C-270 & 271/97) [2000] ECR I-929
369

Deutz und Geldermann, Sektkellerei Breisach
(Baden) GmbH v. Council (Case 26/86)
[1987] ECR 941 *129*

D'Hoop v. Office National de L'emploi
(Case C-224/98) [2002] ECR I-6191 *198*

Di Leo v. Land Berlin (Case C-308/89) [1990]
ECR I-4185 *226*

Dias v. Director da Alfândego do Porto
(Case C-343/90) [1992] ECR I-4673 *152*

Diatta v. Land Berlin (Case 267/83) [1985]
ECR 567, [1986] 2 CMLR 164 *203*

Dillenkofer v. Federal Republic of Germany
(Cases 178 etc./94) [1996] ECR I-4845,
[1996] 3 CMLR 469 *114*

Distillers Co. Ltd v. Commission (Case 30/78)
[1980] ECR 2229, [1980] 3 CMLR 121
134, 283

Ditlev Bluhme (Case C-67/97) [1998]
ECR I-8033, [1999] 1 CMLR 612 *190*

Dona v. Mantero (Case 13/76) [1976]
ECR 1333, [1976] 1 CMLR 26 *225*

Donatella Calfa (Case C-348/96) [1999]
ECR I-11, [1999] 2 CMLR 1138, [1999]
All ER (EC) 850 *206*

Donckerwolcke v. Procureur de la République
(Case 41/76) [1976] ECR 1921, [1977]
2 CMLR 535 *192*

Dorsch Consult Ingenieurgesellschaft mbH
v. Bundesbaugesellschaft Berlin mbH
(Case C-54/96) [1997] ECR I-4961
150

Dorsch Consult Ingenieurgesellschaft mbH v.
Council and Commission (Case C-237/98P)
[2000] ECR I-4549 *144*

Dory v. Germany (Case C-186/01) [2003]
ECR I-2479 *384*

Dow Benelux NV v. Commission
(Case 85/87) [1989] ECR 3137, [1991]
4 CMLR 410 *83, 320*

Dow Chemical Ibérica SA v. Commission
(Cases 97–99/87) [1989] ECR 3156,
[1991] 4 CMLR 410 *320*

Drake v. Chief Adjudication Officer
(Case 150/85) [1986] ECR 1995, [1986]
3 CMLR 42 *392, 393*

Drei Glocken v. USL (Case 407/85) [1988]
ECR 4233 *177, 179*

Dumortier Fils SA v. Council (Cases 64 &
113/76, 167 & 239/78, 27, 28 & 45/79)
[1979] ECR 3091, [1982] ECR 1733 *145*

Duphar BV v. Netherlands (Case 238/82)
[1984] ECR 523, [1985] 1 CMLR 256
178, 179, 186

Dzodzi v. Belgium (Cases C-297/88 &
C-197/89) [1990] ECR I-3763 *152*

Dynamic Medien Vertriebs GmbH v. Avides
Media AG (Case C-244/06) [2008]
ECR 000 *183*

ECSC v. Acciaiera e ferrier Busseni (Case
221/88) [1990] 1 ECR 495 *106*

El Corte Inglés v. Rivero (Case C-192/94)
[1996] ECR I-1281, [1996] 2 CMLR 507
111

Elliniki Radiophonia Tiléorassi v. Dimotiki
Etairia Pliroforissis and others (Greek
Broadcasting) (Case C-260/89) [1991]
ECR I-2925, [1994] 4 CMLR 540 *73, 347,
349*

EMI v. CBS (Case 51/75) [1976] ECR 811,
[1976] 2 CMLR 235 *336*

EMI v. Patricia (Case 341/87) [1989] ECR 79,
[1989] 2 CMLR 413 *334*

Emmott v. Minister for Social Welfare (Case
C-208/90) [1991] ECR I-4269, [1991]
3 CMLR 894 *105, 386*

Enderby v. Frenchay Area Health Authority
(Case C-127/92) [1993] ECR I-5535,
[1994] 1 CMLR 8 *375*

Erauw Jacquery v. La Hesbignonne
(Case 27/87) [1988] ECR 1919, [1988]
4 CMLR 576 *335*

Eridiana v. Commission (Cases 10 & 18/68)
[1969] ECR 459 *133*

Eridiana v. Minister of Agriculture and
Forestry (Case 230/78) [1979] ECR 2749
103

European Night Services and Others v.
Commission (Cases T-374, 375, 384 and
388/94) [1998] ECR II-3141, [1998]
5 CMLR 718 *276, 289, 351*

European Parliament v Council of the
European Union (Case C-540/03) [2006]
ECR I-5769 *59, 77*

Europembellage Corporation and Continental
Can v. Commission (Case 6/72) [1973]
ECR 215, [1973] CMLR 199 *294, 296,
300–302, 307*

Even (Case 207/78) [1979] ECR 2019, [1980]
2 CMLR 71 *223, 228*

EVGF v. Mackprang (Case 2/75) [1975]
ECR 607, [1977] 1 CMLR 198 *82*

Faccini Dori v. Recreb (Case C-91/92)
[1994] ECR I-3235, [1995] 1 CMLR 665
108–111

Fédération Nationale v. France (Case
C-354/90) [1991] ECR I-5505 *354*

Federación Nacional de Empresas de
Instrumentación Científica, Médica,
Técnica y Dental (FENIN) v. Commission
(Case T-319/99) [2003] ECR II-357 *277*

Feldain v. Directeur des Services Fiscaux
(Case 433/85) [1987] ECR 352 *169*

Ferring SA v. Agence centrale des organismes
de sécurité sociale (ACOSS) (Case
C-53/00) [2001] ECR I-9067 *353*

Fidium Finanz AG v. Bundesanstalt
für Finanzdienstleistungsaufsicht
(Case C-452/04) [2006] ECR I-9521 *234*

Fietje (Case 27/80) [1980] ECR 3839, [1981]
3 CMLR 722 *178*

I

Fink Frucht GmbH (Case 27/67) [1968]
ECR 223, [1968] CMLR 228, [1989]
2 CMLR 751, [1989] 2 All ER 758 *168*

Fiorini v. SNCF (Case 32/75) [1975] ECR
1085, [1976] 1 CMLR 573 *223, 224*

Fisscher v. Voorhuis Hengelo (Case C-128/93)
[1994] ECR I-4583, [1995] 1 CMLR 881
376

Foglia v. Novella (No.1) (Case 104/79)
[1980] ECR 745, [1981] 1 CMLR 45 *152*

Foglia v. Novella (No.2) (Case 244/80)
[1981] ECR 304, [1982] 1 CMLR 585 *152*

Ford of Europe v. Commission (Cases 228
& 229/82) [1984] ECR 1129, [1984]
1 CMLR 649 *322*

Foster v. British Gas (Case C-188/89) [1990]
ECR I-3313, [1990] 2 CMLR 833, [1988]
2 CMLR 697 *103, 106*

Foto-Frost v. Hauptzollampt Lübeck Ost
(Case 314/85) [1987] ECR 4199, [1988]
3 CMLR 57 *153, 155*

France v. Commission (Case 102/87) [1988]
ECR 4067 *357*

France v. Commission (Case C-202/88)
[1991] ECR I-1223, [1992] 5 CMLR 552
352

France v. Commission; SCPA & EMC v.
Commission (Cases C-68/94 and 30/95)
[1998] ECR I-1375, [1998] 4 CMLR 829
310, 311

France v. United Kingdom (Re Fishing Net
Mesh Sizes) (Case 141/78) [1979]
ECR 2923, [1980] 1 CMLR 735 *121*

France, Italy and the United Kingdom v.
Commission (the Transparency Directive
Case) (Cases 188–190/80) [1982] ECR
2545, [1983] 3 CMLR 144 *346, 350*

France Télécom SA v. Commission
(Case T-340/04) [2007] ECR II-573 *299*

Francovich & Bonifaci v. Italy (Cases C-6 &
9/90) [1991] ECR I-5357; [1993] ECR 66,
[1993] 2 CMLR 66 *92, 94, 111, 115, 116,*
146

Frascogna (Case 157/84) [1985] ECR 1739
223

Fratelli Cucchi v. Avez SpA (Case 77/76)
[1977] ECR 987 *166*

French Republic v. High Authority
(Case 1/54) [1954] ECR 1 *135*

Fresh Marine Co. A/S v. Commission
(Case T-178/98) [2004] ECR II-3127 *144*

Frilli v. Belgian State (Case 1/72) [1972]
ECR 457, [1973] CMLR 386 *79, 228*

FRUBO v. Commission (Case 71/74) [1975]
ECR 563, [1975] 2 CMLR 123 *275*

GAEC v. Council & Commission
(Case 253/84) [1987] ECR 123, [1988]
1 CMLR 677 *146*

Garcia Avello (Carlos) v. Belgian State
(Case C-148/02) [2003] ECR I-11613 *195*

Garland v. British Rail Engineering Limited
(Case 12/81) [1982] ECR 359 *370*

GB INNO-BM v. Confédération du
Commerce Luxembourgoise Asbl
(Case C-362/88) [1990] ECR I-667,
[1991] 2 CMLR 801 *179*

GBC Echternach and A Moritz v. Netherlands
Minister for Education and Science
(Cases 389 & 390/87) [1989] ECR 723,
[1990] 2 CMLR 305 *217, 226*

Gebhard v. Consiglio dell'Ordine Degli
Avvocati Procurator di Milano
(Case C-55/94) [1995] ECR I-4165,
[1996] 1 CMLR 603 *240, 252*

Geddo v. Ente Nazionale Risi (Case 2/73)
[1973] ECR 865, [1974] 1 CMLR 13 *174*

GEMA v. Commission (Case 125/78) [1979]
ECR 3173, [1980] 2 CMLR 177 *137, 337*

Gencor v. Commission (Case T-102/96)
[1999] ECR II-753, [1999] 4 CMLR 971,
[1999] All ER (EC) 289 *310, 311*

Geraets-Smits v. Stichting Ziekenfonds VGZ;
HTM Peerbooms v. Stichting CZ Groep
Zorgverzekeringen (Case C-157/99)
[2001] ECR I-5473 *248, 249*

Germany v. Commission (Re Tariff Quotas
on Wine) (Case 24/62) [1963] ECR 63,
[1963] CMLR 347 *134*

Germany v. Commission (Cases 281, 283, 284,
285 and 287/85) [1987] ECR 3203 *60*

Germany v. Council (Case C-122/95) [1998]
ECR I-973, [1998] 3 CMLR 570 *97*

Gestoras Pro Amnistía, Juan Mari Olano
Olano and Julen Zelarain Errasti v. Council
(Case C-354/04P) [2007] ECR I-1579 *127*

Gillespie v. Northern Ireland Health and
Social Services Board (Case C-342/93)

[1996] ECR I-475, [1996] 2 CMLR 969
372

Gilli v. Andres (Case 788/79) [1980]
ECR 2071, [1981] 1 CMLR 146 *178*

Giloy (Bernd) v. Hauptzollamt Frankfurt am
Main-Ost (Case C-130/95) [1997]
ECR I-4291 *152*

GlaxoSmithKline Services Unlimited v.
Commission (Case T-168/01) [2006]
ECR II-2969 *280, 284*

Gorgio Domingo Banchero (Case C-387/93)
[1995] ECR I-4663, [1996] 1 CMLR 829
182

Gräbner (see Deutsche Paracelsus Schulen
für Naturheilverfahren GmbH v. Kurt
Gräbner)

Grad v. Finanzamt Traustein (Case 9/70)
[1970] ECR 825, [1971] CMLR *104*

Graham J. Wilson v. Ordre des avocats du
barreau de Luxembourg (Case C-506/04)
[2006] ECR I-8613 *236*

Grandes Distilleries (No.2) (Case 119/78)
[1979] ECR 975, [1980] 3 CMLR 337 *170*

Grandes Distilleries Peureux v. Directeur des
Services Fiscaux (No.1) (Case 86/78)
[1979] ECR 897, [1980] 3 CMLR 337
167, 170

Grant v. South West Trains (Case C-249/96)
[1998] ECR I-621, [1998] 1 CMLR 993
80, 388

Gravier v. City of Liège (Case 293/83) [1985]
ECR 593, [1985] 3 CMLR 1 *235, 247,
249–251*

Grimaldi v. Fonds des Maladies
Professionelles (Case 322/88) [1989]
ECR 4407, [1991] 2 CMLR 265 *58*

Groener v. Minister for Education
(Case 379/87) [1989] ECR 3967, [1990]
1 CMLR 401 *222*

Groupement d'Achat Edouard Leclerc v.
Commission (Case T-19/92) [1996]
ECR II-1961, [1997] 4 CMLR 995 *285*

Grzelczyk v. Centre public d'aide sociale
d'Ottignies-Louvain-la-Neuve (Case
184/99) [2001] ECR I-6193 *197, 205,
224*

Gulling v. Conseils des Ordres des Barreaux
et de Savene (Case 292/86) [1988]
ECR 111, [1988] 2 CMLR 57 *240*

Haegeman v. Belgium (Case 181/73) [1974]
ECR 449, [1975] 1 CMLR 515 *55*

Haegmann Sprl v. Commission (Case 96/71)
[1972] ECR 1005; [1973] CMLR 365 *146*

Hansen (Case 148/77) [1978] ECR 1787,
[1979] 1 CMLR 604 *170*

Harry Franzén (Case C-189/95) [1997]
ECR I-5909 *170*

Hasselblad (GB) Ltd v. EC Commission
(Case 86/82) [1984] ECR 883, [1984]
1 CMLR 559 *285*

Hauer v. Rheinland-Pfalz (Case 44/79) [1979]
ECR 3737, [1980] 3 CMLR 42 *73*

Hercules Chemicals NV v. Commission
(Case T-7/89) [1991] ECR II-1711 *321*

Hermes International v. FHT Marketing Choice
(Case C-53/96) [1998] ECR I-3603 *89*

Hertz v. Dansk Arbejdsgiverforening
(Case 179/88) [1990] ECR I-3979, *380*

Hessische Knappschaft v. Maison Singer et
Fils (Case 44/65) [1965] ECR 965, [1966]
CMLR 82 *138*

Hilti AG v. Commission (Case T-30/89)
[1991] ECR II-1439, [1990] ECR II-163,
[1992] 4 CMLR 16 *300, 302*

HM Customs and Excise v. Schindler
(Case C-275/92) [1994] ECR I-1039 *238*

Hoechst v. Commission (Cases 46/87 &
227/88) [1989] ECR 2859, [1991]
4 CMLR 410 *320*

Hoeckx (Case 249/83) [1985] ECR 973,
[1987] 3 CMLR 638 *223*

Hoekstra (née Unger) v. BBDA (Case 75/63)
[1964] ECR 177, [1964] CMLR 319 *216,
227*

Hoffmann-La Roche (Case 102/77) [1978]
ECR 1139, [1978] 3 CMLR 217 *331, 332*

Hoffmann-La Roche & Co. AG v. Commission
(Vitamins Case) (Case 85/76) [1979]
ECR 461, [1979] 3 CMLR 211 *295, 297,
298, 300, 301, 303*

Hofmann v. Barmer Ersatzkasse
(Case 184/83) [1984] ECR 3047, [1986]
1 CMLR 242 *381, 384*

Höfner v. Macrotron (Case C-41/90) [1991]
ECR I-1979; [1993] 4 CMLR 306 *347*

Home Secretary v. Hacene Akrich
(Case C-109/01) [2003] ECR I-9607
73, 203

Hoogovens v. High Authority (Case 14/61)
[1962] ECR 253, [1963] CMLR 73 *69*

Hugin Kassaregister AB v. Commission
(Case 22/78) [1979] ECR 1869, [1979]
3 CMLR 345 *298*

Humblot v. Directeur des Services Fiscaux
(Case 112/84) [1986] ECR 1367, [1986]
2 CMLR 338 *169, 171*

Hünermund v. Landesapothekemer Baden
Wurttemburg (Case C-292/92) [1993]
ECR I-6787 *181*

Ianelli & Volpi SpA v. Meroni (Case 74/76)
[1977] ECR 557, [1977] 2 CMLR 688
174, 354, 357

IBM v. Commission (Case 60/81) [1981]
ECR 2639, [1981] 3 CMLR 635 *126*

ICI v. Italian Financial Administration
(Case 66/80) [1981] ECR 1191, [1983]
2 CMLR 593 *156*

Impala (see Independant Music Publishers
and Labels Association (Impala,
association internationale) v. Commission)

Imperial Chemical Industries Ltd v.
Commission (Dyestuffs) (Cases 48/69,
49/69, 51–57/69) [1972] ECR 619, [1972]
CMLR 557 *277, 278, 282, 319*

IMS Health (see NDC Health GmbH & Co.
KG and NDC Health Corporation v.
Commission of the European
Communities and IMS Health Inc)

Independant Music Publishers and Labels
Association (Impala, association
internationale) v. Commission (Case
T-464/04) [2006] ECR II-2289 *312, 313*

Inizan v. Caisse primaire d'assurance maladie
des Hauts-de-Seine (Case C-56/01) [2003]
ECR I-12403 *248, 249*

Instituto Chemicoterapico Italiano SpA and
Commercial Solvent Corporation v.
Commission (Cases 6 & 7/73) [1974]
ECR 223, [1974] 1 CMLR 309 *298, 307*

International Fruit Company NV v.
Produktschap voor Groensten en Fruit
(No.3) (Cases 21–24/72) [1972] ECR
1219, [1975] 2 CMLR 1 *55, 107*

International Fruit NV v. Commission (No.1)
(Cases 41–44/70) [1971] ECR 441, [1975]
2 CMLR 515 *59, 129*

International Handelsgesellschaft GmbH
(Case 11/70) [1970] ECR 1125, [1972]
CMLR 255 *70, 71, 77, 90, 91, 100*

Interquell Starke-Chemie GmbH & Co. KG v.
Commission (Cases 261 & 262/78) [1979]
ECR 3045 *145*

Interzuccheri v. Ditta Rezzano e Cassava
(Case 105/76) [1977] ECR 1029 *166*

Inzirillo v. Caisse d'allocations familiales
(Case 63/76) [1976] ECR 2057, [1978]
3 CMLR 596 *223*

Irish Cement Ltd v. Commission
(Case 166/86) [1988] ECR 6473, [1989]
2 CMLR 57 *358*

Italy v. Commission (Re Aids to the Textile
Industry) (Case 173/73) [1974] ECR 709,
[1974] 2 CMLR 593 *355*

Italy v. Commission (Re British Telecom)
(Case 41/83) [1985] ECR 873, [1985]
2 CMLR 368 *348, 349*

Italy v. Council and Commission
(Case 32/65) [1966] ECR 389, [1969]
CMLR 39 *138*

Italy v. Sacchi (Case 155/73) [1974] ECR 409,
[1974] 2 CMLR 177 *102, 170, 276, 345,
349*

Jackson and Cresswell v. Chief Adjudication
Officer (Cases C-63 & 64/91) [1992]
ECR I-4737, [1992] 3 CMLR 389 *393*

Jégo-Quéré & Cie SA v. Commission
(Case T-177/01) [2002] ECR II-2365 *131*

Jenkins v. Kingsgate (Clothing Productions)
Ltd (Case 96/80) [1981] ECR 911, [1981]
2 CMLR 24, [1981] 1 WLR 972 *374, 375*

Jia v. Migrationsverket (Case C-1/05) [2007]
ECR I-1 *203*

John Walker & Sons Ltd v. Ministeriet for
Skatter og Afgifter (Case 243/84) [1986]
ECR 875, [1987] 2 CMLR 275 *168*

Johnson v. CAO (Case C-410/92) [1994]
ECR I-5483, [1995] All ER (EC) 258, [1995]
1 CMLR 725, [1995] IRLR 158 *105, 386*

Johnson v. Chief Adjudication Officer (Case
C-31/90) [1991] ECR I-3723 *392*

Johnston v. Chief Constable of the Royal
Ulster Constabulary (Case 222/84) [1986]
ECR 1651, [1986] 3 CMLR 240, [1986]
3 WLR 1038 *73, 83, 106, 383*

Jongeneel Kaas BV v. Netherlands
(Case 237/82) [1984] ECR 483, [1985]
2 CMLR 649 *176, 185*

Kadi (Yassin Abdullah) v, Council and
Commission (Case T-315/01) [2005]
ECR II-3649 *127*
KB v. National Health Service Pensions
Agency and Secretary of State for
Health (Case C-117/01) [2004] ECR I-541
74
Kaefer and Procacci v. France (Cases C-100/89
and C-101/89) [1990] ECR I-4697 *150*
Kalanke v. Frei Hausestadt Bremen
(Case C-450/93) [1995] ECR I-3051,
[1996] All ER (EC) 66, [1996] 1 CMLR 175
384, 385
Kamer van Koophandel en Fabrieken
voor Amsterdam v. Inspire Art Ltd
(Case C-167/01) [2003] ECR I-10155 *233*
Kampffmeyer v. Commission (Cases 5, 7 &
13–24/66) [1967] ECR 245 *143, 145,
146*
Kapferer v. Schlank & Schick (Case C-234/04)
[2006] ECR I-2585 *91*
Keck & Mithouard (Cases C-267 & 268/91)
[1993] ECR I-6097 *46, 178, 181, 183,
184, 194, 239*
Kelderman (Case 130/80) [1981] ECR 517
175, 179
Keller (Case 234/85) [1986] ECR 2897,
[1987] 1 CMLR 875 *84*
Kempf v. Staatsecretaris van Justitie
(Case 139/85) [1986] ECR 1741, [1987]
1 CMLR 764 *217*
Kenny Roland Lyckeskog (Case C-99/00)
[2002] ECR I-4839 *154, 155*
Keurkoop BV v. Nancy Keane Gifts BV
(Case 144/81) [1982] ECR 2853, [1983]
2 CMLR 47 *335*
Klaus Konle v. Austria (Case C-302/97)
[1999] ECR I-3099 *255*
Klopp (Case 107/83) [1984] ECR 2917,
[1985] 1 CMLR 99 *233*
Kloppenburg (Case 70/83) [1984] ECR 1075,
[1985] 1 CMLR 205 *97*
Knoors v. Secretary of State for Economic
Affairs (Case 115/78) [1979] ECR 399,
[1979] 2 CMLR 357 *236*

Köbler v. Austria (Case C-224/01) [2003]
ECR I-10239 *94, 105, 115, 155*
Kolpinghuis Nijmegen (Case 80/86) [1987]
ECR 3969, [1989] 2 CMLR 18 *109*
Konsumentombudsman v. De Agostini
(Cases C-34–36/95) [1997] ECR I-3843,
[1997] All ER (EC) 687, [1998] 1 CMLR 32
182
Konsumentombudsmannen v. Gourmet
International Products AB (GIP)
(Case C-405/98) [2001] ECR I-1795 *182*
Kreil v. Bundesrepublik Deutschland
(Case C-285/98) [2000] ECR I-69, [2002]
1 CMLR 1047 *383*
Krohn & Co. KG v. Commission
(Case 175/84) [1987] ECR 97, [1987]
1 CMLR 745 *146*
Kunqian Catherine Zhu and Man Lavette
Chen v. Secretary of State for the Home
Department (Case C-200/02) [2004]
ECR I-9925 *199*
Kupferberg (Case 104/81) [1982] ECR 3641
[1983] 1 CMLR 1 *107*
Kupferberg (Case 253/83) [1985] ECR 157,
[1987] 1 CMLR 36 *167*
Kwekerij Gebroeders van der Kooy (Cases 67,
68 & 70/85) [1985] ECR 1315, [1989]
2 CMLR 804 *355, 357*

L'Oreal NV v. de Nieuwe AMCK (Case 31/80)
[1980] ECR 3775, [1981] 2 CMLR 235
285
Läärä v. Finland (Case C-124/97) [1999]
ECR I-6067, [2001] 2 CMLR 257 *238*
Laboratoires Pharmaceutiques Bergaderm SA
and Jean-Jacques Goupil v. Commission
(Case C-352/98P) [2000] ECR I-5291
141–144
Lair (Case 39/86) [1988] ECR 3161, [1989]
3 CMLR 545 *198, 224, 251*
Lancôme v. ETOS BV (Case 99/79) [1980]
ECR 2511, [1981] 2 CMLR 164 *285, 286*
Lassalle v. EP (Case 15/63) [1964] ECR 31,
[1964] CMLR 259 *126*
Lawrie-Blum v. Land Baden-Württemberg
(Case 66/85) [1986] ECR 2121, [1987]
3 CMLR 403 *216, 220, 230*
Leendert van Bennekom (Case 227/82)
[1983] ECR 3883, [1985] 2 CMLR 733 *186*

Lehtonen and ASBL Castors Canada Dry
  Namur-Braine v. ASBL Fédération Royale
  Belge des Sociétés de Basketball (Case
  C-176/96) [2000] ECR I-2681, [2000]
  3 CMLR 409) 225
'Les Verts' (Case 294/83) (see Parti Écologiste
  'Les Verts' v. European Parliament
  (Case 294/83))
'Les Verts' (Case 190/84) (see Parti Écologiste
  'Les Verts' v. European Parliament
  (Case 190/84))
Levin v. Staatsecretaris van Justitie
  (Case 53/81) [1982] ECR 1035, [1982]
  2 CMLR 454 216
Lewen v. Lothar Denda (Case C-333/97)
  [1999] ECR I-7243 371
Lopes da Veiga v. Staatsecretaris van Justitie
  (Case 9/88) [1989] ECR 2989, [1991]
  1 CMLR 217 217
Lorenz GmbH v. Germany (Case 120/73)
  [1973] ECR 1471 354
Ludwigshafener Walzmühle Erling KG v.
  Council & Commission (Cases 197 to 200,
  243, 245 and 247/80) [1981] ECR 3211
  146
Luisi & Carbone v. Ministero del Tesoro
  (Cases 286/82 & 26/83) [1984] ECR 377,
  [1985] 3 CMLR 52 246, 248, 253
Luxembourg v. European Parliament
  (Case 230/81) [1983] ECR 255, [1983]
  2 CMLR 726 127
Luxembourg v. European Parliament and
  Council (Case C-168/98) [2000]
  ECR I-9131 236

Macarthys v. Smith (Case 129/79) [1980]
  ECR 1275, [1980] 2 CMLR 205 374
McDermott & Cotter v. Minister of State for
  Social Welfare (Case 286/85) [1987]
  ECR 1452; [1987] 2 CMLR 607 395
Mackprang v. Commission (Case 15/71)
  [1971] ECR 797, [1972] CMLR 52 137
Magill TV Guide Cases (see RTE, BBC & ITP v.
  Commission) (Cases T-69, etc,/89)
Mahlburg v. Land Meckleburg-Vorpommern
  (Case C-207/98) [2000] ECR I-549, [2001]
  3 CMLR 887 380
Maizena GmbH v. Council (Case 139/79)
  [1980] ECR 3393 135

Maria Pupino (Case C-105/03) [2005]
  ECR I-5285 92, 156
Marks & Spencer plc v. David Halsey
  (Her Majesty's Inspector of Taxes)
  (Case C-446/03) [2005] ECR I-10837 233
Marleasing v. La Commercial Internacional
  de Alimentacion (Case C-106/89) [1990]
  ECR I-4135, [1992] 1 CMLR 305 92, 108,
  109
Marschall v. Land Nordrhein Westfalen
  (Case C-409/95) [1997] ECR I-6363,
  [1998] 1 CMLR 547 385
Marshall v. Southampton and South West
  Area Health Authority (Teaching) (No.1)
  (Case 152/84) [1986] CMLR 688, [1986]
  2 WLR 780 105, 108, 382, 386, 394
Marshall v. Southampton and South
  West Area Health Authority (No.2)
  (Case C-271/91) [1993] ECR I-4367;
  [1993] CMLR 293 106, 108, 386
Martinez Sala v. Freistaat Bayern (Case
  C-85/96) [1998] ECR I-2691 196, 197
Martinez, De Gaulle & Others v. EP
  (Cases T-222, 327 and 329/99) [2001]
  ECR II-2823 24
Mary Carpenter v. Secretary of State for the
  Home Department (Case C-60/00) [2002]
  ECR I-6279 73, 239
Masterfoods Ltd v. HB Ice Cream Ltd (Case
  C-344/89) [2000] ECR I-11369 287, 303
Matteucci v. Communauté Française de
  Belgique (Case 235/87) [1988] ECR 5589,
  [1989] 1 CMLR 357 224
Max Mobile (Commission of the European
  Communities v. T-Mobile Austria GmbH)
  (Case C-141/02P) [2005] ECR I-1283 351
Mayr v. Bäckerei und Konditorei Gerhard
  Flöckner OHG (Case C-506/06) [2008]
  ECR I-000 381
Meilicke v. ADV/ORGA F.A. Meyer AG
  (Case C-83/91) [1992] ECR I-4871 152
Melgar v. Ayuntamiento de Los Barrios
  (Case C-438/99) [2001] ECR I-6915 380
Merci Convenzionali Porto di Genova v.
  Siderurgica (Case C-179/90) [1991]
  ECR I-5889, [1994] 4 CMLR 422 347
Metro-Grossmärkte GmbH v. Commission
  (Case 26/76) [1977] ECR 1875, [1978]
  2 CMLR 1 285

Metronome Musik GmbH v. Musik Point Hokamp GmbH (Case C-200/96) [1998] ECR I-1953, [1998] 3 CMLR 919 *334, 343*

Métropole Télévision SA (M6), Antena 3 de Televisión, SA, Gestevisión Telecinco, SAand SIC – Sociedade Independente de Comunicação, SAv Commission (Cases T-185/00, T-216/00, T-299/00, T-300/00) [2002] ECR II-3805 *289*

Michel S. v. Fonds national de reclassement social des handicappés (Case 76/72) [1973] ECR 457 *226*

Michelin (NV Nederlansche Bander-Industrie Michelin) v. Commission (Case 322/81) [1983] ECR 3461, [1985] 1 CMLR 282 *294, 298, 301*

Micro Leader Business v. Commission (Case T-198/98) [1999] ECR II-3989, [2000] All ER (EC) 361, [2000] 4 CMLR 886 *326*

Microsoft Corp. v. Commission (Case T-201/04) [2007] ECR II-0000 *305, 306, 315*

Middleburgh v. Chief Adjudication Officer (Case C-15/90) [1991] ECR I-4655, [1992] 1 CMLR 353 *217*

Milch-Fett-und Eierkontor v. HZA Saarbrucken (Case 29/68) [1969] ECR 165, [1969] CMLR 390 *155*

Ministre de l'Intérieur v. Aitor Oteiza Olazabal (Case C-100/01) [2002] ECR I-10981 *207*

Ministère Public v. Asjes (Cases 209–213/84) [1986] ECR 1425, [1986] 3 CMLR 173 *276*

Ministère Public v. Tournier (Case 395/87) [1989] ECR 2521, [1991] 4 CMLR 248 *339*

Ministère Public of Luxembourg v. Hein, née Muller (Case 101/71) [1971] ECR 723 *349*

Ministero delle Finanze v. In. Co. Ge. '90 (Cases C-10–22/97) [1998] ECR I-6307, [2001] 1 CMLR 800 *91*

Ministero Fiscal v. Bordessa (Cases C-358 & 416/93) [1995] ECR I-361, [1996] 2 CMLR 13 *253, 255*

Miro BV (Case 182/84) [1985] ECR 3731, [1986] 3 CMLR 545 *179*

Molkerei-Zentrale v. Hauptzollamt Paderborn (Case 28/67) [1968] ECR 143, [1968] CMLR 187 *167*

Morson v. The Netherlands (Cases 35 & 36/82) [1982] ECR 3723, [1983] 2 CMLR 221 *221*

Mouvement contre le racisme, l'antisémitisme et la xénophobie ASBL (MRAX) v. Belgian State (Case C-459/99) [2002] ECR I-6591 *204*

MRAX v. Belgian State (see Mouvement contre le racisme, l'antisémitisme et la xénophobie ASBL v. Belgian State)

Mulder v. Commission & Council (Cases C-104/89 & 37/90) [1992] ECR I-3062 *143, 145*

Müller-Fauré v. Onderlinge Waarborgmaatschappij OZ Zorgverzekeringen UA and EEM van Riet v. Onderlinge Waarborgmaatschappij ZAO Zorgverzekeringen (Case C-385/99) [2003] ECR I-4509 *248, 249*

Municipality of Almelo (Case C-393/92) [1994] ECR I-1477 *348*

Maruko v. Versorgungsanstalt der deutschen Bühnen (Case C-267/06) [2008] ECR I-000 *390*

Murphy v. Bord Telecom Eireann (Case 157/86) [1989] ECR 673, [1988] 1 CMLR 879 *374*

Musik Vertrieb Membran (Cases 55 & 57/80) [1981] ECR 147, [1981] 2 CMLR 44 *334*

Musique Diffusion Française SA v. Commission (Case 100–103/80) [1983] ECR 1825, [1983] 3 CMLR 221 *323*

Nakajima All Precision Co. Ltd v. Council of the European Communities (Case C-69/89) [1991] ECR I-2069 *55*

National Panasonic (UK) Ltd v. Commission (Case 136/79) [1980] ECR 2033, [1980] 3 CMLR 169 *73, 320*

National Pensions Office v. Emilienne Jonkman, Hélène Vercheval and Noëlle Permesaen v. Office national des pensions (Cases C-231, 232 and 233/06) [2007] ECR I-5149 *395*

Navas v. Eurest Colectividades SA (Case C-13/05) [2006] ECR I-6467 *390*

Nazli v. Nürnberg (Case C-340/97) [2000] ECR I-957, [2000] All ER (D) 165 *210*

NDC Health GmbH & Co. KG and NDC
  Health Corporation v. Commission of the
  European Communities and IMS Health
  Inc (Case C-481/01) [2002] ECR I-3401
  304
Neath v. Hugh Steeper Ltd (Case C-152/91)
  [1993] ECR I-6935 *371, 373*
Netherlands v. European Parliament
  (Case C-377/98) [2001] ECR I-7079 *85*
Netherlands v. FNV (Case 71/85) [1986]
  ECR 3855 *391*
Netherlands State v. Reed (Case 59/85) [1986]
  ECR 1283, [1987] 2 CMLR 448 *204*
Ninni-Orasche v. Bundesminister für
  Wissenschaft, Verkehr und Kunst
  (Case C-413/01) [2003] ECR I-13187 *217*
Nold (J) KG v. Commission (Case 4/73)
  [1974] ECR 491, [1974] 2 CMLR 338 *71*
Noordwijk's Cement Accord, Re
  (Cases 8–11/66) [1967] ECR 75, [1967]
  CMLR 77 *126*
Nordsee Deutsche Hochseefischerei GmbH
  (Case 102/81) [1982] ECR 1095 *150*
Nungessor KG v. Commission (Case 258/78)
  [1982] ECR 2015, [1983] 1 CMLR 278
  289
NV Algemene Transport-en Expeditie
  Onderneming (see Van Gend en Loos v.
  Nederlandse Administratie der
  Belastingen)
NV IAZ International Belgium v. Commission
  (Case 96/82) [1983] ECR 3369, [1984]
  3 CMLR 276 *277*

Oebel (Case 155/80) [1981] ECR 1993,
  [1980] 3 CMLR 273 *176, 178, 185*
Officier van Just v. De Peijper (Case 104/75)
  [1976] ECR 613, [1976] 2 CMLR 271 *186*
Officier van Justitie v. Koninklijke Kaasfabriek
  Eyssen (Case 53/80) [1981] ECR 409 *190*
Officier van Justitie v. Sandoz BV (Case
  174/82) [1983] ECR 2445 *191*
Omega Spielhallen- und
  Automatenaufstellungs-GmbH v.
  Oberbürgermeisterin der Bundesstadt
  Bonn. (Case C-36/02) [2004] ECR I-9609
  246
ONEM v. Kziber (Case C-18/90) [1991]
  ECR I-199 *107*

Oosthoek's Uitgeversmaatshappij BV
  (Case 286/81) [1982] ECR 4575, [1983]
  3 CMLR 428 *179, 184*
Openbaar Ministerie v. Van Tiggele
  (Case 82/77) [1978] ECR 25, [1978]
  2 CMLR 528 *175, 356*
Organisation des Modjahedines du peuple
  d'Iran v. Council (Case T-228/02) [2006]
  ECR II-4665 *127*
Orkem (formerly CDM) v. Commission
  (Case 374/87) [1989] ECR 3283 *319*
Oscar Bronner GmbH & Co. KG v.
  Mediaprint Zeitungs- und
  Zeitschriftenverlag GmbH & Co. KG,
  Mediaprint Zeitungsvertriebsgesellschaft
  mbH & Co. KG and Mediaprint
  Anzeigengesellschaft mbH & Co. KG
  (Case C-7/97) [1998] ECR I-7791 *305*
Otto BV v. Postbank NV (Case C-60/92)
  [1993] ECR I-5683 *319*
Ottung v. Klee (Case 320/87) [1989]
  ECR 1177, [1990] 4 CMLR 67 *338*

P v. S and Cornwall County Council
  (Case C-13/94) [1996] ECR I-2143, [1996]
  2 CMLR 247 *80, 379, 388*
Pall Corporation v. P.J. Dahlhausen & Co.
  (Case C-238/89) [1990] ECR I-4827 *333*
Paquay v. Société d'architectes Hoet + Minne
  SPRL (Case C-460/06) [2007] ECR I-8511
  381
Pardini v. Ministero con l'Estero
  (Case 338/85) [1988] ECR 2041 *82*
Parke, Davis & Co. Ltd v. Probel (Case 24/67)
  [1968] ECR 55, [1968] CMLR 47 *337*
Parliament v. Council (Case 13/83) [1985]
  ECR 1513; [1986] CMLR 138 *136, 137*
Parliament v. Council (Comitology) (Case
  302/87) [1988] ECR 5615 *41, 128, 136*
Parliament v. Council (Chernobyl)
  (Case C-70/88) [1990] ECR I-2041,
  [1991]
  ECR I-4529, [1992] 1 CMLR 91 *128*
Parliament v. Council (Case C-295/90)
  [1992] ECR I-4193; [1992] 3 CMLR 281
  136
Parti Écologiste 'Les Verts' v. European
  Parliament (Case 294/83) [1986]
  ECR 1339, [1987] 2 CMLR 343 *127*

Parti Écologiste 'Les Verts' v. European
   Parliament (Case 190/84) [1988]
   ECR 1017 *127*
Patricia v. EMI (Cases C-326/92 and C-92/92)
   ECR I-5145; [1993] CMLR 773 *337*
Patrick v. Ministre des Affaires Culturelles
   (Case 11/77) [1977] ECR 1199, [1977]
   2 CMLR 523 *237*
Paul Corbeau (Case C-320/91) [1993]
   ECR I-2533 *349, 350*
Pharmacia and Upjohn v. Paranova
   (Case C-379/97) [1999] ECR I-6927,
   [1999] All ER (EC) 880, [2000]
   3 WLR 303, [2000] 1 CMLR 51 *332*
Philip Morris (Holland) BV v. Commission
   (Case 730/79) [1980] ECR 2671, [1981]
   2 CMLR 321 *357*
Palacios de la Villa v. Commission
   (Case C-411/05) [2007] ECR I-8531 *77*
PB Groenveld BV v. Produktschap voor Vee
   en Vlees (Case 15/79) [1979] ECR 3409,
   [1981] 1 CMLR 207 *184*
Plaumann & Co v. Commission (Case 25/62)
   [1963] ECR 95, [1964] CMLR 29
   128–133, 141
Portuguese Republic v. Council of the
   European Union (Case C-149/96) [1999]
   ECR I-8395 *55*
Prais v. Council (Case 130/75) [1975]
   ECR 1589, [1976] 2 CMLR 708 *73, 80*
Prantl (Case 16/83) [1984] ECR 217, [1985]
   CMLR 572 *175, 179, 188*
Preston and Othes v. Wolverhampton
   Healthcare NHS Trust and Others and
   Dorothy Fletcher and Others v. Midland
   Bank plc (Case C-78/98) [2000] ECR
   I-3201 *376*
Pretore di Salo v. Persons Unknown
   (Case 14/86) [1987] ECR 2545, [1989]
   1 CMLR 71 *150*
Procureur de la République v. Bouhelier
   (Case 53/76) [1977] ECR 197, [1977]
   1 CMLR 436 *184*
Procureur du Roi v. Dassonville (Case 8/74)
   [1974] ECR 837, [1974] 2 CMLR 436
   174–176, 184, 194
Procureur du Roi v. Royer (Case 48/75)
   [1976] ECR 497, [1976] 2 CMLR 619 *205,
   206*

Pronuptia de Paris GmbH v. Pronuptia de
   Paris Irmgard Schillgallis (Case 161/84)
   [1986] ECR 353, [1986] 1 CMLR 414
   269, 279, 284, 288, 289
Pubblico Ministero v. Flavia Manghera
   (Case 59/75) [1976] ECR 91, [1976]
   1 CMLR 557 *169*
Pubblico Ministero v. Ratti (Case 148/78)
   [1979] ECR 1629, [1980] 1 CMLR 96 *104*
Publishers Association v. Commission
   (Case C-56/89R) [1989] ECR I-1693 *322*
Publishers' Association v. Commission (No. 2)
   (Case T-66/89) [1992] ECR II-1995, [1992]
   5 CMLR 120; on appeal (Case C-360/92P)
   [1995] ECR I-23, (1995) 5 CMLR 33 *277,
   279, 322*

Quietlynn v. Southend Borough Council
   (Case C-23/89) [1990] ECR I-3059, [1990]
   3 CMLR 55 *174, 187*

R. v. Bouchereau (Case 30/77) [1977]
   ECR 1999, [1977] 2 CMLR 800 *207, 208*
R. v. HM Treasury, ex parte Daily Mail and
   General Trust plc (Case 81/87) [1988]
   ECR 5483, [1989] 1 All ER 328 *241*
R. v. Henn and Darby (Case 34/79) [1978]
   ECR 3795, [1981] 1 CMLR 246, [1980]
   2 WLR 597 *154, 174, 186, 187*
R. v. HM Treasury, ex parte British
   Telecommunications plc (Case C-392/93)
   [1996] ECR I-1631 *114*
R. v. Immigration Appeal Tribunal ex parte
   Antonissen (Case C-292/89) [1992]
   ECR I-745; [1991] 2 CMLR 373 *205, 217,
   218*
R. v. Intervention Board for Agricultural
   Produce, ex parte Man (Sugar) Ltd
   (Case 181/84) [1985] ECR 2889, [1985]
   3 CMLR 759, [1986] 2 All ER 115 *78*
R. v. Kirk (Case 63/83) [1984] ECR 2689,
   [1984] 3 CMLR 522 *73, 81*
R. v. Minister of Fisheries and Food, ex parte
   Hedley Lomas (Case C-5/94) [1996]
   ECR I-2553 *113, 114*
R. v. Ministry of Agriculture, Fisheries and
   Food, ex parte Agegate Ltd (Case C-3/87R)
   [1989] ECR 4459, [1990] 1 CMLR 366,
   [1990] 3 WLR 226 *94*

R. v. Pieck (Case 157/79) [1980] ECR 2171, [1980] 3 CMLR 220 *205*

R. v. Royal Pharmaceutical Society of Great Britain (Cases 266 & 267/87) [1989] ECR 1295; [1989] 2 CMLR 751 *173, 189*

R. v. Secretary of State for Employment, ex parte Seymour Smith (Case C-167/97) [1999] ECR I-623, [1999] 2 CMLR 273 *376*

R. v. Secretary of State for Health, ex parte Richardson (Case C-137/94) [1995] ECR I-3407, [1995] All ER (EC) 865, [1995] 3 CMLR 376, The Times 27 Oct 1995 *393, 394*

R. v. Secretary of State for Social Security, ex parte EOC (Case C-9/91) [1992] ECR I-4297, [1992] 3 CMLR 233 *394*

R. v. Secretary of State for Social Security, ex parte Graham (Case C-92/94) [1995] ECR I-2521, [1995] 3 CMLR 169 *394*

R. v. Secretary of State for Social Security, ex parte Smithson (Case C-243/90) [1992] ECR I-467, [1992] 1 CMLR 1061 *393*

R. v. Secretary of State for Social Security, ex parte Taylor (Case C-382/98) [1999] ECR I-8955, [2000] All ER (EC) 80, [2000] 1 CMLR 873 *393*

R. v. Secretary of State for Social Security, ex parte Thomas (Case C-328/91) [1993] ECR I-1247, [1993] 3 CMLR 880 *394*

R. v. Secretary of State for Transport, ex parte Factortame (No. 1) (Case C-213/89) [1990] ECR 2433; [1990] 3 CMLR 1 *94, 95, 99, 120*

R. v. Secretary of State for Transport, ex parte Factortame (No. 2) (Case C-213/89) [1990] 3 WLR 818, [1990] 3 CMLR 375 *91, 95, 99*

R. v. Secretary of State for Transport, ex parte Factortame (No. 3) (Case C-221/89R) [1991] ECR I-3905, [1991] 3 CMLR 589 *91, 95, 99, 112, 113, 116, 143*

R. v. Secretary of State for Transport, ex parte Factortame (No. 4) (Case C-46 and 48/93) [1996] ECR I-1029, [1996] 1 CMLR 889 *95, 99, 358*

R. v. Thompson (Case 7/78) [1978] ECR 2247, [1979] 1 CMLR 47 *163, 188*

R (on the application of Dany Bidar) v. London Borough of Ealing and Secretary of State for Education and Skills (Case C-209/03) [2005] ECR I-2119 *198, 205, 224, 251*

R (on the application of Yvonne Watts) v. Bedford Primary Care Trust and Secretary of State for Health (Case C-372/04) [2006] ECR I-4325 *248, 249*

Raznoimport v. Commission (Case 120/83) [1983] ECR 2573 *145*

Rechberger v. Austria (Case C-140/97) [1999] ECR I-3499, [2000] 2 CMLR 1 *114*

Regione Siciliana v. Commission (Case T-190/00) [2003] ECR II-5051 *130*

Reina v. Landeskreditbank Baden-Württemberg (Case 65/81) [1982] ECR 33, [1982] 1 CMLR 744 *223, 228*

Remia Nutricia v. Commission (Case 42/84) [1985] ECR 2545, [1987] 1 CMLR 1 *284*

Renault (see Consorzio Italiano)

Rewe-Zentral AG Bundesmonopolverwaltung für Branntwein (Cassis de Dijon) (Case 120/78) [1979] ECR 649, [1979] 3 CMLR 494 *170, 176–178, 194*

Rewe-Zentralfinanz (Case 33/76) [1976] ECR 1989, [1977] 1 CMLR 533 *325*

Rewe-Zentralfinanz GmbH v. Landwirtschaftskammer (Case 4/75) [1975] ECR 843, [1977] 1 CMLR 599 *189*

Reyners v. Belgian State (Case 2/74) [1974] ECR 631, [1974] 2 CMLR 305 *232*

Rheinmühlen-Düsseldorf v. Einfuhr- und Vorratsstelle für Getreide und Futtermittel (Case 166/73) [1974] ECR 33 *149*

Richards v. Secretary of State for Work and Pensions (Case C-423/04) [2006] ECR I-3585 *394*

Richez-Parise v. Commission (Cases 19 etc./69) [1970] ECR 325 *142*

Rinner-Kuhn v. FWW Spezial Gebäudereinigung GmbH & Co. KG (Case 171/88) [1989] ECR 2743; [1993] 2 CMLR 932 *371, 376*

Roberts v. Tate & Lyle Industries Ltd (Case 151/84) [1986] ECR 703, [1986] 1 CMLR 714, [1986] 2 All ER 602 *382*

Robertson (Case 220/81) [1982] ECR 2349, [1983] 1 CMLR 556 *178*

Roquette Frères v. Commission (Case 26/74) [1976] ECR 677 *146*

Roquette Frères v. Council (Case 138/79) [1980] ECR 3333 *26, 134*

Rosengren (Klas) and Others v. Riksåklagaren (Case C-170/04) [2007] ECR I-4071 *170*

Royal Scholten-Honig (Holdings) Ltd v. Intervention Board for Agricultural Produce ('Isoglucose') (Cases 103 & 145/77) [1978] ECR 2037, [1979] 1 CMLR 675 *79*

RSV Maschinefabrieken & Scheepswerven NV v. Commission (Case 223/85) [1987] ECR 4617, [1989] 2 CMLR 259 *355*

RTE, BBC & ITP v. Commission (Magill TV Guide) (Cases T-69, 70 & 76/89) [1991] ECR II-485; [1991] 4 CMLR 586; on appeal (Case C-241/91P) [1995] ECR I-743 *304, 338, 339*

Rush Portugesa (Case C-113/89) [1990] ECR I-1417, [1991] 2 CMLR 818 *210*

Rutili v. Ministre de l'Intérieure (Case 36/75) [1975] ECR 1219, [1976] 1 CMLR 140 *73, 207*

Ruzius-Wilbrink (Case 102/88) [1989] ECR 4311, [1991] 2 CMLR 216 *393*

SA Alcan v. Commission (Case 69/69) [1970] ECR 385, [1970] CMLR 337 *130*

SA CNL-Sucal NV v. Hag GF AG ('Hag II') (Case C-10/89) [1990] ECR I-3711, [1990] 3 CMLR 571 *335, 336*

Sabbatini v. European Parliament (Case 20/71) [1972] ECR 345 *80*

Sacchi (see Italy v. Sacchi)

Safir v. Skattemyndighten I Dalarnas Lyn (Case C-118/96) [1998] ECR I-1897, [1998] 3 CMLR 739 *254*

Salgoil SpA v. Italian Minister of Trade (Case 13/68) [1968] ECR 453, [1969] CMLR 181 *174*

Salonia v. Poidomani (Case 126/80) [1981] ECR 1563, [1982] 1 CMLR 64 *152*

Samenwerkende Elektriciteits-Produktiebedrijven (SEP) NV v. Commission (Case C-36/92P) [1994] ECR I-1911 *319*

Samenwerkende Elektriciteits-Produktiebedrijven (SEP) v. Commission (Case T-39/90) [1991] ECR II-1497 *319*

Sandoz Prodotti Farmaceutici SpA v. Commission (Case C-277/87) [1990] ECR I-45 *281*

Sanz de Lera and Others (Cases C-163, 165 and 250/94) [1995] ECR I-4821, [1996] 1 CMLR 631 *253–255*

Sayag v. Leduc (Case 5/68) [1968] ECR 395, [1969] CMLR 12 *142*

Schmidberger (Eugen), Internationale Transporte und Planzüge v. Austria (Case C-112/00) [2003] ECR I-5659 *73, 173, 178*

Schneider Electric SA v. Commission (Case T-310/01) [2002] ECR II-4071 *312, 313, 315*

Schutzverband gegen unlauteren Wettbewerb v. TK-Heimdienst Sass GmbH (Case C-254/98) [2000] ECR I-151 *182*

Scrivner (Case 122/84) [1985] ECR 1027, [1987] 3 CMLR 638 *223*

Sebago and Ancienne Maison Dubois v. GB-Unic (Case C-173/98) [1999] ECR I-4103 *333*

Segers (Case 79/85) [1986] ECR 2357, [1987] 2 CMLR 247 *241*

Sgarlata (Case 40/64) [1965] ECR 215, [1966] CMLR 314 *69*

Silhouette Internationale v. Hartlauer (Case C-355/96) [1998] ECR I-4799, [1998] 2 CMLR 953 *333*

Simmenthal v. Amministrazione della Finanze della Stato (Case 70/77) [1978] ECR 1453, [1978] 3 CMLR 670 *153*

Simmenthal v. Italian Minister of Finance (Case 35/76) [1976] ECR 1871, [1977] 2 CMLR 1 *190*

Simmenthal SpA (No 2) (see Amministrazione delle Finanze dello Stato v. Simmenthal SpA)

Simmenthal SpA v. Commission (Case 92/78) [1979] ECR 777, [1980] 1 CMLR 121 *139*

Sirdar v. The Army Board and the Secretary of State for Defence (Case C-273/97) [1999] ECR I-7403 *383*

Sirena srl v. EDA srl (Case 40/70) [1971] ECR 69, [1971] CMLR 260 *337*

Skoma-Lux sro v. Celní ředitelství Olomouc (Case C-161/06) [2007] ECR 0000 *46*

SNUPAT v. High Authority (Cases 42 & 49/59) [1961] ECR 53 *138*

Social Fonds voor de Diamantarbeiders (Cases 2 & 3/69) [1969] ECR 211, [1969] CMLR 335 *165*

Società Italiana Vetro SpA v. Commission (Cases T-68/89, 77–78/89) [1992] ECR II-1403, [1992] 5 CMLR 302 *294*

Société d'Importation Edouard Leclerc-Siplec v. TFI Publicité SA and M6 Publicité SA (Case C-412/93) [1995] ECR I-179, [1995] 3 CMLR 422 *182*

Société d'Insemination Artificielle (Case 271/81) [1983] ECR 2057 *170*

Société Louis Dreyfus et Cie v. Commission (Case C-386/96P) [1998] ECR I-2309, [1999] 1 CMLR 481 *141*

Société pour l'Exportation des Sucres v. Commission (Case 88/76) [1977] ECR 709 *81*

Société Technique Minière (STM) v. Maschinenbau Ulm GmbH (Case 56/65) [1966] ECR 235, [1966] CMLR 357 *279, 281, 289*

Sofrimport SARL v. Commission (Case C-152/88) [1990] ECR I-2477; [1990] 3 CMLR 80 *131, 142*

Solvay & Co. v. Commission (Case 27/88) [1989] ECR 3255; [1991] 4 CMLR 502 *319*

Sonito (Société Nationale Interprofessionnelle de la Tomate and others) v. Commission (Case C-87/89) [1990 ECR I-1981 *119*

Sotgiu v. Deutsche Bundespost (Case 152/73) [1974] ECR 153 *219, 223*

Spain v. Council (Case C-350/92) [1995] ECR I-1985 *62*

Spain v. UK (Case C-145/04) [2006] ECR I-7917 *74, 121, 200*

Spain, Kingdom of Belgium and Italian Republic v. Commission (Cases C-271, 281 and 289/90) [1992] ECR I-5833 *351*

Spijker Kwasten NV v. Commission (Case 231/82) [1983] ECR 2559, [1984] 2 CMLR 284 *131*

SPUC v. Grogan (Case C-159/90) [1991] ECR I-4685; [1991] 3 CMLR 849 *247, 252*

Staatssecretaris van Financiën v. BGM Verkooijen (Case C-35/98) [2000] ECR I-4071 *255*

Star Fruit v. Commission (Case 247/87) [1989] ECR 291, [1990] 1 CMLR 733 *119*

Stauder v. City of Ulm (Case 29/69) [1969] ECR 419, [1970] CMLR 112 *70*

Steenhorst-Neerings v. Bedrijfsvereniging voor Detailhandel (Case C-338/91) [1993] ECR I-5475, [1995] 3 CMLR 323 *105, 386*

Steinhauser v. City of Biarritz (Case 197/84) [1985] ECR 1819, [1986] 1 CMLR 53 *238*

Steinike und Weinleg (Case 78/76) [1977] ECR 595, [1977] 2 CMLR 688 *355*

Steymann v. Staatsecretaris van Justitie (Case 196/87) [1988] ECR 6159, [1989] 1 CMLR 449 *217*

Stichting Greenpeace Council (Greenpeace International) v. Commission (Case C-321/95P) [1998] ECRI-1651, [1998] 3 CMLR 1 *130, 131*

Stoke-on-Trent City Council v. B & Q plc (Case C-169/91) [1992] ECR I-6635, [1993] 1 CMLR 426 *180*

Suiker Unie v. Commission (Sugar Cartel) (Cases 40–48, 50, 54 to 56, 111, 113 & 114/73) [1975] ECR 1163, [1976] 1 CMLR 295 *278, 300*

Surinder Singh (Case C-370/90) [1991] ECR I-4265; [1992] 3 CMLR 358 *221*

Svenska Journalistförbundet v. Council of the European Union (Case T-174/95) [1998] ECR II-2289 *86*

Svensson and Gustavvson v. Ministre de Logements et de L'Urbanisation (Case C-484/93) [1995] ECR I-3955 *253*

Syndicat National des Fabricants Raffineurs d'Huile de Grassage v. Inter-Huiles (Case 172/82) [1983] ECR 555, [1983] 3 CMLR 485 *349*

T. Port GmbH & Co. KG. v. Bundesanstalt für Landwirtschaft und Ernährung (Case C-68/95) [1996] ECR I-6065, [1997] 1 CMLR 1 *150*

Tankstation't Henkste Vof and Boermans
(Cases C-401 & 402/92) [1994]
ECR I-2199, [1995] 3 CMLR 501 *181*

Tasca (Case 65/75) [1976] ECR 291, [1977]
2 CMLR 183 *175*

Tele Danmark A/S v. Handels- og
Kontorfunktionærernes Forbund i
Danmark (HK) (Case C-109/00) [2001]
ECR I-6993 *380*

Ten Oever v. Stichting Bedrijfspensionfonds
(Case C-109/91) [1993] ECR I-4879,
[1995] 2 CMLR 357 *371*

Terrapin v. Terranova (Case 119/75) [1976]
ECR 1039, [1976] 2 CMLR 482 *330*

Tetra Laval BV v. Commission (Case T-5/02)
[2002] ECR II-4381 *312, 313, 315*

Tetra Pak International SA v. Commission
(No.2) (Case C-333/94P) [1996]
ECR I-5951, [1997] 4 CMLR 662 *299*

Tetra Pak Rausing SA v. Commission
(Case T-51/89) *307*

Tetra Pak Rausing SA v. Commission (No 1)
(Case T-51/89) [1990] ECR II-309,
[1991] 4 CMLR 334 *274, 298, 301,
307*

Teuling (Case 30/85) [1987] ECR 2497,
[1988] 3 CMLR 789 *393*

Tezi Textiel v. Commission (Case 59/84)
[1986] ECR 887 *192*

Theodor Kohl KG v. Ringelham and Rennett
SA (Case 177/83) [1984] ECR 3651,
[1985] 3 CMLR 340 *188, 336*

Thetford Corp. v. Fiamma Spa (Case 35/87)
[1988] ECR 3585, [1988] 3 CMLR 549,
[1989] 2 All ER 801 *331*

Thieffry v. Conseil de l'Ordre des Avocats
à la Cour de Paris (Case 71/76) [1977]
ECR 765, [1977] 2 CMLR 373 *236*

Tiercé Ladbroke v. Commission
(Case T-504/93) [1997] ECR II-923,
[1997] 5 CMLR 309 *305*

Timex Corporation v. Council & Commission
(Case 264/82) [1985] ECR 849, [1985]
3 CMLR 550 *129, 137*

Tipp-Ex GmbH v. Commission (Case
C-279/87) [1990] ECR I-261 *281*

Toepfer KG v. Commission (Cases 106 &
107/63) [1965] ECR 405, [1966]
CMLR 111 *130*

Töpfer v. Commission (Case 112/77) [1978]
ECR 1019 *82*

Torfaen Borough Council v. B & Q plc
(Case 145/88) [1989] ECR 3851, [1990]
1 CMLR 337 *78, 180*

Traghetti del Mediterraneo SpA v. Italy
(Case C-173/03) [2006] ECR I-5177 *115*

Transocean Marine Paint Association v.
Commission (Case 17/74) [1974]
ECR 1063, [1979] 2 CMLR 459 *82, 135*

Trojani (Michel) v. Centre Public d'aide
Sociale de Bruxelles (CPAS) (Case
C-456/02) [2004] ECR I-7573 *199, 217,
228*

Trummer and Mayer (Case C-222/97) [1999]
ECR I-1661 *254, 255*

UAPME v. Council (Case T-135/96) [1998]
ECR II-2335, [1998] 3 CMLR 385 *362*

Überseering BV v. Nordic Construction
Company Baumanagement GmbH
(NCC) (Case C-208/00) [2002]
ECR I-9919 *233*

UK v. Council (Case C-84/94) [1996]
ECR I-5755 *85*

Unilever Italia SpA v. Central Food SpA
(Case C-443/98) [2000] ECR I-7535 *110*

Unión de Pequeños Agricultores (UPA)
v. Council (Case C-50/00P) [2002]
ECR I-6677 *130–132*

Union Départmentale des Syndicats
CGT de l'Aishe v. Sidef Conforama
(Case C-312/89) [1991] ECR I-997 *177, 181*

Union Nationale des Entraîneurs et Cadres
Techniques Professionels du Football
(UNECTEF) v. Heylens (Case 222/86)
[1987] ECR 4097; [1989] 1 CMLR 901 *83*

United Brands v. Commission (Case 27/76)
[1978] ECR 207, [1978] 1 CMLR 429
295, 297, 298, 300–303

URBSFA v. Bosman (Case C-415/93) [1995]
ECR I-4921, [1996] 1 CMLR 645 *225*

Ursula Voß v. Land Berlin (Case C-300/06)
[2007] ECR I-000 *376*

Van Ameyde v. UCI (Case 90/76) [1977]
ECR 1091, [1977] 2 CMLR 478 *346*

Van Binsbergen v. Bestuur van de
Bedrijfsvereniging voor de

Metaalnijverheid (Case 33/74) [1974]
ECR 1299, [1975] 1 CMLR 298 *239–241*

Van den Akker v. Stichting Shell
Pensioenfonds (Case C-28/93) [1994]
ECR I-4527, [1995] 3 CMLR 543 *373*

Van den Bergh Foods Ltd v. Commission
(Case T-65/98R) [2003] ECR II-4653 *303*

Van der Haar (Case 177/82) [1984] ECR
1797, [1985] CMLR 572 *175*

Van Duyn v. Home Office (Case 41/74)
[1974] ECR 1337, [1975] 1 CMLR 1, [1975]
2 WLR 760 *104, 116, 207–209, 214*

Van Gend en Loos v. Nederlandse
Administratie der Belastingen
(Case 26/62) [1963] ECR I, [1963]
CMLR 105 *46, 65, 90, 100, 102, 103,
116, 164, 171*

Van Gend en Loos NV and Expeditiededriff
Wim Bosman BV v. Commission (Cases
98/83 & 230/83) [1984] ECR 3763 *82*

Van Landewyck v. Commission (Cases
209–215 and 218/78) [1980] ECR 3125,
[1981] 3 CMLR 134 *288*

Van Tiggele (see Openbaar Ministerie
Case 82/77)

Van Zuylen Frères v. Hag AG ('Hag I')
(Case 192/73) [1974] ECR 731, [1974]
2 CMLR 127 *335*

Van Zuylen Frères v. Hag AG ('Hag II') (see SA
CNL-Sucal NV)

Vanbraekel and Others v. Alliance nationale
des mutualités chrétiennes (ANMC) (Case
C-368/98) [2001] ECR I-5363 *248, 249*

Varec SA v. Belgian State (Case C-450/06)
[2008] ECR 000 *77*

Verband Sozialer Wettbewerb eV v. Clinique
Laboratoires SNC (Case C-315/92) [1994]
ECR I-317 *183*

Verbond van Nederlandse Ondernemingen
(Case 51/76) [1977] ECR 113 *105*

Verein Gegen Unwesen in Handel und
Gewerbe Köln v. Mars GmbH (Case
C-470/93) [1995] ECR I-1923, [1995]
3 CMLR 1 *183*

Vergani v. Agenzia delle Entrate, Ufficio di
Arona (Case C-207/04) [2005] ECR I-7453
381

Vereinigte Familiapress Zeitungsverlags-
und vertriebs GmbH v. Heinrich Bauer

Verlag (Case C-368/95) [1997] ECR I-3689
178

Vereniging van Cementhandelaren v.
Commission (Case 8/72) [1972] ECR 977,
[1973] CMLR 7 *277, 279*

Viho Europe BV v. Commission (Case
C-73/95P) [1996] ECR I-5457 *277*

Vitamins Case (see Hoffman-La Roche
(Case 85/76))

Vlassopoulos v. Ministerium für Justiz
(Case C-340/89) [1991] ECR I-2357,
[1993] 2 CMLR 221 *240*

Völk v. Etablissements Vervaecke SPRi
(Case 5/69) [1969] ECR 193, [1969]
CMLR 273 *282*

Volvo AB v. Eric Veng (Case 238/87) [1988]
ECR 6211, [1989] 4 CMLR 122 *335, 338*

Von Colson v. Land Nordrhein-Westfalen
(Case 14/83) [1984] ECR 1891, [1986]
2 CMLR 430 *105, 108, 110, 116, 386*

Vroege v. NCIV Institute voor
Volkshuisvesting (Case C-57/93) [1994]
ECR I-4541 *373, 376*

Wagner Miret v. Fonds de Garantie Salarial
(Case C-334/92) [1993] ECR I-6911 *111*

Walloon Regional Executive & Glaverbell
SA v. Commission (Case 67/87) [1989]
3 CMLR 771 *357*

Walrave and Koch v. Association Union
Cycliste Internationale (Case 36/74)
[1974] ECR 1405, [1975] 1 CMLR 320
215

Walter Rau Lebensmittelwerke v. BALM
(Cases 133–136/85) [1987] ECR 2289,
[1987] 12 ELRev. 451 *79*

Walter Rau Lebensmittelwerke v. Commission
(Cases 279, 280, 285 and 286/84) [1987]
ECR 1069, [1988] 2 CMLR 704 *79*

Walter Rau Lebensmittelwerke v. De Smedt
PVBA (Case 261/81) [1982] ECR 3961
177

Warner Brothers v. Cristiansen (Case 158/86)
[1988] ECR 2605, [1990] 3 CMLR 684
334

Watson and Belmann (Case 118/75) [1976]
ECR 1185, [1976] 2 CMLR 552 *246*

Watts v. Bedford Primary Care Trust (see
R (on the application of Yvonne Watts) v.

Bedford Primary Care Trust and Secretary of State for Health)
Webb (Case 279/80) [1981] ECR 3305, [1982] 1 CMLR 719 *238*
Webb v. EMO (Case C-2/93) [1994] ECR I-3567; [1994] 2 CMLR 729 *109, 154, 380*
Werner A Bock KG v. Commission (Case 62/70) [1971] ECR 897, [1972] CMLR 60 *136*
Windsurfing International Inc. v. Commission (Case 193/83) [1986] ECR 611, [1987] 3 CMLR 489 *279, 338*
Wöhrmann v. Commission (Cases 31 & 33/62) [1962] ECR 501, [1963] CMLR 152 *138*
Wood Pulp (Re Wood Pulp Cartel: A Ahlstrom Oy v. EC Commission) (Cases 89, 104, 114, 116–117, 125–129/85) [1988] ECR 5193, [1988] 4 CMLR 901, [1994] ECR I-99, [1993] 4 CMLR 407, [1985] 3 CLR 474 *282*
Worringham & Humphreys v. Lloyds Bank Ltd (Case 69/80) [1981] ECR 767, [1981] 2 CMLR 1, [1981] 1 WLR 950, [1981] 2 All ER 434 *370, 374*

Württembergische Milchverwertung-Südmilch AG v. Ugliola (Case 15/69) [1969] ECR 363, [1970] CMLR 194 *223*

Züchner v. Bayerische Vereinsbank (Bank charges) (Case 172/80) [1981] ECR 2021, [1982] 1 CMLR 313 *278, 348*
Zuckerfabrik Suderdithmarschen AG v. Hauptzollamt Itzehoe (Cases C-143/88 and C-92/89) [1991] ECR I-415, [1995] 3 CMLR 1 *153, 155*
Zhu and Chen (see Kunqian Catherine Zhu and Man Lavette Chen v. Secretary of State for the Home Department)

(EHRR) Table of Cases in the Court of Human Rights

Bosphorus Hava Yollari Turizm Ve Ticaret Anonim Sirketi v. Ireland (Application 45036/98) (2005) 19 BHRC 299, [2005] ECHR 45036/98 *74, 75*

Goodwin v. UK (1996) 22 EHRR 123 *74*

Matthews v. UK (1999) 28 EHHR 361 *74, 121*

Table of cases in the Court of Justice and the Court of First Instance (numerical)

Court of Justice Numerical Cases

1/54 French Republic v. High Authority [1954] ECR 1 *135*

15/57 Chasse [1957 & 1958] ECR 211 *78*

42 & 49/59 SNUPAT v. High Authority [1961] ECR 53 *138*

7/61 Commission v. Italy (Re Ban on Pork Imports, 'Pigmeat' case) [1961] ECR 317, [1962] CMLR 39 *126, 174*

14/61 Hoogovens v. High Authority [1962] ECR 253, [1963] CMLR 73 *69*

16 & 17/62 Confédération Nationale des Productuers de Fruits et Légumes v. Council [1962] ECR 471, [1963] CMLR 160 *59, 128*

24/62 Germany v. Commission (Re Tariff Quotas on Wine) [1963] ECR 63, [1963] CMLR 347 *134*

25/62 Plaumann & Co v. Commission [1963] ECR 95, [1964] CMLR 29 *128–133, 141*

26/62 Van Gend en Loos v. Nederlandse Administratie der Belastingen [1963] ECR I, [1963] CMLR 105 *46, 65, 90, 100, 102, 103, 116, 164, 171*

28–30/62 Da Costa en Schaake NV v. Nederlandse Belastingadministratie [1963] ECR 1, [1963] CMLR 10 *153, 155*

31 & 33/62 Wöhrmann v. Commission [1962] ECR 501, [1963] CMLR 152 *138*

15/63 Lassalle v. EP [1964] ECR 31, [1964] CMLR 259 *126*

75/63 Hoekstra (née Unger) v. BBDA [1964] ECR 177, [1964] CMLR 319 *216, 227*

90 & 91/63 Commission v. Luxembourg and Belgium [1965] ECR 625; [1965] CMLR 58 *164*

106 & 107/63 Toepfer KG v. Commission [1965] ECR 405, [1966] CMLR 111 *130*

6/64 Costa v. Ente Nazionale per l'Energia Elettrica (ENEL) [1964] ECR 585, [1964] CMLR 425 *65, 88, 90, 92, 100, 154, 169, 171*

40/64 Sgarlata [1965] ECR 215, [1966] CMLR 314 *69*

56 & 58/64 Consten and Grundig v. Commission [1966] ECR 299, [1966] CMLR 418 *128, 136, 280, 281, 288, 329, 337*

32/65 Italy v. Council and Commission [1966] ECR 389, [1969] CMLR 39 *138*

44/65 Hessische Knappschaft v. Maison Singer et Fils [1965] ECR 965, [1966] CMLR 82 *138*

48/65 Alfons Lütticke GmbH v. Commission [1966] ECR 19, [1966] CMLR 378 *118, 137, 145*

56/65 Société Technique Minière (STM) v. Maschinenbau Ulm GmbH [1966] ECR 235, [1966] CMLR 357 *279, 281, 289*

5, 7 & 13–24/66 Kampffmeyer v. Commission [1967] ECR 245 *143, 145, 146*

8–11/66 Noordwijk's Cement Accord, Re [1967] ECR 75, [1967] CMLR 77 *126*

24/67 Parke, Davis & Co. Ltd v. Probel [1968] ECR 55, [1968] CMLR 47 *337*

27/67 Fink Frucht GmbH [1968] ECR 223, [1968] CMLR 228, [1989] 2 CMLR 751, [1989] 2 All ER 758 *168*

28/67 Molkerei-Zentrale v. Hauptzollamt Paderborn [1968] ECR 143, [1968] CMLR 187 *167*

5/68 Sayag v. Leduc [1968] ECR 395, [1969] CMLR 12 *142*

7/68 Commission v. Italy (Re Export Tax on Art Treasures) [1968] ECR 423, [1969] CMLR 1 *163, 165, 171, 191, 194*

10 & 18/68 Eridiana v. Commission [1969] ECR 459 *133*

13/68 Salgoil SpA v. Italian Minister of Trade [1968] ECR 453, [1969] CMLR 181 *174*

24/68 Commission v. Italy (Re Statistical Levy) [1969] ECR 193, [1971] CMLR 611 *165*

29/68 Milch-Fett-und Eierkontor v. HZA Saarbrucken [1969] ECR 165, [1969] CMLR 390 *155*

2 & 3/69 Social Fonds voor de Diamantarbeiders [1969] ECR 211, [1969] CMLR 335 *165*

4/69 Alfons Lütticke GmbH v. Commission [1971] ECR 325 *141, 142*

5/69 Völk v. Etablissements Vervaecke SPRi [1969] ECR 193, [1969] CMLR 273 *282*

6 & 11/69 Commission v. France [1969] ECR 523, [1970] CMLR 43 *133*

15/69 Württembergische Milchverwertung-Südmilch AG v. Ugliola [1969] ECR 363, [1970] CMLR 194 *223*

19 etc./69 Richez-Parise v. Commission [1970] ECR 325 *142*

29/69 Stauder v. City of Ulm [1969] ECR 419, [1970] CMLR 112 *70*

48/69, 49/69, 51–57/69 Imperial Chemical Industries Ltd v. Commission (Dyestuffs) [1972] ECR 619, [1972] CMLR 557 *277, 278, 282, 319*

69/69 SA Alcan v. Commission [1970] ECR 385, [1970] CMLR 337 *130*

9/70 Grad v. Finanzamt Traustein [1970] ECR 825, [1971] CMLR *104*

11/70 International Handelsgesellschaft GmbH [1970] ECR 1125, [1972] CMLR 255 *70, 71, 77, 90, 91, 100*

15/70 Chevalley v. Commission [1970] ECR 975 *136*

22/70 Commission v. Council (Re European Road Transport Agreement (ERTA)) [1971] ECR 263, [1971] CMLR 335 *61, 62, 126, 134*

40/70 Sirena srl v. EDA srl [1971] ECR 69, [1971] CMLR 260 *337*

41–44/70 International Fruit NV v. Commission (No.1) [1971] ECR 441, [1975] 2 CMLR 515 *59, 129*

62/70 Werner A Bock KG v. Commission [1971] ECR 897, [1972] CMLR 60 *136*

78/70 Deutsche Grammophon Gesellschaft GmbH v. Metro-SB-Grossmärkte GmbH & Co. KG [1971] ECR 487, [1971] CMLR 631 *330*

80/70 Defrenne v. Belgian State (No.1) [1971] ECR 445, [1974] CMLR 494 *372*

5/71 Aktien-Zuckerfabrik Schöppenstedt v. Council [1971] ECR 975 *142, 143*

15/71 Mackprang v. Commission [1971] ECR 797, [1972] CMLR 52 *137*

20/71 Sabbatini v. European Parliament [1972] ECR 345 *80*

22/71 Béguelin Import Co. v. GL Export-Import SA [1971] ECR 949, [1972] CMLR 81 *277, 282*

96/71 Haegmann Sprl v. Commission [1972] ECR 1005; [1973] CMLR 365 *146*

101/71 Ministère Public of Luxembourg v. Hein, née Muller [1971] ECR 723 *349*

1/72 Frilli v. Belgian State [1972] ECR 457, [1973] CMLR 386 *79, 228*

6/72 Europembellage Corporation and Continental Can v. Commission [1973] ECR 215, [1973] CMLR 199 *294, 296, 300–302, 307*

8/72 Vereniging van Cementhandelaren v. Commission [1972] ECR 977, [1973] CMLR 7 *277, 279*

21–24/72 International Fruit Company NV v. Produktschap voor Groensten en Fruit (No.3) [1972] ECR 1219, [1975] 2 CMLR 1 *55, 107*

70/72 Capalonga v. Azienda Articola Maya [1973] ECR 77, [1973] CMLR *166*

76/72 Michel S. v. Fonds national de reclassement social des handicappés [1973] ECR 457 *226*

81/72 Commission v. Council [1973] ECR 575, [1973] CMLR 639 *136*

2/73 Geddo v. Ente Nazionale Risi [1973] ECR 865, [1974] 1 CMLR 13 *174*

4/73 Nold (J) KG v. Commission [1974] ECR 491, [1974] 2 CMLR 338 *71*

6 & 7/73 Instituto Chemicoterapico Italiano SpA and Commercial Solvent Corporation v. Commission [1974] ECR 223, [1974] 1 CMLR 309 *298, 307*

40–48, 50, 54 to 56, 111, 113 & 114/73 Suiker Unie v. Commission (Sugar Cartel) [1975] ECR 1163, [1976] 1 CMLR 295 *278, 300*

120/73 Lorenz GmbH v. Germany [1973] ECR 1471 *354*

127/73 BRT v. SABAM [1974] ECR 51 & 313, [1974] 2 CMLR 238 *274, 303, 317, 325, 348*

152/73 Sotgiu v. Deutsche Bundespost [1974] ECR 153 *219, 223*

155/73 Italy v. Sacchi [1974] ECR 409, [1974] 2 CMLR 177 *102, 170, 276, 345, 349*

166/73 Rheinmühlen-Düsseldorf v. Einfuhr- und Vorratsstelle für Getreide und Futtermittel [1974] ECR 33 *149*

167/73 Commission v. France (Re French Merchant Seamen) [1974] ECR 359, [1974] 2 CMLR 216 *120, 222*

169/73 Compagnie Continentale v. Council [1975] ECR 177, [1975] 1 CMLR 578 *145*

173/73 Italy v. Commission (Re Aids to the Textile Industry) [1974] ECR 709, [1974] 2 CMLR 593 *355*

181/73 Haegeman v. Belgium [1974] ECR 449, [1975] 1 CMLR 515 *55*

192/73 Van Zuylen Frères v. Hag AG ('Hag I') [1974] ECR 731, [1974] 2 CMLR 127 *335*

2/74 Reyners v. Belgian State [1974] ECR 631, [1974] 2 CMLR 305 *232*

8/74 Procureur du Roi v. Dassonville [1974] ECR 837, [1974] 2 CMLR 436 *174–176, 184, 194*

9/74 Casagrande v. Landeshauptstadt München [1970] ECR 773, [1974] 2 CMLR 423 *226*

15/74 Centrafarm BV v. Sterling Drug Inc. [1974] ECR 1147, [1974] 2 CMLR 480 *331, 332*

16/74 Centrafarm BV v. Winthrop BV [1974] ECR 1183, [1974] 2 CMLR 480 *331, 332, 339*

17/74 Transocean Marine Paint Association v. Commission [1974] ECR 1063, [1979] 2 CMLR 459 *82, 135*

21/74 Airola v. Commission [1975] ECR 221 *80*

26/74 Roquette Frères v. Commission [1976] ECR 677 *146*

33/74 Van Binsbergen v. Bestuur van de Bedrijfsvereniging voor de Metaalnijverheid [1974] ECR 1299, [1975] 1 CMLR 298 *239–241*

36/74 Walrave and Koch v. Association Union Cycliste Internationale [1974] ECR 1405, [1975] 1 CMLR 320 *215*

41/74 Van Duyn v. Home Office [1974] ECR 1337, [1975] 1 CMLR 1, [1975] 2 WLR 760 *104, 116, 207–209, 214*

67/74 Bonsignore v. Oberstadtdirektor of the City of Cologne [1975] ECR 297, [1975] 1 CMLR 472 *207, 208*

71/74 FRUBO v. Commission [1975] ECR 563, [1975] 2 CMLR 123 *275*

74/74 CNTA SA v. Commission [1975] ECR 533, [1977] 1 CMLR 171, [1976] ECR 797 *82, 145*

78/74 Deuka v. EVGE [1975] ECR 421, [1975] 2 CMLR 28 *81*

2/75 EVGF v. Mackprang [1975] ECR 607, [1977] 1 CMLR 198 *82*

4/75 Rewe-Zentralfinanz GmbH v. Landwirtschaftskammer [1975] ECR 843, [1977] 1 CMLR 599 *189*

32/75 Fiorini v. SNCF [1975] ECR 1085, [1976] 1 CMLR 573 *223, 224*

36/75 Rutili v. Ministre de l'Intérieure [1975] ECR 1219, [1976] 1 CMLR 140 *73, 207*

43/75 Defrenne v. SA Belge de Navigation Aérienne (SABENA) (No.2) [1976] ECR 455, [1976] 2 CMLR 98 *81, 103, 369, 370*

48/75 Procureur du Roi v. Royer [1976] ECR 497, [1976] 2 CMLR 619 *205, 206*

51/75 EMI v. CBS [1976] ECR 811, [1976] 2 CMLR 235 *336*

59/75 Pubblico Ministero v. Flavia Manghera [1976] ECR 91, [1976] 1 CMLR 557 *169*

65/75 Tasca [1976] ECR 291, [1977] 2 CMLR 183 *175*

104/75 Officier van Just v. De Peijper [1976] ECR 613, [1976] 2 CMLR 271 *186*

118/75 Watson and Belmann [1976] ECR 1185, [1976] 2 CMLR 552 *246*

119/75 Terrapin v. Terranova [1976] ECR 1039, [1976] 2 CMLR 482 *330*

127/75 Bobie v. HZA Aachen-Nord [1976] ECR 1079 *169*

130/75 Prais v. Council [1975] ECR 1589, [1976] 2 CMLR 708 *73, 80*

13/76 Dona v. Mantero [1976] ECR 1333, [1976] 1 CMLR 26 *225*

26/76 Metro-Grossmärkte GmbH v. Commission [1977] ECR 1875, [1978] 2 CMLR 1 *285*

27/76 United Brands v. Commission [1978] ECR 207, [1978] 1 CMLR 429 *295, 297, 298, 300–303*

33/76 Rewe-Zentralfinanz [1976] ECR 1989, [1977] 1 CMLR 533 *325*

35/76 Simmenthal v. Italian Minister of Finance [1976] ECR 1871, [1977] 2 CMLR 1 *190*

41/76 Donckerwolcke v. Procureur de la République [1976] ECR 1921, [1977] 2 CMLR 535 *192*

46/76 Bauhuis v. Netherlands [1977] ECR 5 *166*

51/76 Verbond van Nederlandse Ondernemingen [1977] ECR 113 *105*

53/76 Procureur de la République v. Bouhelier [1977] ECR 197, [1977] 1 CMLR 436 *184*

63/76 Inzirillo v. Caisse d'allocations familiales [1976] ECR 2057, [1978] 3 CMLR 596 *223*

64 & 113/76, 167 & 239/78, 27, 28 & 45/79 Dumortier Fils SA v. Council [1979] ECR 3091, [1982] ECR 1733 *145*

71/76 Thieffry v. Conseil de l'Ordre des Avocats à la Cour de Paris [1977] ECR 765, [1977] 2 CMLR 373 *236*

74/76 Ianelli & Volpi SpA v. Meroni [1977] ECR 557, [1977] 2 CMLR 688 *174, 354, 357*

77/76 Fratelli Cucchi v. Avez SpA [1977] ECR 987 *166*

78/76 Steinike und Weinleg [1977] ECR 595, [1977] 2 CMLR 688 *355*

83 & 94/76, 4, 15 and 40/77 Bayerische HNL Vermehrungsbetriebe GmbH & Co KG v. Council & Commission [1978] ECR 1209, [1978] 3 CMLR 566 *112, 142, 143*

85/76 Hoffmann-La Roche & Co. AG v. Commission (Vitamins Case) [1979] ECR 461, [1979] 3 CMLR 211 *295, 297, 298, 300, 301, 303*

88/76 Société pour l'Exportation des Sucres v. Commission [1977] ECR 709 *81*

90/76 Van Ameyde v. UCI [1977] ECR 1091, [1977] 2 CMLR 478 *346*

105/76 Interzuccheri v. Ditta Rezzano e Cassava [1977] ECR 1029 *166*

11/77 Patrick v. Ministre des Affaires Culturelles [1977] ECR 1199, [1977] 2 CMLR 523 *237*

30/77 R. v. Bouchereau [1977] ECR 1999, [1977] 2 CMLR 800 *207, 208*

31/77 & 53/77 Commission v. United Kingdom [1977] ECR 921; [1977] 2 CMLR 359 *122*

70/77 Simmenthal v. Amministrazione della Finanze della Stato [1978] ECR 1453, [1978] 3 CMLR 670 *153*

77/77 BP v. Commission [1978] ECR 1513, [1978] 3 CMLR 174 *300*

82/77 Openbaar Ministerie v. Van Tiggele [1978] ECR 25, [1978] 2 CMLR 528 *175, 356*

102/77 Hoffmann-La Roche [1978] ECR 1139, [1978] 3 CMLR 217 *331, 332*

103 & 145/77 Royal Scholten-Honig (Holdings) Ltd v. Intervention Board for Agricultural Produce ('Isoglucose') [1978] ECR 2037, [1979] 1 CMLR 675 *79*

106/77 Amministrazione delle Finanze dello Stato v. Simmenthal SpA [1978] ECR 629; [1978] 3 CMLR 263 91

112/77 Töpfer v. Commission [1978] ECR 1019 82

116 & 124/77 Amylum v. Council & Commission [1979] ECR 3497, [1982] 2 CMLR 590 143

148/77 Hansen [1978] ECR 1787, [1979] 1 CMLR 604 170

149/77 Defrenne v. Société Anonyme Belge de Navigation Aérienne Sabena [1978] ECR 1365 378

156/77 Commission v. Belgium [1978] ECR 1881 122, 133, 138

3/78 Centrafarm BV v. American Home Products Corporation [1978] ECR 1823, [1979] 1 CMLR 326 331, 332

7/78 R. v. Thompson [1978] ECR 2247, [1979] 1 CMLR 47 163, 188

22/78 Hugin Kassaregister AB v. Commission [1979] ECR 1869, [1979] 3 CMLR 345 298

30/78 Distillers Co. Ltd v. Commission [1980] ECR 2229, [1980] 3 CMLR 121 134, 283

86/78 Grandes Distilleries Peureux v. Directeur des Services Fiscaux (No.1) [1979] ECR 897, [1980] 3 CMLR 337 167, 170

92/78 Simmenthal SpA v. Commission [1979] ECR 777, [1980] 1 CMLR 121 139

115/78 Knoors v. Secretary of State for Economic Affairs [1979] ECR 399, [1979] 2 CMLR 357 236

119/78 Grandes Distilleries (No.2) [1979] ECR 975, [1980] 3 CMLR 337 170

120/78 Rewe-Zentral AG Bundesmonopolverwaltung für Branntwein (Cassis de Dijon) [1979] ECR 649, [1979] 3 CMLR 494 170, 176–178, 194

125/78 GEMA v. Commission [1979] ECR 3173, [1980] 2 CMLR 177 137, 337

128/78 Commission v. United Kingdom (Re Tachographs) [1979] ECR 419, [1979] 2 CMLR 45 119

141/78 France v. United Kingdom (Re Fishing Net Mesh Sizes) [1979] ECR 2923, [1980] 1 CMLR 735 121

148/78 Pubblico Ministero v. Ratti [1979] ECR 1629, [1980] 1 CMLR 96 104

153/78 Commission v. Germany (Meat Preparations) [1979] ECR 2555, [1980] 1 CMLR 198 188

170/78 Commission v. United Kingdom (Re Excise Duties on Wine) [1980] ECR 417, [1980] 1 CMLR 716, [1983] CMLR 512 168

207/78 Even [1979] ECR 2019, [1980] 2 CMLR 71 223, 228

209–215 and 218/78 Van Landewyck v. Commission [1980] ECR 3125, [1981] 3 CMLR 134 288

230/78 Eridiana v. Minister of Agriculture and Forestry [1979] ECR 2749 103

232/78 Commission v. France (Re Lamb Wars) [1979] ECR 2729; [1980] 1 CMLR 418 120

258/78 Nungessor KG v. Commission [1982] ECR 2015, [1983] 1 CMLR 278 289

261 & 262/78 Interquell Starke-Chemie GmbH & Co. KG v. Commission [1979] ECR 3045 145

15/79 PB Groenveld BV v. Produktschap voor Vee en Vlees [1979] ECR 3409, [1981] 1 CMLR 207 184

34/79 R. v. Henn and Darby [1978] ECR 3795, [1981] 1 CMLR 246, [1980] 2 WLR 597 154, 174, 186, 187

44/79 Hauer v. Rheinland-Pfalz [1979] ECR 3737, [1980] 3 CMLR 42 73

62/79 Coditel v. Ciné Vog [1980] ECR 881, [1981] 2 CMLR 362 246

73/79 Commission v. Italy (Re Reimbursement of Sugar Storage Costs) [1979] ECR 3837, [1980] 2 CMLR 647 166

90/79 Commission v. France (Re Levy on Reprographic Machines) [1981] ECR 283, [1981] 3 CMLR 1 167

99/79 Lancôme v. ETOS BV [1980] ECR 2511, [1981] 2 CMLR 164 285, 286

104/79 Foglia v. Novella (No.1) [1980] ECR 745, [1981] 1 CMLR 45 152

129/79 Macarthys v. Smith [1980] ECR 1275, [1980] 2 CMLR 205 374

136/79 National Panasonic (UK) Ltd v.
Commission [1980] ECR 2033, [1980]
3 CMLR 169 *73, 320*

138/79 Roquette Frères v. Council [1980]
ECR 3333 *26, 134*

139/79 Maizena GmbH v. Council [1980]
ECR 3393 *135*

149/79 Commission v. Belgium (Re Public
Employees) [1980] ECR 3881, [1981]
2 CMLR 413 *219*

155/79 Australian Mining & Smelting Europe
Ltd v. Commission [1982] ECR 1575,
[1982] 2 CMLR 264 *84, 321*

157/79 R. v. Pieck [1980] ECR 2171, [1980]
3 CMLR 220 *205*

730/79 Philip Morris (Holland) BV v.
Commission [1980] ECR 2671, [1981]
2 CMLR 321 *357*

788/79 Gilli v. Andres [1980] ECR 2071,
[1981] 1 CMLR 146 *178*

789 & 790/79 Calpack v. Commission [1980]
ECR 1949, [1981] 1 CMLR 26 *128*

792/79R Camera Care v. Commission [1980]
ECR 119, [1980] 1 CMLR 334 *321, 322*

27/80 Fietje [1980] ECR 3839, [1981] 3
CMLR 722 *178*

31/80 L'Oreal NV v. de Nieuwe AMCK [1980]
ECR 3775, [1981] 2 CMLR 235 *285*

53/80 Officier van Justitie v. Koninklijke
Kaasfabriek Eyssen [1981] ECR 409 *190*

55 & 57/80 Musik Vertrieb Membran [1981]
ECR 147, [1981] 2 CMLR 44 *334*

66/80 ICI v. Italian Financial Administration
[1981] ECR 1191, [1983] 2 CMLR 593
156

69/80 Worringham & Humphreys v. Lloyds
Bank Ltd [1981] ECR 767, [1981] 2 CMLR
1, [1981] 1 WLR 950, [1981] 2 All ER 434
370, 374

96/80 Jenkins v. Kingsgate (Clothing
Productions) Ltd [1981] ECR 911, [1981]
2 CMLR 24, [1981] 1 WLR 972 *374, 375*

100–103/80 Musique Diffusion Française SA
v. Commission [1983] ECR 1825, [1983]
3 CMLR 221 *323*

113/80 Commission v. Ireland (Re Restrictions
on Importation of Souvenirs) [1981]
ECR 1625, [1982] 1 CMLR 706 *186*

115/80 Demont v. Commission [1981]
ECR 3147 *84*

126/80 Salonia v. Poidomani [1981]
ECR 1563, [1982] 1 CMLR 64 *152*

130/80 Kelderman [1981] ECR 517 *175,
179*

138/80 Borker [1980] ECR 1975, [1980]
3 CMLR 273 *150*

155/80 Oebel [1981] ECR 1993, [1980]
3 CMLR 273 *176, 178, 185*

172/80 Züchner v. Bayerische Vereinsbank
(Bank charges) [1981] ECR 2021, [1982]
1 CMLR 313 *278, 348*

188–190/80 France, Italy and the United
Kingdom v. Commission (the
Transparency Directive Case) [1982]
ECR 2545, [1983] 3 CMLR 144 *346, 350*

197 to 200, 243, 245 and 247/80
Ludwigshafener Walzmühle Erling KG v.
Council & Commission [1981] ECR 3211
146

244/80 Foglia v. Novella (No.2) [1981]
ECR 304, [1982] 1 CMLR 585 *152*

246/80 Broekmeulen v. Huisarts Registratie
Commissie [1981] ECR 2311, [1982]
1 CMLR 91 *150, 236, 237*

279/80 Webb [1981] ECR 3305, [1982]
1 CMLR 719 *238*

8/81 Becker v. Finansamt Munster Innenstadt
[1982] ECR 53; [1982] 1 CMLR 499 *106*

12/81 Garland v. British Rail Engineering
Limited [1982] ECR 359 *370*

19/81 Burton v. British Railways Board [1982]
ECR 555, [1982] 2 CMLR 136, [1982]
3 WLR 387, [1982] 3 All ER 537 *381, 382,
394*

28/81 Commission v. Italy [1981] ECR 2577
118, 119

53/81 Levin v. Staatsecretaris van Justitie
[1982] ECR 1035, [1982] 2 CMLR 454
216

58/81 Commission v. Luxembourg [1982]
ECR 2175; [1982] 3 CMLR 482 *377*

60/81 IBM v. Commission [1981] ECR 2639,
[1981] 3 CMLR 635 *126*

61/81 Commission v. United Kingdom
(Re Equal Pay for Equal Work) [1982]
ECR 2601 *377*

65/81 Reina v. Landeskreditbank Baden-Württemberg [1982] ECR 33, [1982] 1 CMLR 744 *223, 228*

95/81 Commission v. Italy [1982] ECR 2187 *186*

102/81 Nordsee Deutsche Hochseefischerei GmbH [1982] ECR 1095 *150*

104/81 Kupferberg [1982] ECR 3641 [1983] 1 CMLR 1 *107*

115 & 116/81 Adoui and Cornaille v. Belgian State [1982] ECR 1665, 1982 3 CMLR 631 *207–209*

124/81 Commission v. United Kingdom (UHT Milk) [1983] ECR 203, [1983] 2 CMLR 1 *189*

144/81 Keurkoop BV v. Nancy Keane Gifts BV [1982] ECR 2853, [1983] 2 CMLR 47 *335*

220/81 Robertson [1982] ECR 2349, [1983] 1 CMLR 556 *178*

230/81 Luxembourg v. European Parliament [1983] ECR 255, [1983] 2 CMLR 726 *127*

246/81 Bethell v. Commission [1982] ECR 2277, [1982] 3 CMLR 300, [1985] ECR 1, [1985] 2 CMLR 286 *137*

249/81 Commission v. Ireland (Re 'Buy Irish' Campaign) [1982] ECR 4005, [1983] 2 CMLR 104 *173, 174, 352*

261/81 Walter Rau Lebensmittelwerke v. De Smedt PVBA [1982] ECR 3961 *177*

271/81 Société d'Insemination Artificielle [1983] ECR 2057 *170*

283/81 CILFIT Srl [1982] ECR 3415, [1983] 1 CMLR 472 *151–153, 155, 157*

286/81 Oosthoek's Uitgeversmaatshappij BV [1982] ECR 4575, [1983] 3 CMLR 428 *179, 184*

322/81 Michelin (NV Nederlansche Bander-Industrie Michelin) v. Commission [1983] ECR 3461, [1985] 1 CMLR 282 *294, 298, 301*

11/82 AE Piraiki-Patriki v. Commission [1985] ECR 207, [1985] 2 CMLR 4 *131*

35 & 36/82 Morson v. The Netherlands [1982] ECR 3723, [1983] 2 CMLR 221 *221*

40/82 Commission v. United Kingdom (French Turkeys) [1982] ECR 2793, [1982] 3 CMLR 497, [1984] ECR 283 *189*

42/82 Commission v. France (Re Italian Table Wines) [1983] ECR 1013, [1984] 1 CMLR 160 *190*

74/82 Commission v. Ireland (Re Protection of Animal Health) [1984] ECR 317 *189*

86/82 Hasselblad (GB) Ltd v. EC Commission [1984] ECR 883, [1984] 1 CMLR 559 *285*

96/82 NV IAZ International Belgium v. Commission [1983] ECR 3369, [1984] 3 CMLR 276 *277*

132/82 Commission v. Belgium [1983] ECR 1649, [1983] 3 CMLR 600 *166*

165/82 Commission v. United Kingdom (Re Equal Treatment for Men and Women) [1983] ECR 3431, [1984] 1 CMLR 108 *382, 386*

172/82 Syndicat National des Fabricants Raffineurs d'Huile de Grassage v. Inter-Huiles [1983] ECR 555, [1983] 3 CMLR 485 *349*

174/82 Officier van Justitie v. Sandoz BV [1983] ECR 2445 *191*

177/82 Van der Haar [1984] ECR 1797, [1985] CMLR 572 *175*

199/82 Amministrazione della Finanze dello Stato v. San Giorgo [1983] ECR 3595, [1985] 2 CMLR 658 *166*

222/82 Apple and Pear Development Council [1983] ECR 4083 [1984] 3 CMLR 73 *173*

227/82 Leendert van Bennekom [1983] ECR 3883, [1985] 2 CMLR 733 *186*

228 & 229/82 Ford of Europe v. Commission [1984] ECR 1129, [1984] 1 CMLR 649 *322*

231/82 Spijker Kwasten NV v. Commission [1983] ECR 2559, [1984] 2 CMLR 284 *131*

237/82 Jongeneel Kaas BV v. Netherlands [1984] ECR 483, [1985] 2 CMLR 649 *176, 185*

238/82 Duphar BV v. Netherlands [1984] ECR 523, [1985] 1 CMLR 256 *178, 179, 186*

264/82 Timex Corporation v. Council & Commission [1985] ECR 849, [1985] 3 CMLR 550 *129, 137*

286/82 & 26/83 Luisi & Carbone v. Ministero del Tesoro [1984] ECR 377, [1985] 3 CMLR 52 *246, 248, 253*

314/82 Commission v. Belgium (Re Health Inspection Services) [1984] ECR 1543, [1985] 3 CMLR 134 *166*

13/83 Parliament v. Council [1985] ECR 1513; [1986] CMLR 138 *136, 137*

14/83 Von Colson v. Land Nordrhein-Westfalen [1984] ECR 1891, [1986] 2 CMLR 430 *105, 108, 110, 116, 386*

16/83 Prantl [1984] ECR 217, [1985] CMLR 572 *175, 179, 188*

41/83 Italy v. Commission (Re British Telecom) [1985] ECR 873, [1985] 2 CMLR 368 *348, 349*

63/83 R. v. Kirk [1984] ECR 2689, [1984] 3 CMLR 522 *73, 81*

70/83 Kloppenburg [1984] ECR 1075, [1985] 1 CMLR 205 *97*

72/83 Campus Oil v. Minister of State for Industry and Energy [1983] ECR 2727, [1984] 3 CMLR 544 *188*

98/83 & 230/83 Van Gend en Loos NV and Expeditiededriff Wim Bosman BV v. Commission [1984] ECR 3763 *82*

107/83 Klopp [1984] ECR 2917, [1985] 1 CMLR 99 *233*

120/83 Raznoimport v. Commission [1983] ECR 2573 *145*

145/83 Adams v. Commission (No.1) [1985] ECR 3539, [1986] 1 CMLR 506 *145, 323*

177/83 Theodor Kohl KG v. Ringelham and Rennett SA [1984] ECR 3651, [1985] 3 CMLR 340 *188, 336*

184/83 Hofmann v. Barmer Ersatzkasse [1984] ECR 3047, [1986] 1 CMLR 242 *381, 384*

193/83 Windsurfing International Inc. v. Commission [1986] ECR 611, [1987] 3 CMLR 489 *279, 338*

207/83 Commission v. United Kingdom [1985] ECR 1201, [1985] 2 CMLR 259 *178*

229/83 Association des Centres Distributeurs Edouard Leclerc v. 'Au Blé Vert' Sarl [1985] ECR 1, [1985] 2 CMLR 286 *186*

231/83 Cullet v. Centre Leclerc [1985] ECR 306, [1985] 2 CMLR 524 *188*

249/83 Hoeckx [1985] ECR 973, [1987] 3 CMLR 638 *223*

253/83 Kupferberg [1985] ECR 157, [1987] 1 CMLR 36 *167*

261/83 Castelli v. ONPTS [1984] ECR 3199, [1987] 1 CMLR 465 *224*

267/83 Diatta v. Land Berlin [1985] ECR 567, [1986] 2 CMLR 164 *203*

293/83 Gravier v. City of Liège [1985] ECR 593, [1985] 3 CMLR 1 *235, 247, 249–251*

294/83 Parti Écologiste 'Les Verts' v. European Parliament [1986] ECR 1339, [1987] 2 CMLR 343 *127*

42/84 Remia Nutricia v. Commission [1985] ECR 2545, [1987] 1 CMLR 1 *284*

52/84 Commission v. Belgium [1986] ECR 89, [1987] 1 CMLR 710 *355*

59/84 Tezi Textiel v. Commission [1986] ECR 887 *192*

60 & 61/84 Cinéthèque SA [1985] ECR 2605, [1986] 1 CMLR 365 *178*

73/84 Denkavit Futtermittel v. Land Nordrhein-Westfalen [1985] ECR 1013, [1986] 2 CMLR 482 *190*

94/84 Deak [1985] ECR 1873 *223*

101/84 Commission v. Italy [1985] ECR 2629, [1986] 2 CMLR 352 *119, 124*

112/84 Humblot v. Directeur des Services Fiscaux [1986] ECR 1367, [1986] 2 CMLR 338 *169, 171*

122/84 Scrivner [1985] ECR 1027, [1987] 3 CMLR 638 *223*

142, 156/84 British American Tobacco (BAT) & Reynolds v. Commission (The 'Philip Morris' case) [1986] ECR 1899, [1987] ECR 4487, [1987] 2 CMLR 551 *307*

151/84 Roberts v. Tate & Lyle Industries Ltd [1986] ECR 703, [1986] 1 CMLR 714, [1986] 2 All ER 602 *382*

152/84 Marshall v. Southampton and South West Area Health Authority (Teaching) (No.1) [1986] CMLR 688, [1986] 2 WLR 780 *105, 108, 382, 386, 394*

157/84 Frascogna [1985] ECR 1739 *223*

161/84 Pronuptia de Paris GmbH v. Pronuptia de Paris Irmgard Schillgallis [1986] ECR 353, [1986] 1 CMLR 414 *269, 279, 284, 288, 289*

170/84 Bilka-Kaufhaus v. Weber Von Hartz [1986] ECR 1607, [1986] 2 CMLR 701 *370, 371, 373, 376*

175/84 Krohn & Co. KG v. Commission [1987] ECR 97, [1987] 1 CMLR 745 *146*

178/84 Commission v. Germany (Re Beer Purity Laws) [1987] ECR 1227, [1988] 1 CMLR 780 *190, 191*

181/84 R. v. Intervention Board for Agricultural Produce, ex parte Man (Sugar) Ltd [1985] ECR 2889, [1985] 3 CMLR 759, [1986] 2 All ER 115 *78*

182/84 Miro BV [1985] ECR 3731, [1986] 3 CMLR 545 *179*

190/84 Parti Écologiste 'Les Verts' v. European Parliament [1988] ECR 1017 *127*

197/84 Steinhauser v. City of Biarritz [1985] ECR 1819, [1986] 1 CMLR 53 *238*

205/84 Commission v. Germany (Re Insurance Services) [1986] ECR 3755, [1987] 2 CMLR 69 *234, 241*

209–213/84 Ministère Public v. Asjes [1986] ECR 1425, [1986] 3 CMLR 173 *276*

222/84 Johnston v. Chief Constable of the Royal Ulster Constabulary [1986] ECR 1651, [1986] 3 CMLR 240, [1986] 3 WLR 1038 *73, 83, 106, 383*

226/84 British Leyland plc v. Commission [1986] ECR 3263, [1987] 1 CMLR 184 *307*

243/84 John Walker & Sons Ltd v. Ministeriet for Skatter og Afgifter [1986] ECR 875, [1987] 2 CMLR 275 *168*

253/84 GAEC v. Council & Commission [1987] ECR 123, [1988] 1 CMLR 677 *146*

262/84 Beets-Proper v. F. Van Lanschot Bankiers NV [1986] ECR 773, [1987] 2 CMLR 616 *394*

279, 280, 285 and 286/84 Walter Rau Lebensmittelwerke v. Commission [1987] ECR 1069, [1988] 2 CMLR 704 *79*

307/84 Commission v. France (Re French Nurses) [1987] 3 CMLR 555 *220*

311/84 Belgian Telemarketing (Centre Belge d'Études de Marché-Télémarketing (CBEM) v. SA Compagnie Luxembourgeoise de Télédiffusion (CLT) and Information Publicité Benelux (IPB)) [1985] ECR 3261, [1986] 2 CMLR 588 *305, 349*

30/85 Teuling [1987] ECR 2497, [1988] 3 CMLR 789 *393*

53/85 AKZO Chemie BV v. Commission [1986] ECR 1965, [1987] 1 CMLR 231 *322*

59/85 Netherlands State v. Reed [1986] ECR 1283, [1987] 2 CMLR 448 *204*

66/85 Lawrie-Blum v. Land Baden-Württemberg [1986] ECR 2121, [1987] 3 CMLR 403 *216, 220, 230*

67, 68 & 70/85 Kwekerij Gebroeders van der Kooy [1985] ECR 1315, [1989] 2 CMLR 804 *355, 357*

71/85 Netherlands v. FNV [1986] ECR 3855 *391*

79/85 Segers [1986] ECR 2357, [1987] 2 CMLR 247 *241*

89, 104, 114, 116–117, 125–129/85 Wood Pulp (Re Wood Pulp Cartel: A Ahlstrom Oy v. EC Commission) [1988] ECR 5193, [1988] 4 CMLR 901, [1994] ECR I-99, [1993] 4 CMLR 407, [1985] 3 CLR 474 *282*

89/85, 104/85, 114/85, 116/85, 117/85 and 125/85 to 129/85 Ahlström Osakeyhtiö and others v. Commission (No 2) [1993] ECR I-1307 *324*

121/85 Conegate Ltd v. Customs and Excise Commissioners [1986] ECR 1007, [1986] 1 CMLR 739, [1987] 2 WLR 39, [1986] 2 All ER 68 *186, 187, 194*

133–136/85 Walter Rau Lebensmittelwerke v. BALM [1987] ECR 2289, [1987] 12 ELRev. 451 *79*

139/85 Kempf v. Staatsecretaris van Justitie [1986] ECR 1741, [1987] 1 CMLR 764 *217*

150/85 Drake v. Chief Adjudication Officer [1986] ECR 1995, [1986] 3 CMLR 42 *392, 393*

154/85R Commission v. Italy (Re Import of Foreign Motor Vehicles) [1985] ECR 1853, [1986] 2 CMLR 159 *119*

196/85 Commission v. France [1980] ECR, [1988] 2 CMLR 851 *168*

223/85 RSV Maschinefabrieken & Scheepswerven NV v. Commission [1987] ECR 4617, [1989] 2 CMLR 259 *355*

234/85 Keller [1986] ECR 2897, [1987]
1 CMLR 875 *84*

249/85 ALBAKO v. BALM [1987] ECR 2354,
79

281, 283, 284, 285 and 287/85 Germany v.
Commission [1987] ECR 3203 *60*

286/85 McDermott & Cotter v. Minister of
State for Social Welfare [1987] ECR 1452;
[1987] 2 CMLR 607 *395*

293/85 Commission v. Belgium (Re University
Fees) [1988] ECR 305, [1989] 1 CMLR 57
118, 119

314/85 Foto-Frost v. Hauptzollampt Lübeck
Ost [1987] ECR 4199, [1988] 3 CMLR 57
153, 155

338/85 Pardini v. Ministero con l'Estero
[1988] ECR 2041 *82*

407/85 Drei Glocken v. USL [1988] ECR 4233
177, 179

433/85 Feldain v. Directeur des Services
Fiscaux [1987] ECR 352 *169*

14/86 Pretore di Salo v. Persons Unknown
[1987] ECR 2545, [1989] 1 CMLR 71 *150*

24/86 Blaizot v. University of Liège [1988]
ECR 379; [1989] 1 CMLR 57 *250, 251*

26/86 Deutz und Geldermann, Sektkellerei
Breisach (Baden) GmbH v. Council [1987]
ECR 941 *129*

39/86 Lair [1988] ECR 3161, [1989]
3 CMLR 545 *198, 224, 251*

45/86 Commission v. Council [1987]
ECR 1493; [1988] CMLR 131 *134*

62/86 AKZO Chemie BV v. Commission
[1991] ECR I-3359, [1993] 3 CMLR 601
302

63/86 Commission v. Italy (Re Housing
Aid) [1988] ECR 29, [1989] 2 CMLR 601
238

65/86 Bayer & Hennecke v. Süllhöfer [1988]
ECR 5249, [1990] 4 CMLR 182 *338*

66/86 Ahmed Saeed Flugreisen v. Zentrale
Zur Bekämpfung Unlauteren Wettbewerbs
[1989] ECR 803, [1988] 1 CMLR 879
276, 349

80/86 Kolpinghuis Nijmegen [1987]
ECR 3969, [1989] 2 CMLR 18 *109*

104/86 Commission v. Italy [1988]
ECR 1799, [1989] 3 CMLR 25 *120*

157/86 Murphy v. Bord Telecom Eireann
[1989] ECR 673, [1988] 1 CMLR 879 *374*

158/86 Warner Brothers v. Cristiansen [1988]
ECR 2605, [1990] 3 CMLR 684 *334*

166/86 Irish Cement Ltd v. Commission
[1988] ECR 6473, [1989] 2 CMLR 57 *358*

197/86 Brown v. Secretary of State for
Scotland [1988] ECR 3205, [1988]
3 CMLR 403 *198, 224, 251*

222/86 Union Nationale des Entraîneurs
et Cadres Techniques Professionels du
Football (UNECTEF) v. Heylens [1987]
ECR 4097; [1989] 1 CMLR 901 *83*

246/86 Belasco v. Commission [1989]
ECR 2117, [1991] 4 CMLR 96 *279*

263/86 Belgian State v. Humbel and Edel
(Re Higher Education Funding) [1988]
ECR 3565, [1989] 1 CMLR 393 *226, 250*

292/86 Gulling v. Conseils des Ordres des
Barreaux et de Savene [1988] ECR 111,
[1988] 2 CMLR 57 *240*

302/86 Commission v. Denmark (Re
Disposable Beer Cans) [1988] ECR 4607,
[1989] 1 CMLR 619 *178*

3/87R R. v. Ministry of Agriculture, Fisheries
and Food, ex parte Agegate Ltd [1989]
ECR 4459, [1990] 1 CMLR 366, [1990]
3 WLR 226 *94*

27/87 Erauw Jacquery v. La Hesbignonne
[1988] ECR 1919, [1988] 4 CMLR 576
335

30/87 Bodson v. Pompes Funèbres des
Régions Libérées SA [1988] ECR 2479,
[1989] 4 CMLR 984 *276*

35/87 Thetford Corp. v. Fiamma Spa [1988]
ECR 3585, [1988] 3 CMLR 549, [1989]
2 All ER 801 *331*

42/87 Commission v. Belgium (Re Higher
Education Funding) [1988] ECR 5445,
[1989] 1 CMLR 457 *226, 250*

45/87R Commission v. Ireland (Re Dundalk
Water Supply) [1987] ECR 783, [1987]
ECR 1369, [1987] 2 CMLR 197 *163*

46/87 & 227/88 Hoechst v. Commission
[1989] ECR 2859, [1991] 4 CMLR 410
320

53/87 Consorzio Italiano della
Componentistica de Ricambio per

Autoveicoli v. Régie Nationale des Usines Renault [1988] ECR 6039, [1988] 3 CMLR 686 *335, 338*

67/87 Walloon Regional Executive & Glaverbell SA v. Commission [1989] 3 CMLR 771 *357*

81/87 R. v. HM Treasury, ex parte Daily Mail and General Trust plc [1988] ECR 5483, [1989] 1 All ER 328 *241*

85/87 Dow Benelux NV v. Commission [1989] ECR 3137, [1991] 4 CMLR 410 *83, 320*

97–99/87 Dow Chemical Ibérica SA v. Commission [1989] ECR 3156, [1991] 4 CMLR 410 *320*

102/87 France v. Commission [1988] ECR 4067 *357*

142/87 Belgium v. Commission (Re. Tubemeuse) [1990] 1 ECR 959; [1991] 3 CMLR 213 *355*

186/87 Cowan v. French Treasury [1989] ECR 195, [1990] 2 CMLR 613 *247*

196/87 Steymann v. Staatsecretaris van Justitie [1988] ECR 6159, [1989] 1 CMLR 449 *217*

226/87 Commission v. Greece (The Greek Insurance case) [1988] ECR 3611 *350*

235/87 Matteucci v. Communauté Française de Belgique [1988] ECR 5589, [1989] 1 CMLR 357 *224*

238/87 Volvo AB v. Eric Veng [1988] ECR 6211, [1989] 4 CMLR 122 *335, 338*

247/87 Star Fruit v. Commission [1989] ECR 291, [1990] 1 CMLR 733 *119*

266 & 267/87 R. v. Royal Pharmaceutical Society of Great Britain [1989] ECR 1295; [1989] 2 CMLR 751 *173, 189*

277/87 Sandoz Prodotti Farmaceutici SpA v. Commission [1990] ECR I-45 *281*

279/87 Tipp-Ex GmbH v. Commission [1990] ECR I-261 *281*

302/87 Parliament v. Council (Comitology) [1988] ECR 5615 *41, 128, 136*

305/87 Commission v. Greece [1989] ECR 1461, [1991] 1 CMLR 611 *225, 238*

320/87 Ottung v. Klee [1989] ECR 1177, [1990] 4 CMLR 67 *338*

341/87 EMI v. Patricia [1989] ECR 79, [1989] 2 CMLR 413 *334*

344/87 Bettray v. Staatsecretaris Van Justitie [1989] ECR 1621, [1991] 1 CMLR 459 *217*

374/87 Orkem (formerly CDM) v. Commission [1989] ECR 3283 *319*

379/87 Groener v. Minister for Education [1989] ECR 3967, [1990] 1 CMLR 401 *222*

389 & 390/87 GBC Echternach and A Moritz v. Netherlands Minister for Education and Science [1989] ECR 723, [1990] 2 CMLR 305 *217, 226*

395/87 Ministère Public v. Tournier [1989] ECR 2521, [1991] 4 CMLR 248 *339*

C-9/88 Lopes da Veiga v. Staatsecretaris van Justitie [1989] ECR 2989, [1991] 1 CMLR 217 *217*

C-27/88 Solvay & Co. v. Commission [1989] ECR 3255; [1991] 4 CMLR 502 *319*

C-33/88 Allué & Coonan v. Università degli Studi di Venezia [1989] ECR 1591, [1991] 1 CMLR 283 *220*

C-48, 106, 107/88 Achterberg-te Riele and others v. Sociale Verzekeringsbank [1989] ECR 1963, [1990] 3 CMLR 323 *392*

C-49/88 Al-Jubail Fertilizer v. Council [1991] ECR I-3187, [1991] 3 CMLR 377 *83*

C-64/88 Commission v. France [1991] ECR I-2727 *122*

C-70/88 Parliament v. Council (Chernobyl) [1990] ECR I-2041, [1991] ECR I-4529, [1992] 1 CMLR 91 *128*

C-102/88 Ruzius-Wilbrink [1989] ECR 4311, [1991] 2 CMLR 216 *393*

C-109/88 Danfoss (Handels-og Kontorfunktionaernes Forbund v. Dansk Arbejdsgiverforening for Danfoss) [1989] ECR 3199, [1991] 1 CMLR 8 *373, 378*

C-143/88 and C-92/89 Zuckerfabrik Suderdithmarschen AG v. Hauptzollamt Itzehoe [1991] ECR I-415, [1995] 3 CMLR 1 *153, 155*

C-145/88 Torfaen Borough Council v. B & Q plc [1989] ECR 3851, [1990] 1 CMLR 337 *78, 180*

C-152/88 Sofrimport SARL v. Commission [1990] ECR I-2477; [1990] 3 CMLR 80 *131, 142*

C-171/88 Rinner-Kuhn v. FWW Spezial
Gebäudereinigung GmbH & Co. KG
[1989] ECR 2743; [1993] 2 CMLR 932
371, 376

C-177/88 Dekker v. Stichting
Vormingscentrum Voor Jong Volwassenen
[1990] ECR I-3941 *375, 380*

C-179/88 Hertz v. Dansk
Arbejdsgiverforening [1990] ECR I-3979,
380

C-221/88 ECSC v. Acciaiera e ferrier Busseni
[1990] 1 ECR 495 *106*

C-322/88 Grimaldi v. Fonds des Maladies
Professionelles [1989] ECR 4407, [1991]
2 CMLR 265 *58*

C-202/88 France v. Commission [1991]
ECR I-1223, [1992] 5 CMLR 552 *352*

C-262/88 Barber v. Guardian Royal Exchange
Assurance Group [1990] ECR I-1889;
[1990] 2 CMLR 513 *81, 371–373, 378,
382, 395*

C-297/88 & C-197/89 Dzodzi v. Belgium
[1990] ECR I-3763 *152*

C-362/88 GB INNO-BM v. Confédération du
Commerce Luxembourgoise Asbl [1990]
ECR I-667, [1991] 2 CMLR 801 *179*

C-5/89 Commission v. Germany [1990]
ECR I-3437, [1992] 1 CMLR 117 *355*

C-50/89 BPP Industries plc and British
Gypsum Ltd v. Commission [1990]
1 CMLR 34 *303*

C-10/89 SA CNL-Sucal NV v. Hag GF AG
('Hag II') [1990] ECR I-3711, [1990]
3 CMLR 571 *335, 336*

C-23/89 Quietlynn v. Southend Borough
Council [1990] ECR I-3059, [1990]
3 CMLR 55 *174, 187*

C-56/89R Publishers Association v.
Commission [1989] ECR I-1693 *322*

C-69/89 Nakajima All Precision Co. Ltd v.
Council of the European Communities
[1991] ECR I-2069 *55*

C-87/89 Sonito (Société Nationale
Interprofessionnelle de la Tomate and
others) v. Commission [1990] ECR I-1981
119

C-100/89 and C-101/89 Kaefer and Procacci
v. France [1990] ECR I-4697 *150*

C-104/89 & 37/90 Mulder v. Commission &
Council [1992] ECR I-3062 *143, 145*

C-106/89 Marleasing v. La Commercial
Internacional de Alimentacion [1990]
ECR I-4135, [1992] 1 CMLR 305 *92, 108,
109*

C-111/89 Bakker v. Hillegon [1990]
ECR I-1735; [1990] 3 CMLR 119 *166*

C-113/89 Rush Portugesa [1990] ECR I-1417,
[1991] 2 CMLR 818 *210*

C-188/89 Foster v. British Gas [1990]
ECR I-3313, [1990] 2 CMLR 833, [1988]
2 CMLR 697 *103, 106*

C-213/89 R. v. Secretary of State for
Transport, ex parte Factortame (No. 1)
[1990] ECR 2433; [1990] 3 CMLR 1 *94,
95, 99, 120*

C-213/89 R. v. Secretary of State for
Transport, ex parte Factortame (No. 2)
[1990] 3 WLR 818, [1990] 3 CMLR 375
91, 95, 99

C-221/89R R. v. Secretary of State for
Transport, ex parte Factortame (No. 3)
[1991] ECR I-3905, [1991] 3 CMLR 589
91, 95, 99, 112, 113, 116, 143

C-234/89 Delimitis v. Henninger Bräu [1991]
ECR I-935, [1992] 5 CMLR 210 *284, 286*

C-238/89 Pall Corporation v. P.J. Dahlhausen
& Co. [1990] ECR I-4827 *333*

C-246/89R Commission v. United Kingdom
(Re Merchant Shipping Rules) [1989]
ECR 3125, [1989] 3 CMLR 601 *95, 120*

C-260/89 Elliniki Radiophonia Tiléorassi v.
Dimotiki Etairia Pliroforissis and others
(Greek Broadcasting) [1991] ECR I-2925,
[1994] 4 CMLR 540 *73, 347, 349*

C-292/89 R. v. Immigration Appeal Tribunal
ex parte Antonissen [1992] ECR I-745;
[1991] 2 CMLR 373 *205, 217, 218*

C-300/89 Commission v. Council (The
Titanium Dioxide case) [1991] ECR I-2867,
[1993] 3 CMLR 359 *135*

C-308/89 Di Leo v. Land Berlin [1990]
ECR I-4185 *226*

C-309/89 Codorniu v. Council [1994]
ECR I-1853, [1995] 2 CMLR 561 *129*

C-312/89 Union Départmentale des
Syndicats CGT de l'Aishe v. Sidef
Conforama [1991] ECR I-997 *177, 181*

C-332/89 André Marchandise, Jean-Marie Chapuis and SA Trafitex [1991] ECR I-1027, [1993] 3 CMLR 746 *177, 181*

C-340/89 Vlassopoulos v. Ministerium für Justiz [1991] ECR I-2357, [1993] 2 CMLR 221 *240*

C-344/89 Masterfoods Ltd v. HB Ice Cream Ltd [2000] ECR I-11369 *287, 303*

C-2/90 Commission v. Belgium (Re Walloon Waste) [1992] ECR I-4431 *163*

C-6 & 9/90 Francovich & Bonifaci v. Italy [1991] ECR I-5357; [1993] ECR 66, [1993] 2 CMLR 66 *92, 94, 111, 115, 116, 146*

C-15/90 Middleburgh v. Chief Adjudication Officer [1991] ECR I-4655, [1992] 1 CMLR 353 *217*

C-18/90 ONEM v. Kziber [1991] ECR I-199 *107*

C-31/90 Johnson v. Chief Adjudication Officer [1991] ECR I-3723 *392*

C-41/90 Höfner v. Macrotron [1991] ECR I-1979; [1993] 4 CMLR 306 *347*

C-159/90 SPUC v. Grogan [1991] ECR I-4685; [1991] 3 CMLR 849 *247, 252*

C-179/90 Merci Convenzionali Porto di Genova v. Siderurgica [1991] ECR I-5889, [1994] 4 CMLR 422 *347*

C-204/90 Backman v. Belgium [1992] ECR I-249, [1993] 1 CMLR 785 *224*

C-208/90 Emmott v. Minister for Social Welfare [1991] ECR I-4269, [1991] 3 CMLR 894 *105, 386*

C-243/90 R. v. Secretary of State for Social Security, ex parte Smithson [1992] ECR I-467, [1992] 1 CMLR 1061 *393*

C-271, 281 and 289/90 Spain, Kingdom of Belgium and Italian Republic v. Commission [1992] ECR I-5833 *351*

C-294/90 British Aerospace & Rover Group Holdings plc v. Commission [1992] ECR I-493, [1992] 1 CMLR 853 *123*

C-295/90 Parliament v. Council [1992] ECR I-4193; [1992] 3 CMLR 281 *136*

C-343/90 Dias v. Director da Alfândego do Porto [1992] ECR I-4673 *152*

C-354/90 Fédération Nationale v. France [1991] ECR I-5505 *354*

C-370/90 Surinder Singh [1991] ECR I-4265; [1992] 3 CMLR 358 *221*

C-4/91 Bleis v. Ministère de l'Education [1991] ECR I-5627, [1994] 1 CMLR 793 *220*

C-9/91 R. v. Secretary of State for Social Security, ex parte EOC [1992] ECR I-4297, [1992] 3 CMLR 233 *394*

C-45/91 Commission v. Greece [1992] ECR I-2509 *122*

C-63 & 64/91 Jackson and Cresswell v. Chief Adjudication Officer [1992] ECR I-4737, [1992] 3 CMLR 389 *393*

C-83/91 Meilicke v. ADV/ORGA F.A. Meyer AG [1992] ECR I-4871 *152*

C-104/91 Colegio Oficial de Agentes de la Propriedad Inmobiliaria v. José Luis Aguirre Borrell and others [1992] ECR I-3003 *244*

C-109/91 Ten Oever v. Stichting Bedrijfspensionfonds [1993] ECR I-4879, [1995] 2 CMLR 357 *371*

C-152/91 Neath v. Hugh Steeper Ltd [1993] ECR I-6935 *371, 373*

C-169/91 Stoke-on-Trent City Council v. B & Q plc [1992] ECR I-6635, [1993] 1 CMLR 426 *180*

C-200/91 Coloroll Pension Trustees v. Russell [1994] ECR I-4389 *370, 371*

C-267 & 268/91 Keck & Mithouard [1993] ECR I-6097 *46, 178, 181, 183, 184, 194, 239*

C-271/91 Marshall v. Southampton and South West Area Health Authority (No.2) [1993] ECR I-4367; [1993] CMLR 293 *106, 108, 386*

C-320/91 Paul Corbeau [1993] ECR I-2533 *349, 350*

C-328/91 R. v. Secretary of State for Social Security, ex parte Thomas [1993] ECR I-1247, [1993] 3 CMLR 880 *394*

C-338/91 Steenhorst-Neerings v. Bedrijfsvereniging voor Detailhandel [1993] ECR I-5475, [1995] 3 CMLR 323 *105, 386*

T-19/92 Groupement d'Achat Edouard Leclerc v. Commission [1996] ECR II-1961, [1997] 4 CMLR 995 *285*

C-36/92P Samenwerkende Elektriciteits-
Produktiebedrijven (SEP) NV v.
Commission [1994] ECR I-1911 *319*

C-60/92 Otto BV v. Postbank NV [1993]
ECR I-5683 *319*

C-91/92 Faccini Dori v. Recreb [1994]
ECR I-3235, [1995] 1 CMLR 665 *108–111*

C-92/92 and C-326/92 Collins v. Imtrat
Handelsgesellschaft [1993] ECR I-5145;
[1993] 3 CMLR 773 *337*

C-127/92 Enderby v. Frenchay Area Health
Authority [1993] ECR I-5535, [1994]
1 CMLR 8 *375*

C-137/92P Commission v. BASF AG (PVC)
[1994] ECR I-2555 *40, 82*

C-275/92 HM Customs and Excise v.
Schindler [1994] ECR I-1039 *238*

C-292/92 Hünermund v. Landesapothekemer
Baden Wurttemburg [1993] ECR I-6787
181

C-315/92 Verband Sozialer Wettbewerb eV v.
Clinique Laboratoires SNC [1994]
ECR I-317 *183*

C-326/92 and C-92/92 Patricia v.
EMI ECR I-5145; [1993] CMLR 773 *337*

C-334/92 Wagner Miret v. Fonds de Garantie
Salarial [1993] ECR I-6911 *111*

C-350/92 Spain v. Council [1995] ECR I-1985
62

C-393/92 Municipality of Almelo [1994]
ECR I-1477 *348*

C-401 & 402/92 Tankstation't Henkste Vof
and Boermans [1994] ECR I-2199, [1995]
3 CMLR 501 *181*

C-410/92 Johnson v. CAO [1994]
ECR I-5483, [1995] All ER (EC) 258, [1995]
1 CMLR 725, [1995] IRLR 158 *105, 386*

C-2/93 Webb v. EMO [1994] ECR I-3567;
[1994] 2 CMLR 729 *109, 154, 380*

C-7/93 Bestuur van het Algemeen Burgerlijk
Pensioen-fonds v. Beaune [1994]
ECR I-4471 *371*

C-18/93 Corsica Ferries Italia Ltd v. Corpo
dei Piloti del Porto di Genoa [1994]
ECR I-1783 *300, 350*

C-28/93 Van den Akker v. Stichting Shell
Pensioenfonds [1994] ECR I-4527, [1995]
3 CMLR 543 *373*

C-46 and 48/93 R. v. Secretary of State for
Transport, ex parte Factortame (No. 4)
[1996] ECR I-1029, [1996] 1 CMLR 889
95, 99, 358

C-48/93 Brasserie du Pêcheur v. Germany
[1996] ECR I-1029, [1996] 1 CMLR 889,
[1996] All ER (EC) 301, [1996] 2 WLR 506
94, 112, 113, 115, 116, 143, 317

C-57/93 Vroege v. NCIV Institute voor
Volkshuisvesting [1994] ECR I-4541 *373,
376*

C-128/93 Fisscher v. Voorhuis Hengelo
[1994] ECR I-4583, [1995] 1 CMLR 881
376

C-342/93 Gillespie v. Northern Ireland
Health and Social Services Board [1996]
ECR I-475, [1996] 2 CMLR 969 *372*

C-358 & 416/93 Ministero Fiscal v. Bordessa
[1995] ECR I-361, [1996] 2 CMLR 13
253, 255

C-384/93 Alpine Investments BV v. Minister
van a Financien [1995] ECR I-1141, [1995]
3 CMLR 209 *238*

C-387/93 Gorgio Domingo Banchero [1995]
ECR I-4663, [1996] 1 CMLR 829 *182*

C-392/93 R. v. HM Treasury, ex parte British
Telecommunications plc [1996] ECR
I-1631 *114*

C-412/93 Société d'Importation Edouard
Leclerc-Siplec v. TFI Publicité SA and M6
Publicité SA [1995] ECR I-179, [1995]
3 CMLR 422 *182*

C-415/93 URBSFA v. Bosman [1995]
ECR I-4921, [1996] 1 CMLR 645 *225*

C-427, 429 and 436/93 Bristol-Myers Squibb
and Others v. Paranova [1996] ECR
I-3457, [1997] 1 CMLR 1151 *331, 332*

C-450/93 Kalanke v. Frei Hausestadt Bremen
[1995] ECR I-3051, [1996] All ER (EC) 66,
[1996] 1 CMLR 175 *384, 385*

C-470/93 Verein Gegen Unwesen in Handel
und Gewerbe Köln v. Mars GmbH [1995]
ECR I-1923, [1995] 3 CMLR 1 *183*

C-473/93 Commission v. Luxembourg
[1996] ECR I-3207, [1996] 3 CMLR 981
219, 220

C-484/93 Svensson and Gustavvson v.
Ministre de Logements et de
L'Urbanisation [1995] ECR I-3955 *253*

C-5/94 R. v. Minister of Fisheries and Food, ex parte Hedley Lomas [1996] ECR I-2553 *113, 114*

C-13/94 P v. S and Cornwall County Council [1996] ECR I-2143, [1996] 2 CMLR 247 *80, 379, 388*

C-55/94 Gebhard v. Consiglio dell'Ordine Degli Avvocati Procurator di Milano [1995] ECR I-4165, [1996] 1 CMLR 603 *240, 252*

C-63/94 Belgapom v. ITM Belgium SA and Vocarex SA [1995] ECR I-2467 *182*

C-68/94 and 30/95 France v. Commission; SCPA & EMC v. Commission [1998] ECR I-1375, [1998] 4 CMLR 829 *310, 311*

C-84/94 UK v. Council [1996] ECR I-5755 *85*

C-92/94 R. v. Secretary of State for Social Security, ex parte Graham [1995] ECR I-2521, [1995] 3 CMLR 169 *394*

C-120/94 Commission v. Greece [1996] ECR I-1513 *192*

C-120/94R Commission v. Greece [1994] ECR I-3037 *193*

C-137/94 R. v. Secretary of State for Health, ex parte Richardson [1995] ECR I-3407, [1995] All ER (EC) 865, [1995] 3 CMLR 376, The Times 27 Oct 1995 *393, 394*

C-163, 165 and 250/94 Sanz de Lera and Others [1995] ECR I-4821, [1996] 1 CMLR 631 *253–255*

C-178 etc./94 Dillenkofer v. Federal Republic of Germany [1996] ECR I-4845, [1996] 3 CMLR 469 *114*

C-192/94 El Corte Inglés v. Rivero [1996] ECR I-1281, [1996] 2 CMLR 507 *111*

C-194/94 CIA Security International SA v. Signalson SA and Securitel SPRL [1996] ECR I-2201 *110*

C-228/94 Atkins v. Wrekin District Council [1996] ECR I-3633, [1996] 3 CMLR 863 *393*

C-283, 291 & 292/94 Denkavit International v. Bundesamt für Finanzen [1996] ECR I-5063 *114*

C-333/94P Tetra Pak International SA v. Commission (No.2) [1996] ECR I-5951, [1997] 4 CMLR 662 *299*

C-34–36/95 Konsumentombudsman v. De Agostini [1997] ECR I-3843, [1997] All ER (EC) 687, [1998] 1 CMLR 32 *182*

C-68/95 T. Port GmbH & Co. KG. v. Bundesanstalt für Landwirtschaft und Ernährung [1996] ECR I-6065, [1997] 1 CMLR 1 *150*

C-73/95P Viho Europe BV v. Commission [1996] ECR I-5457 *277*

C-120/95 Decker v. Caisse de Maladie des Employés Privés [1998] ECR I-1831, [1998] 2 CMLR 879 *190, 191*

C-122/95 Germany v. Council [1998] ECR I-973, [1998] 3 CMLR 570 *97*

C-130/95 Giloy (Bernd) v. Hauptzollamt Frankfurt am Main-Ost [1997] ECR I-4291 *152*

C-168/95 Arcaro [1996] ECR I-4705, [1997] 1 CMLR 179 *109, 111*

C-185/95P Baustahlgewebe v. Commission [1998] ECR I-8417, [1999] 4 CMLR 1203 *324*

C-189/95 Harry Franzén [1997] ECR I-5909 *170*

C-191/95 Commission v. Germany [1998] ECR I-0000 *118*

C-265/95 Commission v. France [1997] ECR I-6959 *120, 173*

C-321/95P Stichting Greenpeace Council (Greenpeace International) v. Commission [1998] ECR I-1651, [1998] 3 CMLR 1 *130, 131*

C-368/95 Vereinigte Familiapress Zeitungsverlags- und vertriebs GmbH v. Heinrich Bauer Verlag [1997] ECR I-3689 *178*

C-388/95 Belgium v. Spain [2000] ECR I-3123 *121*

C-409/95 Marschall v. Land Nordrhein Westfalen [1997] ECR I-6363, [1998] 1 CMLR 547 *385*

C-53/96 Hermes International v. FHT Marketing Choice [1998] ECR I-3603 *89*

C-54/96 Dorsch Consult Ingenieurgesellschaft mbH v. Bundesbaugesellschaft Berlin mbH [1997] ECR I-4961 *150*

C-85/96 Martinez Sala v. Freistaat Bayern [1998] ECR I-2691 *196, 197*

C-118/96 Safir v. Skattemyndighten I Dalarnas Lyn [1998] ECR I-1897, [1998] 3 CMLR 739 *254*

C-149/96 Portuguese Republic v. Council of the European Union [1999] ECR I-8395 *55*

C-176/96 Lehtonen and ASBL Castors Canada Dry Namur-Braine v. ASBL Fédération Royale Belge des Sociétés de Basketball [2000] ECR I-2681, [2000] 3 CMLR 409 *225*

C-200/96 Metronome Musik GmbH v. Musik Point Hokamp GmbH [1998] ECR I-1953, [1998] 3 CMLR 919 *334, 343*

C-249/96 Grant v. South West Trains [1998] ECR I-621, [1998] 1 CMLR 993 *80, 388*

C-274/96 Bickel and Franz [1998] ECR I-7637, [1999] 1 CMLR 348 *195, 238*

C-328/96 Commission v. Austria [1999] ECR I-7479 *118*

C-348/96 Donatella Calfa [1999] ECR I-11, [1999] 2 CMLR 1138, [1999] All ER (EC) 850 *206*

C-355/96 Silhouette Internationale v. Hartlauer [1998] ECR I-4799, [1998] 2 CMLR 953 *333*

C-386/96P Société Louis Dreyfus et Cie v. Commission [1998] ECR I-2309, [1999] 1 CMLR 481 *141*

C-394/96 Brown v. Rentokil [1998] ECR I-4185, [1998] 2 CMLR 1049 *381*

C-7/97 Oscar Bronner GmbH & Co. KG v. Mediaprint Zeitungs- und Zeitschriftenverlag GmbH & Co. KG, Mediaprint Zeitungsvertriebsgesellschaft mbH & Co. KG and Mediaprint Anzeigengesellschaft mbH & Co. KG [1998] ECR I-7791 *305*

C-10–22/97 Ministero delle Finanze v. In. Co. Ge. '90 [1998] ECR I-6307, [2001] 1 CMLR 800 *91*

C-67/97 Ditlev Bluhme [1998] ECR I-8033, [1999] 1 CMLR 612 *190*

C-124/97 Läärä v. Finland [1999] ECR I-6067, [2001] 2 CMLR 257 *238*

C-140/97 Rechberger v. Austria [1999] ECR I-3499, [2000] 2 CMLR 1 *114*

C-158/97 Badeck [2000] ECR I-1875 *385*

C-167/97 R. v. Secretary of State for Employment, ex parte Seymour Smith [1999] ECR I-623, [1999] 2 CMLR 273 *376*

C-212/97 Centros Ltd v. Erhvervs- og Selskabsstyrelsen [1999] ECR I-1459 *233*

C-222/97 Trummer and Mayer [1999] ECR I-1661 *254, 255*

C-270 & 271/97 Deutsche Post AG v. Sievers and Schrage [2000] ECR I-929 *369*

C-273/97 Sirdar v. The Army Board and the Secretary of State for Defence [1999] ECR I-7403 *383*

C-302/97 Klaus Konle v. Austria [1999] ECR I-3099 *255*

C-309/97 Angestelltenbetriebsrat der Wiener Gebietskrankenkasse [1999] ECR I-2865, [1999] 2 CMLR 1173 *375*

C-323/97 Commission v. Belgium [1998] ECR I-4281 *200*

C-333/97 Lewen v. Lothar Denda [1999] ECR I-7243 *371*

C-340/97 Nazli v. Nürnberg [2000] ECR I-957, [2000] All ER (D) 165 *210*

C-379/97 Pharmacia and Upjohn v. Paranova [1999] ECR I-6927, [1999] All ER (EC) 880, [2000] 3 WLR 303, [2000] 1 CMLR 51 *332*

C-387/97 Commission v. Greece [2000] ECR I-5047 *122*

C-35/98 Staatssecretaris van Financiën v. BGM Verkooijen [2000] ECR I-4071 *255*

C-78/98 Preston and Othes v. Wolverhampton Healthcare NHS Trust and Others and Dorothy Fletcher and Others v. Midland Bank plc [2000] ECR I-3201 *376*

C-168/98 Luxembourg v. European Parliament and Council [2000] ECR I-9131 *236*

C-173/98 Sebago and Ancienne Maison Dubois v. GB-Unic [1999] ECR I-4103 *333*

C-207/98 Mahlburg v. Land Meckleburg-Vorpommern [2000] ECR I-549, [2001] 3 CMLR 887 *380*

C-224/98 D'Hoop v. Office National de L'emploi [2002] ECR I-6191 *198*

C-237/98P Dorsch Consult
Ingenieurgesellschaft mbH v. Council and
Commission [2000] ECR I-4549 *144*

C-254/98 Schutzverband gegen unlauteren
Wettbewerb v. TK-Heimdienst Sass GmbH
[2000] ECR I-151 *182*

C-285/98 Kreil v. Bundesrepublik
Deutschland [2000] ECR I-69, [2002]
1 CMLR 1047 *383*

C-352/98P Laboratoires Pharmaceutiques
Bergaderm SA and Jean-Jacques Goupil v.
Commission [2000] ECR I-5291 *141–144*

C-367/98 Commission v. Portugal (Golden
Share) [2002] ECR I-4731 *255, 257*

C-368/98 Vanbraekel and Others v. Alliance
nationale des mutualités chrétiennes
(ANMC) [2001] ECR I-5363 *248, 249*

C-377/98 Netherlands v. European
Parliament [2001] ECR I-7079 *85*

C-382/98 R. v. Secretary of State for
Social Security, ex parte Taylor [1999]
ECR I-8955, [2000] All ER (EC) 80, [2000]
1 CMLR 873 *393*

C-405/98 Konsumentombudsmannen v.
Gourmet International Products AB (GIP)
[2001] ECR I-1795 *182*

C-407/98 Abrahamsson and Leif Anderson
v. Elisabet Fogelqvist [2000] ECR I-5539
386

C-443/98 Unilever Italia SpA v. Central Food
SpA [2000] ECR I-7535 *110*

C-471/98 Commission v. Belgium [2002]
ECR I-9681 *62*

C-58/99 Commission v. Italy [2000]
ECR I-3811 *256*

C-53/99 Association Eglise de Scientologie de
Paris and Scientology International
Reserves Trust v. the Prime Minister [2000]
ECR I-1335 *255*

C-157/99 Geraets-Smits v. Stichting
Ziekenfonds VGZ; HTM Peerbooms v.
Stichting CZ Groep Zorgverzekeringen
[2001] ECR I-5473 *248, 249*

C-184/99 Grzelczyk v. Centre public d'aide
sociale d'Ottignies-Louvain-la-Neuve
[2001] ECR I-6193 *197, 205, 224*

C-353/99P Council v. Heidi Hautala [2001]
ECR I-9565 *135*

C-385/99 Müller-Fauré v. Onderlinge
Waarborgmaatschappij OZ
Zorgverzekeringen UA and EEM van Riet v.
Onderlinge Waarborgmaatschappij ZAO
Zorgverzekeringen [2003] ECR I-4509
248, 249

C-413/99 Baumbast and R v. Secretary of
State for the Home Department [2002]
ECR I-7091 *197, 198, 214, 226*

C-438/99 Melgar v. Ayuntamiento de Los
Barrios [2001] ECR I-6915 *380*

C-453/99 Courage Ltd v. Bernard Crehan
and Bernard Crehan v. Courage Ltd and
Others [2001] ECR I-6297 *326*

C-459/99 Mouvement contre le racisme,
l'antisémitisme et la xénophobie ASBL
(MRAX) v. Belgian State [2002]
ECR I-6591 *204*

C-483/99 Commission v. France [2002]
ECR I-4781 *257*

C-503/99 Commission v. Belgium [2002]
ECR I-4809 *257*

C-50/00P Unión de Pequeños Agricultores
(UPA) v. Council [2002] ECR I-6677
130–132

C-53/00 Ferring SA v. Agence centrale des
organismes de sécurité sociale (ACOSS)
[2001] ECR I-9067 *353*

C-60/00 Mary Carpenter v. Secretary of
State for the Home Department [2002]
ECR I-6279 *73, 239*

C-99/00 Kenny Roland Lyckeskog [2002]
ECR I-4839 *154, 155*

C-109/00 Tele Danmark A/S v. Handels-
og Kontorfunktionærernes Forbund i
Danmark (HK) [2001] ECR I-6993 *380*

C-112/00 Schmidberger (Eugen),
Internationale Transporte und Planzüge v.
Austria [2003] ECR I-5659 *73, 173, 178*

C-208/00 Überseering BV v. Nordic
Construction Company Baumanagement
GmbH (NCC) [2002] ECR I-9919 *233*

C-280/00 Altmark Trans GmbH and
Regierungspräsidium Magdeburg v.
Nahverkehrsgesellschaft Altmark
GmbH, and Oberbundesanwalt beim
Bundesverwaltungsgericht [2003]
ECR I-7747 *353, 354*

C-294/00 Deutsche Paracelsus Schulen für Naturheilverfahren GmbH v. Kurt Gräbner [2002] ECR I-6515 *243*

C-463/00 Commission v. Spain [2003] ECR I-4581 *254*

C-56/01 Inizan v. Caisse primaire d'assurance maladie des Hauts-de-Seine [2003] ECR I-12403 *248, 249*

C-98/01 Commission v. United Kingdom [2003] ECR I-4641 *257*

C-100/01 Ministre de l'Intérieur v. Aitor Oteiza Olazabal [2002] ECR I-10981 *207*

C-109/01 Home Secretary v. Hacene Akrich [2003] ECR I-9607 *73, 203*

C-117/01 KB v. National Health Service Pensions Agency and Secretary of State for Health [2004] ECR I-541 *74*

C-167/01 Kamer van Koophandel en Fabrieken voor Amsterdam v. Inspire Art Ltd [2003] ECR I-10155 *233*

C-186/01 Dory v. Germany [2003] ECR I-2479 *384*

C-198/01 Consorzio Industrie Fiammiferi (CIF) v. Autorità Garante della Concorrenza e del Mercato [2003] ECR I-8055 *317*

C-224/01 Köbler v. Austria [2003] ECR I-10239 *94, 105, 115, 155*

C-285/01 Burbaud v. Ministère de l'Emploi et de la Solidarité [2003] ECR I-8219 *243*

C-413/01 Ninni-Orasche v. Bundesminister für Wissenschaft, Verkehr und Kunst [2003] ECR I-13187 *217*

C-481/01 NDC Health GmbH & Co. KG and NDC Health Corporation v. Commission of the European Communities and IMS Health Inc [2002] ECR I-3401 *304*

C-36/02 Omega Spielhallen- und Automatenaufstellungs-GmbH v. Oberbürgermeisterin der Bundesstadt Bonn. [2004] ECR I-9609 *246*

C-138/02 Collins v. Secretary of State for Work and Pensions [2004] ECR I-2703 *199, 217, 218*

C-141/02P Max Mobile (Commission of the European Communities v. T-Mobile Austria GmbH) [2005] ECR I-1283 *351*

C-148/02 Garcia Avello (Carlos) v. Belgian State [2003] ECR I-11613 *195*

C-200/02 Kunqian Catherine Zhu and Man Lavette Chen v. Secretary of State for the Home Department [2004] ECR I-9925 *199*

C-263/02P Commission v. Jégo-Quéré & Cie SA [2004] ECR I-3425 *132*

C-304/02 Commission v. France [2005] ECR I-6263 *122*

C-386/02 Baldinger v. Pensionsversicherungsanstalt der Arbeiter [2004] ECR I-8411 *224*

C-456/02 Trojani (Michel) v. Centre Public d'aide Sociale de Bruxelles (CPAS) [2004] ECR I-7573 *199, 217, 228*

C-12/03 Commission v. Tetra Laval [2005] ECR I-987 *312, 313, 315*

C-45/03 Dem 'Yanenko' *156*

C-105/03 Maria Pupino [2005] ECR I-5285 *92, 156*

C-173/03 Traghetti del Mediterraneo SpA v. Italy [2006] ECR I-5177 *115*

C-209/03 R (on the application of Dany Bidar) v. London Borough of Ealing and Secretary of State for Education and Skills [2005] ECR I-2119 *198, 205, 224, 251*

C-446/03 Marks & Spencer plc v. David Halsey (Her Majesty's Inspector of Taxes) [2005] ECR I-10837 *233*

C-503/03 Commission v. Spain [2006] ECR I-1097 *211*

C-540/03 European Parliament v. Council of the European Union [2006] ECR I-5769 *59, 77*

C-27/04 Commission v. Council [2004] ECR I-6649 *262*

C-122/04 Commission v. European Parliament and Council [2006] ECR I-2001 *42*

C-145/04 Spain v. UK [2006] ECR I-7917 *74, 121, 200*

C-170/04 Rosengren (Klas) and Others v. Riksåklagaren [2007] ECR I-4071 *170*

C-196/04 Cadbury Schweppes plc and Cadbury Schweppes Overseas Ltd v.

Commissioners of Inland Revenue [2006]
ECR I-7995 *233*

C-207/04 Vergani *v.* Agenzia delle Entrate,
Ufficio di Arona [2005] ECR I-7453 *381*

C-234/04 Kapferer *v.* Schlank & Schick
[2006] ECR I-2585 *91*

C-354/04P Gestoras Pro Amnistía, Juan Mari
Olano Olano and Julen Zelarain Errasti *v.*
Council [2007] ECR I-1579 *127*

C-372/04 R (on the application of Yvonne
Watts) *v.* Bedford Primary Care Trust and
Secretary of State for Health [2006]
ECR I-4325 *248, 249*

C-423/04 Richards *v.* Secretary of State for
Work and Pensions [2006] ECR I-3585
394

C-452/04 Fidium Finanz AG *v.* Bundesanstalt
für Finanzdienstleistungsaufsicht [2006]
ECR I-9521 *234*

C-503/04 Commission *v.* Germany [2007]
ECR I-6153 *122*

C-506/04 Graham J. Wilson *v.* Ordre des
avocats du barreau de Luxembourg
[2006] ECR I-8613 *236*

C-1/05 Jia *v.* Migrationsverket [2007] ECR I-1
203

C-13/05 Navas *v.* Eurest Colectividades SA
[2006] ECR I-6467 *390*

C-17/05 Cadman *v.* Health & Safety
Executive [2006] ECR I-9583 *376*

C-193/05 Commission *v.* Luxembourg [2006]
ECR I-8673 *236, 237*

C-232/05 Commission *v.* France [2006]
ECR I-10071 *355*

C-411/05 Palacios de la Villa *v.* Commission
[2007] ECR I-8531 *77*

C-161/06 Skoma-Lux sro *v.* Celní ředitelství
Olomouc [2007] ECR 0000 *46*

C-231, 232 and 233/06 National Pensions
Office *v.* Emilienne Jonkman, Hélène
Vercheval and Noëlle Permesaen *v.* Office
national des pensions [2007] ECR I-5149
395

C-244/06 Dynamic Medien Vertriebs GmbH
v. Avides Media AG [2008] ECR 000 *183*

C-267/06 Maruko *v.* Versorgungsanstalt der
deutschen Bühnen [2008] ECR I-000 *390*

C-300/06 Ursula Voß *v.* Land Berlin [2007]
ECR I-000 *376*

C-450/06 Varec SA *v.* Belgian State [2008]
ECR 000 *77*

C-460/06 Paquay *v.* Société d'architectes Hoet
+ Minne SPRL [2007] ECR I-8511 *381*

C-506/06 Mayr *v.* Bäckerei und Konditorei
Gerhard Flöckner OHG [2008] ECR I-000
381

Court of First Instance Numerical Cases

T-7/89 Hercules Chemicals NV *v.* Commission
[1991] ECR II-1711 *321*

T-30/89 Hilti AG *v.* Commission [1991]
ECR II-1439, [1990] ECR II-163, [1992]
4 CMLR 16 *300, 302*

T-51/89 Tetra Pak Rausing SA *v.* Commission
(No. 1) [1990] ECR II-309, [1991]
4 CMLR 334 *274, 298, 301, 307*

T-64/89 Automec *v.* Commission [1990]
ECR II-367, [1991] 4 CMLR 177 *126*

T-66/89 Publishers' Association *v.*
Commission (No. 2) [1992] ECR II-1995,
[1992] 5 CMLR 120; on appeal
(Case C-360/92P) [1995] ECR I-23, (1995)
5 CMLR 33 *277, 279, 322*

T-68/89, 77–78/89 Società Italiana Vetro SpA
v. Commission [1992] ECR II-1403, [1992]
5 CMLR 302 *294*

T-69, 70 & 76/89 RTE, BBC & ITP *v.*
Commission (Magill TV Guide) [1991]
ECR II-485; [1991] 4 CMLR 586; on
appeal (Case C-241/91P) [1995]
ECR I-743 *304, 338, 339*

T-85/89 British Plasterboard Industries plc *v.*
Commission [1992] ECR II-315, [1990]
4 CMLR 464 *298*

T-39/90 Samenwerkende Elektriciteits-
Produktiebedrijven (SEP) *v.* Commission
[1991] ECR II-1497 *319*

T-114/92 BENIM *v.* Commission [1995]
ECR II-147 *326*

T-504/93 Tiercé Ladbroke *v.* Commission
[1997] ECR II-923, [1997] 5 CMLR 309
305

T-194/94 Carvel (John) and Guardian Newspapers Ltd v. Council of the European Union [1995] ECR II-2765 *86*

T-295/94 etc. Buchman v. Commission (Cartonboard) [1998] ECR II-813 *278, 324*

T-374, 375, 384 and 388/94 European Night Services and Others v. Commission [1998] ECR II-3141, [1998] 5 CMLR 718 *276, 289, 351*

T-174/95 Svenska Journalistförbundet v. Council of the European Union [1998] ECR II-2289 *86*

T-102/96 Gencor v. Commission [1999] ECR II-753, [1999] 4 CMLR 971, [1999] All ER (EC) 289 *310, 311*

T-125 and 126/96 Boehringer v. Council [1999] ECR II-3427 *188*

T-135/96 UAPME v. Council [1998] ECR II-2335, [1998] 3 CMLR 385 *362*

T-264/97 D. v. Council [1999] ECR IA-1, [1999] ECR II-1 *388*

T-65/98R Van den Bergh Foods Ltd v. Commission [2003] ECR II-4653 *303*

T-178/98 Fresh Marine Co. A/S v. Commission [2004] ECR II-3127 *144*

T-198/98 Micro Leader Business v. Commission [1999] ECR II-3989, [2000] All ER (EC) 361, [2000] 4 CMLR 886 *326*

T-219/99 British Airways v. Commission [2003] ECR II-5917 *300*

T-222, 327 and 329/99 Martinez, De Gaulle & Others v. EP [2001] ECR II-2823 *24*

T-319/99 Federación Nacional de Empresas de Instrumentación Científica, Médica, Técnica y Dental (FENIN) v. Commission [2003] ECR II-357 *277*

T-342/99 Airtours plc v. Commission [2004] ECR II-1785 *311, 313, 315*

T-185/00, T-216/00, T-299/00, T-300/00 Métropole Télévision SA (M6), Antena 3 de Televisión, SA, Gestevisión Telecinco, SAand SIC - Sociedade Independente de Comunicação, SAv Commission [2002] ECR II-3805 *289*

T-190/00 Regione Siciliana v. Commission [2003] ECR II-5051 *130*

T-168/01 GlaxoSmithKline Services Unlimited v. Commission [2006] ECR II-2969 *280, 284*

T-177/01 Jégo-Quéré & Cie SA v. Commission [2002] ECR II-2365 *131*

T-310/01 Schneider Electric SA v. Commission [2002] ECR II-4071 *312, 313, 315*

T-315/01 Kadi (Yassin Abdullah) v. Council and Commission [2005] ECR II-3649 *127*

T-5/02 Tetra Laval BV v. Commission [2002] ECR II-4381 *312, 313, 315*

T-228/02 Organisation des Modjahedines du peuple d'Iran v. Council [2006] ECR II-4665 *127*

T-218 to 240/03 Boyle and Others v. Commission [2006] ECR II-1699 *132*

T-194/04 Bavarian Lager Co. Ltd v. Commission [2007] ECR 000 *77*

T-201/04 Microsoft Corp. v. Commission [2007] ECR II-0000 *305, 306, 315*

T-340/04 France Télécom SA v. Commission [2007] ECR II-573 *299*

T-464/04 Independant Music Publishers and Labels Association (Impala, association internationale) v. Commission [2006] ECR II-2289 *312, 313*

Table of cases before the national courts

Belgian courts

Minister for Economic Affairs v. Fromagerie Franco-Suisse ('Le Ski') (Cour de Cassation) [1972] CMLR 330 *95*

French courts

Application of Georges Nicolo (Conseil d'Etat) (1989) [1990] CMLR 173 *96*

Boisdet (Conseil d'Etat) [1991] 1 CMLR 3 *97*

Conseil de l'Ordre de Nice Jean-Jacques Rayne (Conseil d'Etat) (1990) Unreported *240*

Directeur Général des Douanes v. Société Café Jacques Vabre (Cour de Cassation) [1975] 2 CMLR 336 *96*

Minister of the Interior v. Cohn-Bendit (Conseil d'Etat) [1980] 1 CMLR 543 *96*

Von Kempis v. Geldof (Conseil d'Etat) [1976] 2 CMLR *96*

German courts

Brunner v. European Union Treaty (Bundesverfassungsgericht) [1994] 1 CMLR 57 *97*

International Handelsgesellschaft (Bundesverfassungsgericht) [1974] 2 CMLR 540 *97*

Wünsche Handelsgesellschaft (1986) *97*

Italian courts

Frontini (Corte Constituzionale) [1974] 2 CMLR 381 *98*

Spa Beca v. Ammistrazione della Finanze (Corte Constituzionale) (1982) cited in Charlesworth and Cullen p. 57 *98*

Polish courts

European Arrest Warrents Case (2005) No. P 1/05 *98*

Polish Membership of the EU Case (2005) K 18/04 *98*

UK courts

Argyll Group plc v. Distillers Co. plc (Court of Session) [1986] 1 CMLR 764 *326*

Brunner v. TEU [1994] 1 CMLR 57 *14*

Bulmer (HP) Ltd v. J. Bollinger SA (CA) [1974] 2 All ER 1190 *152*

Cutsforth v. Mansfield Inns (QBD) [1986] 1 CMLR 1, [1986] 1 WLR 558 *326*

Davidoff v. A & G Imports (High Court) [1999] 2 CMLR 1057 *333*

Duke v. Reliance Systems Ltd (HL) [1988] 2 WLR 359 *110*

Garden Cottage Foods v. Milk Marketing Board (HL) [1983] 2 All ER 770, [1984] AC 130 *325*

Garland v. British Rail Engineering Ltd (HL) [1979] 1 WLR 754, [1982] 2 All ER 402 *93*

Griffin v. South West Water (High Court) [1995] IRLR 15 *106*

Insitu Cleaning Co. v. Heads (EAT) [1995] RLR 4 *367*

Litster v. Forth Dry Dock Co. (HL) [1989] 2 CMLR 194, [1989] 1 All ER 1134 *94, 110*

Megaphone v. BT (QBD) (1989) (unreported) *326*

NUT v. St. Mary's Church of England Junior School (CA) [1997] 3 CMLR 630 *106*

Pickstone v. Freemans plc (HL) [1988] AC 66; [1988] 2 All ER 803 *93*

Plessey v. GEC (QBD) [1992] 4 CMLR 471
326

R. v. Attorney-General, ex parte ICI (CA)
[1987] 1 CMLR 72 354
R. v. Bow Street Magistrates, ex parte
Noncyp Ltd [1989] 3 WLR 467 187
R. v. Chief Constable of Sussex, ex parte
International Trader's Ferry [1998]
3 WLR 1260 (HL) 185
R. v. Human Fertilisation and Embryology
Authority, ex parte Diane Blood (CA)
[1997] All ER 687 247, 248
R. v. Secretary of State for Employment, ex
parte Equal Opportunities Commission
(HL) [1995] 1 AC 1; [1994] 1 All ER 910
377
R v. Secretary of State for Foreign and
Commonwealth Affairs, ex parte Lord Rees
Mogg [1994] QB 552, [1994] 1 All ER 457,
[1994] 2 WLR 115, [1993] 3 CMLR 101
13

R. v. Secretary of State for Transport, ex parte
Factortame (award of interim relief) (HL)
[1990] 3 CMLR 94, 99
R. v. Secretary of State for Transport and ex
parte Factortame (No. 5) (HL) [1999]
3 CMLR 597 94, 99, 115
Rolls-Royce plc v. Doughty (CA) [1992]
1 CMLR 1045, [1992] IRLR 126 106

Stoke-on-Trent Borough Council v. B &
Q plc, The Times, 24 July 1990 95

Thoburn v. Sunderland City Council (the
'Metric Martyrs' case) [2002] EWHC 195
(Admin), [2003] QB 151, [2002] 4 All
ER 156, [2002] 3 WLR 247 93
Three Rivers District Council v. Governor and
Company of the Bank of England [1996]
3 All ER 558 115

USA courts

US v. IE du Pont de Namours & Co
(Cellophane fallacy case) (1956) 297

Table of Commission decisions

ABG Oil, Re (Dec 77/327) OJ L [1977] 117/1, [1977] 2 CMLR D 1 *300*

Aerospatiale-Alenia/De Havilland (Case IV/M053), Re OJ C [1991] 334/42; [1992] 4 CMLR M2 *310*

Aluminium Products, Re (Dec 85/206) OJ L [1985] 92/1, [1987] 3 CMLR D 813 *346*

Application of the Publishers' Association, Re (Dec 89/44) *277*

Benelux Flat Glass Cartel, Re (Dec 84/388) [1985] 2 CMLR D 350 *323*

Binon v. Agence et Messageries de la Presse, Re (Dec 243/83) [1985] 3 CMLR D 8 *285*

British Midland Airways Ltd v. Aer Lingus plc, Re (Dec 92/213) OJ L [1992] 96/34 *276*

Decca Navigator System, Re (Dec 89/113) OJ L [1989] 43/27 *296*

Deere (John), Re (Dec 85/7a) OJ L [1985] 35/58, [1985] 2 CMLR D 554 *324*

Eurocheque/Helsinki Agreement, Re (Dec 92/212) OJ L [1992] 95/50 on appeal (pending) Cases T-39 & 40/92 *278*

Film Purchases by German Television Stations, Re (Dec 89/536) OJ C [1989] 54/2 *276*

Fine Papers Re (Dec 72/291) OJ L 182/24 [1974] CMCL D 94 *288*

'Flat Glass' Re (Dec 89/93) OJ L [1989] L 33 *294*

Franco–Japanese Ball Bearings Agreement, Re (Dec 74/634) OJ L [1974] 343/29 *275*

IBM Personal Computers, Re (Dec 84/233) OJ L [1984] 118/24, [1984] 2 CMLR D 342 *285*

ICI and Tioxide (IV/M4) *301*

Ideal/Standard Agreement, Re (Dec 84/85) OJ L [1985] 20/38, [1988] 4 CMLR D 627 *285*

Kodak, Re (Dec 70/332) OJ L [1970] 147/24, [1970] CMLR D 19 *285*

London European Airways v. Sabena, Re (Dec 88/589) OJ L [1988] 317/47, [1989] *276*

Milchforderungs Fonds, Re (Dec 85/76) OJ L [1985] 35/35, [1985] 3 CMLR D 101 *276*

Murat, Re (Dec 83/610) OJ L [1983] 348/20, [1984] 1 CMLR D 219 *285*

Northumbrian Water/Lyonnaise des Eaux (Dec IV/M567) (not yet reported) *314*

P and I Clubs (see 'Protection and Indemnity Clubs')

Pittsburg Corning Europe, Re (Dec 72/403) OJ L [1972] 272/35, [1973] CMLR D 2 *277*

Polypropylene Cartel, Re (Dec 86/398) OJ L [1986] 230/1, [1988] 4 CMLR D 34 *275*

Protection and Indemnity Clubs Agreement, Re (Dec 85/615) OJ L [1985] 376/2 *275*

Prym/Beka, Re (Dec 73/323) OJ L [1973] 296/24, [1973] CMLR D 250 *288*

Quinine Cartel (Re International Quinine Cartel) (Dec 69/240) OJ L [1969] 192/5 [1969] CMLCR D 41 *275*

Steetley/Tarmac, Re (Case IV/M053) OJ C [1992] 50/25 *314*

Tetra-Pak (BTG Licence), Re (Dec 88/501) OJ L [1988] 272/27 *307*

Table of Commission decisions

Transocean Marine Paint Association, Re
(Dec 67/454) OJ L [1967] 163/19 *288*

UNITEL, Re (Dec 78/516) OJ L [1978]
157/39, [1978] 3 CMLR D 306 *275*

Vacuum Interrupters Ltd, Re (Dec 77/160)
OJ L [1977] 48/32, [1977] 1 CMLR D 67
288

Villeroy & Boch, Re (Dec 1984) OJ L [1985]
OJ 367/15, [1988] 4 CMLR D 461 *285*
Virgin/British Airways (Dec 2000/74) (IV/D
2/34.780) OJ L [2000] 30/1 *301*

Wanadoo, Re (Dec C-2004/1929)
(Comp/C-1/38.233) *299*
Wood Pulp, Re (Dec 85/202) OJ L [1985]
85/1, [1985] 3 CMLR D 474 *324*

Part 1

THE CONSTITUTIONAL LAW OF THE EUROPEAN UNION

1 The development of European Union law

INTRODUCTION

Inspiration

The European Union (EU) as it is today may only be understood by placing it in the context of the development of European integration in the twentieth century. Grand designs for European integration have a long history. Military leaders from Julius Caeser to Adolf Hitler have asserted their territorial claims to integration through force. A more idealistic basis for co-operation between nation states through a 'social contract' may be traced through the writings of the Swiss philosopher, Rousseau, in the late eighteenth and early nineteenth centuries. Political leaders in the 1950s, after two world wars, strongly favoured a co-operative rather than a military approach to the rebuilding of Europe. The failure to resolve the divisions within Europe after the First World War made it imperative to find a lasting solution after the Second World War.

The inspiration for the three institutions that evolved to become the EU derived from the plan devised in 1950 by Robert Schuman, the French Foreign Minister, and Jean Monnet, responsible for overseeing France's economic recovery after the war. At the time, Europe was reliant on US-provided Marshall aid and needed to become self-sufficient. The Schuman plan involved the pooling by France and Germany of their production of coal and steel. Monnet and Schuman believed that Germany should be helped to rebuild, but only if bound politically and economically within an organisation of European states. Such close ties between former adversaries were seen as a step towards prosperity and a deterrent to future military conflict. The period since Monnet and Schuman's original plan has been one of relative prosperity and peace between the Member States. The Union now has 27 Members States, with other applicants waiting in the wings.

The creation of the ECSC, EEC and EURATOM

The Treaty of Paris was signed in 1951 by France, Germany, Italy, Belgium, the Netherlands and Luxembourg. The UK, although invited to participate, did not do so

3

for a number of reasons, including concerns over the nature and powers of the institutional arrangements.[1] As a result of the Treaty, the European Coal and Steel Community (ECSC) was born. Its objective was to create a common market in the production of coal and steel, the raw materials of both military weapons and civilian heavy industry.

> ## Key term
>
> A **common market** is an arrangement under which the participating states agree that goods, persons, services and capital may circulate freely, without any barriers. If goods enter the common market from outside, they face a common tariff or customs duty.

The ECSC proved to be a successful model for further integration; in 1955 the foreign ministers of the six ECSC States met at Messina to discuss the creation of a more wide-ranging common market. The meeting led to the production of the Spaak Report, presented to the six ECSC Member States. In 1957 the same six States signed two further treaties in Rome creating the European Economic Community (EEC) and the European Atomic Energy Community (EURATOM). Like the ECSC, EURATOM was limited to a single sector, atomic energy. In contrast, the EEC was a more ambitious enterprise which the founding states intended from the outset to evolve towards 'ever closer union among the peoples of Europe' (Preamble to the EEC Treaty).

Initially, the ECSC, EEC and EURATOM shared only two institutions, the Assembly (later known as the Parliament) and the Court. This was an inefficient arrangement and in 1965 the Merger Treaty led to the formation of a single Council and a Commission. After the merger the three communities functioned separately but with common institutions. As the ECSC Treaty lapsed in July 2002, its activities are now within the remit of the European Community.

Sovereignty and the Treaty of Rome 1957

The EEC sought integration under the Treaty of Rome (the EEC Treaty) in 1957 by merging the separate interests of the member states into a common market where goods, persons, services and capital could circulate freely. The creation of the EEC required a pooling of sovereignty (see box on p.5) in areas covered by the Treaty.[2] It reflected an ideal reminiscent of Churchill's vision in 1946 of a 'United States of Europe', the purpose of which was to develop Europe as an entity to offset the power of the USA. Unlike the USA, which functions as a single territory under the control of

---

[1] The UK position is considered at p.6.
[2] There is an extensive body of literature on sovereignty. See, for example, Mancini, G. (1998) 'Europe: The Case for Statehood', ELJ 29, and other references cited in Chapter 1 of Chalmers *et al.* (2006).

a federal authority, the EEC was established as a supranational organisation (see box below), capable of making policies and rules that bound the States. The founder members of the EEC, particularly France and Germany, for many years the driving force in European integration, saw the gain in peace, stability and economic development as outweighing the inevitable loss of sovereignty.

Key terms

Sovereignty is a concept which derives from political science and legal theory. It refers to the capability which states have to make their own laws independently. In the context of EU law, 'sovereignty' concerns the authority of EU law over that of the Member States.

Federalism refers to government by aggregation of states where each has conceded a degree of independence in order to share in the decision making of the whole in defined areas.

Supranationalism refers to the practice of decision making at a level over and above that of the states in question, but capable of binding those states.

The role of the Court of Justice in developing the supremacy of EU law over national law is considered in Chapter 4.

Aims of the Community

The Community had ambitious aims from the outset to improve the lives of its citizens through economic co-operation, in particular the creation of a common market and the harmonisation of policies. The original wording may be found in Article 2 of the EEC Treaty which referred to the establishment of a common market and an economic and monetary union (see p.10), progressive approximation (or harmonisation) of the economic policies of Member States. These goals were to be achieved by the promotion of 'a harmonious development of economic activities, a continuous, and balanced expansion, an increase in stability, an accelerated raising of the standard of living and quality of life and closer relations between the states belonging to it' (Article 2, EEC Treaty). They are to be achieved by establishing a common market and an economic and monetary union and, after amendment by the Treaty on European Union (TEU), with the progressive harmonisation of the economic policies of the Member States.

The present version of Article 2 in the Consolidated version of the Treaty establishing the European Community (TEC) incorporates further aims reflecting the changing direction of the Community, namely sustainable development of economic activities, a high level of employment and of social protection between men and women, sustainable and non-inflationary growth, a high degree of competitiveness and convergence of economic performance, a high level of protection and of improvement of the quality of the environment, and economic and social cohesion among the Member States. These aims will be amended further by the Treaty of Lisbon (see p.18), following ratification.

As we shall see in this chapter, throughout its development from EEC to EU, a tension has remained between the parallel themes of widening (broadening the base of the EU to admit more members) and deepening (developing closer ties of integration between existing members).

Position of the UK

At the time the Treaty of Rome was signed the UK was unwilling to sacrifice national sovereignty to join the Communities, seeking to retain its 'special relationship' with the USA and trade links with the Commonwealth. Instead the UK proposed the creation of a free trade area in Europe. In 1959 the European Free Trade Association (EFTA) was founded by the UK, Norway, Denmark, Sweden, Austria and Portugal, later including states such as Ireland and Finland.

> **Key term**
>
> In a **free trade area**, tariff barriers such as customs duties are removed on goods moving between Member States, leaving them free to impose tariffs on goods entering from outside the area. As a result, there is no loss of sovereignty.

When the UK realised its growing economic isolation, it applied in 1961 for full membership of the Communities, a lead followed by most EFTA countries. The UK application was initially unsuccessful as a result of the veto exercised by General de Gaulle, justified at the time on the basis of differences between the UK economy and those of the other Member States, and of problems arising from the UK's ties with the Commonwealth.

WIDENING THE TIES: ENLARGEMENT

First three rounds of enlargement 1973–86

In 1967 the UK reapplied, this time successfully, for membership of the Communities, again followed by Denmark, Norway and Ireland, leading to the signing of the Treaty of Accession in 1972. The UK, Ireland and Denmark joined the Communities, with effect from 1 January 1973. Norway decided not to proceed to membership following a referendum. This negative decision was repeated in 1994 when Norway voted in a second referendum against membership. Greenland[3] withdrew in 1985 after a similar referendum result. Following its return to democracy, Greece joined the EC in 1981, followed by Spain and Portugal in 1986. After the reunification of Germany in

---

[3] Greenland, at the time of the referendum vote in 1982, was an autonomous territory within the Kingdom of Denmark. It is now an overseas territory in association with the EU.

1989, the former East Germany was absorbed into the Communities on 3 October 1990 without the need for formal enlargement.

European Economic Area and enlargement

Austria, Sweden and Finland signed the European Economic Area (EEA) Agreement which came into force on 1 January 1994, extending the application of the single market to the territory of the signatory states. The EEA Agreement set up its own institutions and was seen as a prelude to full membership of the European Union. The EU was enlarged on 1 January 1995 by a further Act of Accession as a result of which Austria, Finland and Sweden became full members of the EU. Unlike previous enlargements, which had involved extensive transitional arrangements, the three EEA states acceded to the *acquis communautaire* with limited temporary exceptions. From 1995, only Switzerland, Norway, Iceland and Liechtenstein remain members of EFTA, although they retain close ties with the EU.

Key term

The *acquis communautaire* is the body of Community law and obligations which bind the Member States.

Enlargement 2004–07

A dramatic enlargement to the EU took place on 1 May 2004, when the EU received 10 new Member States. The catalyst for this immense change was the collapse of communism, a process symbolised by the fall of the Berlin Wall in 1989 after a decade of political upheaval in Eastern Europe. Many of the states previously under Soviet domination looked to the West to provide the way forward, with membership of the EU seen as the badge of a new identity.

The Copenhagen Summit of 1993 paved the way for 'Europe Agreements' which were signed with a number of East European states to promote convergence, integration and regional co-operation, providing for a structured relationship with the EU once economic and political conditions were satisfied. The so-called 'Copenhagen criteria' were agreed at the summit, setting out the conditions for accession to the EU:

- the existence of stable institutions which guarantee democracy, the rule of law, human rights, and respect for and protection of minorities;
- the existence of a functioning market economy, with the capacity to cope with competitive pressures and forces within the Union;
- the ability to take on the obligations of membership, including the *acquis communautaire* and political, economic and monetary union.

Negotiations opened in 1998 for Cyprus, the Czech Republic, Estonia, Hungary, Poland and Slovenia. Six further countries were added by the Helsinki Summit in December 1999: Bulgaria, Latvia, Lithuania, Malta, Romania and the Slovak Republic. To ensure that these States could meet their EU obligations on joining, programmes of financial support paved the way for full membership. In April 2003 a Treaty of Accession was signed with 10 new Member States. Cyprus, the Czech Republic, Estonia, Hungary, Poland, Latvia, Lithuania, Malta, Slovenia and Slovakia joined the EU on 1 May 2004. Bulgaria and Romania joined the EU on 1 January 2007, under a separate Treaty of Accession.

Entry negotiations with Croatia and Turkey began in October 2005. While the Commission envisages that negotiations with Croatia may be concluded within a few years, the position of Turkey remains under consideration. A tentative date of 2015 was proposed for Turkey's accession, but concern remains over Turkey's human rights record, a key Copenhagen criterion. Other potential candidate states from the Western Balkans include the former Yugoslav Republic of Macedonia, Bosnia and Herzegovina, Serbia, Montenegro and Albania.

DEEPENING THE TIES: FURTHER INTEGRATION

The Single European Act 1986

The Single European Act (SEA), signed in 1986, represented the first major revision to the EEC Treaty, following a number of unsuccessful attempts to change the institutional balance within the EC. The Single Market initiative carried the support of all Member States including the UK, although the Conservative government at the time opposed further integration towards economic and political union.

During the 1970s and early 1980s national self-interest predominated in the EC, impeding progress towards integration. If this spirit of protectionism were to be overcome, Member States would have to relinquish barriers such as non-recognition of professional qualifications and exchange control regulations. The rationale for the SEA emerged as a result of a 1985 White Paper on the Completion of the Internal Market issued by the Commission, which showed that many obstacles to trade between Member States remained, to the detriment of the EC's global trading position.

Key point

The emphasis of the White Paper was on **mutual recognition**, by which each Member State accepts the standards of other Member States, rather than **harmonisation**, involving a series of specific directives, a process seen to be too slow. These approaches are considered further in relation to goods in Chapters 11 and 12 and persons in Chapters 14 and 15.

There are differing views as to the dynamics of the process underlying the SEA. Some argue that it was a bargain between the Member States, with the Commission playing a key role. Others stress the role of the European Council and its influence on the Commission.[4] The objective of the SEA was the removal of all barriers to free movement between Member States. These barriers fell into three main types:

1 physical, such as border controls on persons or goods;
2 technical, such as different standards on goods;
3 fiscal, that is, differences in tax treatment.

The previous requirement for unanimity was dropped in favour of qualified majority voting (QMV), a system of weighted voting (see Chapter 2). As a result, the single market programme, a detailed and ambitious programme of directives, was adopted. It was no longer possible for a single State to halt progress. The programme rekindled the enthusiasm of the Member States for European integration.

> ## Key point
>
> The **internal market** is defined by Article 14 (ex 7a) as 'an area without internal frontiers in which the free movement of goods, persons, services and capital is ensured in accordance with the provisions of this Treaty'.

It might appear that the obligation to complete the single or internal market under the SEA did not differ fundamentally from the original provisions in the Treaty of Rome in relation to the common market. However, while the provisions in the Treaty of Rome on the free movement of goods, persons and services were clearly worded, those on capital were not and needed to be strengthened and simplified by the SEA. The main achievement of the single market programme was that it fostered a spirit of goodwill, previously lacking, to promote integration and a timetable for its realisation. By the end of 1992 the single market was largely complete. A single market 'scoreboard' was published on *Europa*, the EC website, and regularly updated. Areas 'scored' until 2000 included veterinary checks, food legislation, forestry, transport and machinery, telecommunication and energy.[5] Member States defaulting on implementation could be subject to action in the Court of Justice (ECJ). Later, the Maastricht Treaty introduced a procedure under Article 228 of the Treaty to impose financial penalties for Member States who continued to default after enforcement proceedings had been brought.

European Union and the Maastricht Treaty 1992

An intergovernmental conference (IGC) was convened in 1990 to consider economic and monetary union, with a second IGC to examine political union.

---

[4] See P. Craig, in C. Barnard and J. Scott (eds) *The Law of the Single Market* (2002: 11).
[5] http://ec.europa.eu/internal_market/sco

Key terms

Intergovernmental conference (IGC): a conference between the governments of the Member States to prepare for revision of the Treaty.

Economic and monetary union (EMU): an advanced form of integration, involving common economic policies and a central bank which issues a common currency.

Economic and political union (EPU): an advanced form of integration, involving common policies and common political institutions.

At the time the Maastricht Treaty or Treaty on European Union was under negotiation, France and Germany were seen as providing the 'motor' for future European integration. They believed firmly that EMU could not be effective without EPU. Other States such as the UK and Denmark were opposed to deeper integration, fearing a further loss of sovereignty. Such differing views could not be fully resolved in the body of a single Treaty. As a result, when the Treaty (the TEU) was signed in December 1991 at Maastricht in the Netherlands, providing for both forms of union, the UK and Denmark 'opted out' of the commitment to EMU in a Protocol.

Key term

Protocol: a separate written instrument annexed to a Treaty. Protocols have been used to enable some Member States to agree to provisions which others do not accept.

The UK further 'opted out' of the Social Chapter[6] in another Protocol, which provided a limited legal basis for employment protection measures, to which the then Conservative government under John Major strongly objected. From the untidy arrangements and political compromises secured to ensure the passage of the TEU we can see the emergence of what Curtin has termed 'a Europe of bits and pieces'.[7] While purists might decry the resulting legal complexities, it could be argued that without such arrangements, progress towards European Union would have ground to a halt. The Treaty of Amsterdam enshrined the concept of 'flexibility' in Articles 43–45, paving the way for the admission of new Member States with differing degrees of integration into the activities of the EU and allowing existing States to advance at different speeds.[8]

[6] Correctly known as the Social Policy Agreement.
[7] Curtin (1993).
[8] See p.15.

● The Three Pillar structure of the EU

The TEU embodied a far-reaching commitment towards European Union. Although some States rejected the commitment to EMU, the obligation to move to political union applied to *all* Member States. EPU was to be achieved through the operation of a new structure comprising three 'pillars'. These were as follows.

(a) The First Pillar, the European Community (EC)

This was made up of the three previous Communities: the ECSC, EURATOM and the EC, as the EEC had been renamed. It was (and is) governed by EC law under the Treaty establishing the EC (TEC or EC).

(b) The Second Pillar, the Common Foreign and Security Policy (CFSP)

The TEU provided for this pillar under Title V (Articles 11–28), covering joint foreign action and security by the Member States. Decisions under the CFSP are reached through inter-governmental co-operation. The CFSP covers political aspects of the EU's external relations: that is, its relations with non-Member States, known as 'third states'. These activities include diplomatic contacts and peace keeping, but not economic activities such as trade or aid agreements which are governed by the EC Treaty.

A unanimous vote in the Council is required under Article 23 TEU for a decision under the CFSP. There is scope under Article 23 for qualified majority voting (see Chapter 2), for example, in adopting joint actions on the basis of a common strategy. The difficulties inherent in achieving unanimity are illustrated by the starkly differing responses of the Member States to US military intervention in Iraq in 2003, when a common response under the CFSP proved impossible. On this occasion the UK supported military intervention by the USA, despite strong opposition by France and Germany.

(c) The Third Pillar, Police and Judicial Co-operation in Criminal Matters (PJCC)

The third pillar was originally entitled Co-operation in Justice and Home Affairs under the Maastricht Treaty, the title being changed to Police and Judicial Co-operation in Criminal Matters by the Treaty of Amsterdam. The Third Pillar is governed by Title VI (Articles 29–42) of the TEU. It covers some aspects of the regulation of external borders and the free movement of persons, such as asylum and immigration policies, as well as co-operation between judicial, police and customs authorities.

> ### Key point
>
> The Second and Third Pillars were not seen at the time of the Maastricht Treaty as suitable for regulation by law. As a result they were administered through inter-governmental co-operation under the Treaty on European Union (TEU) and were not subject to review by the Court of Justice. A significant trend from the Treaty of Amsterdam onwards has been the gradual removal of certain areas from the Third Pillar to the First (see below).

As we have seen (p.10), the TEU provided for the adoption of a new legal base for social policy, set out in a Protocol, as the UK refused to participate. The Social Chapter was incorporated into the body of the Treaty by the Treaty of Amsterdam after a change of government in the UK. The TEU also provided for the principle of subsidiarity.

Key term

The principle of **subsidiarity** governs the allocation of competences (or responsibilities) in areas where the EC shares the role with the Member States rather than being responsible alone. The principle was introduced by the TEU, and is set out in Article 5 (ex 3b) of the Treaty. Examples of areas governed by the principle include protection of the environment and consumer protection.

Article 5 provides that the EC should act either where it is given the power to do so under the Treaty or where it can achieve a particular objective more effectively than a Member State (see Chapter 4). The UK supported the inclusion of subsidiarity at Maastricht, believing that it would act as a check on the EC institutions and the growth of federalism. In practice it has proved hard to rely on the principle as the basis for an action in judicial review (see Chapter 8).

Objectives of the Union

The objectives of the Union are set out in Article 2 of the TEU, reflecting the activities to be pursued under the three pillars. In addition the Union is to maintain in full and build on the *acquis communautaire*. The Maastricht Treaty added a commitment to the establishment of an Economic and Monetary Union to the original list of tasks in Article 2, along with the 'strengthening of social cohesion' (Article 3).

Other changes introduced by the Treaty on European Union

Important institutional changes were made by the TEU, particularly the introduction of the co-decision procedure, strengthening the role of the European Parliament without giving it direct legislative power. This procedure, now the main legislative mechanism of the EC, involves the adoption of legislation jointly by the Council and the European Parliament. It is considered further in Chapter 2.

The European Council, made up of the heads of state or government and the President of the Commission, is required under Article 4 TEU to meet at least twice a year. It must provide the Union with 'the necessary impetus for its development' in order to define the general political guidelines.

A new category of Citizenship of the Union was established for EU nationals under Article 17 (ex 8) EC. Union citizenship is not merely symbolic. Citizens enjoy residence rights throughout the EU, as well as democratic rights such as the right to stand and vote in European Parliamentary elections. There is an expanding body of case law on citizenship built on the principle of non-discrimination (see Chapter 13). Citizens' rights are of great significance to individuals outside the established economic categories of free movers.

The TEU enabled the Union to declare its allegiance to human rights, though the provisions were placed in the TEU rather than the legally enforceable EC Treaty. Fundamental rights in EU law may be understood as those rights guaranteed by the European Convention on Human Rights and Fundamental Freedoms (ECHR) and those resulting from the constitutional traditions common to the Member States (see Chapter 4).

Titles and terminology

Following ratification of the TEU in 1993, the European Union was established as an over-arching entity covering the EC, ECSC and EURATOM. The TEU dropped the word 'Economic' from the title to signify the Community's evolution from an economic community to the present-day European Union, with its wide-ranging sphere of interests. The other name change was to the Council of Ministers, which became known as the Council of the European Union.

Key terms

EC law and **EU law**: The expression 'EC law' refers to the legal regulation of activities under the First Pillar. While some commentators restrict the term 'EU law' to activities under the Second and Third Pillars, others use it as an 'umbrella' term to denote the regulation of all three pillars. The title of this book reflects the latter approach, although the main emphasis remains on the law of the First Pillar, the EC. Once the Treaty of Lisbon (see p.17) has been ratified, there will be no need to distinguish between these terms, as the term 'European Community' will be subsumed into the 'European Union'.

Ratification of the Treaty on European Union

Key term

Ratification is the act by which a national government or parliament formally approves an international treaty.

Ratification proved to be a fraught process. There was strong opposition in the UK from an alliance of Conservative 'euro-sceptics' and some Labour MPs. An unsuccessful legal challenge led to further delay (*R* v. *Secretary of State for the Foreign and Commonwealth Office, ex parte Lord Rees Mogg*). The Danish people rejected the Treaty in a referendum, only accepting it in a second referendum. Ratification in Germany was delayed by a challenge to the Treaty in the Constitutional Court (*Brunner* v. *TEU*). The Treaty finally came into force on 1 November 1993 when the ratification process was complete in all Member States.

The Treaty of Amsterdam 1997

An IGC between 1996 and 1997 reviewed the Maastricht Treaty prior to further enlargement. The Treaty of Amsterdam (TOA) was signed in October 1997 and took effect on 1 May 1999. Many commentators considered that the Treaty lacked a 'big idea', as it failed to make significant changes to the institutions. Instead it made modest alterations to the decision-making structure, simplifying and extending the co-decision-making procedure.

The Treaty of Amsterdam kept the three-pillar structure introduced at Maastricht, but began the process that has continued with later Treaty revisions of moving activities from the Third Pillar to the First Pillar, bringing them within the jurisdiction of the ECJ. The Schengen Agreement providing for a gradual relaxation of border controls on the movement of persons between participating states was brought into the legal regime of the First Pillar by a Protocol. The UK and Ireland did not sign the Schengen Agreement or the Protocol, owing to concern over immigration, terrorism and drug trafficking. Some aspects of immigration policy were also moved to the First Pillar by the TOA, with the UK and Ireland again opting out.

Under the Second Pillar (CFSP), Member States were required by Articles 11–28 TEU to ensure that their national policies complied with the EU model in areas such as the common defence policy and peace keeping.

The Third Pillar was renamed Police and Judicial Co-operation in Criminal Matters to reflect the stated intention in Article 29 TEU to provide citizens with a high level of safety within an area of freedom, security and justice. EC rules were to be drawn up on common action on asylum, visas, immigration and controls at external borders.

Policies and tasks under the Treaty of Amsterdam

New tasks were provided under Article 2 of the Treaty including:

- the promotion of equality between men and women;
- a high level of protection and improvement of the quality of the environment;
- promotion of a high degree of competitiveness; and
- economic development which must be 'sustainable' as well as 'balanced and harmonious'.

These tasks are reflected in changes to the substantive provisions of the Treaty, as follows:

(a) **Non-discrimination**. The introduction of a legal base under Article 13 EC for action to combat discrimination marked the Union's move away from an economics-based approach to one covering many different types of discrimination (see Chapter 22).

(b) **Transparency**. The principle of transparency was acknowledged in Article 255, providing that EU citizens have a right of access to the European Parliament, Council and Commission documents.

(c) **Flexibility**. Articles 43–45 TEU enable Member States to use the institutional framework to establish closer co-operation between themselves (see Chapter 16 in relation to Economic and monetary union).

(d) **Human rights**. Article 6(1) TEU sets out the Union's commitment to human rights and fundamental freedoms, with the possible suspension under Article 7 TEU of a Member State from the European Council where there is a persistent and serious breach. So far it has not been necessary to invoke Article 7 against an individual Member State (see Chapter 4).

(e) **Environment**. The commitment to the environment was strengthened by Article 6 (ex 3c), requiring the integration of environmental policies into the definition and implementation of EC policies, with a view to promoting sustainable development.

Key point

The TOA renumbered almost all provisions of the EC Treaty as part of the process of simplification and consolidation. Law reports of pre-TOA case law use the old numbering, whereas reports of cases arising post-TOA use the new. Taking the Treaty provision for preliminary rulings as an example, a renumbered provision should be cited by reference to the new numbering first, followed by the old numbering in brackets, i.e. Article 234 (ex 177) EC. References in this book are to the EC Treaty, that is the Treaty of Rome as amended by later treaties, up to and including the Treaty of Nice, unless otherwise specified.

The Treaty of Nice 2001

The next IGC was convened at the Cologne Summit in June 1999 to address the issues left unresolved by the TOA, particularly institutional reform prior to enlargement. As Craig and De Burca observe,[9] the Communities had existed without a single IGC from 1957 until 1985, when the integration process begun by the SEA prompted an almost continuous process of Treaty revision. The Treaty of Nice (TON) was agreed by the Member States in December 2000 and signed in February 2001 despite the dissatisfaction of many citizens who felt isolated from the EU institutions and the process of integration.

A Protocol to the Treaty of Nice provided methods for introducing changes to the EC institutions. These changes were complex, involving weighted voting in the Council, an upper limit on the number of MEPs and a reduction in the number of Commissioners (see Chapter 2). The Treaty extended the co-decision procedure and reformed the judicial system. It provided more detailed procedures on the use of

[9] Craig and De Burca (2007: 42).

Article 7 of the TEU, suspension of voting rights in the Council for a serious and persistent breach of human rights.

Changes were made to the Second Pillar, the CFSP, particularly to the security and defence policy in Article 17. New provision under the Second Pillar was made in Article 43 TEU for 'enhanced co-operation', replacing the previous expression 'closer co-operation' (see p.15). Under Article 43 enhanced co-operation may only be invoked where eight[10] Member States agree to participate, subject to a series of conditions including the need to respect the *acquis communautaire*. Military and defence matters are excluded.

Although ratification of the TON proceeded fairly smoothly in 14 of the 15 Member States, the Irish people rejected the Treaty in a referendum in June 2001, refusing to ratify. A second referendum in Ireland in October 2002 secured the requisite majority, and the Treaty came into force on 1 February 2003, just over a year before enlargement of the Union to 25 Member States on 1 May 2004.

> **Key point**
>
> The Consolidated Version of the Treaty establishing the European Community, i.e. the EC Treaty as amended by the Treaty of Nice, remains the current version of the Treaty, until the Treaty of Lisbon is ratified (see below).

The Charter of Fundamental Rights 2000

The Charter was signed by the 15 Member States at the European Council meeting at Nice in December 2000. It is not yet legally binding, but takes the form of a declaration annexed to the Treaty. Its status will change under the Treaty of Lisbon (see p.17), when it will become legally binding. The Charter has been invoked on a number of occasions by the Court of First Instance and by the Advocates General of the ECJ. The current non-binding status of the Charter resulted from the differing positions of the Member States, with the UK arguing in the Treaty negotiations that it was unnecessary, while the majority of other Member States supported it as a formal element within the Treaty. A Protocol recognises the position of the UK and Poland. The Charter incorporates rights drawn from a number of international sources, particularly the European Convention on Human Rights. It recognises these rights under six headings: dignity, freedom, equality, solidarity, citizens' rights and justice. The Charter is considered further in Chapter 4.

The failed Constitutional Treaty 2004

The Convention on the Future of Europe was set up following the Laeken Summit of the European Council in December 2001 to explore the areas identified by the Nice

---

[10] Nine, under the Treaty of Lisbon.

IGC as requiring further action: subsidiarity, the status of the Charter of Fundamental Rights, simplification of the Treaties and the role of national and regional parliaments in relation to the EU. The Convention under the Chairmanship of the former President of France, Valéry Giscaird d'Estaing, drew up the Treaty establishing a Constitution for Europe or Constitutional Treaty (CT) in July 2003. The CT was signed by the Member States in October 2004. However, popular unease and frustration over the role and function of the EU led to resounding 'no' votes in referenda in 2005 in France and the Netherlands. The ratification process stalled, and the CT was eventually abandoned.

Despite the failure of the CT, it was clear that a new Treaty was essential to the future operation of the Union. While the EC Treaty in its present form, supplemented by the decisions of the ECJ, operates as a 'constitution' for the EU and its institutions, it does not contain all the primary rules, for example in relation to the composition of the institutions, where reference to the relevant Accession Treaty (2003 or 2005) is needed. The Member States convened an IGC in 2007, which identified the need for greater efficiency in decision making, increased democracy through a greater role for the European Parliament and national parliaments, and increased external coherence. The Reform Treaty (Treaty of Lisbon) was signed in December 2007, with a target date for ratification of January 2009.

The Treaty of Lisbon 2007: a summary of key changes

When the Treaty of Lisbon (TOL) is ratified, it will introduce significant changes intended to simplify the structure and organisation of the European Union. It amends the Treaty on European Union (TEU) and the EC Treaty, which is renamed the Treaty on the Functioning of the Union (TFU). The 'European Union' will continue as a single combined entity and the 'European Community' will disappear. Article I of the TEU provides for the establishment of the Union, and that both Treaties will have the same legal value. The three-pillar structure will be merged into one, 'the Union', although special procedures in foreign policy, security and defence will be retained.

The Charter of Fundamental Rights will not be incorporated into the body of the Treaty by the TOL, as it would have been under the CT. Instead Article 6 of the TEU provides for the recognition of the rights, freedoms and principles set out in the Charter of Fundamental Rights, which is stated to have the same legal value as the Treaties. The provisions of the Charter 'shall not extend in any way the competences of the Union as defined in the Treaties'. A Protocol on the application of the Charter to the UK and Poland provides that the Charter does not extend the ability of the ECJ or any court or tribunal of the UK or Poland to find that the laws, regulations or administrative provisions are inconsistent with the fundamental rights and principles in the Charter. It could be argued that the Protocol was unnecessary, as the Charter was not intended to introduce new rights. It remains to be seen how the Protocol will be interpreted in the future.

Key point

Before the Treaty of Lisbon, the Union lacked legal personality, preventing it from acceding to international treaties such as the ECHR. This deficiency is rectified by Article 46A of the TFU which provides that the Union shall have legal personality. Article 6(2) TEU requires the Union to accede to the ECHR.

A new set of aims

A new Article 1a, of the TEU provides for the Union to be founded on the values of 'respect for human dignity, freedom, democracy, equality, the rule of law and respect for human rights'. Article 2, TEU provides for a new set of aims, including:

- the promotion of peace, its values and the well-being of its peoples;
- an area of freedom, security and justice without internal frontiers, in conjunction with external border controls;
- the establishment of an internal market: the Union is required to work for the sustainable development of Europe, to combat social exclusion and discrimination, to promote social justice and equality and to respect cultural and linguistic diversity;
- the establishment of economic and monetary union;
- the upholding and promotion of its values in its relations with the wider world;
- the pursuit of its objectives by appropriate means commensurate with its competences conferred on it by the Treaties.

The Union is required to develop a 'special relationship with neighbouring countries', founded on the values of the Union and 'characterised by close and peaceful relations based on co-operation' (Article 7a, TEU).

Key term

Competence is the capacity to act. The EU has capacity to act only where the Treaty confers it (the principle of 'conferral').

The distribution of competences between the EU and the Member States will be clarified. Article 2F of the TFU provides that the limits of Union competences are governed by the principle of conferral. Such competences may be either 'exclusive', i.e. conferred on the Union alone or 'shared with the Member States'. Where the Union has exclusive competence, only the Union may legislate unless empowered to act by the Union. Where competence is shared, both the Union and Member states may legislate. The Member States shall exercise their competence to the extent that the Union has not done so. The areas in which the Union has exclusive competence are listed in Article 2B, with areas of shared competence listed in Article 2C, TFU. This is considered further in Chapter 3.

There is no provision in the TEU or TFU for the primacy of Union law over national law (unlike the CT). Instead, a Declaration appended to the Treaty of Lisbon recalls that, in accordance with well-settled case law of the Court of Justice, the Treaties and secondary legislation have primacy over the law of Member States under the conditions laid down by the ECJ. The TOL will make many changes to the institutional framework, intended to make the EU more workable with 27 Member States. These are considered in Chapter 2. Qualified majority voting will be extended to many additional areas, with a new definition of qualified majority in Article 205 which will take effect in 2014.

An elected President of the European Council will replace the rotating presidency. The European Council is recognised as an institution in the legal order. The position of High Representative of the Union for foreign affairs and security policy has been strengthened by combining this existing role with that of the Vice-President of the Commission, to raise the EU's profile in the world. The High Representative will act in foreign policy matters only where there is unanimous support from the 27 Member States, and not as a replacement of the foreign policy of Member States.

The Treaty of Lisbon will amend both the Treaty on European Union and the Treaty establishing the European Community:

- **The Treaty on European Union**: includes new provisions for the Common Foreign and Security Policy.
- **The Treaty on the Functioning of the Union** (previously the Treaty establishing the European Community): includes many new or amended provisions. A new Title IV Area of Freedom, Security and Justice covers border checks, asylum and immigration, replacing the previous Title IV on Visas, Asylum and Immigration.

Provision is made in the Treaty to replace the words 'Community' and 'European Community' with 'Union', and to replace 'common market' with 'internal market'.

The substantive changes under the Treaty of Lisbon are considered, where relevant, throughout the book.

Ratification of the Treaty of Lisbon

As this book goes to press, the EU faces a crisis over the ratification of the Treaty of Lisbon. In June 2008, the Irish people voted against ratification of the Treaty in a referendum. While 19 Member States, including the UK, had ratified by July 2008, the Treaty can only come into effect once it has been ratified by *all* the Member States. Ireland was the only Member State committed to holding a referendum. Other States, such as Poland and the Czech Republic, now appear reluctant to complete the ratification process. Resolving the deadlock poses a huge challenge for the incoming French Presidency of the Council. It is not yet clear how resolution will be achieved. Ireland may be encouraged to hold a second referendum, although the outcome of such a vote may lead to a second rejection. Reform is essential if the EU is to function effectively with 27 or more Member States, but it must have the support of the peoples of those States. Further information on the ratification process will be provided on the website accompanying this book.

QUESTIONS

1 Why did the EEC Treaty require Member States to pool their sovereignty in certain areas? How were the objectives of the EEC to be achieved?

2 Why was the single market programme necessary and how was it achieved?

3 How do the changes resulting from the Treaties of Maastricht, Amsterdam and Nice reflect the parallel themes of 'widening' and 'deepening' the European Union?

Further reading

Chalmers, D., Hadjiemmanuil, C., Monti, G. and Tomkins, A. (2006) *European Union Law,* Cambridge University Press, Chapters 1 and 2.

Craig, P. (2002) 'The Evolution of the Single Market' in C. Barnard and J. Scott (eds), *The Law of the Single Market,* Hart Publishing.

Craig, P. and De Burca, G. (2007) *EU Law: Text, Cases and Materials,* 4th edition, Oxford University Press, Chapter 1.

Curtin, D. (1993) 'The Constitutional Structure of the Union: A Europe of Bits and Pieces', (1993) 30 CMLRev. 17.

Dell, E. (1995) *The Schuman Plan and the British Abdication of Leadership in Europe,* Oxford, Clarendon.

O'Keefe, D. and Twomey, P. (eds) (1994) *Legal Issues of the Maastricht Treaty,* Wiley Chancery.

Lenaerts, K. and Gerard, D. (2004) 'The Structure of the Union according to the Constitution for Europe: the emperor is getting dressed', (2004) 29 ELRev. 289.

Weatherill, S. (2004) in T. Tridimas and P. Nebbia (eds), *European Union Law for the Twenty First Century,* Hart Publishing, Chapter 2.

Visit **http://www.mylawchamber.co.uk/kent** to access answer guidance to questions in the book to test yourself on this chapter.

2

The institutions of the EU: the Parliament, the Council, the Commission and the Court of Justice

INSTITUTIONS

As we have seen in Chapter 1, the EC Treaty is a legal framework, providing for broadly stated objectives and obligations. It follows that the enactment of detailed rules is left to the institutions of the EC, acting within the limits of powers conferred on them by the Treaty. Successive revisions of the Treaty have amended these powers and the rules on composition of the institutions. The recent enlargements of the EU to 27 Member States have created a patchwork of further amendments, to which will be added the changes under the Treaty of Lisbon. The present rules may thus be found in EC Treaty, as amended by the Treaty of Nice and by the Acts of Accession of 2003 and 2005.

Five principal institutions

Article 7 (ex 4) of the Treaty provides that the tasks entrusted to the Community are to be carried out by five institutions, namely:

1 a European Parliament,
2 a Council,
3 a Commission,
4 a Court of Justice,
5 a Court of Auditors.

Process of evolution over the years

The changing role and composition of each institution is considered below in this chapter. It should be remembered that the dynamics of the relationships between the main EC institutions have evolved over the years. Initially, the European Parliament (EP) tended to align itself with the Commission against the Council in promoting European integration. However, in recent years, tensions have arisen in the relations between the EP and the Commission, as the EP sought to exercise the powers in has been given by successive Treaty revisions. The role of the European Court of Justice (ECJ) is particularly significant, as it has interpreted its role creatively to develop the

21

Community legal order in a way which may appear 'political' to observers from a common law tradition.

THE EUROPEAN PARLIAMENT

The European Parliament (EP) provides a forum to consider legislation and to review the activities of other institutions such as the Commission. Its role differs from that of a national parliament as it lacks the power to legislate unless acting with the Council (see below), which has traditionally been seen as the source of political power in the EU. The limited legislative powers have led to criticisms of a 'democratic deficit' in EU decision making. In order to appreciate whether there is indeed such a deficit, it is necessary to assess the roles of the EP and the other EU institutions involved in the decision-making process.

The EP is based in Strasbourg, with some sessions held in Brussels, where committee meetings are also usually held. Members (MEPs) are elected for five years. The EP has been directly elected since 1979, after which its stature and influence have steadily increased.

The TEU introduced co-decision under Article 251 to enable legislation to be adopted jointly by the EP and the Council, referring to it clumsily as 'the procedure under Article 251'.

Key term

Co-decision procedure: the procedure under Article 251 EC by which legislation is adopted jointly by the EP and the Council.

The introduction of co-decision making may be seen as recognition that the EP, the only elected body in the Union, should play an equal part in the process of decision making. Most secondary legislation is now adopted under this procedure, as successive Treaty reforms have expanded the areas subject to co-decision making.

The Treaty of Lisbon

The status of co-decision as the main mechanism for the adoption of legislation is reflected in its renaming under the Treaty of Lisbon (TOL) as 'the ordinary decision-making procedure'. The TOL will introduce a 'special decision-making procedure' which will enable the EP to adopt legislation alone after participation by the Council in areas of the Treaty covered by the procedure under new Article 249A(2). There is also a procedure enabling the Council to adopt laws alone after participation by the EP. The special decision-making procedure is not spelt out in the TOL. However, provisions which invoke it such as Article 18b (measures concerning social security or social protection) require the Council to act unanimously after consulting the EP.

Key point

The introduction of the special decision-making procedure appears to represent a significant change to the inter-institutional balance, as the EP has never previously possessed the power to make laws alone. However, there are few areas in the Treaty where special decision-making applies to the EP (see, for example, Article 190(5) regulations for MEPs).

Composition of the Parliament

After enlargement in 2007 the number of MEPs is as follows: Germany (99); France, Italy and the UK (78 each); Spain and Poland (54 each); Romania (35); Netherlands (31); Belgium, Hungary, the Czech Republic, Greece and Portugal (24 each); Sweden (19); Austria (18); Bulgaria (18); Denmark, Finland, Slovakia (14 each); Ireland (13); Latvia and Lithuania (nine each); Slovenia (seven); Cyprus, Estonia, Luxembourg (six each); and Malta (five). The distribution of MEPs between the 27 Member States will have to be recalculated during the 2009–14 Parliamentary term. Under the Treaty of Lisbon, the number of MEPs is reduced to 751 plus the President. Numbers of MEPs from a single country cannot exceed 96 and must not be less than six for each Member State.

It should be noted that seats in the Parliament are not distributed evenly according to population. Citizens in smaller Member States are better represented than those in larger States, with Luxembourg, for example, enjoying a representation of one MEP for about 65,550 citizens, compared with Germany, where the ratio is one MEP for about 400,000 citizens.[1] Although there have been common electoral procedures requiring the use of proportional representation (PR)[2] in the Member States since 2002, there is considerable discretion for Member States in the choice of PR system and in the size of constituencies.

Political groups

Most MEPs sit in one of the eight cross-national political groupings, reflecting traditional ideological divisions. The 'left' is represented by the Socialist Group, and the 'right' by the Group of the European People's Party and the European Democrats. MEPs do not receive instructions on voting from their home state but vote on an individual and personal basis, with alliances which transcend political and national groupings. Recognition as a group in the EP requires a strong level of political affinity between the members. Lack of a sufficiently strong affinity caused the Technical

---

[1] Chalmers *et al.* (2006: 111).
[2] Proportional representation covers a range of electoral systems whereby seats are allocated roughly in proportion to votes cast, unlike the 'first-past-the-post' system used in the Westminster Parliament.

Group of Independent Members to fail in its action to annul a decision on recognition in Joined Cases T-222, 327 and 329/99 *Martinez, De Gaulle & Others* v. *EP*.

European political parties are seen as an important element in integration, contributing to 'forming a European awareness and to expressing the political will of the citizens of the Union' under Article 191 of the Treaty. However, their existence has done little so far to awaken the interest of the voters in European rather than national issues. Although Union citizenship carries political rights including the right to vote in EP and local elections, Union citizens tend not to identify themselves as part of a European people (a *demos*) but as nationals of their own Member State. As Joseph Weiler points out: '[E]urope's political architecture has never been validated by a process of constitutional adoption by a European constitutional *demos* and, hence, . . . does not enjoy the same kind of authority that may be found in federal states where their federalism is rooted in a classic constitutional order.'[3]

Functions of the Parliament

The EP has important functions, including the following:

- the Budget,
- supervision of the Commission,
- legislation.

Parliament and the Budget

The EP has significant powers to amend and delay the Budget under Article 272 (ex 203) EC. While the Council has the last word over obligatory expenditure (expenditure which is required under the Treaty, such as under the Common Agricultural Policy), the EP's budgetary powers over non-obligatory expenditure (expenditure on discretionary fields of activity, such as culture and education) are considerable, enabling it to amend or even reject the budget. Non-obligatory expenditure has increased greatly since 1988 through doubling expenditure on structural funds and financial support for former Eastern bloc countries prior to accession.[4] The Treaty of Lisbon will reform the budgetary procedures and increase the role of the Parliament in relation to the budget, abolishing the distinction between obligatory and non-obligatory expenditure (new Article 272).

Supervision of the Commission

The Parliament exercises a degree of supervision over the activities of the Commission, which submits a report of its activities annually to the EP for debate in open

---

[3] J. Weiler, 'A Constitution for Europe? Some Hard Choices', in J. Weiler, I. Begg and J. Peterson (eds) (Blackwell, 2003).

[4] See Arnull *et al.* [Hereafter Wyatt and Dashwood] (2006: 47).

session (Article 200). The EP may pass a motion of censure on the Commission under Article 201, enabling it to dismiss all members of the Commission, although it cannot dismiss individual Commissioners. The censure motion is a cumbersome mechanism requiring a two-thirds majority of votes cast. It has been threatened on eight occasions, though never pursued to a conclusion.

Key point

A censure motion was tabled in the EP in 1999, following publication of a highly critical report by a Committee of Experts into allegations of fraud, mismanagement and nepotism on the part of the Commission. In March 1999, the day before the vote was due to be taken, all members of the Commission, led by President Jacques Santer, resigned.[5] The motion was dropped.

Even if a vote of censure had been passed and the Commission required to resign, Article 210 provides for the Commission to remain in place to deal with EC business until a new Commission is appointed under Article 214. Although those who resigned in 1999 declared that they would act in a limited capacity pending replacement, they did not in practice limit their dealings. A new President, Romano Prodi, was introduced in September 1999, with a 'new' Commission which nevertheless included some Commissioners who had resigned.

The Parliament has a major role to play in the nomination of the President of the Commission under Article 214 and in the final approval of the Commission as a whole. As a result, the Commission has increased its accountability to the Parliament, with the two institutions in office for the same length of term. The use of the EP's powers under Article 214 to approve the Commission is illustrated by the Parliament's near rejection of the Commission proposed by José Barroso, President of the Commission, in 2004. The EP objected to the offensive views expressed by the nominee for the Justice, Freedom and Security portfolio, which included responsibility for anti-discrimination policy. The problem was resolved without rejection of the whole Commission following a compromise involving the replacement of two of the Commissioners by nominees more acceptable to the Parliament.[6]

Parliament's role in the legislative process

Under the present version of the EC Treaty, the Parliament cannot legislate alone, although it may adopt laws jointly with the Council under Article 251 EC. This procedure is considered in more detail below. As we have seen (p. 22), the Treaty of Lisbon will allow the EP to adopt legislation under the special procedure where applicable, though it remains to be seen how the procedure will operate in practice.

---

[5] For an assessment of the Santer Presidency, see J. Peterson, 'The Santer Era: the European Commission in Normative, Historical and Theoretical Perspective' (1999) 6 JEPP 46.

[6] Wyatt and Dashwood (2006: 39).

Progressive Treaty reforms have strengthened the Parliament's influence on the adoption of legislation while increasing the number of areas to which the co-decision procedure applies under Article 251, as the legal base on which legislation is adopted determines which procedure which applies.

There are currently three legislative procedures, as follows:

1 consultation,
2 co-decision,
3 assent.

> ## Key point
>
> The Treaty of Lisbon will repeal Article 252 (consultation procedure) and replace it with new Article 252a which requires the EP, Council and Commission to consult each other and agree to make arrangements for co-operation. They are empowered, to that end, to conclude binding interinstitutional agreements (i.e. agreements between institutions).

Consultation procedure

The consultation procedure is governed by Article 252, until it is repealed by the Treaty of Lisbon. Proposed legislation is submitted by the Commission to the Council. Where the Treaty requires, the draft must be laid before the EP for the first reading. The draft is then considered in a committee of the EP before an opinion is delivered. Any proposed amendments are referred back to the Council. The Council adopts the final act after discussion in the Committee of Permanent Representatives (COREPER). Consultation with the Economic and Social Committee and the Committee of the Regions may be required in some cases. (See pp.48–49 for an explanation of the role of these bodies.)

The Council cannot ignore the need to consult the Parliament where consultation is an essential procedural requirement under the Treaty. Failure to consult may lead to annulment of the act, as Case 138/79 *Roquette Frères SA* v. *Council* illustrates. Here the Court annulled a regulation adopted under what is now Article 37(2) by the Council without waiting for the EP's opinion, which had been sought several months earlier. The Court emphasised that consultation with the Parliament was an 'essential factor in the institutional balance intended by the Treaty', reflecting the EP's role as a representative assembly. [7]

The co-decision procedure

The co-decision procedure under Article 251 was introduced by the Treaty of Maastricht and simplified by the Treaty of Amsterdam, replacing the co-operation procedure for single market measures.

[7] At p.3360.

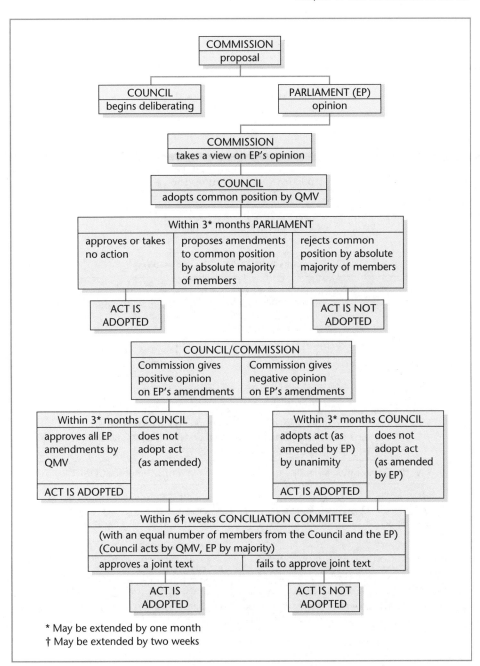

Figure 2.1 The co-decision procedure in the EC

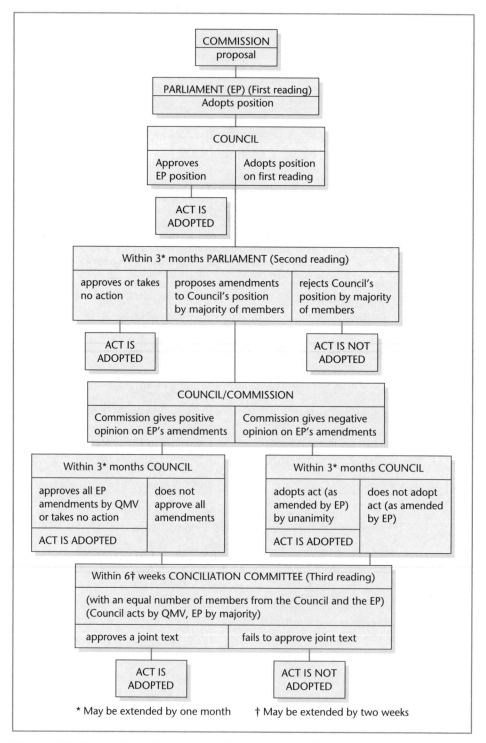

Figure 2.2 The ordinary decision-making process in the Union under the Treaty of Lisbon

Key point

The objective of the co-decision procedure was to provide a new mechanism which recognised the joint involvement of the Parliament and the Council in the legislative process.

Co-decision was extended by the Treaties of Amsterdam and Nice to include areas such as measures to combat discrimination (Article 13), social exclusion (Article 37), transport (Article 71), culture (Article 151), consumer protection (Article 152), incentive measures in relation to public health (Article 152(4)) and the environment (Article 175). A full list of the 40 legal bases to which co-decision currently applies may be found on the Parliament's website.[8]

Key point

Under the Treaty of Lisbon, the co-decision procedure will be known as the 'ordinary procedure' and will become the norm for legislation.

Under Article 251(2) the Commission drafts the proposal for submission to the EP and Council of Ministers at the same time. Ultimately, if the proposal passes successfully through its various stages, it will be adopted by a joint act of the EP and the Council, signed by the President of each institution. In 1999 the institutions adopted the Joint Declaration on practical arrangements for the new co-decision procedure,[9] providing that the institutions: 'Shall co-operate in good faith with a view to reconciling their positions as far as possible so that wherever possible acts can be adopted at first reading.' The Parliament's statistics for 1999–04 reveal only limited progress, with 28 per cent of proposals agreed at first reading, and 50 per cent agreed at second reading.[10]

The Declaration has led to the introduction of 'trilogues', a practice of holding preparatory meetings of representatives to facilitate the decision-making process, developed in response to the complexities arising from recent enlargements. The trilogue has been criticised by some commentators as lacking formality and transparency, as well as avoiding checks and balances. Chalmers *et al.* declare that: 'The trilogue is the biggest challenge to democratic legitimacy, for it centralizes power in those actors who represent the Council at the trilogue.'[11]

---

[8] http://www.europarl.europa.eu/code/information/legal_bases_en.pdf

[9] OJ1999 C148/1.

[10] EP Activity Report for the 5th Parliamentary Term, PE 287.644,12–13, cited in Chalmers *et al.* (2006: 154–155).

[11] Chalmers *et al.* (2006: 154) (citing H. Farrell and A. Héritier (2004), 'Interorganizational Negotiations and Intraorganisational Power in Shared Decision-Making: Early Agreements under Codecision and their Impact on the European Parliament and the Council', *Comparative Political Studies* 37, 1184, 1200–4).

Key term

Trilogue: a preparatory meeting during the legislative process, usually between a representative from the Council, a senior Commission official and several MEPs.

Under Article 251, if the EP proposes amendments to the original proposal, the Council may adopt either the original or the amended proposal. If the Council does not accept the original proposal, it must adopt a common position, which it conveys to the EP, with full reasons for its decision. The EP must then decide whether to amend or reject the Council's common position. In the event of rejection of the common position or refusal by the Council to accept the EP's amendments, the act is not adopted. Amendments to the common position by the EP result in the amended text being sent to the Council and the Commission.

Key point

Under the Treaty of Lisbon, the Commission drafts the proposal which is submitted to the EP for consideration at the first reading. It adopts a position which is communicated to the Council. If the Council approves, the act is adopted in the wording of the EP's position. If not, it adopts a position at first reading and communicates it to the EP. The Council must inform the EP fully of its reasons, and the Commission must inform the EP of its position.

If the Council does not agree all amendments, a Conciliation Committee composed of equal representation of the Council and of the EP must be specially convened. Failure to agree on a joint text in the Committee is rare, and leads to the act not being adopted. According to the EP's own website, 'Conciliation procedures are almost always successful.'[12] A recent example of the use of the successful conciliation procedure may be found in Directive 2006/7 on bathing water quality, in which the Conciliation Committee resolved differences between the Parliament and the Council as to the wording of the standard to be adopted.

Key point

Under the Treaty of Lisbon, at the second reading, the EP has three months in which to approve the Council's position or take no action, in which case the act is adopted according to the wording of the Council's position. If it rejects the position by majority of its component members, the act is not adopted. If the EP amends the Council's position by majority, it must send the text to the Council

---

[12] http://www.europarl.europa.eu/news/public/story_page/008-11420-275-10-40-901-20

and the Commission, which must deliver an opinion on the amendments. The Council has three months in which it may approve the amended text by QMV, in which case the act is adopted. If not, the President of the Council and President of the EP shall convene the Conciliation Committee. The Council is required to act by unanimity if the Commission delivers a negative opinion.

After amendment by the TOA, the EP lost its right to reject the final draft of legislation by an absolute majority. It used the power of veto only once, in 1995, when it rejected the draft text agreed by the Conciliation Committee on the Directive on the protection of biotechnological inventions. A modified version of the Directive was adopted in 1998.

Key point

Under the Treaty of Lisbon, the Conciliation Committee stage is known as the third reading. The procedure at this point otherwise remains as before.

Assent procedure

The assent procedure requires the positive approval of both the EP and the Council before a measure may be adopted. Areas under the Treaty for which the assent procedure is required include various categories of international agreements (Article 310), accession of new Member States (Article 49 TEU) and sanctions over a persistent and serious breach of human rights (Article 7 TEU). It is best suited to straightforward issues that do not require complex interaction between the institutions.

The Treaty of Lisbon has dispensed with the Assent Procedure. Until the Treaty is ratified, assent is required for measures to facilitate the rights of Union citizens (Article 18). This will move to the special legislative procedure under the TOL. Most other areas will move to the ordinary legislative procecure.

Other bodies

Various changes were introduced as a result of the Maastricht Treaty in an effort to bring the Union closer to the citizen. Article 193 EC enables the Parliament to set up temporary Committees of Inquiry to investigate alleged contraventions or maladministration in the implementation of EC law. Under Article 194 any EU citizen or resident may petition the Parliament on any EC matter affecting him directly. Article 195 enables the Parliament to appoint an Ombudsman to receive complaints about maladministration by the EC institutions other than the ECJ. There are, however, no powers to enforce any findings of maladministration.

Plate 1 The European Parliament in Strasbourg (Getty Images)

Key point

Under the Treaty of Lisbon, not less than one million citizens of a significant number of Member States may invite the Commission to submit a proposal to implement the Treaties (Articlce 8B TEU).

National parliaments under the Treaty of Lisbon

For the first time, national parliaments will be given a direct role in the legislative process under Article 8C of the TEU. They will be entitled to be forwarded the draft legislative acts of the Union in accordance with a Protocol on the role of national parliament in the EU to ensure that they comply with the principle of subsidiarity. There is also provision for national governments to evaluate mechanisms to implement policies in the area of freedom, security and justice, in accordance with Article 61 of the TFU.

Under the TOL, national parliaments may also participate in the new procedures to revise the Treaty. Article 48 of the TEU sets out the ordinary revision procedure whereby the government of any Member State, the EP or the Commission may submit proposals to the Council to amend the Treaties. If the European Council decides by simple majority to examine the proposals, the President of the European Council will convene a convention to adopt a recommendation to a conference of representatives of governments, which will determine by common accord the amendments to be made to the Treaties, for ratification in the normal way.

A simplified revision procedure is also created under Article 48 TEU, enabling the governments of Member States, the EP or Commission to submit proposals to the European Council relating to the internal policies and actions of the Union. Acting by unanimity after consulting the EP and Commission, the European Council may then adopt a decision adopting all or part of the provisions of Part Three of the TFU. In either case, the European Council must inform national parliaments. If any national parliament objects within six months of notification, the decision will not be adopted.

Key point

The Treaty of Lisbon makes provision for the first time for any Member state to decide to withdraw from the Union in accordance with its own constitutional requirements: Article 49A TEU.

THE COUNCIL OF THE EUROPEAN UNION

Composition and functions

The Council is the powerhouse of the EU. It is composed of ministers from the Member States, with a variable membership depending on the subject matter under consideration. The task of the Council is 'to ensure that the objectives set out in this Treaty are attained': Article 202 (ex 145). It has a 'duty to ensure co-ordination of the general economic policies of the Member States' and has the 'power to take decisions', as well as the power to delegate implementation to the Commission: Article 202. In these areas the Council must act unanimously, acting on a proposal of the Commission, after obtaining the opinion of the Parliament.

The Council operates by adopting policy, legislation and the budget (in conjunction with the EP). It concludes agreements with non-Member States. Despite the wording of Article 202, it is through the Council that Member States tend to express their national interests, for example over matters such as contribution to the budget. The Council is authorised to commit the government of each Member State under Article 203 EC.

In practice the Council meets in certain recognized formations: Economic and Financial Affairs (ECOFIN) deals with economic policy coordination, and the General Affairs and External Relations Council (consisting of foreign ministers) handles issues which transcend policy boundaries such as enlargement. The General Affairs Council also has responsibility for preparing and following up meetings of the Heads of Government in the European Council.

There are also seven specialised formations with the following responsibilities:

1 Justice and Home Affairs,
2 Agricultural and Fisheries,
3 Environment,
4 Competitiveness (including the internal market),
5 Employment, Social Policy and Consumer Affairs,
6 Transport, Telecommunications and Industry,
7 Education, Youth and Culture.

Some activities, notably the decision as to whether Member States have satisfied the criteria to move to the third stage of EMU (see Chapter 16) are reserved under Article 121 for the Council 'meeting in the composition of the Heads of State or Government' of the Member States. Such a meeting should be distinguished from the Heads of State meeting with the President of the Commission, in which case the meeting is one of the European Council (see below).

Only one voting delegate per member state is allowed. Meetings are held in private unless the Council unanimously decides otherwise. The office of the President is held by each state in turn for six months. The Council is assisted by a General Secretariat under the responsibility of a Secretary-General, whose office is combined with that of 'High Representative of the CFSP' (Article 26 TEU).

Key point

Although the Council is clearly a political body, which may reflect the national interests of Member States in legislative matters, it normally acts on a proposal from the Commission and is usually required to consult Parliament and the Economic and Social Committee. Decisions taken under the co-decision procedure are adopted jointly by the Council and the EP. Parliamentary objections may be overcome only where there is unanimity within the Council. This will continue under the Treaty of Lisbon.

Voting procedures

Under Article 205 (ex 148) voting may be by one of the following:

- **Simple majority**: a simple majority of votes cast by ministers present, where each member has one vote. This method is used only rarely, mainly in relation to procedural areas. The Treaty of Lisbon will amend Article 205 to define simple majority as a majority of the component members of the Council.
- **Qualified majority (QMV)**: a system of weighted voting (see below). Each Treaty revision has extended the number of areas requiring QMV, to the point where it has become the most usual method of voting.

• **Unanimity**: where a single state may veto proposals. Despite the extension of QMV, unanimity is still required in many important areas including strengthening the rights of Union citizens under Article 22 (ex 8), changing the number of judges in the ECJ (Article 221), the amendment of a Commission proposal (Article 250) and the general power to pass laws coming within the objectives of the Community (Article 308).

Key point

The Treaty of Lisbon will move most of these areas to the ordinary legislative procedure, though amending a Commission proposal will still require unanimity. Article 308 will be repealed and replaced by a new Article 308, which requires special legislative procedure.

Qualified majority voting

The arrangements for qualified majority voting (QMV) have been the subject of intense negotiation, particularly in the context of recent enlargements, as Member States sought to ensure that their interests were represented to their satisfaction. Until the enlargements in 2004 and 2007, weighting of votes approximately reflected population size. The Treaty of Nice introduced changes in response to concerns of the larger states about dilution of control (see below). The present arrangements are set out in principle in Article 205 of the Treaty, with further provision in the 2003 and 2005 Accession Treaties. Following enlargement to 27 Member States, voting in the Council has been weighted as follows:

Germany, France, Italy, UK	29 votes
Spain, Poland	27
Romania	14
Netherlands	13
Belgium, Czech Republic, Greece, Hungary, Portugal	12
Austria, Sweden, Bulgaria	10
Denmark, Ireland, Lithuania, Slovenia, Slovakia, Finland	7
Estonia, Cyprus, Latvia, Luxembourg, Slovenia	4
Malta	3

The TON (as amended by the two accession treaties) introduced a new requirement under Article 205 EC for reaching a qualified majority threshold, namely:

(a) 255 votes in favour, cast by a majority of Members, where the Treaty requires adoption on a proposal from the Commission;
(b) 232 votes in favour, cast by at least two thirds of the Members, in other cases.

As there are very few matters where a proposal from the Commission is not required, it can be assumed that the first method will be the norm.

One of the most controversial issues surrounding the weighting of votes has always been its relationship with the population of the Member States. Before the 2004 enlargement the allocation of votes approximated very roughly to population,[13] although small states had greater weighting relative to their populations than did larger states such as Germany. These large states feared a further dilution of their influence with the influx of the 2004 accession states, most of which were small. This fear was well founded, as the weighting of votes agreed by the Treaty of Nice was a compromise, which deferred a final decision on weighting to a later date which has not yet been reached. To avoid unfairness, a verification procedure was introduced, enabling a Member of the Council to request verification that the Member States constituting the qualified majority represent at least 62 per cent of the total population of the Union.

Concern from some Member States, particularly Poland and Spain, led to an agreement to postpone the new provision until 31 October 2009, supplemented by a Declaration which would enable small states to make alliances to prevent a vote being taken.

Key point

Qualified majority voting under the Treaty of Lisbon

A new approach will be provided by Article 205 which will come into effect in November 2014. This redefines a *qualified majority* as at least 55 per cent of the members of the Council, comprising at least 15 of them, and representing at least 65 per cent of the population of the Union. A *blocking majority* would require at least the minimum number of Council members representing more than 35 per cent of the population of the participating states, plus one member, failing which the qualified majority will be deemed to have been reached. Provision is made under Article 205 for derogations from 2014 where the Council does not act on a proposal from the Commission or High Representative for Foreign Affairs.

Unanimity

Under the original Treaty provisions many important areas, such as Article 94 (ex 100) on the approximation of laws, required a unanimous vote. The intention of the Treaty was to move towards voting by qualified majority at the end of the transitional period.[14] Instead, in response to a political crisis caused by a French boycott of Council meetings after Common Agricultural Policy (CAP) negotiations broke down, the Luxembourg Accords were drawn up in 1966. Under the Accords, which do not have the force of law, Member States may insist on a unanimous vote where vital national interests are at stake. The Accords have only rarely been invoked formally,[15] and have

---

[13] Germany, France, Italy and the UK had 10 votes each; Spain had 8 votes; Belgium, Greece, the Netherlands and Portugal had 5 votes each; Austria and Sweden had 4 votes each; Finland, Denmark and Ireland had 3 votes each; Luxembourg had 2 votes.

[14] 31 December 1965.

[15] For example, the German government's use of the Accords to block a cereal price decrease in 1985.

fallen gradually into disuse since the 1980s. The trend with each Treaty revision has been to reduce the number of areas requiring unanimity.

The European Council

The European Council, not to be confused with the Council of the EU, is a regular summit meeting of Heads of State and their Foreign Ministers, who are required to meet at least twice a year under Article 4 TEU. The President of the Commission and one other Commissioner may attend. The summit provides an important mechanism for European political leaders to agree the agenda for change within the EU, to be put into action by the Council of the EU. The process may be illustrated by the Copenhagen Council of 1992, which laid down the entry criteria for enlargement in central and Eastern Europe, and the Laeken Council of 2001, which led to the Convention process to prepare for the failed Constitutional Treaty.

Committee of Permanent Representatives

Since Council membership varies and is combined with full-time responsibilities in the home state, much of the work is carried out by the Committee of Permanent Representatives (COREPER). The Committee's function under Article 207(1) of the Treaty is to examine and sift Commission proposals before a final decision is made by the Council. COREPER is the only body that can exercise an overview of the full range of the Council's activities. The Committee operates on two levels, COREPER II (permanent representatives from the Member States at ambassadorial level) to reflect the political dimension and COREPER I (deputy permanent representatives), the technical dimension. In addition, specialised committees such as the Economic and Finance Committee also undertake preparatory work. The risk of overlap with the activities of COREPER is addressed by Article 207 that states that the activities of these bodies is 'without prejudice to Article 207'.

COREPER is responsible for preparing the agenda of the Council, dividing the list into 'A Points', which may be adopted by the Council without discussion, and 'B Points', requiring discussion. This responsibility enables COREPER to influence what is discussed and agreed within the Council.

THE EUROPEAN COMMISSION

Features

The role of the Commission is primarily to promote further integration in the EU. Its function is wider than that of a traditional civil service, as it encompasses the formulation and execution of EU policies and legislation. The Commission operates on the principle of collegiality, with the College of Commissioners taking collective responsibility for all decisions. The Commission, which employs over 24,000 staff, meets weekly in private and takes decisions by simple majority.

Composition

The current rules on composition are found in Article 213. Commissioners must be nationals of Member States. They are appointed by agreement of the governments of the Member States and must 'neither seek nor take instructions from any government or from any other body'. Commissioners are chosen on the basis of general competence and their 'independence is beyond doubt'. If they infringe their duties, the Council or Commission may apply to the ECJ for their dismissal.

Key point

The Treaty of Lisbon will replace Article 213 with a new provision as follows: 'The Members of the Commission shall refrain from any action incompatible with their duties. Member States shall respect their independence and shall not seek to influence them in the performance of their tasks.'

Prior to the two most recent enlargements, each Member State had a single Commissioner and five States had two. It was accepted that a reduction in the number of Commissioners was essential if the Commission were not to become unmanageably large. A Protocol on Enlargement attached to the Treaty of Nice enabled the number of Commissioners to be specified in the Treaty of Accession. As a result, the Accession Treaty of 2003 altered the number of Commissioners without formally amending Article 213, which states that the Commission consists of 20 members. The 2003 Treaty provides that there should be a national from each new Member State appointed to the Commission from the date of accession. Numbers were reduced to one Commissioner per Member State from November 2004, the start of the term of the present Commission under President Barros. The Commission's term of office expires on 31 October 2009.

The next time the EU enlarges it will be necessary to reduce the number of Commissioners in accordance with Article 4(3) of the Protocol on Enlargement 2003. The responsibility for deciding on the number of Commissioners will fall to the Council acting unanimously.

Members of the Commission are appointed for a term of five years: Article 214.

Key point

The Treaty of Lisbon repeals many of the provisions of the EC Treaty in relation to the Commission. It provides in Article 211a for the selection of members of the Commission on a rota system, whereby Member States are treated on a 'strictly equal footing', subject to which each successive Commission will be composed 'to reflect satisfactorily the demographic and geographical range of all the Member States' (as in the 2003 Protocol on Enlargement).

● The President of the Commission

The President of the Commission is nominated under Article 214, holding office for a renewable term of two years. His role is a significant one: the President is responsible for the political direction of the Commission, setting its priorities during his term of office. Following confirmation of his own appointment, which requires approval of the Member States and of the EP, the President chooses his Commission. His choice of the Commission as a whole is subject to approval by the European Parliament. As we have seen, the EP's initial rejection of the Barroso Commission led to the withdrawal and replacement of two proposed Commissioners before the whole Commission was approved by the EP.

The President allocates portfolios to individual Commissioners, each assisted by his own Cabinet, a group of officials appointed by and responsible to him. The President may also withdraw portfolios, dismissing an individual Commissioner provided he has agreement from the College of Commissioners.

The Commission is divided into Directorates General (DGs) covering matters such as external relations, competition and the internal market. There are also various specialised services such as the Legal Service which advises all the DGs and represents the Commission in legal proceedings.

> **Key point**
>
> The Treaty of Lisbon will repeal Article 214. New provision is made under amended Article 215 for the appointment of Commissioners and of the High Representative in the event of retirement or resignation. It also provides that, in the event of resignation of the entire Commission, they shall remain in office until replaced.

● Functions

The Commission has three main functions:

1 **Initiator**. It initiates Community legislation. Most Council legislation must be made on the basis of a proposal from the Commission subject to the special power under Article 208 (ex 152) EC, which enables the Council to request the Commission to make a proposal to attain the Treaty objectives. The Commission may draft proposals on any matter covered by the Treaty, either where power is specifically provided or under the general power under Article 308 (ex 235).

2 **Guardian of the Treaties**. The Commission acts as the guardian of the Treaties. Under Article 10 EC, Member States must take all necessary steps to implement obligations imposed by the Treaty or by the institutions and to refrain from measures which could jeopardise the operation of the Treaty. The Commission has a duty to investigate and bring to an end infringements of EC law by the Member States. It has the power to bring an action against a Member State under

Article 226. The Commission has an administrative and enforcement role in relation to competition policy, and is empowered to investigate alleged breaches. Much of its previous role has, however, been devolved to national competition authorities (see Chapter 19).

3 **Executive**. The Commission acts as the executive of the Community, implementing policies decided on by the Council. This often involves drawing up detailed legislation which may require a final decision by the Council. Decisions may only be delegated under strict limits. Failure to observe these rules may result in annulment by the Court, as in Case C-137/92P *Commission v. BASF AG* (PVC). In this case the ECJ upheld a decision by the Court of First Instance (CFI) to annul a Commission decision which was defective in the way it had been adopted. The Competition Commissioner had adopted a number of translations additional to the original decisions adopted by the Commission. The CFI held that the whole Commission itself should have adopted an authenticated version.

Where powers have been delegated by the Council to the Commission some measure of control is retained through the system of committees known as *comitology* (see below). The Commission also possesses its own power of decision under Article 211 where no reference to the Council is necessary, for example in the reinforcement of competition policy.

In addition the Commission possesses various representative and financial functions:

4 **Representative**. In external relations it acts as the negotiator in the treaty-making process, although agreements are concluded by the Council after consultation with the Parliament: Article 300.

5 **Financial**. The Commission draws up the preliminary draft Budget.

Comitology

Comitology refers to the practice of decision making by the Commission in committee under powers delegated by the Council. Typically the Council will adopt a framework regulation, to be followed by detailed regulations or directives in a technical area by the Commission. Since 1987 the Commission's legislative activities have been supervised by the Council under a series of comitology decisions.[16] The system requires the Commission to submit its draft measure for consideration to a committee composed of representatives of the Member States and chaired by the Commission. There are about 300 committees in areas such as industry, social affairs, agriculture, the internal market, research and development, consumer protection and food safety.[17]

Both the Commission and the EP have long objected to the scope provided by comitology for intervention by the Council. The system was unsuccessfully challenged

---

[16] The First Comitology Decision 87/373 was replaced by the Second Comitology Decision 1999/468, which was amended by Decision 2006/512/EC of 17 July 2006.

[17] Source: http://europa.eu/scadplus/glossary/experts_committees_en.htm.

Plate 2 The Commission building in Brussels: 'the Berlayment' (Getty Images)

before the ECJ in Case 302/87 *Parliament* v. *Council.* (No ruling was made as the EP had failed to establish that it had standing to bring an action.)

The comitology system was simplified in 1999 by Council Decision 468/99 and amended in 2006 by Decision 2006/512, placing the EP and the Council on an equal basis for all comitology procedures related to co-decision acts. The EP may now block implementing measures under co-decision legislation, with the result that the Commission will have to propose a new comitology decision or a new legislative act under the co-decision procedure.

Key point

The Treaty of Lisbon will go further than Decision 2006/512 by empowering the EP or the Council to revoke the delegation of authority rather than simply blocking it. The delegated act may enter into force only if no objection has been expressed by the EP or Council within the period set for approval: Article 249B(2).

To avoid problems and delay, draft measures are sent by the Commission to the EP for information before implementation. Guidelines are laid down in Article 2 on identifying the correct procedure. Transparency was improved with the publication of a list of committees and a public register of all committee documents. Three categories of committee have been used since 1987, with a fourth added under the 2006 Decision, as follows:

1 **Advisory committee.** The committee is composed of representatives of the Member States and chaired by the Commission. Decisions of the committee do not bind the Commission but must be considered: Article 3 of the Decision. The procedure is used 'where it is considered most appropriate' under Article 2.

2 **Management committee.** The committee is composed in the same way as in 1. Under Article 4 the proposal of the Commission requires the approval of the committee, which must give its decision on the draft within a time period. If the Commission follows the opinion, it may adopt the measure. If it does not, the Commission may still adopt the draft, but it must inform the Council. The Commission may also defer application of the measure for up to three months, in which case the Council may substitute its own decision for that of the committee of that period. If the committee votes against the measure, it will be referred back to the Council. The procedure is used for management measures (e.g. under the CAP).

3 **Regulatory committee.** The committee is again composed as in 1. Under Article 5 the proposal of the Commission requires approval in the committee in the same way as the management procedure. However, if it wishes to depart from the decision, it must put a draft before the Council and inform the EP. The Commission cannot adopt a measure against the Council's decision. The procedure is used for measures of general scope, such as health and safety.

   The Commission unsuccessfully challenged the use of the regulatory procedure in Case C-122/04 *Commission* v. *EP and Council* on the 'Forest Focus' Regulation (monitoring of forests and environmental interactions). The Court found that, as the Regulation created a wide and general framework for the scheme, there was no breach of the criteria in Article 2.

4 **Regulatory committee with scrutiny:** The committee is once more composed as in 1. Under Article 5a (introduced by the 2006 amendment) the Council and the EP may scrutinise a measure of general scope before adoption. The procedure enables the EP to play a greater role in relation to measures designed to amend non-essential elements of a basic instrument adopted by co-decision, in relation to measures adopted by co-decision after July 2006 and which specify the new procedure. Earlier measures will have to be amended to enable the new procedure to apply. Under Article 5a if either the Council or the EP objects, the Commission cannot adopt the proposed measure, although it may submit a new or amended proposal. The intention of the new procedure is to give the EP and the Council equal powers on matters covered by co-decision, in relation to the monitoring of the Commission's exercise of implementation powers.

Article 8 enables the EP to pass a resolution that draft implementing measures submitted to a committee under a basic instrument adopted under co-decision would exceed the implementing powers of that instrument. This requires the Commission to re-examine the draft and either amend it or submit a new proposal. This Article will become redundant as a result of new Article 5a.

In the past, the EP has rarely exercised its powers of scrutiny under the 1999 Decision, and when it has sought to do so, the Commission has not necessarily been prevented from implementation. See, for example, the EP's Resolution of July 2000 on safe harbour privacy principles in which the EP objected to the Commission's draft, calling for it to be reviewed. The Resolution was ignored as the Commission proceeded to adopt the implementing Decision 2000/520. In contrast, the EP was successful in its Resolution of 22 September 2002 on the postponement of the ban on the marketing of cosmetics that had been tested on animals; the Commission did not go ahead with the implementing measures.[18] The EP in December 2007 delayed final agreement on a regulation on aviation security under the new regulatory procedure with scrutiny, in order to ensure that security measures that are 'unforeseen today' can be included in the regulation.[19]

> **Key point**
>
> Despite limited reform, the basic objection to comitology remains: it is undemocratic, and enables the Council and the Commission to control the process of law making. The EP's role, even under the new procedure in Article 5a, continues to be limited. It remains to be seen how widely its scope to veto legislation is interpreted.[20]

THE COURTS

There are two courts:

1 The Court of Justice (ECJ), as the Court is officially known in the Treaty, is the highest court providing rulings on Community law.
2 The Court of First Instance (CFI), which has a limited but expanding role, and is subject to appeal to the Court of Justice. The Treaty of Lisbon will rename this court the General Court. Judicial panels may be attached to the CFI (see p.47).

In addition, the Court of Auditors exercises specific functions in relation to financial control. This chapter provides an overview of the composition and functions of the ECJ. The jurisdiction of the Court is examined in more detail in Chapters 7–10.

---

[18] Resolution of 5 July 2000: see EP news press service at http://www.europa.eu/news/expert/background_page/001-9281-178-06-26-9

[19] EP news press service at http://www.europarl.eu/news/expert/infopress_page/062-15678-351-12-51-91

[20] See Craig and De Burca (2007: 123).

Main functions

The main functions of the Court of Justice (ECJ) are:

- to provide a uniform interpretation of Community law throughout the Member States;
- to ensure that Community law is enforced;
- to provide a forum for the resolution of disputes between Member States and the EC institutions, as well as between the institutions themselves;
- to review acts of the institutions where these acts have legal effect;
- to protect individual rights.

Composition

Judges

Article 221 currently provides that the Court of Justice shall consist of one judge from each Member State (i.e. 27 judges). This provision will be deleted by the Treaty of Lisbon which does not prescribe a specific number.

Judges must be 'persons whose independence is beyond doubt' (Article 233), either as judges or academics in their own country. The Judges appoint a President for three years from among their own ranks and are assisted by eight Advocates-General: Article 222. Judges are appointed by 'common accord' of the governments of the Member States for staggered terms of six years. The Treaty of Lisbon will add the requirement to consult the new panel on suitability, to be set up under Article 224a (see below). A Judge may only be removed under the Statute of the Court of Justice if all the other Judges and Advocates-General agree that he is no longer qualified or fit to hold office. This has never happened in all the years of the Court's existence. Judges must not be influenced by their own national origins but must strive for a Community approach in reaching a decision.

Key point

Under the Treaty of Lisbon, a panel will be set up under Article 224a to assess the suitability of candidates to become Judges and Advocates-General in the Court of Justice and General Court, before the governments of the Member States make appointments under Articles 223 and 225. The panel will comprise seven members drawn from former members of the ECJ and General Court, members of national supreme courts and lawyers of recognised competence, one of whom will be proposed by the EP. The Council will adopt a decision to establish the panel's rules of operation. It will act on the initiative of the President of the Court of Justice.

Full Court, Grand Chamber and Chamber

One of the problems resulting from the accession of new States has been that it is no longer practical for all cases to be heard by a full court of 27 judges. Recourse to the full court is now regarded as unusual, being required in cases involving the removal of members of the Commission, the Court of Auditors and the Ombudsman. It may also be used in cases of exceptional importance, such as an action brought by a Member State.[21] Article 221 provides that the ECJ may sit in chambers or in a Grand Chamber of 13 judges, with a quorum (minimum number) of nine judges, in accordance with the rules laid down in the Statute of the Court of Justice. Straightforward actions may be heard in a chamber consisting of three or five judges.

Advocates-General

Advocates-General must be qualified in the same way as judges under Article 223. Their role is to assist the Court by presenting reasoned submissions on the facts, as well as recommendations for a decision. These submissions are objective and do not represent the views of either party. The Advocate-General's submissions are the only part of the written record in which the legal issues are fully examined and may assist the common lawyer unfamiliar with continental pleadings. While the submissions are persuasive they do not bind the judges. As it is now accepted that some cases may be decided without the benefit of the Advocate-General's submission, the Statute of the Court was amended to permit the Court to dispense with the submission where it considers that the case raises no new points of law.

Judicial style

Procedures in the ECJ derive from the continental tradition and are mainly inquisitorial, with the emphasis on written rather than oral pleadings. However, the adversarial skills of the common lawyers have made an impact on the Court. The judges operate as a judicial college to produce a single judgment, formally and briefly expressed. There is no dissenting judgment, although some insight into an alternative view may be gained from the Advocate-General's submissions where these have *not* been followed in the judgment. Decisions of the ECJ are not subject to review. The Court hears appeals from the Court of First Instance: see below.

Role of the Court of Justice

As the EC Treaty is a framework treaty, substance had to be given to its provisions by the decisions of the ECJ. In its early years the Court actively promoted European integration in its judgments, making full use of the opportunities provided by preliminary reference from the national courts under Article 234 (see Chapter 10) to clarify the law with binding effect on all the Member States. The Court's vision is

---

[21] Article 16, Statute of the Court.

clearly demonstrated in bold decisions such as Case 26/62 *Van Gend en Loos* in which the Court declared that, 'The Community has created a new legal order in international law.'[22]

Key point

While the Court does not operate a formal doctrine of precedent, it normally follows its own previous decisions. Where it intends to depart from an earlier judgment, it will usually make the position very clear. A good example of this is provided by Cases C-267 and 268/91 *Criminal Proceedings against Keck and Mithouard* where the Court stated that it was necessary to re-examine its approach to the use of Article 30 (now 28) as the basis for a challenge to national rules on arrangements on how goods are sold. It signalled its new approach with the words, 'Contrary to what has previously been decided . . .' and went on to rule that Member States are free to adopt their own rules on selling goods, provided they do not contravene EC law. (See Chapter 12.)

While the preliminary reference procedure, Article 234, continues to be one of the main mechanisms used by the Court to develop Community law, the procedures under Articles 226 and 230 are important. They are examples of what is known as 'direct actions' where the procedure begins and ends in the Court. Under Article 226 proceedings may be brought by the Commission in the Court against a Member State in breach of its obligations under the Treaty. Article 230 provides for the review of the legality of acts of the Council and the Commission other than recommendations or opinions.

Cases may be conducted in any of the 23 official languages.[23] The working language of the Court itself remains French, a legacy of the early years when continental procedures dominated the development of the Court. After translation into the 'authentic' language, usually that of the applicant, the judgment will be translated into the remaining official languages, before publication in the European Court reports.

In Case C-161/06 *Skoma-Lux sro* v. *Celní ředitelství Oloumuc* the ECJ held that a regulation which is not published in the *Official Journal of the European Union* (see Appendix II) in all the official languages of a Member State cannot be enforced against individuals in that State, even where they could have learned of the legislation by other means.

The Court of First Instance

The Court of First Instance (CFI) was established under Article 224 (ex 168) in 1989, after amendment by the SEA to ease the workload of the Court of Justice. Unlike the

---

[22] See Chapter 6.
[23] Rules also permit cases to be conducted in Irish.

ECJ, which is limited under Article 221 to one judge per Member State, the CFI is not so limited and 'shall comprise at least one judge per Member State' under Article 224(1). The number of CFI judges is determined by the Statute of the Court, which may also provide for the appointment of Advocates-General.

Key point

The Treaty of Lisbon will rename the CFI the 'General Court' and will repeal Article 224(1), so that there will no longer be at least one Judge per Member State. As with judges to the ECJ, Judges of the General Court will be appointed by a panel under Article 224a.

The jurisdiction of the CFI was initially limited to disputes between the EC and its staff ('staff cases'), competition and anti-dumping cases and certain matters relating to the ECSC and EURATOM, other than preliminary rulings under Article 234. Since 1993 (Decision 93/350) the CFI has heard all cases brought by individuals or under-takings, including actions for judicial review and actions for damages against the EC institutions, but not actions brought by the EC institutions or the Member States. The CFI was given jurisdiction by the Treaty of Nice to hear and determine proceedings at first instance relating to actions under Articles 230, 232, 235, 236 and 238 of the EC Treaty, apart from those already assigned to a judicial panel.

Judicial panels

Article 220 of the Treaty provides for judicial panels to be attached to the CFI where the Council unanimously decides under Article 225a. The first of these panels, the EU Civil Service Tribunal, was set up in November 2004 to handle staff cases. There is a right of appeal on points of law to the CFI.

Key point

The Treaty of Lisbon will repeal Article 220. Cases previously assigned to a judicial panel will, under the TOL, be assigned to a specialised court set up under Article 225a. New Article 225a provides that the EP and the Council may, under the ordinary legislative procedure, establish specialised courts attached to the General Court to hear certain cases at first instance. Appeal on points of law to the CFI will continue.

Preliminary rulings

The CFI may hear preliminary rulings under Article 234 in specific areas provided by the Statute of the Court, following amendment by the Treaty of Nice. Previously the ECJ had resisted the extension of the CFI's jurisdiction in this way, but pressures resulting from enlargement proved overwhelming. Where the CFI considers that the case involves the unity or consistency of EC law, it may refer it to the ECJ for a ruling under Article 225(3). The ECJ may also hear appeals from preliminary rulings of the CFI where there is a serious risk to the unity or consistency of EC law. There is a right of appeal to the ECJ which may, if the appeal is allowed, give the final judgment itself or send the case back to the CFI. The CFI may sit in plenary session, in chambers of three or five Judges or (since May 1999) as a single Judge in some cases where no difficult questions of law or fact are raised.

The Court of Auditors

The Court of Auditors was set up in 1975 under the Budgetary Powers Treaty to control and supervise the implementation of the Budget and to audit the accounts of the EC institutions. It became a full institution under the Treaty of Maastricht.

OTHER BODIES IN THE DECISION-MAKING PROCESS

The Economic and Social Committee (ESC)

The ESC plays a consultative role within the decision-making process of the EC and EURATOM (Articles 257–262). Its members, who are appointed by the Council, consist of representatives of groups such as farmers, trade unionists, producers and the general public. Consultation, where provided in the Treaty, is an essential procedural requirement. This means that failure to consult is a ground for annulment of a measure (see Chapter 8).

The ESC gives its opinion by an absolute majority of members. The Committee may also be consulted by the Council and the Commission wherever they consider it appropriate and may advise the Council and Commission on its own initiative.

Key point

The Treaty of Lisbon will repeal Articles 257 and 261, and delete Article 258(2) on membership. Instead, new Article 258 provides for the Council acting unanimously on a proposal from the Commission to adopt a decision determining the Committee's composition. The term of appointment will increase from four to five years: Article 259(1).

The Committee of the Regions

The Committee of the Regions (COR) was set up in 1994 as an advisory committee by the Maastricht Treaty under Articles 263–265 (ex 198a–c) EC to provide an opinion in matters of local or regional interest within the EU. Its 344 members are drawn from individuals who have been elected to local and regional authorities, or who are politically accountable to a democratically elected assembly. Members of the

Committee are appointed by the Council for a term of four years. The Committee must be informed whenever an opinion is sought from the ESC. Consultation with the Committee is required in matters of education, vocational training and youth, culture, public health, trans-European networks, economic and social cohesion and environmental policy.

Key point

The Treaty of Lisbon will amend Article 263, deleting paragraph one on membership. Instead, new Article 263(1) provides for the Council acting unanimously on a proposal from the Commission to adopt a decision determining the Committee's composition. Members will be appointed for five, not four years. Article 265(4) which currently authorises the Committee to issue an opinion where specific regional interests are involved is deleted, though other references in Article 265 to the provision of an opinion are retained.

The European Central Bank

The European Central Bank (ECB), based in Frankfurt, acts as the Central Bank of the EU within the European System of Central Banks (ESCB), with responsibility for monetary policy within the EU since the beginning of the third stage of Economic and Monetary Union (EMU) on 1 January 1999. It conducts foreign exchange operations, holds and manages the official reserves of the Member States, and promotes the smooth operation of the payments systems The ECB is the only body entitled to issue euro banknotes under Article 106. It may adopt regulations on monetary policy, take decisions, make recommendations and deliver opinions. The role of the ECB is considered further in Chapter 16.

QUESTIONS

❶ What are the powers of the EP to adopt legislation, following the Treaty of Nice? Do you think the problems caused by the recent enlargements of the EU have been addressed, as far as the legislative process is concerned? How will the position change under the Treaty of Lisbon?

❷ What are the respective roles of the Commission and the Council in decisions adopted under 'comitology'? Does the use of this procedure undermine the role of the EP?

❸ What are the distinctive features in the approach of the Court of Justice which distinguish it from a national court?

Further reading

Arnull, A., Dashwood, A., Dougan, M., Ross, M., Spaventa, E. and Wyatt, D. (2006) *Wyatt and Dashwood's European Union Law*, 5th edition, Thomson, Sweet and Maxwell Chapters 2 (Council, Commission and EP), 3 (The Legislative Process) and 12 (The ECJ).

Bradley, St.J. (2001) 'Institutional Design in the Treaty of Nice', (2001) 38 CMLRev. 1095.

Brown, L.N. and Kennedy, T. (2000) *Brown and Jacobs' The Court of Justice of the European Communities*, 5th edition, Sweet and Maxwell.

Chalmers, D., Hadjiemmanuil, C., Monti, G. and Tomkins, A. (2006) *European Union Law*, Cambridge University Press, Chapters 3 and 4.

Craig, P. (2008) 'The Treaty of Lisbon: Process, Architecture and Substance', 33 ELRev 137.

Craig, P. and De Burca, G. (2007) *EU Law: Text, Cases and Materials*, 4th edition, Oxford University Press, Chapters 2–4.

Hayes-Renshaw, F. and Wallace, H. (2006) *The Council of Ministers*, 2nd edition, Palgrave.

Kreppel, A. (1999) 'What Affects the European Parliament's Legislative Influence? An Analysis of the Success of EP Amendments' 37 JCMS 521.

Nugent, N. (2001) *The European Commission*, Palgrave.

Nugent, N. (2006) *The Government and Politics of the European Union*, 6th edition, Palgrave, Chapter 2.

Shaw, J. (2005) 'Europe's Constitutional Future', (2005) PL 132.

Tridimas, T. (1997) 'The Court of Justice and Judicial Activism', 22 ELRev 199.

Walker, N. (2005) 'Europe's Constitutional Momentum and the Search for Political Legitimacy', (2005) 3 *International Journal of Constitutional Law* 211.

Weiler, J. (2003) 'A Constitution for Europe? Some Hard Choices?' in J. Weiler, I. Begg and J. Peterson (eds), *Integration in an Expanding Europe*, Blackwell Publishing.

Visit **http://www.mylawchamber.co.uk/kent** to access answer guidance to questions in the book to test yourself on this chapter.

Use **Case Navigator** to read in full some of the key cases referenced in this chapter:

- C-267 and 268/91 **Criminal Proceedings against Keck and Mithouard** [1993] ECR I-6097
- 26/62 **Van Gend en Loos**

2

The institutions of the EU

The sources of EU law: competences of the EC and EU

INTRODUCTION

The study of EU law

EU law at first sight may appear unfamiliar to the student of English law. The origins of EU law lie in the codes of continental Europe, which in turn derive from Roman law. In the case of EU law, the 'code' is the Treaty establishing the European Community. This provides a framework which requires fleshing out with more detailed rules in the form of secondary legislation and the decisions of the Court of Justice. The attempt in the Constitutional Treaty to transform the Treaty into the EU's official 'constitution', as we have seen in Chapter 1, was doomed to failure.

Thus, the main sources of EU law are the treaties creating the institutions, and subsidiary treaties, above all the treaties creating the communities. These are: the EC Treaty (under the Treaty of Lisbon to be renamed the Treaty on the Functioning of the Union), the Euratom Treaty and the Treaty on European Union (TEU). Before 23 July 2002 when the ECSC was wound up, the ECSC Treaty was also a primary source. These treaties are the result of international agreement between sovereign states, and so only came into effect when they were ratified by the Member States. Depending on the national procedure for the incorporation of treaties, ratification will be by the national parliaments or by referendum. Ratification of the 1972 Act of Accession in the UK was achieved by the European Communities Act 1972.

Strictly speaking, it is more accurate to refer to sources of Community (or EC) law than to EU law, as the laws which can be invoked by individuals are adopted within the First Pillar which is governed by law under the TEC, whereas EU law may be taken to refer to all three pillars. This book follows the current trend in legal writing, which is to use the term 'EU law' to reflect the main focus on the EU since the Maastricht Treaty (TEU). The distinction will vanish along with the three-pillar structure when the Lisbon Treaty is ratified, as the EU alone will remain (see Chapter 1).

The TEU which established the three-pillar model created structures for intergovernmental co-operation rather than law to cover the Second and Third Pillars. This approach was seen as more suitable for areas of high political sensitivity in which the Member States wished to preserve their powers of independent decision making.

The provisions for the Second and Third Pillars are contained in a separate Treaty, the Treaty on European Union (TEU), which exists alongside the TEC. At present, three Titles of the TEU cannot be enforced before the Community Courts; these are Title I Common Provisions, Title V on the CFSP and Title VI Police and Judicial Co-operation in Criminal Matters. After ratification of the TOL, only the CFSP will remain outside the legal regime.

Detailed rules may be found in the legislation adopted by the EU institutions and in the decisions, opinions and general principles of the Court of Justice (ECJ). With the Treaties, these sources of EU law provide a *system* of law. Unlike English law, which has evolved haphazardly over many centuries, EU law is of recent origin. Its coherence lies in the commitment to underlying themes such as the principles of free movement of goods, persons, services and capital.

TREATIES

Treaties creating the institutions

The two principal founding treaties are:

1 the **Treaty establishing the European Community (TEC)**, to be renamed the **Treaty on the Functioning of the Union (TFU)** by the Treaty of Lisbon, and
2 the **Treaty on European Union (TEU)**.

These constitutive treaties provide the legal framework of the Community as primary sources of EU law, taking priority over conflicting legal obligations contained in subsidiary treaties or in secondary legislation. The current version of the TEC, until ratification of the Treaty of Lisbon (TOL), is known as the Consolidated Version of the Treaty establishing the European Community. It incorporates amendments from a number of earlier treaties up to and including the Treaty of Nice and the Acts of Accession.

> **Key point**
>
> The Treaty of Lisbon, as we have seen in Chapter 1, was signed in 2007, but has not been fully ratified. When ratified, the three-pillar structure will largely disappear, to be replaced by a single body, the European Union, though some separate procedures would continue for the CFSP under the TEU.

The Treaty establishing the European Community (TEC)
The current legal position is represented by the TEC, i.e. the EC Treaty as amended by later Treaties including the following:

- **The Acts of Accession.** These treaties provided the arrangements for the accession of new Member States:
  - **1972** (in force 1 January 1973): UK, Ireland, Denmark,
  - **1979** (in force 1 January 1981): Greece,
  - **1985** (in force 1 January 1986): Spain and Portugal,
  - **1994** (in force 1 January 1995): Austria, Finland and Sweden,
  - **2003** (in force 1 January 2004): Czech Republic, Estonia, Cyprus, Latvia, Lithuania, Hungary, Malta, Poland, Slovenia and Slovakia,
  - **2005** (in force 1 January 2007): Bulgaria and Romania.
- **The Single European Act (SEA) 1986** (in force 1 July 1987). The SEA provided for the completion of the internal market by the end of 1992. It introduced the co-operation procedure which enabled the adoption of directives to complete the single (or internal) market, providing a spur for the 'relaunch' of the Community (see Chapter 1).
- **The Treaty on European Union (TEU) 1992** (in force 1 January 1993). The TEU, otherwise known as the Treaty of Maastricht, introduced the new entity known as the European Union, with its three-pillar structure (see above). The TEU provided for both legal and political union, as well as economic and monetary union for participating states (see Chapter 1). In addition, the TEU reformed elements of the First Pillar, notably by introducing the co-decision procedure for the adoption of legislation (see Chapter 2).
- **The Treaty of Amsterdam (TOA) 1997** (in force 1 May 1999). The TOA began the process of reform of the institutions prior to enlargement (see Chapter 1). It moved a number of areas previously within the remit of the Third Pillar (renamed Police and Judicial Co-operation in Criminal Matters) to the First Pillar. In addition it provided for the principle of 'closer co-operation' between participating Member States. It also renumbered the provisions of the EC Treaty and the TEU.
- **The Treaty of Nice (TON) 2001** (in force 1 February 2003). The TON addressed important issues left unresolved by the TOA, in particular the size and composition of the Commission and the weighting of qualified majority voting (QMV) in the Council. As extensive enlargement was about to take place, the TON could not make exact provision, and so focused on establishing a template for future enlargement. In order to see the current institutional arrangements, it is necessary to refer to the two later Acts of Accession adopted in 2003 and 2005, which introduced changes to the institutions without formally amending the Treaty itself (see Chapter 2).

The **Constitutional Treaty (CT)** would have provided for the Constitution of the Union in a single Treaty but was dropped after opposition in the Member States. The **Treaty of Lisbon 2007**, once ratified, will amend the existing Treaty on European Union and the TEC, to be renamed the Treaty on the Functioning of the Union. It does not set out to be a constitutional document in the same way as the CT, but seeks to make the necessary amendments to provide for an enlarged Union while increasing the democratic involvement of the citizen, as well as allowing for greater transparency in decision making (see Chapter 2).

Subsidiary treaties

Subsidiary treaties (or conventions) form 'an integral part of Community law': Case 181/73 *Haegeman* v. *Belgium*. Such agreements may be concluded in the following ways:

(a) **By the EC exclusively under powers conferred by the EC Treaty.** Where the Treaty provides for the EC to exercise exclusive powers, the consequence is that Member States no longer have the power to act in this area, and must leave all action to the EC. See, for example, commercial agreements under Article 133 (ex 113).

(b) **By the EC on succession to an earlier agreement.** The most significant example remains the General Agreement on Tariffs and Trade (GATT) 1947. In Cases 21–24/72 *International Fruit* the Court held that the EEC took over the powers of the Member States in relation to GATT 1947. While GATT 1947 is not regarded as directly effective, the ECJ accepted in Case C-69/89 *Nakajima* that where the EC adopts legislation to comply with international obligation such as GATT 1947, any provisions of the legislation inconsistent with that obligation will be regarded as in breach of the Treaty or a rule relating to its application for the purpose of judicial review. In contrast, World Trade Organisation (WTO) agreements may not be relied on for judicial review: Case C-149/96 *Portugal* v. *Council*. The ECJ found that WTO agreements differ substantially from the GATT 1947 in terms of the mechanism for dispute resolution between the parties.

(c) **By individual Member States under Article 204 (ex 220).** For example, the Convention on Jurisdiction and Enforcement of Judgments in Civil and Commercial Matters 1968). The category has only rarely been regarded as a source of EU law by the ECJ, presumably due to the possibility of such agreements undermining the EU legal order.

ACTS OF THE INSTITUTIONS

Legislative powers of the Council and the Commission

In order to carry out their task in accordance with the provisions of the EC Treaty, the Council and the Commission are empowered 'to make regulations, issue directives, take decisions, make recommendations or deliver opinions'. The measures, known as 'acts', are defined in Article 249 (ex 189), and are considered individually below.

The legislative process under which measures are adopted is outlined in Chapter 2, either under the co-decision procedure[1] in Article 251, or under the consultation procedure in Article 252. Where Article 251 applies, the procedure starts with a proposal

---

[1] To be renamed 'the ordinary legislative procedure' under the Treaty of Lisbon.

from the Commission. After a complex sequence of consultations, it ends, if success-ful, with the joint adoption of the measure by the Council and the European Parliament. Under Article 252 the procedure also starts with a proposal from the Commission, but ends, if successful, with the measure adopted by the Council alone, after consultation with the EP.

> ## Key point
>
> Following ratification of the Treaty of Lisbon, the first paragraph of Article 249 will be amended as follows:
>
> 'To exercise the Union's competences, the institutions shall adopt regulations, directives, decisions, recommendations or opinions.'

The direct effect of these measures, that is the extent to which such rules may be enforced directly before the courts of the Member States, is considered in Chapter 6.

Regulations

Article 249 states that a regulation has 'general application', and is 'binding in its entirety and directly applicable in all Member States'. This means that regulations set out rules that apply to all the Member States. The expression 'direct applicability' means that regulations take effect throughout the EU without the need for national implementing legislation. The ECHR has found that they are also 'directly effective', which means that they may be relied upon by individuals before the national courts (see Chapter 6).

Regulations tend to be the preferred form of secondary legislation in areas such as the Common Agricultural Policy where the EC adopts detailed rules which apply uniformly across the Community.

Regulation 1612/68 on freedom of movement for workers within the Community serves to illustrate a typical Regulation. Although some of its provisions have been repealed by a later Directive (Directive 2004/38: see Chapter 13), Articles 1–9 con-tinue to provide rules for workers and their families in relation to eligibility for employment, employment and equality of treatment. Article 9 of the Regulation on entitlement to housing provides as follows:

1 A worker who is a national of a Member State and who is employed in the territory of another Member State shall enjoy all the rights and benefits accorded to national workers in matters of housing, including ownership of the housing he needs.
2 Such worker may, with the same rights as nationals, put his name down on the housing list in the region where he is employed, where such lists exist; he shall enjoy the resultant benefits and priorities.

Directives

Article 249 states that a directive is 'binding, as to the result to be achieved, upon each member state to which it is addressed', but leaves to the national authorities 'the choice of form and methods'. This means that a directive states the requirement to be reached, leaving the Member States to decide how to achieve it. Implementation may be by legislation or administrative action

The Product Liability Directive 85/374, for example, imposed a requirement (the 'result to be achieved') on Member States to introduce strict liability for defective products. Article 1 of the Directive provides that: 'The producer shall be liable for damage caused by a defect in his product.' Directive 85/374 was implemented in the UK by the Consumer Protection Act 1987.

The flexibility of the directive makes it attractive to the EU institutions which do not want to prescribe detailed rules, for example in relation to the single market programme under the Single European Act where a programme of 282 directives enabled the Community to achieve its goal of the removal of barriers to free movement by the deadline of December 1992.

Key point

Although directives may be addressed to a limited number of Member States, in practice they are normally addressed to all Member States, usually with a deadline for implementation. Directives are seen as flexible and appropriate to advance European integration without recourse to unnecessarily detailed rule making by the EC authorities. The process of the adoption of common standards through directives in known as *harmonisation* or *approximation*. Directives were the preferred form of secondary legislation adopted to complete the internal market in 1992.

Examples of selectively addressed directives may be found in the measures adopted under the Agreement on Social Policy (or 'Social Chapter') which was annexed to the Maastricht Treaty. The Social Chapter was not supported at the time by the UK government, which remained outside the arrangements until the Chapter was incorporated in the Treaty by the Treaty of Amsterdam (see Chapter 1). As a result, directives such as Directive 94/95 establishing a European Works Council, were addressed to Member States other than the UK.

Decisions

Article 249 provides that a decision shall be 'binding in its entirety upon those to whom it is addressed'. Decisions are made by the Council or Commission. As they are addressed to specified persons, either states or individuals, they do not apply across the EC as a whole. No further implementation is required. A typical example of a decision on competition would be made by the Commission and would be addressed to an undertaking to cease an anti-competitive practice or to impose a fine (see Chapter 8).

Key point

The Treaty of Lisbon will amend Article 249 as follows: 'A decision shall be binding in its entirety. A decision which specifies those to whom it is addressed shall be binding only on them.'

Framework decisions are decisions adopted under the Third Pillar, not under Article 249. Article 34 of the TEU empowers the Council to adopt framework decisions for the purpose of approximation of the law and regulations of the Member States. They are similar to directives in that they bind the Member States as to the result to be achieved but leave the choice of form and method to the national authorities. Article 34 specifies that framework decisions shall not entail direct effect. The ECJ is empowered under Article 35 to give preliminary rulings on the validity and interpretation of framework decisions and to review their legality.

Binding nature of secondary legislation

Only regulations, directives and decisions are legally binding. Article 253 requires that these measures must 'state the reasons on which they are based'. They must also 'refer to any proposals or opinions which were required to be obtained pursuant to this Treaty'. These procedural requirements are regarded as essential. Failure to comply may lead to annulment in the Court under Article 230 (see Chapter 8).

Soft law

Article 249 provides that: 'Recommendations and opinions shall have no binding force.' Non-binding instruments such as recommendations, opinions and guidelines are sometimes known as 'soft law', though this expression does not appear in the Treaty. The use of soft law has grown exponentially since the European Council met at Lisbon in 2000 where ambitious goals were set to achieve economic growth with greater cohesion by 2010. Soft law is seen as possessing advantages over traditional law making, including flexibility and scope for diversity, but also disadvantages in that it may be unclear, ineffective or unaccountable.[2]

The absence of legally binding status does *not* enable national courts to ignore soft law. In Case C-322/88 *Grimaldi* v. *Fonds des Maladies Professionelles* the ECJ stated

---

[2] See C. Sabel and J. Zeitlin, in D. Trubeck, P. Cottrell and M. Nance (2005).

that national judges must consider relevant recommendations in dealing with cases before them, particularly where they clarify the interpretation of other provisions of national or EC law. The Charter of Fundamental Rights, as a declaration, has the status of soft law, but has on a number of occasions been cited for the purpose of clarification in relation to fundamental rights. See, for example, Case C-540/03 *European Parliament* v. *Council of the EU*, a case involving immigration policy and the right of family reunification, in which the Directive 2003/86 was considered in the light of the Charter.

> **Key point**
>
> The Treaty of Lisbon will empower the Council to adopt recommendations under Article 249D, on a proposal from the Commission, where provided in the Treaty. The Commission and the ECB may also adopt recommendations where provided by the Treaty.

Classification

The classification of acts is not as straightforward as it appears from Article 249. The formal designation of an act as regulation, directive or decision should not be taken at face value as the ECJ considers the *substance* of the act rather than its *form*. The distinction is significant in the context of judicial review under Article 230 (see Chapter 8), as individuals can only challenge a measure if it is a decision addressed to them or a measure which is equivalent to a decision and in which they are directly and individually concerned.

In Cases 16 and 17/62 *Confédération Nationale des Productions de Fruits et Légumes* v. *Council* the ECJ concluded that where a regulation 'fails to lay down general rules', it may be relabelled a 'disguised decision'. The Court's finding in this case meant that the act was open to challenge by an individual. A similar conclusion was reached in Cases 41–44/70 *International Fruit Co.* v. *Commission* where a 'regulation' was held to be a 'bundle of decisions'.

CHANGES UNDER THE TREATY OF LISBON

Legislative and non-legislative acts

> **Key point**
>
> Under the Treaty of Lisbon, acts of the Union will be divided into legislative acts and non-legislative acts (Article 249A).

Legislative acts

These will be acts which have been adopted by legislative procedure. Article 249A provides for the adoption of regulations, directives and decisions under Article 251 under the *ordinary legislative procedure*, as co-decision will be known.

A new procedure known as the *special legislative procedure* will be introduced under Article 249A(2). For the first time, where provision is made in the Treaty, the European Parliament will be able to adopt regulations, directives and decisions directly, with participation of the Council. The Council is similarly empowered to act, with participation of the EP (see Chapter 2).

Non-legislative acts

Article 249B enables the delegation of power under a legislative act to the Commission to adopt acts of general application (i.e. non-legislative acts) to supplement or amend a legislative act. The legislative act must define the scope and conditions of the delegation. Either the EP or the Council may decide to revoke the delegation. A delegated act will enter into force only if the Council or EP do not object within the time stated in the legislative act. The word 'delegated' will appear in the title of the legislation. Member States will be required to adopt measures of national law necessary to implement legally binding acts under Article 249C. The word 'implementing' will be inserted in the title of implementing acts.

THE COMPETENCE OF THE COMMUNITY

Express and implied powers

Under Article 5 (ex 3b) EC, the Community is empowered to act within the limits of the powers conferred on it by the Treaty and of the objectives assigned to it therein. This is sometimes called the principle of conferral (see Chapter 1) and is a reference to the express powers of the Community. The Treaty cannot provide for every eventuality, however, and there may be scope for action in other circumstances. The theory of implied powers may provide support for such action.

The theory of implied powers, which derives from the common law traditions of the UK and USA, may take either a narrow or wide form. In its narrow form, the existence of an express power implies the existence of any other power which is reasonably necessary to exercise the express power. An example of the exercise of the narrow form may be seen in Cases 281 etc./85 *Germany* v. *Commission* arising out of Article 137 EC. At the time this provision gave the Commission the task of promoting social co-operation in the social field but did not provide the necessary powers. When the Commission adopted a decision in this area, it was challenged by Germany. The ECJ held that the provision must be regarded as impliedly conferring on the Commission the powers which are 'indispensible in order to carry out that task'.[3] In

---

[3] See Hartley (2003: 106).

its wide form, the existence of a given function or objective implies the existence of a power which is necessary to achieve it. This is supported by the general power in Article 308 (see below).

The external competence of the Community

The EC's treaty-making powers may be divided into two categories: powers which are expressly provided by the Treaty and powers which are implied on the basis that the treaty-making or external competence of the EC should reflect its internal powers. The Community's external competence is a highly complex area. Considerations of space do not permit detailed treatment in a book of this kind.[4] The two most clearly defined express powers related to:

1 **Commercial agreements under the Common Commercial Policy: Article 133.** These powers cover the EC commercial policy as a whole, including tariff and trade agreements, export aids, credit, finance and development policy.
2 **Association agreements: Article 310.** Association agreements are concluded with third countries either in preparation for full membership or as an alternative to membership.

As these powers are exclusive to the Community, Member States are no longer competent to conclude such agreements themselves. Under the Treaty international agreements are negotiated by the Commission and concluded by the Council, normally after consultation with the EP.

The theory of implied powers has been applied to the Community's external competence, particularly its capability to enter into treaties. The underlying reasoning is that if the Community possesses the powers to legislate internally (i.e. adopt secondary legislation such as regulations or directives) it should also be competent to enter into international agreements in the same fields. The theory of implied powers gained the recognition of the EC in Case 22/70 *Commission* v. *Council (Re European Road Transport Agreement)*.

Key case

In 1962 five of the then six Member States had signed an agreement known as the first European Road Transport Agreement (ERTA) with certain other European states. As the agreement was not ratified by enough of the contracting states the Member States began negotiations to conclude a second ERTA. Meanwhile the Council issued a regulation deriving from its internal power covering the same areas. The Commission objected to the Council's decision to allow negotiations →

---

[4] For further discussion of external competence, see Hartley (2003: 160–177).

> to continue and sought to annul the resolution to that effect in the ECJ. The second ERTA was nevertheless concluded in 1970.
>
> The ECJ held that the EC had authority to enter into such an agreement. Authority may arise not only out of express provision in the Treaty but also from other Treaty provisions and from secondary legislation. When the EC had adopted common rules to implement a transport policy in 1960 Member States lost their competence to conclude international agreements in this area: Case 22/70 *Commission* v. *Council.*

The presumption of implied powers does not necessarily operate in reverse. In the bilateral 'open skies' agreements cases, the ECJ held that it was *not* necessary for the EC to have external competence (i.e. the authority to make treaties) in relation to air transport to exercise internal competence in providing services: see for example Case C-471/98 *Commission* v. *Belgium.*

General powers under Article 308

The Community can be regarded as possessing wide-ranging treaty-making powers. After the ERTA decision particular use has been made of the so-called general powers provided by Article 308 which states that if action by the EC should prove necessary to attain, in the course of the operation of the common market, one of the objectives of the EC and that the Treaty has not provided the necessary powers, the Council shall, acting unanimously on a proposal from the Commission and after consulting the EP, take the necessary measures.

Article 308 provided a useful base to develop legislation in areas such as environmental protection before Treaty amendment made this unnecessary. As the ECJ usually adopts a 'purposive' approach to interpretation of the Treaty (i.e. interpreting the provision according to the spirit or purpose of the Treaty), the wording of the Article has not proved particularly limiting. However, in Opinion 2/94 on Accession by the EC to the ECHR, the Court of Justice found that Article 308 could not be relied on to extend the scope of the powers of the EC beyond the framework provided by the Treaty as a whole. The Article could not be used to circumvent the normal procedure to amend the Treaty.

The Court's main objection to the use of Article 308 as a legal base has been that it reduces the role of the European Parliament in the legislative process. In consequence, Article 308 should only be used where there is no other possible legal base. The Court has made it clear that it will examine closely the use of Article 308 when an alternative legal base is available which would provide for greater involvement of the EP: Case C-350/92 *Spain* v. *Council.*[5]

---

[5] See Craig and De Burca (2007: 94).

Legal proceedings under Article 300

Article 300(6) EC provides a procedure under which the Council, the Commission, Parliament or a Member State may obtain an opinion of the ECJ on the compatibility of a proposed agreement with the Treaty. An adverse opinion ensures that the agreement may only come into force in accordance with Article 48 of the TEU, the procedure for amending the Treaty, requiring ratification by all Member States.

In Opinion 1/91 on the *Draft Agreement on the European Economic Area (EEA)* the ECJ objected to the existence and jurisdiction of the proposed EEA Court, holding that the EEA should not be able to determine the respective competences of the EC and the Member States, as these matters were covered by the exclusive jurisdiction of the ECJ (see below) under Article 292 (ex 219). The draft EEA was revised to comply with Opinion 1/91 and found to be compatible with EC law in Opinion 1/92.

The principle of subsidiarity

The principle of subsidiarity was introduced by the Treaty on European Union to govern the allocation of competences (i.e. powers or authority) where responsibility is shared between the EC and Member States. It was seen by the treaty-drafters as offsetting the tendency for 'competence creep', that is the gradual increase in the number and range of areas within the EU's exclusive competence. Where the Treaty provides that the Community has exclusive competence, Member States lose the power to act. As a result, Members States forcefully contest the classification of exclusive competence. Examples of exclusive competence include the free movement provisions of the internal market, and the common commercial policy under Article 133.

Under Article 5(1) of the EC Treaty the Community may 'take action, in accordance with the principle of subsidiarity, only if and so far as the objectives of the proposed action cannot be sufficiently achieved by the Member States and can therefore, by reason of the scale or effects of the proposed action, be better achieved by the Community'. This Article creates a presumption which can be rebutted in favour of action by the Member States in areas of shared competence.

Article 5(2) provides that the action should not exceed what is necessary to achieve the objective in question. In other words, the action should accord with the principle of proportionality.

COMPETENCE OF THE UNION UNDER THE TREATY OF LISBON

The principles of conferral, subsidiarity and proportionality

The TOL provides for the principle of conferral in new Article 3a of the TEU (repealing the existing Article 3). Under Article 3a competences not conferred on the Union in the treaties remain with the Member States.

> **Key point**
>
> The TOL makes a distinction in Article 3b between the *limits* of Union competences, which are governed by the principle of conferral, and their *use*, which is governed by the principles of subsidiarity and proportionality.

Article 3b(1) provides that under the principle of conferral, the Union shall act only within the limits of the competences conferred on it by the Member States in the treaties to attain the objectives therein. Article 3b(2) provides that competences not conferred upon the Union in the TOL remain with the Member States.

The TOL will repeal Article 5 and replace it with Article 3b of the TEU, which covers the principles of conferral, subsidiarity and proportionality. Article 3b(3) repeats the wording of Article 5, but adds a requirement that national parliaments shall 'ensure compliance with the principle of subsidiarity' in accordance with the procedure set out in the Protocol on Subsidiarity. The principles of subsidiarity and proportionality are considered in more detail in Chapter 4, in the context of general principles of EU law.

> **Key point**
>
> Uncertainty over the scope of exclusive and non-exclusive competences should be resolved by the Treaty of Lisbon which provides a list of competences in two new Articles in Title I, Articles 2B and 2C.

Exclusive competences under the Treaty of Lisbon

Exclusive competences are listed under Article 2B as follows:

(a) the customs union;
(b) the establishment of the competition rules necessary for the functioning of the internal market;
(c) monetary policy for the Member States whose currency is the euro;
(d) the conservation of marine biological resources under the common fisheries policy;
(e) the customs union;
(f) common commercial policy.

Article 2B also provides for exclusive competence for the Union to conclude an international agreement where provided for in a legislative act of the Union or where necessary to enable the Union to exercise its internal competence, or in so far as its conclusion may affect common rules or alter their scope.

Shared competences under the Treaty of Lisbon

Article 2C provides that the Union shall share competence with the Member States where the treaties confer on it a competence which does not relate to the areas referred to in Articles 2B and 2E. Article 2E provides the Union with competence to support, co-ordinate or supplement the action of Member States in relation to the protection and improvement of human health, industry, culture, tourism, education, vocational training and sport, civil protection and administrative co-operation.

Under Article 2C the areas of shared competence are as follows: internal market; social policy for aspects defined in the Treaty; economic, territorial and social cohesion; environment; consumer protection; transport; trans-European networks; energy; area of freedom, security and justice; and common safety concerns in public health matters, for the aspects defined in this Treaty.

DECISIONS OF THE COURT OF JUSTICE

Decisions of the Court of Justice are an important source of EC law, binding on all the Member States. The Court is made up of:

- the **Court of Justice (ECJ)**, established by the original EC Treaty, which sets out its jurisdiction. It is the senior court and hears appeals from the Court of First Instance. (See Chapter 2 for further information on the Court.)
- the **Court of First Instance (CFI)**, established after the SEA to relieve the ECJ of some of its workload. The CFI deals with specialised areas such as staff cases and competition. It will be renamed the **General Court** by the TOL.

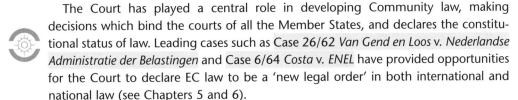

The Court has played a central role in developing Community law, making decisions which bind the courts of all the Member States, and declares the constitutional status of law. Leading cases such as Case 26/62 *Van Gend en Loos* v. *Nederlandse Administratie der Belastingen* and Case 6/64 *Costa* v. *ENEL* have provided opportunities for the Court to declare EC law to be a 'new legal order' in both international and national law (see Chapters 5 and 6).

The Court has relied on the preliminary reference procedure under Article 234 to interpret the law. This mechanism enables national courts to refer questions to the ECJ for clarification and rulings on validity (see Chapter 10). Under this procedure, the Court has recognised *general principles of law* as a source of EC law. These principles derive from international law such as the European Convention on Human Rights and Fundamental Freedoms and from the laws of the Member States. Examples include the principles of equality (or non-discrimination) and legal certainty. General principles and the related concept of fundamental rights are considered in Chapter 4.

Where to find the law

Please see Appendix 2 for further information, including useful websites.

QUESTIONS

1 (a) Which treaty most recently amended the EC Treaty: the Treaty of Amsterdam, the Treaty of Nice or the Single European Act?

(b) What is the status of the Treaty of Lisbon?

(c) Why does a directive provide greater flexibility as a legal act than a regulation?

(d) What is a framework decision and how does it differ from regulations, directives and decisions?

(e) How will the Treaty of Lisbon change the classification of secondary legislation?

2 How has the EC used its internal powers under the EC Treaty to develop its external competence to adopt international agreements?

3 What is the relationship between the principles of conferral, subsidiarity and proportionality under the Treaty of Lisbon?

Further reading

General

Chalmers, D., Hadjiemmanuil, C., Monti, G. and Tomkins, A. (2006) *European Union Law*, Cambridge University Press, Chapter 4.

Craig, P. and De Burca, G. (2007) *EU Law: Text, Cases and Materials*, 4th edition, Oxford University Press, Chapter 3.

Hartley, T. (2003) *The Foundations of European Community Law*, 5th edition, Oxford, Chapters 3 and 4.

Sabel, C. and Zeitlin, J. in D. Trubeck, P. Cottrell and M. Nance, 'Soft Law, Hard Law and European Integration: toward a theory of hybridity', Jean Monnet Working Paper 02/05, 19, cited in Chalmers *et al.*, at p.139.

Competence

Craig, P. (2004) 'Competence, clarity, conferral, containment and consideration', (2004) 29 ELRev. 323.

Heffernan, L. and McAuliffe, C. (2003) 'External relations in the air traffic sector: the Court of Justice and the "Open Skies" Agreements', (2003) 28 ELRev. 601.

Weatherill, S. (1995) *Law and Integration in the European Union*, Oxford University Press, pp.38–57.

Visit **http://www.mylawchamber.co.uk/kent** to access
answer guidance to questions in the book to test
yourself on this chapter.

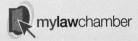

Use **Case Navigator** to read in full some of the key cases referenced
in this chapter:

- Case 6/64 **Costa** *v.* **ENEL** [1964] ECR 585
- C-540/03 **European Parliament** *v.* **Council of the EU**
- 26/62 **Van Gend en Loos** *v.* **Nederlandse Administratie
  Belastingen**

4 General principles of law

INTRODUCTION

The term 'general principles of law' refers to the body of principles developed by the ECJ through its interpretation of EC primary and secondary legislation. The principles themselves derive from international law and from principles that are common to the Member States. The incorporation of general principles of law within the body of EC law is one of the distinguishing features of the jurisprudence of the ECJ, reflecting a high level of judicial activism, necessitated by the gaps left by the Treaty on European Union (TEU) and by secondary legislation.

The legal authority for the incorporation of general principles of law derives from three provisions of the Treaty:

1 Article 220 provides that the ECJ shall ensure that in the interpretation and application of the Treaty 'the law' is observed. It is generally accepted that the word 'law' has a meaning which goes beyond the law in the Treaty, entitling the ECJ to take account of general principles formulated outside the Treaty.
2 Article 230 gives the ECJ power to review the legality of acts of the Council and the Commission on grounds which include infringement of the Treaty or of any rule relating to its application.
3 Article 288 provides that liability of the EC in tort is determined in accordance with the general principles common to the laws of the Member States.

The growing significance of general principles, particularly fundamental rights, as a source of law is recognized in Article 6(1) of the TEU which provides that: 'The Union is founded on the principles of liberty, democracy, respect for fundamental rights and fundamental freedoms, and the rule of law, principles which are common to the Member States.'

Sources of general principles of law

General principles of law are found in international law, particularly in the European Convention on Human Rights and Fundamental Freedoms (ECHR), in the domestic legal systems of the Member States and in the decisions of the ECJ. These three 'sources' are not mutually exclusive. What is regarded as a 'general principle' in the Member States may represent a principle of international law, and may, in time, find its way into the jurisdiction of the ECJ.

To be accepted as a general principle by the ECJ the principle in question need not be common to all the Member States. It is sufficient if the principle is accepted by the legal systems of most of the Member States or conforms with the direction of legal developments in the Member States. In the words of Advocate-General Lagrange in Case 14/61 *Hoogovens* v. *High Authority*: 'The Court . . . is not content to draw on more or less arithmetical "common denominators" between different national solutions, but chooses from each of the member states those solutions which, having regard to the objects of the Treaty, appear to be the best or . . . the most progressive.'[1]

General principles in the legal systems of the Member States

General principles are familiar to lawyers in continental legal systems: French administrative law has long been regulated by the general principles of law. In Germany the courts have held the principles of proportionality to underline Articles 2 and 25 (ex 12) of the Basic Law. To the UK lawyer at first sight the doctrine of general principles of law appears unfamiliar. However, the concept of reasonableness, the maxims of equity and the rules of natural justice are of equivalent importance in the UK and have influenced the development of general principles in the ECJ.

Role of general principles in EC law

The general principles of law have become an independent and important source of law. General principles include:

(a) Fundamental rights
(b) Proportionality
(c) Equality
(d) Legal certainty
(e) Procedural rights.

Each of these is considered below.

> **Key point**
>
> General principles may be invoked to interpret EC law. They cannot prevail over the express provisions of the Treaty: Case 40/64 *Sgarlata*.

---

[1] At pp.283–4.

FUNDAMENTAL RIGHTS

The protection of fundamental human rights within the EU has developed through various mechanisms. Initially, the Court of Justice played the lead role, as it developed a body of case law on the subject. The importance of fundamental rights has also been acknowledged in the TEU (Articles 6 and 7), but these provisions cannot be legally enforced. In addition, the EU adopted the Charter of Fundamental Rights which was annexed as a Declaration to the Treaty of Nice. The Charter would have been incorporated into the body of the Treaty under the Constitutional Treaty (CT). While this will not happen under the Treaty of Lisbon (see below), the Charter will nevertheless become legally binding.

Key point

'Fundamental rights' should not be seen as a self-contained legal principle but as an *approach* reflecting other general principles such as proportionality in order to assess validity.

The protection of fundamental rights in the ECJ

The development of fundamental rights in the Court of Justice has been influenced by the fundamental rights entrenched in the post-war German constitution which empowers the Federal Constitutional Court to determine the constitutionality of legislation. German litigants in their national courts and in the ECJ argued that EC law should comply with the fundamental rights provisions of the constitution.

As a response to the German constitutional arguments, the ECJ formulated its own doctrine of fundamental rights by which it declared that the ECJ would annul any provision of EC law which contravened human rights. This declaration was made in Case 29/69 *Stauder* v. *City of Ulm*, a case which arose out of a Community scheme to provide cheap butter for recipients of welfare benefits. The applicant objected to the requirement to divulge his name and address on a coupon to obtain the butter and challenged the law as a violation of human rights (equality of treatment) in the German courts. A reference was made to the ECJ to determine the validity of the EC decision creating the scheme. The Court held that the scheme did not require the applicant's name on the coupon and found nothing in the scheme 'capable of prejudicing the fundamental human rights enshrined in the general principles of Community law and protected by the Court'.

Key case

Case 11/70 *International Handelsgesellschaft* concerned a dispute arising out of the Common Agricultural Policy (CAP) under which exports of certain agricultural products were only permitted if the exporter had first obtained an export licence and paid a deposit. The applicants objected to the forfeiture of their deposit for failure to carry out the export within the period of validity of the licence as contrary to the German constitution, particularly the principle of proportionality. The ECJ decided that such a scheme did not infringe fundamental rights and stated that Community measures may only be judged according to Community criteria and not by national standards, even those relating to fundamental human rights.

The *Handelsgesellschaft* decision provided an opportunity for the ECJ to affirm the importance of fundamental rights, with the Court declaring that:

> Respect for fundamental rights forms an integral part of the general principles of law protected by the Court of Justice. The protection of such rights, whilst inspired by the constitutional traditions common to the Member States, must be ensured within the framework of the structure and objectives of the Community.

The scope of fundamental rights was extended further in Case 4/73 *J. Nold* v. *Commission*. The applicant, a coal wholesale company in Germany, challenged a Commission decision under the ECSC Treaty on the ground that it violated the company's fundamental human rights, in this case the right to the free pursuit of economic activity and property rights. While the ECJ considered that there was no breach of fundamental rights on the facts which concerned 'mere commercial interests or opportunities', it reiterated the principle that fundamental principles form an integral part of the general principles of law and continued:

> In safeguarding these rights, the Court is bound to draw inspiration from constitutional traditions common to the Member States, and it cannot therefore uphold measures which are incompatible with fundamental rights recognised and protected by the constitutions of those states.
>
> Similarly, international treaties for the protection of human rights on which the member states have collaborated or of which they are signatories, can supply guidelines which should be followed within the framework of Community law.

Key points

- EC measures conflicting with fundamental rights enshrined in national constitutions should be annulled.
- International law is an important source of EC law.

European Convention on Human Rights and Fundamental Freedoms

The European Convention on Human Rights and Fundamental Freedoms (ECHR), an international Treaty signed by all the EU Member States, has been given special significance by the ECJ, although the Convention has not been formally incorporated into EU law. In 1977 the institutions of the EC issued a Joint Declaration affirming their adherence to the principles of the ECHR. The commitment to respect human rights was recognised by Article 6(1) of the TEU which declares that: 'The Union is founded on the principles of liberty, democracy, respect for human rights and fundamental freedoms, and the rule of law, principles which are common to the Member States.' Article 6(2) provides that the EU shall respect fundamental rights, as guaranteed by the ECHR and as they result from the constitutional traditions common to the Member States, as general principles of Community law. The EU is required by Article 6(3) to respect the national identities of its Member States, and is empowered by Article 6(4) to provide itself with the necessary means to attain its objectives and carry through its policies.

Under Article 7 of the TEU the Council may determine the existence of a persistent and serious breach of human rights by a Member State of the principles in Article 6(1). The procedure involves the European Council acting unanimously on a proposal by one third of the Member States or by the Commission, after obtaining the assent of the EP. Where such a determination has been made, the Council may, by qualified majority vote under Article 6(2), decide to suspend the rights of the Member State under the Treaty, including voting rights in the Council. So far, the procedure has not been invoked.

Key point

The Treaty of Lisbon will amend Article 7, replacing the word 'assent' with 'consent' and the reference to 'breach of principles' to 'breach of values referred to in Article 1a'.

The values of the Union

New Article 1a of the TEU, as amended by the TOL, will provide that: 'The Union is founded on the values of respect for human dignity, the rule of law and respect for human rights, including the right of persons belonging to minorities. These values are common to the Member States in a society in which pluralism, non-discrimination, tolerance, justice, solidarity and equality between women and men prevail.'

Accession to the ECHR

Until recently, accession to the Convention by the EU was ruled out following ECJ Opinion 2/94 that the Community lacked the necessary competence to become a party to the ECHR, leading to criticism that the EU was neglecting human rights.[2]

---

[2] See, for example, White (2000).

Key point

The Treaty of Lisbon, in a new Article 6(2) of the TEU, will require the EU to accede to the ECHR. The Union's former lack of legal competence is remedied by Article 46A of the TFU which provides that the Union will have legal personality. Accession is stated not to affect the Union's competences as defined in the Treaties: Article 6(1). A Protocol to the Treaty provides that the accession of the EU to the ECHR must be agreed unanimously.

The provision for accession to the ECHR under the TOL repeats the wording of the failed CT. In addition Article 6(1) of the amended TEU provides for the Charter of Fundamental Rights of the EU declared at Nice to have 'the same legal value as the Treaties' (see below).

The ECHR and the ECJ

The ECJ decisively acknowledged the significance of the Convention in Case 36/75 *Rutili*, after which it has proceeded to recognise a number of specific rights under the ECHR as directly enforceable on a case-by-case basis. Examples of the Court approach include:

- the right to property (First Protocol Article 1): Case 44/79 *Hauer* v. *Rheinland-Pfalz*;
- non-retroactivity of penal provisions (Article 7): Case 63/83 *R.* v. *Kirk*;
- right to family life, home and correspondence (Article 8): Case C-60/00 *Mary Carpenter*; Case C-109/01 *Home Secretary* v. *Akrich*; Case 136/70 *National Panasonic* Case 136/79 (investigation by Commission of alleged anti-competitive practices);
- freedom of religion (Article 9): Case 130/75 *Prais* v. *Council*;
- freedom of expression (Article 10): Case C-112/00 *Schmidberger* v. *Austria*; Case C-260/89 *Elleneki Radiophonia Tileorasi*;
- freedom of assembly (Article 11): *Schmidberger* v. *Austria*;
- right to an effective judicial remedy before the national courts (Article 13): Case 224/84 *Johnston* v. *Chief Constable of the RUC* Case 222/84.

The Court's dynamic approach to the recognition of individual Articles of the Convention has enabled the protection of fundamental human rights in EC law to keep pace with social change. This is illustrated by Case 117/01 *KB* on the right to marry under Article 12 of the ECHR.

Key case

This case arose as a result of the denial of a new birth certificate under UK law to a transsexual following gender reassignment surgery. The lack of the certificate prevented KB from marrying a post-operative man, with consequential loss of →

4

General principles of law

pension rights in the event of the partner's death. After the decision of the European Court of Human Rights (ECtHR) in *Goodwin* v. *UK*, it was clear that the UK law in question infringed Articles 8 and 12 of the ECHR. The ECJ found that, in principle, Article 141 on equal pay for men and women precluded legislation which denied such individuals the right to marry, in contravention of the ECHR: Case 117/01 *KB* v. *NHS Pensions Agency and the Secretary of State for Pensions*.

The European Court of Human Rights (ECtHR) demonstrated in *Matthews* v. *UK* that it regards matters of EC law as admissible, contrary to previous practice. In this case the applicant, a resident of Gibraltar, brought an action in the ECtHR relying on Article 3 of Protocol 1 of the ECHR (right of free election) when she found herself excluded from the right to vote in the elections to the EP. Her claim that the limited status accorded to the residents of Gibraltar under Annex 2 of the EC Act on Direct Elections 1976 infringed Article 3 of Protocol 1 was upheld by the Court. The ECtHR ruled that the ECJ was unable to provide a remedy as it lacked the capacity to review the 1976 Act (itself a Treaty). The UK sought to rectify the situation by adopting the European Parliament (Representation) Act in 2003. Spain, for whom the constitutional status of Gibraltar is a sensitive political issue, brought proceedings against the UK in the ECJ in Case C-145/04 *Spain* v. *UK* , alleging that the 2003 Act infringed various provisions of the Treaty including Article 17 on citizenship. The Court found against Spain, holding that the UK could not be penalised for compliance with the case law of the ECtHR, particularly the judgment against the UK.

For a further example of a ruling of the ECtHR on the relationship between EC law and the ECHR, see *Bosphorus* v. *Ireland*, App. No. 45036/98.

Key case

Ireland seized an aircraft leased by Bosphorus Airways (BosA) from Jugoslav Airlines under Regulation 990/03 of the Council of the EU, which had been adopted pursuant to UN Resolution 820 (1983) to impose sanctions against the Federal Republic of Yugoslavia. BosA challenged the seizure, claiming that the Regulation did not apply to aircraft. The Supreme Court of Ireland referred the case to the ECJ to clarify the meaning of the Regulation. The ECJ found that the interference with the right to property was justified by the general interest. Parallel proceedings were also brought in the ECtHR which found that the Irish government had *not* infringed Article 1 of Protocol 1 of the ECHR (peaceful enjoyment of possessions). EC law was seen to provide equivalent protection to the protection of human rights under the Convention. The presumption of equivalent protection could have been rebutted if the protection of Convention rights were manifestly deficient. In this case, it was not and the presumption was not rebutted: *Bosphorus* v. *Ireland*, App. No. 45036/98.

The *Bosphorus* decision demonstrates that the ECtHR continues to regard itself as the primary protector of Convention rights, willing to review the protection of rights by the EU when this is strictly necessary.[3]

The Charter of Fundamental Rights

As we have seen, the initial responsibility for identifying and clarifying fundamental rights in EC law fell to the Court of Justice, with the result that the development of fundamental rights was piecemeal. In addition, progressive Treaty amendments referred to the strengthening of fundamental rights, leading to the decision by the Cologne Council in 1999 that these rights should be consolidated in a single instrument.

The Charter of Fundamental Rights was drafted under the 'Convention' process which was also followed in relation to the Constitutional Treaty, a radical approach to governance involving a 'Convention' of 62 people, its membership drawn from representatives from Heads of State of Governments, the Commission, the EP and national parliaments (see Chapter 1). The Convention proposed a draft Charter of Fundamental Rights in 2000, providing for rights which overlap with the ECHR rights. This was agreed by the European Council who approved the Charter in October 2000. The final version of the Charter was annexed to the Treaty of Nice as a Declaration in December 2000. If the CT had been ratified, the Charter would have been incorporated into the body of the Treaty.

> ### Key point
>
> Under the Treaty of Lisbon the Charter will be given 'the same legal effect as the Treaties', as set out in a new Article 6(1) TEU. As a result the Charter will have legal force in the ECJ and the national courts.

The UK and Poland (see Chapter 1) signed a Protocol to the TOL declaring that the Charter does not extend the ability of the Court of Justice or these Member States to find that laws or administrative provisions conflict with the fundamental rights under the Charter.

Protection of fundamental rights under the Charter

The rights recognised by the Charter take their inspiration from the ECHR, but in a form which reflects the legal order of the EU and the changes in society since the Convention was adopted. The Charter is arranged under six Chapters:

- **Chapter I Dignity**: This chapter provides for respect for human dignity (Article 1), right to life (Article 2), right to the integrity of the person (Article 3), prohibition of torture (Article 4) and prohibition of slavery and forced labour (Article 5).

[3] See Parga (2006).

- **Chapter II Freedoms**: This chapter provides for the right to liberty and security (Article 6), respect for private and family life (Article 7), protection of personal data (Article 8), right to marry and found a family (Article 9), freedom of thought, conscience and religion (Article 10), freedom of expression and information (Article 11), freedom of assembly and association (Article 12), freedom of the arts and sciences (Article 13), right to education (Article 14), freedom to choose an occupation and the right to engage in work (Article 15), freedom to conduct a business (Article 16), right to property (Article 17), right to asylum (Article 18), protection in the event of removal, expulsion or extradition (Article 19).
- **Chapter III Equality**: This chapter provides that everyone is equal before the law (Article 20), for the prohibition of discrimination on grounds of race, sex, colour, etc. (Article 21), respect for cultural, religious and linguistic diversity (Article 22), equality between men and women (Article 23), the rights of the child (Article 23), the rights of the elderly (Article 24) and the integration of persons with disabilitities (Article 26).
- **Chapter IV Solidarity**: This chapter provides for various rights in employment including the right for workers or their representatives to be consulted (Article 27), the right of collective bargaining and action (Article 28), protection from unjustified dismissal (Article 30), fair and just working conditions (Article 31), prohibition of child labour and protection of children at work (Article 32), legal, economic and social protection for the family, as well as the right to reconcile family and professional life (Article 33), respect for social security and social assistance (Article 34), right of access to health care (Article 35), integration of a high level of environmental protection into the policies of the Union (Article 37) and of consumer protection (Article 38).
- **Chapter V Citizens' Rights**: This chapter provides for the right for Union citizens to vote and stand as a candidate in EP elections (Article 39) and municipal elections (Article 40). It also covers the right of good administration (Article 41), access to documents (Article 42), access to the Ombudsman (Article 43), right to petition the EP (Article 44), freedom of movement and residence (Article 45) and diplomatic and consular protection (Article 46).
- **Chapter VI Justice**: This chapter provides for the right to an effective remedy and to a fair trial (Article 47), the presumption of innocence and right of defence (Article 48), the principles of legality and proportionality of criminal offences and penalties (Article 49) and the right not to be tried twice in criminal proceedings for the same offence (Article 50).

Chapter VII provides in Article 52 for *derogation* from the rights recognised by the Charter subject to the principle of proportionality, only if necessary and 'genuinely' to meet objectives of general interest recognised by the Union or to protect the rights and freedoms of others. Article 53, which is similar to Article 53 of the ECHR, provides that nothing in the Charter will be interpreted as restricting or adversely affecting human rights and fundamental freedoms under EU or international law.

Current reliance on the Charter of Fundamental Rights

Until the Treaty of Lisbon is ratified, the Charter will continue to be regarded as 'soft law'. Since its adoption it has been cited on many occasions by Advocates-General in their submissions without being taken up by the Court. In the past six years, however, the Court has made frequent reference to the importance of the Charter, while acknowledging that is not legally binding: Case C-540/03 *EP* v. *Council*.[4] See, for example:

- Case C-411/05 *Palacios de la Villa* v. *Commission* where the Court referred to the Charter in relation to the need to combat discrimination, for action to integrate elderly and disabled people when interpreting Directive 2000/78 in the context of age discrimination.
- Case C-450/06 *Varec SA* v. *Belgian State*, in which the Court referred to Article 7 of the Charter (respect for private life) in relation to the protection of business secrets.
- Case T-194/04 *The Bavarian Lager Co.* v. *Commission*, in which the CFI referred to Articles 7 and 8 of the Charter (protection of personal data) in successful proceedings to annul a Commission decision to refuse access to full minutes of a meeting.

The *Bavarian Lager* case also illustrates the use made by the European Ombudsman of reliance on the Charter in reports to the EP and the Commission on data protection. The Ombudsman has made frequent critical reference to the failure of the EC institutions to observe the rights in the Charter.[5] The Commission, too, has issued reports on the impact of the Charter on legislative proposals.[6] Given the prospect of legal status in the future, it is to be expected that references to the Charter in judgments of the ECJ before the Treaty of Lisbon is ratified will increase greatly.

PROPORTIONALITY

Principle of proportionality

The principle of proportionality is one of the most important of the general principles recognised by EC law. After making provision for subsidiarity (see below), the principle of proportionality is now incorporated in the Treaty in Article 5, which requires that action by the Community 'shall not go beyond what is necessary to achieve the objectives of this Treaty'. Directive 2004/38 also provides for the principle of proportionality under Article 27 when Member States seek to derogate from free movement rights for Union citizens (see Chapter 13).

Proportionality is derived from German law, where it is regarded as one of the rights underlying the constitution: *International Handelsgesellschaft* (see above). The

---

[4] See comments by Craig and De Burca (2007), pp.417–418.
[5] See www.ombudsman.europa.eu/speeches/en/2006-04-028.htm, cited in Craig and De Burca (2007), pp.417–418.
[6] COM (2005)172.

principle of proportionality is applied to administrative law. It operates as a constraint on public authorities, which may not impose obligations beyond those which are appropriate and necessary to achieve the objective of the measure. The principle implies a clear relationship between the means and the ends of legislation: the means must be reasonably likely to achieve the objective, and the advantage to the public must be greater than the disadvantage. The principle of proportionality is similar to the concept of reasonableness but arguably involves more stringent criteria. The ECJ has on occasion referred specifically to reasonableness: in Case 15/57 *Chasse* the ECJ held that the High Authority must not exceed what is reasonable and must avoid, as far as possible, causing harm. Proportionality has been invoked frequently before the ECJ, particularly under Article 230 under which an administrative act may be annulled.

Key case

An export company paid the Intervention Board for Agricultural Produce a deposit of £1,670,000 to support its application for an export licence. When the application was submitted to the Commission four hours late, the Commission ruled that the entire deposit was forfeit, as it was required to do under EC regulation. The EC ruled that forfeiture of the entire deposit for a trivial breach of the deadline was a disproportionate act: Case 181/84 *R. v. Intervention Board for Agricultural Produce, ex parte Man (Sugar)*.

Internal market

Proportionality has also been applied in relation to the provisions for limitation of the free movement of labour and persons which must be justified under Article 30 (ex 36) or Article 39(3) (ex 48(3)). The ECJ in various cases has held that the measure must not exceed what is necessary to achieve the objective. The proportionality principle was invoked in relation to Case 145/88 *Torfaen Borough Council* v. *B&Q*[7] in which the ECJ held that national measures banning Sunday trading must not exceed what was necessary to achieve the objectives in question.

Freedom of commercial activity

The principle of proportionality reflects the broader concept of freedom of commercial activity, a freedom which underlines the EC Treaty and which is protected in the German constitution. Freedom of commercial activity is a wide-ranging freedom which encompasses not only the principle of proportionality but also the freedom to pursue a trade or profession, the freedom from unfair competition and a general freedom to act where no legal prohibition applies.

[7] See Chapter 12.

All four principles were unsuccessfully invoked in Cases 133–136/85 *Walter Rau* v. *BALM* and Case 249/85 *ALBAKO* v. *BALM* in a dispute arising out of a Commission scheme in 1985 to increase butter consumption. Under the scheme the inhabitants of West Berlin were offered two blocks of butter for the price of one. Rau, an aggrieved margarine manufacturer, challenged the Commission decision before the ECJ under Article 230 and brought parallel proceedings in the German courts against BALM. The ECJ held that none of the four principles had been infringed, upholding its own earlier decisions on a cheap 'Christmas butter' scheme also involving Cases 279, 280, 285 and 286/84 *Walter Rau*.

EQUALITY

The principle of equality implies that persons in similar situations should be treated in the same way unless there is objective justification for different treatment. The EC Treaty prohibits discrimination:

- on grounds of nationality: Article 12 (ex 6);
- on grounds of sex, in the context of equal pay for men and women: Article 141 (ex 119);
- against producers or consumers under the CAP: Article 34(3) (ex 40(3)).

The Treaty of Amsterdam introduced a legal base under Article 13 of the Treaty which gave the Council new powers to combat discrimination on grounds of sex, racial or ethnic origin, religion or belief, disability, age or sexual orientation. These grounds mark a departure from the previous areas in which discrimination is prohibited, as there is little or no economic basis for the action. Two important directives were introduced under Article 13:

1 Directive 2000/43 implementing the principle of equal treatment irrespective of racial or ethic origins (with effect from July 2003);
2 Directive 2000/78 establishing a general framework for equal treatment and occupation (with effect from December 2003).

These directives are considered further in Chapters 23 and 24.

A general principle of non-discrimination

The ECJ has held that EC law recognises a general principle of equality or non-discrimination. This is apparent from its case law such as Cases 103 and 145/77 *Royal Scholten-Honig ('Isoglucose')*, where the Court held that the production levy system for Isoglucose 'will offend against the general principle of equality of which the prohibition on discrimination set out in Article 40(3) . . . is a specific expression'. In Case 1/72 *Frilli* the ECJ held that equality of treatment is one of the fundamental principles of EC law.

Examples of the decisions of the ECJ on non-discrimination

1 A female official at the EP was denied an allowance because she was not the 'head of the family'. Under the relevant provision of EC law it was only possible for a

woman to be defined as a 'head of the family' in exceptional circumstance such as incapacity of the husband through illness. HELD: The provision was discriminatory and could not be upheld: Case 20/71 *Sabbatini* v. *European Parliament*.

2 A female EC official lost her expatriation allowance on marriage to an Italian under an EC rule which did not permit payment of the allowance to an official who acquired the nationality of the country in which she worked. Foreign women marrying Italian men automatically acquired Italian nationality on marriage although foreign men marrying Italian women did not. HELD: EC law may not take account of nationality which has been involuntarily acquired under a discriminatory national law: Case 21/74 *Airola* v. *Commission* .

3 A Jewish woman sought annulment of a Council decision to hold a competitive examination for a post as an EC official on a Jewish festival. The applicant had not mentioned her religion on the application form and there was no specific evidence of religious discrimination. The Council accepted that freedom of religion was a general principle of EC law but argued that it was not in breach. HELD: The appointing authority was not obliged to avoid holding the examination on a religious holiday since it had not been informed of the fact in advance. Where advance information is given, the appointing authority should try to avoid such dates: Case 130/75 *Prais* v. *Council*.

4 A transsexual was dismissed following gender reassignment surgery. On a reference from the industrial tribunal hearing the ensuing claim for unfair dismissal, the ECJ held that the Equal Treatment Directive was 'simply the expression of the "principle of equality which is one of the fundamental principles" of EC law. The Directive should be liberally interpreted and not limited to discrimination on grounds of gender': Case C-13/94 *P.* v. *S.* (see Chapter 24).

The ECJ took a more conservative line in Case C-249/96 *Grant* v. *S. W. Trains*, refusing to extend equal treatment to sexual orientation to enable same-sex partners to benefit from travel facilities for spouses. It should be noted that this decision was made before amendment of the Treaty to include new Article 13 as a base for action to combat discrimination.

LEGAL CERTAINTY

Principle of legal certainty

Legal certainty is a wide-ranging and important principle underlying EC law and the legal systems of many of the Member States. The concept can be sub-divided into two specific principles: non-retroactivity and legitimate expectations.

Retroactivity

Two rules govern the principle of non-retroactivity in EC law:

1 In the absence of clear evidence to the contrary, there is a rule of interpretation that legislation is presumed not to be retroactive. The principle prevents EC secondary legislation from taking effect before publication.

In Case 88/76 *Société pour l'Exportation des Sucres* v. *Commission* the Commission had passed a regulation on 30 June 1976 removing the right of exporters to cancel their export licences. The regulation was dated 1 July, the expected date of publication of the *Official Journal*. Owing to a strike the *Journal* did not appear until 2 July. The applicant applied for cancellation on 1 July but was refused on the basis of the regulation. The ECJ ruled that the regulation did not come into force until 2 July, the date of actual publication.

2 Under substantive EC law, retroactivity is prohibited unless the measure may not otherwise be achieved, provided there is respect for legitimate expectations.

Examples

1 A regulation establishing a system of levies and quotas for the production of isoglucose had been annulled for non-consultation with the EP. Following the correct consultation procedure a further regulation was issued retrospectively regulating isoglucose. HELD: The ECJ upheld the regulation on the basis that isoglucose producers should reasonably have expected the measure: Case 88/76 *Société pour l'Exportation des Sucres* v. *Commission*.

2 The captain of a Danish fishing vessel was charged with infringement of UK fisheries legislation. The ECJ held that a later regulation could not retrospectively validate national penal provisions which were otherwise invalid: Case 63/83 *R.* v. *Kirk*.

Key point

In some cases the ECJ has limited the temporal effect of its own judgments. In Case 43/75 *Defrenne* v. *Sabena* (No. 2) the ECJ ruled that considerations of legal certainty required that claims based on Article 119 (now 141) could only be brought from the date of the judgment unless proceedings had already commenced. The *Defrenne* approach was reserved for exceptional cases where the ECJ introduced a new principle or when the judgment might cause serious difficulties in relation to past events, such as substantial claims for back pay: Case C-262/88 *Barber* v. *Guardian Royal Exchange* (see Chapter 24).

Legitimate expectations

The principle of legitimate expectations (originally translated into English as 'protection of legitimate confidence') is another concept originating in German law. Under the principle, EC measures must not violate the legitimate expectations of those concerned, in the absence of overriding public interest. The principle may be invoked as a rule of interpretation: Case 78/74 *Deuka* v. *EVGE*; in an action in tort for damages:

Case 74/74 *CNTA* v. *Commission* (see Chapter 9); and as a basis for annulment of an EC measure: Case 112/77 *Töpfer* v. *Commission* (see Chapter 8).

In Case C-137/92P *Commission* v. *BASF AG and others* the ECJ upheld a decision of the CFI in which legal certainty had been invoked as a reason to annul a Commission measure. The Commission had failed to create an authenticated version of the measure in contravention of its own procedural rules.

Key point

An expectation will only be legitimate if it is reasonable, i.e. *within the contemplation of a prudent person acting within the course of business*. It does not cover speculative profiteering: Case 2/75 *EVGF* v. *Mackprang*.

In *Mackprang* a German grain dealer was prevented by a Commission decision from taking advantage of a fall in the value of the French franc which had made it profitable to buy grain in France and resell it to EVGF, the German grain intervention agency. M brought proceedings against EVGF in the German courts, claiming that he had a legitimate expectation of being able to sell the grain to the agency. The ECJ ruled (under Article 234) that the Commission decision did not infringe the principle of legitimate expectations but was a justified precaution against speculative activities. See also: Case 338/85 *Pardini* v. *Ministero con l'Estero*.

A legitimate expectation does not arise from:

- incorrect acceptance by an official of a defective document: Joined Cases 98/83 and 230/83 *Van Gend en Loos NV and Expeditiebedriff Wim Bosman BV* v. *Commission*;
- incorrect calculation by an EC institution of a trader's previous profit: Case 112/77 *Töpfer* v. *Commission*.

Few cases claiming legitimate expectations have been successful.

PROCEDURAL RIGHTS

Procedural rights in EC law are usually provided in the relevant secondary legislation. Where they are not provided, the person affected may rely on general principles in the following areas:

(a) **The right to a hearing**. The right to a hearing derives from the English principle of natural justice. It was first raised in the ECJ in Case 17/74 *Transocean Marine Paint Association* v. *Commission* , a competition case under Article 81 (ex 85). The Commission had addressed a decision to the applicants without referring to a condition which was later applied. The applicants sought annulment of the decision as far as it related to this condition. The ECJ held that there is a general principle of EC law that a person whose interests are perceptibly affected by a decision taken by a public authority must be given the opportunity to make his views known. As this had not been done, the condition was annulled. The decision was followed by the ECJ in Case 85/87 *Dow Benelux* v. *Commission*; see also: Case C-49/88 *Al-Jubail Fertilizer* v. *Council*. The ECJ annulled a regulation imposing anti-dumping duty on certain products made in Libya and Saudi Arabia after a complaint by the applicants, Saudi Arabian manufacturers, that they had been denied a fair hearing.

(b) **The duty to give reasons**. The duty to give reasons was established in Case 222/86 *Union Nationale des Entraîneurs et Cadres Techniques Professionels du Football (UNECTEF)* v. *Heylens*. M. Heylens was a Belgian national, holding a Belgian football trainers' diploma. His application to the French authorities for recognition of the diploma was refused without any reason for the decision. M. Heylens was charged with practising in France as a football trainer without the necessary French diploma (or recognised equivalent). On a preliminary reference the ECJ held that the right of free movement under Article 39 EC requires that there should be legal redress from a decision affecting access to employment and that reasons for the decision should be given.

(c) **The right to an effective judicial remedy**. The right to an effective judicial remedy in the national courts was upheld in Case 222/84 *Johnston* v. *Chief Constable of the Royal Ulster Constabulary*.

Key case

Case 222/84 *Johnston* v. *Chief Constable of the Royal Ulster Constabulary*:

The case arose out of a refusal by the RUC to renew contracts of women members of the RUC Reserve. A decision had been taken that full-time Reserve members were to be fully armed, but women were neither issued with firearms nor trained to use them. Mrs Johnston, a full-time member, claimed that the measure contravened Directive 76/207 providing equal treatment for men and women in employment. The Secretary of State for Northern Ireland issued her with a certificate stating that the purpose of the refusal was to safeguard national security and public order, 'conclusive evidence' of purpose under Article 53(2) of the Sex Discrimination (Northern Ireland) Order.

The ECJ held that Article 6 of Directive 76/207 requiring Member States to pursue their claims by judicial process after recourse to the competent authorities reflected a general principle laid down in Articles 6 and 13 of the ECHR. Further, Member States must ensure effective judicial control of directly applicable EC law and national implementing legislation. The ECJ held that national legislation stating that a compliance certificate was conclusive deprived the individual of access to the courts to assert his or her rights under EC law, contrary to Article 6 of the Directive.

Other general principles

A number of other general principles have been identified by the ECJ, including the right to be assisted by counsel: Case 115/80 *Demont*; confidentiality of communication between lawyer and client: Case 155/79 *AM&S*; and the right to exercise a profession: Case 234/85 *Keller*.

SUBSIDIARITY

The principle of subsidiarity derives from theological and natural law traditions. It has not developed through the case law of the ECJ, but was inserted into the EC Treaty by the Treaty of Maastricht. Subsidiarity is essentially concerned with the allocation of competences (see Chapter 1). Article 5(1) EC states that 'the Community shall act within the limits of the powers conferred upon it by this Treaty and of the objectives assigned to it therein'. In Article 5(2) it provides that in areas outside its exclusive competence, the Community shall take action, in accordance with the principle of subsidiarity, only where this cannot be sufficiently achieved by the Member States and can therefore, by reason of the scale or effects of the proposed action, be better achieved by the Community. Article 5 (3) EC states that: 'Any action by the Community shall not go beyond what is necessary to achieve the objectives of the Treaty.' The Treaty of Lisbon will repeal Article 5 and substitute a new provision (see below).

Protocol on subsidiarity

To decide whether action can be better achieved by the Member States or the EC the following considerations were set out as guidelines in a Protocol to the TOA:

● whether the issues in question have transnational aspects which cannot be satisfactorily regulated by the Member States; and/or
● whether actions by member states alone would conflict with the requirements of the Treaty; and/or
● whether the Council is satisfied that action at EC level would produce clear benefits by reason of scale or effects compared with action at the level of Member States.

The guidelines also make it clear that directives are to be preferred to regulations and framework directives to detailed directives.

Application of subsidiarity to legislation

Under the Protocol the Council must examine every Commission proposal for compliance with the principle of subsidiarity. The Commission is required to submit an annual report on the application of the principle to the European Council and the EP. The first full report was presented in December 1993. After the first two reports, the Commission decided to extend the scope of the reports to cover *all* action to improve legislation. 'Better Lawmaking' Reports have been issued annually since 1995. As the 1999 Report states: '"Better Lawmaking" does not simply mean applying the principles of subsidiarity and proportionality correctly; it also involves making legislation simpler, more understandable and more accessible. The result is greater effectiveness and acceptability of Community actions.'[8] This project (known as the 'SLIM' initiative) has led to a substantial reduction in legislative activity and a willingness to consider alternatives to legislation (e.g. agreements with the oil industry in 1999 to reduce vehicle emissions). The Commission has stated that its contribution takes the form of better drafting, simplification, consolidation, recasting, and improvements in access to legislation.

Can subsidiarity be successfully invoked before the ECJ?

While subsidiarity has been raised before the ECJ, it has yet to lead to the annulment of any piece of secondary legislation. For examples of unsuccessful challenges raising subsidiarity as a ground, see Case C-84/94 *UK* v. *Council* (a challenge by the UK over the 'Working Time' Directive) and Case C-377/98 *Netherlands* v. *EP and Council* (a challenge by the Netherlands in relation to Directive 98/44 on the legal protection of biotechnological inventions).

Key point

The Treaty of Lisbon will repeal Article 5 EC, replacing it with a new Article 3b which covers the principles of subsidiarity, proportionality and conferral (see Chapter 3). Article 3b will add an important new dimension by adding the requirement for national parliaments to scrutinise draft legislation to ensure compliance with the principle of subsidiarity.

A new Protocol on Subsidiarity and Proportionality provides for the Commission to forward its proposals to the national parliaments at the same time as the Union legislator. If by a majority of 55 per cent of members of the Council or a majority of votes cast in the EP, the legislator is of the opinion that the proposal is not compatible with the principle of subsidiarity, the proposal will be given no further consideration.

---

[8] COM (1999) 562 final.

TRANSPARENCY

Transparency is usually taken to refer to access to documents. The principle was recognised as a right and incorporated in the TEU by the Treaty of Amsterdam and is now recognised by Article 42 of the Charter of Fundamental Rights. Article 1 of the TEU provides for decisions to be taken as closely as possible to the citizen. Article 255(1) EC gives Union citizens and businesses with registered offices in a Member State the right of access to EP, Council and Commission documents, subject to conditions to be defined by the Council under Article 255(2). The Council duly adopted Regulation 1049/2001 providing detailed rules for access.

Although the ECJ and CFI have not set out a general right of transparency, they stressed in Case T-194/94 *Carvel* and Case T-174/95 *Svenska Journalist* v. *Council* the need to balance the needs of the citizen against the need for confidentiality.

Key point

The Treaty of Lisbon will strengthen the principle of transparency by introducing new Article 2B. Under Article 2B(1) the institutions are required to give citizens and representative associations 'the opportunity to make known and publicly exchange their views in all areas of Union action' and to 'maintain an open, transparent and regular dialogue with representative associations and civil society' (Article 2B(2)). The Commission is required to carry out 'broad consultations' with parties concerned to ensure that the Union's actions are coherent and transparent (Article 2B(3)). Scope is also provided for a citizens' initiative where one million citizens invite the Commission to submit a proposal (Article 2B(4)).

QUESTIONS

1 How are the general principles of EC law recognised and what is their relevance?

2 To what extent are fundamental rights protected by EU law? Discuss by reference to the provision in the Treaties as well as the decisions of the Court of Justice. How will ratification of the Treaty of Lisbon alter the position?

3 When may the principle of subsidiarity be invoked? Is it possible to rely on the principle to annul a legislative act?

Further reading

Chalmers, D., Hadjiemmanuil, C., Monti, G. and Tomkins, A. (2006) *European Union Law*, Cambridge University Press, Chapter 10, pp.440–463.

Craig, P. and De Burca, G. (2007) *EU Law: Text, Cases and Materials*, 4th edition, Oxford University Press, Chapters 4 and 15.

Eekhout, P. (2002) 'The EU Charter of Fundamental Rights and the Federal Question', (2002) 39 CMLRev. 945.

Parga, A.H. (2006) '*Bosphorus* v. *Ireland* and the protection of fundamental rights in Europe', (2006) 31 ELRev. 251.

Tridimas, T. (2006) *The General Principles of EC Law*, 2nd edition, Oxford University Press.

White, R.C.A. (2000) 'Editorial – Making Rights Visible', (2000) 25 ELRev. 97.

Visit **http://www.mylawchamber.co.uk/kent** to access answer guidance to questions in the book to test yourself on this chapter.

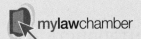

Use **Case Navigator** to read in full some of the key cases referenced in this chapter:

- 11/70 **International Handelsgesellschaft** v. **EVGF** [1970] ECR 1125
- C-84/94 **United Kingdom** v. **Council** (Working Time Directive) [1996] ECR I-5755

General principles of law

5 The supremacy of Community law

INTRODUCTION

The Treaty establishing the European Community makes no explicit provision for the supremacy of Community law over national law, although some support is provided by Article 10 (ex 5), the principle of solidarity or effectiveness. This omission has not deterred the Court of Justice from recognising the primacy of EC law. Relying on concepts such as direct applicability under Article 249 EC, the Court has constructed a 'new legal order' characterised by the supremacy of EC law over national law and by direct effect. In Case 6/64 *Costa* v. *ENEL* the Court declared that the precedence of EC law is confirmed by Article 189 (now 249) which would be 'quite meaningless if a state could unilaterally nullify its effects by means of a legislative measure which could prevail over Community law'.

> **Key terms**
>
> **Direct applicability**: a provision takes effect in the legal system of the Member States without the need to pass a law to give it effect.
> **Direct effect**: a directly applicable provision which creates rights on which individuals may rely before the national courts (see Chapter 6).

The debate over the status of Community law has continued in the 50 years since the signing of the Treaty of Rome, as the Community advanced towards ever closer union. While the doomed Constitutional Treaty would have provided for the primacy of Community law in the body of the Treaty, the Treaty of Lisbon merely recalls in a Declaration that the Treaties and law adopted under them have primacy over the laws of the Member States 'in accordance with well settled case law of the Court of Justice'. This shift of position in the TOL makes no significant difference in law but may be seen as a response to the popular suspicion of constitutionalism which found its voice in the rejection in the two referenda on the CT in France and the Netherlands.

The EC Treaty and TEU as international treaties

The Treaty establishing the European Communities and the Treaty on European Union are international agreements entered into by sovereign states requiring *incorporation* into the domestic legal systems of the Member States. There are two main approaches in the Member States to the incorporation of international law.

1 **The monist approach**. The international obligation takes effect in the domestic legal system as soon as the treaty is ratified, as for example, in France and the Netherlands.
2 **The dualist approach**. The international obligation takes effect in the domestic legal system only when it is incorporated by statute, as, for example, in Germany, Italy, Belgium and the UK.

EC law must comply with international law, and thus be capable of being interpreted consistently with it: Case C-53/96 *Hermes International* v. *FHT Marketing Choice*. In this case, the ECJ held that Regulation 40/94 providing for a Community trade mark had to be interpreted in accordance with Article 50 of the 'TRIPS'[1] agreement. The relationship between EC law and international law has also raised important questions in the context of the protection of human rights, particularly under the European Convention on Human Rights and Fundamental Freedoms (ECHR). This area is considered further in Chapter 4.

Where an EU Member State has a written constitution, it may also be necessary to refer to the constitution and to the practice of the courts to establish the status of the Treaties in domestic law. Although the French Constitution, for example, provides that Treaties or agreements which have been ratified have authority superior to any national law, the Conseil d'Etat only moved towards acceptance of this position in 1989 in the *Nicolo* case (see p.96).

ROLE OF THE COURT OF JUSTICE

Need for a uniform approach

To avoid disparities between national approaches to the incorporation of EC law and to ensure uniformity in its application, the ECJ has developed its own jurisprudence on the supremacy of EC law. In so doing, the Court has made extensive use of the preliminary reference procedure under Article 234, which enables the ECJ to issue rulings on the meaning and validity of Community law binding on all the Member States (see Chapter 10).

---

[1] The Agreement on Trade-Related Aspects of International Property Rights (TRIPS) is an international treaty set out as an Annex to the World Trade Organisation (WTO) Agreement.

The first statement of the Court on supremacy was made in Case 26/62 *Van Gend en Loos* decision. The principle was reiterated and developed in later cases, particularly Case 6/64 *Costa* v. *ENEL* and Case 11/70, decisions which are considered below.

A new legal order

The Court used the opportunity afforded by a request for a preliminary reference from a Dutch court in *Van Gend en Loos* to make an important pronouncement about the nature of Community law. The case arose out of a clash between Article 25 (ex 12) EC which prohibits the imposition of any new customs duty and a Dutch law imposing a new duty. The Court held that Article 25 was directly effective, enabling individuals to rely on it directly in the national courts. The significance of the case lies in the Court's words about the nature of Community law on the nature of the legal order.

> **Key point**
>
> 'The Community constitutes a new legal order in international law, for whose benefits the States have limited their sovereign rights, albeit within limited fields': *Van Gend en Loos*.

The legal order was new in terms of *international law* as it created the European Community, an entity was recognised in international law. It was new in terms of *national law* as the EC Treaty created rights and duties which can be enforced in the national courts. The ECJ developed its reasoning on the legal order in *Costa* v. *ENEL*.

> **Key case**
>
> Case 6/64 *Costa* v. *ENEL*: Mr Costa was a shareholder in the Italian electricity company which had been nationalised by a statute passed after the Italian Ratification Act incorporating EC law into Italian law. He refused to pay his electricity bill, claiming that the nationalising statute contravened various provisions of the EC Treaty. The Italian court referred the question of priority to the ECJ. The Court held that the reception of Community law into the legal system of the Member States made it impossible for the Member State to give priority to a unilateral, subsequent national measure over EC law. The Court further stated that:
>
> > The transfer, by Member States, from their national orders in favour of the Community order of the rights and obligations arising from the Treaty, carries with it a clear limitation of their sovereign right upon which a subsequent unilateral law, incompatible with the aims of the Community, cannot prevail.

EC law may not be invalidated by national law

The dispute in Case 11/70 *International Handelsgesellschaft* v. *EVGF* arose out of an apparent clash between a requirement under the CAP for an export licence and German fundamental rights. The applicant sought annulment of the regulation in the German court, claiming that the German constitution which enshrines fundamental rights took precedence over EC law. The EC rejected this claim, declaring that:

> Recourse to the legal rules or concepts of national law in order to judge the validity of measures adopted by the institutions . . . would have an adverse effect on the uniformity and efficacy of Community law. The validity of such measures can only be judged in the light of Community law.

Conflicting national legislation should not be applied

5

The supremacy of Community law

Key case

Case 106/77 *Simmenthal SpA (No. 2)* arose out of a conflict between an Italian statute passed after the Ratification Act and Article 28 (ex 30) EC on the free movement of goods. The Italian judge referred a question to the ECJ to find out whether he should wait for the Italian constitutional court to declare the measure void (as it had declared it would do if the Italian law conflicted with EC law) or give immediate priority to EC law. The ECJ replied that a national court in such circumstances must refrain from applying the conflicting national legislation even if adopted subsequently and should not wait for the decision of a higher court before action.

It should be noted that the ECJ reconsidered *Simmenthal* in Joined Case C-10–22/97 *Ministero della Finanze* v. *In. Co. Ge. '90*. In this case the ECJ held that it could *not* be inferred from *Simmenthal* that the incompatibility of a later national law with EC law rendered the national law (here, a tax law) non-existent. Any reclassification was a matter for the national court. The national court should disapply the national rule. In so doing, the principle of co-operation (or solidarity) under Article 10 of the Treaty does *not* require a national court to disapply its internal rules of procedure in order to review and set aside a decision which conflicts with EC law: Case C-234/04 *Kapferer* v. *Schlank & Schick*.

National statutes may be set aside

In Case C-213/89R *R.* v. *Secretary of State for Transport, ex parte Factortame (No. 2)*, the ECJ followed *Simmenthal* and allowed an action for interim relief even though it meant setting aside a national statute. The Court declared that:

> The full effectiveness of Community law would be . . . impaired if a rule of national law could prevent a court seised of a dispute governed by Community law from granting interim relief

in order to ensure the full effectiveness of the judgment to be given on the existence of those rights claimed under Community law. It follows that a court which in those circumstances would grant interim relief were it not for a rule of national law, is obliged to set aside that rule.

> **Key point**
>
> The problems posed by supremacy may, on occasion, be avoided by recourse to the principle of indirect effect in Case C-106/89 *Marleasing* (see Chapter 6). This principle requires national courts to interpret national legislation so as to comply with EC obligations whether the national law is passed before or after the relevant EC law.

State liability

The *Francovich* decision, as developed by later case law, sets out the circumstances in which a state may be liable to its citizens in damages for breach of EC law (see Chapter 6). The decision may be seen in part as an application of the supremacy of EC law over national law and reminds Member States of the financial implications of failing to fulfil their obligations under Community law. It also establishes that direct effect is not required for state liability.

Supremacy and the Second and Third Pillars

The case law on supremacy has been developed by the ECJ in relation to the First Pillar, EC law. It has been suggested[2] that the reasoning of the ECJ in *Costa* v. *ENEL* on supremacy should be applied to the Second and Third Pillars as well, even where the law in question is not directly effective. As Craig and De Burca point out[3], the ECJ has already considered indirect effect in the context of the Third Pillar in Case C-105/03 *Criminal Proceedings against Maria Pupino* (see Chapter 10 for the facts). The Court held in that case that Article 34(2)(b) of the TEU confers a binding character on framework decisions, as with directives under Article 249 EC. It follows that national courts must interpret national law, as far as possible, in the light of the wording and purpose of the framework decision. Such an approach is consistent with the commitment of the Member States to European Union. It would not be difficult to develop the reasoning further to include supremacy.

EC LAW IN THE UK

The European Communities Act 1972 (ECA) was enacted to give effect to UK obligations under the EEC Treaty and came into force on 1 January 1973. Later Treaties have been ratified in the UK by Acts amending the ECA.

[2] By Leanerts and Corthaut (2006), cited in Craig and De Burca (2007: 351–352).
[3] At p.352.

Direct applicability, direct effect and indirect effect

Section 2(1) ECA provides for the direct applicability and direct effect of EC law in the UK:

> All such rights, powers, liabilities, obligations and restrictions from time to time created or arising by or under the Treaties, as in accordance with the Treaties, are without further enactment to be given legal effect or used in the United Kingdom and shall be recognised and available in law, and be enforced, allowed and followed accordingly, and the expression 'enforceable Community right' and similar expressions shall be read as referring to one to which this subsection applies.

Section 2(2) ECA provides for the implementation of EC obligations which are not directly applicable by means of secondary legislation, subject to the provisos of Schedule 2.

Section 2(4) ECA deals with the relationship between EC law and national law without expressly providing for the supremacy of EC law over national law, stating:

> any enactment passed or to be passed . . . shall be construed and have effect subject to the foregoing provisions of this section.

Occasional challenges continue to occur, as the case of the 'Metric Martyrs' shows.

Key case

In *Thoburn* v. *Sunderland County Council* (2002) (the 'Metric Martyrs' case) the applicant challenged the requirement that produce that was not already packaged must be sold in metric rather than imperial measures. The High Court dismissed the application that the Weights and Measures Act 1985 should be regarded as having impliedly repealed the European Communities Act 1972 (ECA). The High Court dismissed the application, finding that the ECA has a 'constitutional quality' and so cannot be subject to implied repeal.

Approach of the House of Lords

The 'rule of construction approach' to s. 2(4) was adopted by the House of Lords in *Garland* v. *British Rail Engineering Ltd*, a case involving a clash between the Equal Pay Act 1970 and Article 119 (now 141), this time over the exemption of death and retirement from the equal pay provision under s. 6(4) of the Act. The House of Lords (HL) held that s. 6(4) must be construed so as to conform with Article 119. In *Pickstone* v. *Freemans plc* (1988), the HL went further, interpreting the regulations amending the Equal Pay Act 1970 *against* their literal meaning in order to comply with EC law. [4]

---

[4] See Steiner, Woods and Twigg-Flesner (2006), Chapter 4.

Key point

It is not open to a Member State to enact legislation deliberately in breach of Community law. To do so would be a clear infringement of state liability (see Chapter 6).

Lord Bridge, applying the *Factortame* ruling of the ECJ in the House of Lords, stated unequivocally that, under the terms of the ECA 1972, 'It has always been clear that it was the duty of a United Kingdom court, when delivering final judgment, to override any rule of national law found to be in conflict with any directly enforceable rule of Community law': R. v. *Secretary of State for Transport, ex parte Factortame* (No. 5) (1999).

Where the EC legislation in question is not directly effective the House of Lords has indicated in *Litster* v. *Forth Dry Dock Engineering Co. Ltd* (1989) that UK courts may give priority to EC law by interpreting the UK law 'purposively' to comply with the spirit and purpose of the relevant EC law.

After the decisions of the ECJ in *Francovich, Brasserie du Pêcheur* and Case C-224/01 *Köbler* v. *Austria* (that national courts may be liable for breaches of EC law where the conditions for state liability are satisfied: see Chapter 6), this duty clearly extends to *all* obligations of EC law where the conditions for state liability are satisfied.

The *Factortame* series of decisions

The dispute in Case C-213/89 R. v. *Secretary of State for Transport, ex parte Factortame*[5] arose out of the introduction by the UK government of the Merchant Shipping Act 1988. The statute introduced strict rules against fishing in UK waters by vessels not registered as British. Under the nationality and evidence requirements of the new rules many Spanish vessels previously registered as British failed to qualify for registration and were thus unable to share the UK catch quota. The Queen's Bench Divisional Court referred several questions to the ECJ to enable the UK Court to determine the compatibility of the new requirements with EC law. As a reference under Article 234 usually takes about two years and with major commercial interests at stake, the Divisional Court ordered the temporary suspension of the controversial provisions of the Merchant Shipping Act until the ruling was made.

The Court of Appeal quashed the order for the temporary suspension of the legislation. An appeal against the decision was made to the House of Lords which referred further questions to the ECJ, reformulated by the ECJ as an enquiry as to whether a national court may disregard a national rule which precludes it from granting interim relief. The ECJ ruled that a national law should be set aside where it prevents the granting of interim relief in a dispute governed by EC law: see above. This ruling has proved to be of great constitutional significance.

---

[5] For another case on similar facts, raising comparable issues, see Case C-3/87 R. v. *Ministry of Agriculture, Fisheries and Food, ex parte Agegate Ltd.*

> ### Key point
>
> As a result of the decision in Case C-213/89 *R. v. Secretary of State for Transport, ex parte Factortame*, national courts have jurisdiction temporarily to suspend any provisions of domestic law which may be in breach of EC law.

By the time the ruling was received the offending parts of the Merchant Shipping Act had already been suspended as a result of parallel proceedings brought by the Commission against the UK government: *Commission* v. *UK Re Merchant Shipping Rules* (Case 246/89R) (see Chapter 7). For the decision of the House of Lords applying the ruling of the ECJ: see *R. v. Secretary of State for Transport, ex parte Factortame* (1990): (see above). The ECJ ruled on the substantive issues (on the right of the establishment) under Article 43 (ex 52) EC in Case C-221/89 *R. v. Secretary of State for Transport ex parte Factortame*.

In Case 48/93 *R. v. Secretary of State for Transport, ex parte Factortame* the ECJ clarified the requirements for state liability, in particular that the breach must be 'sufficiently serious': see Chapter 6. The House of Lords (1999) held that the breach in question *was* sufficiently serious and that the UK government was liable in damages. In this case the breach was the deliberate adoption of legislation by the UK government which was clearly discriminatory under the EC Treaty.

Acceptance of the supremacy of EC law over national law is further demonstrated in *Stoke-on-Trent* v. *B&Q plc* (1990, Chancery Division of the High Court), one of the Sunday trading cases (see Chapter 12). Hoffman J declared that that the EC Treaty is, 'the supreme law of our country, taking precedence over Acts of Parliament. Our entry into the Community meant that Parliament had surrendered its sovereign rights to legislate contrary to the provisions of the Treaty on matters of social and economic policy which it regulated.'

EC LAW IN OTHER MEMBER STATES

Belgium

It is not entirely clear whether Belgium adopts a monist or dualist approach to international law. EC law is incorporated into Belgian law by statute. However, there is no provision in the constitution giving supremacy to international law. Thus the constitutional status of EC law in Belgium was uncertain until the decision of the Cour de Cassation in *Minister for Economic Affairs* v. *Fromagerie Franco-Suisse 'Le Ski'* (1972). The ECJ had ruled in Article 226 (ex 169) proceedings that import duties on dairy products contravened Article 25 (ex 12) of the EEC Treaty. The Belgian Parliament abolished the duties but passed a statute preventing the return of money already paid. The retention of the money was challenged in the Belgian courts. The Cour de Cassation ruled that the normal rule that a later statute repeals an earlier one did not apply to an international treaty, being a higher legal norm. It followed that in the event of a conflict between the EEC Treaty and domestic law, the Treaty must prevail.

France

There has been reluctance in the French courts to recognise the supremacy of EC law. For many years, the Cour de Cassation, the highest court of appeal, displayed a greater preparedness than the Conseil d'Etat, the supreme administrative court, to find legal solutions to the problems posed by EC law. Two cases illustrate these differing approaches:

1 *Directeur Général des Douanes* v. *Société Café Jacques Vabre* (1975, Cour de Cassation): Vabre, a coffee importer, had imported soluble coffee extract into France from the Netherlands. Under a French statute passed after membership of the EC, Vabre was required to pay customs duties, while coffee extract produced in France was taxed at a lower rate. Vabre claimed that the payment of these duties was contrary to that of Article 90 (ex 95) EC. The Cour de Cassation upheld his claim, holding that the EEC Treaty had created a separate legal order binding on the Member States. Further, any apparent lack of reciprocity in enforcement by the Netherlands was not a ground for refusing to apply EC law.

   This approach was followed a year later by the Cour de Cassation in *Von Kempis* v. *Geldof* (1976) which held that the EEC Treaty also takes precedence over earlier French legislation.

2 *Cohn-Bendit* (1975, Conseil d'Etat): Daniel Cohn-Bendit was a German citizen permanently resident in France where he was a student. As one of the leaders of the student uprising in 1968 he was deported following an order from the Minister of the Interior on the ground that he represented a threat to public policy (*ordre public*). In 1975 he sought to return to France to take up an offer of employment. The Minister, however, without giving any proper reason, refused to rescind the deportation order. Cohn-Bendit challenged this decision in the Tribunal Administratif which stayed the proceeding pending the result of a reference to the ECJ to determine the scope of the public policy proviso under Directive 64/221. The Minister appealed to the Conseil d'Etat against the order of reference. Before judgment was given, the Minister revoked the deportation order. Despite the revocation, the Conseil d'Etat delivered its judgment and allowed the appeal. HELD: Under the EEC Treaty directives may not be invoked by individuals to challenge administrative decisions. Thus as Cohn-Bendit could not invoke the directive, its interpretation was irrelevant.

While the Cour de Cassation acknowledged the full supremacy of EC law over French law, doubt remained after the *Cohn-Bendit* decision over the recognition of the direct effect of directives by the French administrative courts until the judgment (published on 20 October 1989) in a series of cases before the Conseil d'Etat: *Application of Georges Nicolo* (1989).

The cases concerned alleged irregularities in the elections to the EP. The Conseil d'Etat declared that it was prepared to accept the supremacy of the EEC Treaty over the law of 7 July 1977 on the election of representatives to the EP. See also: *Boisdet* (Conseil d'Etat, 1991) where acceptance of the supremacy of EC law was based on the case law of the ECJ.

Germany

Initially, membership of the EC posed constitutional problems for Germany, exemplified in the *International Handelsgesellschaft* decision (1974): see above and Chapter 4. A potential challenge to the supremacy of EC law was posed by the Constitutional Court's statement that until fundamental rights were adequately protected in EC law, EC measures would be subject to the provisions of the German constitution. No such measures were in fact found to contravene the German constitution and in 1986 the Constitutional Court ruled in *Wünsche Handelsgesellschaft* that provided the general protection of human rights in EC law remained adequate, it would hear no further test cases involving a comparison of EC law with the German constitution.

However, the supremacy of EC law is not universally recognised throughout the German courts. Apart from the Federal Constitutional Court, the final authority on constitutional matters, Germany has five separate systems of courts: the ordinary courts and specialised courts dealing with administrative matters, social security, labour and tax, each headed by a Federal Supreme Court.

The Federal Tax Court has refused on two occasions, in 1981 and 1986, to recognise the direct effect of directives. Both cases arose out of claims by taxpayers for a tax exemption provided under a VAT directive which had not been implemented in Germany. In the second of these cases, Case 70/83 *Kloppenburg* the Federal Tax Court contradicted a ruling of the ECJ in the same case that the directive was directly effective and refused the exemption. Kloppenburg appealed to the Constitutional Court which upheld the supremacy of EC law, annulling the decision of the Federal Tax Court as violating the German constitution which provides that no one shall be deprived of his 'lawful judge' (in this case, the ECJ). The Tax Court should either have followed the ECJ ruling or made a second reference.

Further constitutional turmoil was experienced in Germany over the ratification of the Maastricht Treaty. In 1993, in *Brunner* v. *European Union Treaty* the Constitutional Court accepted that the ECJ holds primary responsibility for protecting fundamental rights, but indicated that it reserved the right to review the legal measures of the EC institutions if they appear to be outside the Treaty.

Germany has also sought to challenge EC law in the long-running saga of the EC banana regime. In 1998, in Case C-122/95 *Germany* v. *Council*, the ECJ annulled part of a Council decision concluding the framework agreement on bananas within the World Trade Organisation agreement for breach of the principle of non-discrimination.

Italy

The leading case on the constitutional position of EC law in Italy in recent years is *Frontini* (1974). In this case a cheese importer claimed that a levy imposed by an EC regulation contravened Article 23 of the Italian constitution which states that taxes may only be imposed by statute. Since Article 241 of the EEC Treaty provides for the direct applicability of regulations, he argued that the EEC Treaty was incompatible with the Italian constitution, with the result that the Italian incorporation statute was unconstitutional. The Italian Constitutional Court ruled that EC law is separate from international law and from Italian law, and that the Italian constitution does not apply to legislation enacted by the EC institutions. Thus, Article 23 of the Italian constitution does not apply to EC measures. In subsequent decisions such as *Spa Beca* v. *Ammistrazione della Finanze* (1982) the Italian courts have shown clear support for the supremacy of EC law.

Poland

The position of the Polish courts resembles that adopted by the German courts in the early years of membership of the Community, when the German Constitutional Court considered the protection of fundamental rights in the EC to be lower than under German law (see above).[6] Poland's membership of the EU under the Accession Treaty was challenged before the Polish Constitutional Tribunal (2005) in Case K 18/04. Although the Constitutional Tribunal found that the Accession Treaty conforms to the Polish Constitution, it held that, in the event of 'irreconcilable inconsistency' between the Constitution and the EC Treaty, the 'autonomous decision' to resolve the inconsistency 'belongs to the Polish constitutional legislator'. The Tribunal did not accept that the Communities and EU are 'supranational organisations', a category not recognised under the Polish Constitution which refers to 'international organisations'. Emphasising the 'relative autonomy' of both EC law and national law, the Tribunal identified areas in which an inconsistency might arise between the two systems. Were this to happen, the Tribunal stated that the principle of interpreting national law in a way which is 'sympathetic to European law' has limits, and may *not* lead to a result which would conflict with a 'minimum guaranteed function' under the Constitution. Further, it found, the Member States retain the right to assess whether or not EC institutions acted within their delegated competences in issuing particular legal decisions and in accordance with subsidiarity and proportionality.

The Tribunal went further in the *European Arrest Warrants* Case (2005) No. P 1/05. It held that the domestic law implementing a Framework Decision creating the European Arrest Warrant (EAW) was incompatible with the Polish Constitution which prohibited the extradition of a Polish citizen. Given that the time limit for implementation had passed, the Tribunal deferred cancellation of the implementing legislation to allow enough time to amend the Constitution. It is clear that the Polish courts do not accept the supremacy of EU law over the Polish Constitution. However, the

[6] See Sadurski (2006) cited in Craig and De Burca (2007: 373–374).

Constitutional Tribunal has shown some flexibility in deferring the cancellation of domestic law implementing the EAW.

ACADEMIC COMMENTARY ON SUPREMACY

Academic commentators have fallen into two main schools of thought on the supremacy of Community law. On the one hand there are the pluralists such as MacCormick who acknowledge that not all legal problems have a legal solution.[7] In his view (1995), both the ECJ and the national courts should not interpret Community law without regard for the political consequences of the judgment. National courts likewise should not reach decisions without reference to their position in the Union. MacCormick later modified his position (1999),[8] advocating the referral of a conflict between national courts and the ECJ to international arbitration or adjudication.

Other commentators such as Kumm (2005)[9] adopt a different approach, emphasising the underlying commitment to constitutionalism of both EU law and the laws of the Member States. This commitment, he argues, is based on four central elements: commitment to the rule of law, protection of fundamental rights, federalism and a commitment to the specific nature of the national community. Kumm's perspective may be a useful approach to the resolution of disputes between the national courts and the ECJ. However, it fails to take account of the broader questions that surround such disputes, particularly where long-established traditional practices are overtaken by EU requirements.[10]

QUESTIONS

1 **What would be the legal position if a Member States adopted legislation which contravened EC law? Would it make any difference whether the national law was adopted before or after the relevant EC law?**

2 **To what extent have the UK courts accepted the supremacy of EC law over national law? What is the constitutional significance of the *Factortame* series of cases?**

3 **How have different academic commentators sought to explain the relationship between EC law and national law? Do you consider that any of these theories offers an explanation for conflicts between EC law and national law?**

---

[7] MacCormick (1995) cited in Chalmers *et al.* (2006: 206–207).
[8] MacCormick (1999) cited in Craig and De Burca (2007: 376).
[9] Kumm (2005) cited in Chalmers *et al.* (2006: 208–209).
[10] See Chalmers *et al.* (2006: 208–209).

Further reading

Chalmers, D., Hadjiemmanuil, C., Monti, G. and Tomkins, A. (2006) *European Union Law*, Cambridge University Press, Chapter 5.

Craig, P. and De Burca, G. (2007) *EU Law: Text, Cases and Materials*, 4th edition, Oxford University Press, Chapter 10.

Hadzopoulos, V. (2008) 'With or without you . . . judging politically in the field of Area of Freedom, Security and Justice', (2008) 33 ELRev. 44.

Kumm, M. (2005) 'The Jurisprudence of Constitutional Conflict: Constitutional Supremacy in Europe before and after the Constitutional Treaty', (2005) ELJ 262, 299–300.

Laenaerts, K. and Corthaut, T. (2006) 'Of Birds and Hedges: The Role of Primacy in invoking Norms of EU Law', (2006) 31 ELRev. 287, cited in Craig and De Burca (2007: 351–352).

MacCormick, N. (1995) 'The Maastricht *Urteil*: Sovereignty Now', (1995) 1 ELJ 259, 264–265, cited in Chalmers *et al.* (2006: 206–207).

MacCormick, N. (1999) *Questioning Sovereignty*, Oxford University Press, cited in Craig and De Burca (2007: 376).

Sadurski, W., ' "Solange Chapter 3": Constitutional Courts in Central Europe – Democracy – European Union', EUI Working Papers, Law No. 2006/40, 6–10, cited in Craig and De Burca (2007: 373–374).

Steiner, J., Woods, L. and Twigg-Flesner, C. (2006) *EU Law*, 9th edition, Oxford, Chapter 4.

Walker, N. (2002) 'The Idea of Constitutional Pluralism', (2002) 65 MLR 317.

Visit **http://www.mylawchamber.co.uk/kent** to access answer guidance to questions in the book to test yourself on this chapter.

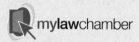

Use **Case Navigator** to read in full some of the key cases referenced in this chapter:

- 6/64 **Costa** *v.* **ENEL** [1964] ECR 585
- 11/70 **International Handelsgesellschaft** *v.* **EVGF** [1970] ECR 1125
- 48/93 **R** *v.* **Secretary of State for Transport, ex parte Factortame (Factortame III)** [1996] ECR I-1029
- 26/62 **Van Gend en Loos**

6

The principles of direct effect, indirect effect and state liability

INTRODUCTION

As we have seen in Chapter 5, the Court of Justice established the principles of the supremacy of EC law and direct effect in order to give effect to the objectives of the Community. The Court has maintained its active role as the legal order developed, elaborating the principles of indirect effect (the duty of 'consistent interpretation') and state liability to complete the protection of individual rights under EC law in the national courts. This chapter examines the principles of direct effect, indirect effect and state liability. It is essential to appreciate the inter-relationship of these concepts which underpin Community law today.

DIRECT APPLICABILITY AND DIRECT EFFECT

Key terms

The terms are not defined in the EC Treaty and are often used interchangeably. However, it may be helpful to distinguish them as follows:[1]

- **Directly applicable** means those provisions of EC law which take effect in the legal systems of the Member States without the need for further enactment.
- **Directly effective** means those provisions of EC law which give rise to rights or obligations on which individuals may rely before their national courts.

The EC Treaty provides in Article 249 (ex 189) that regulations are 'directly applicable'. Although Article 249 does not make provision for the direct applicability of other provisions of secondary legislation, the ECJ has ruled that not only regulations but also Treaty articles, directives and certain provisions of international Treaties create direct effect: see below.

---

[1] See Winter (1983).

The principle of direct effect is incorporated into UK law by s. 2(1) of the European Communities Act 1972 (see Chapter 5).

Treaty articles

The first ruling of the ECJ on the direct effect of Treaty provisions was the seminal case of *Van Gend en Loos*, in which the Court introduced the concepts of the 'new legal order' and of direct effect (see Chapter 5).

Key case

Case 26/62 *Van Gend en Loos* v. *Nederlands Administratie de Belastige*: A firm of importers in the Netherlands was required to pay a customs duty on the importation of ureaformaldehyde, an essential component in making glue, under a law adopted by the Dutch government after joining the EC. The firm challenged the law in the Dutch courts on the basis that it infringed Article 25 (ex 12), which prohibits Member States from introducing new customs duties between themselves. The Dutch court referred questions for interpretation to the ECJ under Article 234. The ECJ held that Article 25 was directly effective, creating rights which the national courts must respect.

Key point

The Court in *Van Gend en Loos* stated the requirements for direct effect. These requirements have been modified by later decisions and can now be stated as follows:

- the provision must be clear and unambiguous;
- it must be unconditional;
- it must take effect without further action by the EC or Member States.

The ECJ has found most of the Treaty provisions at the heart of the Community legal order to be directly effective, enabling individuals to enforce them before the national courts. Directly effective provisions include those on citizenship (Article 18), the free movement of persons (Article 39), services (Article 43), establishment (Article 49) and goods (Articles 28–30), equal pay (Article 141) and competition (Articles 81 and 82). As we shall see in the later chapters of this book, these rights are expounded in straightforward, direct and often brief terms. In contrast, Articles 1–4 EC expounding aims and purposes for the EC have been held to be incapable of conferring individual rights: Case 155/73 *Sacchi*.

Vertical and horizontal direct effect

Where a Treaty obligation falls on a Member State itself, the provision may create *vertical direct effect*, reflecting the relationship between the individual and the state.

Such a provision may, therefore, only be enforced against the state and not horizontally against individuals. The definition of 'the state' includes public bodies, such as the Dutch customs authority in *Van Gend en Loos*. The expression 'public body' (also known as 'organ' or 'emanation' of the state') has been clarified by the ECJ in Case C-188/89 *Foster* v. *British Gas*: see below.

Horizontal direct effect arises where an obligation falls on individuals, reflecting the relationship between individuals.

Key point

While the scope of horizontal direct effect remains controversial, it is clear from *Defrenne (No.2)* that Treaty provisions are horizontally effective. This means that individuals can rely on them to bring and defend actions against other individuals in the national courts.

Key case

Gabrielle Defrenne, an air hostess, invoked Article 119 (now Article 141) in an equal pay claim before the Belgian Courts against her employers, Sabena, a private airline. She was paid less than a male steward and required to retire earlier. While Article 119 was intended to be implemented by the end of the transitional period (December 1961), the deadline was moved to the end of 1964, when it remained unmet by several Member States including Belgium. The Court held that Article 119 was directly effective. It was not limited to public authorities but also covered the relationship between individuals. Resolutions purporting to alter the implementation timetable were ineffective: Case 43/75 *Defrenne* v. *Sabena (No. 2)*.

Regulations

Article 249 (ex 189) states that a regulation is of 'general application . . . binding in its entirety and directly applicable in all Member States'. As a result, a regulation takes effect without further enactment (i.e. without the need to pass another law to implement it at national level) and may be invoked either vertically or horizontally before the national courts if the requirements for direct effect are met.

A regulation will not be regarded as directly effective if it is formulated too vaguely, leaving important features to be devised and implemented by the Member States. The general rule is that implementation measures should not be required except where 'necessary': see Case 230/78 *Eridiana*. Here the ECJ held that the directly applicable nature of regulations does not prevent them from containing provisions for implementation by the Member States.

Directives and decisions

Article 249 states that a directive is 'binding, as to the result to be achieved, upon each Member State to which it is addressed, but shall leave to the national authorities the choice of form and methods'. A decision is binding 'in its entirety upon those to whom it is addressed'. Unlike regulations, neither directives nor decisions are described in the Treaty as 'directly applicable' under Article 249.

The ECJ held in *Grad* that where the criteria for direct effects are satisfied decisions and (by implication) directives may be directly effective. Doubt remains, however, as to whether a decision can create horizontal effects when addressed to a Member State.

Key case

A German company challenged a tax imposed by the German government which the company argued contravened an EC directive requiring Member States to amend their VAT systems and a decision which set a time limit for implementation of the Directive. The ECJ ruled that it would be incompatible with the binding nature of decisions (and, by implication, directives) to exclude the possibility of direct effect. Although the Directive required implementation, once the time limit for implementation had expired, the Directive could be directly effective: Case 9/70 *Grad* v. *Finanzamt Traustein*.

Where a *time limit* has not expired a directive is not directly effective. In Case 148/78 *Pubblico Ministero* v. *Ratti*, R, an Italian solvent manufacturer, sought to defend himself against charges brought under Italian legislation on the labelling of dangerous products. He claimed that the products were labelled in accordance with two directives which had not been implemented by the Italian government. The time limit for implementation had expired in relation to one of the two directives. The ECJ held that only the directive in which the deadline had expired could be directly effective.

Key point

A directive may only be enforced directly before the national courts after the deadline for implementation has expired.

Where implementation is not required a directive may take effect at once provided the criteria for direct effect are met: Case 41/74 *Van Duyn* v. *Home Office*. Here the ECJ held that Article 3 of Directive 64/221, the public policy proviso, was directly effective. The Court's reasoning was based on the consideration that to deny direct effect to directives would weaken their useful effect (*l'effet utile*) and because it would be incompatible with the binding effect of directives under Article 249. After implementation a directive may be invoked to allow individuals access to the courts to determine whether the implementing authorities have acted within their powers: Case 51/76 *Verbond van Nederlands Ondernemingen.*

Key point

Limitation periods under national law do not begin to run until full implementation of the relevant directive: Case C-208/90 *Emmott* v. *Minister for Social Welfare.*

In Case C-338/91 *Steenhorst-Neerings* the ruling in *Emmott* was justified on the facts, as the time bar had deprived the applicant of the opportunity to rely on the Directive. The ECJ held in Case C-410/92 *Johnson* v. *CAO* that a national rule limiting the period in which arrears of benefit may be claimed under Directive 79/7 was compatible with EC law although the Directive had not been properly implemented within the transposition period.

How far is it possible to rely on a directive?

For many years the ECJ avoided ruling on whether a directive may create horizontal direct effect. The Court found an alternative approach in *Von Colson*, based on the principle of indirect interpretation (see below). The question of the direct effect of directives came to a head in Case 152/84 *Marshall* v. *Southampton and South West Area Health Authority* (*Teaching*) (*No. 1*), and this time the Court did not evade the issue.

Key case

Ms Marshall challenged the different retirement ages, 65 years for men and 60 for women, permissible under the Sex Discrimination Act 1975 but forbidden under Article 5 of the Equal Treatment Directive 76/207. The ECJ, in an Article 234 reference from the Court of Appeal, ruled that a directive may produce vertical but not horizontal direct effects.

The ruling has created anomalies. Ms Marshall succeeded in her claim under the Directive because she was employed by an area health authority which was deemed to be a public body. Had she been employed in the private sector (that is by an employer who was not a 'public body') her claim based on the Directive would have failed.

Key point

An action for equal pay based on Article 141 provides a stronger basis in the national courts than a claim based on a directive, such as for equal treatment under Directive 76/207, since a right deriving from the Treaty may be enforced horizontally against either the State or a private body, whereas a directive may only be enforced vertically.

In Case C-271/91 *Marshall (No. 2)* the Court held that the amount of damages available under a directly effective right in EC law may not be limited under a national statute. In the UK this led to the removal of upper limits to claims in employment tribunals based on EC law.

Public bodies

The harshness of the decision in Marshall was to some degree tempered by the Court's adoption of a broad approach to what constitutes a 'public body'. Aware of the imminent programme to privatise public utilities in the UK, the ECJ took the opportunity to provide guidance on the meaning of 'public body' in *Foster* v. *British Gas*. This case arose out of a claim for equal treatment under Article 5 of Directive 76/207 brought while British Gas was still in public ownership. *Foster* has been criticised by some commentators as providing only limited assistance with what constitutes a public body.

Key point

'A body made responsible for providing a public service under state control and which possessed special powers exceeding those normally applicable in relations between individuals' will be regarded as a public body: Case C-188/89 *Foster* v. *British Gas.*

It is clear that most of the privatised utilities in the UK such as British Telecom and the providers of water, gas and electricity are within the ruling in *Foster*. (See, for example, *Griffin* v. *South West Water* (1995) where the High Court held that a privatised water company was covered.) The Court of Appeal, however, found that Rolls-Royce was not a public body as it did not possess the necessary special powers and responsibilities, despite being wholly owned by the Crown at the time: *Rolls-Royce plc* v. *Doughty* (1992). The Court of Appeal was asked to rule once more on what constitutes a public body in *NUT* v. *St Mary's Church of England Junior School* (1997). It held that the governors were a public body 'charged by the state with running the school'. Other bodies held to be public bodies include: the Royal Ulster Constabulary: Case 222/84 *Johnston* v. *RUC*; local or regional authorities: Case C-221/88 *ECSC* v. *Acciaiera e ferrier Busseni*; and tax authorities: Case 8/81 *Becker.*

International treaties

No general rule may be formulated about the possible direct effect of international treaties. In Case 104/81 *Kupferberg*, in a case before Portuguese accession, the ECJ found that Article 1 of the Free Trade Agreement between Portugal and the EC was directly effective. In Case 87/75A *Bresciani* Article 2(1) of the Yaoundé Convention between the EC and developing countries was also found to be directly effective. Similar decisions were reached in relation to parts of several association agreements: see, for example, the agreement between the EC and Portugal: Case C-18/90 *ONEM v. Kziber*.

Although international agreements are judged by the same criteria as Treaty provisions they may be more strictly interpreted: see, for example, Opinion 1/91 on the Draft *EEA Agreement* in which the ECJ stated that the Agreement was intended only to create rights and obligations between the contracting parties (States) and provided no transfer of sovereign rights. In an earlier case, Cases 21–24/72 *International Fruit*, the ECJ had found Article XI of the GATT not to be directly effective.

General principles of law

The general principles of EC law do not usually bind the Member States. They may be regarded as directly effective only in very limited circumstances, for example:

- in an action brought by an individual to challenge the use of a derogation such as the public policy proviso under Article 39 EC or Article 30 EC on the basis that it contravenes a general principle of EC law;
- where a party to proceedings claims that an EC measure is invalid because it contravenes a general principle of EC law. Determination of such an issue would require a reference to the ECJ.

INDIRECT EFFECT

We have already seen in this chapter that only those provisions of Community law which satisfy the requirements laid down by the ECJ will be regarded as directly effective. The Court relied on the principle of solidarity under Article 10 (ex 5) of the Treaty to develop the principle of indirect effect in order to deal with provisions which were not directly effective.

Key point

Under Article 10 EC, Member States are required to 'take all appropriate measures, whether general or particular, to ensure fulfilment of the obligations arising out of this Treaty . . .'.

The duty of consistent interpretation

The ECJ established the principle that national legislation should be interpreted in light of the wording and purpose of the directive which it implements in *Von Colson*. This decision was taken before the Court's ruling in *Marshall* that directives may only be enforced vertically and not horizontally, and represents an alternative way to ensure that Community law may be enforced in the national courts.

> **Key case**
>
> Ms Von Colson had applied for a job with the prison service in a men's prison. She was not appointed and brought a claim for damages in the German courts. The national court found that the rejection was based on sex but was justifiable and awarded damages limited to travelling expenses. The applicant claimed that this award contravened Article 6 of the Equal Treatment Directive 76/207 (requiring Member States to introduce the necessary remedies to enable equal treatment claims to be pursued through the judicial process). The ECJ found that Article 6 was not directly effective as it did not prescribe a specific sanction. Relying on Article 10, the Court held that the obligation to observe Community law applies to all authorities, including the courts in the Member States. National courts are also bound under Article 249 to achieve the result stated in the Directive. It followed that the national courts must apply national law so as to ensure an effective remedy under Article 6. As a result, Member States are obliged to interpret national law so as to give effect to the obligations under the Directive: Case 14/83 *Von Colson* v. *Land Nordrhein-Westfalen*.

Von Colson upheld

The duty of consistent interpretation has been maintained since the *Von Colson* decision in cases such as *Marleasing* and *Faccini Dori*, both of which also show the determination of the ECJ not to extend horizontal direct effects to directives.

> **Key case**
>
> Marleasing SA, a Spanish company, brought an action before the Spanish courts to annul the memorandum and articles of association of the defendant company, La Comercial. The applicant claimed that the La Comercial had been established in order to put its assets beyond the reach of creditors including Marleasing, and that the company was null and void as it infringed various provisions of the Spanish Civil Code due to 'lack of cause'. The defence of La Comercial was based on the fact that lack of cause was not specified in Directive 68/151 which lists exhaustively the grounds for the invalidity of a company. The Court held that a national court must interpret national law as far as it is possible to do so in the light of the wording and purpose of the Directive, and this applies whether the

law was adopted before or after the directive. This obligation derives from the need to achieve the result required by the Directive according to Article 249 (ex 189) of the Treaty: *Marleasing SA* v. *La Comercial Internacional de Alimentacion* (Case C-106/89).

It followed from the decision of the ECJ in *Marleasing* that the Spanish court was obliged to interpret the Civil Code so as to rule out a declaration of nullity on grounds other than those listed in the directive.

The Court followed the same approach in Case C-91/92 *Faccini Dori* v. *Recreb Srl*. Ms F.D. had entered into a contract for a language correspondence without prior arrangement at Milan Station. She changed her mind four days later and sought to cancel the contract within the seven-day cooling off period provided by Directive 85/577, a consumer protection measure applying to contracts concluded away from business premises which had not been implemented by Italy. The ECJ held that although the relevant parts of the Directive were sufficiently clear, precise and unconditional they could not create horizontally enforceable rights. The ECJ then repeated its formulation in *Marleasing* on the duty of interpretation.

This duty may pose problems for national courts obliged to interpret a national statute which long predates a directive. Lord Slynn, a former Advocate-General and judge in the ECJ, expressed the view that it would be straining the English language too far to interpret a nineteenth-century statute in the light of a 1991 Directive. In his view, any conflict should be resolved by Parliament.[2]

It should be noted that the ECJ has imposed limits on the duty of consistent interpretation. In Case 80/86 *Kolpinghuis Nijmegen* it held that a directive cannot have indirect effect in criminal proceedings when it would cause the accused to be convicted where he would otherwise have been acquitted. Nor can a directive indirectly aggravate guilt. In Case C-168/95 *Arcaro* the ECJ held that the obligation to interpret national law in line with a directive reaches a limit where the obligation has not been transposed. In this case Italian law had failed to implement directives requiring prior notification of *all* discharges of cadmium (a highly poisonous substance), rather than merely new discharges. Without the directive, criminal liability could not be imposed without implementation of the directive.

Incidental horizontal effect

While the Court's position that directives do not create horizontal direct effects has been maintained in decisions such as *Marleasing* and *Webb* v. *EMO*, some commentators[3] have seen later decisions of the ECJ as supporting the possibility that directives may incidentally create horizontal effects for third parties.

---

[2] Slynn (1999: 124).
[3] For differing explanations of the status of directives, see Tridimas (2001) and Dougan (2000).

Key case

CIA Security brought an action in the Belgian courts against Signalson and Securitel to compel them to cease their unfair trading practices. CIA argued that it had been libelled by the two companies when they claimed that the alarm system marketed by CIA had not been approved under Belgian law. While acknowledging that it had not sought approval, CIA claimed that the Belgian regulation contravened Article 28EC and had not been notified to the Commission as required by Directive 83/189. The Court held that the Directive was intended to protect the free movement of goods from preventive control. As the regulation had not been notified it would enhance the effectiveness of the control if the provision of national law was not applied to individuals. (The Court's decision would have provided the applicant with an incidental benefit, effectively enabling it to rely on the Directive in the national courts in the action for unfair trading practices): Case C-194/94 *CIA Security International SA* v. *Signalson SA and Securitel SPRIL*.

The ECJ followed CIA Security with a similar ruling in Case C-443/98 *Unilever Italia SpA* v. *Central Food SpA*. Here the Court was asked to consider the status of technical regulations which had been notified to the Commission but which infringed Directive 83/189. The parties had a contract to deliver olive oil. The plaintiff delivered oil which complied with the Directive in terms of labelling but not with the Italian regulations. While acknowledging that directives cannot create horizontal effects, the Court found that case law such as *Faccini Dori* does not apply where a technical regulation is rendered inapplicable by non-compliance. A national court, the Court ruled, must refuse to apply a technical regulation adopted contrary to the Directive. The Directive creates neither rights nor duties for individuals.

UK decisions on indirect effect

In *Duke* v. *Reliance Systems Ltd* (HL, 1987) the plaintiff sought damages under the Sex Discrimination Act 1975 which had been amended to comply with the Equal Treatment Directive 76/207. As the amendment was retrospective the House of Lords refused to allow a claim arising out of the period before amendment on the basis that the language of the statute was clear. The *Von Colson* approach was rejected as the basis for interpretation of a UK statute.

However, in *Litster* v. *Forth Dry Dock Engineering* (HL, 1989) the House of Lords interpreted a UK regulation implementing Directive 77/187 (which safeguards employees' rights if the undertaking is transferred) so as to comply with the Directive. Thus, it follows that where the national legislation is enacted to give effect to EC obligations the national courts should adopt a 'purposive' approach to statutory interpretation: that is, they should, wherever possible, construe the English law so as to comply with EC law, even if this involves departing from a strict, literal approach.

STATE LIABILITY

The landmark decision in Cases C-6, 9/90 *Francovich and Bonfaci* v. *Italy* mitigated to some extent the lack of horizontal effect of directives. In reaching its decision the Court was conscious of the need to fill the gaps in legal protection left by direct and indirect effect.

Key case

The case arose out of Italy's failure to implement Directive 80/987 on the protection of workers on the insolvency of their employer. Francovich and Bonfaci had brought claims in the Italian courts against their employers, a company later declared to be insolvent. The ECJ found that the Directive was insufficiently precise in identifying the institution which was to guarantee compensation to beneficiaries, and so it could not be regarded as directly effective. However, it held that the principle of effectiveness (or solidarity) under Article 10 EC requires Member States to compensate individuals for a breach of EC law where the fault is attributable to the Member State, where three conditions are satisfied:

1 The directive must confer rights for the benefit of individuals.
2 The content of the rights must be identifiable from the directive.
3 There is a causal link between the damage suffered and the breach.

Cases C-6 and 9/90 *Francovich and Bonfaci* v. *Italy.*

The scope of the decision in *Francovich* is potentially very wide. It removes any incentive for a Member State not to implement a directive on time and it provides a remedy, when conditions for state liability are satisfied, for individuals to claim against the State under directives which are not directly effective. *Francovich* has been upheld in decisions including Case C-91/92 *Faccini Dori*, Case C-334/92 *Wagner Miret*, Case C-192/94 *El Corte Inglés SA* v. *Rivero* and in Case C-168/95 *Arcaro.*

It is the responsibility of Member States to determine the procedures and of courts to enable individuals to pursue claims against the state. These must not make a remedy impossible and should be no less favourable than procedures for similar claims under national law.

Clarification of conditions for State liability

While *Francovich* established the principle of state liability it left many points unanswered, including the question of whether state liability was restricted to non-implementation of a directive or whether it could be applied more widely to a breach of EC law. The opportunity to clarify the position was provided by a request for a preliminary ruling in relation to two long-running breaches of EC law which raised similar issues. The ECJ ruled on the two referrals together in *Brasserie du Pêcheur* and *Factortame III*.

Key case

Joined Cases C-46/93 and 48/93 *Brasserie du Pêcheur* v. *Federal Republic of Germany* and *R.* v. *Secretary of State for Transport, ex parte Factortame (Factortame III)*.

Brasserie du Pêcheur had its origins in the German 'beer purity laws', the effect of which was to exclude beer containing additives produced in other Member States. The dispute had already given rise to a finding against Germany in enforcement proceedings brought by the Commission. Beer importers in Germany sought damages against the German government.

Factortame arose out of the exclusion from the UK catch quota of Spanish nationals as a result of UK legislation designed to make it difficult for them to register their fishing vessels in the UK. This dispute, too, had led to successful enforcement proceedings against the Member State by the Commission. The Spanish trawler owners sought exemplary damages from the UK government for their lost profits.

Breach must be sufficiently serious

The ECJ held that the principles which should apply to the establishment of liability by Member States should be the same as those governing the liability of the EC institutions in decisions such as Cases 83/76, etc. *Bayerische HNL* v. *Council and Commission* (*see* Chapter 9). This meant that the breach should be *sufficiently serious* if it is to lead to liability. (Other expressions used in this context include 'manifest and grave'.) Liability is not restricted to failure to implement a directive, but covers responsibility of the national legislature for acts and omissions contrary to EC law.

Key point

It follows from *Brasserie du Pêcheur/Factortame III* that there are now three conditions to satisfy, to establish that a breach of EC law gives rise to state liability, namely:

1 the rule of law breached must be intended to confer rights on individuals;
2 the breach must be sufficiently serious;
3 there must be a direct causal link between the breach and the damage suffered by the injured party.

Other aspects of the ruling

Brasserie du Pêcheur/Factortame also established that reparation may not be made conditional on fault which is greater than a 'sufficiently serious breach' of EC law. Reparation must be commensurate with the loss or damage suffered, and should be determined by national law in the absence of EC law. Specific (e.g. exemplary) damages may be awarded if this is available in similar claims in national law. This means that actions for state liability should be brought in the national courts under national law, and not in the ECJ (although most cases so far have led to preliminary rulings by the ECJ). The obligation of Member States to compensate for breaches of EC law cannot be limited to damages sustained after the delivery of a judgment by the ECJ finding the infringement in question.

Clarifying 'sufficiently serious breach'

In Case C-5/94 *R. v. Minister of Fisheries and Food, ex parte Hedley Lomas* the ECJ upheld the three conditions for liability set out in *Brasserie du Pêcheur* and ruled that the mere infringement of EC law may constitute a sufficiently serious breach where the Member State is in no position to make legislative choices and has little or no discretion. In this case the Ministry of Agriculture, Fisheries and Food (MAFF) had refused to grant licences to export live animals to Spain owing to UK concern over conditions in slaughter houses there. The Commission did not accept that the UK view was justified, in the light of its own inspection which led to a finding that pre-slaughter conditions complied with EC standards set out in a directive.

> **Key point**
>
> The ECJ held in *Hedley Lomas* that the decisive test for a sufficiently serious breach is whether the Member State has manifestly and gravely disregarded the limits of its discretion.

The Court provided guidelines in *Hedley Lomas* for national courts which should consider whether:

(a) the EC rule breached is clear and concise;
(b) Member States have any discretion;
(c) the breach or damage was intentional;
(d) the mistake was excusable;
(e) the EC institutions may have contributed to the breach;
(f) any national measures contrary to EC law have been retained.

Breach where Member States have exercised discretion

It does not follow that each time a Member State has infringed EC law the breach will be serious enough to result in state liability. On occasion Member States do their best to implement EC law, with little help from the EC institutions, in areas where there is considerable national discretion, only to find that their implementation measures fall short of what is required. An example may be found in the case of Case C-392/93R. v. *HM Treasury, ex parte British Telecommunications plc*. Here, the UK had sought to implement an ambiguously worded directive on procurement in telecommunications. BT claimed that the company had failed to win an order as a result of the approach to implementation taken by the UK. The ECJ ruled that, while the UK had not implemented the breach correctly, the breach was not sufficiently serious. Following the guidelines in *Hedley Lomas* the ECJ found that the UK's interpretation had been made in good faith, was in keeping with the aims and wording of the Directive, and that no guidance had been made available to the UK government from the Commission or from previous decisions of the ECJ.

Similar reasoning was adopted by the ECJ in Case C-283, 291 and 292/94 *Denkavit International* v. *Bundesamt für Finanzen* where the German government had incorrectly transposed a directive on taxation. The ECJ was influenced by the fact that most other Member States had adopted the same approach as Germany; there was no case law on the subject. As a result, the breach was not sufficiently serious.

Failure to implement a directive on time or correctly

In Cases 178, etc./94 *Dillenkofer* v. *Federal Republic of Germany*, Germany had failed to implement the package holidays Directive by the deadline specified. The ECJ held that failure to implement a directive on time amounted to a sufficiently serious breach. In Case C-140/97 *Rechberger* v. *Austria*, another case involving the package holidays Directive, the ECJ found that incorrect transposition of a directive into national law may be sufficiently serious where the Member State has no discretion as to how to implement it.

Liability of national courts

In Case C-224/01 *Köbler* v. *Austria*, an Austrian professor claimed recognition of time spent working in another Member State towards a long-service increment. The question for the ECJ was whether the Austrian court had 'manifestly infringed' EC law by failing to make a second referral which would effectively have determined the compatibility of the national provision with Article 39 EC. The Austrian court had originally referred the matter to the ECJ but had withdrawn it on the advice of the ECJ Registrar who assumed that the question had been resolved by another ECJ ruling that such an increment conflicted with Article 39. The Austrian court then reclassified the increment as a 'loyalty bonus', resulting in the loss of the payment to the applicant who sued the Austrian government. The ECJ considered that it had enough information to rule on the facts, and held that the breach was not sufficiently manifest to result in state liability.

Key point

The main significance of the decision in *Köbler* lies in the Court's ruling that national courts of last resort may infringe rights which give rise to state liability where the court has manifestly infringed the law.

Köbler was followed in Case C-173/03 *Traghetti del Mediterraneo*, a case arising out of the attempt by the Italian government to restrict the state liability of courts of last resort. The Court held that under no circumstances may a national law impose criteria for state liability in relation to courts of last resort which are stricter than that of a 'manifest infringement of the applicable law', as set out in *Köbler*.

Approach of the national courts to cases of State liability

It has proved difficult in practice to succeed in an action in the national courts to establish state liability, despite the growing case law of the ECJ on the subject. Most of the cases turn on whether the breach was sufficiently serious. However, in *Three Rivers District Council* v. *Governor and Company of the Bank of England* (1996) the High Court held that the First Banking Directive did not intend to confer rights on individuals, which would otherwise have imposed a duty on the Bank of England to protect the depositors in Bank of Credit and Commence International (BCCI). No action for state liability, therefore, arose.

In *Francovich* itself the Italian courts found (1992) that the applicant was outside the group on whom the Directive conferred rights, and so was unable to claim.

The German Bundesgerichtshof (Federal Supreme Court) in *Brasserie du Pêcheur* v. *Germany* (1997) found that the breach was insufficiently serious to make an award of damages. It considered that the act causing loss to the applicants was denying them the right to sell beer containing additives, and that there was no causal connection between this act and their loss. In the UK, however, Spanish trawler owners were successful in obtaining damages against the UK government in *R.* v. *Secretary of State for Transport, ex parte Factortame* (No. 5). The House of Lords confirmed liability, holding that the adoption of legislation which was discriminatory on grounds of nationality in relation to the registration of British fishing vessels was sufficiently serious to give rise to liability to individuals who had suffered loss as a result.

QUESTIONS

1 To what extent do the directly effective rights of individuals under directives differ from those under the Treaty?

2 When does the duty to interpret national law in accordance with a directive come to an end?

3 Why did the Court of Justice develop the principle of State liability? Which conditions have to be satisfied before an action for State liability may succeed?

Further reading

Chalmers, D., Hadjiemmanuil, C., Monti, G. and Tomkins, A. (2006) *European Union Law*, Cambridge University Press, Chapter 9, pp.365–408.

Craig, P. and De Burca, G. (2008) *EU Law: Text, Cases and Materials*, 4th edition, Oxford University Press, Chapter 8 and 10.

Dougan, M. (2000) 'The *Francovich* Right to Reparation: Reshaping the Contours of Community Remedial Competence', (2000) 6 EPL 103.

Lenz, M. (2000) 'Horizontal what? Back to Basics', (2000) 20 ELRev. 502.

Slynn, G. (1999) *Introducing a European Legal Order*, Stevens, p.124.

Tridimas, T. (2001) 'Liability for Breach of Community Law: Growing up and Mellowing Down?', (2001) 38 CMLRev. 301.

Winter, T. A. (1983) 'Direct Applicability and Direct Effects', (1983) 8 ELRev. 425.

Visit **http://www.mylawchamber.co.uk/kent** to access answer guidance to questions in the book to test yourself on this chapter.

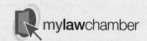

Use **Case Navigator** to read in full some of the key cases referenced in this chapter:

- C-46/93 and 48/93 **Brasserie du Pêcheur** v. **Federal Republic of Germany** and **R.** v. **Secretary of State for Transport, ex parte Factortame (Factortame III)** [1996] ECR I-1029
- C-6, 9/90 **Francovich and Bonfaci** v. **Italy** ECR I-5357
- 41/74 **Van Duyn** v. **Home Office** [1974] ECR 1337
- 26/62 **Van Gend en Loos**
- 14/83 **Von Colson** [1984] ECR 1891

7

Enforcement actions against Member States: Articles 226 to 228, 88, 95 and 298

INTRODUCTION

In Chapters 7 and 8 the key procedures involved in the enforcement of EU law against Member States, and in the judicial review of the acts of the institutions, are outlined. The main procedure for enforcement of EC law against Member States by the Commission is provided in Article 226. A parallel procedure for action by Member States is provided by Article 227. Remedies to support the enforcement procedures under Articles 226 and 227 are provided by Article 228. Other specific enforcement provisions arise under Articles 88, 95 and 298.

DIRECT ACTION UNDER ARTICLE 226

Power of the Commission under Article 226

Article 226(1) (ex 169) provides that if the Commission considers that a Member State has failed to fulfil an obligation under the Treaty, it shall deliver a reasoned opinion on the matter after giving the State concerned the opportunity to submit its observations. Under Article 226(2), if the State concerned does not comply with the opinion within the period laid down by the Commission the latter may bring the matter before the ECJ.

Function of Article 226

Article 226 serves three main functions:

1 It seeks to ensure that Member States comply with their EC obligations.
2 It provides a useful mechanism to resolve disputes without necessarily involving proceedings before the ECJ.
3 Where the ECJ is involved, it provides general guidance on EC law.

Failure to implement an obligation

Proceedings may be brought against any State or state agency. 'Failure' covers any breach of EC law, whether under the EC Treaty, international agreements to which the EC is a party, secondary legislation or general principles of law. Such a breach may take the form of either act or omission, including non-implementation of EC law and retention of national laws which conflict with EC law.

Procedure

There are two stages to procedure under Article 226: the first stage, which is administrative, and the second stage, which is judicial.

Key point

It should be appreciated that both the Commission and the Member State involved have an interest in resolving the dispute at an early stage, rather than letting a dispute runs its course to the judicial stage.

The administrative stage

Having informed the Member State concerned of the grounds of complaint, the Commission invites it to submit its observations. The Commission issues a reasoned opinion recording the infringement and requiring the State concerned to take action to end the breach. This opinion is not a binding act capable of annulment, merely a step in the proceedings: Case 48/65 *Alfons Lütticke GmbH* v. *Commission*.

If the Member State will not accept the opinion it may move on to the second stage, before the ECJ. In deciding whether or not to issue a reasoned opinion, and to commence proceedings in the ECJ, the Commission acts as a college. In other words, such decisions cannot be taken by a Commissioner alone but 'must be the subject of collective deliberation by the college of Commissioners': Case C-191/95 *Commission* v. *Germany*.

The Commission usually imposes a time limit for compliance in the reasoned opinion. If not, a Member State should comply within a reasonable time. While the ECJ may dismiss an action where the Commission has allowed insufficient time, as it did in *Commission* v. *Belgium (Re University Fees)* (Case 293/85), in urgent cases, the period may be much shorter (seven days to respond to the formal letter and 14 to the reasoned opinion were accepted in Case C-328/96 *Commission* v. *Austria*). The ECJ is not empowered to change the limit imposed by the Commission Case 28/81: *Commission* v. *Italy*.

> ### Key point
>
> It should be appreciated that the decision to proceed is the Commission's alone. No party may require the Commission to act under Article 226. Failure to act is not a breach of Article 232 (ex 175): *Star Fruit* v. *Commission* (Case 247/87).

See also Case C-87/89 *Sonito* v. *Commission* (dismissal of action by an applicant who had requested the Commission to bring enforcement proceedings against France).[1]

The judicial stage

If a Member State fails to comply with the reasoned opinion within the stated time limit, the Commission continues to have complete discretion as to whether to bring proceedings before the ECJ. The Court conducts a full examination into the case and may review the legality of the Commission's action: Case 293/85 *Commission* v. *Belgium*. While interested States have the right to be heard, individuals do not: Case 154/85R *Commission* v. *Italy (Re Import of Foreign Motor Vehicles)*.

Defences

Defences to actions under Article 226 rarely succeed, as the statistics of the Court in its report for 2006 show.[2] The main reason is that the pre-judicial stages act as a filter, so that only the more serious (and hard to defend) cases reach the ECJ. Member States are required by Article 10 (ex 5) to implement EC law fully. Occasionally, a Member State establishes that it is not bound by the obligation: for example, where the deadline for implementation of a directive has not yet expired or where the Commission has introduced grounds not cited in the reasoned opinion: Case 101/84 *Commission* v. *Italy*.

Unsuccessful defences have included:

- *force majeure*: Case 101/84 *Commission* v. *Italy* (a bomb attack on the office of the Italian Ministry of Transport was held to be no justification for Italy's failure to submit statistical returns on carriage of goods by road);
- difficulties of a constitutional, institutional or administrative nature: Case 28/81 *Commission* v. *Italy*, or of a political nature: Case 128/78 *Commission* v. *United Kingdom (Re Tachographs)*;

---

[1] For further consideration of the Commission's discretion under Article 226, see Craig and De Burca (2007: 434–438).

[2] Annual Report for 2006 of the Court of Justice, Tables and Statistics http://curia.europa.eu/en/instit/presentationfr/rapport/stat/06_cour_stat.pdf. The report shows that, of the 111 cases concerning failure of a Member State to fulfil its obligations (most of which were brought under Article 226), the action was dismissed in only eight cases (7 per cent), compared with 103 cases (93 per cent) where an infringement was declared.

- introduction of the obligation in practice but not in law: Case 167/73 *Commission v. France (Re French Merchant Seamen)*;
- failure to implement an obligation which is directly effective: Case 104/86 *Commission v. Italy*;
- reciprosity, i.e. failure by another State to comply with EC law: Case 232/78 *Commission v. France (Lamb Wars)*.

Key case

Case C-265/95 *Commission* v. *France*: The Commission brought enforcement proceedings against France following the failure of the French authorities to respond adequately to violent action by French farmers. During this period the farmers had systematically disrupted the movement in France of agricultural produce from other Member States and had intimidated retailers, as part of a campaign to persuade them to stock only French goods. During 1993 the campaign focused on strawberries from Spain and tomatoes from Belgium.

The French government claimed that it had condemned the violent acts by the farmers and that it had taken preventive measures, such as surveillance, which had reduced the number of incidents. The Commission considered that these steps were insufficient and issued a reasoned opinion under Article 226, stating that by failing to take necessary and proportionate action to prevent the obstruction of the free movement of fruit and vegetables, France was in breach of its duties in relation to the common organisation of the market in agricultural products and Articles 8 and 10 EC. The ECJ upheld the decision.

Parallel proceedings

It is becoming increasingly common for proceedings to be brought before a national court in which a question of EC law is raised leading to a referral to the ECJ under Article 234. At the same time, the Commission may instigate proceedings under Article 226 where it considers that there has been a breach of EC law. Interim measures may be ordered at the request of the Commission where there is a *prima facie* case and the matter is urgent.

Example

Case C-213/89 *R.* v. *Secretary of State for Transport, ex parte Factortame*: ECJ ruling on an Article 234 referral from the House of Lords, and Case 246/89R *Commission v. UK (Re Merchant Shipping Rules)*: Article 226 proceedings ordering the suspension of the Merchant Shipping Act 1988.

ACTION UNDER ARTICLE 227

Action by Member States: Article 227

Under Article 227(1) a Member State which considers that another Member State has failed to fulfil an obligation under the Treaty may bring the matter before the ECJ. Member States bringing an action are subject to a similar procedure to that created by Article 226, namely notification to the Commission (Article 227(2)), followed by the delivery of a reasoned opinion by the Commission (Article 227(3)), with the right to bring the matter before the ECJ.

Under Article 227(3) both parties have the right to submit their case orally and in writing. Failure by the Commission to deliver an opinion within three months does not prevent the matter being brought before the ECJ.

Actions before the ECJ

Few cases have been brought to judgment under Article 227 (ex 170), as Member States prefer to avoid direct confrontation. There is only one example of a ruling under this Article: Case 141/78 *France* v. *United Kingdom*. In this case, France brought an action against the UK in the ECJ over fishing net mesh sizes. The Commission intervened in support of France and the ECJ upheld the Commission opinion.

The Court rejected actions under Article 227 in the following cases:

- Case C-388/95 *Belgium* v. *Spain* based on a claim by Belgium that a Spanish law requiring Rioja wine to be bottled in the area where it is grown and forbidding bulk exportation of the wine contravened Articles 28–30 EC.
- Case C-145/04 *Spain* v. *UK* concerning the voting rights of residents of Gibralter in the European Parliament. This case arose as a result of the implementation by the UK of the judgment by the ECHR in *Matthews* v. *UK* (See Chapter 4). The Commission declined to issue a reasoned opinion, given the sensitivity of the long-standing political dispute between the two countries over Gibraltar. The Court found that the UK could not, in the circumstances, be criticised for compliance with the judgment of the ECHR.

Voluntary procedure: Article 239

Article 239 provides an alternative mechanism for the resolution of disputes under which States may agree to submit any dispute concerning the subject matter of the Treaty to the ECJ.

Sanctions against Member States under Article 228

Article 228 (ex 171) was amended by the Maastricht Treaty to provide for the imposition of a sanction for non-compliance with a decision of the ECJ. (Previously, an order under Article 228 was declaratory only.)

Under Article 228 the Commission may issue a reasoned opinion specifying non-compliance with a judgment of the ECJ after giving the Member State the opportunity to submit its observations. The Commission may initiate proceedings in the ECJ if the State fails to take the necessary measures to comply within the time limit laid down by the Commission. If the ECJ finds that the State has not complied it may impose a lump sum or penalty payment.

The Commission is becoming more active in seeking the imposition of a penalty under Article 228, although the number of judgments remains low. It provided guidance in Memorandum 96/C 242/07 as to the factors to be taken into account in assessing the penalty, namely the seriousness of the infringement, its duration and the need to ensure deterrence. The Court applied the Commission's guidance in Case C-387/97 *Commission* v. *Greece*, while making it clear that it did not regard itself as bound, imposing a periodic penalty on Greece for failure to comply with the judgment in Case C-45/91 (over non-implementation of directives on the disposal of waste).

In some cases the Court has imposed a different penalty from that requested by the Commission. See, for example, Case C-304/02 *Commission* v. *France*, in which the Court imposed both a lump sum and a periodical penalty on France for non-implementation of its decision in Case C-64/88 over failure to observe fisheries conservation. The Commission had requested a periodical payment only. In Case C-503/04 *Commission* v. *Germany* the Commission once more asked the Court to impose a periodical penalty. This time the Court decided that, as the breach had been rectified by the time of the Article 228 hearing, it was inappropriate to impose a financial penalty, instead making a declaration only of failure to comply in time with the reasoned opinion under Article 228.

SPECIFIC ENFORCEMENT PROCEDURES: ARTICLES 88(2), 298 AND 95(4)

State aids: Article 88(2)

Under Article 88(2) (ex 93(2)) the Commission may issue a decision which requires the State concerned to change or abolish the illegal aid within a set time. Failure to comply entitles the Commission or any other interested State to bring the matter before the ECJ. Decisions under Article 88(2), unlike opinions under Articles 226 or 227, may be challenged before the ECJ under Article 230: Case 156/77 *Commission* v. *Belgium*. See, for example, Cases 31/77 and 53/77R *Commission* v. *United Kingdom* in which the Commission issued a decision to UK pig producers to end a subsidy forthwith. In the absence of action by the UK, the Commission brought the matter before the ECJ under Article 88(2). The ECJ upheld the Commission decision in the same terms: cf. Case C-294/90 *British Aerospace and Rover Group Holdings plc* v. *Commission* in which failure by the Commission to observe the rights of interested third parties led to annulment of the Commission decision. This decision had required the UK to recover payments which the Commission considered were illegally made to Rover in the takeover by British Aerospace.

Measures to prevent internal disturbances: Article 298

Article 298 empowers the Commission to challenge the action of a Member State under Articles 296 and 297, following an expedited procedure, where it considers that the State concerned is acting improperly. The ruling of the ECJ is given in camera. (Articles 296 and 297 enable Member States to disregard obligations under the Treaty in the essential interests of its security, internally or internationally, where these interests involve arms production or the withholding of information.)

> ### Key point
>
> The ECJ is empowered under Article 243 in any cases before it to prescribe any necessary interim measures. This power may be used, for example, in conjunction with Articles 88 (ex 93) or 298 to enable the ECJ to grant an interim injunction.

Improper use of powers under Article 95(4)

Article 95(4) (para. 1) empowers a Member State after adoption of a harmonisation measure to apply stricter national measures under Article 30 or relating to the protection of the environment or working environment. Article 95(4) (para. 3) enables the Commission or a Member State to use a similar procedure to that under Article 298 where it considers that a State is making improper use of its powers under Article 95(4).

QUESTIONS

1 What is the main purpose of the enforcement procedure under Article 226?

2 Assume that the Council and European Parliament have adopted Directive 2006/1 on synchronised timetables for cross-border bus and train travel, for implementation throughout the EU by December 2007. The Directive was not implemented on time by Utopia and Nirvana (both new Member States). Utopia argues that it cannot afford to implement the Directive due to the costs of joining the EU. Nirvana argues that it is unfair to expect new Member States to implement a directive which was being openly ignored by several Member States.

Transalpina, an established Member State, implemented the Directive but complains that it has increased the costs of running its transport network. It wants to see all Member States incur the same level of costs, claiming that the additional costs deter tourists from visiting Transalpina.

Advise the government of Transalpina whether:

(a) the Commission has the power to resolve the problem without recourse to the Court of Justice;

(b) it (the government of Transalpina) may bring proceedings in the Court of Justice against Utopia and Nirvana or whether it would be better to leave enforcement to the Commission;

(c) a financial penalty may be imposed on Utopia or Nirvana if they fail to comply with a judgment of the Court of Justice.

3 To what extent, if any, do you consider that enforcement of EU law would be more effective if the procedures under Articles 226–228 were simplified?

Further reading

Craig, P. and De Burca, G. (2007) *EU Law: Text, Cases and Materials*, 4th edition, Oxford University Press, Chapter 12.

Harlow, C. and Rawlings, R. (2006) 'Accountability and law enforcement: The centralized EU infringement procedure', (2006) 31 ELRev. 447.

Rawlings, R. (2006) 'Engaged Elites, Citizen Action and Institutional Attitudes in Commission Enforcement', (2006) 6 ELJ 4.

Theodossiou, M., (2002) 'An Analysis of the Recent Response of the Community to Non-Compliance with Court of Justice Judgments: Art.228', (2002) 27 ELRev. 25

Wenneras, P. (2006) 'A New Dawn for Commission Enforcement under Arts. 226 and 228: General and Persistent (GAP) Infringements, Lump Sums, and Penalty Payment', (2006) 43 CMLRev. 31

Visit **http://www.mylawchamber.co.uk/kent** to access answer guidance to questions in the book to test yourself on this chapter.

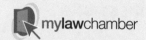

Use **Case Navigator** to read in full some of the key cases referenced in this chapter:

- 101/84 **Commission** *v.* **Italy** [1985] ECR 2629

8

Judicial review: annulment under Article 230, failure to act under Article 232, and indirect review under Article 241

INTRODUCTION

Under Article 230 (ex 173) the ECJ may examine the activities of the institutions to determine the validity of their legislation, whereas under Article 232 (ex 175) the ECJ may consider the inactivity of the institutions when they are under a legal duty to act. Article 241 (ex 149) provides a means of indirect review where an applicant challenges the legality of a general act on which a later act or omission is based. All three procedures derive from French administrative law.

ACTION FOR ANNULMENT: ARTICLE 230

Scope of Article 230

> **Key point**
>
> Article 230(1) provides that the ECJ shall review the legality of acts adopted jointly by the European Parliament and the Council, of acts of the Council, of the Commission and of the ECB, other than recommendations and opinions, and of acts of the European Parliament intended to produce legal effects *vis-à-vis* third parties: Article 230(1).

The Treaty of Lisbon will replace 'acts' under Article 230(1) with 'legislative acts' and will add the European Council to the list of bodies whose acts may be challenged. Provision is made to 'review the legality of acts of bodies, agencies of the Union intended to produce legal effects *vis-à-vis* third parties', extending the scope for review beyond the acts of the EP.

The ECJ has jurisdiction under Article 230(2) in actions brought by Member States, the European Parliament, the Council or the Commission on grounds of lack of competence, infringement of an essential procedural requirement, infringement of the Treaty or of any rule of law relating to its application, or misuse of powers.

Article 230(4) provides for a restricted right of challenge for natural or legal persons, provided the proceedings are instituted within the time limits specified in Article 230(4). Actions brought by applicants under Article 230(2) ('privileged applicants') and Article 230(3) are heard in the ECJ. Actions brought by applicants under Article 230(4) ('non-privileged applicants') are heard in the CFI, with the possibility of appeal to the ECJ.

Five essential questions

Five questions must be considered in relation to Article 230, namely:

1 Which acts may be challenged?
2 Who has the right to challenge?
3 What are the relevant time limits?
4 On which grounds may the acts be challenged?
5 What are the effects of annulment?

ACTS WHICH MAY BE CHALLENGED

Reviewable acts

Reviewable acts are not limited to regulations, directives and decisions.

> **Key point**
>
> The ECJ is concerned with substance rather than form and will consider all measures taken by the institutions which are designed to have legal effect: Case 22/70 *Commission* v. *Council (Re European Road Transport Agreement)*.

The following have been held to be reviewable acts:

- 'Discussions' of guidelines before the signing of the ERTA: *Commission* v. *Council (Re ERTA)*.
- A 'communication' in the form of a registered letter from the Commission issued under the competition rules stating that the company was no longer immune from fines: Cases 8–11/66 *Re Noordwijk's Cement Accord*.
- A notice of vacancy for a post in the EP, stating that a 'perfect knowledge of Italian' was required (i.e. restricting the post to Italian nationals): Case 15/63 *Lassalle* v. *European Parliament*.

The following have been held not to be reviewable acts:

- A reasoned opinion under Article 226 (ex 169): Case 7/61 *Pigmeat*.
- A letter from the Commission to an undertaking under Regulation 17 containing a statement of objections: Case 60/81 *IBM* v. *Commission*.
- Preliminary observations by the Commission in a competition investigation: Case T-64/89 *Automec* v. *Commission*.

The TEU amended the wording of Article 230 (2) which previously referred only to acts of the Council and the Commission so that the EP's acts may be challenged where they were intended to produce legal effects *vis-à-vis* third parties. This reflects the following decisions:

- Case 230/81 *Luxembourg* v. *European Parliament* (a challenge by Luxembourg to the EP's resolution to move from Luxembourg to Brussels and Strasbourg); and
- Case 294/83 *Partie Ecologiste ('Les Verts')* v. *European Parliament* (a challenge to the allocation of campaign funds to the Green Party for the 1984 elections). Previously, old Article 173 referred only to acts of the Council and the Commission.

Where an act of the EP had only internal effect (authorisation and implementation of expenditure), it was found to be inadmissible: Case 190/84 *'Les Verts'* v. *European Parliament*. Here a further challenge to the budget, already the subject of a challenge in Case 294/83, was rejected.

The CFI considered the possibility of reviewing acts under the Second Pillar (CFSP) in two cases involving sanctions against persons suspected of supporting Al-Qaeda. Following a UN Security Council Regulation the EU adopted a regulation to identify individuals whose assets should be frozen. The CFI declined to admit the challenge to the regulation brought by Kadi, who was identified on the list, maintaining that this would have amounted to indirect review of international law: Case T-315/01 *Kadi* v. *Council and Commission*. In contrast, a challenge was found to be admissible in Case T-228/02 *Organisation des Modjahedines du Peuple d'Iran* where an individual identified for sanctions was permitted to challenge the regulation, again adopted pursuant to a UN resolution. The difference between the two cases was that the UN had not named the organisation in *Modjahedines*, whereas it had done so in *Kadi*.

The ECJ has been empowered since the TOA to review the legality of framework decisions and decisions under the Third Pillar (Police and Judicial Co-operation in Criminal Matters). Actions by the police or law enforcement agencies, and by Member States to maintain law and order or internal security, are excluded under Article 35(5) TEU. In Case C-354/04P *Gestoras pro Amnistia, Olano and Errasti* v. *Council* the ECJ considered the questions arising from an action brought by an individual identified on an annex to a Council common position adopted pursuant to a UN resolution on co-operation between States to combat the financing of terrorism. The annex listed the groups affected. While making it clear that a common position is not itself an act which can be challenged, the ECJ found that a national court with serious doubts as to whether a common position was intended to create legal effects may seek clarification from the ECJ by means of a preliminary reference.[1]

RIGHT TO CHALLENGE

The right to challenge depends on whether the applicant is regarded as privileged or non-privileged.

---

[1] See Craig and De Burca (2007: 507–508).

> **Key point**
>
> Privileged applicants under Article 230(2) enjoy full rights of challenge, whereas non-privileged applicants have restricted rights under Article 230(4).

Privileged applicants

The ECJ has jurisdiction under Article 230(2) in actions brought by Member States, the European Parliament, the Council or the Commission on grounds of lack of competence, infringement of an essential procedural requirement, infringement of the Treaty or of any rule of law relating to its application, or misuse of powers.

Before amendment by the TEU, the EP did not enjoy privileged status. Its position changed as a result of the decision in Case C-70/88 *Parliament* v. *Council ('Chernobyl')*, partially overruling the decision in Case 302/87 *Parliament* v. *Council ('Comitology')*. In *Chernobyl* the ECJ recognised that the EP had limited rights to safeguard its own prerogatives, typically where a measure was adopted under an incorrect legal base, as this restricted the EP's involvement in the legislative process. The Treaty of Nice accorded the EP full rights to challenge, putting it on a par with the other privileged applicants.

The ECB and the Court of Auditors are covered by Article 230(3) and so only entitled to challenge in response to a threat to their prerogatives. The Treaty of Lisbon will add the Committee of the Regions to existing 'semi-privileged' applicants under Article 230(3).

Non-privileged applicants

A natural or legal person is only entitled to challenge a decision addressed to him or herself or a decision in the form of a regulation or a decision addressed to another person, which is of direct and individual concern to him or herself.

Many successful challenges to decisions concerning individuals have been brought in competition cases: see, for example, Cases 56 and 58/64 *Consten and Grundig* v. *Commission*. However, it is difficult to establish standing where the decision is addressed to another person, which, for these purposes, has been held to include the Member States: Case 25/62 *Plaumann*. In such a case or where a regulation is involved it is essential to satisfy two criteria for an action to be admissible:

1 The measure must be equivalent to a decision.
2 It must be of direct and individual concern to the person himself.

Measure must be equivalent to a decision

A 'true' regulation may not be challenged under Article 226 Cases 789 and 790/79 *Calpack*. The ECJ has stressed that the nature and content of an act rather than its form should be considered: Cases 16 and 17/62 *Confédération Nationale des Producteurs de Fruits et Légumes* v. *Council*. A regulation applies generally and objectively to categories of persons whereas a decision binds those to whom it is addressed, i.e. named or identifiable individuals. In some cases the ECJ has found that an act described as a regulation has the characteristics of a decision. For example:

- where the regulation prescribed the number of import licences for a particular period on the basis of previous applications and so applied only to a finite number of people: Cases 41–44/1970 *International Fruit NV v. Commission (No. 1)*.
- where the behaviour of a company exporting watches had been taken into account in a regulation imposing anti-dumping duties: Case 264/82 *Timex v. Commission*.

Even where a regulation is deemed to be a 'true' regulation, it may be of direct and individual concern to the applicant where a right has been infringed.

Key case

Case C-309/89 *Codorniu* v. *Council*: The applicant sought to challenge a regulation reserving the word '*crémant*' for high-quality sparkling wines from certain parts of France and Luxembourg. The applicant was a major producer of sparkling wines in Spain and the largest producer of quality sparkling wines in the EU, holding a Spanish trade mark for one of its products. The ECJ held that the regulation was a true regulation of general application. Although Codorniu was not part of a fixed and ascertainable group, the company was held to be individually concerned because the regulation affected it in a different way from other producers by removing its trade mark rights.

While the decision in *Codorniu* was welcomed by lawyers and commentators as a relaxation of the approach to individual concern, it did not provide a basis for the ECJ to develop its case law on standing. Instead we must turn to the interpretation provided by the ECJ in *Plaumann*.

Measure must be of direct and individual concern to the applicant

It is hard, if not impossible, for most applicants to establish standing in relation to a measure which is not addressed to them. The test for direct and individual concern continues to be represented in the *Plaumann* formula, as follows :

Key point

'In order for a measure to be of individual concern to the person to whom it applies, it must affect their legal position because of a factual situation which differentiates them from all other persons and distinguishes them individually in the same way as the person to whom it is addressed' (the *Plaumann* formula, as restated in Case 26/86 *Deutz under Geldermann* v. *Council*).

The test was criticised as too restrictive, notably by Advocate-General Jacobs in *UPA* who proposed a wider definition which was rejected by the Court (see below).[2]

> ## Key case
>
> The applicant, a major importer of clementines, claimed to be individually concerned in a Commission decision addressed to the German government. The decision refused permission to the government to reduce customs duties on clementines from outside the EC. The ECJ refused to accept that the applicant had standing. It held that the test to establish individual concern requires the applicant to prove that the decision affects him because of factors which are peculiarly relevant to him, and not merely because he belongs to a class affected by the act. In this case, the class was that of importer of clementines and, in principle, anyone could import clementines: Case 25/62 *Plaumann & Co. v. Commission*.

As Craig and De Burca point out,[3] it is both unrealistic and unfair to maintain that anyone may import clementines as it would take time for a new trader to enter the market. The authors also criticise the Court's reasoning in conceptual terms, as the wording of the test in *Plaumann* makes it almost impossible for an applicant to succeed in establishing standing, given that an unidentified trader may always appear at a later stage.

A measure is of direct concern to the applicant when his or her position is decided by the act itself, without the exercise of further discretion: Case 69/69 *SA Alcan* v. *Commission*. As a result, the exercise of discretion by a third party will be fatal to admissibility. In Case T-341/02[4] *Regione Siciliana* v. *Commisssion* the Region of Sicily sought annulment of a Commission decision addressed to the Italian government ending financial assistance for a motorway project on the island. The CFI in a decision upheld by the ECJ on appeal refused to admit the application, finding that the national government had significant discretion in implementing the measure.

For many years following the *Plaumann* decision the ECJ failed to adopt a consistent line on standing. The following provide examples where direct and individual concern was recognised:

- Cases 106 and 107/63 *Toepfer KG* v. *Commission*: The applicant, an importer of cereals, had applied unsuccessfully to the German government for a licence to import cereals from France into Germany. The refusal was confirmed in a Commission decision. As the decision affected only existing applicants it was found to be of individual concern to the applicant.

---

[2] See also Arnull (1995 and 2001).
[3] Craig and De Burca (2007: 512).
[4] On appeal, Case C-417/04P.

- Case 11/82 *AE Piraiki-Patriki* v. *Commission*: The applicants, who manufactured and exported cotton yarn, sought to challenge a decision addressed to the French government of general application authorising the imposition of an import quota on Greek cotton yarn. The ECJ held that the decision *was* of individual concern to those who had entered into contracts before the decision for performance subsequently.
- Case C-152/88 *Sofrimport SARL* v. *Commission*: The ECJ held that importers whose goods were in transit at the time a Commission regulation was adopted were individually concerned. The regulation banning the importation of fruits into the EC had been adopted under a Council regulation which required the EC to have regard for the interests of importers with goods in transit.

By contrast, the Court adopted a restrictive view on individual concern in the following cases and did not recognise the standing of the applicants:

- Case 231/82 *Spijker Kwasten NV* v. *Commission*: The Commission had issued the Dutch government with a decision requiring it to ban the import of Chinese brushes. Despite the fact that the applicant had previously applied for an import licence for Chinese brushes, the ECJ held that the decision was *not* of individual concern to the applicant.
- Case C-321/95P *Stichtung Greenpeace Council (Greenpeace International)* v. *Commission*: The applicants, an alliance between an environmental group and local residents, fishermen and farmers, sought to annul a Commission decision to provide financial aid to build two power stations on the Canary Islands. The ECJ applied the *Plaumann* formula to the applicants and found that they could not be differentiated from residents generally, or others working in the area. It upheld the decision of the CFI not to recognise individual concern.

Back to the *Plaumann* formula

The CFI set off a short-lived flurry of excitement in 2002 in Case T-177/01 *Jégo Quéré* by adopting a more liberal approach to individual concern. The applicants ('JQ') sought to challenge an EU regulation imposing a fishing net mesh size which would have prevented them from using their nets to fish off Ireland where they had been fishing for some time. As the Regulation was a measure of general application, it would not normally have been open to a challenge by a non-privileged applicant. However, the Court found the action to be admissible, holding that the applicants would otherwise be deprived of a remedy under Articles 6 and 13 of the ECHR. In a decision given after the submissions of Advocate-General Jacobs in *UPA* but before the judgment (see below), the CFI formulated a new test for individual concern, namely that an individual should be regarded as individually concerned in a measure of general application where it 'affects his legal position in a manner which is both definite and immediate, by restricting his rights or by imposing obligations on him'.

A few months later, the ECJ reached a different conclusion in Case C-50/00P *Unión de Pequenos Agricultores (UPA)*.

Key case

The applicants, the UPA, were a trade association seeking to challenge a regulation on the common organisation of the market in olive oil. They claimed that, as they could not readily use Article 234 to challenge the regulation, they should be able to challenge it under Article 230 if they were not to be deprived of a judicial remedy. Advocate-General Jacobs argued that the time had come for the Court to depart from its narrow interpretation of standing in the interests of effective judicial protection. Accordingly, he submitted that the only satisfactory solution was to recognise that the applicant was individually concerned by a EC measure 'where the measure has, or is liable to have a substantial effect on his interests'.[5]

This liberal interpretation was *not* accepted by the Court, which held that it continued to be necessary for a natural or legal person to establish direct and individual concern in order to challenge a measure under Article 230. It found that to adopt a more liberal interpretation would set aside the condition in Article 230(4), and would exceed the jurisdiction of the Court. To make such a change to the system of judicial review would require amendment to the Treaty by the Member States: Case C-50/00P *Unión de Pequeños Agricultores (UPA)* v. *Council.*

The ECJ followed *UPA* when considering the appeal in *Jégo Quéré*.[6] It explicitly rejected the test for standing put forward by the CFI, finding that the rules could not be relaxed even where national law would provide no remedy. As a result, it is clear that the standing of non-privileged applicants continues to be governed by the strict requirements of the *Plaumann* test. The CFI applied the test in its recent decision in Joined Cases T-218 to 240/03 *Boyle and others v. Commission*. This case arose out of a request to the Commission by a group of individuals including the applicants who owned fishing vessels in the Irish fleet to increase the objectives of the Multilateral guidance for the Irish fishing fleet ('MAGPI IV'). The Commission refused this request in a decision addressed to Ireland. As the number and identity of the vessel owners could be established before the decision was made, the CFI found that it affected a closed group of identified persons within the meaning of the *Plaumann* formula. As a result, the applicants were permitted to challenge the decision.

● Treaty reform

The Treaty of Lisbon has followed the wording of the Constitutional Treaty in providing for a replacement for Article 230(4) as follows:

> Any natural or legal person may . . . institute proceedings against an act addressed to that person or which is of direct and individual concern to them, and against a regulatory act which is of direct concern to them and does not entail implementing measures.

[5] At para. 102(4).
[6] In Case C-263/02P.

The notable feature of this amendment is in the addition of challenges to regulatory acts. Such a challenge will require a non-privileged applicant to demonstrate only 'direct concern', without the need to show individual concern. Such a change falls a long way short of Advocate-General Jacob's call for standing to be extended to those whose interests are adversely affected by a measure. Nevertheless, it may possibly indicate the beginning of a process of gradual relaxation of the rules on standing, but it does not alter the need for individuals to satisfy the *Plaumann* test where they seek to challenge a decision addressed to someone else.

TIME LIMITS

What are the relevant time limits?

Under Article 230(3) an applicant, whether a privileged applicant or an individual, must bring a claim for annulment within two months of:

- publication of the measure; or
- notification of the measure to the applicant; or
- the day in which it came to the knowledge of the applicant (in the absence of notification).

As Article 254 (ex 191) requires regulations to be published, time will run from the date of publication. In the case of directives and decisions time will run from the date of notification. The date of knowledge is the date on which the applicant became aware of the measure. A limited extension of the two-month limitation period takes account of the distance of the applicant's place of residence from the ECJ (10 days in the case of the UK).

After the expiry of the two-month period, the measure may not be challenged by other means such as Article 241 (ex 184): Case 156/77 Commission v. *Belgium* or Article 175: Cases 10 and 18/68 *Eridania* v. *Commission*. But see Cases 6 and 11/69 *Commission* v. *France* in which a late action after two months was permitted under Article 230.

GROUNDS FOR CHALLENGE

Grounds for annulment

Article 230 provides four grounds for annulment:

1 lack of competence;
2 infringement of an essential procedural requirement;
3 infringement of the EC Treaty or of any rule relating to its application;
4 misuse of power.

These actions derive from French administrative law where they are known respectively as *incompetence, vice de forme, violation de la loi* and *détournement de pouvoir*. The grounds for annulment are not mutually exclusive but overlap, making it possible to plead more than one ground.

Lack of competence

This ground is the equivalent of the English doctrine of *ultra vires* in substantive law. The institutions may adopt measures only where they are empowered to act by the EC Treaty or secondary legislation. Thus, a measure may be challenged on the ground that the adopting institution lacked the necessary legal authority. See Case 22/70 *Commission* v. *Council, re European Road Transport Agreement (ERTA)* in which the Commission brought an action against the Council over the latter's participation in the formulation of the Road Transport Agreement, where Article 300 (ex 228) gives the Commission the power to negotiate and the Council power to conclude international agreements. The application was unsuccessful on the facts (see pp.61–62).

Infringement of an essential procedural requirement

This ground, the equivalent of *ultra vires* in procedural matters, is based on the requirement that institutions adopting binding measures must follow the correct procedures. Procedures may be laid down either in the EC Treaty or in secondary legislation. A number of actions have invoked Article 253 (ex 190) which provides that decisions of the Commission shall state the reasons on which they are based.

Key case

An application by Germany to the Commission to import wine for blending for domestic consumption was partially unsuccessful, the Commission giving as its reason that information showed a sufficient production of such wines already within the EC. The ECJ annulled the decision on the ground of vagueness. HELD: Reasons must not be too vague or inconsistent. They must set out in a clear and relevant manner the main issues of law and fact on which they are based to enable: (i) the parties to defend their rights, (ii) the ECJ to exercise its supervisory functions and (iii) Member States and interested nationals to be informed: Case 24/62 *Germany* v. *Commission (Re Tariff Quotas on Wine)*.

See also Case 45/86 *Commission* v. *Council* in which the Commission challenged two regulations adopted by the Council under the General System of Preferences (tariffs to developing countries). It was held that failure to state the legal basis infringed an essential procedural requirement under Article 253 (ex 190).

It should be noted that no action lies where the result of applying the measure is unaffected by the defect, nor where the defect is trivial: Case 30/78 *Distillers Co. Ltd* v. *Commission*.

Failure to consult the EP where this is required by the Treaty has been held to constitute an essential procedural requirement: Case 138/79 *Roquette Frères SA* v. *Council* and Case 139/79 *Maizena GmbH* v. *Council*. Consultation with the EP has been denied by choice of an incorrect legal basis for the legislation. In Case C-300/89 *Commission* v. *Council* ('*Titanium Dioxide*') the Council based a measure to harmonise the regime for titanium dioxide waste on former Article 130 (now repealed) rather than on Article 95 (ex 100a). Article 130 required unanimity, whereas Article 95 (the co-operation procedure) required a qualified majority. The ECJ held that a single legal base, Article 95, should have been used enabling the EP to influence decision making in environmental issues.[7]

It is arguable whether choice of incorrect legal basis is an infringement of an essential procedural requirement or an infringement of the Treaty. Aspects of both are present. The choice of legal base has become less controversial as a result of the extension of the co-decision procedure to most areas of legislation.

Infringement of the Treaty or of any rule relating to its application

This ground for annulment is widely drafted to cover the provisions of *all* relevant Treaties, secondary legislation adopted under the Treaties and general principles common to the laws of the Member States: see, for example, Case 17/74 *Transocean Marine Paint Association*, in which the principle of natural justice was recognised as a general principle. Any of the general principles recognised by the ECJ may be invoked as a ground for annulment. Proportionality is frequently invoked: see, for example, Case C-353/99P *Council v. Hautala* in which a journalist sought access to a Council document on arms exports. Access was refused under Regulation 731/93 (access to documentation) on the basis that it might damage relations with third countries. The ECJ found that the decision on access was subject to the principle of proportionality which required the Council to consider partial access. It also required that the derogation was appropriate and necessary for the objectives of the measure.

For further examples relating to general principles: see Chapter 4.

Misuse of powers

This ground is known in English law as abuse of power, misuse of power or bad faith. However, the term has been interpreted by the ECJ to include improper (though not illegal) use of powers. In Case 1/54 *French Republic* v. *High Authority* the High Authority of the ECSC took several decisions under Article 60 ECSC which could have had the effect of reducing prices generally although the stated purpose was to prevent price discrimination. The ECJ held that where the main purpose of the act complained of was legitimate, there was no abuse of powers even if an improper

---

[7] After amendment by the TEU, environmental measures were governed by the co-decision procedure under Article 251.

object were incidentally achieved. See also: Case 62/70 *Werner A. Bock KG v. Commission* in which a decision was annulled for breach of the principle of proportionality.

EFFECTS OF ANNULMENT

Article 233 (ex 176) requires the institutions whose act has been declared void to take the necessary measures to comply with the judgment of the ECJ. In some cases, only part of the measure is declared invalid: see, for example, Cases 56 and 58/64 *Consten and Grundig v. Commission*. Where the act for annulment is a regulation, Article 231 (ex 174(2)) empowers the ECJ to declare which parts of the measure annulled shall be considered as definitive: see, for example, Case 81/72 *Commission v. Council* in which the ECJ ordered that staff salaries should still be paid under a regulation which had been annulled until a new regulation was issued.

In Case C-295/90 *Parliament v. Council* the EP obtained annulment of Directive 90/366, which provided for the right of residence for students, on the grounds of an incorrect legal base. Nevertheless, the ECJ ordered that the provisions of the Directive should remain in force until correctly based legislation was adopted. This was achieved by Directive 93/96 (now replaced by Directive 2004/38).

ACTION FOR INACTIVITY UNDER ARTICLE 232

Article 232 (ex 175) complements Article 230 by providing a remedy where an EC institution has failed to act. Inconsistency between the provisions of Articles 230 and 232 may be resolved by applying the 'unity principle', i.e. the same approach to both Articles: *Chevalley v. Commission* (Case 15/70). But see Case 302/87*Parliament v. Council 'Comitology'* in which this approach was rejected.

Provision

Article 232(1) EC states that if the EP, the Council or the Commission fail to act in infringement of the Treaty, the Member States and the other institutions of the EC may bring an action before the ECJ to have the infringement established. Prior to amendment by the TEU no specific provision was made to the EP. No claims for inactivity against the EP were brought in the ECJ.

Scope of Article 232

Failure to act must be an infringement of the Treaty. Such a failure includes failure to act where the institution was under a legal obligation. In Case 13/83 *Parliament v. Council* the EP brought an action under Article 232 complaining of the Council's failure to implement a common transport policy. The ECJ upheld the action in part but rejected the complaint where the obligation was too vague to be enforceable.

RIGHT TO COMPLAIN (STANDING)

'Privileged applicants'

As privileged applicants under Article 232(1) the EC institutions, including the EP after amendment by the Maastricht Treaty, may challenge any omission on the part of the Council or the Commission to adopt a binding act where there is a legal duty to act. While the Council and the Commission were specifically accorded this right under the EEC Treaty the ECJ recognised that the EP as one of the 'other institutions' is also privileged: Case 13/83 *Parliament* v. *Council*.

Individuals

Article 232(3) gives natural and legal persons the right to complain to the ECJ that an institution had failed to address to that person any act other than a recommendation or an opinion.

Where the decision is addressed to a third party the legal position is not clear. By analogy with Article 230, it would be consistent if an applicant could challenge an omission in relation to a third party where he or she is directly and individually concerned. Such a right was implied by the ECJ (although the claim failed) in Case 246/81 *Bethell* v. *Commission* in which the requirement was stated to be that the institution had failed to adopt a measure which the applicant was legally entitled to claim. See also Case 15/71 *Mackprang* v. *Commission*.

Where the applicant succeeds in establishing his or her right to complain, resulting in a decision addressed to a third party, he will be considered to be directly and individually concerned in that decision with entitlement to review under Article 230: Case 264/82 *Timex Corporation* v. *Council and Commission*.

Procedure

No action may be brought under Article 232 unless the institution in question has first been called upon to act. Following such a call, the institution has two months in which to act in accordance with the request or to define its position. If the institution fails to comply, the applicant may bring an action before the ECJ within two months.

Where the institution has defined its position but has not adopted a measure, the applicant may not invoke Article 230. No further action may be taken under Article 232. In Case 48/65 *Alfons Lütticke GmbH* v. *Commission* the ECJ held that a definition of position by the institution ends its failure to act.[8]

---

[8] See also: Case 125/78 *GEMA* v. *Commission*.

Effects of successful action

Article 233 lays down the effects of a successful action under both Articles 230 and 232. In both cases the institution concerned will be required to take the necessary measures to remedy its failure in accordance with the judgment of the ECJ. No sanctions are available, although a further action may be brought under Article 232.

INDIRECT REVIEW UNDER ARTICLE 241

Like the grounds for annulment under Article 230, the plea of illegality (or *exception d'illégalité*) also derives from French law. Under Article 241 (ex 184) an applicant may challenge the legality of a general act on which a subsequent act or omission is based without restrictive time limits.

Provision

Article 241 provides that, notwithstanding the expiry of the time limit laid down in Article 230(3), any party may, in proceedings in which a regulation of the Council or the Commission is in issue, plead the grounds specified in Article 230(1), in order to invoke before the ECJ the inapplicability of that regulation.

Scope of the provision

The plea of illegality does not give rise to an independent cause of action but may only be invoked in the context of proceedings already before the ECJ: Cases 31 and 33/62 *Wöhrmann* v. *Commission*, for example under Article 230 (or in equivalent provision, Article 35 ECSC: *SNUPAT* v. *High Authority* (Cases 42 and 49/59)). However, the ECJ refused to consider a plea under Article 241 in the context of Article 234 proceedings: Case 44/65 *Hessische Knappschaft* v. *Maison Singer et Fils*.

A plea under Article 241 may be brought by either the applicant, or by the defendant provided there is a direct judicial link between the act or omission affecting the applicant and the general measure in question: Case 32/65 *Italy* v. *Council and Commission*.

Standing

Article 241 gives the right to bring an action to 'any party'. Doubt remains over the entitlement of the institutions to bring an action. While the issue has not been decided by the ECJ it has been raised in cases such as Case 32/65 *Italy* v. *Council and Commission* and Case 156/77 *Commission* v. *Belgium* . It appears likely, however, that the liberal wording of Article 241 would enable the institutions to act.

Reviewable acts

Article 241 is stated to apply only to regulations. However, to be consistent with the approach adopted under Article 230, where the substance rather than the form determined the remedy, the ECJ held in Case 92/78 *Simmenthal SpA* v. *Commission* that a general notice of invitation to tender (the basis of a decision to the Italian government in which the applicant was directly interested) could be challenged. As a result the decision was annulled.

Grounds of review

The grounds of review under Article 241 are the same as those for annulment under Article 230.

Effects of a successful action

A successful action under Article 241 will result in the regulation in question being declared inapplicable. Any subsequent measure based on the inapplicable regulation will be void.

QUESTIONS

1 How does the capability of the European Parliament to challenge an act and to face a challenge to its own acts reflect its changing status in EC law?

2 How has the Court of Justice sought to limit the access of non-privileged applicants to judicial review? Do you think the Court has achieved the right balance in its current position?

3 Will the Treaty of Lisbon increase the access of individuals to judicial review?

Further reading

Arnull, A. (1995) 'Private Applicants and the Action for Annulment under Article 173 of the EC Treaty', (1995) 32 CMLRev. 7.

Arnull, A. (2001) 'Private Applicants and the Action for Annulment since *Codorniu*', (2001) 38 CMLRev. 7.

Chalmers, D., Hadjiemmanuil, C., Monti, G. and Tomkins, A. (2006) *European Union Law*, Cambridge University Press, Chapter 10.

Craig, P. and De Burca, G. (2007) *EU Law: Text, Cases and Materials*, 4th edition, Oxford University Press, Chapters 14 and 15.

Harlow, C. (1009) 'Towards a Theory of Access for the European Court of Justice', (1992) 12 YEL 213.

Visit **http://www.mylawchamber.co.uk/kent** to access answer guidance to questions in the book to test yourself on this chapter.

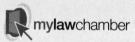

9 Liability of the Community institutions

NON-CONTRACTUAL LIABILITY OF THE EC INSTITUTIONS

Article 235 EC gives the Court of Justice jurisdiction in disputes relating to compensation for damage provided for in Article 288 EC. Article 288(2) provides that the Community shall make good any damage caused by its institutions or its servants in the performance of their duties, in accordance with the general principles common to the laws of the Member States.

The legal position changed significantly as a result of the decision in Case C-352/98P *Laboratoires Pharmaceutiques Bergaderm et Goupil* v. *Commission* (see pp.143–144). As a result, the Court focuses on a test for liability based on the exercise of discretion rather than the nature of the act or omission.

Standing and limitation

> **Key point**
>
> There are no restrictions on the standing of the persons who may bring an action under Article 288(2), in marked contrast to position under Article 230 (see Chapter 8).

The Court's liberal position on standing under Article 288(2) was established in Case 4/69 *Alfons Lütticke GmbH* v. *Commission* in which it found an action to be admissible under Article 288(2) despite the refusal of standing under Article 232. *Lütticke* represents a departure from the earlier restrictive approach in Case 25/62 *Plaumann & Co* v. *Commission* where the Court had refused to admit a claim under Article 288(2) following denial of standing under Article 230. A claim under Article 288 may thus be admissible following failure to establish standing under Article 230 unless this constitutes an abuse of process: Case C-386/96P *Société Louis Dréfus et Cie* v. *Commission*.

A five-year limitation period starts to run from the event giving rise to liability: Article 46, Statute of the Court of Justice. Claims by natural and legal persons have been heard in the Court of First Instance since 1988.

Elements of non-contractual liability

It is always necessary to demonstrate that the basic rules for liability, established in the context of liability for administrative acts, have been satisfied. The decision in Case C-352/98P *Bergaderm* (see p.143) removed the artificial distinction between acts intended to have legal consequences and administrative acts.

Key point

Liability in damages for loss arising from administrative acts arises where there has been:

- a wrongful act or omission by a Community institution or its servants;
- damage to the plaintiffs;
- a causal connection between the two: Case 4/69 *Alfons Lütticke GmbH* v. *Commission*.

Acts are divided into failures of administration and negligent acts by a servant in performance of his duties. An example of the first type may be seen in Cases 19 etc./69 *Richez-Parise* v. *Commission* in which the applicants, EC officials, had resigned after relying on incorrect information about their pensions. The ECJ held that the failure to correct the information was a failure of administration under Article 288(2).

The second type of failure has proved hard to establish. For an example of an unsuccessful action see Case 5/68 *Sayag* v. *Leduc*, where an engineer employed by EURATOM caused an accident while driving to work. The ECJ held that the use of a private car only constituted performance of his duty in exceptional circumstances such as a serious emergency.

Where the act or omission was intended to have legal consequences, liability was restricted under the criteria in Case 5/71 *Aktien-Zuckerfabrik Schöppenstedt* v. *Council* (known as the 'Schöppenstedt' formula), as restated in Cases 83 and 94/76 etc. *Bayerische HNL Vermehrungsbetriebe GmbH & Co. KG* v. *Council and Commission*. Liability only arose in areas involving choices of economic policy (in practice, often in the context of the Common Agricultural Policy).

Requirements of the Schöppenstedt formula

The formula lays down three essential requirements:

1 There must be a breach of a superior rule of law.
2 The superior rule of law must be for the protection of the individual.
3 The breach must be 'sufficiently serious'.

The first two requirements have been interpreted by the ECJ as including the general principles of EC law such as proportionality, equality or legal certainty. The principle of legitimate expectations was successfully invoked in Case C-152/88 *Sofrimport SARL* v. *Commission*. Here, an EC measure had failed to provide for goods in transit, depriving importers affected by it of the opportunity to mitigate their loss by making alternative arrangements for apples entering the EC from Chile.

In contrast with Article 230, 'individual' may include a class of people where legislation was designed to protect that class: Cases 5, 7 and 13–24/66 *Firma E. Kampffmeyer* v. *Commission*.

A 'sufficiently serious breach' was defined in *Schöppenstedt* as meaning a sufficiently flagrant violation of a superior rule of law for the protection of the individual. The requirement was narrowly construed in *Bayerische HNL* and depends on the scope of the institution's discretion.

> **Key point**
>
> Where the institution possesses a wide discretion, it will only be liable where it has manifestly and gravely disregarded the limits on the exercise of its power (*Bayerische HNL*).

The requirements of the '*Schöppenstedt*' formula are so strict that few cases succeeded on the merits. In Cases 116 and 124/77 *Amylum* v. *Council and Commission* only conduct 'verging on the abnormal' was found to be covered.

An example of an unsuccessful application may be seen in Cases C-104/89 and 37/90 *Mulder* v. *Commission and Council* where an exemption on levies on dairy products was decided by reference to the previous year's sales figures. As no products had been sold the previous year the applicants were refused an exemption. While the breach was sufficiently serious, a later change in EC rules prevented actual loss. The application failed.

> **Key point**
>
> The conditions for liability for the EC institutions are the same as those under which the Member States are liable: *Brasserie du Pêcheur/Factortame III*. Avoiding the risk of anomalies between the criteria, ie a breach of a superior rule of law for the protection of individuals, which is sufficiently serious and which caused the damage. See Case C-352/98P *Bergaderm* for an application of this approach.

EXTENDING LIABILITY: THE IMPORTANCE OF DISCRETION

It was clear from the *Schöppenstedt* formula that liability arose only in relation to loss arising from acts or omissions which were intended to have legislative consequences. The position changed as a result of Case C-352/98P *Laboratoires Pharmaceutiques Bergaderm and Goupil* v. *Commission*, from which it may be seen that it is the use of discretion which is significant. In practice, legislative acts normally involve at least some degree of discretion.

Key point

The distinction between legislative and administrative is irrelevant when considering the possible liability of the EC institutions. What matters is whether the act involves the use of discretion. The test is whether the EC institution manifestly and gravely disregarded the limits on its discretion: *Bergaderm*.

Key case

Case C-352/98P *Laboratoires Pharmaceutiques Bergaderm and Goupil* v. *Commission*.

The Commission adopted a directive which prohibited the use of a particular substance in suntan lotions as it was considered to cause cancer. Bergaderm, the only company to use the substance in question, claimed that it was driven into liquidation as a result. It sued the Commission unsuccessfully for damages in the CFI. On appeal to the ECJ Bergaderm argued that the measure was an administrative rather than a legislative act as it related to the applicant alone, and that, in consequence, it should only be necessary to establish that the act was illegal without showing that the breach was sufficiently serious.

The ECJ found that it was immaterial whether the act was legislative or administrative. What was significant was whether the act involved the use of discretion. Thus the test for whether the breach is sufficiently serious is whether the EC institution manifestly and gravely disregarded the limits on its discretion. This will be difficult to establish where the discretion is broad, but more likely when the EC institution had little discretion.

For a recent example of imposition of damages on the Commission, see Case T-178/98 *Fresh Marine* v. *Commission*. In this case the Commission misread a report and imposed anti-dumping penalties on a company for selling salmon within the EC below the price on the Norwegian market. The Court found the Commission liable in damages, holding that the mere infringement of EC law was enough to result in liability where there was little or no discretion.

● Liability arising from a lawful act

Claims for losses arising from a lawful act have been made on several occasions before the ECJ, but have never succeeded. It is clear from Case C-237/98P *Dorsch Consult* v. *Council* that unusual and special damage must be established. The applicant had entered into a construction contract with the government of Iraq in 1975. After the invasion of Kuwait by Iraq the EC adopted a regulation banning trade with Iraq, pursuant to a UN resolution. The government of Iraq froze the assets of companies doing business in Iraq. The ECJ found that the loss was caused by the UN resolution, rather than the EC regulation. Where loss arose from a lawful act, it was necessary to establish unusual and special damage. As Iraq was regarded as a 'high risk' country, the risks of doing business with it were inherent in the sector concerned.

CAUSATION AND DAMAGES

Causation

The damage suffered must not be too remote (*Lütticke*) and must be a sufficiently direct consequence of the unlawful conduct of the institution in question: Cases 64 and 113/76, 167 and 239/78, 27, 28 and 45/79 *Dumortier Fils SA* v. *Council* (refunds withheld as a result of an illegal regulation were recovered but not damages for reduced sales). Applicants must act as reasonably prudent business people: Case 169/73 *Compagnie Continentale* v. *Council*, in this case in relation to handling misleading information.

Contributory negligence

The ECJ does not usually take contributory negligence into account. However, it did so in Case 145/83 *Adams* v. *Commission (No. 1)* where damages for financial loss and emotional distress arising out of a breach of confidence by the Commission were reduced by 50 per cent as a result of the plaintiff's failure to protect himself (see Chapter 20).

There is a duty on the applicant to mitigate his loss: Case 120/83 *Raznoimport* v. *Commission*. In Cases C-104/89 and C-37/90 *Mulder* v. *Commission and Council* damages were reduced by the amount the applicants would have earned from alternative commercial activities while they were unable to produce and sell dairy products.

The applicant is unable to recover a loss which he could have passed on to his customers: Cases 261 and 262/78 *Interquell Stark-Chemie GmbH* v. *Commission*.

Recoverable damage

Actual damage, or imminent damage which is foreseeable with sufficient certainty, must be established: Cases 5, 7 and 13–24/66 *Kampffmeyer* v. *Commission*. Damages for economic loss are recoverable, but only where such losses are specific, such as those arising out of cancelled contracts already concluded: *Kampffmeyer*. Damages were *not* recovered in the following cases:

- A regulation which infringed the principle of legitimate expectations deprived the plaintiff of export refunds. Currency fluctuations prevented actual loss: Case 74/74 *CNTA SA* v. *Commission*.

9

Liability of the Community institutions

- Alleged losses of French farmers arising from German farm subsidies following a Council decision as prices had already fallen: Case 253/84 *GAEC* v. *Council and Commission*.

ROLE OF THE NATIONAL COURTS

Concurrent liability

It has been possible to bring an action against a Member State in the national courts for state liability since the decision in *Francovich*. Alternatively, it may be possible to bring an action in the CFI under Article 288(2) against the EC institutions. Such a choice raises the question as to whether the applicant is required to exhaust national remedies before bringing proceedings in the CFI. The decisions in *Kampffmeyer* and Case 96/71 *Haegemann Sprl* v. *Commission* support the need for exhaustion. In Case 175/84 *Krohn* v. *Commission* the ECJ held that where the national authority is primarily at fault (e.g. refusal to issue a licence) the action should be brought in the national courts. However, loss directly caused by an EC institution which cannot be attributed to a national body should be the subject of a claim in the ECJ.

Where a remedy is needed from both the national courts and the ECJ, applicants should bring actions before both courts: Case 26/74 *Roquette* v. *Commission*. If no effective remedy exists at national level, failure to bring an action before the national courts is not a bar to an action before the ECJ under Article 288(2): Cases 197 etc./80 *Ludwigshafener Walzmühle Erling KG* v. *Council and Commission*.

QUESTIONS

1 In May 2007 the European Parliament and the Council adopted Regulation 15/00 (imaginary) on financial assistance for hill farmers after an outbreak of foot and mouth disease in sheep. Under the Regulation hill farmers within the EU were permitted to apply for funding to replenish their stock. The deadline for applications was January 2008. Owing to a strike, the Regulation was never published in the *Official Journal*. As a result, most hill farmers remained unaware of the Regulation.

The Agriculture Commissioner, Paul, a national of Orchadia (a fictional Member State), was closely involved in formulating the original proposal for the legislation. He passed on information to the government of Orchadia about the measure and encouraged applications from farmers in his home state. As a result, the only applications received for funding were from farmers in Orchadia.

Tom is a hill farmer in Candida, a new Member State. He had to cull his entire flock of sheep during the foot and mouth outbreak and is desperate to replenish his stock

before he goes out of business. Tom was unaware of the scheme set up under Regulation 15/00 until he read about the number of successful applications from farmers in Orchadia.

Advise Tom whether he has any remedy against:

(a) Paul;

(b) the EU institutions;

(c) the government of Candida.

2 To what extent does the liability of the EC institutions in damages depend on the exercise of discretion?

3 Assume that, following a recent UN resolution on climate change, the Commission adopted a Regulation forbidding farmers from spraying their crops with pesticides and insecticides. The Preamble to the Regulation refers to research which establishes a link between the use of crop sprays and climate change. Provision is made in the Regulation for application to the Commission for exemption in cases of hardship.

Bob, a wheat farmer in the UK, consulted the National Farmers' Association which advised him that the link is not established and that it would have been more appropriate for the EU to limit the use of sprays rather than to impose a ban. Despite the imminent ban on crop spraying, Bob invested in new equipment to spray his crops. He applied for an exemption from the Commission but was refused. His crops are now suffering from plagues of insects as well as mildew.

Bob seeks your advice as to whether he can recover compensation from the Commission for his loss of profits from the damaged crops as well as the costs of the spraying equipment he can no longer use.

Further reading

Chalmers, D., Hadjiemmanuil, C., Monti, G. and Tomkins, A. (2006) *European Union Law*, Cambridge University Press, pp. 457–464.

Craig, P. and De Burca, G. (2007) *EU Law: Text, Cases and Materials*, 4th edition, Oxford University Press, Chapter 16.

Hilson, C. (2005) 'The Role of Discretion in EC Law on on-Contractual Liability', (2005) 42 CMLRev. 677.

Tridimas, T. (2001) 'Liability for Breach of Community Law: Growing Up and Mellowing Down?' (2001) 38 CMLRev. 301.

Wills, W. (1992) 'Concurrent Liability of the Community and Member State', (1992) 17 ELRev. 191.

Visit **http://www.mylawchamber.co.uk/kent** to access answer guidance to questions in the book to test yourself on this chapter.

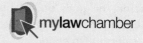

Use **Case Navigator** to read in full some of the key cases referenced in this chapter:

- C-46/49 and 48/93 **Brasserie du Pêcheur** v. **Federal Republic of Germany** and **R.** v. **Secretary of State for Transport, ex parte Factortame (Factortame III)** [1996] ECR I-1029

10 Preliminary rulings under Article 234

PROCEDURE

The procedure for obtaining a preliminary ruling on the interpretation or validity of Community law is of great significance. Most decisions of major importance by the Court of Justice have been made as a result of references under Article 234 (ex 177). By this means uniformity in the interpretation of EC law throughout the Member States has been achieved, as the Court declared in Case 166/733 *Rheinmühlen-Düsseldorf* v. *Einfuhr und Vorratsstelle Getreide*:

> Article 177 is essential for the Community character of the law established by the Treaty and has the object of ensuring that in all circumstances this law is the same in all states in the Community.

The procedure provides a means by which a national court, in need of guidance on a point of interpretation or validity of EC law, may formulate a question or questions for clarification by the ECJ. At this stage, national proceedings are suspended until a ruling is given by the ECJ. The ECJ does *not* apply the law. It is the function of the national court, with the benefit of the ECJ ruling, to apply the law and reach a decision on the facts.

Article 234: the provision

Article 234(1) provides that the ECJ shall have jurisdiction to give preliminary rulings concerning:

(a) the interpretation of the EC Treaty;
(b) the validity and interpretation of acts of the institutions of the Community and of the European Central Bank (ECB);
(c) the interpretation of the statutes of bodies established by an act of the Council, where those statutes so provide.

Under Article 234(2), where such a question is raised before any court or tribunal of the Member State, that court or tribunal may, if it considers that a question is necessary to enable it to give judgment, request the ECJ to give a ruling on it.

Under Article 234(3), where any such question is raised in a case pending before a court or tribunal of a Member State, against whose decisions there is no judicial remedy under national law, that court or tribunal shall bring the matter before the ECJ.

Key point

The Treaty of Lisbon will remove the reference to the ECB from Article 234(b) as well as the whole of point (c) (interpretation of statutes, etc.). It will add a new paragraph (4):

> If such proceedings are raised in a case pending before a court or tribunal of a Member State with regard to a person in custody, the Court of Justice will act with the minimum of delay.

Key point

The jurisdiction of the ECJ under Article 234 is restricted to questions of EC law. Thus, it may not interpret domestic law, nor may it rule on the validity of a particular national provision under EC law.

The ECJ is not empowered under Article 234 to consider questions concerning alleged failure to act on the part of the EC institutions: Case C-68/95 *T. Port GmbH & Co. KG* v. *Bundesanstalt für Landwirtschaft und Ernährung*.

What is a 'court or tribunal'?

Article 234 provides that 'any court or tribunal of a Member State' has the power to make a reference. It does not matter how the body making the reference is named. The criteria that the Court may take into account to establish whether the body is a 'court or tribunal' were set out in Case C-54/96 *Dorsch Consult*, namely whether the body is established by law, is permanent, has compulsory jurisdiction, its procedure is *inter partes*, it applies rules of law and is independent.

The following were held by the ECJ to be a 'court or tribunal' for the purposes of Article 234:

- an appeal committee (in this case, the Dutch medical body which had refused the applicant registration as a GP): Case 246/80 *Broekmeulen*;
- a magistrate acting as both prosecutor and investigating judge: Case 14/86 *Pretore di Salo* v. *Persons Unknown*;
- an administrative tribunal in a French overseas territory: Cases C-100/89 and C-101/89 *Kaefer and Procacci* v. *France*.

A key factor appears to be the element of public control or participation lacking in the following, which were held by the ECJ *not* to constitute a court or tribunal:

- the Council of the Paris Bar (in an action arising out of a request for a declaration that a member of the Paris Bar denied access to a court in Germany was entitled to provide legal services under EC law): Case 138/80 *Borker*;
- an arbitrator appointed under a private contract (without consideration by the ECJ of the significance of excluding recourse to the courts): Case 102/81 *Nordsee Deutsche Hochseefischerei GmbH*.

Courts with a discretion to refer

Any court or tribunal not covered by the obligation to refer under Article 234(3) has a discretion to refer to the ECJ when it considers that a reference is *necessary*. In reaching a decision the national courts must exercise their discretion, subject to the *CILFIT* criteria.

When is a reference necessary?

In general terms a reference will be necessary when a national court requires a ruling from the ECJ in order to give judgment. The ECJ provided guidelines in Case 283/81 *CILFIT Srl*, a reference from the Italian Supreme Court, as to when a reference is *not* 'necessary'. These guidelines were drawn up in relation to the mandatory jurisdiction of the national courts, but apply also to their discretionary jurisdiction.

Key case

A group of textile firms in Italy challenged an EC levy on wool imported from outside the EC. The central question was whether wool should be regarded as an animal product. (Animal products were outside the scope of the Regulation applying the levy.) The Italian Minstry of Health argued that there was no need to refer the matter to the ECJ as it was obvious that wool was an animal product. The Court of Cassation (highest civil court in Italy) decided, however, to make a reference to the ECJ. The decision of the ECJ is of great importance for the guidance it provides to the national court as to when it is appropriate for a national court to refer. The decision is expressed in the negative.

The ECJ held that a reference is not necessary where:

- The question of EC law is irrelevant.
- The question has already been decided by the ECJ.
- The correct interpretation is so obvious as to leave no scope for doubt.

This question must be examined on the basis of the special features of EC law, in particular the need for a uniform interpretation despite the existence of texts in different languages and the use of concepts and terminology which differ from the national legislation: Case 283/81 *CILFIT Srl*.

It has been argued by some commentators[1] that the *CILFIT* criteria are almost meaningless. What matters is the spirit of the decision as encouragement to national courts to reach their own decisions on matters of EC law (Chalmers *et al.*, 2006: 300). In practice many national courts of last resort have exercised their independence by failing to refer questions that were necessary to resolve a dispute.[2]

---

[1] E.g. Rasmussen (1989).

[2] There were no referrals made by such courts between 1999 and 2002 in various Member States including Germany, the Netherlands, France and Italy (Chalmers *et al.*, 2006: 301).

Lord Denning sought to guide the UK courts in *Bulmer* v. *Bollinger* as to the factors that should be taken into account when deciding to refer. The guidelines (considerations of time, delay, cost, workload of the ECJ, the wishes of the parties) were influential in the UK but have been overtaken by the *CILFIT* criteria.

There must be a genuine question of EC law

Key point

The ECJ will not rule on a question which has been artificially fabricated by the parties in order to obtain an ECJ ruling: Case 104/79 *Foglia* v. *Novella (No. 1)* and Case 244/80 *(No. 2)*.

The question must involve genuine issues of EC law, which have been raised before the national court, either by one of the parties or by the court itself: Case 126/80 *Salonia* v. *Poidomani*. In Case 244/80 *Foglia* v. *Novella (No.2)* the ECJ stated that its function under Article 234 was to assist in the administration of justice in the Member States, not to give advisory opinions on general or hypothetical questions.

The ECJ refused to rule in Case C-83/91 *Meilicke* on an academic, artificially constructed question. This approach was confirmed in Case C-343/90 *Dias* v. *Director da Alfandego do Porto* in which the ECJ held that it will not rule where the question appears to be 'manifestly irrelevant' to the decision.

In order to ensure the uniform interpretation of EC law, the ECJ has jurisdiction to give a preliminary ruling on the interpretation of a provision of EC law where the national law of a Member State referred to the content of that provision in order to determine the rules applicable to a purely internal situation in that state: Joined Cases C-297/88 and C-197/89 *Dzodzi* v. *Belgium*, a case involving the application of EC social security rules outside the EC where national law referred to EC rules. This approach was confirmed in Case C-130/95 *Giloy* where the Court held that it will only reject a request for a reference from a national court 'if it appears that the procedure laid down in Article [234] has been misused and a ruling elicited from the Court by means of a contrived dispute, or it is obvious that Community law cannot apply'[3] to the circumstances of the case.

Notes for guidance on references by national courts for preliminary rulings

The following Notes for guidance were issued by the ECJ in 1996 to provide a summary of advice from the case law of the Court on the necessity of making a reference.

---

[3] At paragraph 22 of the judgment.

They are reproduced in full as they continue to provide a useful summary of the Court's position:

1 While any court or tribunal of a member state may ask for an interpretation, courts or tribunals against whose decision there is no judicial remedy must refer unless the ECJ has already ruled on the point or unless the application of the rule of EC law is obvious: Case 283/81 *CILFIT*.

2 The ECJ may rule on the validity of acts of the EC institution. Where a national court intends to question the validity of an EC act, it must refer: Case 314/85 *Foto-Frost*. Where the national court has serious doubts about the validity of an EC measure on which a national measure is based, it may suspend the national measure (or provide other interim relief) and must refer: Cases C-143/88 and C-92/89 *Zuckerfabrik*.

3 Questions for referral must be limited to the interpretation or validity of a provision of EC law. The national courts apply the law, in the light of the ruling.

4 The order referring a question may be in any form permissible under national law. Pending the ECJ ruling, national proceedings are usually suspended.

5 The order for reference must be translated by the ECJ into the other official languages.

6 The order for reference should include a statement of reasons (facts, national law, reasons prompting the referral, statement of reasons and, where relevant, summary of the parties' arguments). This must be succinct but complete enough to provide an understanding of the factual and legal content to enable the ECJ to provide a helpful answer.

7 The national court may refer as soon as it finds that a ruling from the ECJ is necessary, but preferably not before the national court has defined the factual and legal context, and both parties have been heard: Case 70/77 *Simmenthal*.

Acte clair and acte éclairé

Acte clair is a doctrine deriving from French administrative law according to which no question of interpretation is taken to arise from a provision where the meaning is clear. *Acte éclairé* refers to the entitlement of national courts not to refer when the ECJ has already pronounced on a materially identical point.

Limited endorsement of the principle of *acte clair* was given by the ECJ in Cases 28–30/62 *Da Costa en Schaake NV* (national courts should refer every question for interpretation to the ECJ unless a previous ruling had been made on a materially identical question) and in *CILFIT*.

Courts for which referral is mandatory

While any court or tribunal *may* make a reference to the ECJ, Article 234(3) provides that, where a question of interpretation is raised before any court or tribunal of a member state against whose decisions there is no judicial remedy under national law, that court or tribunal *shall* bring the matter before the ECJ.

Abstract or concrete theory?

The scope of Article 234(3) has given rise to controversy over the years. According to the 'abstract' or 'narrow' view, only courts of final resort such as the House of Lords in the UK and the Conseil d'Etat in France are covered. However, in many circumstances there may be no right of appeal from a decision of a lower court (e.g. the Court of Appeal when leave to appeal to the House of Lords is refused). The UK courts tended to favour the abstract view, with the result that referrals were left to the House of Lords in some significant cases: see, for example *R. v. Henn and Darby*[4] and *Webb v. EMO*.[5]

Unlike various national courts, the ECJ itself has long followed the 'concrete' or 'wide' view of which courts are obliged to refer. This is illustrated by Case 6/64 *Costa v. ENEL*, a referral from an Italian small claims court from which there was no right of appeal due to the low sum claimed. The ECJ held that national courts from whose decisions there is no judicial remedy, as in the present case, *must* refer the matter to the ECJ.

Key point

National courts against whose decisions there is no judicial remedy are covered by the obligation to refer cases to the ECJ under Article 234(3).

Until the decision in *Lyckeskog,* the ECJ had not ruled on the position of a national court from which an appeal was available to a higher court, provided it was found to be admissible.

Key case

Lyckeskog was convicted by a district court in Sweden of attempting to smuggle 500 kg of rice from Norway into Sweden. The court found that the quantity of rice showed that he was a commercial importer, as the permissible level for importation was only 20 kg. Lyckescog appealed to the Court of Appeal for Western Sweden. An appeal brought in an action by an individual lay from this court to the Supreme Court, provided the Supreme Court found it to be admissible. The Appeal Court, despite taking the view that it could rule on the merits of the case, decided to refer to the ECJ questions to determine whether a court in its position was covered by the obligation to refer under Article 234(3), as well as questions on customs duties.

The ECJ held that decisions of a national appellate court which can be challenged before a supreme court are not covered by the obligation to refer under Article 234(3) even where an appeal on the merits of the case is subject to a declaration of admissibility. If a question arises as to interpretation or validity, the supreme court should refer a question to the ECJ either at the stage when it examines admissibility or at a later stage: Case C-99/00 *Kenny Roland Lyckeskog.*

[4] See Chapter 12.
[5] See Chapter 24.

Applying the *Lyckeskog* decision to the UK courts, it may be seen that the Court of Appeal will not be covered by the obligation to refer under Article 234(3). The House of Lords will be obliged to refer, either when considering an application for leave to appeal or when hearing the appeal itself. It does not follow that the House of Lords will be the only court covered by the obligation to refer. Instead, it is necessary to see whether an appeal lies to a higher court and whether leave to appeal is required.

However, it should be remembered that the *acte clair* and *acte éclairé* principles apply to Article 234(3). A national court of last resort need not make a reference under Article 234(3) where one of the three criteria in *CILFIT* is satisfied.

National courts wrongly refusing to refer cases to the ECJ under Article 234 may be accountable for breach of state liability, following the decision in Case C-224/01 *Kobler* v. *Austria*. The Court found that damages may be available where it was manifestly apparent that a court had failed to observe its duties under Article 234, where neither *acte clair* nor *acte éclairé* applied. In the particular case, the ECJ did not find Austria liable, as it wrongly (but in good faith) considered that the matter was covered by a previous ruling.

Rulings on validity

The ECJ has jurisdiction under Article 234 to provide rulings on the validity of secondary legislation. In Case 314/85 *Foto-Frost* v. *Hauptzollamt Lubeck-Ost* the Court of Justice held that national courts cannot declare the acts of the EC institutions invalid under Article 234. Only the ECJ may do so. The Court indicated that there may perhaps be scope for a national court to grant an interim injunction, though it did not rule.

This point came up in Joined Cases C-143/88 and C-92/89 *Zuckerfabrik Suderdithmarschen AG* v. *Hauptzollamt Itzehoe*. The Court held that the power of national courts to order the suspension of an administrative act of a national authority based on an EC measure whose validity is in doubt was equivalent to the power of the ECJ to suspend a contested act under Article 242 of the Treaty in interim proceedings. A national court may thus suspend a national measure implementing an EC regulation where:

- The national court entertains serious doubts as to the validity of the EC measure and itself refers the question of validity to the ECJ, if this has not already been done.
- There is urgency and the threat of irreparable damage to the applicant.
- The national court takes due account of the interests of the EC.

Effect of an Article 234 ruling

An Article 234 ruling by the ECJ binds the national court in the case in which the reference was made: Case 29/68 *Milch-Fett-und Eierkontor* v. *HZA Saarbrucken* and any other national court considering the same point of EC law. It is, however, open to another national court to request a fresh interpretation: Joined Cases 28–30/62 *Da*

Costa, though not on a question of validity: Case 66/80 *ICI* v. *Italian Financial Administration*.

Third-Pillar competence

The Treaty of Amsterdam (TOA) moved a number of areas covered by the Third Pillar, relating to Police and Judicial Co-operation in Criminal Matters to the First Pillar, the EC. As a result, the ECJ has been given jurisdiction to deal with certain measures under the preliminary reference procedure under Title IV of the EC Treaty and Title VI of the TEU.

Title IV of the EC Treaty (Visas, Asylum, Immigration, etc.)
The Council is empowered under Title IV to adopt measures to establish progressively an area of freedom, security and justice, as well as measures in relation to asylum, immigration, judicial co-operation relating to civil matters with cross-border implications such as visas, measures to encourage and strengthen administrative co-operation and measures of police and judicial co-operation to combat crime.

Article 68 EC provides for referral under Article 234 to the ECJ, but only by national courts against whose decisions there is no judicial remedy where the national court considers that a referral is necessary to enable it to give judgment. The wording of Article 68 is narrower than Article 234 as it precludes requests from the lower courts: Case C-45/03 *Dem 'Yanenko'*.

Under Article 68(3) the Council, Commission or a Member State may request the ECJ to give a ruling on a question of interpretation or validity under the Title.

Title VI of the TEU (Police and Judicial Co-operation)
The TOA brought Title VI (Police and Judicial Co-operation) within the remit of the ECJ, but only where each Member State involved accepts the Court's jurisdiction: Article 35 TEU.

The jurisdiction of the ECJ extends to giving preliminary rulings on various Third Pillar measures, namely the 'validity and interpretation of framework decisions and decisions on the interpretation of conventions established under this Title and on the validity and interpretation of the measures implementing them'. Framework decisions are decisions to harmonise the laws of the Member States to promote the objectives of the Third Pillar. Their form is similar to directives, though they lack direct effect. It would appear that the ECJ still expects the doctrine of indirect effect to apply to framework decision, as may be seen from the *Pupino* decision.

Key case

Pupino was a nursery school teacher who was accused of having mistreated children in her care in Italy. The Italian Public Prosecutor sought to take evidence from the children at the first stage of criminal proceedings, contrary to the normal practice of waiting until the second part of proceedings. The Italian court acknowledged that it could not grant the request as the circumstances were beyond those permitted by Italian law. It made a preliminary referral to the ECJ to seek clarification on the status of a Council Framework Decision on the standing of victims. The ECJ held that framework decisions bind the Member States as to the result to be achieved. The duty to interpret national law with EC law applies to framework decisions: Case C-105/03 *Pupino*.

Member States may choose, by making a declaration, to limit the possibility of referral to the ECJ to national courts against whose decisions there is no judicial remedy. The ECJ has no jurisdiction under Article 35 to review the legality or proportionality of operations carried out by the police or other national law enforcement agencies.

Reforming the preliminary reference procedure

For many years concern has been expressed that the ever-increasing workload of the ECJ made it impossible for the Court to act sufficiently expeditiously. Various solutions have been proposed, including handing over some of the Court's workload under Article 234 to the CFI and encouraging the national courts to act more effectively as a filter for references. For the first time, under the Treaty of Amsterdam, the CFI was empowered to give preliminary rulings in areas prescribed by the Statute of the Court. The CFI may remit the case directly to the ECJ where it considers there is a decision of principle which may affect the unity or consistency of EC law. Alternatively, the ECJ may review a decision of the CFI where such considerations apply.

The ECJ has been entitled since 2000[6] to use a simplified procedure for preliminary references where the question referred is identical to one referred earlier, where the answer may clearly be deduced from the case law or where the answer admits of no reasonable doubt. It is concluded by a reasoned order after national courts have been informed and interested parties heard. There are no oral arguments or Advocate-General's submissions. The new procedure has enabled the Court in some cases to provide a response in as little as five months rather than two years or so. In 2006 it was used in 33 per cent of all preliminary references.[7] Whether the simplified procedure brings real benefit should be considered in the context of the *CILFT* criteria, as it may be argued that the national courts could have reached their own decisions in these circumstances without referring a question to the ECJ. An accelerated procedure for urgent cases is also available following a similar route.

---

[6] Under Article 104 of its Rules of Procedure.
[7] Proceedings of the Court of Justice, Annual Report 2006.

QUESTIONS

1 How has the preliminary reference procedure under Article 234 provided the Court of Justice with a mechanism to develop Community law? Explain with particular reference to the Court's role in relation to interpretation of the Treaty and secondary legislation.

2 Assume that the UK requires fruit growers who are producing pears for export to the rest of the EU to obtain an export licence from the Panel of Pear Producers (PPP), a committee of local growers. The Panel is mainly concerned with the quality and size of the pears. Anyone selling pears for export without a licence may be prosecuted. An appeal lies against its decision to the Fruit Licensing Board (FLB), which is composed of government agricultural experts and other public officials, and from there to the High Court. In the event of a dispute, the parties may resolve any disagreements through arbitration (ARB), if both agree.

Sally, a pear grower in East Anglia, has recently produced a new strain of pear for export throughout the EU. The pear is smaller than most, but has a delicate flavour. She is worried that her application for a licence to the PPP may be turned down, and considers that the requirement for a licence is in breach of EU law.

If there is any doubt about the legal position, Sally would like the body dealing with her application to make a reference to the Court of Justice.

Advise Sally, in principle, which of the following would have either a discretion or a duty to refer any question for interpretation to the Court of Justice:

(a) the PPP;

(b) the FLB;

(c) the ARB;

(d) the High Court;

(e) the House of Lords.

3 How did the Treaty of Amsterdam extend the competence of the ECJ to give preliminary rulings on matters previously within the Third Pillar? Are there any drawbacks resulting from limitations to the Court's jurisdiction in this area?

Further reading

Chalmers, D., Hadjiemmanuil, C., Monti, G. and Tomkins, A. (2006) *European Union Law*, Cambridge University Press, Chapter 7.

Craig, P. and De Burca, G. (2007) *EU Law: Text, Cases and Materials*, 4th edition, Oxford University Press, Chapter 13.

Rasmussen, H. (1989) 'The European Court's *Acte Clair* Strategy in CILFIT', (1989) 9 ELRev. 242.

Rasmussen, H. (2000) 'Remedying the Crumbling EC Judicial System', (2000) 37 CMLRev. 1071.

Tridimas, T. (2003) 'Knocking on Heaven's Door: Fragmentation, Efficiency and Defiance in the Preliminary Reference Procedure', (2003) 40 CMLRev. 9.

Visit **http://www.mylawchamber.co.uk/kent** to access answer guidance to questions in the book to test yourself on this chapter.

Part 2

FREE MOVEMENT WITHIN THE SINGLE MARKET

Customs duties and discriminatory internal taxation; State monopolies of a commercial nature

INTRODUCTION

The EC Treaty provides for an internal market comprising an area within which the free movement of goods, persons, services and capital are ensured in accordance with the Treaty: Article 14 (ex 7A). A common tariff (rate of duty) is applied to imports entering the Community from outside: Article 23 (ex 25). Discriminatory taxation is prohibited: Article 90 (ex 95). The Treaty requires that all quantitative restrictions and measures having equivalent effect on the free movement of goods must be eliminated: Articles 28–30 (ex 30–36) (see Chapter 12). State monopolies of a commercial nature may also disturb the free movement of goods and must be 'adjusted' under Article 31.

Key term

The term **goods** is not defined in the Treaty and is used interchangeably with 'products'. In Case 7/68 *Commission* v. *Italy (Re Export Tax on Art Treasures)* the ECJ defined 'goods' as meaning anything capable of money valuation and of being the object of commercial transactions. It may even have a negative value (e.g. shipments of non-recyclable waste): Case C-2/90 *Commission* v. *Belgium (Walloon Waste)*. The term was held to cover goods supplied in a contract for work and materials as well as goods in a contract of sale: Case 45/87 *Commission* v. *Ireland (Re Dundalk Water Supply)*. In Case 7/78 *R.* v. *Thompson*, gold and silver collectors' coins were found to be 'goods' provided the coins were not in circulation as legal tender.

Customs union

A customs union is a limited form of integration between the participating States involving the removal of tariff barriers between participating States (see below). It involves little loss of sovereignty and was achieved early in the development of the EC in 1968. Article 23 (ex 9) of the EC Treaty requires Member States to form a customs union involving:

- the prohibition between the Member States of customs duties on imports and exports and of charges having an equivalent effect;
- the adoption of a common customs tariff in relation to third countries (i.e. non-Member States).

Key term

The **Common Customs Tariff (CCT)** is the rate at which customs duty is applied to goods entering the EU from outside. It is governed by Article 26 (ex 28) of the EC Treaty, requiring the Council by a qualified majority to fix the rate. The CCT is published by the Commission and regularly updated.

In a customs union the abolition of duties is not limited to goods originating in the contracting States. It also covers goods coming from third countries which are in free circulation in the Member States: Article 23(2). The application of a common tariff to third countries prevents goods produced outside the EC from entering the internal market at a lower tariff than EC produced goods.

PROHIBITION OF CUSTOMS DUTIES ON IMPORTS AND EXPORTS WITHIN THE EC AND OF ALL CHARGES OF EQUIVALENT EFFECT: ARTICLE 25

Article 25 (ex 25) prohibits customs duties on imports and exports and charges having equivalent effect between Member States. The prohibition is stated also to apply to customs duties of a fiscal nature.

Under the original Treaty provisions on the customs union, old Article 12 prohibited the imposition of new customs duties and equivalent charges, whereas old Article 13 required Member States to abolish existing duties within the transitional period in accordance with old Articles 15–16. Old Articles 12–17 were repealed, as the distinction between new and existing duties had become outdated. Article 25 (ex 12) now provides for the prohibition in a single Article for both imports and exports, as well as for equivalent charges. Old Article 12 was held to be directly effective in the well-known case of *Van Gend en Loos*. It was applied equally to agricultural goods: Cases 90 and 91/63 *Commission* v. *Luxembourg and Belgium*.

Key case

Ureaformaldehyde, an essential element in the making of glue, was reclassified under Dutch law, as a result of which it attracted a higher rate of duty. Such a reclassification was held by the ECJ to contravene old Article 12: Case 26/62 *Van Gend en Loos*.

Exceptions to the rule in Article 25 are not permitted: Case 7/68 *Commission* v. *Italy (Re Export Tax on Art Treasures)* in which the ECJ held that old Article 36 (now 30) could not be invoked to justify an illegal tax levied by the Italian government to protect the national artistic heritage. The position may be contrasted with that of Article 28 (ex 30) and 29 (ex 34) on the free movement of goods, which permit derogations under Article 30 (ex 36).

'Charges having equivalent effect'

Abolition of charges

Article 25 provides for the abolition of charges having an effect equivalent to import duties. Such charges must be interpreted in the spirit of the Treaty, particularly the provisions on free movement of goods.

In Case 24/68 *Commission* v. *Italy* ('Statistical Levy') the Italian government had levied a charge for the compilation of statistical data in trade patterns. The ECJ held that the advantage to individual traders was too uncertain to be an identifiable benefit. As a result there had been a breach of old Articles 9–16. The ECJ declared that:

> any pecuniary charge . . . which is imposed unilaterally on domestic or foreign goods by reason of the fact that they cross a frontier and which is not a customs duty in the strict sense constitutes a charge having equivalent effect within the meaning of Articles 9, 12, 13 and 16 of the Treaty, even if it is not imposed for the benefit of the State, is not discriminatory or protective in effect and if the product on which the charge is imposed is not in competition with any domestic product.

Disguised charges

Charges having equivalent effect come in many forms and may be disguised as a tax or levy.

Key case

Cases 2 and 3/69 *Social Fonds voor de Diamantarbeiders* arose out of a levy on imported diamonds imposed by the Belgian government. The levy was not protectionist as Belgium did not produce diamonds, but was intended to provide social security benefits for diamond workers. The ECJ ruled that customs duties on goods between Member States are prohibited independently of their purpose and destination. The imposition of any charge on goods crossing a frontier amounts to an obstacle to the free movement of goods.

A **genuine tax**, however, is permissible provided it complies with Article 90: see below.

> **Key point**
>
> A charge levied as a payment for services is permissible but is limited in scope. Such charges are carefully considered by the Court and are not readily accepted.

The difficulties for the State in establishing the right to recover the charges are illustrated by the case law of the Court. A mandatory inspection charge under a common EC scheme may be recovered: Case 46/76 *Bauhuis* v. *Netherlands*, but not an inspection merely *permitted* under EC law: Case 314/82 *Commission* v. *Belgium (Re Health Inspection Service)*, or a storage charge imposed by Belgium on imported goods temporarily stored for customs clearance under an EC transit scheme: Case 132/82 *Commission* v. *Belgium*.

There will be no breach of Article 25 unless all three conditions set out in Case 77/76 *Fratelli Cucchi* v. *Avez SpA* (see below) are fulfilled. However, there may be a breach of Article 90 (discriminatory taxation) or of Article 87 (state aids): Case 73/79 *Commission* v. *Italy (Re Reimbursement of Sugar Storage Costs)*.

Sums paid under an illegal charge must be repaid by the Member State, since Article 23 is directly effective. National law must not be allowed to frustrate recovery: Case 199/82 *Amministrazione della Finanze dello Stato* v. *San Giorgio*.

Non-discriminatory charges

A non-discriminatory charge taxed at the same rate regardless of source should be reviewed in the light of Article 90. However, if the proceeds of the charge are applied to the exclusive benefit of the domestic product, there may still be a breach of Article 25: Case 70/72 *Capalonga* v. *Azienda Articolo Maya*, in which Italy introduced a charge on both imported and domestically produced egg boxes to finance the domestic production of paper and cardboard. The ECJ held that the charge was discriminatory. The decision was modified by the ECJ in *Fratelli Cucchi* and *Interzuccheri*.

> **Key cases**
>
> *Fratelli Cucchi* and *Interzuccheri* concerned the legality of a levy on imported and domestically produced sugar, intended for the exclusive benefit of national sugar refineries and sugar beet producers. In both cases the ECJ ruled that such a charge would be of equivalent effect to a customs duty if:
>
> - it has the sole purpose of providing financial support for the specific advantage of the domestic product;
> - the taxed product and the domestic product benefiting from it are the same;
> - the charges imposed on the domestic product are made good in full.
>
> Case 77/76 *Fratelli Cucchi* v. *Avez SpA* and Case 105/76 *Interzuccheri* v. *Ditta Rezzano e Cassava*.

PROHIBITION OF DISCRIMINATORY TAXATION: ARTICLE 90

A 'genuine tax'

The importance of the distinction between a genuine tax and a charge having equivalent effect has already been considered: see above.

> **Key term**
>
> A **genuine tax** was defined by the Court in Case 90/79 *Commission* v. *France (Re Levy on Reprographic Machines)* as a measure relating to a system of internal dues applied systematically to categories of products in accordance with objective criteria irrespective of the origin of the products.

Genuine taxes are subject to Article 90 (ex 95) which provides:

> No Member State shall impose, directly or indirectly, on the products of the other member states any internal taxation of any kind in excess of that imposed directly or indirectly on similar domestic products.
>
> Furthermore, no Member State shall impose on the products of other member states any internal taxation of such nature as to afford indirect protection to other products.

Article 90 allows Member States the freedom to establish the taxation system for each product provided there is no discrimination against imported products or indirect protection of domestic products.

> **Key point**
>
> The purpose of Article 90 is to abolish discrimination against imported products, not to accord them tax privileges: Case 253/83 *Kupferberg*.

Thus, internal taxation may be imposed on imported products where the charge relates to the whole class of products, irrespective of origin, even in the absence of a domestically produced counterpart: Case 90/79 *Commission* v. *France*. Article 90 does not prohibit the imposition of a higher rate of tax on domestic than on imported products: Case 86/78 *Grandes Distillerie Peureux* v. *Directeur des Services Fiscaux*. In Case 28/67 *Molkerei-Zentrale* v. *Hauptzollamt Paderborn*, the ECJ ruled that the words 'directly or indirectly' must be construed broadly to include all taxation actually and specifically imposed on the domestic products at earlier stages of the manufacturing process.

'Similar' products

> **Key point**
>
> To be covered by Article 90 it is not necessary that products are identical. It is enough if they are **similar**, an expression which the ECJ has held must be widely interpreted.

Most cases alleging discrimination under Article 90 have arisen in the context of the taxation of alcoholic drinks.

Examples
1 A comparison was made between fruit liqueur wines and whisky. The ECJ held that it was not enough that both products contained alcohol. To be 'similar', alcohol would have to be present in more or less equal quantities. As whisky contained twice as much alcohol as fruit liqueur wines it was not similar, within the meaning of old Article 95(2) (now Article 90(2)): Case 243/84 *John Walker*.
2 In the UK wine is more highly taxed and less widely drunk than beer. Allowing for changing habits and the growing popularity of wine, the ECJ held that it was possible to compare beer with certain categories of lighter, cheaper wines: Case 170/78 *Commission* v. *UK (Re Excise Duties on Wine)*.

It is permissible to tax 'similar' products differently where the difference is based on objective criteria to achieve acceptable economic objectives: *see* Case 196/85 *Commission* v. *France* in which 'traditional' natural sweet wines were taxed at a lower rate than ordinary wine. The ECJ accepted as justified the purpose of the differential (to provide economic assistance to rural areas dependent on wine production). There was no contravention of EC law without protectionist or discriminatory motives.

Indirect discrimination against imports

Internal taxation contravenes Article 90(2) if it discriminates against imports. Unlike Article 90(1), Article 90(2) does not provide for a direct comparison between domestic and imported products. Indirect protection will occur where the imported products are taxed more heavily than their domestic competitors: *Fink Frucht GmbH* (Case 27/67). See also Case 170/78 *Commission* v. *UK* (above), in which the ECJ held that whichever criteria for comparison were adopted, the tax system benefited domestic production.

> **Key point**
>
> Particular risk of indirect discrimination arises from the use of a sliding scale of taxation which distinguishes between imports and exports.

Examples

1 The German government taxed small brewers, normally German, on a scale which benefited them to the detriment of larger brewers, normally importers, who were charged at a fixed rate. The ECJ held that the possibility of discrimination under such a system amounted to a breach of old Article 95: Case 127/75 *Bobie* v. *HZA Aachen-Nord*.

2 The French government applied road tax on a sliding scale with a significantly higher rate payable on cars exceeding 16 c-v (horsepower) rating. No cars exceeding 16 c-v were made in France. A French taxpayer who imported a 36 c-v Mercedes from Germany sought repayment in the French courts of the tax differential. The ECJ held that such a system of taxation amounted to indirect discrimination based on nationality, contrary to old Article 95: Case 112/84 *Humblot* v. *Directeur des Services Fiscaux*.

3 In an attempt to remedy the discrimination found in *Humblot* the French government amended the taxation system to introduce nine new categories under the sliding scale for tax purposes. The rate of taxation increased sharply at 16 c-v. The ECJ found that the discrimination had merely been modified but not removed: Case 433/85 *Feldain* v. *Directeur des Services Fiscaux*.

STATE MONOPOLIES UNDER THE EC TREATY

Adjustment of State monopolies: Article 31

Under Article 31(1) (ex 37)(1) Member States must adjust any state monopolies of a commercial character to ensure that no discrimination exists between nationals of Member States affecting conditions under which goods are procured and marketed. Article 31(1) has been directly effective from the end of the transitional period: Case 59/75 *Pubblico Ministero* v. *Flavia Manghera*. Article 31(2) also provides for a 'standstill' on the introduction of any new measures contrary to Article 31(1). This provision has been directly effective from the entry into force of the Treaty: Case 6/64 *Costa* v. *ENEL*.

> **Key term**
>
> To be considered a **state monopoly**, the organisation in question need not enjoy exclusive control over the market in particular goods. It will be covered if the object of the organisation is to enter into transactions involving a commercial product which is capable of being traded between Member States, and to play an effective part in such trade: Case 6/64 *Costa* v. *ENEL*.

Article 31 does not prohibit the existence of monopolies. Its purpose is to prevent the discriminatory use of monopolies, with resulting obstruction to the free movement of goods and distortion of competition. (A parallel may be drawn with Article 82 EC which does not prohibit the holding of a dominant position, merely the abuse

169

of dominance.) State monopolies in the provision of services are not prohibited by Article 31: Case 155/73 *Italy* v. *Sacchi*. But see Case 271/81 *Société d'Insemination Artificielle* in which the ECJ recognised that a monopoly over the provision of services may indirectly influence trade in goods. State monopolies in relation to services may contravene other Treaty provisions: Article 12 (non-discrimination), Articles 49–55 (services) and Article 82 (competition).

STATE MONOPOLIES AND OTHER PROVISIONS OF THE TREATY

There is little need today to invoke Article 31 in relation to differential taxation, where Article 90 is to be preferred, although it is still relevant in the context of Articles 28–30.

Key point

In Case 148/77 *Hansen*, a case arising out of differential rates of tax applied by the German Federal Monopoly Administration, the ECJ decided that it was preferable to consider the issue from the perspective of Article 90 rather than Article 31.

This emphasis is supported by later decisions in Case 120/78 *Cassis* and the first *Grandes Distilleries* case (Case 86/78) concerning the French alcohol monopoly. The ECJ held that at the end of the transitional period internal taxes were subject exclusively to old Article 95. Old Article 37 was held to apply only to activities intrinsically connected with the specific business of the monopoly. These activities must be capable of affecting trade between Member States. In the second of the *Grandes Distilleries* cases (Case 119/78), the ECJ held that old Article 37 required the adjustment but not the abolition of state monopolies. However, the distinction between alcohol produced domestically from national raw materials and alcohol produced domestically from raw materials from other Member States contravened Articles 30 and 37 (now Articles 28 and 31). It follows that internal charges after the transitional period are regulated by Article 90, not Article 31.

Article 31 may, however, still be applied in conjunction with the other provisions on the elimination of quantitative restrictions, customs duties and charges having equivalent effect. In Case C-189/95 *Harry Franzén* the Court of Justice found that provisions restricting the sale of alcohol to a state monopoly of retail outlets such as those in force in Sweden did not contravene Article 31. The Court considered the monopoly provisions again in Case C-170/04 *Rosengren and others*. The Court found that the ban on direct imports of alcoholic drinks into Sweden by private individuals did not constitute a rule relating to the existence or operation of the monopoly relating to the sale of alcohol. As a result the restriction was outside Article 31 and had to be assessed under Article 28. The Court held that the ban was disproportionate and unjustifiable under Article 30 EC.

QUESTIONS

1 What is the underlying purpose of Article 90 (ex 95) in relation to genuine taxes?

2 What is the meaning of 'similar' products under Article 90 (ex 95)? When is it permissible to tax similar products at a differential rate?

3 How, following the end of the transitional period, has the scope of Article 31 been limited in relation to State monopolies?

Further reading

Arnull, A., Dashwood, A., Dougan, M., Ross, M., Spaventa, E. and Wyatt, D. (2006) *Wyatt and Dashwood's European Union Law*, 5th edition, Thomson, Sweet and Maxwell, pp.631–634.

Eason, A. (1980) 'The Spirits, Wine and Beer Judgments: A Legal Mickey Finn?', (1980) 5 ELRev. 318.

Craig, P. and De Burca, G. (2007) *EU Law: Text, Cases and Materials*, 4th edition, Oxford University Press, Chapter 18.

Snell, J. (2007) 'Non-Discriminatory Tax Obstacles in Community Law', (2007) 56 ICLQ 339.

Visit **http://www.mylawchamber.co.uk/kent** to access answer guidance to questions in the book to test yourself on this chapter.

Use **Case Navigator** to read in full some of the key cases referenced in this chapter:

- 7/68 **Commission** v. **Italy (Italian Art Treasures)** [1968] ECR 423
- 6/64 **Costa** v. **ENEL** [1964] ECR 585
- Case 112/84 **Humblot** [1985] ECR 1367
- 26/62 **Van Gend en Loos**

12 Quantitative restrictions and measures having equivalent effect

INTRODUCTION

Non-tariff barriers and the need for elimination of quantitative restrictions and measures having equivalent effect

While the EC was successful in removing tariff barriers between States as well as the more obvious non-tariff barriers such as quotas, many other obstacles to interstate trade remained.

> **Key term**
>
> A **quantitative restriction** or **quota** is a measure which restricts the import of a product by amount or by value. Measures having equivalent effect (MEQR) are usually administrative measures which, like quotas, are capable of restricting the free movement of goods to an even greater extent than tariff barriers.

Principal Treaty provisions

The principal provisions are:

- Article 28 (ex 30) prohibiting quantitative restrictions, and all measures having equivalent effect, on imports;
- Article 29 (ex 34) prohibiting quantitative restrictions, and all measures having equivalent effect, on exports;
- Article 30 (ex 36) providing that the prohibitions in Articles 28 and 29 (ex 30–34) will not apply to import and export restrictions justified on various specific grounds.

The renumbering of Treaty provisions as a result of the TOA has had a particularly unfortunate effect on the provisions on free movement of goods. Old Article 30 became Article 28; Articles 31 and 32 were repealed; Article 34 became Article 29.

Most confusingly, Article 36 became (new) Article 30. Thus any reference to Article 30 should be treated with care, to see whether it applies to the pre- or post-TOA numbering.

'Measures taken by Member States'

While these Articles are addressed to measures taken by Member States, the expression has been interpreted widely to cover the activities of any public or semi-public body, such as measures adopted by professional bodies on which national legislation has conferred regulatory powers: Cases 266 and 267/87 *R. v. Royal Pharmaceutical Society of Great Britain*. See also: Case 222/82 *Apple and Pear Development Council*, in which the ECJ held that a body established and funded by the government was covered. In Case 249/81 *Commission* v. *Ireland* the ECJ held that a Member State could not avoid liability under Article 28 by relying on the fact that the campaign 'Buy Irish' was conducted by a private undertaking. No binding decisions were involved but the Irish Goods Council was capable of influencing traders through its promotional activities.

A Member State may infringe Article 28 by failing to act as well as by acting. In Case C-265/95 *Commission* v. *France* the Commission brought enforcement proceedings against France for failing to act against private individuals for disrupting the free movement of goods (agricultural products such as Spanish strawberries) from other Member States. Lorries transporting the goods were intercepted, loads destroyed and lorry drivers threatened. The ECJ held that, by failing to adopt all necessary and proportionate measures to prevent the free movement of goods being obstructed, France was in breach of Article 28, Article 10 (ex 5) and the provisions on the common organisation of the markets in agricultural products.

When considering omissions, it is, however, important to examine the degree of discretion which the Member State may exercise.

Key case

The Austrian government decided not to ban a demonstration by an environmental group, resulting in the closure of the Brenner motorway for 30 hours. Schmidberger, a German-based undertaking transporting steel and timber between Germany and Italy, brought an action against the Austrian authorities for State liability relating to their losses from the closure of the motorway. The ECH held (Article 234) that the decision not to ban the road closure was an MEQR. However, it found that the Austrian authorities had a wide margin of discretion in the area. That discretion had been exercised in accordance with the principle of proportionality in terms of its legitimate objectives, the protection of fundamental rights (this was a lawful demonstration). As a result, the decision did not infringe Article 28: Case C-112/00 *Schmidberger* v. *Austria*.

PROHIBITION OF QUANTITATIVE RESTRICTIONS ON IMPORTS AND OF MEASURES HAVING EQUIVALENT EFFECT: ARTICLE 28

Prohibition

The prohibition in Article 28 was held in Case 74/76 *Ianelli & Volpi* to be directly effective. It covers both quantitative restrictions and measures equivalent to quantitative restrictions.

Quantitative restrictions

The ECJ interpreted 'quantitative restrictions' in Case 2/73 *Geddo* v. *Ente Nazionale Risi* as measures which amount to a total or partial restraint on imports, exports or goods in transit. Examples include a quota system: Case 13/68 *Salgoil SpA* v. *Italian Minister of Trade*; a ban: Case 7/61 *Commission* v. *Italy (Re Ban on Port Imports)*; and *R.* v. *Henn and Darby* (Case 34/79) involving a ban on pornographic materials. However, a national prohibition on the sale of sex articles from unlicensed premises, applied without distinction to domestic and imported products, is not a quantitative restriction: Case C-23/89 *Quietlynn* v. *Southend Borough Council*.

Measures having equivalent effect to quantitative restrictions on imports

This expression has been more widely interpreted than quantitative restrictions. It may be applied to domestic goods as well as imports and exports. It covers regulatory measures such as standards on size, quality and weight as well as inspection or certification requirements: Case 249/81 *Commission* v. *Ireland*.

Distinctly and indistinctly applicable measures

Directive 70/50 was issued by the Commission to guide Member States by providing a non-exhaustive list of measures equivalent to quantitative restrictions. Measures are divided under the Directive into:

(a) Measures other than those applicable equally to domestic or imported products (i.e. distinctly applicable measures) that hinder imports which could otherwise take place, including those 'which make importation more difficult than the disposal of domestic production': Article 2(1).
(b) Measures which are equally applicable to domestic and imported products (i.e. indistinctly applicable measures): Article 3. These measures only contravene Article 28 'where the restrictive effect of such measures on the free movement of goods exceeds the effect intrinsic to trade rules': Article 3.

Dassonville Formula

In Case 8/74 *Procureur du Roi* v. *Dassonville* the Court defined measures having equivalent effect in broad terms.

Key point

All trading rules enacted by Member States which are capable of hindering directly or indirectly, actually or potentially, intra-Community trade are to be considered as measures having an effect equivalent to quantitative restrictions (the 'Dassonville formula').

Key case

The defendants had imported into Belgium a consignment of Scotch whisky purchased from French distributors without the certificate of origin required by Belgian law, arguing as a defence to criminal proceedings that the requirement contravened Article 28. In a preliminary ruling arising from the proceedings against the importers, the ECJ held that a requirement such as that laid down by Belgian law constituted a measure having equivalent effect in favouring direct imports from the country of origin over imports from another Member State where the goods were in free circulation: Case 8/74 *Procureur du Roi* v. *Dassonville*.

⬤ ECJ decisions after *Dassonville*

The definition in *Dassonville* has been confirmed and applied in numerous subsequent decisions: see, for example:

- In *Tasca* the defendant was charged with selling sugar above the national maximum price in Italy. HELD (ECJ): Fixing a maximum price is not a measure equivalent to a quantitative restriction unless it is fixed at such a level that it makes the sale of imported goods more difficult: Case 65/75 *Tasca*.
- In *Van Tiggele* the defendant was charged with selling gin below the national minimum price in the Netherlands. HELD: A minimum price may contravene (old) Articles 30–34 by preventing imports from being sold at a price below the fixed price: Case 82/77 *Van Tiggele*.

The ECJ has consistently rejected the argument that although a measure contravenes Articles 28 and 29 it is administered with sufficient flexibility to allow exceptions, holding that freedom of movement is a right which may not be made dependent upon the discretion of a national authority: Case 130/80 *Kelderman*.

It is not necessary to show that a measure has an *appreciable* effect on trade between Member States. It is sufficient to show that the measure is *capable of producing such effect*: Case 16/83 *Prantl*, even where the hindrance is slight: Case 177/82 *Van der Haar*. A measure which is incapable of hindering trade between Member States will not contravene Articles 28 and 29 even where the sale of domestic goods is affected. The following measures were held by the ECJ *not* to contravene Article 28:

- A Belgian law, intended to improve working conditions, banned the production and delivery of bread during the night. Competing bakers in adjoining Member States were not similarly controlled: Case 155/80 *Oebel*.
- A Dutch law regulated the permitted ingredients in cheese produced in the Netherlands but not outside: Case 237/82: *Jongeneel Kaas BV* v. *Netherlands*.

Cassis de Dijon

The next significant development came in the *Cassis de Dijon* decision, a ruling of immense importance to the development of the law on free movement of goods. The Court in *Cassis* identified the *principle of recognition* which underpinned the completion of the single market in goods, as well as the grounds on which Member States may adopt *indistinctly applicable* measures to restrict free movement.

The ruling does not apply to distinctly applicable measures. It should be remembered that indistinctly applicable measures apply to domestically produced goods as well as to imports and therefore pose less of a threat to the operation of the market than do distinctly applicable measures which, by definition, discriminate against imports.

Key case

German law laid down a minimum alcohol content of 25 per cent for spirits including cassis, a blackcurrant-flavoured liqueur, a requirement which was satisfied by cassis produced in Germany but not in France where the alcohol level was only 15 to 20 per cent. The effect of the measure, although indistinctly applicable, was to exclude French cassis from the German market. The measure was challenged by German importers in the German court who referred the case for interpretation to the ECJ. The Court applied the *Dassonville* formula and held that a requirement such as that in the German law contravened Article 28.

While the ECJ rejected German claims relating to public health (that a higher alcohol level would prevent increased consumption), the fairness of commercial transactions (that weak imported cassis would have an unfair commercial advantage over the more expensive German product) and protection of the consumer, the Court nevertheless acknowledged that it may be possible to justify a departure from Article 28 where it is *necessary* to do so to satisfy one of the *mandatory requirements* relating in particular to the effectiveness of fiscal supervision, the protection of public health, the fairness of commercial transactions and the defence of the consumer: Case 120/78 *Rewe-Zentral AG* v. *Bundesmonopolverwaltung für Branntwein* ('Cassis de Dijon')

This principle established whereby a restriction may be upheld where certain conditions are satisfied is sometimes known as *'the rule of reason'*. It was set out by the Court in *Cassis* as follows:

> Obstacles to movement within the EC arising from disparities between national laws relating to the marketing of the product in question must be accepted in so far as those provisions may be recognized as being necessary in order to satisfy the mandatory requirements relating in particular to the effectiveness of fiscal supervision, the protection of public health, the fairness of commercial transactions and the defence of the consumer.

The measure in *Cassis*, though mandatory, failed because the ECJ found that it was not *necessary*. The objectives could have been achieved by other less restrictive means such as labelling. It follows that 'necessary' means *no more than is necessary* and is subject to the principle of proportionality (see below).

The *Cassis* decision is important because it displaced the previous assumption that Article 28 did not apply to a national measure unless it could be shown that the measure discriminated between imports and domestic products or between different forms of intra-Community trade. After *Cassis*, it may be seen that the Court applied the prohibition under Article 28 to indistinctly applicable rules, as follows:

- **Indistinctly applicable measures**. The rule of reason may be applied to establish a breach of Article 28. Where a measure is necessary to protect a mandatory requirement there will be no breach of Article 28.
- **Distinctly applicable measures**. Distinctly applicable measures will normally contravene Article 28 but may be justified under Article 30.

Some commentators have made further distinctions, such as that made by Weatherill and Beaumont[1] between 'dual-burden' and 'equal burden' rules. Dual-burden rules are those rules applied to imported goods by the host State, even though they have already been subject to regulation in the home State. The decision of the ECJ in *Cassis* meant that such a requirement could only be applied if it could be justified as necessary to satisfy a mandatory requirement. Rules relating to the product itself, such as to packaging, clearly involve a dual burden, as the producer or seller has to satisfy the rules of both the home State and the host State. See, for example, a requirement to sell margarine in cube-shaped boxes: Case 261/81 *Walter Rau*. A similar dual burden is experienced as a result of rules relating to the composition of the product, such as the permitted ingredients in pasta in Italy: Case 407/85 *Drei Glocken* v. *USL*.

Equal burden rules apply to all goods, regardless of origin and are not protectionist. The Court has not been entirely consistent in its treatment of equal burden cases. It has tended to treat equal burden rules concerned with the conditions under which goods are sold as outside the scope of Article 28. See, for example, a ban on the employment of labour on Sundays in France: Case C-312/89 *Union Départmentale des Syndicats CGT* v. *Sidef Conforama* and Case C-332/89. However, in some cases the ECJ

---

[1] Weatherill and Beaumont (1999) and see further commentary by Craig and De Burca (2007: 681–684).

has found that an equal burden rule is within Article 28, but justifiable under *Cassis*. See, for example, Cases 60 and 61/84 *Cinéthèque SA*, in which a French rule designed to protect the cinema industry by prohibiting the distribution of video-cassettes within one year of release of the film in question was not expressly held to be a mandatory requirement. The ECJ nevertheless held that the rule was justifiable and did not contravene Article 28. Uncertainty over equal burden cases was not addressed by the Court until its decision in Cases C-267 and 268/91 *Keck and Mithouard* on selling arrangements: see below.

Decisions since *Cassis*

The list of mandatory requirements in *Cassis* is not exhaustive. Various national rules have been held by the ECJ to be mandatory requirements under the *Cassis* formulation, including:

- improvement of working conditions by limiting night working: Case 155/80 *Oebel*;
- protection of the environment: Case 302/86 *Commission* v. *Denmark (Re Disposable Beer Cans)*;
- protection of fundamental rights: Case C-112/00 *Schmidberger* v. *Austria* (see above);
- pluralism of the press: Case C-368/95 *Vereinigte Familiapress Zeitungsverlags und vertriebs GmbH* v. *Heinrich Bauer Verlag* (prizes offered in magazines could eliminate competition from smaller papers which could not afford to offer such prizes).

A justification based on purely economic grounds was held by the ECJ *not* to be a mandatory requirement: Case 238/82 *Duphar BV* v. *Netherlands*.

The ECJ has held that certain other rules contravene the *Cassis* formulation, though they may be considered for justification under Article 30:

Examples
1 Imposition of a labelling requirement: Case 27/80 *Fietje*.
2 Requirement that silver goods be hallmarked: Case 220/81 *Robertson*.
3 Prohibition on retail sale of certain products unless marked with their country of origin: Case 207/83 *Commission* v. *United Kingdom*.

> **Key point**
>
> The approach of the ECJ in *Cassis* was modified in *Gilli* v. *Andres*. Italian law prohibited the selling of vinegar containing acetic acid unless it was produced by the fermentation of wine, thus excluding vinegar made from cider. The ECJ suggested a modification to the *Cassis* principle, namely that the principle applied only where national rules do not discriminate in application between domestic and imported goods. The Court found that legislation such as the Italian law in relation to vinegar contravened Article 28 because it discriminated against goods which did not satisfy the national requirement for vinegar: Case 788/79 *Gilli* v. *Andres*.

Failure to establish 'necessity'

In a number of instances, the governments in question have failed to show that the measure was necessary.

Examples

1 P was charged with breach of a German law intended to prevent unfair competition. He had imported Italian wine in a traditional Italian bulbous bottle of similar shape and design to a traditional German quality wine. HELD: As long as the imported wine conformed with fair and traditional practice in its state of origin, its exclusion from Germany could not be justified: Case 16/83 *Prantl*.

2 In the Netherlands the name 'jenever' was restricted to gin with a minimum 35 per cent alcohol level. HELD: The name could not be reserved for one national variety provided the import (Belgian 'jenever' with a 30 per cent alcohol level) had been lawfully produced and marketed in the exporting state: Case 182/84 *Miro BV*.

Other prohibited restrictions include Dutch requirements on the permitted ingredients in bread: Case 130/80 *Kelderman* and Italian requirements for pasta: Case 407/85 *Drei Glocken* v. *USL*.

Justification in the interests of consumers

Justification in the interests of consumers was clarified by the Court in Case 238/82 *Duphar*.

Key case

The Dutch government adopted a regulation that listed approved drugs which may be paid for out of public funds. Duphar, a drug company, challenged its exclusion from the list in the Dutch courts. The ECJ, under Article 234, ruled out economic justification but accepted that such a measure may be necessary in the interests of consumers provided the choice of drugs on the list did not discriminate against imports. The ECJ stated that the list must be drawn up according to objective criteria, without reference to the origin of products, both requirements being verifiable by the importer: Case 238/82 *Duphar BV* v. *Netherlands*.

See also Case 286/81 *Oosthoek's Uitgeversmaatschappij BV*, in which the ECJ upheld national consumer protection measures which restricted the giving of free gifts as a sales promotion, despite the fact that such legislation could impede inter-member trade. In Case C-362/88 *GB INNO-BM* v. *Confédération du Commerce Luxembourgoise*, a Belgian company had distributed leaflets advertising cut-price products. The leaflets were lawful in Belgium but not in Luxembourg, where they were seized and the supermarket prosecuted. The company invoked Article 28 as a defence. In a preliminary reference the ECJ ruled that the ban was unlawful under Article 28, as it was not justifiable as a consumer protection measure. The Court considered the ban prejudicial to small importers who were denied a particularly effective means of advertising.

Principle of mutual recognition

To clarify the implications of the *Cassis* decision the Commission issued a statement in 1980 recognising the need for mutual recognition. They stated: 'There is no valid reason why goods which have been lawfully produced and marketed in one of the Member States should not be introduced into any other Member State.'

This means that goods which have been lawfully marketed in one Member State will comply with the mandatory requirements of the State into which they are being imported unless it can be shown that the measure is necessary. The ECJ adopts a rigorous approach to determining what is 'necessary' and will not allow any measure which is disproportionate.

The principle of mutual recognition has operated as the cornerstone of the Commission's internal market programme through the harmonisation of identified sectors of the market. It has been applied outside the free movement of goods, particularly to the recognition of professional qualifications (see Chapter 15).

Article 28 as a defence

As the cases above show, Article 28 has frequently been invoked, not always successfully, as a defence in charges involving regulatory offences before the national courts.

The most controversial use of the Article 28 defence in recent years has probably been in relation to prosecutions in England and Wales for breaches of the law on Sunday trading, prior to the limited liberalisation of the law by the Sunday Trading Act 1994. The first ruling from the ECJ on the subject was in *Torfaen BC* v. *B&Q plc*.

Key case

A DIY retail company in the UK was charged with trading on a Sunday contrary to s. 47 of the Shops Act 1950. The company argued that the measure was unlawful under Article 28. HELD (ECJ, Article 234): Such measures constitute a legitimate part of social and economic policy to accord with national or regional socio-cultural characteristics and do not contravene Article 28 provided their restrictive effect is not disproportionate: Case 145/88 *Torfaen Borough Council* v. *B&Q plc*.

In other words, Sunday trading is a legitimate area for legislation by Member States provided the measure complies with the principle of proportionality. The emphasis on proportionality was maintained in other cases on Sunday trading such as Case C-169/91 *Stoke-on-Trent City Council* v. *B&Q plc*, as well as in similar 'equal burden' rulings in relation to bans on employment on Sundays in France and Belgium: Case

C-312/89 *Union Départmentale des Syndicats CGT* v. *Sidef Conforama* and Case C-332/89 *Criminal Proceedings* v. *Marchandise*, see above. The ECJ held that the restrictive effects on trade which might stem from national rules in shop opening hours were not disproportionate to rules designed to arrange working hours to accord with national or regional socio-cultural characteristics.

The position after the Sunday trading cases need clarifying. While a prohibition on selling goods on a Sunday reduced turnover, it did not discriminate against imports. The ECJ nevertheless treated such prohibitions as contrary to Article 28 unless they could be justified.

Selling arrangements: calling 'time' on Article 28 as a defence

After the Sunday trading cases there was a danger that Article 28 was being overused in attempts to undermine national legislation with little or no relevance to imports. The Court of Justice signaled its determination to identify the limits of Article 28 in Joined Cases C-267 and 268/91 *Keck and Mithouard* in relation to selling arrangements. Once a measure was identified as a selling arrangement, it was outside Article 28. Guidance on what constitutes a selling arrangement may be obtained from the Court's decisions in *Keck* and its aftermath.

Key case

K and M resold goods at a loss contrary to French law. They argued that the law infringed Article 28 as it restricted the volume of imported goods. After expressing the need to reappraise its previous jurisprudence under the Article the ECJ ruled that:

> The application to products from other Member States of national provisions restricting or prohibiting certain selling arrangements is not such as to hinder directly or indirectly, actually or potentially, trade between Member States, provided that the provisions apply to all affected traders operating within the national territory and provided that they affect in the same manner, in law and in fact, the marketing of domestic products and those from other Member States.

Joined Cases C-267 and 268/91 *Keck and Mithouard*.

When is a selling arrangement outside Article 28?

After *Keck* it is clear that Member States are free to determine their own selling arrangements where there is no effect on imports and no discrimination. The following provide examples of selling arrangements held to be outside Article 28 and so enforceable within the national jurisdiction:

- Dutch restrictions on the opening hours of petrol stations: Cases 401 and 402/92 *Tankstation't Heukste Vof and Boermans*.
- German restrictions on the promotion of para-pharmaceutical products outside pharmacies: Case C-292/92 *Hünermund* v. *Landesapothekemer Baden-Wurttemburg*.

- Italian rules reserving the retail sale of tobacco products to approved suppliers: Case C-387/93 *Gorgio Domingo Banchero.*
- Belgian rules prohibiting sales at very low profit margins: Case C-63/94 *Belgapom.*
- A French ban on televised advertising of the distribution sector: Case C-412/93 *Société d'Importation Edouard Leclerc-Siplec* v. *TFI Publicité SA and M 6 Publicité SA.*

Other decisions on *advertising as a selling arrangement* are less clear. In Cases C-34–36/95 *Konsumentombudsman* v. *De Agostini* the Court considered a Swedish ban on certain types of television advertising. Actions had been brought against traders in the Swedish courts for infringing the restrictions, in one case by advertising a magazine entitled *Everything you Need to Know about Dinosaurs* contrary to a ban on advertising to children under 12 years, and in the other for marketing a soap called 'Body de Lite' which was considered to be misleading advertising. The Court found that an outright ban on advertising would have infringed Article 28. However, it left the national court to decide whether the restriction actually operated unequally on imported goods relative to domestic products, when television advertising was virtually the only way for a new entrant to break into the market in question. In Case C-405/98 *Konsumentombudsmannen* v. *Gourmet International Products* the Court again had to consider an advertising ban in Sweden, this time in relation to alcoholic drinks above 2.25 per cent alcohol. Gourmet International Products had published three pages of advertisements of whiskey and red wine in a magazine largely intended for the restaurant trade. This time the Court decided that such a ban infringed Article 28 as it affected the marketing of products from other Member States more severely than home products and was thus an obstacle to trade between Member States.

A national restriction will not be regarded as a selling arrangement when it imposes a 'dual burden' of regulation, both where the goods are produced and where they are sold. In such a case, the purpose and context of the relevant national legislation should be assessed to see whether it infringes Article 28 or not.

Key case

Austrian law required that bakers, butchers and grocers were only permitted to sell their goods in a given district if they traded from a permanent establishment in the same district. The ECJ found that the requirement imposed an additional burden on traders from outside Austria. The Court did not accept that the measure was justified on grounds of public health, as it was seen as disproportionate (refrigeration in the delivery vans would have avoided deterioration): Case C-254/98 *Schutzverband gegen unlauteren Wettbewerb.*

Product requirements

A 'dual burden' often arises in the context of a specific requirement in relation to the product. The problems of dual burdens may be illustrated by two cases where a national law on unfair competition made it necessary for importers to repackage the goods.

Key cases

1 German law prohibited the use of the name 'Clinique' for cosmetics. The effect of the prohibition was that lawfully produced cosmetics produced outside Germany would have to be repackaged if they were to be sold there. The German government was unable to convince the ECJ that customers were misled into thinking that the goods possessed pharmaceutical properties: Case C-315/92 *Verband Sozialer Wettbewerb eV* v. *Clinique Laboratoires SNC*.

2 Mars GmbH had increased the quantity of ice cream in an individual packet by 10 per cent as a publicity promotion. The company was prevented under German law from distributing its products in Germany with the words 'plus 10%'. Again, the effect was to require the company to repackage in order to sell the product in Germany. The ECJ held that such a requirement infringed Article 28 as it compelled the importer to incur additional costs: Case C-470/93 *Verein gegen Unwesen in Handel und Gewerbe Köln* v. *Mars GmbH*.

In Case C-244/06 *Dynamic Median Vertriebs GmbH* v. *Avides Media AG* the Court found that German requirements that image storage media (e.g. photographs) must be subject to examination and classification to protect young persons was not a selling arrangement. Such rules did not infringe Article 28 provided the procedure was transparent and the decision open to challenge.

As the case law on selling arrangements continues to build, it may be seen that the ECJ has tended to leave most issues in this area to the discretion of the national authorities where there is no obvious discrimination or effect on trade between Member States.

Criticisms of the Court's approach to indistinctly applicable measures

Academic commentators have commented extensively on the Court's case law on indistinctly applicable measures, particularly in relation to selling arrangements. An article by White,[2] a legal adviser at the Commission, proved to be influential in the Court's approach. He proposed a distinction between indistinctly applicable laws relating to the characteristics of the goods which would be covered by Article 28 and those relating to selling arrangements, which would be outside the prohibition. The Court went on to make this distinction in *Keck*, a decision which has generated further academic criticism.[3]

Two particular lines of criticism post *Keck* have been identified by Chalmers *et al.*[4]

---

[2] White (1989).
[3] See, for example, Steiner (1992).
[4] Chalmers *et al.* (2006: 687–699).

1 That the *Keck* approach is too formal, particularly in the context of product require-ments, to protect the interests of the exporting state.[5]

2 That the *Keck* approach fails to protect market integration. As a result, some authors[6] have proposed a new test, namely whether the measure imposed a direct or substantial restriction on trade within States, thus enabling selling arrangements such as those on advertising which restrict access to the market to be covered.[7]

The case law of the Court continues to evolve, and there is every indication that the Court is responding flexibly, both to academic commentary and to new types of selling arrangements as they emerge.

PROHIBITION BETWEEN MEMBER STATES OF QUANTITATIVE RESTRICTIONS ON EXPORTS AND OF MEASURES OF EQUIVALENT EFFECT: ARTICLE 29

The principles relating to imports under Article 28 also apply to exports under Article 29 (ex 34), except that indistinctly applicable measures will not contravene Article 29 unless they discriminate against exports. Thus measures will only breach Article 29 if they have as their object or effect the restriction of export patterns, providing an advantage to the home product or market to the disadvantage of the EC import: Case 15/79 *P.B. Groenveld BV*.

The *Dassonville* test will be applied to distinctly applicable measures against exports which will usually contravene Article 29.

> **Key case**
>
> Manufacturers of meat products banned the possession of horsemeat to prevent its export to countries where such trade was prohibited. The ECJ held that the measure did not contravene Article 29, contrary to the opinion of Advocate-General Capotorti. It is clear from the Court's decision that the *Dassonville* test does not apply to exports where the measures in question are indistinctly applic-able: Case 15/79 *P.B. Groenveld BV*.

The following restrictions were found to infringe Article 29:

- A prohibition on free gifts as sales promotion: Case 286/81 *Oosthoek's*.
- A requirement under French law that watches for export underwent a quality inspection in order to obtain an export licence. HELD (ECJ): Such a requirement con-travened Article 29 as it was not imposed on watches for the home market: Case 53/76 *Bouhelier*.

---

[5] See Maduro (1997).
[6] See, for example, Weatherill (1996).
[7] Greaves (1998).

The following were found *not* to infringe Article 29:

- Indistinctly applicable Dutch rules on the content and quality of Dutch cheeses. While not overtly protectionist, the rules gave an advantage to importers not bound by the same standards. HELD (ECJ): There was no breach of Article 29 as the rules were not intended to give advantage to domestic production: Case 237/82 *Jongeneel Kaas BV.*
- Restrictions on night working in bakeries: Case 155/80 *Oebel.*

Approach of the House of Lords

The decision of the House of Lords in *International Traders' Ferry*, a case in which no reference was made to the Court of Justice, provides insight into the approach of the UK courts to Article 29.

> **Key case**
>
> In *R. v. Chief Constable of Sussex, ex parte International Traders' Ferry Ltd* (HL, 1999) the House of Lords considered the legality under Article 29 of policing arrangements for the port of Shoreham in Sussex. International Trader's Ferry (ITF) had been operating out of Shoreham since 1995, transporting live animals across the Channel. A long protest campaign by animal rights groups made it difficult for lorries to reach the port facilities without police protection. The Chief Constable, after some time, reduced the level of policing for the operation, stating that the deployment of police at the port was significantly affecting his resources to police other areas. He informed ITF that lorries seeking access to the port at times when policing was not available would be turned away. ITF sought judicial review in the UK courts of the decision to reduce the level of policing on grounds of unreasonableness (in English law) and as a measure having equivalent effect under Article 29.
>
> Without referring to the ECJ under Article 234 the House of Lords held that:
>
> - The Chief Constable had not acted unreasonably in English law, there being no absolute right to trade lawfully or to protest lawfully.
> - Assuming the Chief Constable's acts to be 'measures equivalent to quantitative restrictions' under Article 29, the measures were justified under Article 30 on grounds of public policy. This justification arose not only where there was something inherently bad about the activity itself justifying the restriction, but also where the broader requirements of public policy such as the maintenance of public order justified steps being taken. The Chief Constable's actions were both proportionate and reasonable, having regard to the resources available to him.

12

DEROGATION FROM ARTICLES 28 AND 29

Main principle for derogation: Article 30

Article 30 (ex 36), the main principle for derogation, provides:

> The provisions of Articles 28 and 29 shall not preclude prohibitions or restrictions on imports, exports or goods in transit justified on grounds of public morality, public policy or public security; the protection of health and life of humans, animals or plants; the protection of national treasures possessing artistic, historic or archaeological value; or the protection of industrial and commercial property. Such prohibitions or restrictions shall not, however, constitute a means of arbitrary discrimination or a disguised restriction on trade between Member States.

Grounds of derogation

As an exception to one of the basic freedoms of the common market Article 30 (ex 36) must be interpreted strictly. The list of exceptions is exhaustive: Case 95/81 *Commission* v. *Italy*. The following have been held by the ECJ *not* to justify derogation since they are not listed in Article 30:

- Consumer protection or the fairness of consumer transactions: Case 113/80 *Commission* v. *Ireland*, in which the Irish government unsuccessfully sought to justify its origin-marking rules as consumer protection measures.
- Protection of cultural diversity: Case 229/83 *Association des Centres Distributeurs Edouard Leclerc* v. *'Au Blé Vert' Sarl.*
- Economic policy: Case 238/82 *Duphar.*

Justification and arbitrary discrimination

Member States may derogate from the free movement of goods to the extent that a measure is justified to achieve the objectives in Article 30. 'Justified' is to be interpreted as meaning 'necessary': Case 227/82 *Leendert van Bennekom*, with the onus of demonstrating necessity resting on the national authorities. Thus, Article 30 may only be invoked subject to the principle of proportionality. It may not be relied upon to facilitate administrative tasks or to reduce public expenditure, unless alternative arrangements would place an excessive burden on the authorities: Case 104/75 *Officier van Just* v. *De Peijper*.

Measures must not only be necessary. They must not amount to a means of arbitrary discrimination or a disguised restriction on inter-member trade, for example, by providing an advantage to the marketing of one State, including the domestic State, over the other State.

Public morality

There have been three Article 234 references to the ECJ from UK courts in which the public morality ground was raised: Case 34/79 *R.* v. *Henn and Darby*, Case 121/85

Conegate Ltd v. *Customs and Excise Commissioners* and Case C-23/89 *Quietlynn* v. *Southend Borough Council*.

Key case

R. v. *Henn and Darby* (Case 34/79): This case arose out of a prosecution under customs legislation of importers who had attempted to bring pornographic materials from the Netherlands into the UK. The customs legislation banned material which was 'indecent or obscene' whereas domestic legislation prohibited material only where it was likely to 'deprave or corrupt', a distinction apparently discriminating against imported goods since indecency is a less rigorous concept than obscenity. A reference to the ECJ was made on appeal to the House of Lords. HELD: **(a)** There was a breach of Article 28 but the breach was justified under Article 30. A Member State is permitted under Article 30 to prohibit imports from another Member State of articles which are of an obscene or indecent nature in accordance with its domestic laws. **(b)** If a prohibition on the importation of goods is justifiable on the ground of public morality and is imposed for that purpose, enforcement of the prohibition cannot constitute a means of arbitrary discrimination or a disguised restriction on trade contrary to Article 30 unless there is a lawful trade in the same goods within the Member States concerned.

R. v. *Henn and Darby* should be contrasted with Case 121/85 *Conegate Ltd* v. *Customs and Excise Commissioners*. In this case Customs and Excise in the UK seized a number of inflatable rubber 'love dolls' on the ground that they were indecent and obscene. The importers claimed that the seizure of the goods contravened Article 28, the sale of such objects being restricted but not banned in the UK. HELD: The seizure was not justified, in the absence of a general prohibition on the manufacture and marketing of the goods in the UK and of effective measures to restrict domestic distribution.

In *R.* v. *Bow Street Magistrates, ex parte Noncyp Ltd* (1989) the Court of Appeal decided *not* to refer to the ECJ the question of whether seizure of a book deemed to be obscene but published in the public interest was permitted by Article 30. The Court held that such books remained 'obscene' and liable to forfeiture under Article 30 in the absence of lawful UK trade.

In Case C-23/89 *Quietlynn* v. *Southend Borough Council* the ECJ held (in an Article 234 reference from the Crown Court arising out of a prosecution under UK licensing legislation) that Article 28 should be construed as meaning that national provisions prohibiting the sale of lawful sex articles from unlicensed sex establishments did not constitute a measure having equivalent effect to a quantitative restriction on imports.

Public policy

To date public policy has succeeded on one occasion only as a derogation under Article 30.

Key case

In Case 7/78 *R.* v. *Thompson and others* the ECJ held that silver alloy coins minted before 1947 were not legal tender and thus not a 'means of payment'. They should therefore be regarded as 'goods'. Restrictions on the exportation of such coins to prevent their being melted down were found to be justified on grounds of public policy.

The public policy exception in relation to goods has been strictly construed by the ECJ which has ruled that it may *not* be invoked:

- to serve economic ends: Case 231/83 *Cullet* v. *Centre Leclerc*;
- to restrict criminal behaviour: Case 16/83 *Prantl*;
- to protect consumers: Case 177/83 *Kohl.*

Public security

Public security was successfully invoked by the Irish government in *Campus Oil*.

Key case

The Irish government invoked public policy to justify an order instructing petrol importers to purchase up to 35 per cent of their requirements from INPC (the Irish National Petroleum Co.) at government-fixed prices. The ECJ found that, although petroleum products were of fundamental national importance, they were not automatically exempt from Article 28 and ruled that the measure, being clearly protectionist, contravened Article 28. While rejecting the validity of claims based on public policy or purely economic objectives, the ECJ held that the measure was, however, justified on grounds of public security, to maintain the continuity of essential oil supplies in times of crisis: Case 72/83 *Campus Oil* v. *Minster of State for Industry and Energy.*

Protection of the health and life of humans, animals and plants

The protection of public health outweighs all other considerations, particularly economic concerns, as the CFI declared in Cases T-125 and 126/96 *Boehringer* v. *Council* (a decision upholding a directive which prohibited the administration of growth-promoting drugs to food-producing animals). Discriminatory measures on public health grounds include import bans, import licences, health inspections and prior authorisation requirements. Import bans are hard to justify as they are usually unnecessary to protect health: *see* Case 153/78 *Commission* v. *Germany (Meat Preparations)*.

When may a restriction be justified on health grounds?

For a restriction to be justified under Article 30, the Court held in Case 40/82 *Commission* v. *UK (French Turkeys)* that:

- there must be a real, not a slight, health risk;
- the measure must form part of a seriously considered health policy;
- the measure must not operate as a disguised restriction on trade.

Key case

A licensing system had been established by the UK government to exclude poultry imported from countries following a policy of vaccination rather than slaughter in response to Newcastle disease, a contagious poultry disease. The measure had been adopted by the government in the run-up to Christmas, after lobbying by UK poultry producers. The ECJ held that such a ban could not be justified on grounds of animal health. It did not form part of a seriously considered health policy but operated as a disguised restriction on inter-member trade: Case 40/82 *Commission* v. *UK (French Turkeys)*.

A requirement to obtain an import or export licence constitutes an MEQR: Case 124/81 *Commission* v. *UK (UHT Milk)*. In this case the ECJ accepted the UK argument that an import licensing system was necessary to regulate the heat treatment of imported milk and to trace the origins of infected milk, but held that the system which involved retreating and repackaging imported milk was not justified since milk in all the Member States was subject to equivalent controls. In Case 74/82 *Commission* v. *Ireland (Re Protection of Animal Health)*, a case involving similar licensing requirements was accepted as justified by the ECJ because British poultry did not match the high standards of Irish poultry, demonstrating the need to examine each case on its merits to assess whether the restriction is justifiable.

Examples where restrictions were found to be justified under Article 30

1 A plant health inspection to control a plant pest applied to imported but not domestically produced apples was found by the ECJ to be justified as only imported apples posed a threat: Case 4/75 *Rewe-Zentralfinanz GmbH*.
2 The rules of a national pharmaceutical society prohibiting the substitution by pharmacists of equivalent drugs instead of proprietary prescribed brands was found to discriminate against imports. However, the ECJ accepted that the prohibition was necessary to avoid anxiety caused by product substitution and to maintain confidence: Cases 266 and 267/87 *R.* v. *Royal Pharmaceutical Society of Great Britain*.

3 A national measure restricting the keeping of bees on a Danish island to a particular species was an MEQR. However, it was justified under Article 30 in order to preserve an endangered sub-species: Case C-67/97 *Ditlev Bluhme*.

> ### Key point
>
> Health inspections carried out at national frontiers may constitute an MEQR. Such inspections at times may be an appropriate way to protect the health and life of humans, animals and plants. However, they are only justified if they are reasonably proportionate to the aim pursued and health protection may not be achieved by less restrictive means. Random but not systematic checks are permitted: Case 42/82 *Commission v. France*.

In Case 42/82 *Commission v. France (Re Italian Table Wines)* the ECJ found that excessive delays in the customs clearance of wine imported from Italy into France caused by analyses of goods sampled for checks were disproportionate and discriminatory. 'Random' checks on three out of four consignments were seen by the ECJ to be systematic. The requirement to produce a health or other certificate contravenes Article 28: *Denkavit* Case 73/84 *Denkavit Futtermittel* v. *Land Nordrhein-Westfalen*, but may be justified under Article 30 as it is less restrictive than a system of licensing or inspection.

> ### Key point
>
> Where harmonisation over prior authorisation or inspection has occurred, the importing State may no longer carry out systematic inspections.

A national system of prior authorisation for marketing food imported from other Member States was found to contravene Article 28 in Case 35/76 *Simmenthal* as a Directive had placed the responsibility for inspection on the exporting State. In the absence of harmonisation, justification under Article 30 is likely, as Member States continue to exercise considerable discretion in the degree of protection to be accorded to the health and life of humans, animals and plants. National authorisation schemes have been upheld on pesticides, fungicides, bacteria and additives. Factors which may be taken into account include the harmful effect of the substance, the eating habits of the importing country and national storage habits: Case 53/80 *Officer van Justitie* v. *Koninklijke Kaasfabriek Eyssen*. Where a national requirements for prior authorisation is disproportionate, it will not be justified under Article 30, as the decisions in *Decker* and the *German Beer Purity* case illustrate.

Key cases

1 Case C-120/95 *Decker* v. *Caisse de Maladie des Employées Privés*: The ECJ considered a preliminary reference in relation to a requirement by the Luxembourg government for prior authorisation before claiming the cost of spectacles made outside Luxembourg. The ECJ found that such a requirement acts as a barrier to the free movement of goods, since it curbs the importation of spectacles, and that it was not justified on grounds of public health, since spectacles may only be purchased on prescription from a qualified ophthalmologist.

2 Case 178/84 *Commission* v. *Germany (Re Beer Purity Laws)*. The German government banned all additives in beer, not merely a particular additive which could have been justified by German drinking habits. The ECJ held the ban to be disproportionate. It was not justified to satisfy mandatory health or consumer protection requirements.

The precautionary principle in relation to health

Where scientific opinion is divided as to the health risk, a Member State is entitled to decide on the degree of protection for its citizens, in the absence of harmonisation: Case 174/82 *Officier van Justitie* v. *Sandoz BV*. In this case, the Dutch authorities had refused to allow the sale of muesli bars with added vitamins, on the ground that they were dangerous to health, although the bars were freely sold in Germany and Belgium. It was unclear from scientific evidence at which point the addition of vitamins (seen to be beneficial to some degree) could cause harm. The Court held that a requirement for prior authorisation to sell foodstuffs where vitamins had been added did not infringe Article 28 provided it was not disproportionate. However, it added that where the addition of vitamins meets a need, especially a technical or nutritional one, the Member State must authorise its marketing.

Protection of national treasures possessing artistic, historic or archaeological value

These grounds have not yet been invoked to justify a derogation under Article 30. Italy was unsuccessful in its attempt to rely on Article 30 to justify a special tax on the exportation of works of art in Case 7/68 *Commission* v. *Italy (Re Export Tax on Art Treasures)*. While the case law of the ECJ remains undeveloped in this area, two measures were adopted as part of the internal market programme. Regulation 3911/92 on exports of cultural goods seeks to impose uniform controls at borders on the export of protected goods. Categories of protected goods are listed in the Annex to the Regulation and in Directive 93/7, which also provides that Member States retain the right to define their national treasures unlawfully removed from States and for co-operation between national authorities.

Protection of industrial and commercial property

The protection of industrial and commercial property, such as trade marks, copyright and patents, an area of great commercial importance, is one of the exceptions listed in Article for derogation from Articles 28 and 29. This area is considered separately in Chapter 21.

Internal market measures

Member States applying national provisions relating to major needs specified in Article 30 or to protection of the environment or working environment must notify the Commission who may confirm the provisions if they do not constitute a means of arbitrary or disguised restriction on inter-member trade. Measures must be proportionate. Member States must also notify the grounds for maintaining these provisions. Strict procedures for the Commission are laid down in Article 95(4). Improper use of these powers entitles the Commission or another Member State to bring an action in the ECJ.

Derogation outside Article 28

Derogation from Article 28 outside Article 30 is provided in the form of measures to meet deflections of trade capable of obstructing EC commercial policy, or economic difficulties in any Member State arising out of the implementation of the common commercial policy: Article 134 (ex 115): see Case 41/76 *Donckerwolcke* v. *Procureur de la République*.

Such measures may be taken by the Commission or the Council on a proposal from the Commission and are subject to the principle of proportionality. In Case 59/84 *Tezi Textiel* v. *Commission* the ECJ insisted on a strict interpretation of Article 134 as a departure from the purpose of the common market.

> **Key point**
>
> Article 134 will be repealed by the Treaty of Lisbon.

Derogation may also take place in the interests of national security under Articles 296–297 (ex 223 and 224). Article 296 (ex 223) enables a State to take the measures it considers necessary to protect national security by producing arms provided competition within the EC in non-military products is not affected. Article 297 (ex 224) provides for a consultation procedure to counteract measures taken by another Member State in wartime, threat of war or serious internal disturbances, or to carry out peace-keeping or international security. Improper use may lead to action by the Commission before the ECJ under Article 298 (ex 225).

In a case in relation to the closure by Greece of its frontier with the former Yugoslavian Republic of Macedonia: Case C-120/94 *Commission* v. *Greece*, the ECJ refused the Commission's application for interim relief (Case C-120/94R) owing to uncertainty over the interpretation of Articles 296–298.

QUESTIONS

1 Antonio, a wineseller in Italy, reduced the prices on some of his stock as a 'loss leader'. As a result, he was charged with reselling wine at a loss, contrary to Italian law. Advise Antonio whether the charge is valid under Community law.

2 Compare and contrast the treatment of the Court of Justice of distinctly and indistinctly applicable measures restricting the free movement of goods in relation to health.

3 Following discovery of a new disease in pigs which, it is suspected, may have an adverse effect on the health of consumers, the UK government has imposed a licensing system on pork importers. Michael, an importer, complains that the requirements are so stringent that they are impossible to satisfy. Advise Michael.

Further reading

Chalmers, D., Hadjiemmanuil, C., Monti, G. and Tomkins, A. (2006) *European Union Law*, Cambridge University Press, Chapters 15 and 19.

Craig, P. and De Burca, G. (2007) *EU Law: Text, Cases and Materials*, 4th edition, Oxford University Press, Chapter 19.

Greaves, R. (1998) 'Advertising Restrictions and the Free Movement of Goods and Services', (1998) 23 ELRev. 305.

Macmaolain, C. (2001) 'Free Movement of Foodstuffs, Quality Requirements and Consumer Protection: Have the Court and the Commission Both Got it Wrong?', (2001) 26 ELRev. 413.

Maduro, M. (1997) 'Reforming the Market or the State? Article 30 and the European Constitution: Economic Freedom and Political Rights', (1997) 3 ELJ 51.

Steiner, J. (1992) 'Drawing the Line: Uses and Abuses of Art.30 EEC', (1992) 29 CMLRev. 749.

Weatherill, S. (1996) 'After Keck: Some Thought on how to Clarify the Clarification' (1996) 33 CMLRev. 885.

Weatherill, S. and Beaumont, P. (1999) *EU Law*, 3rd edition, Penguin.

White, E. (1989) 'In Search of the Limits to Article 30 of the EEC Treaty', (1998) 26 CMLRev. 235.

Visit **http://www.mylawchamber.co.uk/kent** to access
answer guidance to questions in the book to test
yourself on this chapter.

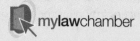

Use **Case Navigator** to read in full some of the key cases referenced
in this chapter:

- 7/68 **Commission** *v.* **Italy (Re Export Tax on Art Treasures)**
  [1968] ECR 423
- 121/85 **Conegate** [1986] ECR 1007
- 8/74 **Dassonville** [1974] ECR 837
- C-267 and 268/91 **Keck and Mithouard** [1993] ECR I-6097
- 120/78 **Rewe-Zentral AG** *v.* **Bundesmonopolverwaltung für
  Branntwein ('Cassis de Dijon')** [1979] ECR 649

13 Union citizenship

INTRODUCTION

Before the Maastricht Treaty the rights of Union nationals to move around the Community and reside outside the home State depended largely on economic status. Their rights as workers, self-employed persons or in relation to the exercise of the right of establishment have been clearly defined under the Treaty as follows:

- Articles 39–42 (ex 48–51) on the free movement of workers: see Chapter 14;
- Articles 43–48 (ex 52–58) on the right of establishment: see Chapter 15;
- Articles 49–55 (ex 59–66) on the freedom to provide services: see Chapter 15.

Provision was made for the rights of their families under secondary legislation.

To accord with the move to political union, the TEU introduced the category of Union citizenship under Articles 17–22 of the Treaty. These provisions enabled citizens to exercise rights of movement and residence, as well as political rights. Detailed provision to implement the free movement rights of citizens was made in Directive 2004/38 (with effect from 30 April 2006). The Court of Justice, after a slow start, began to develop a body of case law on Union citizenship, extending existing rights under Community law by applying the principle of non-discrimination. See, for example, Case C-148/02 *Garcia Avello* (the right to change surnames) and Case C-274/96 *Bickel and Franz* (the right to the use of the German language in criminal proceedings in a border area).

Who is a Union citizen?

The introduction of Union citizenship was one of the most significant changes under the TEU. The category of 'Union citizens' is determined by national not EU law.

Article 17 of the EC Treaty provides:

1 Citizenship of the Union is hereby established. Every person holding the nationality of a Member State shall be a citizen of the Union. Citizenship shall complement and not replace national citizenship.
2 Citizens of the Union shall enjoy the rights conferred by this Treaty and shall be subject to the duties imposed thereby.

Article 18(1) provides:

> Every citizen shall have the right to move and reside freely within the territory of the Member States, subject to the limitations and conditions laid down in the Treaty and by the measures adopted to give it effect.

The second sentence of Article 17(1) on complementary citizenship was added by the TOA. The word 'complement' will be replaced by the words 'be additional to' under the Treaty of Lisbon which will provide a new Article 17(2), as follows:

> Citizens of the Union shall enjoy the rights and be subject to the duties provided for in the Treaties. They shall have, *inter alia*: (a) the right to move and reside freely within the territory of the Member States'. . . . These rights shall be exercised in accordance with the conditions and limits defined by the Treaties and the measures adopted thereunder.

The Treaty of Lisbon does not replace Article 18(1), though it appears to duplicate it. Measures to attain the objectives under Article 18(1) will be taken under the ordinary legislative procedure, with a new Article 18(3) empowering the Council to adopt measures on social security or social protection under the special legislative procedure.

At first sight it would appear that the introduction of Union citizenship under Articles 17 and 18 severed the link between economic status and the freedom to move and reside. However, the reference to 'limitations and conditions' and 'measures adopted to give it effect' was initially interpreted by Member States as support for the continued application of financial restrictions on the residence of Union citizens. While the words 'limitations and conditions' clearly encompass the derogations on grounds of public policy, public security and public health (see below), it is unclear whether they were intended to cover limitations such as the financial and insurance requirements of the Single Market directives for the economically inactive under Directives 93/96, 90/354 and 90/366 (now replaced by Directive 2004/38).

In the early years after the TEU, the Court did little to indicate that Union citizenship rights were more than symbolic. Academic commentators began to query whether Union citizenship added anything new or whether it merely gave a new name to rights which already existed. However, in Case C-85/96 *Martinez Sala* v. *Freistaat Bayern* the Court identified a rationale to develop the rights of citizens, thereby signalling its recognition of citizenship as a significant right.

Martinez Sala: a blueprint for citizenship

Key case

The case arose out of the refusal by the German authorities to pay child-rearing allowance to Ms Sala, a Spanish national who had been resident for many years in Germany, working intermittently before she gave birth. Her claim for the allowance was rejected as she did not have a current residence permit, although she had applied for one. The ECJ (Article 234) held that where a Union citizen is lawfully resident in the territory of the host State, he or she may rely on the principle of non-discrimination in all areas within the material scope of the Treaty. The effect of the ruling was that any lawfully resident Union citizen would be able to claim a benefit such as the child-rearing allowance: Case C-85/96 *Martinez Sala* v. *Freistaat Bayern*.

Citizenship as a 'fundamental status'

The Court applied a similar reasoning in Case C-184/99 *Grzelczyk* v. *Centre Public de l'Aide Sociale d'Ottignies-Louvain-la-Neuve*, a case arising out of a claim for financial relief by a French national studying in Belgium. The applicant claimed it was discriminatory to refuse him relief on the grounds that he was outside the scope of the applicable secondary legislation, Regulation 1612/68. The Court found that the rule in relation to 'sufficient resources' merely required the student to make a declaration at the start of the period of study as to resources. It held that a Member State may rely on Directive 93/96 to decide that a student who has recourse to social assistance no longer fulfils the conditions for residence, and may withdraw his residence permit. Such withdrawal should not, however, be the automatic result of an application for social assistance.

The Court then made an important declaration about the status of Union citizenship, which it repeated in later decisions:

Key point

'Union citizenship is destined to be the fundamental status of nationals of the Member States, enabling those who find themselves in the same situation to enjoy the same treatment, irrespective of nationality, subject to such exceptions as are expressly provided for': Case C-184/99 *Grzelczyk*.

A directly effective right

The Court developed its reasoning further in Case C-413/99 *Baumbast and R.* v. *Secretary of State for the Home Department*, where it held that Article 18(1) is directly effective.

Key case

B, a German national, lived in the UK with his wife, a Colombian national, and their two children, first as an employed and then as a self-employed person. When his business failed, B worked outside the EU, while the rest of the family stayed on in the UK, travelling to Germany for medical treatment, where they had comprehensive medical cover. B appealed against the UK government's refusal to renew the residence permits for himself and his family. The ECJ (Article 234) held that a Union citizen who no longer enjoys residence rights as a migrant worker →

> may enjoy a right of residence by direct application of Article 18(1). While the exercise of the right is subject to limitations and conditions, they must be applied in accordance with the general principles of Community law, particularly the principle of proportionality: Case C-413/99 *Baumbast and R.*

Baumbast demonstrates that the introduction of Union citizenship has strengthened the rights of those who are covered by it, creating a right which is directly effective and moving the rights of some categories previously covered only by secondary legislation (e.g. students under Directive 93/96) to the protection of a substantive right under the Treaty, which must be read subject to the general principles of Community law.[1]

The need for integration

The rights of students arose again in the Case C-209/03 *Dany Bidar*, in the context of a decision to refuse an application for a student loan to a French national who had attended school in the UK for three years before taking up a university place at the London School of Economics. The Court held that the introduction of Union citizenship had changed the position of students, whose requests for assistance had previously been found to be outside the Treaty (see Case 197/86 *Brown* and Case 39/86 *Lair*).

> **Key point**
>
> The Court ruled in *Bidar* that lawfully resident students were covered after the TEU by the principle of non-discrimination and could claim financial assistance provided they could demonstrate a sufficient degree of integration into the society of that State, for example by having lived there for a certain length of time.

In *Bidar* the Court seems to have been willing to go further than Directive 2004/38 (not then in force) which makes no specific provision regarding student loans or maintenance grants. It does not follow, however, that students from across the EU will readily gain access to financial support such as student loans outside the home State, as establishing the necessary degree of integration will be difficult.

Jobseekers and the economically inactive

The need for a suitably developed link was also a factor in claims brought by Union citizens for jobseekers' allowances. In Case C-224/98 *D'Hoop* v. *Office Nationale de l'Emploi* a Belgian applicant was refused a 'tideover' allowance (payable when seeking a first job) because she had completed her secondary education in France. In this case, the link required was seen to be disproportionate. The link with the host State

---

[1] See Craig and De Burca, (2007: 852–853).

was weaker in Case C-138/02 *Collins* v. *Secretary of State for Work and Pensions*. In this case an Irish national who had moved to the UK to look for work unsuccessfully claimed a jobseeker's allowance. The Court found that a jobseeker was entitled to a financial benefit which was intended to facilitate access to the labour market of another Member State. The residence requirement imposed by the UK, which had defeated the claim by *Collins*, had to be interpreted in accordance with the principle of proportionality.

In Case C-456/02 *Trojani* v. *CPAS* the Court found that a Union citizen who is lawfully resident but not economically active may rely on the principle of non-discrimination in a claim for social assistance. While it was open to the host State to find that reliance on social assistance infringed the right of residence, any decision to deport was subject to the principle of proportionality.

13

Union citizenship

The rights of children and their parents

The case of *Zhu and Chen*, arising from a residence claim in very specific circumstances, demonstrates the reality of the right under Article 18. It shows us clearly that the beneficiary of the right need exercise the right consciously (as a young child), and that parents may derive rights from such a child who needs to be cared for.

Key case

Mrs Chen came to the UK from China in order to escape the Chinese 'one child' policy. She moved to Northern Ireland from Wales to give birth, so that the child would acquire Irish nationality. After the birth, Mrs Chen and the child moved back to Wales, where the family had sufficient resources to avoid becoming a burden on the state. The UK government refused Mrs Chen residence rights, a decision which Mrs Chen challenged. The ECJ (Article 234) stated that even though the child had never left the UK this was not a 'wholly internal situation' as she had the nationality of another Member State, Ireland. It rejected the view that Mrs Chen's temporary move to Northern Ireland was an abuse of EU law, ruling that the child was capable of exercising free movement rights and that her mother's rights derived from the fact that her child needed to be cared for by her: Case C-200/01 *Zhu and Chen*.

Political rights of Union citizens

Union citizenship bestows the following political rights on Union citizens under Articles 19–21:[2]

- The right to vote and stand as a candidate in municipal elections and elections to the EP in a Member State in which the Union citizen is resident but not a national (*Article 19*). The right has been implemented in relation to municipal elections by

---

[2] The Treaty of Lisbon will renumber these provisions as Article 17(b), (c) and (d).

Directive 94/80 since 1996 and to EP elections by Directive 93/109 since 1993. The ECJ found that Belgium had infringed this Directive in Case C-323/97 *Commission v. Belgium* when it failed to allow EU citizens other than Belgian nationals to vote or stand in municipal elections. See also Case C-145/04 *Spain* v. *UK* in relation to the voting rights in the EP of the residents of Gibraltar (see p.74).

- The right to receive diplomatic and consular protection in the State in which the Union citizen is resident on the same terms as a national of that State (*Article 20*), implemented by Directive 95/533 from May 2002.
- The right to petition the EP and the Community Ombudsman (*Article 21*), and to write to the EC institutions in any of the official languages (rights already recognised in practice by the EP).

The Commission is required to report on the application of the Citizenship provisions to the EP, Council and Economic and Social Committee every three years (Article 22(1)), while the Council must adopt provisions which it recommends to Member States. So far, the interest of its citizens in participation in EP elections has been very low.[3] However, the Treaty of Lisbon provides encouragement to citizens to participate in the decision-making process, particularly through the citizens' initiative (see Chapter 2) under Article 8B of the TEU. Further provision will be made for this in an amendment to Article 21.

DIRECTIVE 2004/38

Directive 2004/38 of the Council and the EP came into effect on 30 April 2006 in implementation of Article 18 EC after many years of delay. It provides detailed rights for Union citizens and their family members, particularly the right to move freely and reside throughout the territories of the Member States. Directive 2004/38 introduces some new elements, but is mainly a consolidating piece of legislation, amending Regulation 1612/68, and repealing Directives including 68/360, 90/364 and 365, and 93/96, and replaces Directive 64/221. The freedom of movement and residence of EU citizens and their families may be restricted on grounds of public policy, public health or public security: Article 27, see below.

Three categories of residence rights

The Directive introduces three categories of residence rights:

1 residence rights up to three months;
2 residence rights for more than three months;
3 permanent residence rights.

Residence rights up to three months

Union citizens and their families have the right of residence in another Member State for up to three months on production of a valid identity card or passport under

---

[3] COM (2003) 174.

Article 6(1), provided they do not become a burden on the social assistance of the host State.

Residence rights for more than three months

In order to establish residence rights after three months, the individual will need to demonstrate under Article 7(1) that he or she falls within one of the following categories (all previously recognised under Community law and of an essentially economic nature):

(a) Union citizens who are workers or self-employed in the host State.
(b) All other Union citizens with sufficient resources to avoid becoming a burden on the social assistance system of the host State and comprehensive sickness cover in that State while they are resident.
(c) Union citizens following a course of study in the host State, provided they have comprehensive sickness cover in that State and give an assurance to the relevant authority, by means of a declaration or equivalent means, that they have sufficient resources for themselves and their family members not to become a burden on the social assistance system of the host Member State during their period of residence.
(d) The family members accompanying or joining an EU citizen who satisfies the conditions in (a), (b) or (c).

The right of residence for longer than three months is subject to the requirement that the Union citizen and family members must continue to meet the conditions in Article 7: Article 14(2). Applying the principle of proportionality, the Directive provides in Article 14(3) that failure to do so should not lead automatically to deportation. The host State should consider whether the case is one of temporary difficulties, taking into account duration of stay, personal circumstances and the amount of aid granted. Persons with a genuine chance of finding employment or self-employment should not be expelled unless considerations of public policy or public security apply. Registration may be required for stays over three months.

Permanent residence rights

Permanent residence rights are granted to citizens who have resided lawfully for five years or more (Article 16) and are not subject to the conditions otherwise imposed under Chapter III (Articles 6 to 15). Family members who are not nationals of a Member State but who have legally resided with the Union citizen in the host State for a continuous period of five years also benefit from permanent residence rights: Article 16(2).

> ### Key point
>
> Once permanent residence rights have been established, it is extremely difficult for a Member State to remove the Union citizen or family member, as it is necessary to establish that there are serious grounds of public policy or public security under Article 28: see p. 209. Permanent resident rights may only be lost through absence from the host Member State for a period exceeding two years: Article 16(4).

A shorter continuous period of three years' lawful residence may be sufficient for workers or the self-employed who reach the age of entitlement to a state pension in the host State provided they have worked for at least 12 months there (Article 17(1)(a)). An exceptions is also made for individuals who suffer industrial accidents, who only require two years' lawful residence (Article 17(1)(b)) and frontier workers living in the host State but working in another after three years' continuous residence, provided they return to the host State at least once a week (Article 17(1)(c)).

Definition of 'family members'

The Directive repealed Article 10 Regulation 1612/68 and broadened the definition of 'family member' to include registered partners. Family members are defined by Article 2(2) of the Directive as:

(a) the spouse;
(b) the partner with whom the EU citizen has contracted a registered partnership, on the basis of the legislation of a Member State, if the legislation of the host Member State treats registered partnerships as equivalent to marriage and in accordance with the conditions laid down in the relevant legislation of the Member State;
(c) the direct descendants who are under the age of 21 or are dependants and those of the spouse or partner, as defined in (b);
(d) the dependent direct relatives in the ascending line and those of the partner or spouse, as defined in (b).

Who is a 'spouse'?

An individual who is married to a Union citizen and who is not separated is certainly covered by the term 'spouse'. In some cases, however, it may be necessary to consider whether the marriage is recognised as providing residence rights by one of the Member States. Such a right would then be recognised by the other Member States, in accordance with the principle of mutual recognition.

The position of non-EU nationals married to Union citizens can be complex, as the pre-Directive case law of the ECJ illustrates, particularly where the third country national is not lawfully resident in the EU.

Key case

Akrich, a Moroccan national, entered the UK illegally in 1989 on a tourist visa. He was convicted of theft, was refused leave to remain and deported. Akrich re-entered the UK illegally in 1992, marrying a British national in 1996. He failed to regularise the marriage with the British authorities and moved to Ireland, before applying unsuccessfully for revocation of the deportation order in order to re-enter the UK, relying on Article 10 of Regulation 1612/68, which provided a right of installation in the Member State in which the other spouse resided. The UK authorities considered that Akrich was deliberately taking advantage of EU rights of free movement.

The ECJ held (Article 234) that the intention of the parties was irrelevant, unless there was an abuse of EU law, such as in the case of a marriage of convenience. The Court also found that the non-EU spouse could only benefit from EU rights where he was lawfully resident (which Akrich was not): Case C-109/01 *Secretary of State for the Home Department* v. *Akrich.*

The position was clarified in Case C-1/05 *Jia* v. *Migrationsverket* in which the Court held that a third country national may acquire rights under EU law without having been previously resident in another Member State, enabling a non-EU national to move directly to the host state from a third country.

Marriages of convenience

Member States are entitled to question whether the marriage is 'real': Article 35. Rights conferred by the Directive may be refused, withdrawn or terminated by Member States in the case of abuse of rights or fraud such as a marriage of convenience. This usually arises where a non-EU national marries an EU national to acquire residence and other rights.

Effect of divorce and separation

Before implementation of Directive 2004/38, the position was unclear, as there were no decisions of the ECJ as to the effect of divorce on family rights. Some guidance was provided by the decision in Case 267/83 *Diatta* v. *Land Berlin* (on the entitlement of a Senegalese woman separated from her German husband) where the Court ruled that separation does not dissolve the marital relationship as it has not been terminated by the competent authorities.

Key point

Directive 2004/38 introduced new provision for the consequences of divorce and separation under Article 13(2) that, 'Divorce, annulment of marriage or termination of the registered partnership . . . shall not entail loss of the right of residence of a Union citizen's family members who are not nationals of a Member State' in specific circumstances.

Under Article 13(2) there will be no loss of residence rights as follows:

(a) before initiation of the divorce proceedings or termination of the registered partnership . . . the marriage or registered partnership has lasted at least 3 years, including one year in the host Member State; or
(b) by agreement . . . the spouse or partner who is not a national of a Member State has custody of the Union citizen's children; or

(c) it is warranted by particularly difficult circumstances, such as having been the victim of domestic violence while the marriage or registered partnership was subsisting.

Cohabitees and registered partners

Before Directive 2004/38 cohabitees enjoyed no general right of residence under EU law, although entitlement might arise in specific instances under the principle of non-discrimination in Article 12 EC. See Case 59/85 *Netherlands* v. *Reed*, where a residence right arose for a UK national cohabiting with another UK national in circumstances which would have given rise to residence rights if one of the parties had been a Dutch national.

Key point

Registered partners under Article 2(2) of Directive 2004/38 acquired the same residence and other rights as spouses, provided that the partnership is recognised as equivalent to marriage in the host State.

A partnership which is validly registered in one Member State but not recognised by the host State will not, therefore, be covered by Article 2(2). Such an individual, along with certain other family members, may gain some rights from Article 3(2) of the Directive, depending on the durability of the relationship. Article 3(2) requires the host Member State, in accordance with national legislation, to facilitate entry and residence of:

(a) any other family members, irrespective of their nationality, not falling under the definition in point 2 of Article 2 who, in the country from which they have come, are dependants of members of the household of the Union citizen having the primary right of residence, or where serious health grounds require the personal care of the family member by the Union citizen;
(b) the partner with whom the Union citizen has a durable relationship, duly attested.

The wording of Article 3(2) is likely to be the subject of future referrals to the ECJ under Article 234 to clarify the host State's commitment to 'facilitate entry and residence', as well as its obligation to undertake an extensive examination of the personal circumstances' and to 'justify any denial of entry or residence to these people'. Meanwhile, the scope of the right under Article 3(2) remains uncertain, but should be read subject to the fundamental right of family reunification.

Union citizens and family members who are not EU nationals, lacking necessary travel documents or visas, should not be excluded by Member States but given a reasonable opportunity to obtain the necessary documentation or have them brought to them within a reasonable time: Article 5(4) of the Directive, incorporating the decision in Case C-459/99 *MRAX* v. *Belgium*.

Equality of treatment

Under Article 24(1), Union citizens and their families, including third country nationals, are entitled to equal treatment, as follows:

> Subject to such specific provisions as are expressly provided for in the Treaty and secondary law, all Union citizens residing on the basis of this Directive in the territory of the host Member State shall enjoy equal treatment with the nationals of that Member State within the scope of the Treaty. The benefit of this right shall be extended to family members who are not nationals of a Member State and who have the right of residence or permanent residence.

Article 24(2) gives effect to the principle of equal treatment set out in cases such as *Grzelczyk*. There is no duty on the host State to confer entitlement to social assistance during the first three months of residence: Article 24(2). Union citizens are not entitled to a student loan or maintenance grant under the Directive unless they are workers, self-employed or their families. This contrasts with the position in *Bidar* where the Court found that such an entitlement would arise where the applicant has demonstrated a sufficient level of integration with the society of the host State (see p.198).

Rights of exit and entry

Key point

Union citizens with a valid identity card or passport and their family members who are not EU nationals are entitled to leave the territory of a Member State to travel to another Member State under Article 4. A similar right of entry is provided by Article 5. Administrative formalities for Union citizens are set out in Article 8 and for family members who are not EU nationals in Article 9 of Directive 2004/38.

The right to residence derives from the Treaty, not from the possession of a residence permit. In Case 157/79 *R. v. Pieck* the ECJ held that the public policy proviso did not justify *general* formalities at the frontier beyond the production of a valid identity card or passport. Article 39(3) is a means of taking measures against *individuals* who may pose a threat.

In Case 48/75 *Procureur du Roi v. Royer* the ECJ held that the right to enter includes the right to enter in search of work. This right is not, however, of unlimited duration, as the host State may be entitled to deport the Union citizen after a reasonable period of time. In Case C-292/89 *R v. Immigration Appeal Tribunal ex parte Antonissen* a period of six months before deportation was found to be sufficient where there was no evidence of a continuing genuine attempt to find work. (The UK was keen to deport as the applicant would have been entitled to state benefits after six months.) The right of entry and residence should now be read subject to Article 7 of the Directive (right of residence for more than three months: see above).

LIMITATIONS JUSTIFIED ON GROUNDS OF PUBLIC POLICY, PUBLIC SECURITY OR PUBLIC HEALTH

Scope of the limitation

Directive 2004/38 provides in Chapter VI, Articles 27 to 33 for restrictions on the right of entry and residence of Union citizens and their family members on grounds of public policy, security or public heath under the Directive. The restrictions under Directive 2004/38 apply regardless of the category in which the individual exercises free movement rights.

Directive 2004/38 repeals Directive 64/221 which previously applied to measures taken by Member States restricting entry and residence on grounds of public policy, public health or public security. 'Public policy' is a translation of the French expression *l'ordre public*, perhaps better translated as 'public order'. 'Public security' was not defined in Directive 64/221, but was often invoked as an alternative to public policy. 'Public health' was defined in relation to diseases listed in the Annex to the Directive; sufferers from these diseases might be refused entry or residence. These provisions have been consolidated into Directive 2004/38 along with the case law of the ECJ on Directive 64/221, and some new elements. The case law is considered in relation to the new provisions under Directive 2004/38.

> **Key point**
>
> Article 27(2) specifies in paragraph 1 that measures taken on grounds of public policy or public security shall comply with the *principle of proportionality*, and shall be based exclusively on the personal conduct of the individual concerned.
>
> Criminal connections do not in themselves constitute grounds for taking such measures.

The reference to proportionality in Article 27(2) reflects the decision of the ECJ in Case 48/75 *Procureur du Roi* v. *Royer* where the Court held that failure to comply with administrative requirements (e.g. to renew a passport or ID card) does not justify deportation although it may lead to a penalty, provided the penalty is not disproportionate.

In Case C-348/96 *Donatella Calfa* an Italian national on holiday on Crete was convicted of possession and use of prohibited drugs and sentenced to three months' imprisonment, as well as to expulsion for life from Greece. (Expulsion was an automatic penalty under Greek law, unless there were compelling reasons for not doing so.) The ECJ held that automatic expulsion following conviction failed to take account of the individual's personal conduct and the extent to which it posed a threat.

Personal conduct

Article 27(2) provides in paragraph 3 that:

> The personal conduct of the individual concerned must represent a genuine, present and sufficiently serious threat affecting one of the fundamental interests of society. Justifications that are isolated from the particulars of the case or that rely on considerations of general elements shall not be accepted (Article 27(2)).

Article 27(2) reflects decisions including Case 36/75 *Rutili* v. *Ministre de l'Intérieur* where the Court held that restrictions on the movement of an EC national under Article 39(3) may not be imposed unless the behaviour of the individual constitutes a genuine and sufficiently serious threat to public policy. Rutili, an Italian political activist, had challenged the French Minister of the Interior's decision to restrict his activities to certain *départements*. The Court held under Article 234 that only a total ban may be considered under the public policy proviso, as a partial ban may only be imposed where a similar restriction may be placed on a national of the host State. It also held that restrictions may not be placed on a worker's rights to enter another Member State, live and move freely unless his presence constituted a genuine and sufficiently serious threat to public policy, in accordance with Articles 8–11 of the ECHR. These Articles do not permit restrictions in the interests of national security or public safety unless they are necessary to protect those interests in a democratic society.

In Case C-100/01 *Ministre de l'Interieur* v. *Olazabal*, unlike the decision in *Rutili*, the Court held that partial restrictions on residence rights may be imposed on nationals of other Member States, provided the host State imposes punitive measures 'or other genuine and effective measures' against its own nationals to combat that conduct.

The area of discretion left to national authorities in relation to the public policy/public security proviso, particularly in relation to convictions, may be examined by reference to decisions of the ECJ such as *Rutili* (above), *Bouchereau*, *Bonsignore*, *Van Duyn* and *Adoui*.

Convictions

Measures taken on grounds of public policy will not be justified on the basis of criminal convictions alone unless the convictions show there is a present threat to public policy: Case 30/77 *R* v. *Bouchereau*. 'Measures' were defined in *Bouchereau* as 'any action affecting the rights of persons coming within the field of application of Article 39 to enter and reside freely in a Member State on the same conditions as the nationals of the host state'.

Key case

Bouchereau, a French national, came to work in the UK in 1975. He was convicted of unlawful possession of drugs in June 1976, having pleaded guilty to a similar offence in January 1976. The magistrates' court referred to the ECJ questions to determine to what extent previous convictions may be considered as a ground for exclusion. The ECJ held that restrictions on the movement of an EC national may not be imposed unless the individual's behaviour constitutes a genuine and sufficiently serious threat to one of the fundamental interests of society. A previous criminal conviction may only be taken into account as evidence of personal conduct where it constitutes a present threat to the requirements of public policy, by indicating a likelihood of recurrence. Past conduct alone, however, may constitute a present threat where the conduct is sufficiently serious: Case 30/77 *R. v. Bouchereau.*

The need to assess the threat on an individual basis is illustrated by the case of *Bonsignore B.* an Italian working in Germany, accidentally shot his brother with a pistol. He was convicted and fined for unlawful possession of a firearm and was ordered to be deported. He challenged the deportation order in the German courts, which made a referral to the ECJ. HELD (ECJ): The public policy requirement may only be invoked to justify a deportation for breaches of the peace and public security which may be committed by the individual concerned and not for reasons of a general preventive nature: Case 67/74 *Bonsignore v. Oberstadtdirecktor of the City of Cologne.*

While the concept of public policy varies from State to State, its scope may not be unilaterally determined by Member States without control by the EC institutions: Case 41/74 *Van Duyn v. Home Office.*

Key case

Van Duyn, a Dutch woman was prevented by the Home Office from taking up employment in the UK with the Church of Scientology, an organisation which was not illegal but which was regarded as socially harmful by the UK government. The ECJ found that present but not past association may be considered as personal conduct. While holding that Member States may not unilaterally determine the scope of public policy, the Court nevertheless permitted a stricter standard to be applied to an EC national in these circumstances than would have been applied to a UK national where the government deemed it to be necessary: Case 41/74 *Van Duyn v. Home Office.*

It is difficult to reconcile the decision in *Van Duyn* with the later ruling in Cases 115 and 116/81 *Adoui and Cornaille v. Belgian State,* where two prostitutes, both EC nationals, were denied residence permits in Belgium, despite the fact that prostitution is not illegal there. The ECJ held that Member States may *not* refuse residence to EC nationals on account of conduct which is not illegal or controlled in the nationals of the host state. The Court did not, however, seek to distinguish or overrule its previous decision in *Van Duyn*. Arguably, *Adoui* better represents the present approach of the Court's interpretation of departures from the single market provisions of the Treaty.

Supply of information

Provision is made in Article 27(3) for supplying of information by the Member State of origin to the host Member Sate in order to ascertain whether the person concerned represents a threat. Where a person is expelled, he or she is entitled to re-enter the Member State issuing the passport or ID card without formality (Article 27(4)).

Protection against expulsion

Key point

Article 28 provides for protection against expulsion. Host Member States must take account of considerations such as length of residence, family and economic considerations, social and cultural integration into the host State and limits with the country of origin: Article 28(1).

Union citizens with a permanent right of residence or their family members, irrespective of nationality, may not be expelled unless there are *serious* grounds of public policy or public security: Article 28(2).

Expulsion decisions may not be taken against Union citizens, unless the decision is based on imperative grounds of public security, as defined by the Member States, if they:

(a) have resided in the Member State for the previous ten years; or
(b) are a minor, unless the expulsion is necessary for the best interests of the child under the UN Convention on the Rights of the Child 1989: Article 28(3).

Notification of decisions: procedural safeguards

Key point

Article 30 provides for notification in writing of any decision taken under Article 27(1). This must be in clear language, informing the persons concerned of the grounds on which the action is taken and the relevant appeals mechanisms.

Article 31 provides for procedural safeguards, including access to judicial and administrative redress.

Duration of exclusion orders: expulsion as a penalty of legal consequence

Article 32 provides that persons excluded on grounds of public policy, public security or public health may submit an application to have the order lifted after a reasonable period or three years from the enforcement of the final exclusion order.

Article 32 provides that expulsion orders may not be issued by the host State as a penalty or legal consequence of a custodial penalty unless they conform to the requirements of Articles 27, 28 and 29.

The public health exception

Article 29 covers the public health exception. It is wider than the provisions under the Annex to Directive 64/221 in terms of the diseases covered.

Under Article 29(1) the only diseases justifying measures which restrict freedom of movement are diseases with epidemic potential as defined by the World Health Organisation and other infectious or contagious parasitic diseases where there are controls on the nationals of the host state.

Article 29(2) provides that diseases occurring after a three-month period from the date of arrival do not constitute grounds for expulsion. Article 29(3) provides that where there are serious grounds that it is necessary, Member States may, within three months from the date of arrival, require persons entitled to the right of residence to undergo, free of charge, a medical examination to certify that they are not suffering from any of the conditions in para. 1. Such medical examinations are not required as a matter of routine.

Nationals of third countries

Considerations of space do not permit detailed treatment of the rights of third-country nationals in this book. Such nationals enjoy rights under various legal arrangements including association agreements. Case C-340/97 *Nazli* v. *Nurnberg* provides an example. In this case a Turkish national was detained for a year in custody pending criminal proceedings after being lawfully employed in Germany for four years. The ECJ held that the national of a third country does not, in such circumstances, lose his or her status as a lawful member of the EU workforce under an association agreement and may claim an extension of his or her residence permit to enable him or her to continue to claim right of access to paid employment.

Nationals of third countries who are employed by undertakings established within the EU may rely on rights derived from their employers. Thus, they must be allowed to move with the undertaking with no greater restriction than would be applied to nationals in the state of origin: Case C-113/89 *Rush Portugesa*.

Third-country nationals may be required to obtain a visa, but the host State should give them 'every assistance' to do so under Article 5(4) of Directive 2004/38.

Nationals of third countries married to a Union citizen are entitled to reside in the Member State of their spouse under Article 2(2) Directive 2004/38: see above.

Nationals from Iceland, Norway and Liechtenstein enjoy full rights of free movement within the EU under the European Economic Area Agreement.

Third country nationals will gain some rights under the Treaty of Lisbon: see below.

The Schengen Agreement

The Schengen Agreement is an example of the 'enhanced co-operation' by which some Member States have pursued a deeper level of integration. Five of the EU Member States (France, Germany, Belgium, Luxembourg and the Netherlands) entered the Schengen Agreement in 1985 to create an area within which border formalities would be removed. Gradually the area was extended to include all Member States except the UK and Ireland, which remained outside due to concern about terrorism, drug trafficking and illegal immigration. Under the Schengen Information System (SIS) an information network was established at border posts, police stations and consular agents to enable Member States to access information about individuals, vehicles or objects.

The Schengen Agreement and its implementing convention (the Convention Implementing the Schengen Agreement (CISA)) were brought within the First Pillar of the EU by the TOA. The UK has participated since 1999 in aspects of the Schengen Agreement (police and judicial co-operation in criminal matters, the fight against drugs and the SIS), with Ireland following suit in 2000. Iceland and Norway agreed to play a limited role in Schengen decision making, as has Switzerland since 2004.

13

Union citizenship

Key case

Commission v. *Spain* concerned the relationship between CISA and Community law. The proceedings arose out of the refusal of the Spanish authorities to allow two third-country nationals (Algerians) who were married to Spanish nationals to enter the country because their names were included on the SIS list of persons to be excluded under an alert. The Court made it clear that the Schengen *acquis* (i.e. the body of law surrounding the Schengen Agreement) must comply with Community law. Any restriction on movement must accord with the requirements of Directive 64/221 (in force at the time). As a result, the Court held that a country participating in the Schengen arrangements may issue an alert only after establishing that the individual represents a genuine and sufficiently serious threat to one of the fundamental rights of society. If that country consults the SIS, it must be able to prove that the individual's presence in the area poses such a threat. The Court found against Spain, as it had failed to verify that the individuals posed such a threat before refusing them entry: Case C-503/03.

● Changes under the Treaty of Lisbon

The Treaty of Lisbon will introduce new Article 7a into the TEU, requiring the Union to develop a 'special relationship with neighbouring countries, aiming to establish an area of prosperity and good neighbourliness, founded on the values of the Union and characterized by close and peaceful relations based on co-operation'.

Key point

A new Title IV will be provided under the Treaty of Lisbon, covering the *Area of Freedom, Security and Justice*, replacing Article 61 EC. New Article 61(1) of the TFU states:

> The Union shall constitute an area of freedom, security and justice with respect for fundamental rights and the different legal systems and traditions of the Member States.

The old Title IV, introduced into the EC Treaty by the TOA, required Member States to create an area of freedom, security and justice, within which the free movement of persons would be secured within five years (i.e. by 2004). The Treaty of Lisbon will go further and is more specific.

New Article 61(2) requires the Union to ensure the absence of border controls and to frame a common policy on asylum, immigration and border control, based on solidarity between Member States. Stateless persons are to be treated as third-country nationals.

New Article 61(3) states that the Union will 'endeavour to ensure a high level of security through measures to combat crime, racism and xenophobia' and through co-operation between the police, judicial and other competent authorities, the mutual recognition of judgments in criminal matters and, if necessary, through the approximation of criminal law.

New Article 61(4) provides that the Union 'shall facilitate access to justice', particularly through the mutual recognition of judicial and other decisions in civil matters.

The European Council is required to adopt strategic guidelines under Article 61A for legislative and operational planning within the area of freedom, security and justice.

National Parliaments must ensure that the proposals and legislative initiatives submitted under Chapters 4 and 5 (judicial and police co-operation) comply with the principles of proportionality and subsidiarity.

New Article 61E makes it clear that Title IV does not affect the duty of Member States to maintain law and order and to safeguard national security.

Key point

New Article 62(1) requires the Union to develop a policy with a view to:

(a) ensuring the absence of border controls on persons, whatever their nationality;

(b) carrying out checks on persons and efficient monitoring of the crossing of external borders;

(c) the gradual introduction of an integrated management system for external borders.

New Article 62(2) empowers the EP and the Council under the ordinary legislative procedure to adopt measures to achieve the policy in Article 61(1). If the Treaty has not provided the necessary powers and further action is necessary, Article 61(3) enables the Council, under the special legislative procedure, to act by unanimity after consulting the EP.

Article 62(4) makes it clear that the competence of Member States in relation to the geographical demarcation of their borders in accordance with international law is not affected.

Article 63 requires the Union to develop a common policy on asylum, subsidiary protection and temporary protection in accordance with the international law on the status of refugees.

Article 63A requires the Union to develop a common immigration policy aimed at ensuring the efficient management of migration flows, fair treatment of third-country nationals residing legally in Member States, and the prevention of, and measures to combat, illegal immigration and trafficking in human beings.

QUESTIONS

1 To what extent did the introduction of European citizenship under the Treaty of Maastricht create a new right of residence throughout the EU on which individuals may rely?

2 How has the implementation of Directive 2004/38 strengthened the rights of Union citizens against deportation or other restrictions of movement and residence within the EU?

Further reading

Chalmers, D., Hadjiemmanuil, C., Monti, G. and Tomkins, A. (2006) *European Union Law*, Cambridge University Press, Chapter 13.

Closa, G. (1992) 'The Concept of Citizenship in the Treaty on European Union', (1992) 29 CMLRev. 1137.

Craig, P. and De Burca, G. (2007) *EU Law: Text, Cases and Materials*, 4th edition, Oxford University Press, Chapter 23.

Dougan, M. (2006) 'The Constitutional Dimension to the Case law on Union Citizenship', (2006) 31 ELRev. 613.

Hatzopoulos, V. (2008) 'With or without you. . . . Judging politically in the field of Area of Freedom, Security and Justice' (2008) 33 ELRev. 45, pp.57–58 (on The Schengen Convention).

O'Leary, S. (1999) 'Putting Flesh on the Bones of European Citizenship', (1999) 24 ELRev. 68.

Tomuschat, C. (2000) 'Casenote on Case C-85/96 *Maria Martinez Sala* v. *Freistaat Bayern*', (2000) 37 CMLRev. 449.

Toner, H. (2000) 'Judicial Interpretation of European Union Citizenship: Consolidation or Transformation?', (2000) 7 MJ 158.

Visit **http://www.mylawchamber.co.uk/kent** to access answer guidance to questions in the book to test yourself on this chapter.

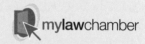

Use **Case Navigator** to read in full some of the key cases referenced in this chapter:

- C-413/99 **Baumbast** [2002] ECR I-7091
- 41/74 **Van Duyn** v. **Home Office** [1974] ECR 1337

14 Free movement of workers

INTRODUCTION

Article 3(c) of the EC Treaty requires 'the abolition, as between Member States, of obstacles to freedom of movement of persons'. The free movement of persons remains one of the cornerstones of the single market. Specific provision for the free movement of workers is made in Articles 39–42 (ex 48–51), for the right of establishment in Articles 43–48 (ex 52–58) and for the freedom to provide services in Articles 49–55 (ex 59–66). The free movement of workers is essentially an individual, economic right, enabling the worker to live and work in a State other than the home State.

Article 40 empowers the Council to adopt secondary legislation to achieve the objectives in Article 39. Most of this secondary legislation was consolidated from April 2006 by Directive 2004/38 which recognises the rights of the members of the workers' families, as well as other categories, to reside with the worker in the host State. The free movement of workers is subject to derogations under Article 39(3) and Directive 2004/38 on grounds of public policy, public security and public health: see Chapter 13. Employment in the public service (Article 39(4)) and activities connected with the exercise of state authority under Article 66 (ex 55) are excluded from the right of free movement.

Non-discrimination

Article 12 (ex 6) EC which prohibits any discrimination on grounds of nationality underlies much of the case law of the ECJ on person. The Article only applies within the scope of the Treaty, that is, in relation to economic activity: Case 36/74 *Walrave and Koch* v. *Association Union Cycliste Internationale*.

Treaty provision

Article 39(1) of the EC Treaty provides that freedom of movement of workers shall be secured within the Community. This freedom under Article 39(2) requires the abolition of any discrimination based on nationality between workers of the Member States in relation to employment, remuneration and other conditions of work and employment. Under Article 39(3) freedom of movement entails the right, subject to limitations justified on grounds of public policy, public health or public security:

- to accept offers of employment actually made;
- to move freely within the territory of Member States for this purpose;
- to stay in a Member State for the purpose of employment under the same provisions laid down by law, regulation or administrative action governing employment of nationals of that State;
- to remain in the territory of a Member State after employment in that State, subject to conditions to be contained in secondary legislation.

Secondary legislation

The main secondary legislation is now Directive 2004/38, which is examined in Chapter 13. Directive 2004/38 consolidated previous secondary legislation, repealing Directive 68/360, Regulation 1251/70 and Directive 64/221, and amending Regulation 1612/68: see below. Workers and their families benefit from rights under the Directive, including the right of permanent residence after five years of residence under Article 16 and entitlement to a state pension after three years of lawful residence in certain circumstance under Article 17(1)(a): see Chapter 13. Administrative formalities over the issuing of a permanent residence certificate are covered by Articles 19–21. Regulation 1408/71 continues to apply to social security.

SCOPE OF ARTICLE 39

'Workers'

The Treaty does not define the word 'worker'. The Court has interpreted the term liberally and has held that the concept of 'worker' is a Community one, which may not be determined by the laws of Member States: Case 53/81 *Levin* v. *Staatsecretaris van Justitie*.

> **Key point**
>
> The essential characteristic of a worker was defined by the ECJ to be the performance of services for and under the direction of another in return for remuneration during a certain period of time: Case 66/85 *Lawrie-Blum* v. *Land Baden-Württemberg*.

The term 'worker' has been construed by the ECJ to include the following:

1 A worker who had lost his job but was capable of finding another: Case 75/63 *Hoekstra* (*née Unger*) v. *BBDA* (see below: Jobseekers and the unemployed).
2 A part-time worker, provided the work was 'real' work of an economic nature and not nominal or minimal: Case 53/81 *Levin*.

3 A part-time music teacher (from Germany) receiving supplementary benefit (in the Netherlands) to bring his income up to subsistence level: Case 139/85 *Kempf* v. *Staatsecretaris van Justitie*.

4 A member of a religious community paid 'keep' and pocket-money but not formal wages where commercial activity was a genuine and inherent part of membership: Case 196/87 *Steymann* v. *Staatsecretaris van Justitie*.

5 A Portuguese national employed prior to Portuguese accession on board ship of another Member State, provided the employment relationship had a sufficiently close link with the territory of that state: Case 9/88 *Lopes da Veiga* v. *Staatsecretaris van Justitie*.

6 An EC national employed by an international organisation in a Member State other than his state of origin, even if the rules of entry and residence are governed by an international agreement between the organisation and the host state: Cases 389 and 390/87 *GBC Echternach and A. Moritz* v. *Netherlands Minister for Education and Science*.

To qualify as a 'worker', the activities performed must serve some economic purpose. In Case 344/87 *Bettray* v. *Staatsecretaris van Justitie* the Court held that paid activities carried out as part of a state-run drug rehabilitation scheme in Belgium did not (unlike *Steymann*) amount to real and genuine economic activity. In Case C-456/02 *Trojani* the individual performed various tasks in return for his keep in a hostel run by the Salvation Army, which was required to promote his reintegration into the community. The ECJ left the national court to determine whether he was in fact a worker. A self-employed person working in another Member State, however, is not a 'worker' under Article 39, but is covered by Articles 43–49: Case C-15/90 *Middleburgh* v. *Chief Adjudication Officer*.

Jobseekers and the unemployed

Union citizens who were formerly workers but lost their job are now protected by Article 7(3) of Directive 2004/38: see Chapter 13. Under the Article, Union nationals who are unemployed as a result of illness or accident retain the status of workers, as do those who become involuntarily unemployed after being employed for more than one year and who have registered as jobseekers. Citizens who have been employed for less than a year must register as jobseekers also and retain the status of worker for six months, unless the individual embarks on vocational training related to the previous employment. In Case C-413/01 *Ninni Orasch* the Court held that a Union citizen whose fixed-term contract came to an end would not be regarded as voluntarily unemployed.

The Directive does not provide for rights in the event of voluntary unemployment, but such persons would benefit from the ruling in *Antonissen* that they are entitled to reside in the host State for a reasonable period of time to look for work. The Court held in *Collins* that they are also entitled to benefits which are intended to facilitate access to the labour market. However, it ruled that the status of worker is not an indefinite one. As a result, Collins could not rely on having been a worker 17 years previously: see Chapter 13 for further information on the position of jobseekers and the decisions in *Antonissen* and *Collins*.

Workers from the Accession States

Unlike previous enlargements, workers from most of the new Member States that joined the EU in 2004 and 2007 have been subjected to transitional arrangements limiting their access to the labour markets of the rest of the EU. As a result, these workers require a work permit if they wish to work in one of the Member States where there are restrictions. The first phase of transitional measures ran from 1 May 2004 to 1 May 2006. Restrictions in the second phase may be extended until 1 May 2009, but after that date, in the third phase, only for a further two years, with the permission of the Commission and where there are serious disturbances to the labour market. Current information on the position in the various Member States may be found on the *Europa* website.[1]

Key point

There is an absolute cut-off date for transitional measures of April 2011 when workers from the new Member States joining in 2004 will enjoy full access to the labour market of the EU. For workers from States joining in 2007, the cut-off date is 2014. Until then, workers from the new Member States must be given priority over third-country nationals. Where workers from new Member States are entitled to gain access to the labour market, they must be treated equally with the nationals of the host State.

Workers from the Czech Republic, Estonia, Latvia, Lithuania, Hungary, Poland, Slovenia and Slovakia who joined on 1 May 2004 were restricted by the arrangements set out in their Treaty of Accession 2003. During the first phase until May 2006, access to the labour market depended on the national laws and policies of the 15 EU Member States. The UK, Ireland and Sweden granted full access immediately. Spain, Finland, Greece and Portugal did so from May 2006, with Italy following suit from July 2006. Workers from **Cyprus** enjoy full access to the EU labour market as no restrictions were imposed under their Treaty of Accession. Workers from **Malta** may be subject to a safeguard clause.

Workers from Romania and Bulgaria, which joined the EU on 1 January 2007, are subject under their Treaty of Accession to transitional restrictions. While, in principle, the limitations follow the pattern of the 2004 enlargement, in practice they are significantly more restrictive, reflecting concern over the impact on the labour market of the 2007 enlargement. However, the previous 25 Member States must not impose

---

[1] http://ec.eua.eu/employment_social/free_movement/docs/pr_en.pdf

more restrictons than applied at the date of signing the Accession Treaty (25 April 2005). The position is complex and varies considerably from State to State. The UK, for example, imposed strict transitional restrictions on workers from Bulgaria and Romania, who are required to have work permits.[2] The current scheme distinguishes between skilled and low-skilled migrant workers. Skilled workers have to show that there are no suitable British nationals for the job. Low-skilled workers may apply for a work permit for up to six months only under schemes applying to certain sectors of the economy, such as agriculture, and are subject to a quota and have no entitlement to social assistance such as housing benefits. Self-employed Bulgarians and Romanians are not subject to restrictions in the UK, provided they can prove that they are genuinely self-employed. Bulgarian and Romanian students may work part time while studying, but require a work authorisation document.

EMPLOYMENT IN THE PUBLIC SERVICE

Exclusion of public service employment

Article 39(4) of the EC Treaty permits Member States to deny or restrict access to workers employed in the public service on the basis of nationality.

The exception has proved controversial, as many Member States have sought to rely on it to preserve jobs for their own nationals. In most cases they have not succeeded. Attempts by Member States to exclude jobs in the 'public sector' have not been accepted: see, for example, Case C-473/93 *Commission* v. *Luxembourg*. The exclusion has been narrowly interpreted by the ECJ. The Court held in Case 152/73 *Sotgiu* v. *Deutsche Bundespost* that Article 39(4) does not apply to all employment in the public service, only to certain activities connected with the exercise of official authority. The claim had arisen in the context of an allowance for post office workers living apart from their families in Germany. It was argued that this discriminated against non-nationals by denying the allowance to workers resident abroad at the time of recruitment. The Court also held in *Sotgiu* that the exception covers access to employment, but not conditions of employment.

Key case

A Belgian law reserving posts in the public service for Belgian nationals, including posts as nurses, plumbers and architects employed in central and local government, was found to contravene Article 39. The exception under Article 39(4) was intended to apply only to the exercise of public authority in order to safeguard the general interests of the state. The exercising of authority at junior level was not covered: Case 149/79 *Commission* v. *Belgium (Re Public Employees)*.

---

[2] http://http://ec.europa.eu/eures/main.jsp?acro=free&lang=en&countryId=UK&fromCountry
…ec.europa.eu/eures/main.jsp?acro=free&lang=en&countryId=UK&from

There is no secondary legislation on the exception. The Commission issued a Notice in 1988 announcing that certain sectors of employment were only rarely to be regarded as covered by the exception in Article 39(4). The list is only indicative and is not enforceable. The sectors identified include:

- public health services,
- teaching in state educational establishments,
- research for non-military purposes in public establishments,
- public bodies responsible for administering commercial services.

Further insight into the exception may be obtained from the decisions of the Court. The following were found to be outside the exception in Article 39(4):

- nurses in public hospitals in France: Case 307/84 *Commission* v. *France (Re French Nurses)*;
- a training scheme within the civil service in Germany: Case 66/85 *Lawrie-Blum*;
- lecturers at state universities in Italy, as they are not charged with the exercise of powers conferred by public law and are not responsible for safeguarding the interests of the state: Case 33/88 *Allué & Coonan* v. *Università degli studi di Venezia*;
- secondary school teachers: Case C-4/91 *Bleis* v. *Ministère de l'Education*;
- restrictions on the employment of non-nationals in Luxembourg, irrespective of the level of responsibility, in teaching, health, inland transport, telecommunications, water, gas and electricity: Case C-473/93 *Commission* v. *Luxembourg*.

Key point

The implication of these decisions is that the exception only covers high-level posts in which the post-holder owes a particular allegiance to the state, such as the armed forces, police, judiciary and high-ranking civil servants.

RIGHTS ENJOYED BY WORKERS AND THEIR FAMILIES

Regulation 1612/68 and Directive 2004/38

Prior to the implementation of Directive 2004/38, Regulation 1612/68 provided most of the substantive rights which were relevant to workers and their families. The rights of family members were covered by Articles 10 and 11 of the Regulation. These two Articles were repealed by Directive 2004/38 (see Chapter 13), but other provisions of the Regulation were retained.

The members of a worker's family, as defined by Article 2(2) of the Directive, are entitled under Article 7(1) to reside in another Member State for more than three months. As their rights are 'parasitic' (i.e. dependent) on those of the worker, the family members will benefit in the same way as the worker if he or she gains permanent residence rights under Article 16 through lawful residence for five or more years.

Family members who are dependent on the Union citizen but who are outside the definition in Article 2(2) benefit from the obligation on the host State to 'facilitate entry and residence' under Article 3(2). Similar considerations apply to individuals where there are serious health grounds requiring the personal care of the Union citizen.

Key point

Provision for family members under Article 2(2) of Directive 2004/38 (see Chapter 13) consolidates the previous law under Regulation 1612/68, with the addition of registered partners who now have rights to reside in countries where the partnership is recognised as equivalent to marriage. The Directive also provides more extensive rights for divorced and separated spouses than the previous case law.

Internal situations

In order to rely on the free movement and non-discrimination rights of EU nationals under Articles 39 and 12 of the Treaty, there must be a cross-border element. In Cases 35 and 36/82 *Morson* v. *the Netherlands* parents with Surinamese nationality were not permitted to join their son, a Dutch national living and working in the Netherlands. In Case C-370/90 *Surinder Singh* the ECJ held that Article 10(1) of Regulation 1612/68 (see now Directive 2004/38) covered family members where a worker who had worked outside his home State returned to the home State.

Regulation 1612/68

Article 39(2) of the Treaty provides for the abolition of any discrimination based on nationality between workers of the Member States in employment, remuneration and other conditions of work and employment. Regulation 1612/68 implements Articles 39(2) and 3(a) and (b). The Regulation requires equality of treatment in all matters relating to the actual pursuit of activities of employed persons and the elimination of obstacles to the mobility of workers, particularly the right to be joined by family members and integration of the family into the host country: Fifth Recital.

Two Titles within Part I of the Regulation continue to apply:

- Title I (Articles 1–6) on eligibility for employment;
- Title II (Articles 7–9) on equality of treatment within employment.

Title III previously included Articles 10 and 11, but these Articles were repealed and replaced by the provisions of Directive 2004/38 on workers' families: see above. Part II (continuing) provides for co-operation between employment agencies within the Member States and the Commission. Part III (continuing) set up an Advisory Committee and a Technical Committee to ensure close co-operation on matters relating to free movement and employment.

EQUALITY OF TREATMENT

Eligibility for employment

Under Regulation 1612/68 EC nationals are guaranteed the right to take up and pursue employment in the territory of another Member State under the same conditions as nationals of that State: Article 1. Member States are prohibited from discriminating, either overtly or covertly, against non-nationals by limiting applications and offers of employment under Article 3(a), by prescribing special recruitment procedures or limiting advertising or in any other way hindering recruitment of non-nationals: Article 3(2). Restriction by number or percentage of foreign nationals employed in any particular activity or area is also forbidden: Article 4.

Key case

A ratio of three French to one non-French crew laid down in the Code du Travail Maritime 1926 was held by the ECJ to contravene Article 4, even though the French government had given oral instructions not to apply the ratio: Case 167/73 *Commission v. France (Re French Merchant Seamen)*.

Non-nationals must be offered the same assistance as nationals in seeking employment: Article 5. Engagement or recruitment of non-nationals must not depend on discriminatory medical, vocational or other recruitment criteria: Article 6(1). Vocational tests when expressly requested on making a job offer to a non-national are permitted: Article 6(2). States are also permitted to impose on non-nationals conditions relating to linguistic knowledge required by the nature of the post: Article 3(1).

Key case

The Irish government required that teachers in vocational schools should be proficient in the Irish language. The ECJ held that such a requirement was permissible under Article 3(1) in the light of national policy on the promotion of the Irish language: Case 379/87 *Groener v. Minister for Education*.

Equality in employment

Conditions of employment

Equality in employment is expressly granted to workers by Article 7(1) of Regulation 1612/68, which provides that an EC worker may not, in the territory of another Member State, be treated differently from national workers on account of his nationality in relation to conditions of employment and work, and in particular in relation to remuneration, dismissal and reinstatement or re-employment on becoming unemployed.

Examples are as follows:

1 Legislation which recognised periods of national service in the home State but not in another Member State for calculating seniority was held to be unlawful: Case 15/69 *Ugliola*.
2 A decision to increase separation allowances only to those living away from home in the State in question was held capable of breaching Article 7(1): Case 152/73 *Sotgiu* v. *Deutsche Bundespost*.

Entitlement to social and tax advantages

Under Article 7(2) non-national EC workers are entitled to 'the same social and tax advantages as national workers', a right interpreted liberally by the ECJ.

Key case

An Italian widow living in France claimed the special fare reduction card issued to the parents of large families. During his lifetime the Italian husband had claimed the card. HELD: Article 7(2) covers all social and tax advantages, whether or not deriving from contracts of employment. Since the family had the right to remain in France under Regulation 1251/70, they were entitled to equal 'social advantage' under Article 7(2): Case 32/75 *Fiorini* v. *SNCF*.

Fiorini was followed in Case 207/78 *Even* in which the ECJ held that Article 7(2) applies to any benefit whether or not linked to a contract of employment, payable by virtue of an individual's status as a worker or by virtue of residence on national territory. The *Even* ruling has been applied in a number of subsequent cases, with the following examples held to be a 'social advantage'.

Examples

1 An interest-free discretionary loan payable to German nationals living in Germany to increase the birth rate was granted to an Italian couple resident in Germany on the basis of the claimant's status as a worker or a resident: Case 65/81 *Reina*.
2 An allowance to handicapped adults: Case 63/76 *Inzirillo*.
3 An old-age benefit system for those not entitled to a pension under the national social security system: Case 157/84 *Frascogna*.
4 A special unemployment benefit for young people: Case 94/84 *Deak*.
5 Claims in Belgium to qualify for a minimum income allowance (the 'minimex') by family members of a worker: Case 249/83 *Hoeckx*, and the family of an unemployed worker: Case 122/84 *Scrivner*.

6 A guaranteed minimum income paid for old persons, paid to an Italian widow living with her retired son in Belgium: Case 261/83 *Castelli* v. *ONPTS*.

7 A scholarship to study abroad under a reciprocal scheme between Belgium and Germany, paid to the child of an Italian worker in Belgium: Case 235/87 *Matteucci* v. *Communauté Française de Belgique*.

But see Case C-204/90 *Backman*, in which the ECJ held that while in principle national legislation making pension contributions in the home territory tax-deductible contravened Article 39, it could be justified where the resulting pensions were liable to be taxed.

In contrast, an allowance to former prisoners of war payable only to the nationals of the Member State was held to be outside Article 7(2) of the Regulation, as it was intended to compensate the nationals of the Member State for hardships endured for that country during the War, rather than to individuals in a category such as workers: Case C-386/02 *Baldinger*.

Key case

In Case 197/86 *Brown* the applicant had a place at Cambridge to study engineering and in Case 39/86 *Lair* the place was for languages at the University of Hanover. Brown, who held dual UK/French nationality and had worked for a UK engineering company for eight months before university under sponsorship from the company, sought the UK government maintenance grant. Lair sought a similar grant from the German government after working for five years in Germany with periods of involuntary unemployment. The refusal of a grant in both cases led to challenge under Article 7(2) and (3) of Regulation 1612/68. Judgments in the two cases were delivered on the same day. It was held by the ECJ that, while neither course constituted vocational training, a grant for university education was a social advantage. The word 'worker' must have an EC meaning. While Brown was regarded as a worker, he had acquired that status purely as a consequence of his university place. A migrant worker such as Lair, however, was entitled to equal treatment if involuntarily unemployed and legitimately resident. A worker who gave up a job to pursue further training in the host State was only eligible for a grant when there was a link between the work and the subject studied: Cases 197/86 *Brown* and 39/86 *Lair*.

It should be noted that the decisions in *Brown* and *Lair* were made before the introduction of Union citizenship, a factor to which the Court alluded in *Grzelczyk* (in relation to *Brown*). While Directive 2004/38 does not provide for access to maintenance grants, the decision of the Court in *Bidar* supports the right of the student as Union citizen to claim financial support in another Member State where a sufficient degree of integration has been established: see Chapter 13.

Rights relative to trade union activities, sport and housing

Migrant workers are entitled to equality of treatment in trade union membership: Article 8. They may be excluded from the management of bodies governed by public law but may sit as workers' representatives in such bodies.

Professional and semi-professional sporting activities are regulated by the EC Treaty in so far as they constitute economic activity: Case 13/76 *Dona* v. *Mantero*. Exclusion of a non-EU national on non-economic grounds from a national team would not appear to contravene Article 39.

> ### Key case
>
> The position of professional footballers was considered in *Bosman*. The ECJ interpreted Article 39 and Article 4 of Regulation 1612/68 prohibiting quotas based on nationality, in the context of football transfer rules. Bosman, a Belgian national, wished to move from a Belgian to a French club. He was prevented from doing so by his club's refusal to accept a transfer fee, without which a move was impossible. The ECJ held that transfer rules such as those affecting Bosman infringe Article 39 and Article 4 of Regulation 1612/68: Case C-415/93 *URBSFA* v. *Bosman*.

A further ruling on professional sport, this time on professional basketball, was made in Case C-176/96 *Lehtonen and ASBL Castors Canada Dry Namur-Braine* v. *ASBL Fédération Royale Belge des Sociétés de Basketball*. National rules by sporting associations such as those prohibiting basketball clubs from fielding players from other Member States in national championships, where a different rule is applied relating to the timing of transfer to players from non-Member States, infringed Article 39 in the absence of objective justification.

Migrant workers enjoy the same rights and benefits in matters of housing including ownership as nationals of the host State: Article 9. Restrictions on foreigners' rights to acquire property were held by the ECJ to be unlawful: Case 305/87 *Commission* v. *Greece*.

Children's access to educational training

Article 12 of Regulation 1612/68 provides that children of migrant workers shall be admitted to the host State's general educational, apprenticeship and vocational training courses under the same conditions as the nationals of the host State. This case law has now been confirmed by Article 12(3) of Directive 2004/38.

Key case

S, the mentally handicapped son of an Italian who had been employed, before his death, in Belgium, was refused benefit from a fund set up to assist people whose employment prospects were seriously affected by handicap. HELD: Article 12 entitled the handicapped child of a foreign worker to take advantage of rehabilitation benefits on the same basis as nationals of the host state: Case 76/72 *Michel S.* v. *Fonds national de reclassment social des handicappés*.

In Case 9/74 *Casagrande* v. *Landeshauptstadt München*, the son of a deceased Italian who had worked in Germany was refused an educational grant. The Court held that Article 12 entitles migrant workers not only to admission to courses but also to general measures of support such as grants and loans. This financial support was held to include study abroad on the same basis as nationals of the host state: Case C-308/89 *Di Leo* v. *Land Berlin*. In Case 42/87 *Commission* v. *Belgium*, the ECJ held that the children of migrant workers, including workers who have retired or died in the State, are entitled to equal treatment in access to all forms of state education. However, in Case 263/86 *Belgian State* v. *Humbel and Edel* the ECJ ruled that Article 12 did not preclude a Member State from charging a fee for admission to ordinary schooling, if it was classified as non-vocational, within its territory to the children of migrant workers residing in another Member State, where no such fee was charged to the nationals of that other Member State. The scope of entitlement was extended in *Echternach and Moriz* and, more recently, in *Baumbast*: see Chapter 13.

Key case

The child of a German migrant worker who had returned to Germany after working in the Netherlands sought an educational allowance from the Dutch authorities to study there because the German authorities refused to recognise his Dutch diploma. HELD (Article 234): Taking into account the need for integration of migrant workers in the host State and for continuity in education, a child did not lose his status as a 'child of the family' under Regulation 1612/68 on his parent's return to the country of origin. Such a child is entitled to continue his education in the host State where his parent (the worker) has returned to his country of origin if the educational systems are incompatible: Cases 389 and 390/87 *GBC Echternach and A. Moritz* v. *Netherlands Minister for Education*.

In Case C-413/99 *Baumbast* v. *R.* the Court decided that Article 12 should not be interpreted so as to restrict the entitlement of the children (in this case, of divorced parents, only one of whom was an EU national) to complete their education in the host State to circumstances where they could not do so in their country of origin. Article 12(3) of Directive 2004/38 now embodies this right (and the rights of parents as carers) to stay on to complete their education after the divorce or death of a parent.

SOCIAL SECURITY

Considerations of space no longer permit a chapter on social security in this edition. Readers may wish to refer to the chapter on this topic in the third edition (2001). It is, however, useful to be aware of the general principles underlying this area.

It is important to appreciate that there is no EU-wide system of social security. The Council was required under Article 42 (ex 51) of the EC Treaty to adopt measures to ensure the implementation of two principles:

1 aggregation, for the purpose of acquiring and retaining the right to benefit and of calculating the amount of benefit, of all periods taken into account under the laws of several Member States;
2 payment of benefit to persons resident in the territories of Member States.

Regulation 1408/71

Regulation 1408/71, as amended, was adopted to implement these objectives, in order to co-ordinate the different national schemes of social security in accordance with the principles in Article 42. Article 2(1) of the Regulation provides that it applies to the employed, the self-employed and their families, terminology which does not correspond exactly with the Treaty terminology referring to 'workers', beneficiaries of the right of establishment and the providers of services. The Regulation takes a pragmatic approach to coverage, defining employed and self-employed persons in Article 1(1)(a) (as amended) by reference to whether a person is insured for one or more of the contingencies covered by the branches of a social security scheme for employed or self-employed persons: Case 75/63 *Hoekstra*. It is irrelevant whether the national scheme is voluntary or compulsory.

Regulation 1408/71 embodies five *general principles* of social security:

1 non-discrimination on grounds of nationality: Article 3(1);
2 payment regardless of residence: Article 10(1);
3 no entitlement to double benefits: Article 12(1);
4 the single state principle: Article 13 (a worker covered by the Regulation is subject to the legislation of a single state only);
5 aggregation: applied to individual benefits and takes account of periods of contribution in all Member States where the worker has worked in order to determine eligibility to benefit.

Article 4(1) provides that the Regulation applies to legislation on sickness and maternity benefits, invalidity benefits, old-age benefits, survivors' benefits, benefits in relation to accidents at work and occupational diseases, death grants, unemployment benefits and family benefits. Under Article 4(2)(a) the Regulation applies to all general and special social security schemes, whether contributory or non-contributory. The Article extends the benefits under legislation other than that under Article 4(1) where such benefits supplement or substitute for social benefits under the Regulation, and are intended solely to protect the disabled or to guarantee a minimum income.

Social assistance

Article 4(4) provides an exception: the Regulation does *not* apply to social and medical assistance, benefit schemes for the victims of war or to special schemes for civil servants. The term 'social assistance' is not defined in the Regulation but has been narrowly interpreted by the ECJ. Social assistance tends to be based on need and is discretionary whereas social security benefits are available as of right. Some benefits have elements of both, in which case they have been treated by the Court as social security, applying a 'double function' test: see Case 1/72 *Frilli* v. *Belgian State* involving a non-contributory minimum income, which was based on need but was treated as social security, being assimilated into the old-age pension.

> ### Key point
>
> The double function test remains important, as benefits which are categorised as 'social security' can be exported to other Member States, whereas 'social assistance' is only available in the host State.

Social advantages

During the 1980s the Court moved from finding most benefits to be social security under Regulation 1408/71 to regarding them as a 'social advantage' under Regulation 1612/68, the scope of 'social advantage' having been extended in cases such as Case 207/78 *Even* and Case 65/81 *Reina*: see above. Claims which might previously have failed as social security stood more chance of success as a social advantage.

Union citizenship and social advantages

The restrictive approach to social security and social advantage underlying the Regulations, particularly the exclusion of social and medical assistance from Regulation 1408/71, seems out of step with the rights of Union citizens, even though these rights are subject to 'limitations and conditions' under Article 18(1) of the Treaty. Member States remain preoccupied with preventing 'benefits tourism'. However, the position of the non-working Union citizen is beginning to be acknowledged by the Court: for example, in Case C-456/02 *Trojani* where the Court found that the economically inactive may claim social assistance by applying the principle of non-discrimination provided they are lawfully resident.

Regulation 883/2004

The Council and EP adopted Regulation 883/2004 in April 2004. It is not yet in force, being dependent on implementation by a further regulation, which has not yet been adopted. Regulation 883/2004 is intended to co-ordinate social security systems in the EU to make it easier for workers and their families to move around the EU without loss of social security entitlement. The new Regulation should provide an approach which is simplified, modernised and transparent. Healthcare benefits will be aligned. Jobseekers will be able to extend the period in which they are looking for work from three to six months. The rights of the economically inactive will be included and co-operation between Member States improved to make it easier for individuals to receive their benefits. Regulation 883/2004 will repeal Regulation 1408/71, except in relation to third country nationals in some circumstances.

14

Free movement of workers

QUESTIONS

1 What are the main features of equality of treatment for a worker and his family under Article 39 of the Treaty and Regulation 1612/68? How has the Court of Justice used the concepts of 'social and tax advantages' to extend equality of treatment?

2 To what extent are jobseekers and the economically inactive entitled to benefits under:

(a) Regulation 1408/71

(b) Directive 2004/38?

How will the position change under Regulation 883/2004?

Further reading

Arnolfini, A. (2005) 'Free Movement and Access to Work of Citizens of the New Member States: the Transitional Measures', (2005) 42 CMLRev. 469.

Barnard, C. (2004) *The Substantive Law of the EU: the Four Freedoms*, Oxford University Press.

Carrera, S. (2005) *'What Does Free Movement Mean in Theory and in Practice in an Enlarged EU?'*, (2005) ELJ 699.

Chalmers, D., Hadjiemmanuil, C., Monti, G. and Tomkins, A. (2006) *European Union Law*, Cambridge University Press, Chapter 16.

Craig, P. and De Burca, G. (2007) *EU Law: Text, Cases and Materials*, 4th edition, Oxford University Press, Chapter 21.

O'Leary, S. (1999) 'The Free Movement of Persons and Services' in Craig P. and De Burca G. (eds), *The Evolution of EU Law*, Oxford University Press, Chapter 11.

Rogers, N. and Scannell, R. (2004) *Free Movement of Persons in the Enlarged European Union*, Sweet and Maxwell.

Shaw, J., Hunt, J., Wallace, C. (2007) *Economic and Social Law of the European Union*, Palgrave Macmillan, Chapter 12.

Visit **http://www.mylawchamber.co.uk/kent** to access answer guidance to questions in the book to test yourself on this chapter.

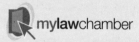

Use **Case Navigator** to read in full some of the key cases referenced in this chapter:

- 66/85 **Lawrie-Blum** [1986] ECR 2121

15

The right of establishment and the freedom to provide services

INTRODUCTION

The right of establishment and the freedom to provide services are both essential requirements of the single market. Both rights envisage the pursuit of business or professional activity. The right of establishment refers to the right of EC nationals (individuals and companies) to set up a business in a Member State other than their own. Establishment is seen as a permanent (or near permanent) right. Freedom to provide services is the right of persons established in one Member State to provide services in another State. The provision of services is, however, seen as a temporary right, not necessarily involving residence.

The provisions in the EC Treaty on the right of establishment are contained in Articles 43–48 (ex 52–58) and on the freedom to provide services in Articles 49–55 (ex 59–66).

The law on both establishment and services is complementary. Both rights are subject to the limitation in Directive 2004/38 on grounds of public policy, public security and public health. However, there are differences between the rights of workers and the self-employed in certain areas, as there is no equivalent provision to Regulation 1612/68 (see Chapter 14) for the self-employed. The differences have been reduced by the adoption of Directive 2004/38 which repealed and replaced previous Directives 73/148 on entry and residence and Directive 75/34 on the right to remain after employment for the self-employed and their families.

RIGHT OF ESTABLISHMENT

Article 43(1) provides for the prohibition of restrictions on the freedom of establishment of the nationals of a Member State in the territory of another Member State within the framework provided in the Treaty.

Article 43(2) provides that freedom of establishment includes the right to take up and pursue activities as self-employed persons and to set up and manage undertakings, in particular companies or firms within the meaning of Article 48(2) under the same conditions as are applied to nationals of the host State, subject to the provisions of the Treaty relating to capital.

The reference in Article 43 to Article 48 means that freedom of establishment applies to both natural and legal persons (i.e. individuals and companies). Article 48 provides that companies or firms formed and having their registered office, central administration or principal place of business within the EC shall be treated in the same way as natural persons for the purpose of establishment.

The exercise of State authority is excluded from the right of establishment under Article 45. The Court held in *Reyners* (see below) that the profession of advocate was not connected with the exercise of State authority.

The General Programme

The law regulating companies differs between Member States, depending on where the company is incorporated. The Council and Commission drew up the General Programme in 1961 to abolish restrictions on freedom of establishment, as required by Article 44. Under the General Programme companies incorporated under the law of one of the Member States but having their principal place of business outside the EC must maintain an effective and continuing link with the economy of a Member State. A link provided by nationality, particularly the nationality of partners or the members of the managing or supervisory body, was excluded, preventing an organisation from gaining access to the single market merely by registering a company in one of the Member States while the real business is carried out outside the Community. An extensive programme of directives harmonising company law was adopted under the General Programme.

Beneficiaries of the right of establishment

Article 43 has been directly effective from the end of the transitional period (December 1961): Case 2/74 *Reyners* v. *Belgian State* (ECJ).

Key case

R was a Dutch national, born, educated and resident in Belgium, with a doctorate in Belgian law. He was refused admission to the Belgian bar because he was not a Belgian national. The Court found that the General Programme and implementing Directives were merely intended to facilitate legislation under Article 43. It held that Article 43 was directly effective from the end of the transitional period as an application of the principle of non-discrimination in Article 12 EC: *Reyners* v. *Belgian State* (Case 2/74).

Article 43 has been interpreted by the Court as creating a distinction between persons not yet established in a Member State and those who are already established. Persons in the first category are merely entitled to establish themselves in any Member State, whereas persons already established have the right to set up agencies and branches in any Member State, subject to the observance of professional rules of conduct: Case 107/83 *Klopp*.

Registration of a branch or subsidiary may enable a company to take advantage of a more liberal regime, as the case of *Centros* illustrates.

> ### Key case
>
> Centros was a company incorporated in the UK, where there was no legal require-ment for a minimum share capital. The company did not trade in the UK but conducted its business in Denmark, which operated stricter rules on company formation. When Centros sought to establish a branch in Denmark its applica-tion was refused by the Danish Board of Trade and Companies, which claimed that the company was in fact trying to establish a principal place of business rather than a branch and had registered in the UK in order to circumvent Danish rules on company formation. The ECJ found that the refusal of a Member State to register a branch or subsidiary infringed Articles 43 and 48 of the Treaty: Case C-212/97 *Centros Ltd.* v. *Ervervs-og Selskabsstyreisen*.

Commentators expressed surprise at the judgment, that a deliberate choice to estab-lish in one Member State with less demanding requirements and transact business in another was not seen as an abuse by the Court but as the exercise of a legitimate right in the absence of harmonisation.[1] However, the Court stayed firm, developing its reasoning in later case law. In Case C-208/00 *Überseering* v. *NCC* the Court held that a company which is legitimately incorporated in one Member State and moves its administration to another Member State cannot be denied legal personality by the State to which it moves. In *Inspire Art* it found that Dutch legislation imposing minimum share capital and other requirements on a company registered in the UK, while capable in principle of objective justification, were disproportionate and unneces-sary: Case C-167/01 *Kamer van Koophandel en Fabriekenvoor Amsterdam* v. *Inspire Art Ltd.* In Case C-196/04 *Cadbury Schweppes and Cadbury Schweppes Overseas* the Court again found that it was not an abuse for a company to take advantage of more favourable national legislation, but that a measure restricting freedom of establish-ment may be justified to prevent wholly artificial arrangements which do not reflect economic reality in order to escape the payment of tax on profits.

Article 43 is often considered in relation to the taxation of companies operating across various Member States. See, for example, Case C-446/03 *Marks & Spencer* v. *Hasley*, where the Court found that while a State may, in appropriate circum-stances, treat non-resident companies differently from resident companies in terms of direct taxation (in this case in relation to the deductibility of losses incurred by a subsidiary in another Member State), such treatment is subject to the principle of proportionality.

[1] See Craig and De Burca (2007: 808–811).

Establishment or services?

It is not always clear whether the rules on establishment or those on services should apply. In *Commission* v. *Germany (Re Insurance Services)* (Case 205/84) the ECJ held that an enterprise would be regarded as an establishment rather than as the provider of services where there was no branch or agency within the EC but only an office managed by the enterprise staff or other authorised independent person. It appears to be a question of degree rather than of principle which determines whether the activities of an undertaking are governed by the provisions on establishment or on services.

FREEDOM TO PROVIDE SERVICES

Article 49(1) provides for the abolition of restrictions on the freedom to provide services in respect of EC nationals who are established in a Member State other than that of the person for whom the services are intended, within the framework of the Treaty. In Case C-452/04 *Fidium Finanz* the Court held that a company established outside the Community was not entitled to provide services within it.

Key point

The provision of services is a *temporary* right.

Under Article 50(3) a person providing a service may temporarily pursue his activity in the State where the service is provided under the same conditions as the State imposes on its own nationals.

Services

'Services' are defined under Article 50(1) as those 'normally provided for remuneration, in so far as they are not governed by the provisions relating to the freedom of movement of goods, capital and persons'. They include industrial and commercial services and the activities of craftsmen and professionals, but not transport, insurance or banking, for which there is a separate provision in the Treaty.

Limitation on establishments and the provision of services

The right of establishment and provision of services are subject to express exceptions under:

- Articles 45 (exercise of state authority);

- Article 46 (public policy, public security and public health) – Directive 2004/38 makes further provision for this exception: see Chapter 13;
- Article 55 (capital and payments).

Both rights are subject to the same conditions as govern nationals of the host State: Article 43(2) covers establishment and Article 50(3), services. The conditions laid down by law or by trade or professional bodies in relation to education or training and rules of professional conduct may provide a barrier, indirectly discriminating against the nationals of other Member States who find them harder to satisfy than do the nationals of the home State: see below.

General programme on the abolition of restrictions on the freedom to provide services 1961

The Council adopted a general programme in 1961 on the abolition of restrictions on services, in parallel with the programme relating to the right of establishment. Both programmes have been invoked before the courts for the purpose of interpretation (Case 293/83 *Gravier*), although they are not legally binding. The Commission had parallel responsibilities in this area, as it was under a duty under Article 47 to draft directives to harmonise professional qualifications: see below.

Elimination of barriers to the free movement of professional persons

Before the adoption of directives on mutual recognition of qualifications, there were two distinct approaches to this problem:

1 harmonisation of professional qualifications under Article 47;
2 application of the principle of non-discrimination under Article 12.

Harmonisation of professional qualifications

A number of Directives were issued under Article 47 covering specific professions. It has been easier to harmonise where the professionals in question possessed skills which were failry readily transferable through the EU, such as health professionals. Directives were adopted to harmonise the qualifications of doctors, nurses, dentists, pharmacists and veterinary surgeons. Architects are also the subject of a Directive. Where basic training and qualifications have been harmonised, professionals have the right to establish and practise throughout the EU. A degree of harmonisation has also taken place in the fields of agriculture, the film industry, mining, gas services and catering.

It has been more difficult to harmonise professional qualifications where training requires the acquisition of detailed knowledge specific to particular Member States, for example in relation to lawyers and accountants. Directive 77/249 enables lawyers to provide services but not to establish themselves in other Member States. Directive 98/5 seeks to facilitate the practice of the profession of lawyer on a self-employed or salaried basis in a State other than that in which the professional qualification was achieved. It was unsuccessfully challenged by Luxembourg in Case C-168/98 *Luxembourg v. EP and Council.*

Key case

The Commission brought proceedings under Article 226 to enforce Directive 98/5 against Luxembourg over its requirements for lawyers to satisfy a test to establish proficiency in the three national languages before being permitted to practise: Case C-193/05 *Commisison v. Luxembourg.* The Court considered in parallel a preliminary reference on the same point in Case C-506/04 *Graham Wilson v. Ordre des Avocats du barreau de Luxembourg.* The Court heard both cases on the same day and gave a single ruling in relation to both – that Luxembourg was in breach of the Directive by making registration subject to a prior language test.

Beneficiaries of the right of establishment and the freedom to provide services

A person who possesses recognised or equivalent qualifications is entitled to exercise the right of establishment and the freedom to provide services even where he or she is a national of the State in question: Case 115/78 *Knoors*; Case 246/80 *Broekmeulen*: see below. In the absence of a specific directive recognising the mutual recognition of professional qualifications, the refusal of permission to practise a profession to a person whose qualifications have been recognised as equivalent contravenes Articles 43 or 49 and Article 12: *Thieffry.*

Key case

T, a Belgian national with a Belgian law degree, sought to challenge the decision of the French Bar Council refusing to allow him to undertake practical training for the French bar. His law degree had been recognised by the University of Paris and he held a further qualification certificate in France for practising as an 'avocat'. HELD (Article 234): When a national of one Member State wishes to practise a profession such as advocate in another Member State, having obtained a qualification in his own country recognised as equivalent by the other Member State, it contravenes Article 43 to demand the national diploma as a further prerequisite to the special qualifying examination: Case 71/76 *Thieffry v. Conseil de l'Ordre des Avocats à la Cour de Paris.*

The Court made a similar ruling in Case 11/77 *Patrick* v. *Ministre des Affaires Culturelle*. P, a UK national who had trained as an architect in the UK, was prevented from practising as an architect in France. At the time there was neither a directive on architectural qualifications, nor a diplomatic convention. P's qualifications had, however, been recognised as equivalent to the corresponding French qualification under a Ministerial Decree of 1964. The Court again held that the effect of recognition was to enable the person to practise in that state. However, that an individual's qualifications from another Member States are neither harmonised nor recognised may be subject to discrimination without contravention of the Treaty.

Additional requirements

In Case 246/80 *Broekmeulen* a doctor qualified in Belgium was refused permission to practise as a GP in the Netherlands because he had not undertaken a further three-year training as a GP, which was not required under Directive 75/362 on the training of GPs. Such a requirement was found to be unenforceable. See also Case C-193/05 *Commission* v. *Luxembourg* (*above*).

> ### Key point
>
> Where a directive has been issued in relation to a particular profession, that profession may no longer insist on compliance with its own requirements from persons qualified in another Member State, even where the individual in question is a national of the Member State in which he seeks to practise: Case 246/80 *Broekmeulen*.

Application of the principle of non-discrimination

There is no secondary legislation on the right of establishment and the freedom to provide services comparable to Regulation 1612/68 (providing for co-operation between national authorities on the free movement of labour and for equal treatment). Thus, the principle of non-discrimination or equality under Article 12 of the Treaty is particularly important.

By applying this principle where recognition and harmonisation have not been achieved in a particular profession it has been possible to invoke Articles 12, 43, 49 and 50 to challenge a traditional rule which is discriminatory. 'Discrimination' has been liberally construed to cover both the taking up and pursuit of a particular activity.

Examples

1 A German artist living in France applied to the local authority to rent a 'crampotte' (a fisherman's hut used to exhibit paintings). The application was refused because city regulations stated that the huts could only be rented by French nationals. HELD

(Article 234): freedom of establishment under Article 43 covered not only taking up activity as a self-employed person but also the pursuit of that activity in the broadest sense: Case 197/84 *Steinhauser* v. *City of Biarritz*.

2 A cheap mortgage facility available only to Italian nationals was held by the ECJ to contravene Article 7 (now Article 12 EC). It should have been available to all EC nationals providing services who required a permanent dwelling in the host State: Case 63/86 *Commission* v. *Italy: Re Housing Aid*.

3 Discrimination under Greek law against land-owning by non-Greek nationals was held by the ECJ to contravene Articles 43–49: Case 305/87 *Commission* v. *Greece*.

4 The manager of a company incorporated and established in the UK held a licence in the UK for the provision of manpower but not in the Netherlands where the company recruited and supplied temporary staff. He was charged with supplying manpower without the necessary licence. HELD (Article 234): such restrictions were only permissible where justified by the common good and to the same extent as applied to the nationals of the host State. The provision of manpower was identified as 'specially sensitive' from the occupational and social point of view, enabling a Member State to impose a licensing system provided the scheme is not excessive in relation to the aim pursued: Case 279/80 *Webb*.

5 Two German-speaking individuals were charged with criminal offences in Italy where the residents of a particular area were entitled to the use of German in legal proceedings. This entitlement did not cover the individuals in question as both were German-speakers from outside Italy (namely, Germany and Austria). The ECJ held that the right to have criminal proceedings conducted in a language other than the principal language of the state concerned was covered by the principle of non-discrimination in Article 12 of the Treaty. A national rule providing such an entitlement to the residents of a particular area, without conferring the same right on EU nationals travelling or staying in the area, infringed Article 12: Case C-274/96 *Bickel and Franz*.

6 The promotion of lotteries across state boundaries. In Case C-275/92 *HM Customs and Excise* v. *Schindler* the defendants were Dutch-based agents acting on behalf of public bodies responsible for administering the state lottery in Germany. They had written to individuals in the UK and the Netherlands inviting them to buy tickets for the German lottery. The UK Customs and Excise authorities seized the letters, claiming that they breached UK law on gambling and lotteries. The ECJ ruled that the sending of the letters amounted to providing a service within Article 49. It follows that lotteries may be regulated by Member States in this way provided they act proportionately and without discrimination on grounds of nationality. See also Case C-124/97 *Läärä* v. *Finland*, in which the ECJ held that the grant of exclusive rights to a single public body to operate slot machines does not infringe Article 49 in view of the public interest objectives which justify it (control of gambling, prevention of risk or fraud from gambling).

7 A Dutch ban on 'cold calling' (unsolicited telephoning of potential customers): Case C-384/93 *Alpine Investments BV* v. *Minster van a Financien*. Such a measure in

principle infringed Article 49 as it denied the applicant, a UK company providing financial services, access to the Dutch market. On the face of it such a restriction operates against the principles of the internal market. However, the ECJ considered that the measure was necessary to protect consumers and the Dutch securities market and was not disproportionate. The ECJ distinguished the case from *Keck* (see Chapter 12) which it found to be concerned with goods rather than with services.

Human rights and the provision of services

In a departure from its previous approach to the provision of services as an essentially economic right, the Court in the *Carpenter* case read Article 49 as subject to Article 8 of the ECHR, respect for family life. It is clear from this decision that any measure restricting freedom of movement must respect fundamental human rights. While such thinking is novel in relation to the provision of services, it has been extensively developed in relation to Union citizenship: see Chapter 13.

Key case

Mrs Carpenter, a national of the Philippines, had entered the UK on a six-month visa. After the expiry of the visa, she stayed on without permission and married Mr Carpenter, a UK national, looking after the children from his first marriage. The UK government served a notice of deportation on her, against which she appealed to the Immigration Appeals Tribunal. Mr Carpenter ran a business selling advertising space and providing publishing services to medical and scientific journals. The business was based in the UK, but involved much cross-border activity. Mr Carpenter claimed that his business would be affected if his wife were deported to the Philippines as he would either have to accompany her there or remain in the UK, which would separate the family. In a preliminary ruling the ECJ read Article 49 on the provision of services as subject to Article 8 of the ECHR (respect for family life), holding that a decision to deport in such circumstances would infringe Article 8 and was therefore precluded: Case C-60/00 *Mary Carpenter* v. *Secretary of State for the Home Department*.

Professional rules of conduct

Professional rules of conduct may also provide barriers to the free movement of persons, particularly where a residential qualification is required.

The ECJ ruled in *Van Binsbergen* that a residential qualification in a properly qualified person is not a legitimate condition of exercising a specific profession, unless it is necessary to ensure the observance of professional rules of conduct. It also held that Article 49 was directly effective from the end of the transitional period in 1961.

Key case

Van Binsbergen was the client in a case before the Dutch courts, in which he was represented by an unqualified legal adviser, Kortman. When Kortman moved from the Netherlands to Belgium he was told he could no longer represent Van Binsbergen as he was not resident in the Netherlands. HELD (Article 234): A residence requirement infringed Article 49 unless it was objectively justified. Case 33/74 *Van Binsbergen*.

Subsequent case law follows a similar approach, emphasising the principle of proportionality. In Case 292/86 *Gulling* v. *Conseils des Ordres des Barreaux et de Savene* a registration requirement by the German bar for barristers wishing to establish themselves in Germany, which was applied equally to nationals of the host State, was held by the ECJ to be permissible. However, in *Conseil de l'Ordre de Nice* v. *Jean-Jacques Raynel* (1990, Conseil d'Etat) the Conseil d'Etat decided that refusal of permission to an advocate of the Nice bar by his circuit leader to open chambers and to join the Brussels bar contravened Article 43. The Court also ruled that the freedom of establishment of an advocate in another Member State does not permit a distinction between the practice of an advocate in a principal or second set of chambers.

In Case C-340/89 *Vlassopoulos* v. *Ministerium für Justiz* a Greek lawyer challenged the German rules on qualification which excluded him from practising. HELD (ECJ): Article 43 entitled the national authorities to examine the qualifications of non-nationals for equivalence. Further guidance was given by the ECJ in *Gebhard*.

Key case

The reference arose out of disciplinary proceedings brought by the Milan bar against a German member of the Stuttgart for using the term 'avvocato' contrary to Italian law. The ECJ held that where national measures restrict one of the fundamental freedoms under the Treaty, they must:

- be applied in a non-discriminatory manner;
- be justified by imperative requirements in the general interest;
- be suitable to attain the objective;
- not exceed what is necessary to achieve the objective.

Case C-55/94 *Gebhard* v. *Consiglio dell'Ordine Degli Avvocati Procurator di Milano*.

Respect for the legitimate rules and standards of Member States

The law may not be invoked to undermine the legitimate rules and standards of Member States in education and training and professional rules.

Key case

Under UK government rules Treasury consent was required before a company could transfer its head office to another Member State. The Court held, contrary to the submissions of Advocate-General Darmon, that freedom of establishment was a fundamental right. However, in the absence of directives, Articles 43 and 48 do *not* confer on a company incorporated under the legal system of a Member State in which its registered office is situated the right to transfer its management and control to another Member State: *R. v. HM Treasury, ex parte Daily Mail and General Trust plc* (Case 81/87).

By contrast, in Case 79/85 *Segers*, a company registered in one Member State but operating entirely through an agency in another Member State was held entitled to establish itself in the State in which it operated.

'Insurance' cases

Actions were brought by the Commission under Article 226 against four Member States as a result of national rules requiring insurance undertakings to conduct their business in those States through persons already established and authorised to practise there: *see Commission* v. *Germany* (Case 205/84). Three further cases were decided against Ireland, France and Denmark.

Key case

In *Commission* v. *Germany* the ECJ followed *Van Binsbergen* and distinguished between establishment and services. 'Establishment' was held to cover an office managed by the staff of the enterprise or by an independent person authorised to act on behalf of an enterprise. An enterprise established outside the EC but whose activities are largely directed towards the Member State where services are provided (in an attempt to escape the rules of conduct of that State) is also covered. The ECJ held that Articles 49 and 50 require, in addition to the removal of discrimination based on nationality, the abolition of restrictions on the freedom to provide services imposed as a result of establishment in a Member State other than that in which the services are provided. The establishment requirement was held to be unjustified but the authorisation requirement was justified in so far as it was necessary to protect policy-holders and insured persons: Case 205/84 *Commission* v. *Germany*.

THE SINGLE MARKET PROGRAMME

Financial services

The Commission developed a new approach to the right of establishment and the provision of service in its harmonisation of financial services within the single market programme. A number of Directives were adopted, including banking (Directive 89/646), insurance (Directive 88/357), non-life insurance (Directive 88/357) and life insurance (Directive 90/619). The internal market in financial services is now regarded as complete. The approach reflects the Commission's commitment to harmonisation of essential safeguards and relevant standards and the acceptance of the standards of other Member States within that framework, on the principle of control and supervision by the home State. A single licence is issued, enabling an institution licensed in one Member State to offer its services to another Member State (by establishing a branch or agency, or supplying its services in the other State).

A fresh initiative on qualifications

It became clear to the Commission that the sectoral approach to the harmonisation of professional qualifications was too slow. The Commission, therefore, decided to speed up the recognition process by creating a single system of mutual recognition of higher education qualifications based on the principle of non-discrimination, entitling an individual to practise a vocation or profession.

Directive 89/48 on the mutual recognition of qualifications was adopted in December 1988, with effect from 1991. It covered workers as well as the self-employed, did not apply to those professions which are already subject to a harmonising directive, and left unchanged the rules of particular professions in the Member States. The central element was the mutual recognition throughout the EC of higher education diplomas requiring professional education or training of three or more years' duration. Diplomas were defined as qualifications awarded by a competent authority in a Member State that established that the holder had successfully completed a post-secondary period of education and training of at least three years' duration at a university or higher education establishment and had the professional qualifications required to take up a regulated profession in that Member State. Directive 92/51 extended recognition to programmes of less than three years, thus covering all post-secondary education and training. Directive 99/42 replaced various sectoral directives in industrial and professional areas.

Directive 2005/36 on the recognition of professional qualifications

Directive 2005/36, which came into effect in October 2007, consolidated the three directives of 1989, 1992 and 1999, as well as the 12 sectoral directives on health professionals, but not Directives 77/249 and 98/5 on lawyers' rights concerning authorisation to practise rather than recognition of qualifications: see above.

Directive 2005/36 distinguishes between the right of establishment and the provision of services, depending on duration, frequency, regularity and continuity of the services, in accordance with the case law of the ECJ. It contains six Titles:

- Title I on General Provisions,
- Title II on Provision of Temporary Services,
- Title III on Establishment,
- Title IV on Knowledge of Language and Use of Titles,
- Title V on Administrative Co-operation, and
- Title VI on Other Provisions.

The Directive continues to be based on mutual recognition. Under Article 2 the principle of mutual recognition applies to any EU nationals wishing to pursue a regulated profession in a self-employed or employed capacity, including those belonging to the liberal professions, other than that in which they obtained their qualifications.

One of the innovations introduced is the idea of *common platforms* under Title III, defined in Article 15 as a set of criteria making it possible to compensate for the widest range of substantial differences identified between the training requirements of at least two-thirds of the Member States, including all the Member States which regulate that profession. If such a platform would make recognition of qualifications easier, the Commission may submit it to the Member States and adopt an implementing measure. Member States will then waive any compensating measures for applicants who meet the conditions of the platform.

Key point

Recognition of professional qualifications enables the beneficiary to practise his or her profession in another Member States on the same terms as the national of the host State under Article 4(1) of Directive 2005/36.

A 'regulated profession'

A 'regulated profession' is defined in Article 1(a) of Directive 2005/36 as covering any professional activity where the possession of a diploma is required in the Member State, either directly or indirectly. As Directive 2005/36 consolidates previous case law, the Court's decisions on the earlier directives remain relevant. In Case C-285/01 *Burbaud* the ECJ found that employment in the public service could be covered by Directive 89/48, contrary to the claim of the French government, as the definition of a 'regulated profession' was a matter of Communiy, not national law. In contrast the Court found in Case C-294/00 *Gräbner* that 'health practitioner' was not a regulated profession and so was outside Directive 92/51.

Routes to recognition under the Directive

There are three routes to recognition:

1 **The general system for the recognition of qualifications**. Under Article 13(1), where access to a regulated profession requires specific qualifications, the host State will allow access to and pursuit of that profession on the same terms as the nationals of the State concerned where the applicant has the attestation of competence or evidence of formal qualifications. Access will also be granted to persons who have pursued the profession in question on a full-time basis for two of the previous 10 years. Attestations of competence will have been issued by the competent authority of a Member State. Member States may require applicants to take an aptitude test or complete an adaptation period of less than three years where:
   - the training is substantially different from the host State;
   - the regulated profession in the host State comprises one or more regulated activities which do not exist in the corresponding home State;
   - the difference consists of specific training required by the host State which is substantially unlike anything covered by the applicant's home State.

   Under Article 14 the applicant may choose whether to take an aptitude test or undergo an adaptation period, unless the activity requires a precise knowledge of national law, in which case the host State may choose.

2 **Activities requiring only general or commercial knowledge**. Under Article 16, the Member State will recognise previous pursuit of the activity in another Member State as sufficient proof of such knowledge and aptitude.

3 **Professionals covered by previous sectoral directives** (doctors, nurses, pharmacists, architects and dentists). Under Article 21 such professionals require evidence that the applicant has satisfied minimum training requirements, in addition to holding formal qualification.

These categories presuppose a new and arguably less coherent approach to recognition.[2]

Cases outside the legislation

Where qualifications are not covered by a specific directive and are outside Directive 2005/36, Member States may specify the knowledge and qualifications required: Case C-104/91 *Colegio Oficial de Agentes de la Propriedad Immobiliara* v. *Aguirre*, where a UK national had been prosecuted for practising as estate agent in Spain without a Spanish qualification, although he was a member of the Royal Institute of Chartered Surveyors in the UK. As the facts had arisen before the implementation date for Directive 89/48, Spain could specify its own qualifications.

---

[2] See Chalmers *et al.* (2006: 721–722).

THE SERVICES DIRECTIVE: DIRECTIVE 2006/123

After prolonged discussion, Directive 2006/123 on services in the internal market was adopted in 2007 for implementation by December 2009. Often known as the 'Bolkenstein Directive', after the Commissioner who introduced the original proposal, the Directive covers both the right of establishment and the temporary provision of services, and aims to remove the remaining barriers to setting up a business anywhere in the EU and providing services. The Directive has provoked criticism that it represents a compromise, with the loss of key features such as the 'country of origin principle' after years of negotiation.[3] Although it is intended to simplify the law, it is a complex and confusing document.

Articles 1–3 provide a series of exclusions (e.g. social services, criminal law). Article 4 provides definitions. Articles 5–8 deal with procedural simplification, particularly the creation of the 'single point of contact' under Article 6 to facilitate access to service activities. Articles 9–15 deal with the freedom of establishment, including authorisation schemes, conditions for the granting of authorisations, duration of authorisation, selection and authorisation procedures, and requirements which are prohibited or need to be evaluated. Articles 16–18 provide a set of highly complex derogations, subject to the usual requirements of non-discrimination, necessity and proportionality (Article 16). Article 19 covers the rights of recipients of services. Articles 22–27 cover provisions on the quality of services, including information on providers and their services, and the settlement of disputes. Articles 28–36 provide administrative co-operation including mutual assistance and alert mechanisms.

Restrictions on the provision of services

Article 49 is now subject to Directive 2004/38 in terms of restrictions on grounds of public order, public policy and public morality: see Chapter 13. Previously, it was covered by Directive 64/221. The *Omega* case provides a rare example of a decision clarifying the restriction of services under the Directive.

Key case

A German company operated a laser installation in Germany, inspired by the film *Star Wars*, featuring laser targeting devices and tags fixed in the firing corridors or on jackets worn by the players. The German authorities prohibited the company from operating on human targets, on the basis that entertainment games which featured simulated killings were contrary to human dignity and so constituted a threat to public order. The German company in its appeal argued ➜

---

[3] See de Witte (2007) extracted in Craig and De Burca (2007: 842).

that the ban infringed Article 49 as the installation in question used equipment and technology supplied by a British company. The Court held (Article 234) that the services in question were covered by Article 49, but that such a derogation could be justified in order to protect fundamental rights even though equipment was not prohibited in the UK provided the prohibition was necessary and proportionate: Case C-36/02 *Omega*.

Industrial property rights and the freedom to provide services

The legitimate exercise of industrial property rights cannot be prevented by invoking Article 49 on the freedom to provide services: Case 62/79 *Coditel* v. *Ciné Vog*. In this case a Belgian film distributor, SA Ciné Vog Films, owned the performing rights in various films including one called *Le Boucher*. Ciné Vog tried to prevent Coditel, a cable television service, from picking up *Le Boucher* from German television and transmitting it in Belgium. Coditel argued before the national court that preventing transmission amounted to a breach of the freedom to provide services in Article 49. The ECJ held that Article 49 cannot be invoked to prevent a legitimate exercise of industrial property rights unless a disguised restriction on trade is involved.

FREEDOM TO RECEIVE SERVICES

Articles 49 and 50 are worded in terms of the freedom to *provide* services. There is no explicit mention of the receipt of services. However, the ECJ has extended the freedom to include the freedom to *receive* services. The issue first came before the ECJ in Case 118/75 *Watson and Belmann* where the Commission submitted that the freedom to receive services was the essential corollary to the freedom to provide services. The ECJ adopted this approach in *Luisi and Carbone* v. *Ministero del Tesoro*.

Key case

These cases arose out of the criminal prosecutions of Luisi and Carbone for taking currency out of Italy in amounts greater than currency regulations permitted, the money being payments for tourism and medical services. The ECJ held that the freedom to provide services included the freedom to receive services. This freedom was found to entitle the recipient to visit another Member State to receive services without obstruction by restrictions. Tourists, persons receiving medical treatment and persons travelling for the purpose of education or business were regarded as the recipients of services: Joined Cases 286/82 and 26/83 *Luisi and Carbone* v. *Ministero del Tesoro*.

Principle of non-discrimination

The principle of non-discrimination or equality under Article 12 EC may also be invoked in the context of the receipt of services, such as the payment of fees for education: see, for example, Case 293/83 *Gravier* in which the ECJ held that a discriminatory registration fee to gain access to vocational training courses contravened Article 12. The Court applied the principle again in the case of *Cowan*, this time in relation to the receipt of services as a tourist.

Key case

In this case the plaintiff had been attacked and robbed in the Paris Metro while on holiday. The French Criminal Injuries Compensation Board refused to pay him compensation for injuries since French law only provided for the payment of compensation out of public funds to French nationals. Cowan argued that, as his claim was based on the receipt of tourist services, the French rule contravened old Article 12. The ECJ held that the recipient of services was entitled to equal protection from, and compensation for, the risks of assault as a corollary of the right to receive services: Case 186/87 *Cowan* v. *French Treasury*.

The ruling in *Cowan* may be contrasted with *SPUC* v. *Grogan*, where the lack of an economic element prevented the Court from treating the case as one of receipt of services.

Key case

The case arose in the context of the protection of the right of the unborn child to life, a right which was recognised by the Irish constitution. The ECJ considered an Irish ban which prevented a student union from distributing information on abortion. The ECJ held that as no economic activity was involved there was no breach of Community law: Case C-159/90 *SPUC* v. *Grogan*.

Subsequently the Irish government applied for an injunction to prevent an Irish citizen from leaving the country to obtain an abortion abroad. While the Irish Court upheld the woman's right to travel, the Irish government sought to amend the protocol of the Maastricht Treaty (which contained a declaration recognising that Community law does not affect the right to life) to permit the right to travel. In 1992 the Irish people voted in a referendum in favour of the amendments and supported the right to travel.

The Court of Appeal in the UK considered the scope of Article 49 in *Diane Blood* in relation to the receipt of services without making a reference to the ECJ.

Key case

A British woman had been refused fertility treatment using her dead husband's sperm, as the deceased man had not given his consent under UK law. She sought an order allowing her to take the sperm sample to another EU State for treatment. The Court of Appeal without referral to the ECJ, granted the order on the basis that to have refused permission would have been an unreasonable restriction on her right to travel to receive medical services: *R. v. Human Fertilisation and Embryology Authority, ex parte Diane Blood*.

Medical treatment

It was clear from the decision in *Luisi* and *Carboni* that the freedom to receive services clearly covered private healthcare, where there is an obvious economic element, More problematic, however, is the question of health services such as the NHS in the UK which are 'free at the point of delivery'. The Court has addressed the question of medical treatment abroad in a series of cases: *Gerait Smits* and *Peerbooms, Müller Fauré, Inizan, Vanbraekel* and *Watts*.

Key case

The referral arose in relation to two Dutch citizens who had been treated in other Member States. In the Netherlands citizens could be treated abroad if the treatment was approved in advance by the appropriate sickness insurance fund for which it had to be seen as both 'normal' and 'necessary'. G-S had sought treatment in Germany for Parkinson's disease. P sought treatment in Austria after he fell into a coma. In both cases, applications to the sickness fund were rejected, as it was considered that the applicants did not meet the criteria. The ECJ found that the requirement for prior authorisation did not breach Community law provided it was objectively justifiable and proportionate. The Court held that the requirement that the treatment be 'normal' should be interpreted with reference to international medical standards. The requirement for 'necessity' could be justified where it was interpreted to mean that authorisation would only be refused where the same or equally effective treatment may be obtained without undue delay from an establishment with which the insured person's sickness fund has arrangements: Case C-157/99 *Geraets-Smits* v. *Stichting Ziekenfonds VGZ; HTM Peerbooms* v. *Stichting CZ Groep Zorgverzekeringen*.

In Case C-385/99 *Müller Fauré*, the Court distinguished between hospital and non-hospital care, finding that requirements for prior authorisation did not infringe Community law if they were necessary and proportionate, whereas restrictions on non-hospital care were held to be incapable of being objectively justified. The Court in *Inizan* followed its previous approach in *Geraets-Smits* and *Müller Fauré*. In Case C-368/98 *Vanbraekel and others* v. *Alliance Nationale des Mutualites Chretiennes* the applicant sought reimbursement of her expenses for an operation outside her home State. The ECJ held (Article 234) that reimbursement should take place on terms no less favourable than would have applied in the applicant's home State.

Key case

Mrs Watts sought approval from her primary healthcare trust in the UK for authorisation for hip replacement surgery abroad under the E112 scheme, an EU scheme enabling authorisation to travel to another Member State for medical treatment. Such authorisation cannot be refused where treatment in the Member State cannot be provided without undue delay. The Trust classified her application as 'routine', which would have led to a waiting period of one year. It rejected her application, stating that as treatment could be provided within the government's target period, it did not involve 'undue delay'. In the meantime the arthritis from which Mrs Watts was suffering deteriorated, as a result of which her period of waiting was reduced to three months, but the refusal of authorisation was sustained. Her application for judicial review of the refusal in the High Court was unsuccessful, and she appealed to the Court of Appeal which made a preliminary referral to the ECJ. During this period she went to France where the operation was carried out.

The Court held that circumstances such as those in question were covered by Article 49. There was no need to determine whether the provision of hospital treatment in the context of a national health service such as the NHS was a service within the meaning of Article 49: Case C-372/04 *Watts* v. *Bedford Primary Health Care Trust*.

The ruling in *Watts* treats all services, including public services, as covered by Articles 49–50, provided they are *paid* services. State-funded healthcare services are therefore included as being 'provided for remuneration'. As long as there is a cross-border element, it follows from *Watts* and the previous case law that Union citizens are treated as consumers of services for which the national healthcare providers may seek reimbursement from the citizen's home state. The practical consequence of *Watts* in the UK is that Union citizens are likely to seek to obtain medical treatment abroad in areas and claim reimbursement subsequently, where the waiting lists is considered to be too long and the treatment has been authorised.

Education and vocational training: *Gravier*

The issue of the access of EC nationals to education and vocational training arose in *Gravier*.

Key case

Gravier, a French national, had applied and had been accepted for a four-year course at the Liège Académie des Beaux-Arts in the art of the strip cartoon. She was treated by the Académie as a foreign student and was required to pay the *minerval*, a special fee not payable by Belgian nationals. Ms Gravier argued, first, that the *minerval* was an obstacle to her freedom to receive services and, secondly, that to charge a higher fee for a vocational course to an EC national was discriminatory under Article 12. The Court held that vocational training was covered by old Article 12, without ruling on the first argument. It also held that 'vocational training' covered all forms of teaching leading to a particular profession, trade or employment, or which provides the necessary skills for such a profession, even if the programme involves an element of general education: Case 293/83 *Gravier* v. *City of Liège.*

The reasoning which enabled the ECJ in *Gravier* to rule that vocational training was covered by Article 12 derives from an imaginative interpretation of Article 150, empowering the Council to lay down general principles to implement a common vocational training programme, and from the provisions on workers and their children in Regulation 1612/68, Articles 7(3) and 12. The Court held that this general provision brought vocational training within the scope of coverage of EC law, as a result of which such training was subject to the equality principle of Article 12. Article 150 was thus treated as directly effective.

Education and training after *Gravier*

The scope of 'vocational training' was not clear after *Gravier*. However, it was clarified by the decisions in *Blaizot, Humbel* and *Commission* v. *Belgium.*

Following the decision in *Gravier,* a number of university students of veterinary studies claimed reimbursement of the *minerval* in Case 24/86 *Blaizot* v. *University of Liège.* The Court held that a university course may be considered vocational training not only where the final examinations constitute the required qualification but also where the course provides specific training in the form of the knowledge necessary to practise a trade or profession, even in the absence of a formal requirement for such knowledge.

Two further cases involving higher education in Belgium were decided on the same day: *Humbel* and *Commission* v. *Belgium.* In Case 263/86 *Belgian State* v. *Humbel* the Belgian authorities claimed the payment of the *minerval* for a one-year vocational course in Belgium which formed part of general secondary education received by the son of a French national living in Luxembourg. The Court held under Article 234 that such a course must be regarded as 'vocational' if it forms an integral part of an overall programme of education. Case 42/87 *Commission* v. *Belgium* involved enforcement proceedings against Belgium where national rules limited access to higher education to only 2 per cent of non-nationals. The Court held that the rules contravened Article 12 in so far as they applied to vocational training.

Key point

As a result of the decision in *Gravier*, *Blaizot* etc., EC nationals were granted access to courses which (overall) are vocational on terms equivalent to those granted to the nationals of the host State, including courses subsidised by that State. Most university undergraduate courses qualify as 'vocational'. Only those courses designed to improve general knowledge (e.g. a general arts degree) rather than preparation for an occupation are excluded. Thus, those degrees such as medicine and veterinary studies involving an academic and vocational stage are effectively considered as a single 'vocational' stage.

In Case 197/86 *Brown* and Case 39/86 *Lair* (see Chapter 14) the ECJ held that maintenance grants fell outside the scope of the EC Treaty, being a matter of educational and social policy, and were thus not subject to Article 12.

Key point

The entitlements of students have changed as a result of the introduction of Union citizenship and the Title on Education under the Maastricht Treaty. In *Bidar* the Court effectively overturned *Brown* and *Lair*. It is, of course, essential for students claiming financial support to be able to establish the necessary degree of integration with the host State: see Chapter 13.

QUESTIONS

① How has the principle of non-discrimination been used to develop the right of establishment and the provision of services, in the absence of specific secondary legislation, to enable the beneficiaries of these rights to claim equal treatment in Member States other than their own?

② Assess the role of the Court of Justice in developing the right to receive services from the provision in the Treaty in Article 49 for the provision of services. How has the Court's case law progressed to include publicly-funded healthcare provision?

Further reading

Barnard, C. (2004) *The Substantive Law of the EU: the Four Freedoms*, Oxford University Press, Chapter 13.

Cabral, P. (2004) 'The Internal Market and the Right to Cross-Border Medical Care', (2004) 29 ELRev. 673.

Chalmers, D., Hadjiemmanuil, C., Monti, G. and Tomkins, A. (2006) *European Union Law*, Cambridge, Chapters 16 and 17.

Craig, P. and De Burca, G. (2007) *EU Law: Text, Cases and Materials*, 4th edition, Oxford University Press, Chapter 22.

de Witte, B. (2007) *'Setting the Scene-How did Services get to Bolkenstein and why?'*, (2007) European University Institute Working Papers of the Law Department.

Dyrberg, P. (2003) 'Full Free Movement of Companies in the European Community at Last', 28 (2003) ELRev. 528.

Hatzopoulos, V. (2002) 'Killing National Health Systems but Healing Patients' (2002) 39 CMLRev. 683.

Hatzopoulos, V. and Do, T. (2006) 'The Caselaw of the ECJ concerning the Free Provision of Services 2000–2005' (2006) 43 CMLRev. 923.

Spaventa, E. (2004) 'From Gebhard to Carpenter: Towards (Non)-Economic European Constitution' (2004) 41 CMLRev. 743.

Van Nuffel, P. (2005) 'Patients' Free Movement Rights and Cross-Border Access to Health-care' (2005) 12 MJ 253.

Visit **http://www.mylawchamber.co.uk/kent** to access answer guidance to questions in the book to test yourself on this chapter.

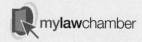

Use **Case Navigator** to read in full some of the key cases referenced in this chapter:

- C-55/94 **Reinhard Gebhard** *v.* **Consiglio dell'Ordine Degli Avvocati Procurator di Milano** [1995] ECR I-4165
- C-159/90 **SPUC** *v.* **Grogan** [1991] I-4685

16

Capital movements and economic and monetary union

INTRODUCTION

The free movement of capital has only been a directly effective right since the completion of the internal market. The wording of the original provisions in the Treaty of Rome in (old) Articles 67–73 was vague and unenforceable, unlike provisions relating to the free movement of goods, persons and services, all of which were recognised by the ECJ to be directly effective at an early stage. Member States were reluctant to abandon exchange control regulations as an instrument of economic policy. Early case law reflected the distinction between the provisions on capital, which required further implementation, and provisions on payments, which were directly effective as they derived from other directly effective rights under the Treaty such as the right to receive services: Cases 286/82 and 26/83 *Luisi and Carbone* v. *Ministero del Tesoro*.

Completion of the internal market

Significant progress in removing barriers to the movement of capital was made in the internal market programme with the adoption of Directive 88/361 on capital movements and Directive 89/646 in relation to home-country control of credit institutions. Other Directives in areas such as tax harmonisation and financial services also contributed to the completion of the internal market in this area. Directive 88/361 provided for the abolition of restrictions on the transfer of capital, with capital transfers to be effected on the same terms as payments. The Directive was held to be directly effective from July 1990 in Cases C-358 and 416/93 *Ministero Fiscale* v. *Bordessa*; it could thus be relied upon to provide a defence to a criminal charge under national exchange control regulations which did not comply with the Directive. However, the Court held in Cases C-163, 165 and 250/94 *Criminal Proceedings against Sanz de Lera and Others*, that Article 4 of the Directive, providing for derogation from free movement of capital, was non-exhaustive. As a result, Member States remained free to take action in non-specified areas relating to public policy and public security.

The provisions on capital movements should be seen in terms of their relationship with other provisions of the Treaty, particularly the provisions on services. In Case C-484/93 *Svensson and Gustavvson* a national condition on the grant of interest rate subsidy on housing obtainable only from a credit organisation approved in that Member State was found to infringe both the Directive and Treaty provisions on the free movement of services. In Case C-18/96 *Saffir* v. *Skattemyndighten I Dalarnas Lyn*, the ECJ ruled that a Swedish measure on the payment of tax on capital life assurance premiums to a British company based in Sweden could be considered in relation to the provision of services under Article 49.

Treaty of Maastricht

The Maastricht Treaty replaced the original provisions in the EC Treaty on capital with new ones, incorporating the wording of Directive 88/361. The Treaty provisions were renumbered Articles 56–60 by the Treaty of Amsterdam.

Key point

As a result of the amendment by the Treaty of Maastricht, the EC Treaty provided for the first time an integrated right of free movement of both capital and payments in abolishing a distinction which had persisted, even after the completion of the single market.

Article 56(1) provides that all restrictions on the movement of capital between Member States, and between Member States and third countries, shall be prohibited. Article 56(2) provides a similar prohibition in relation to restrictions on payments. Article 56(1) and (2) were held to be directly effective in Cases C-163, 165 and 250/94 *Sanz de Lera and Others*. In Case C-463/00 *Commission* v. *Spain* the ECJ recognised that free movement of capital is a fundamental principle of the Treaty which can only be restricted in accordance with Article 58(1) or by 'overriding requirements of the general interest'. In addition, any restriction must comply with the principle of proportionality.

What constitutes a restriction on the movement of capital?

The Treaty does not define either movement of capital or restrictions on it, although the Court found in Case 222/97 *Trummer and Mayer* that it is appropriate to refer to the illustrative list in the Annex to Directive 88/361: see above. This is a long list which sets out 13 groups of transactions to be considered as capital movements, now covered by Article 56(1), and is summarised by Chalmers *et al.* as follows: 'direct investments, such as investments in a company or finance provided by an entrepreneur; investments in real estate, such as a purchase of a house; operations in securities, be it trading in bonds, shares and other money market instruments; financial loans and sureties; operations in current and deposit accounts with financial institutions; transfers relating to insurance contracts, and finally, personal capital movements such as gifts, inheritances or personal loans' (Chalmers *et al.* 2006: 509).

The Court has found the following to involve capital movement:

- investments in real property: Case C-302/97 *Klaus Konle* v. *Austria*;
- mortgages to secure loans to purchase real estate: *Trummer and Mayer*;
- acquisition of securities on the capital markets: Case C-367/98 *Commission* v. *Portugal (Golden share)*;
- banknotes or coins: Case C-358 and 416/93 *Bordessa*;
- receipt of dividends from a third country: Case C-35/98 *Staatsecretaris van Financien* v. *Verkooijen*.

In contrast, in Case C-163 and 165/94 *Sanz de Lera*, the Court found that taking a car filled with money out of the country was *not* a movement of capital.

Exceptions to the free movement of capital under the Treaty

Restrictions existing on 31 December 1993 under national or EC law in relation to the movement of capital from the EC to third countries involving direct investment, establishment, the provision of financial services or the admission of securities to capital markets may continue to be applied: Article 57. After that date, measures compatible with the free movement of capital in these areas between Member States and third countries may be adopted by QMV in the Council. Under the Treaty of Lisbon, such measures will be adopted by the EP and Council under the ordinary legislative procedure.

Where such a measure constitutes a step back from the liberalisation of free movement of capital, unanimity is required. Under the Treaty of Lisbon, such a 'step back' may only be taken under the special legislative procedure, after consultation with the EP.

Article 58(1)(b) allows certain exceptions in relation to tax law and residence where they are necessary to prevent infringements of national law, etc. or are justified on grounds of public policy or public security, provided:

- the measures do not infringe the provisions of the Treaty on establishment (Article 58(2));
- they do not constitute a means of arbitrary discrimination or a disguised restriction on the free movement of capital and payments: Article 58(3).

The exception under Article 58(1)(b) has proved difficult for Member States to invoke successfully.

Key case

The ECJ considered the compatibility with Treaty provisions on capital movements of a French requirement for prior authorisation of direct foreign investments. It held that Article 58 precludes a national authorisation for foreign investment which is defined in such general terms as investments representing a threat to public policy and public security. Such a requirement may only be justified in order to identify the specific circumstances in which prior authorisation is required: Case C-53/99 *Association Eglise de Scientologie de Paris and Scientology International Reserves Trust* v. *the Prime Minister*.

Where, in exceptional circumstances, capital movements to third countries cause or threaten to cause serious difficulties for the operation of EMU (see below), the Council may by QMV take safeguard measures of up to six months, after consulting the European Central Bank (ECB): Article 59. In an emergency, measures may be taken by a Member State against a third country, informing the Commission and the other Member States: Article 60. Such measures may later be amended or abolished by QMV in the Council.

> ## Key point
>
> The Treaty of Lisbon will add a new paragraph 4 to Article 58:
>
> > In the absence of measures pursuant to Article 57(3), the Commission or, in the absence of a Commission decision within three months from the request of the Member State concerned, the Council may adopt a decision stating the restrictive tax measures adopted by a Member State concerning one or more third countries shall be considered compatible with the Treaties insofar as they are justified by one of the objectives of the Union and compatible with the proper functioning of the internal market. The Council shall act unanimously on application by a Member State.

Restrictions on capital from 'special' or 'golden' shares

In recent years many undertakings previously controlled by the state in various Member States have been moved wholly or partly into private ownership. This may require the creation of a new undertaking in which both public authorities and private investors participate, with safeguards to protect the interests of the public in the 'privatised' undertaking. Such safeguards sometimes involve the issuing of 'special' or 'golden' shares under which the government is entitled to appoint directors or to approve important decisions relating to the company.

The Commission issued a Communication in 1997 listing various national arrangements which it considered were unlawful restrictions on the free movement of capital, including:

- a prohibition on the number of shares which may be owned by investors from another EU country;
- measures such as a general authorisation requirement for the acquisition of a stake in a domestic company above a certain level;
- the right to veto major company decisions or to impose a nomination of a director.

It was not clear from the Commission Communication of 1997 whether special or golden shares constituted a restriction on capital movements. In order to establish the position, as it perceived the use of special shares as damaging to cross-border trade, the Commission initiated enforcement proceedings under Article 226 against Italy, France, Belgium, Portugal and the UK. While the Italian government conceded in Case C-58/99 *Commission* v. *Italy*, the other four Member States vigorously contested the proceedings. The case against the UK may be taken as an example.

Key case

The Commission brought enforcement proceedings against the UK in relation to the Articles of Association of the British Airports Authority (BAA). The BAA, previously responsible for the ownership and management of airports in the UK, was privatised by the Airports Act 1986. Under the Articles of Association, the Secretary of State held a £1 special share which entitled him to veto the winding up of BAA and the sale of a 'designated airport' such as Heathrow. The articles prohibited any shareholder from owning more than a 15 per cent holding in the company. The Court of Justice held that the veto power and the equity limitation were restrictions on the movement of capital, rejecting claims by the UK that the provisions were non-discriminatory. In the Court's view, such provisions were likely to deter investors from other Member States and therefore affected access to the markets. The Court was equally dismissive of the UK's claim that the restrictions were purely a matter of private company law, again finding that they were restrictions on the movement of capital: Case C-98/01 *Commission* v. *UK*.

In Case C-483/99 *Commission* v. *France*, the Commission challenged the rights attaching to the 'golden share' of the French government in Elf-Acquitaine, the national oil company. In this case, the special share prevented the acquisition of shares above a certain level unless approved by the relevant minister in the French government, as well as the sale or use as a security of the four subsidiaries of Elf. The Court found that the use of a 'golden share' where the State reserves the right to interfere with the management of the company is a restriction on the free movement of capital. While the safeguarding of oil supplies was seen to be a legitimate objective, the mechanism in the golden share was seen to confer wide discretionary power and to be too vague.

In Case C-367/98 *Commission* v. *Portugal* the Commission accepted that Member States may be justified in retaining a degree of control over undertakings where they provide services in the public interest or strategic services.

By contrast in Case C-503/99 *Commission* v. *Belgium* the Court considered rules giving a golden share to Belgium in SNTC and Distrigaz, as a result of which the Belgian government was entitled to oppose the sale or transfer of the company's strategic assets and to be involved in various management decisions. It found that, although the rules were a restriction on the movement of capital, they were justified in order to maintain energy supplies, and were not disproportionate as they did not involve the use of excessive powers.

ECONOMIC POLICY BEFORE THE TREATY OF MAASTRICHT

European Monetary System

The provision on economic and monetary policy under the Treaty of Rome failed to provide for a mechanism for exchange rate management between the currencies of the Member States. An attempt to regulate European currencies was made in 1972 by means of the 'snake', a scheme which permitted limited currency fluctuation. This first scheme was not entirely successful and was abandoned. In 1979 the nine Member States, prior to the second accession, formed the European Monetary System (EMS), to create closer monetary co-operation leading to a zone of monetary stability in Europe. There were two main elements in the EMS: the exchange rate mechanism (ERM), and the creation of the European currency unit (the ECU). The UK joined the ERM in 1990 but, with Italy, suspended membership after a currency crisis in 1992.

Exchange Rate Mechanism

Each Member State participating in the ERM had a central currency rate set against the ECU. This central rate could be realigned if the participants agreed. Under the ERM participating States were required to control their exchange rates, for example by adjusting interest rates, so that the value of the currency moved within fixed limits, originally within a narrow band, but widened in 1993 after currency speculation (see below).

European currency

The first EC currency was known as the European unit of account, a gold-based currency used to express the operations of the European Monetary Co-operation Fund. From 1979 the Fund's activities were expressed in a unit of account known as the ECU, defined as the sum of specified amounts of the currencies of Member States. This meant that the ECU was based on a 'basket of currencies', including the deutschmark and the pound sterling. On 1 January 1999, the ECU was replaced by the euro, the single currency of the EU, when the third stage of EMU began. The Council decided in December 1995 that references in the Treaty to the ECU should be regarded in future as references to the euro.

ECONOMIC AND MONETARY UNION

The introduction of the EMS was the first step towards economic and monetary union (EMU). Adoption of the Single European Act represented a further step in that direction by the Member States. The European Council at its meeting in Hanover in June 1988 appointed a Committee chaired by Jacques Delors, the President of the Commission, to make proposals on stages for achievement of EMU for consideration by the meeting of the European Council in Madrid in June 1989. The Report of the Delors Committee was issued in May 1989. It proposed that the Treaty should be amended to make the institutional changes necessary to achieve full EMU. Progress towards union should be seen as a single process, involving three stages. The first stage would involve greater convergence of economic and monetary policy. In the second stage the economic and institutional basis for EMU including a European

Central Bank would be set up. In the third stage of full EMU the single currency would be introduced, fixed at an irrevocable exchange rate.

Treaty on European Union

Intergovernmental conferences were convened to consider EMU (and, in parallel, political union). By December 1990 agreement on the terms of EMU was reached, but only after two Member States, the UK and Denmark, had secured 'opt outs' from the commitment to EMU through Protocols annexed to the Treaty enabling them to decide whether they wished to participate in EMU at a later date. The Treaty on European Union was signed at Maastricht in February 1991 and ratified in November 1993: see Chapter 1.

Legal basis of EMU

The legal foundation for EMU was incorporated into the EC Treaty by the Maastricht Treaty. It requires 'the close co-ordination of economic policies' (Article 3(1) EC) to be established as a matter of common concern within the framework of policy guidelines set by the Council following the decision of the European Council: Articles 98 (ex 102a) and 100 (ex 103a). It is based on the three-stage approach of the Delors plan as follows:

Stage 1

Member States were required to comply with the provisions of the Treaty on the free movement of capital; liberalise their financial institutions: Article 101 (ex 104); and work towards lasting convergence in economic policy: Article 116 (ex 109e). The first stage began on 1 July 1990 and finished on 31 December 1993. During that time the Exchange Rate Mechanism, seen as a cornerstone of economic policy, suffered from speculative pressures on the international currency market. As a result of falling values of the pound sterling and the lira, the UK and Italy had to leave the ERM in 1992. The EU permitted a wider band for currency fluctuation, effectively suspending the ERM from 1993. Nevertheless, the completion of the internal market in capital and payments required by the Maastricht Treaty was largely achieved by the end of the first stage.

Stage 2

This began on 1 January 1994 as a preparation for full EMU in Stage 3. The European Monetary Institute (EMI), the forerunner of the ECB, was established in Frankfurt in 1994 to prepare for the introduction of the third stage. The EMI was required to specify the regulatory and organisation structure of the ECB by December 1996.

Stage 3

This began on schedule on 1 January 1999, the date fixed by Article 121(4) (ex 109j(4)) of the EC Treaty. On this date the ECB and European System of Central Banks were established, and the euro was introduced as the single currency, its value fixed irrevocably by the unanimous decision of the participating states. The EMI went into liquidation.

Any Member State wishing to be admitted to Stage 3 has to satisfy strict convergence criteria which include limits on inflation, avoidance of excessive government budgetary deficits, observance of the narrow band of the ERM for two years and restrictions on average long-term interest rates. The European Council decided by qualified majority in May 1998 which States had fulfilled the convergence criteria to proceed to Stage 3. The UK, Denmark and Sweden chose to stay outside EMU, although only the UK and Denmark negotiated an 'opt out' from EMU at Maastricht. At present 15 Member States have adopted the euro: Austria, Belgium, Cyprus, Finland, France, Germany, Greece, Ireland, Italy, Luxembourg, Malta, Netherlands, Portugal, Slovenia and Spain.

● European Central Bank

The European Central Bank is based in Frankfurt, like its predecessor, the European Monetary Institute. It has legal personality under Article 107(2). The ECB operates as an independent bank, similar to the Bundesbank on which it is modelled, within the European System of Central Banks (ESCB). The ESCB is composed of the ECB and the national central banks under Article 107(1).

The ECB is responsible for controlling the euro, and is the only bank which may authorise the issue of euro banknotes. Euro notes and coins were introduced into the participating States on 1 January 2002, with all national notes and coins withdrawn by 1 July 2002. The main duty of the ECB is to maintain price stability in relation to the euro and to support the general economic activities of the EU, as set out in Article 2 of the Treaty. Under Article 105(2) the ECB has the following tasks:

- to define and implement the monetary policy of the participating States;
- to conduct foreign exchange operations;
- to hold and manage the foreign reserves of participating States;
- to promote the smooth operation of the payments system.

It is empowered to make legislation in the form of regulations and decisions in certain areas and may impose fines or periodic payments on defaulting states: Article 110. ECB legislation may be reviewed in the normal way under Article 230. The ECB is, to some degree, accountable to the other EC institutions, although there has been considerable criticism that the Bank is not sufficiently accountable. It must produce an annual Report on its activities to the EP, the Council, the European Council and the Commission.[1] The President may be called to explain the Report to a committee of the EP. However, the ECB may refuse to answer the committee's questions.

The Council retains some legislative powers and may enter into exchange-rate agreements for the euro with third countries (Article 111), and may alter the central rate within the exchange mechanism by QMV. The Council may also amend parts of the Statute of the ESCB, but may not affect the independence of the system.

[1] See, for example, Gormley and de Haan (1996).

Management of EMU

Under Article 98, Member States participating in EMU are obliged to conduct their economic policies with a view to contributing to the achievement of the objectives of the Community and in accordance with the guidelines under Article 99, in accordance with the principle of an open market economy.

Article 99 requires Member States to regard their economic policies as a matter of common concern and to co-ordinate them with the Council. It creates a system of multilateral surveillance to enable the Commission and the Council to oversee the fiscal position of Member States. Article 104 obliges Member States to avoid excessive government deficits. It sets specific limits on the extent to which Member States may rely on deficit financing which are the same as those set for the convergence criteria for joining EMU. As a result, a deficit of more than 3 per cent is only acceptable in exceptional or temporary circumstances.

> **Key point**
>
> Member States participating in EMU are subject not only to obligations in the Treaty and Protocol, but also to the Stability and Growth Pact 1997. The objective of the system is to avoid situations where a national government would become financially unstable as a result of an unsustainable fiscal position, as this would pose a threat to the operation of EMU.

Member States participating in the EMU are subject to major constraints on fiscal management. Under Article 101 EC the ECB and national central banks are prohibited from providing credit to public bodies or from buying government bonds. Article 102 prohibits any EC or national measure other than one aimed at the safety and soundness of the financial sector, where the effect would give the public sector preferential access to the credit of the commercial sector. Article 103 prohibits Member States from 'bailing out' another Member State by taking on their public sector liabilities. While this rule appears harsh, it is unlikely that it would ever need to be invoked. As Chalmers *et al.* (2006: 531) point out: 'It is quite inconceivable that the EC would allow a Member State to reach the point of insolvency. Especially if it appeared to be triggered by the Treaty straightjackets, such a national insolvency would create extremely bad feelings against the European project itself, as well as dramatic economic instability within the European Union.'

Under the 1997 Stability Pact, Member States in the eurozone must submit an annual stability programme. Non-participating states seeking to join EMU submit a convergence programme. Participating states under Article 104 should avoid excessive budget deficits, normally taken to mean deficits exceeding 3 per cent of the state's gross domestic product (GDP) or public debt exceeding 60 per cent of GDP. Under the Pact, sanctions should be imposed on States breaking the rules. However, despite adverse reports on France, Germany, Italy and Poland in 2004, the Council failed to take action. In the belief that that Council's failure to act would weaken EMU, the

Commission began proceedings under Article 230 against the Council in the Court: Case C-27/04 *Commission* v. *Council*. Although the Court annulled the Council's conclusions on procedural grounds, the Court stated that nothing could be done to enforce the Stability Pact.

Key point

The Treaty of Lisbon will make a number of amendments to the provisions on economic and monetary policy. It will strengthen Article 99 providing a new para. 4, enabling the Commission to address a warning to a Member State whose economic policies are not consistent with the guidelines in Article 99(2). The Council is empowered to make recommendations to the Member State concerned.

Article 104 will be amended, enabling the Commission, where it considers that an excessive deficit in a Member State exists or may occur, to address an opinion directly to the Member State concerned and inform the Council. At present, the Commission addresses an opinion to the Council which may act by QMV under Article 104(6).

Article 115A will empower the Council to adopt measures to ensure the proper functioning of EMU, for those Member States whose currency is the euro.

A two-speed Europe

It has not proved possible for all Member States to participate in full EMU so far, either because of 'opt-outs' or through failure to meet the convergence criteria, demonstrating the continuation of a 'two-speed Europe' or 'Europe of variable geometry'. A two-tier approach to European integration may be seen as the inevitable result of the political compromises agreed at Maastricht on the single currency and other issues. A flexible approach in the future will continue to be needed in an EU of 27 (or more) Member States with different levels of development and commitment to integration.

QUESTIONS

1 Why were the provisions on the free movement of capital recognised to be directly effective long after those relating to goods, persons and services?

2 In what circumstances have 'special' or 'golden' shares been found to constitute a restriction on the free movement of capital?

3 What restrictions are placed on Member States participating in EMU in terms of the regulation of economic and monetary policies? To what extent have the restrictions been enforced?

Further reading

Barnard, C. (2004) *The Substantive Law of the EU: the Four Freedoms*, Oxford University Press, Chapter 17.

Beaumont, P. and Walker, N. (1999) *The Legal Framework of the Single European Currency*, Hart.

Chalmers, D., Hadjiemmanuil, C., Monti, G. and Tomkins, A. (2006) *European Union Law*, Cambridge, Chapter 12.

Craig, P. and De Burca, G. (2007) *EU Law: Text, Cases and Materials*, 4th edition, Oxford University Press.

Flynn, L. (2002) 'Coming of Age: the Free Movement of Capital Caselaw 1993–2002', (2002) 39 CMLRev. 773.

Gormley, L. and de Haan, J. (1996) 'The Democratic Deficit of the European Central Bank', (1996) 21 ELRev. 95.

Louis, J. V. (2004) 'The Economic and Monetary Union: Law and Institutions' (2004) 41 CMLRev. 575.

Usher, J. (1994) *The Law of Money and Financial Services in the European Community*, Oxford University Press.

Visit **http://www.mylawchamber.co.uk/kent** to access answer guidance to questions in the book to test yourself on this chapter.

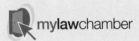
mylawchamber

Part 3

COMPETITION LAW
AND POLICY

17 Introduction to competition

UNDERSTANDING COMPETITION

Terminology

It is useful to become familiar with some of the economic terms in competition policy:

Economic terms

- *Barriers to entry*: Legal restrictions (e.g. patents, licensing requirements) on entering the market.
- *Cartel*: A combination of undertakings which agree to restrict competition (e.g. by fixing prices).
- *Concerted practice*: A practice falling short of an actual agreement which is illegal under Article 81 (ex 85).
- *Dominance*: The enjoyment by an undertaking of market power; abuse of a dominant position is illegal under Article 82 (ex 86).
- *Duopoly*: Where market power is held by two sellers who react to each other's conduct.
- *Exclusive dealing*: An arrangement for the distribution of goods within an identified area, usually involving supply by a producer to a single franchised dealer who agrees not to sell competing goods.
- *Horizontal agreement*: Agreement or merger between undertakings operating at the same level in the chain of distribution (e.g. a cartel between distributors).
- *Information agreement*: Agreement to provide competitors with advance information on prices.
- *Market power*: The extent to which an undertaking may influence prices and output in a particular market.
- *Monopoly*: Where market power is held by a single undertaking.

➜

- *Oligopoly*: Where a few sellers hold market power and react to each other's conduct.
- *Parallel imports*: Situation which arises where the price of goods is much higher in one Member State than another, making it cost effective to buy goods in the State where they are cheapest and sell in the State(s) where the price is highest. Eventually, this practice should lead to price equalisation.
- *Quantitative restriction (quota)*: A restriction on the quantity of goods to be produced or imported, including an absolute prohibition (nil quota) on production or importation.
- *Vertical agreement*: Agreement between firms operating at different levels in the chain of distribution (e.g. agreement between a producer and a supplier or between a supplier and customer).

Theory of competition: perfect competition

The modern approach to competition from the latter part of the nineteenth century onwards derives from the theory of perfect competition. As a model rather than an account of what happens in real life, perfect competition assumes various factors: that all markets contain a large number of buyers and sellers, that the sellers produce identical (or interchangeable) products, that resources can flow freely from one area of economic activity to another, and that there are no 'barriers to entry or exit' (i.e. restrictions on new businesses entering or existing businesses leaving the market).

Applying the theoretical model, any producer will be able to sell its product at a price no higher than the market will bear. Because there are many producers, no single producer will be able to dictate prices. Under conditions of perfect competition an efficient distribution of resources is achieved. A producer acting rationally has an incentive to make more profits by expanding production up to the point where it costs more to produce a further unit than the price of the product (the 'marginal cost'). Output would be maintained at this point (the 'optimal level'). Consumers would be free to buy as many goods as they need at the price they are willing to pay (an efficient allocation of resources).

Without regulation, according to the traditional view, market power would be concentrated in the form of monopoly or oligopoly. As a result, the monopolist would prosper at the expense of the consumer, whose choice of products would be restricted. There would be little pressure to keep down prices, and resources would be misallocated because it is in the interest of the monopolist to limit output, using 'too few' of society's resources, while more resources are channelled into the production of less valuable goods. Similar objections may be levelled against oligopolies where undertakings tend to behave as if acting in a cartel by responding rapidly to the behaviour of rival undertakings with similar behaviour ('conscious parallelism').

> **Key point**
>
> The traditional view of economists was based on an acceptance that perfect competition does not exist in the real world. State intervention was, therefore, necessary if economic activity was to be brought closer to perfect competition, thus protecting both consumer choice and opportunities for small businesses (now known within the EC as 'small and medium-sized enterprises').

This approach underlay much early anti-trust (competition) law in the USA, such as the Sherman Act 1890. It was also adopted in Europe after the Second World War, particularly in Germany, where it was seen as a means of avoiding dominance by larger producers and, to a lesser degree, in France.

An opposing view of competition: the Chicago school

An opposing view has emerged through the writings of the Chicago school of economists who believe that perfect competition *is* reflected in the real world, rendering state intervention largely unnecessary. It follows that only the most serious anti-competitive activities need to be controlled. Even monopolies are not necessarily to be prohibited unless they prevent competition from new entrants to the field.

A compromise approach: 'workable competition'

Some economists have adopted a compromise approach based on the idea of 'workable competition'. These economists accept that perfect competition is impossible, but consider that firms should strive to attain the most competitive structure which can be achieved, i.e. a workable competitive structure, which would benefit production and performance. The theory of workable competition has been invoked on a number of occasions by the EC Commission and by the ECJ (e.g. in Case 161/84 *Pronuptia* v. *Schillgallis*: see Chapter 18). Following the theory of workable competition, competition rules are needed to deal with certain problems, including the need to prevent firms from entering into agreements which restrict competition without any beneficial features and the need to control the abuses of their position by monopolists or those in a dominant position. Workable competition will have to be maintained in industries in which there are only a few sellers, and mergers controlled to avoid a concentration of market power.

Theory of 'contestable competition'

According to the theory of 'contestable competition', the best allocation of resources is achieved by ensuring that firms operate only in a 'contestable' market. This theory emphasises the need for freedom to enter and leave the market without incurring costs. Such a market need not be perfectly competitive. While the importance of this theory in EC competition law is hard to assess at present, its likeliest application would appear to be in relation to deregulation (e.g. of the airline industry).

COMPETITION LAW AND POLICY IN THE EC

Purpose of competition law in the EC

Competition law in the EC and elsewhere does not aim solely to maximise consumer welfare by drawing up legal rules to provide for the most efficient allocation of resources and the maximum reduction of costs.

> **Key point**
>
> There is no single competition policy. Instead, competition law and policy within the EC reflect changing values and social aims and cannot be restricted to the narrow application of any one economic theory.

Article 2 refers to the task of the EC as the promotion of the harmonious development of economic activities by the creation of a common market and the progressive approximation of the economic policies of the Member States. The main objectives of competition policy within the EC may be summarised as follows:

- to create and maintain a single market for the benefit of producers and consumers ('market integration');
- to prevent large undertakings from abusing their power ('equity');
- to persuade firms to rationalise production and distribution and to keep up to date with technical progress ('efficiency').

Legal framework of competition law in the EC

Competition law and policy in the EC are based on Article 3(g) of the EC Treaty which requires the institution of a system ensuring that competition in the internal market is not distorted. The competition rules are seen as an essential adjunct to the provisions on the free movement of goods in Articles 28–30. Articles 81 and 82 (ex 85 and 86) of the Treaty provide a framework for competition rules on concerted practices in Article 81 (ex 85), and abuse of a dominant position in Article 82 (ex 86). Article 86 (ex 90) provides for similar rules to be applied to public undertakings. State aids are covered in Article 87(1) (ex 92(1)). Mergers have been regulated by the Commission since 1990 when Regulation 4064/89 took effect. The current merger Regulation is Regulation 139/2004.

Before May 2004, the main secondary legislation on competition was found in Regulation 17/62. Under the old regime, the Commission played a central role in the administration and enforcement of competition law and policy, and was the only body able to grant exemptions under Article 81(3) where an agreement was otherwise invalid under Article 81(2). On 1 May 2004 Regulation 1/2003 came into force, heralding a new approach. As a result, much of the administration of competition law was devolved to national competition authorities (NCAs) which apply Articles 81 and 82 directly: see below.

Criticism of EC competition policy

The competition policy of the EC has long been criticised for failing to distinguish between to different types of agreement. The traditional approach adopted by the Commission was to treat all agreements which restrict competition as illegal unless they are covered by a joint or individual exemption. This approach did not distinguish between horizontal and vertical agreements. While horizontal agreements are usually perceived to be damaging, vertical agreements may not necessarily operate against the interests of consumers.

Key term

Horizontal agreements are agreements between undertakings operating at the same level in the chain of distribution, e.g. an agreement between retailers to fix prices. Vertical agreements are agreements between undertakings at different levels (e.g. an agreement between a wholesaler and a retailer for the exclusive distribution of goods).

The Commission adopted a new Regulation on Vertical Agreements, Regulation 2790/99, to apply for 10 years from 1 June 2000 to answer this criticism. The Regulation covers suppliers holding no more than 30 per cent of the relevant market. It enables such suppliers (with some exceptions) to benefit from a block exemption for vertical agreements.

Modernisation

In response to the need to update the competition rules to meet changing circumstances, the Commission published a White Paper in 1999 for consultation throughout the EU on modernising the competition rules. These circumstances included the completion of the single market, the introduction of the euro, enlargement of the EU and the trend towards globalisation. Regulation 1/2003 was adopted as a lynchpin of the strategy competition law for the future. One significant change was the dropping of the notification procedure. Notification of agreements to the Commission, in order to apply for exemption from Article 81(1), had previously been the practice under Regulation 17/62. As a result of the adoption of Regulation 1/2003,

17

Introduction to competition

the enforcement of competition law was devolved to the national competition authorities (NCAs), leaving the Commission free to concentrate on the most serious cases.

Competition law in the UK

The UK adopted the Competition Act in 1998, with effect from 2 March 2000. The Act instituted a new regime based on the principles in Articles 81 and 82 of the EC Treaty. Section 60 of the Act requires the UK competition authorities to ensure consistency with the principles of the EC Treaty, the case law of the European Courts and the decisions and statements of the Commission. The prohibitions against anti-competitive agreements and abuse of a dominant position in the UK are enforced primarily by a new body, the Office of Fair Trading, established under the Enterprise Act 2002 which repealed the previous UK law on monopolies and mergers in the Fair Trading Act 1973. The 2002 Act made involvement in cartels a criminal offence and created a new specialist tribunal knows as the Competition Appeal Tribunal (CAT). Further significant changes were made under the Competition Act 1998 and other Enactments (Amendment) Regulations 2004 to give effect to the devolution of responsibilities at EC level.

Competition law is a highly specialised branch of EC law, with a large body of case law. Considerations of space in this book permit only coverage of the main principles of Community law. Administration of competition law at national level is not considered in detail.

QUESTIONS

1 Why, in relation to 'perfect competition', do economists consider is it necessary to regulate the operation of market power? Which theory (or theories) of competition have influenced the development of competition law and policy within the EC?

2 How does competition law in the EC recognise the fact that not all forms of anti-competitive agreements are detrimental to consumers?

Further reading

Rodger, B. J. and MacCulloch, A. (2004) *Competition Law and Policy in the EC and the UK*, 3rd edition, Cavendish Publishing, Chapter 1.

Chalmers, D., Hadjiemmanuil, C., Monti, G. and Tomkins, A. (2006) *European Union Law*, Cambridge University Press, pp.927–940.

Furse, M. (2004) *Competition Law of the EC and UK*, 4th edition, Oxford University Press.

Jones, A. and Sufrin, B. (2008) *EC Competition Law: Text, Cases and Materials*, 3rd edition, Oxford University Press, Chapter 1, pp.1–55.

Korah, V. (2007) *An Introductory Guide to EC Competition Law and Practice'*, 9th edition, Hart Publishing, Chapter 1.

Van den Bergh, R. J. and Camesasca, P. D. (2006) *European Competition Law and Economics: A Comparitive Perspective'*, 2nd edition, Thomson, Chapters 1–3.

Visit **http://www.mylawchamber.co.uk/kent** to access answer guidance to questions in the book to test yourself on this chapter.

17

Introduction to competition

18   Article 81

INTRODUCTION

Articles 81 and 82 (ex 85 and 86) are the two principal provisions in the Treaty covering competition law. Both provisions are directly effective: Case 127/73 *BRT* v. *SABAM*. As we have seen in Chapter 17, the Articles provide a framework which is supplemented by detailed rules in secondary legislation, particularly Regulation 1/2003 (from May 2004). Articles 81 and 82 are complementary in their pursuit of a common objective under Article 3(g) (providing a system to ensure that competition in the internal market is not distorted): Case T-51/89 *Tetra Pak Rausing SA* v. *Commission*. However, it should be noted that the two provisions may also be read independently of each other, as legal instruments addressing different situations: Article 81 concerns agreements, decisions of associations of undertakings and concerted practices; Article 82 concerns unilateral activity of one or more undertakings.

Article 81: the prohibition

Article 81(1) prohibits all agreements between undertakings, decisions by associations of undertakings and concerted practices which may affect trade between Member States and which have as their object or effect the prevention, restriction or distortion of competition within the common market. This general prohibition is followed by examples of anti-competitive practices in Article 81(1)(a) to (e) such as price fixing and market sharing. Article 81(2) provides that any agreement in breach of Article 81(1) shall be automatically void.

Article 81(3) provides that Article 81(1) may be declared inapplicable if certain conditions are satisfied. Before 1 May 2004, only the Commission was permitted to apply Article 81(3), which it did under Regulation 17/62 through the granting of exemptions and decisions on negative clearance, following the notification of specific agreements between undertakings. Regulation 1/2003, a key element in the modernisation programme, introduced a radically different approach based on devolution to the national competition authorities (NCAs). Notification to the Commission was abandoned , leaving the Commission free to focus on cases of greater complexity or which raised strategic issues. Article 81(3) became directly applicable. As a result, the

NCAs were empowered to reach their own decisions as to whether individual agreements or practices infringed Article 81(1), though provision is made for co-operation between the Commission and the NCAs.

INFRINGEMENT

Infringement of Article 81(1)

The basic elements which must be present for there to be an infringement of Article 81(1) are considered under the following headings:

- Agreements
- Undertakings
- Decisions by associations of undertakings
- Concerted practices
- Effect on trade between Member States
- Prevention, restriction or distortion of competition
- Object or effect
- Within the EC: the 'effects' doctrine

Agreements

The word 'agreement' is not defined in the Treaty. However, it has been widely interpreted by the Commission to include an agreement not normally regarded as a contract, such as a 'gentlemen's agreement': Dec. 69/240 *Quinine Cartel*[1] because it was enforceable through arbitration, and a voluntary undertaking to limit freedom of action without a contract: Dec. 74/634 *Franco–Japanese Ball Bearings Agreement*. An agreement may be oral or in writing.

Undertakings

(a) Undertakings generally

'Undertaking' is not defined but, like 'agreement', has been liberally interpreted by the Commission and the ECJ to include any legal or natural person engaged in economic or commercial activity involving the provision of goods or services: Dec. 86/398 *Polypropylene*. This activity need not be pursued for a profit: Dec. 85/615 *P and I Clubs*. The following have been considered to be 'undertakings':

- Individuals engaged in sporting or cultural activities, e.g. opera singing: Dec. 78/516 *Re UNITEL*.
- Trade associations: *FRUBO* v. *Commission* (Case 71/74).

---

[1] Competition decisions are cited as follows: Commission decisions: Dec. year/number; CFI decisions: Case T-number/year ('T' stands for 'Tribunal'); ECJ decisions: Case C-number/year. Where the citation is followed by 'P', this indicates a *pourvoi*, or appeal.

- State-owned corporations: Case 155/73 *Italian State* v. *Sacchi*. (The competition rules are extended to the public sector by Article 86(1): see Chapter 22.)
- Undertakings related to agriculture: Dec. 85/76 *Milchforderungs Fonds*.
- Coal, steel and atomic energy, where the matter is not already covered.

(b) Transport undertakings

It is clear from the decision of the ECJ in Cases 209–213/84 *Ministère Public* v. *Asjes* that Articles 81 and 82 apply in principle to air and sea transport. Action may not be taken by individuals in their national courts until implementation measures have been taken by the EC institutions or the Member States. Regulations 3975/87 and 3976/87 enabled the Commission to enforce competition rules in the air transport sector. Regulation 2410/92 extended the application of EC competition rules to air transport within a single State. Regulation 3975/87 does not, however, apply to air transport between an EC and non-EC airport. Regulation 2672/88 enabled the Commission to issue block exemptions in this field. In Case 66/86 *Ahmed Saeed Flugreisen* v. *Zentrale Zur Bekämpfung Unlauteren Wettbewerbs* the ECJ held that tariff agreements for flights to destinations outside the EC remained covered by Articles 84 (ex 88) and 85 (ex 89), being outside the implementing regulations. Flights within the EC are covered by the Regulation, with the result that agreements relating to such flights which infringe Article 81(1) will automatically be void. Article 82 was held to apply to air transport without distinction.

In Dec. 88/589 *London European Airways* v. *Sabena* the Commission fined Sabena €100,000, the first time the competition rules had been invoked against an airline. In 1992 Aer Lingus was found by the Commission to have breached Articles 81 and 82 by making it difficult for British Midland to compete on the Heathrow to Dublin route: Dec. 92/213 *British Midland* v. *Aer Lingus*. This decision was annulled by the CFI in Joined Cases T-374, 375, 384 and 388/94 *European Night Services and others* v. *Commission* on the basis of inadequate reasoning by the Commission on market share and effect on competition. Completion of the internal market in air transport was largely achieved following several packages of measures between 1987 and 1995. Regulation 4056/86 applied the competition rules to sea transport.

(c) Public authorities

Agreements and concerted practices entered into by public authorities engaged in commercial activities would appear to be covered by Article 81(1). In Case 30/87 *Bodson* v. *Pompes Funèbres des Régions Libérées SA* the ECJ held that Article 81 did not cover a licensing arrangement over certain funeral services to the Société des Pompes Funèbres, where the local authority was acting in its capacity as a public authority. If it had been acting in the course of commercial activities, the authority should have been covered. In Dec. 89/536 ARD/Nefico (*Film Purchases by German Television Stations*) the Commission held that an association representing a number of German television companies, a public institution under national law, constituted an undertaking under Article 81(1).

In contrast, the CFI in Case T-319/99 *FENIN* confirmed that a healthcare authority buying services from the private sector were not undertaking when acting in the exercise of public activities. As Korah (2007) observes, the rules on public procurement are concerned with the integration of the internal market rather than competition, and do not usually affect trade between Member States.

(d) The 'economic entity' principle

Agreements between undertakings which form a single economic unit do not infringe Article 81(1). Thus an agreement between a parent company and its subsidiary over a matter controlled by a parent is covered by the 'economic entity' principle and is not regarded as a decision between undertakings: Case C-73/95P *Viho Europe BV* v. *Commission*. A parent company may, however, be liable for the acts of its subsidiary in relation to third parties when the subsidiary is acting on the instructions of the parent: Case 22/71 *Béguelin Import Co.* v. *G.L. Export–Import SA*. The Commission may examine the relationship between the parties to determine its true nature: Dec. 72/403 *Pittsburg Corning Europe*.

Decisions by associations of undertakings

The most usual type of 'association' covered by Article 81(1) is the trade association: Case 8/72 *Vereniging van Cementhandelaren* v. *Commission*. Where trade associations co-ordinate their activities, there may be an anti-competitive effect without a formal agreement. The expression 'decisions by associations of undertakings' has been widely interpreted by the ECJ.

Examples
- A non-binding recommendation of trade association: Case 96/82 *NV IAZ International Belgium* v. *Commission*.
- A non-binding code of conduct: Dec. 89/44 *Re The Application of the Publishers' Association*, upheld by the CFI but overruled by the ECJ on a different point in 1995 in Case C-360/92P *Publishers' Association* v. *Commission*.

Concerted practices

Concerted practices arise where positive steps short of an agreement have been taken to align the activities of undertakings, for example, following a recommendation to exchange advance information on intended prices. In Case 48/69 etc. *Imperial Chemical Industries Ltd* v. *Commission (Dyestuffs)* the ECJ defined a concerted practice as a form of co-operation between undertakings which have not entered into a formal agreement but which have 'knowingly substituted practical co-operation . . . for the risks of competition'.

Key case

On three occasions in 1964, 10 major producers of dyestuffs, including ICI and CIBA, who produced 80 per cent of the dyes sold in the EC, announced price rises of about 10 per cent. Similar price rises occurred on two further occasions. There was evidence of collusion: on the first occasion four of the parent companies had sent telex messages to their subsidiaries within an hour of each other. Two further messages had been sent within the next two hours, all messages being similarly worded. The ECJ upheld the decision of the Commission, holding that their behaviour contravened Article 81(1), and imposed heavy fines on the undertakings concerned. It held that parallel behaviour does not necessarily amount to a concerted practice under Article 81(1) unless it leads to competition which does not accord to normal conditions of the market: Cases 48/69, etc. *Imperial Chemical Industries Ltd* v. *Commission*.

The decision in *Dyestuffs* has been criticised on the ground that in a market dominated by a few sellers normal price increases involving parallel pricing without co-operation may result in a breach of Article 81(1). In Cases 40 etc./73 '*Suiker Unie*' *(Sugar Cartel)* the ECJ held that the Commission must consider the characteristics of the market in deciding whether the parallel behaviour is an independent response to the market or the result of intentional co-operation (i.e. 'a concerted practice').

Collusion in a pricing cartel involving a number of producers of carton board was found by the CFI in Cases T-295/94 etc. *Buchmann* v. *Commission* etc.). The CFI confirmed the Commission's decision, as far as the majority of producers was concerned. It laid down conditions for holding an undertaking responsible for participation in an overall cartel as follows:

> The Commission must demonstrate that each undertaking concerned either consented to the adoption of an overall plan comprising the constituent elements of the cartel or that it participated directly in all those elements during that period.

On a number of occasions the Commission has issued decisions which recognise the distinction between genuine, independent price rises and concerted practices. It is more likely that a concerted practice will be identified in the context of a distribution agreement with emphasis placed by the Commission and the ECJ on the spirit rather than the letter of a practice, as the decision in *Züchner* demonstrates. In Case 172/80 *Züchner* v. *Bayerische Vereinsbank* an EC national challenged the service charge made for transferring funds to Italy, arguing that the charge amounted to a concerted practice, even though it was apparently uniformly applied by a number of banks. The Court held that such a charge could be a concerted practice where co-operation could be shown provided there was a sufficient effect on competition. This decision should be contrasted with Dec. 92/212 the *Eurocheque* case where uniform bank charges under the Eurocheque system were approved due to the clear advantages to tourists and other travellers.

Effect on trade between Member States

The agreement, decision or concerted practice must affect inter-Member trade to infringe Article 81(1). Thus an agreement which is concerned with trade within one Member State or with exports outside the EC is, on the face of it, not covered by Article 81(1).

> **Key point**
>
> The test defining the circumstances in which an agreement is brought within Article 81(1) was stated by the ECJ in Case 56/65 *Société Technique Minière* v. *Maschinenbau* as follows:
>
> 'It must be possible to foresee with a sufficient degree of probability on the basis of a set of objective factors of law or of fact that the agreement in question may have an influence, direct or indirect, actual or potential, on the pattern of trade between Member States.'

This test has been applied on a number of occasions, for example, in Case 193/83 *Windsurfing International Inc.* v. *Commission* where the ECJ emphasised the need to look at restrictions in the context of the agreements as a whole.

Examples

- An attempt to partition the market on national lines: Case 161/84 *Pronuptia*. In this case a franchising agreement between Pronuptia in France, the franchisor, and the franchisee in Germany, limiting the franchisee's power to operate outside a defined territory, was found by the ECJ to contravene Article 81(1). There was no evidence that the franchisee intended to operate outside the area of restriction. However, a potential effect on trade was enough.
- A scheme fixing the price of cement in the Netherlands contravened Article 81(1) by strengthening existing division of the market: Case 8/72 *Vereniging van Cementhandelaren*.
- The operators of a cartel in the Belgian roofing-felt sector were fined for contravention of Article 81(1). Although the agreement was limited to sales in one Member State, it was capable of affecting inter-member trade: Case 246/86 *Belasco* v. *Commission*.

  However, in Case C-360/92P *Publishers' Association* v. *Commission* the ECJ set aside part of the decisions of the Commission and CFI. The Court held that the refusal of exemption to the net book agreements in the UK (a system of price maintenance for books) had failed to take sufficient account of the single language area formed by the British and Irish book markets.

Prevention, restriction or distortion of competition

Competition law in the EC is concerned with distortion of competition rather than the question of whether inter-member trade has been increased or decreased. This, and a number of other important principles, were established in the case of *Consten and Grundig* v. *Commission*.

> ## Key case
>
> Grundig, a German manufacturer of electronic goods, entered into an exclusive dealing agreement with Consten SA. Under the agreement Consten had the sole right to distribute Grundig products in France and also exclusive use of the Grundig trademark (GINT) in that country. In return Consten agreed not to re-export Grundig products into any of the other Member States, effectively banning parallel imports and exports. However, another French undertaking, UNEF, purchased Grundig products in Germany and resold them in France, under-cutting Consten's prices. As a result, Consten brought an action against UNEF in the French courts for trademark infringement. UNEF applied for and obtained a decision that the decision between Grundig and Consten contravened Article 81(1). HELD (ECJ): The object of the agreement was to eliminate competition at the level of supply by the wholesaler to the distributor (i.e. inter-brand competition): Cases 56 and 58/64 *Consten and Grundig* v. *Commission*.

Principles established by the *Consten and Grundig* decision

(a) The list of examples in Article 81(1)(a) to (e) is illustrative not exhaustive. The general words in Article 81(1) govern the particular words in the examples.
(b) The prohibition applies to vertical as well as horizontal agreements.
(c) An agreement should be examined in the light of the whole network of agreements where such a network exists.
(d) Only those parts of the agreement which restrict competition and affect trade between Member States should be prohibited.
(e) A particular agreement may be condemned without a full market analysis of actual effects where the object of the agreement is to restrict competition: see below.
(f) Trade mark rights may not be enforced where their use partitions the market. An absolute territorial ban will be seen as partitioning the market.

The decision was criticised for bringing vertical agreements (such as those between producers and distributors, or distributors and retailers) clearly within the scope of Article 81(1). It has been argued that vertical agreements are often beneficial to consumers since they lead to improvements in the promotion and distribution of products. However, such agreements are equally capable of partitioning the market. In *Consten and Grundig* the ECJ found that the agreement aimed to insulate the French market for Grundig products.

The CFI reached a different view on partitioning the market in Case T-168/01 *Glaxo Smith Klein Services Unlimited* v. *Commission*, where it exceptionally held that an agreement to limit parallel trade in pharmaceuticals could only be considered to have as its object the restriction of competition when it deprived the final consumers of advantage. In the very specialised and heavily regulated pharmaceuticals market, no assumption could be made that parallel trade would reduce prices and increase consumer welfare. As a result, the Court found that an agreement containing an export ban, dual pricing system or other limitation of parallel trade would not necessarily have a negative effect on competition.

> **Key point**
>
> After many years of sustained criticism that its approach to vertical agreements was too restrictive, the Commission adopted Regulation 2790/99, providing a single block exemption for vertical agreements, on condition that the party being protected has a market share which does not exceed 30 per cent: see below.

Object or effect

The decision of the ECJ in *Consten and Grundig* that a market analysis is not necessary where the object of an agreement is clearly to restrict competition was followed in Case 56/65 *Société Technique Minière (STM)* v. *Maschinenbau Ulm GmbH (MU)*. The words 'object or effect' should thus be read disjunctively; it is not necessary to establish both elements.[2] An analysis would only be required in the case of an overtly anti-competitive agreement to confirm that the agreement was incapable of restricting competition. This approach was confirmed in Case C-277/87 *Sandoz* v. *Commission*, in which imports were stamped 'Export prohibited'. The invoices were held to constitute agreements: see also Case C-279/87 *Tipp-Ex* v. *Commission*.

Where an agreement does not have the restriction of competition as its object (e.g. a research and development agreement) a market analysis is required to establish whether effects of the agreement infringe Article 81(1). The issues to be covered in such an analysis were set out in Case 56/65 *Société Technique Minière* v. *Maschinenbau Ulm GmbH*, an Article 234 reference from the Court d'Appel in Paris out of a claim by STM that the distribution agreement into which they had entered contravened Article 81(1). The issues under consideration in an exclusive dealing agreement include:

- the nature or quantity of the products to which the agreement relates;
- the position and size of the parties in the market of the producer and the exclusive dealer;
- whether the agreement is isolated or part of a network;
- the severity of the restrictions;
- whether the agreement allows re-exportation and parallel importation of the products concerned.

[2] Odudu (2006).

As a result of such an analysis, the agreement between STM and MU was found not to contravene Article 81(1).[3]

Within the EC: the 'effects' doctrine

While Article 81(1) specifically bans agreements between undertakings located within the EC, undertakings situated outside the EC are within the scope of Article 81(1) if the *effects* of their agreements or practices are felt within the EC: *Béguelin Import Co. v. G.L. Export-Import SA*. In Cases 48/69 *Dyestuffs* four of the parties were established outside the EC. Because the effects of their concerted practices were felt within the EC they were held liable by the Commission for infringements of Article 81(1), a decision upheld by the ECJ. It should be noted that ICI (UK) Ltd was found liable for the acts of its subsidiary in the Netherlands at a time prior to UK membership of the EC. The *Dyestuffs* decision does not, therefore, represent total commitment to the 'effects' doctrine: action against subsidiaries established in the EC circumvented the issue.

Key point

An agreement may be covered by Article 81 where its effects are felt within the EC, even where the undertakings concerned are located outside the EC.

In Cases 89, 104, 114, 116–117, 125–129/85 *Wood Pulp-A Ahlström OY and others v. Commission* the ECJ supported the 'effects' doctrine. It upheld a Commission decision in relation to a number of undertakings established outside the EC, not acting through subsidiaries, but who supplied two-thirds of the EC consumption of wood pulp. The ECJ held that the key factor was the place where the agreement or concerted practice was *implemented*. As the agreement in question had been implemented within the EC, the undertakings were fined for a breach of Article 81(1).

Minor agreements: the *de minimis* principle

Only agreements which affect competition to a noticeable extent are covered by Article 81(1). An insignificant effect will escape the prohibition under Article 81(1): Case 5/69 *Völk v. Etablissements Vervaecke SPRL*. In this case, Völk, a manufacturer of washing machines in Germany, and Vervaecke, a Dutch distributor of electrical goods, entered into an agreement giving Vervaecke exclusive rights to distribute Völk's products in Belgium and Luxembourg, reinforced by a ban into these countries of parallel

---

[3] See Whish (1998: 216–221).

imports by third parties of Völk's products. Völk produced only 0.2 to 0.5 per cent of washing machines in the German market and its share of the Belgian and Luxembourg market was even smaller (about 200 machines sold annually). The ECJ held that, taking into account the position of the parties in the Belgian and Luxembourg market, there was no noticeable effect on competition.

> **Key point**
>
> Once an agreement is found to fall within the *de minimis* rule there will be no breach of Article 81(1), even if the parties clearly intend to restrict competition.

In 1986 the Commission issued a Notice on Minor Agreements (amended in 1994), providing that some minor agreements did not contravene Article 81(1). The Notice was replaced by a fresh Notice 1997, and again, most recently, in 2001, in the context of the Commission's modernisation of competition rules. Guidelines on the 'effect on trade' condition was provided by the Commission on 31 March 2004, as part of the Modernisation Package.[4] The Notice provides that agreements between undertakings concerned with production or distribution do not infringe Article 81(1) where the market share of the undertakings does not exceed 10 per cent (horizontal agreement) and 15 per cent (vertical agreement). A 5 per cent threshold applies to parallel networks of similar agreements. Such networks were previously outside the Notice where their cumulative effect was taken to restrict competition (e.g. in the supply of beer).

Notices are not legally binding, although they do indicate the likely approach of the Commission. Where an agreement covered by the Notice contravenes Article 81(1) because of its effect on competition, the Commission will not normally fine the undertaking. The Notices raise a presumption that agreements between undertakings below a certain level do not affect trade. This presumption can be rebutted, as Case 30/78 *Distillers Co. Ltd.* v. *Commission* illustrates. In that case, there was evidence that distribution and production were in the hands of a large undertaking.

Agreements likely to infringe Article 81(1)

Article 81(1)(a) to (e) provides a list of examples (not exhaustive) of agreements likely to infringe Article 81(1), including the following: price-fixing; control of production, markets or technical development; application of dissimilar trading terms; and the application of extraneous obligations. Where the agreement is not covered by the *de minimis* principle and has an effect on inter-member trade, it infringes Article 81(1). Agreements relating to those matters listed in Article 81(1)(a) to (e) are usually automatically void. Certain agreements may, however, be found not to infringe Article 81(1),

---

[4] http://ec.europa.eu/comm/competition/antitrust/legislation/

in which case they will benefit from negative clearance. Other agreements will be found to infringe Article 81(1) but to be eligible for exemption under Article 81(3) on either an individual or a block basis.

Rule of reason

The rule of reason is a concept borrowed from US anti-trust law. Under s. 1 of the Sherman Act 1890 contracts in restraint of trade in the USA were prohibited without definition or exemption. The US courts compromised on the harshness of the statute by applying the 'rule of reason', i.e. by weighing the pro- and anti-competitive effects of the agreement to decide whether the agreement was permissible.[5]

Under Article 81(3) of the EC Treaty, agreements which restrict competition may be permissible where they satisfy certain conditions. It should be noted, however, that in Case T-168/01 *Glaxo Smith Klein* (under appeal, Case C-501/06P), the CFI did not accept the existence of a 'rule of reason'. Under Regulation 17/62, it was necessary to notify agreements in order to obtain exemption under Article 81(3). To reduce its workload, the Commission decided to issue block exemptions categorising practices deemed to be acceptable, thus avoiding the need for individual applications where the conditions were satisfied: see below.

An alternative approach may be seen in the practice of identifying elements of an agreement deemed essential although restrictive. The following restrictions have been found by the ECJ to be essential and therefore justifiable under Article 81(1).

Examples
- Provisions in franchising agreements to protect the intellectual property rights of the franchisor and to maintain the identity of the franchise system: Case 161/84 *Pronuptia* v. *Schillgalis*.
- Restrictive covenants on a vendor of a business and its goodwill which were considered necessary to the transfer in question: Case 42/84 *Remia Nutricia* v. *Commission*.
- An exclusive purchasing obligation in an agreement between a brewery and tenant was not illegal if, in its economic and legal context, it did not prevent access to the market by competitors: Case C-234/89 *Delimitis* v. *Henninger Bräu*.

Distribution agreements

The rule of reason is particularly relevant to distribution agreements.[6] Many benefits flow from opening up new markets through distribution agreements, provided strong competition remains between brands. While block regulations cover exclusive distribution and franchising agreements, selective distribution agreements have, before Regulation 2790/99 on vertical agreements, only been exempted on an individual basis. It remains to be seen how they are treated under the new regime by NCAs.

---

[5] See Whish (2003, Chapter 4).
[6] See Weatherill and Beaumont (1999: 821–823).

Key point

Selective distribution systems do not infringe Article 81(1), provided dealers are chosen on the basis of objective criteria of a qualitative nature relating to the technical qualification of the dealer and his staff and the suitability of his trading premises, and that such conditions are laid down uniformly and not applied in a discriminatory fashion: Case 26/76 *Metro-Grossmärkte GmbH* v. *Commission*.

The Court also emphasised that price competition is not the only form of competition, basing its analysis on the concept of 'workable competition': see Chapter 17, defined as 'the degree of competition necessary to ensure the observance of the basic requirements and the attainments of the objectives of the Treaty, in particular the creation of a single market'.

The ruling in *Metro* was upheld in a number of subsequent decisions: e.g. Case 99/79 *Lancôme* v. *ETOS BV* and Case 31/80 *L'Oréal NV* v. *de Nieuwe AMCK*. However, it is clear that the *Metro* principle applies only to the type of goods in relation to which it is appropriate to restrict outlets for distribution.

Examples
- Technically complex products, e.g. cameras: Dec. 70/332 *Kodak*; computers: Dec. 84/233 *IBM Personal Computers*.
- Products where the brand image is significant, e.g. ceramic tableware: *Villeroy & Boch* (D1984); gold and silver jewellery: Dec. 83/610 *Murat*.
- Luxury goods such as certain cosmetics and fine fragrance: Case T-19/92 *Groupement d'Achat Edouard Leclerc* v. *Commission*.
- Newspapers, since the short shelf-life necessitates effective distribution: Dec. 243/83 *Binon* v. *Agence et Messageries de la Press*; unlike plumbing fittings where selective distribution was not seen as appropriate: Dec. 84/85 *Re Ideal/Standard Agreement*.

Any restrictions imposed in a selective distribution agreement must go no further than is necessary to protect the quality of the product: Case 31/80 *L'Oréal*. In Case 86/82 *Hasselblad* the Commission objected to provisions enabling the producers to supervise advertising by distributors, as the control would have included price cuts.

The ECJ in *Metro* distinguished between qualitative and quantitative restrictions.

Key point

In a selective distribution system, qualitative restrictions of an objective nature such as those relating to the suitability of premises are permissible where they are justifiable. Quantitative restrictions are only permissible where they do not exceed the requirements of a selective distribution system.

A selective distribution agreement is a form of vertical agreement and will be covered by the block exemption of vertical agreements provided it satisfies the conditions of the Regulation 1216/99: see below.

Invalidity under Article 81(2)

Under Article 81(2) any agreements or decisions prohibited pursuant to this Article shall be automatically void. Before Regulation 1/2003 came into force, powers of enforcement were vested solely in the Commission, which was empowered under regulation 17/72 to grant exemptions to agreements where the conditions in Article 81(3) were satisfied. This practice caused complications for national courts which were obliged to avoid giving decisions that could conflict with those of the Commission: Case C-234/89 *Delimitis*.

Regulation 1/2003 was adopted in the context of the Commission's White Paper on modernisation of the competition rules. As a result of the Regulation, Article 81(3) became directly applicable, enabling national competition authorities (NCAs) to apply Article 81 directly. The Commission continues to play a role in major cases: see Chapter 20.

Guidance letters and Notices

Under the previous regime provided by Regulation 17/62, undertakings were required to notify agreements to the Commission if exemption was sought. The procedure for exemption was slow, sometimes involving delays of up to three years, as the Commission was required to give a fully reasoned decision in each case. In cases not considered to be especially important, the Commission sometimes issued a 'comfort letter' stating that the agreement did not infringe Article 81(1) or that it was within an exempt category. Such letters were not legally binding: e.g. see Case 99/79 *Lancôme* v. *ETOS*, and so had only limited utility.

Key point

The Commission no longer issues comfort letters from 1 May 2004, under Regulation 1/2003. It is, however, able to issue a 'guidance letter' in accordance with its Notice on Informal Guidance in 2004.[7]

Under the Notice, the Commission may provide a guidance letter in cases of genuine uncertainty which present novel or unresolved questions for the application of Articles 81 and 82. The Commission may provide a written statement in a guidance letter in response to a request from an individual undertaking under para. 6 of the

---

[7] Notice on Informal Guidance relating to novel questions concerning Articles 81 and 82 EC Treaty that arise in individual cases (guidance letters) OJ 2004 C 101/78.

Guidance. The Commission will not consider a request for guidance where the questions raised are identical to or similar to those raised in a case pending before the ECJ or CFI, or when the agreement in question is subject to proceedings before the Commission, a national court or an NCA.

The 2004 Notice is an example of another form of non-binding guidance: the Commission Notice (e.g. the Notice on Minor Agreements 2001) and the Guidelines on the Effect on Trade 2004. Such notices are increasingly important in the post-2004 regime.

EXEMPTIONS AND EXCEPTIONS

The power exists under Article 81(3) to declare that Article 81(1) does not apply to any agreement or category of agreement between undertakings, or any decision or category of decision by associations of undertakings which contributes to improving the production or distribution of goods or to promoting technical or economic progress, while allowing consumers a fair share of the resulting benefit, provided the agreement, etc. does not:

- impose on the undertakings concerned restrictions which are not indispensable to the attainment of objectives;
- afford such undertakings the possibility of eliminating competition in respect of a substantial part of the products in question.

The Commission used to grant individual exemptions under Regulation 17 before May 2004. As we have seen, the power to enforce competition law has largely been devolved to the NCAs and the notification procedure dropped. The Commission continues to issue block exemptions to cover various common commercial practices which are not considered damaging to competition, such as agreements over research and development: see below.

Individual exceptions

NCAs do not enjoy the degree of discretion previously exercised by the Commission when applying Article 81(3). It is clear from Article 16 of Regulation 1/2003 and from the decision in Case C-344/98 *Masterfoods* (see p. 303) that NCAs are not authorised to make decisions which conflict with those made or pending by the Commission. It will become easier to sue for breach of contract (see Korah, 2007), without the delays previously suffered as a result of applications for exemption. If the parties to an agreement are involved in litigation, the national court will have to consider whether to apply Article 81(3) directly and issue a declaration. The burden remains on the parties to establish that the conditions in Article 81(3) are satisfied.

A declaration under Article 81(3) made by an NCA or a national court will state that Article 81(1) did not apply to the agreement at the date in issue. If conditions change, the declaration will cease to apply. Thus it may be seen that a declaration is *not* an exemption, as before, providing a guarantee to the parties that no action will be taken provided they complied with the terms of the exemption for a fixed period of time. As a result, Korah considers that the word 'exception' is more appropriate to the new regime.[8]

Article 81(3): the conditions

There are four conditions which must be satisfied before Article 81(3) may be relied upon, as follows:

1 The agreement must contribute to improving the production or distribution of goods or to promoting technical or economic progress. See, for example, Dec. 73/323 *Prym Beka*, where the Commission granted an exemption where one party agreed to stop manufacturing needles and sold its plant to the other in return for shares, undertaking to buy all its needles in future from the other company. The resulting improvement led to a reduction in the price of needles.
2 The agreement must allow consumers a fair share of the resulting benefit. Consumers may benefit from a reduction in price or an increased range of products.
3 There must be no unnecessary restrictions. An absolute territorial restriction will be unacceptable: *Grundig*, see above. However, limited territorial protection for a franchisee may be acceptable: *Pronuptia*.
4 There must be no elimination of competition. Where there is lively competition, the market may be the EC as a whole: Dec. 72/291 *Re Fine Papers*, or the world market: Dec. 77/160 *Re Vacuum Interrupters*. Where competition is more limited, it may be the territory of a single member state where the agreement is performed: Cases 209–215 and 218/78 *Van Landewyck v. Commission*.

The *Transocean* case provides a typical example of the approach of the Commission when considering an application for exemption in the past.

Key case

Various small and medium-sized manufacturers of marine paint in the EC collaborated to rationalise the production and marketing of marine paints on the world market. The Commission granted an exemption, accepting that a global distribution network was established and that the gain in international competition outweighed the reduction in competition between members: Dec. 67/454 *Transocean Marine Paint, Association*.

[8] Korah (2007: 95–96).

The relationship between Article 81(1) and 81(3)

The CFI in *Métropole* sought to establish whether the weighing of pro- and anti-competitive effects should be undertaken in relation to Article 81(1) or 81(3).

> **Key case**
>
> The Commission had granted an exemption to a joint venture, the European Broadcasting Union (EBU), between the majority of the European state-owned broadcasting companies. Using the Eurovision link, members were entitled to transmit sports and other programmes. Various private television companies which were excluded from the venture appealed to the CFI against the exemption. The CFI held that the applicants had standing as they were individually concerned in the proceedings. (They competed directly with the EBU members.) For the first time the CFI annulled a Commission decision granting an exemption. The Court found that the Commission had erred in its interpretation of Article 81(3) by failing to examine whether the membership rules of the EBU were objective and non-discriminatory, in order to assess whether they were indispensable: Case T-112/99 *Métropole Télévision (MT)* v. *Commission*.

The Court did not accept that the earlier case law in decisions including *STM, Nungessor, Pronuptia* and *European Night Services* supported the existence of a 'rule of reason' approach (weighing the pro- and anti-competitive effects of the agreement). Instead, account should be taken of the context of the agreement, particularly the economic context. As Jones and Sufrin[9] observe (2008), the CFI seems to favour an approach 'which divides the substantive appraisal between Article 81(1) and 81(3). In their analysis, the appraisal should be divided into five parts:

1 The Commission (or person seeking to establish the position) must show that the agreement restricts competition.
2 The person seeking to benefit from Article 81(3) must establish that the agreement achieves pro-competitive objectives.
3 Consumers must attain a fair share of the benefits.
4 The agreement must be indispensable to the attainment of those benefits.
5 There is no possibility that competition may be eliminated.

Commission guidelines on the application of Article 81(3)

The Commission adopted guidelines on the application of Article 81(3)[10] as part of the Modernisation Package, in order to provide guidance to businesses on consistent

---

[9] Jones and Sufrin (2008: 215–218).
[10] Commission Notice on the application of Article 81(3) of the Treaty, OJ2004, C101/97: http://ec.europa.eu/comm/competition/antitrust/legislation/

application. These guidelines complement other notices and guidelines, such as those on vertical restraints: see below.

BLOCK EXEMPTIONS

The practice of issuing block exemptions developed as the Commission's response to the need to focus on unusual or complex agreements and the uncertainty of firms about to enter into agreements over the validity of those agreements. A series of regulations was issued in areas where agreements are generally beneficial rather than anti-competitive. As a result, many undertakings draft their agreements in order to take advantage of the provisions of these block exemptions. While block exemption regulations may be retained, they may be withdrawn in an individual case under Regulation 1/2003 by the Commission or by an NCA: Article 29.

Regulations have been issued granting exemptions in a number of areas since 1983. Some regulations have been amended or replaced. The following provide examples:

- Specialisation: Regulation 2658/2000, replacing Regulation 417/85.
- Research and development: Regulation 2659/2000, replacing Regulation 418/85.
- Franchising: Regulation 4087/88.
- Technology Transfer: Regulation 240/96 (replacing the Patent Licensing Regulation 2349/84 and the Knowhow Licensing Regulation 556/89).
- Vertical Restraints Regulation 2790/99: see below, replacing the block exemption regulations for exclusive distribution agreements under Regulation 1983/83, exclusive purchasing agreements under Regulation 1984/83 and franchising agreements under Regulation 4078/88.

Pattern of the Regulations

Prior to the modernisation changes, the practice was for the regulations to lay down the permitted restrictions deemed essential to the agreement (the 'white' list), followed by a list of forbidden restrictions (the 'black' list). In some cases there was a further category of restrictions subject to the 'opposition' procedure (the 'grey' list) under which restrictions had to be notified to the Commission. If they were not opposed within six months they are considered to be exempt.

A new approach was taken in relation to more recent regulations, such as Regulation 2790/99 on vertical agreements. The new block exemption is drafted in wide terms to cover all types of agreement between undertakings at different levels of production or distribution which contain conditions relating to the sale or purchase of goods. There is no white list. As a result, any provisions not specified on the black list of 'hardcore' restrictions are permissible.

Block exemption Regulation on vertical agreements

The block exemption Regulation on vertical agreements, Regulation 2790/99, was adopted by the Commission in December 1999, running for 10 years from 1 June 2000. The Regulation defines 'vertical agreements' broadly under Article 2 as 'agreements or concerted practices entered into between two or more undertakings, each of which operates, for the purpose of the agreement, at a different level of the production or distribution chain, and relating to the conditions under which the parties may purchase, sell or resell certain goods or services'.

(a) Scope of the block exemption

The block exemption is limited to suppliers holding no more than 30 per cent of the relevant market on which it sells goods or services: Article 3. (For exclusive supply agreements, the threshold is 30 per cent of the relevant market on which it purchases goods or services.) The block exemption will not apply to competitors unless:

- the buyer's annual turnover does not exceed €1,000 million; or
- the supplier is a manufacturer and a distributor, while the buyer is a distributor but not a manufacturer of competing products; or
- the supplier is a provider of services at several levels of trade where it purchases the contract services.

The Regulation does not apply to vertical agreements which are covered by other block exemption regulations.

(b) Forbidden ('hardcore') restraints

Article 4 lists restraints which are forbidden as they are outside the Regulation. Such restraints may not be severed from the agreement. (This means that the whole agreement containing such a restraint will be invalidated.) They are:

- resale price maintenance (unless it relates to a maximum price);
- restrictions on resales (e.g. refusal to supply), with some exceptions, including the restriction on resales to unauthorised distributors in selective distribution;
- restrictions on sales to users in selective distribution agreements (a prohibition from operating out of an unauthorised place of distribution is permissible);
- restriction on cross-supplies between distributors in a selective distribution system (with the result that selective distribution may not be combined with any other vertical restraints);
- restriction on sale of spare parts.

Other restraints

The following restraints are forbidden but are severable from the agreement under Article 5:

- Non-compete obligations longer than five years. (A 'non-compete obligation' is defined in Article 1 as any direct or indirect obligation causing the buyer not to manufacture, purchase, sell or resell goods or services which compete with the contract goods or services; or any direct or indirect obligation on the buyer to purchase from the supplier or designated undertaking more than 80 per cent of the buyer's total purchases of the contract goods or services and their substitutes on the relevant market.)

- Post-termination non-compete clauses (except to protect know-how).
- Obligations relating to specified competitor brands imposed on selective distribution.

The Commission may withdraw the benefits of the block exemption (including withdrawal from the territory of a Member State) when an agreement does not fulfil the criteria of Article 81(3), particularly where the market is being reduced by a network of parallel vertical agreements. The Regulation may be disapplied by the Commission by a separate regulation, where parallel agreements cover more than 50 per cent of the network.

While there are a number of benefits under the new scheme, in particular the use of a single block exemption relying on a 'black list' approach, the list of forbidden agreements is long and technical. The Regulation does not provide for a 'grey' list (see above), unlike previous block exemptions. Other advantages relate to selective distribution agreements, which may no longer require notification to ensure validity in certain circumstances. It is helpful that the Regulation covers agreements between several undertakings, and includes goods as well as services. The use of thresholds for determining coverage has been criticised.

QUESTIONS

1 How has the US concept of the 'rule of reason' influenced the development of competition law in the EC?

2 A SA is the largest producer of apple juice in France. A intends to enter into an agreement with B plc, a UK company manufacturing tins and cartons for drinks. Under the agreement A SA will stop making its own containers and will instead purchase all its containers from B plc. The agreement will enable A SA to penetrate the UK fruit juice market and B plc the French food-packaging market. There will be a reduction in price which will be passed on to the consumer who, in the words of A SA and B plc, will be offered a 'superior product'. Advise A SA and B plc of the legality of the agreement under Community law.

3 How has the modernisation of competition law affected the approach to block exemptions? Consider this question with particular reference to the block exemption on vertical restraints.

Further reading

Chalmers, D., Hadjiemmanuil, C., Monti, G. and Tomkins, A. (2006) *European Union Law*, Cambridge University Press, Chapter 22.

Craig, P. and De Burca, G. (2007) *EU Law: Text, Cases and Materials*, 4th edition, Oxford University Press, Chapter 25.

Harding, C. and Gibbs, A. (2005) 'Why go to Europe? An analysis of cartel appeals 1995–2004' (2005) 30 ELRev. 349.

Hawk, B. (1995) 'System failure: Vertical Restraints and EC Competition Law', (1995) 32 CMLRev. 973.

Jones, A. and Sufrin, B. (2008) *EC Competion Law: Text, Cases and Materials*, 3rd edition, Oxford University Press, Chapters 3 and 4.

Korah, V. (2007) *An Introductory Guide to EC Competition Law and Practice'*, 9th edition, Hart Publishing, Chapters 2 and 3.

Nazzini, R. (2006) 'Article 81 EC between present and time past: A normative critique of "restriction of competition" in EU Law', (2006) 43 CMLRev. 497.

Odudu, O. (2006) *The Boundaries of EC Competition Law: the Scope of Article 81*, OUP Studies in European Law, Oxford University Press.

Weatherill, S. and Beaumont, P. (1999) *EC Law*, 3rd edition, Penguin.

Whish, R. (2003) *Competition Law*, 5th edition, Oxford University Press.

18

Article 81

Visit **http://www.mylawchamber.co.uk/kent** to access answer guidance to questions in the book to test yourself on this chapter.

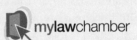

mylawchamber

19 Article 82

INTRODUCTION

Article 82 (ex 86) regulates the activities of undertakings in a dominant position, whereas Article 81 (ex 85) controls the activities of independent undertakings which collude: see Chapter 18.

Article 82: the prohibition

Under Article 82 any abuse by one or more undertakings of a dominant position within the common market or in a substantial part of it is prohibited as incompatible with the common market in so far as it may affect trade between Member States. This prohibition is followed by an illustrative list of abusive practices.

It is important to note that it is not *dominance* but *abuse of a dominant position* which is illegal under Article 82: Case 322/81 *Michelin NV Nederlandsche Bander-Industrie Michelin* v. *Commission*. Such abuse must be controlled because it is anti-competitive and leads to the inefficient distribution of resources; the customer of a monopolist charging high prices cannot obtain alternative goods or services from another supplier. The monopolist, on the other hand, may be able to profit excessively from its market position.

'Undertakings' and the control of oligopoly

Prior to the Dec. 89/93 *Flat Glass* decision it was generally thought that Article 82 did not apply to the activities of independent undertakings but only to those covered by the 'enterprise entity' concept, i.e. where parent and subsidiary are treated as indivisible: Case 6/72 *Continental Can*. Thus oligopolies could be controlled under Article 81, which required proof of an agreement or concerted practice, but not Article 82. In *Flat Glass* the Commission decided that a group of undertakings held a dominant position in the flat glass market in Italy. Although the CFI in Cases T-68/89, T-77/89 *Società Italiana Vetro SpA* v. *Commission*, and T-78/89 partly annulled the Commission's decision it did not rule against the relevance of Article 82 for oligopolies.

Commission discussion paper and reform of Article 82

The Commission has issued a discussion paper in 2005[1] as part of an internal review of the application of Article 82 to exclusionary abuses. It received over 100 responses and held a public hearing in June 2006. A draft text is expected which may take the form of guidance. The limitation of the review to exclusionary abuses (i.e. abuses which exclude undertakings from a market), has been criticised, as it does not cover exploitative abuses such as excessive pricing.

Essential elements for a breach of Article 82

There are three essential elements in establishing a breach of Article 82:

1 a dominant position,
2 abuse of that position,
3 an effect on inter-member trade caused by the abuse.

Under Article 82 there was no procedure equivalent to the (repealed) Regulation 17/62 to provide for exemption negative clearance, unlike Article 81. A negative clearance procedure does, however, exist for mergers and concentrations under Regulation 139/2004: see below.

DOMINANCE

Dominance was defined in Case 27/76 *United Brands* v. *Commission* as 'the position of economic strength enjoyed by an undertaking which enables it to prevent effective competition being maintained on the relevant market by giving it the power to behave to an appreciable effect independently of its competitors, and ultimately of its consumers'.

This definition of dominance was repeated in Case 85/76 *Hoffman-la Roche* (the Vitamins case), and extended as follows:

> Such a position does not preclude some competition . . . but enables the undertaking which profits by it, if not to determine, at least to have an appreciable effect on the conditions under which that competition will develop, and in any case to act largely in disregard of it so long as such conduct does not operate to its detriment.

Where there is effective competition from alternative products or from a challenge to the undertaking's market share by another firm, there will be no breach of Article 82.

To prove dominance it is necessary to establish the relevant market. This is identified by examining the product market, the geographical market and, sometimes, the temporal market. The task is assisted by the Commission's Notice of 1997 on the definition of the relevant market for the purpose of EC competition law: see below. The Notice is largely based on the case law of the ECJ, CFI and Commission.

[1] http://ec.europa.eu/comm/competition/antitrust/art82/index.html

Product market

It is in the interests of an undertaking whose activities are being investigated under Article 82 to argue that the market should be defined as widely as possible, since this reduces the opportunity for dominance. A producer of, say, wheels for sports cars will hold a smaller share of the market if the product market is wheels for cars generally rather than for sports cars. Where services are in issue the 'relevant service market' should be identified: Dec. 89/113 *Decca Navigator System*. The importance of identifying the relevant product market in establishing dominance was shown in the first case to come before the ECJ under Article 82: Case 6/72 *Europemballage Corp.* v. *Continental Can*. The Commission's failure to identify the product market in this case led to the annulment of its decision by the ECJ.

Key case

Continental Can (CC), a powerful US multinational company, through its wholly owned subsidiary, Europemballage (E), held 86 per cent of the shares in Schmalbach (S). S had a dominant position in Germany for tins of meat and fish and for metal lids for glass containers. E proposed to take over a Dutch packaging firm, Thomassen (T). At the time of the proposed takeover S and T were operating in adjacent areas but were not competitors. E offered for the shares held in T by third parties, as a result of which the CC holding in T rose to 91 per cent. The dominance of S was imputed under the enterprise entity concept to CC. The Commission held that CC (and S) had a dominant position in three separate markets: cans for meat, cans for fish, and metal tops. The elimination of *potential* competition between S and T and the reduction in consumer choice in the supply of products amounted to an abuse. The Commission decided that the takeover of T by CC (through E) amounted to a breach of Article 82. While agreeing in principle with the Commission that the takeover could be an abuse, the ECJ held that the Commission had failed to identify the relevant product market and had not given reasons for its decision. The Commission decision was annulled: Case 6/72 *Continental Can*.

Product substitution

Continental Can provides an example of the need to consider possible product substitution on the *supply* side, that is, the scope for suppliers to offer alternative products. The ECJ rejected the Commission's reasoning that there were three separate markets for the different types of metal container for food packaging, rather than a single market. It found that the Commission had not considered why competitors were unable to enter the market by adapting their production methods.

The product market is more frequently defined by reference to the question of product substitution on the *demand* side, that is, whether there is 'a sufficient degree of interchangeability between all the products forming part of the same market in so far as a specific use of such products is concerned': Case 85/76 *Hoffman-La Roche*. Thus, the product market covers goods which are identical or are regarded by customers as interchangeable or similar in relation to the characteristics of the product, its price, quality or use.

The 1997 Notice on Market Definition defines the relevant product market as 'all those products and/or services which are regarded as interchangeable or substitutable by the consumer, by reason of the products' characteristics, their prices and their intended uses'.

Key point

The Notice adopts the US-based approach known as the SSNIP test.[2] This involves asking whether a small (i.e. 5–10 per cent) but non-transitory increase in price of one product will cause buyers to purchase sufficient of another product as a substitute to make the price rise unsustainable (para. 17).

One of the problems of the SSNIP test is the so-called *Cellophane fallacy*. The name derives from a US case involving a producer of cellophane: *US* v. *IE du Pont de Namours & Co.*, 1956, in which the Supreme Court considered whether there were substitutes for cellophane without considering whether substitutes would have existed if the price had been competitive. The problem occurs in relation to Article 82 because the SSNIP approach is based on the prevailing price which may already be too high due to existing dominance. The Commission claims that a market decision will usually be based on a number of criteria and different items of evidence (Market Definition Notice, note 11). In paras 38–43 of the Notice, the following factors are identified as relevant to deciding whether products may be considered as substitutes :

- evidence of substitution in the recent past;
- quantitative econometric tests;
- views of customers and competitors;
- consumer preferences and marketing studies;
- barriers and costs associated with switching demand to possible substitutes;
- different categories of customers and price discrimination.

Decisions on the product market

Product substitution has been the main factor in defining the product market, as the following cases demonstrate. In *United Brands*, the question was whether the market was bananas or fresh fruit.

---

[2] SSNIP stands for a small but significant non-transitory increase in price.

Key case

The Commission alleged that United Brands, one of the world's largest producers of bananas, with 40 per cent of the EC trade in bananas marketed under the brand name 'Chiquita', had infringed Article 82 in various ways. The Commission claimed that the product market was bananas (branded and unbranded). United Brands, on the other hand, claimed that the market was fresh fruit. The ECJ upheld the Commission definition, accepting that there was a separate market for bananas. Bananas were consumed particularly by the very young, the old and the sick, consumption being little affected by pricing or consumption of other fruits: Case 27/76 *United Brands* v. *Commission*.

In *Commerical Solvents*, the question for the Court was whether the product market was the raw materials or the end product.

Key case

Commercial Solvents Corporation (CSC) and its Italian subsidiary refused to supply Zoja, an Italian company, with aminobutanol, the best and cheapest raw material used to make ethambutol, a drug for treating tuberculosis. CSC had a near monopoly in ethambutol. Other substitutable drugs existed but were less satisfactory. Zoja could not readily adapt its production process to these alternatives. The ECJ upheld the Commission decision that the product market was aminobutamol (the end product), not the raw materials for making ethambutol: Cases 6, 7/73 *Instituto Chemicoterapico (Commercial Solvents)*.

⬤ Other examples of the product market

The following provide examples of product markets identified by the ECJ or CFI:

- Tyres for heavy vehicles, as distinct from tyres for cars and light vans, because production processes were different, and customers came from separate groups: Case 322/81 *Michelin (NV Nederlandsche Bander-Industrie Michelin)* v. *Commission*.
- Vitamins, each of which occupied a separate market depending on its properties and functions: Case 85/76 *Hoffman-la Roche*: see above.
- Spare parts for independent repair of cash registers. The parts were supplied by a Swedish firm to a firm in the UK through its subsidiary, illustrating how small the relevant market may be in contrast with, for example, Case 27/76 *United Brands*; Case 22/78 *Hugin Kassaregister AB* v. *Commission* .
- Different types of cartons for fresh pasteurised milk and UHT (ultra high temperature) treated milk. Fresh and UHT milk taste different and were not regarded by consumers as interchangeable: Case T-51/89 *Tetra Pak (No. 1)*.
- Plasterboard and wet plaster, the latter requiring to be laid by skilled, trained plasterers: Case T-85/89 *British Plasterboard Industries plc* v. *Commission*.

● Internet services based on ADSL[3] technology, which allows broadband access over traditional telephone wires: Comp/38.233 *Wanadoo.*

Key case

The *France Télécom* case arose as an appeal to the CFI from the Commission's decision in *Wanadoo.* The Commission had considered differences in performance between high- and low-speed internet access, concluding that there was a separate market for high-speed connections, for which customers were prepared to pay more. France Télécom which had taken over Wanadoo Interactive (WIN) claimed on appeal that the Commission should have considered the market as comprising both high- and low-speed access. The Court found that there were significant differences between high- and low-speed access. Some internet-based applications were unfeasible with low-speed access. Similar differences existed in technical features and performance, for example, in relation to modem usage. (A high-speed modem could not be used with a low-speed internet access and vice versa.) The differences in features in performance were reflected in the price of high-speed and low-speed access.

The CFI found little evidence of migration from high-speed access to low-speed, as most migration went in the opposite direction, despite the difference in price between the two services. It accepted, in accordance with para. 17 of the Notice, the evidence in a survey carried out on behalf of the Commission that 80 per cent of subscribers would retain their subscription to high-speed access in the event of a price increase in the range of 5–10 per cent, which it saw as 'a strong indication of the absence of demand-led substitution'. As a result, it upheld the Commission decision that there was insufficient substitutability between high- and low-speed access, and that the relevant market was that of high-speed access for residential customers: Case T-340/03 *France Télécom SA* v. *Commission* (under appeal Case C-202/07P).

Geographical market

Article 82 is only infringed where dominance occurs within the common market or a substantial part of it. Thus it is essential to determine the geographical market. The 1997 Notice provides the following definition of the geographical market:

> The relevant geographical market comprises the area in which the undertakings concerned are involved in the supply and demand of products and services, in which the conditions of competition are sufficiently homogeneous and which can be distinguished from neighbouring areas because the conditions of competition are appreciably different on those areas. (Case C-333/94P *Tetra Pak* v. *Commission*)

---

[3] Asynchronous Digital Subscriber Line.

A useful point to start the identification of the geographical market is by reference to the sales area. However, the geographical market is not necessarily synonymous with the sales area and is influenced by such factors as:

- **Costs and feasibility of transportation.** Where the product is easy and cheap to transport, such as nail cartridges in Case T-30/89 *Hilti* v. *Commission*, the market may be the whole of the EC. By contrast, highly perishable products such as fresh seafood will have a more restricted local market.
- **Consumer preferences.** The pattern and volume of consumption may be examined to determine whether the territory of a Member State may be a substantial part of the common market. In Case T-219/99 *British Airways plc* v. *Commission* the geographical market was found to be the United Kingdom, for the purpose of air travel agency services provided by agents established in that country. In Cases 40/73, etc. *SuikerUnie*, Belgium and Luxembourg were considered sufficiently large to amount to a substantial part of the common market. It is now generally accepted that the territory of each Member State, or even part of such a territory, such as the port of Genoa: Case C-18/93 *Corsica Ferries*, may be a substantial part of the common market. However, the geographical market is not necessarily identical with the physical size of the market. It is possible for the market to be the whole of the EC or even of the whole world where competition is on a global scale.

Temporal market

Seasonal considerations affecting opportunities for product substitution may be a factor. Although the Commission did not define the banana market according to the time of year in *United Brands*, it did consider the time factor in Dec. 77/327 *Re ABG Oil*. In this case the Commission limited the oil market to the crisis period after the OPEC action in the early 1970s, during which companies had a particular responsibility to supply customers on fair terms. Although this decision was annulled by the ECJ Case 77/77 in *BP* v. *Commission*, the annulment was based on abuse, rather than the definition of the market.

Assessing dominance

Key point

To assess dominance a detailed economic analysis is required.

The main elements of the economic analysis involve examination of the following:

- **Market share of the undertaking.** This is a key feature in establishing dominance. In *Continental Can* the share of the German market held by CC was 70–80 per cent. The share of three of the seven vitamin markets held by Roche in *Hoffman-la Roche* was more than 80 per cent. Such a high market share will be regarded by the ECJ as proof of dominance.

- **Market share of competitors**. A relatively low market share by the undertaking (such as 40–45 per cent in *United Brands*) may indicate dominance where the market is fragmented by competitors (in that case holding 10 and 16 per cent). The lowest share seen as establishing dominance under Article 82 was 39.7 per cent in *Virgin/British Airways*.
- **Financial and technical resources**. Ready access to the international capital market was significant in *Continental Can*. Possession of superior technology has been identified by the ECJ in several cases (e.g. *Michelin, United Brands*, etc.).
- **Control of production and distribution**. Control of production and distribution (sometimes called 'vertical integration') was regarded as significant in *United Brands* where the undertaking owned the plantations and the means of transport and also marketed the bananas itself. Roche's highly developed sales network in *Hoffman-la Roche* amounted to a similar commercial advantage over competitors.

    In Case IV/M4 *ICI and Tioxide*, notified under the Merger Regulation (see below), the Commission found that ICI's acquisition of Tioxide did not contravene Article 82. Before the acquisition Tioxide supplied most of ICI's requirement for titanium dioxide in paint manufacturing. The acquisition did not affect access to markets, titanium dioxide and paints being seen as separate markets.
- **Conduct and performance**. An undertaking's conduct and performance may provide evidence of dominance (e.g. discriminatory pricing): *Michelin*. Economic performance may also indicate dominance (e.g. where it shows that there is 'spare' or 'idle' capacity): *Hoffman-la Roche*. A temporary loss made by United Brands did not prevent a finding of dominance in the light of the undertaking's success in retaining its market share.

19

Article 82

ABUSE OF A DOMINANT POSITION

Key point

Article 82 does not prohibit dominance, merely abuse of a dominant position.

The list of abusive practices which follows the prohibition in Article 82 provides examples including unfair prices, limiting production, discrimination in contractual terms and the imposition of supplementary obligations.

Comparison with Article 81

There are many parallels between the types of behaviour prohibited under Article 81 and Article 82. Both Articles must be interpreted in the light of the objectives of Article 3(g) of the Treaty. However, Article 82 provides no equivalent to the previous mechanism under Article 81(3) for exemption or negative clearance. In Case T-51/89 *Tetra Pak Rausing*, the CFI held that the grant of exemption under Article 81(3), either as a result of individual or block exemption, could not render inapplicable the prohibition under Article 82. The Commission has developed the concept of 'objective justification' where behaviour which is apparently anti-competitive is found not to constitute an abuse. In most cases the behaviour has not been found to be objectively justified (see e.g. *Hilti*).

Categories of abuse

Two main categories have been identified by the Commission and the ECJ (see Whish, 1998: Chapter 18). These are:

1 **Exploitative abuses**. Where the dominant undertaking takes advantage of its position by imposing harsh or unfair trading conditions (e.g. unfair pricing).
2 **Anti-competitive abuses**. Abuses which are not harsh or unfair but which reduce or eliminate competition, such as refusal to supply. In these circumstances the undertaking uses its market dominance to undermine or eliminate competitors or to prevent new entrants from entering the market. Since the decision in *Continental Can*, mergers have been regarded as exploitative abuses within the scope of Article 82. However, since its adoption mergers have increasingly been considered under the Merger Regulation (Regulation 139/2004).[4] Mergers (or 'concentrations' as they are known under the Regulation) are examined separately: see below.

These categories should not be regarded as sacrosanct. Many types of abuse, such as price discrimination, fall into both categories. If the undertaking's activities are considered by the Commission to be without objective justification and thus abusive, there is a breach of Article 82.

Examples of abuse

Unfair prices
An unfair price was defined in *United Brands* as a price which bears no reasonable relation to the economic value of the product. Such prices may be excessively high or (occasionally) excessively low as a result of pressure from a dominant purchaser.

Discriminatory prices
Discriminatory prices arise where different customers are charged different prices without objective justification. Differential pricing based on national markets was rejected in *United Brands* as the basis for objective justification. Price discrimination may take many different forms, for example, predatory pricing (undercutting a rival product at below cost price): Case C-62/86 *AKZO Chemie BV*; loyalty rebates:

---

[4] Previously under Regulation 4064/89, as amended.

Hoffman-la Roche; discounts intended to keep imports outside a dominant firm's territory: Case 50/89 *BPP Industries plc* v. *Commission*.

Unfair trading conditions

Conditions imposed by a copyright society on its members could be unfair if they exceeded what was necessary for the society to manage its rights effectively: Case 127/73 *BRT* v. *SABAM*.

Refusal to supply

Refusal to supply has been considered an abuse on a number of occasions by the Commission and the Court, for example, *Commercial Solvents* (see above), in which a competitor was driven out of business as a result; and *United Brands*, in which the undertaking refused to supply a Danish wholesaler who had taken part in a sales campaign by a rival supplier. In some cases, refusal to supply has involved the practice of 'tying', whereby goods or services are supplied under contract which is tied to the fulfilment of supplementary obligations unconnected to the subject of the contract. Such arrangements are specifically prohibited under Article 82(d) and have frequently been found to be abusive by the Commission and the Court, as the case of *Van den Bergh Foods* demonstrates.

> ## Key case
>
> Van den Bergh Foods Ltd., formerly known as HB Ice Cream Ltd. (HB), an ice cream manufacturer, supplied retailers in Ireland with freezer cabinets, either free or at a nominal charge, on condition that the freezers were used exclusively for HB products. At least 40 per cent of retailers supplying single wrapped 'impulse' ice creams had been supplied with freezer cabinets by HB. The CFI upheld the decision of the Commission that the exclusive dealing agreements were an abuse of a dominant position, in that they prevented competitors from gaining access to the market: Case T-65/98R *Van den Bergh Foods Ltd.* v. *Commission*.

The initial proceedings by the Commission against HB did not lead to an order as HB had changed its contractual terms following settlement to allow retailers to free themselves from the tie if they bought the freezers on reasonable terms. HB obtained an injunction in the Irish courts to prevent retailers from stocking their freezers with ice creams supplied by Mars, a competitor, unless the freezer had been purchased from HB. Mars complained to the Commission that few retailers had availed themselves of the opportunity to buy the freezers, with the result that they could not stock Mars' products. The Commission reopened proceedings and adopted a decision against HB prohibiting the freezer tie. When Masterfoods, which had taken over HB, tried to enforce the injunction, the ECJ ruled (under Article 234) in Case C-344/98 *Masterfoods Ltd.* v. *HB Ice Cream* that the courts should not enforce an injunction which was incompatible with a decision of the Commission, even if adopted later.

Key point

The 2005 Discussion Paper indicates that the Commission is likely to treat exclusive dealing arrangements as an abuse, but will do so by considering the effects of such agreements rather than on a 'per se' approach (presumed illegality).[5]

In the *Magill TV Guide* cases the refusal by television companies to supply information about weekly programme listings to a competing producer of a guide was an abuse: Cases C-241/91P and C-242/91P *RTE, BBC and ITP* v. *Commission*. Refusal to supply also arose in the case of *IMS Health*, which followed the *Magill* case.

Key case

The case arose in relation to the use of a system known as the '1860 brick structure'. The system was based on a map of Germany on to which a series of geographical areas ('bricks') was superimposed, with information on postcodes, administrative boundaries and the location of doctors and pharmacies. IMS held the copyright in the 1860 brick structure which the Commission accepted was an industry standard. It used the system to provide its clients, pharmaceutical laboratories, with localised data. To prevent NDC and another company from infringing its copyright in the bricks, IMS obtained an interim injunction in the German courts which made a preliminary referral to the ECJ. The Commission required IMS in an interim decision to license its copyright. An appeal was brought in the CFI, but the case was dropped after the German appeal court quashed the interim injunction.

The ECJ then considered the request under Article 234 from the German court. The Court held that three conditions must be satisfied before a refusal to grant a licence may be considered to be an abuse. The refusal must:

- prevent the emergence of a new product for which there is potential demand;
- be unjustified;
- exclude competition on any secondary market.

The Court held that it was the responsibility of the national court to decide whether access to the brick structure was essential and whether the undertaking seeking the licence intended to duplicate existing goods or services, or to produce new goods or services for which there was a potential demand: Case C-481/01 *IMS Health* v. *Commission*.

[5] See Jones and Sufrin (2008: 480).

Refusal to supply a service was also considered an abuse in Case 311/84 *Belgian Telemarketing*. However, it should be noted that the CFI held that a refusal to supply only infringes Article 82 where supply is essential to the activity in question or where refusal prevents the introduction of a new product for which there is growing demand: Case T-504/93 *Tiercé Ladbroke* v. *Commission*.

Refusal to supply sometimes arises in the context of what has been called the 'essential facilities doctrine'. The *Oscar Bronner* case demonstrates how the duty to supply is only recognised by the Court in relation to supply of an essential facility, although the Court has tended to avoid using the expression 'essential facilities'.

Key case

Oscar Bronner published a newpaper, *Der Standard*, with a low circulation (about 3.6 per cent of the daily newspaper market in Austria). He wanted access to the nationwide home delivery services of Mediaprint, which held about 36.8 per cent of the circulation market for the newspapers which it distributed. Mediaprint refused to include *Der Standard* in its distribution scheme. Bronner brought proceedings in the Austrian courts, requiring Mediaprint to cease abusing its dominant position on the home delivery market, and to include *Der Standard*, for a reasonable fee. Although the matter in question was confined to a single Member State, the Austrian court sought guidance from the ECJ under Article 234 in order to avoid possible conflict between EC law and Austrian law. The ECJ found the reference admissible.

The ECJ found that it was not enough for a facility to be merely desirable. It must be essential. While it might be desirable for *Der Standard* to be delivered to the homes of customers, it was not essential as it could be sold in other ways, for example, through shops and kiosks. It held that the refusal of a publisher to allow access to a competitor to its distribution network was not an abuse of a dominant position. The Court identified four factors which would have to be satisfied for there to be an abuse:

- The refusal would be likely to eliminate all competition in the downstream market from the person requesting access.
- The refusal must be incapable of objective justification.
- The access must be indispensable to carrying on the other person's business.

There must be no actual or potential substitute for it: Case C-7/97 *Oscar Bronner & Co.* v. *Mediaprint*.

Tying

Tying (see p. 303) and the related concept of 'bundling' were in issue in the *Microsoft* decision by the Commission. Bundling is used to increase the appeal of a product by selling it in conjunction with a second product (e.g. a colour supplement to boost the sale of a newspaper).

Key case

Microsoft supplied its Windows Media Player (WMP) as a package with its desktop operating system, with the result that customers purchasing their software found WMP already installed. The Commission considered that this excluded competition from other media suppliers such as RealPlayer, stifling innovation and reducing consumer choice. There was no doubt that Microsoft was dominant in the market for operating systems for PCs. In fact, the company enjoyed a market share of more than 90 per cent, and so was approaching a complete monopoly position. This position of 'overwhelming dominance' carried special responsibilities. The Commission also found Microsoft to be dominant over work operating systems for group servers, where it held a share of at least 60 per cent.

The Commission found that by tying WMP, Microsoft had abused its dominant position. It had extended its dominance over Windows to adjacent markets in worktop servers (which cover everyday tasks like allocating work to printers) and media players to the detriment of consumers. The Commission also found that Microsoft's refusal to supply 'interoperability' information to customers was an abuse. Prior to the introduction of Windows 2000, Microsoft had freely provided information to other providers of workplace servers. Its change of practice made it difficult, if not impossible, for competitors to provide workplace servers.

The Commission imposed a fine of €497,196,304 on Microsoft for the abuse including failure to supply information. It also ordered the company to offer PC manufacturers a version of Windows without WMP. In 2007 the CFI upheld the Commission decision in Case T-201/04, except for the requirement for Microsoft to submit a proposal to appoint a monitoring trustee with independent access to documents. The fine imposed was upheld, with the CFI finding that the Commission had not erred in relation to the gravity and duration of the infringement: Case T-201/04 *Microsoft* v. *Commission*.

While the Commission was investigating, the US competition authorities charged Microsoft with illegal tying by bundling its own browser, Internet Explorer, with its Windows Operating System. This charge was eventually withdrawn, and the matter examined under a 'rule of reason' approach. The US courts found that the bundling was in the interests of consumers, who like the convenience of being able to buy a computer with the browser already installed, a very different approach from the one adopted by the Commission, which considers that such arrangements are anti-competitive.

Key point

The 2005 Discussion Paper, in reviewing tying and bundling in the aftermath of the *Microsoft* decision, identifies four elements required for a practice to be seen as abusive under Article 82: dominance in the tying market, two distinct products, a likely market distorting foreclosure effect, and no justification objectively or by efficiencies.

Import and export bans

Import and export bans constitute an abuse, not only restricting competition but also hindering market integration see Whish (1998: Chapter 8). In Case 226/84 *British Leyland* v. *Commission* the ECJ upheld the Commission's finding that BL's pricing policy requiring type approval certificates on cars reduced imports into the UK and constituted an abuse.

EFFECT ON INTER-MEMBER TRADE

For an infringement of Article 82 an effect on inter-member trade must be proved. The phrase has the same meaning as applied to Article 81. It is important to note that alterations in the competitive structure of the common market amount to an effect on inter-member trade: *Commercial Solvents*.

MERGERS AND CONCENTRATIONS

Merger control under Article 82

Article 82 was invoked for the first time in the context of merger control in Case 6/72 *Continental Can*: see above. The ECJ ruled, in principle, that mergers which eliminate competition infringe Article 82, without the need to show a causal link between dominance and abuse. It should be noted, however, that the Commission decision that there was a breach of Article 82 was annulled for failure to examine the relevant product market.

For a further example of the application of Article 82 to mergers prior to the Merger Regulation, see Dec. 88/501 *Tetra Pak 1 (BTG Licence)*. Here the Commission held that it was an abuse to take over a firm to acquire an exclusive licence for patents and know-how which had the effect of excluding other operators from the market. The subsequent appeal to the CFI was withdrawn on this point although it went ahead on a number of other issues. While holding that the acquisition of an exclusive licence is not itself an abuse, the CFI recognised that the acquisition had strengthened Tetra Pak's market dominance and was likely to delay competition from fresh entrants: (on appeal) Case T-51/89 *Tetra Pak Rausing SA* v. *Commission*.

Merger control under successive merger regulations

The possibility of a merger infringing Article 81 arose for the first time in Cases 142 and 156/84 *BAT & Reynolds* v. *Commission*. This case provided the stimulus to revive the proposal for a regulation to control mergers. Regulation 4064/89 was adopted in 1989, with effect from October 1990. It was amended by Regulation 1310/97, and then repealed and replaced by Regulation 139/2004.

Under Regulation 139/2004 the Commission is obliged to investigate mergers, known as 'concentrations', where certain threshold levels are involved: see below. Mergers above these thresholds must be notified to the Commission which has to decide whether it would 'significantly impede competition within the Common Market', particularly as a result of the creation of strengthening of a dominant position: Article 2. Mergers outside the regulation are regulated by the national competition authorities. There has been discussion about alteration of the threshold levels since the introduction of the first merger regulation in 1989. The Commission proposed a lowering in 1996, but this was rejected by the Council, which put forward an alternative proposal, adopted in Regulation 139/2004, whereby the regulation would apply where turnover is lower but achieved in more than two Member States.

Key point

A 'concentration' is deemed to arise under Article 3(1) of the regulation 'where a change of control on a lasting basis results from:

(a) the merger of two or more previously independent undertakings or parts of undertakings, or
(b) the acquisition by one or more persons already controlling at least one undertaking, or by one or more undertakings, whether by purchase of securities or assets, by contract or by other means of direct or indirect control of the whole or parts of one or more undertakings.'

Article 3(4) of the merger regulation extends the scope of a concentration to include a joint venture where it performs on a lasting basis the functions of an autonomous economic entity. Joint ventures not covered by this definition will be considered to be 'co-operative' and are covered by Articles 81 and 82.

A merger has a community dimension when the turnover of the parties exceeds the thresholds specified in Article 1(2) where:

(a) The undertakings concerned have a combined worldwide turnover exceeding €5,000 million; and
(b) the aggregate Community-wide turnover of each of at least two of the undertakings concerned is no more than €250 million.

Article 1(3) provides that a concentration which does not meet the thresholds in Article 1(2) will have a Community dimension where:

(a) the combined aggregate worldwide turnover of all the undertakings concerned is more than €2,500 million;
(b) in each of at least three three Member States, the combined aggregate turnover of all the undertakings concerned is more than €100 million;
(c) in each of at least three three Member States included for the purpose of point (b), the aggregate turnover of each of at least two of the undertakings concerned is more than €25 million; and
(d) the aggregate Community-wide turnover of each of at least two of the undertakings concerned is more than €100 million.

Procedures under Regulation 139/2004

Participating undertakings are required by Article 4 of the regulation to notify the Commission of concentrations with a Community dimension prior to their implementation and following the conclusion of the agreement, announcement of public bid or acquisition of a controlling interest. They are not permitted to put the concentration into effect before notification and the Commission has either completed its assessment under Article 7(2) or should have done so.

Article 2(1) of the regulation requires the Commission to make an appraisal of the proposed merger, taking into account:

(a) the need to maintain and develop effective competition within the common market in view of, among other things, the structure of all the markets concerned and the actual or potential competition from undertakings located either within or out with the Community;

(b) the market position of all the undertakings concerned and their economic and financial power, the alternatives available to suppliers and users, their access to suppliers or markets, any legal and other barriers to entry, supply and demand trends for the relevant goods and services, the interests of intermediate and ultimate consumers, and the development of technical and economic progress provided that it is to the consumers' advantage and does not form an obstacle to competition.

Key point

Where a concentration would not significantly impede effective competition in the common market or a substantial part of it, particularly as a result of the creation or strengthening of a dominant position, it will be declared compatible with the common market under Article 2(2). Conversely, a concentration which would significantly impede competition in the common market by creating or strengthening a dominant position will be declared incompatible with the common market under Article 2(3).

Appraisals are divided into two stages:

- **Stage I**: Decisions must be taken within 25 working days under Article 10(1) of notification. The Commission may declare the concentration compatible with the common market. Most notified agreements are cleared at this stage, sometimes with commitments to avoid anti-competitive effects which are negotiated and agreed with the parties.

- **Stage II**: Decisions must be taken within 90 working days of initiating proceedings for Stage II under Article 8, or the concentration will be deemed to have been approved under Article 6(2). Where the parties offer commitments, the period may be increased to 105 days. A further extension of 15 working days is available at the Commission's request, with the consent of the parties. The Commission is empowered under Article 8 to attach conditions and obligations to a decision under Stage II.

The possibility of obtaining commitments with a view to reducing market power resulting from the concentration has enabled the Commission to clear mergers in 140 cases after Stage I and 79 cases after Stage II, with only 19 outright prohibitions at the end of 2006.[6] The Commission may obtain information under Article 11, and may request NCAs to conduct investigations under Article 12. It may also conduct investigations itself under Article 13. The Commission is empowered to impose fines in various circumstances, most notably of up to 10 per cent of aggregated turnover of the undertakings concerned under Article 14(2) for failure to suspend or end a concentration, or for failure to notify a concentration within a week. The CFI may review decisions on the merits under Article 230 of the EC Treaty and has unlimited jurisdiction to impose fines under Article 229 EC, with a further appeal to the ECJ.

Of the concentrations notified to date only a few have been found to be incompatible with the common market. One of few such decisions was *Aerospatiale-Alenia/De Havilland* (1991) in which the Commission based its analysis on the world market for commuter aeroplanes. The parties would have increased their market share to 50 per cent of the world market without economies of scale, depriving consumers of choice and creating barriers to new entrants. The decision was criticised by governments, which saw the decision as reducing national control in the sector.

Collective dominance and the merger regulation

The CFI held in Case T-102/96 *Gencor* v. *Commission* that Regulation 4064/89 applies to collective dominant positions. As a result, it upheld a Commission decision prohibiting a concentration between Gencor Ltd and Lonrho plc. If the merger had gone ahead it would have led to a dominant oligopoly in the world market between the resulting body and another company in relation to platinum and rhodium, significantly reducing competition in the EC.

In Joined Cases C-68/94 and C-30/95 *France* v. *Commission/SPCA and EMC* v. *Commission* the ECJ annulled the Commission decision on the merger between Kali and Salz and the Mitteldeutsche Kali AG (a subsidiary of the Treuhand, a German public body) as the decision had failed to establish that the merger would lead to a collective dominant position. The decision was unusual in that the CFI declined jurisdiction to enable the ECJ to rule.

Key case

These cases arose out of a decision by the Commission under Regulation 4064/89 that a concentration in the potash market between Kali und Salz AG, Mitteldeutsch Kali AG was compatible with the common market. The proposed

---

[6] See House of Lords, European Union Committee, 15th report of Session 2006–7, cited in Korah (2007: 309).

concentration was approved by the Commission despite acknowledging that the concentration would lead to a position of collective dominance in the EC market outside Germany. The ECJ held that collective dominant positions do not fall outside the scope of Regulation 4064/89. However, it also ruled that the Commission had misapplied the concept of collective dominance, by failing to establish that the concentration in question would in fact give rise to a collective dominant position in the relevant market. (There was a failure to establish a lack of effective competition to the undertakings in the proposed concentration.) The ECJ annulled the Commission decision: Joined Cases C-68/94 and C-30/95 *France* v. *Commission; SCPA and EMC* v. *Commission*.

19

Further decisions under the merger regulation

The decision in Case T-342/99 *Airtours* was the first occasion on which the CFI overturned a decision of the Commission to block a proposed merger, essentially as a result of the Commission's failure to undertake a full economic analysis before reaching a decision. The case was decided under Article 2(3) of Regulation 4064/89 (as amended), but remains relevant as it was largely repeated in Article 2(3) of Regulation 139/2004.

Key case

Airtours, a UK company, sold holidays to 'short-haul' destinations such as Spain and Italy. It launched a bid to take over First Choice, one of its main competitors in the UK, the others being Thomsons and Thomas Cook. The bid was notified to the Commission. Concerned with possible tacit collusion between the three undertakings, the Commission decided in 1999 that the merger was incompatible with the common market, as it would have given the merged undertaking collective dominance, along with Thomsons and Thomas Cook. The merger would have increased their combined share of the short haul market from 68 per cent to 78 per cent. Airtours appealed to the CFI.

The CFI repeated the earlier approach in *Gencor*, holding that three conditions must be established before the Commission could find that there was collective dominance:

1 Each undertaking must be able to monitor the activities of the others.
2 There must be an incentive not to depart from the common policy, i.e. members of the oligopoly must be able to retaliate.
3 The policy must be able to withstand challenge by other competitors, potential competitors or customers.

→

The CFI considered that the Commission had failed to undertake a full economic analysis, and had wrongly identified the market. It overturned the Commission's finding that customers did not switch between short and long haul holidays. The CFI found that, in fact, customers had significant buying power and switched both destinations and tour operators and destinations when prices rose. It also found that the Commission had failed to establish that the three undertakings would have had an incentive to cease competing with each other: Case T-324/99 *Airtours*.

Two further decisions by the Commission to prohibit mergers were reversed by the CFI on the basis of inadequate economic analysis: Case T-5/02 *Tetra Laval BV* v. *Commission* and Case T-310/01 *Schneider Electric*. In *Tetra Laval* the CFI held that where the Commission seeks to prohibit a merger because it will create or strengthen a dominant position, it must produce convincing evidence. This was particularly important in the case of a conglomerate-type merger, where the effects were usually considered to be neutral or even beneficial for competition. The CFI's decision in *Tetra Laval* was upheld by the ECJ in Case C-12/03 *Commission* v. *Tetra Laval*, although the Court did not accept all of the CFI's reasoning on the extent of the economic analysis.

Key term

A 'conglomerate' merger is a merger which brings together unconnected types of business, frequently held in a portfolio of company purchases by a holding company.

The CFI annulled a further decision of the Commission in *Impala*,[7] on this occasion a decision to clear rather than block a proposed merger.

Key case

Sony and Bertelsmann notified the Commission of their proposed merger. In May 2004 the Commission objected on the basis that the merger would strengthen the parties' collective dominance in the recorded music market. However, after considering evidence from the parties, the Commission changed its view, deciding in July 2004 that the merger was compatible with the common market. In December 2004, a third party, Impala (an international music organisation), applied for the decision clearing the merger to be annulled.

---

[7] Independent Music Publishers and Labels Association (Impala).

The CFI quashed the Commission's decision for failure to give sufficient reasons for the decision. It found that, while it might be possible to infer collective dominance in the recorded music market in accordance with the three conditions in *Airtours* (transparency, scope for retaliation and third-party pressure) they may be established indirectly from a mixed set of indicators, particularly where there was close alignment of prices over a long period. The Court found that the Commission's analysis was flawed and inadequate for a number of reasons including its reliance on the absence of retaliatory measures when it would have been sufficient to establish the existence of an effective mechanism for deterrence: Case T-464/04 *Impala* v. *Commission*, under appeal Case C-413/06P.

The merger was returned to the Commission to reconsider. The Commission cleared the merger, stating that the concerns have been removed through commitments.[8] The decision of the CFI in *Impala* was criticized for its lack of consistency with earlier decisions in *Airtours, Tetra Laval* and *Schneider*.[9]

Effect of decisions in Airtours, etc.

The effect of the three CFI's actions to quash the Commission decisions in *Airtours, Tetra* and *Schneider*, and the criticisms of the Commission's approach to economic analysis led to the introduction of a comprehensive package of merger reforms, particularly the introduction of new merger Regulation 139/2004, which clearly applied to situations of oligopoly or collective dominance. However, the continuing uncertainties resulting from the *Impala* decision above, taken *after* the introduction of Regulation 139/2004, show that the problems may have not all have been resolved. Other elements of the merger package included an improved system in relation to the timing of applications, as well as a simplified system for transfer of cases between the Commission and the NCAs (see above). Greater flexibility was introduced into the system, particularly over the investigation of complex cases. A Chief Competition Economist was appointed within the Commission, to provide economic advice on mergers.

'One-stop shopping'

Part of the purpose of the merger regulation was to provide a single forum for the examination of concentrations within the EC, as parties to mergers above the thresholds are not required to notify NCAs. However, as Article 82 is directly effective, considerations relating to concentrations may be raised before the national courts. Provision is made for involvement by the national authorities where there are distinct national markets or legitimate notifiable interests.

---

[8] IP/07/695 Press release, 22 May 2007.
[9] See Volcker and O'Daly 2006.

Distinct national markets

A Member State is entitled under Article 9(2) of the Regulation within three weeks of receiving a copy of a notification of a concentration to inform the Commission that a concentration threatens to strengthen a dominant position, significantly impeding competition in a distinct national market.

If the Commission decides that there is both a threat and a distinct market, it may either consider the case itself or refer it to the Member State's competition authorities. A Member State, in the event of a referral, must within four months reach a decision, limiting itself to measures necessary to safeguard competition. The Commission and Council declared in 1990 that the procedure should only be invoked in exceptional circumstances.

The procedure was invoked in Case IV/M75 *Steetley/Tarmac* when a notification relating to brick and clay tiles was referred back to the UK authorities. If the concentration were allowed to go ahead it would give the new company a dominant position where previously three undertakings had been active. The concentration was likely to cause significant barriers to entry in the relevant market in the UK, while having little impact on other parts of the EC. In the circumstances it was appropriate for the issues to be decided by the UK authorities. Conversely a Member State may invoke a procedure under Article 22(1) requesting the Commission to apply the Regulation to a concentration in its own territory without a Community dimension.

The protection of legitimate interests

Although Article 21(1) of the Regulation states that Member States shall not apply their national legislation on competition to a concentration with a Community dimension it must be read subject to para. 3, which entitles Member States to take appropriate measures to protect legitimate interests outside the Regulation, provided they are compatible with EC law.

Under para. 4 Member States may intervene at their own instigation in three areas:

1 'public security' (i.e. defence interests),
2 'plurality of the media' (i.e. the need to maintain diversified information and news),
3 'prudential rules' (i.e. surveillance of financial bodies, e.g. solvency rules).

Member States wishing to intervene to protect legitimate interests in other matters of public interest must notify the Commission.

The procedure (then under Article 21(3) of Regulation 4064/89) was invoked for the first time by the UK in Dec. IV/M567 *Northumbrian Water/Lyonnaise des Eaux*. The UK was allowed to exercise strict control over mergers in the water industry in order to preserve competition between firms under a regulatory system based on price comparisons.

The 'Dutch' clause

Under Article 22(1) a Member State may request the Commission to investigate a concentration which does not have an EC dimension where that concentration creates or strengthens a dominant position as a result of which effective competition on the territory of that State would be impeded. It is unlikely that this provision will be invoked often, as it was intended to cover the position where a Member State lacked a national system of merger control.

QUESTIONS

1 How have the Commission and the Court used the concept of product substitution to define the product market?

2 What does the *Microsoft* decision demonstrate in terms of the approach of the Commission to tying and bundling?

3 To what extent has Regulation 139/2004 addressed the concerns raised by the decisions in *Airtours, Tetra Laval* and *Schneider* in relation to mergers?

Further reading

Chalmers, D., Hadjiemmanuil, C., Monti, G. and Tomkins, A. (2006) *European Union Law,* Cambridge University Press, Chapters 23 and 24.

Commission Discussion Paper 2005 on Exploitative Abuses http://ec.europa.eu/comm/competition/antitrust/art82/index.html

Craig, P. and De Burca, G. (2007) *EU Law: Text, Cases and Materials,* 4th edition, Oxford University Press.

Doherty, B. (2001) 'Just What Are Essential Facilities?', (2001) 38 CMLRev. 397.

House of Lords (2007) European Union Committee, 15th report of Session 2006–7.

Jones, A. and Sufrin, B. (2008) *EC Competion Law: Text, Cases and Materials,* 3rd edition, Oxford University Press, Chapters 5, 6 and 7 (Article 82) and 12 (mergers).

Kent, P., Allsopp, V. and English, P., (2004) 'The Future of Merger Control in the EC' in Tridimas, T. and Nebbia, P. (eds) *European Union Law for the Twenty First Century: Rethinking the New Legal Order* (Volume 2), Hart Publishing.

Korah, V. (2007) *An Introductory Guide to EC Competition Law and Practice*, 9th edition, Hart Publishing, Chapters 4 and 5 (Article 82) and 12 (mergers).

Spector, D. (2006) 'From Harm to Competitors to Harm to Competition: One More Effort, Please!' (2006) 2 ECJ 145.

Vickers, J. (2006) 'Market Powers in Competition Case', (2006) 2 ELJ 3.

Volcker, S. and O'Daly, C. (2006) 'The CFI's IMPALA Judgment: a Judicial Counter-reformation in EU Merger Control?' (2006) ECLR 589.

Whish, R. (2003) *Competition Law*, 5th edition, Oxford University Press.

Visit **http://www.mylawchamber.co.uk/kent** to access answer guidance to questions in the book to test yourself on this chapter.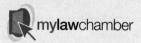

Articles 81 and 82: enforcement and procedure

INTRODUCTION

The Commission has a duty under Article 85(1) (ex 89(1)) to ensure that the principles laid down by Articles 81 and 82 are applied. It is required to investigate suspected infringement of these principles and to propose measures to bring it to an end. Where the infringement is not ended, the Commission is required under Article 85(2) to record the details of the infringement in a reasoned decision. The powers and procedures of the Commission in enforcing EC competition law were originally laid down in Regulation 17/62, under which the Commission alone was empowered to grant exemptions or negative clearance, following notification by the undertakings concerned. Mergers were covered by a separate procedure under the merger regulation: see Chapter 19. Articles 81 and 82 have long been recognised in decisions such as Case 127/73 *BRT* v. *SABAM* to be directly effective in the national courts. As a result, it is clear that conflicting national competition laws should be disapplied: Case C-198/01 *Consorzio Industries Fiammiferi (CIF)* v. *Autorità Garante della Concorrenza e del Mercato*. Infringements of Articles 81 and 82 may also give rise to State liability where the conditions in *Brasserie du Pêcheur* are satisfied: see Chapter 6.

Regulation 1/2003

In 1999 the Commission published its White Paper on the application of the competition rules, proposing decentralisation, with a greater involvement of the national competition authorities (NCAs), as well as the simplification of procedures, in the light of changes such as enlargement of the EU and globalisation. Regulation 1/2003 was adopted in accordance with the principles in the White Paper, with effect from 1 May 2004.

> **Key point**
>
> Article 1 of Regulation 1/2003 provides that agreements, decisions and concerted practices caught by Article 81(1) EC which do not satisfy the conditions of Article 81(3) shall be prohibited, no prior decision to that effect being required.

Decentralisation was achieved largely by making Articles 81 and 82 directly applicable in their entirety. Legal certainty is maintained by allowing undertakings to enforce their agreements through the national courts provided the agreements are not anti-competitive. Notification of agreements to the Commission is no longer required, leaving the Commission free to concentrate on major competition decisions and the most serious breaches of competition rules, although it may remove a case from the consideration of national authorities where it consider this appropriate.

Competition policy continues to be directed by the Commission through the adoption of regulations and notices. One regulation has been adopted under Regulation 1/2003: Regulation 773/2004 on the conduct of proceedings by the Commission pursuant to Articles 81 and 82 EC. Seven non-binding Notices have been adopted. These will be considered, where relevant, during this chapter.

Applications by parties to a possible infringement

Previously, under Regulation 17, the parties to an agreement which might breach Article 81(1) could apply to the Commission under Article 81(3) for negative clearance or exemption. If the application was found not to infringe Article 81(1), the Commission would provide negative clearance. If it infringed Article 81(1) but was justified under the conditions set out in Article 81(3), the Commission could grant an individual exemption. Responding to such applications was time-consuming and not the best use of the Commission's resources.

> ### Key point
>
> Under Regulation 1/2003, the Commission no longer receives applications for negative clearance or exemption. However, where public interest in the Community requires, the Commission may make a finding of inapplicability under Article 10 of the Regulation in relation to either Article 81 or 82, acting on its own initiative.

The Commission may make an Article 10 ruling where the conditions of Article 81(1) are not fulfilled, or because the conditions under Article 81(3) are satisfied. Such rulings should not be seen as equivalent to decisions on negative clearance or exemptions, as they merely provide a declaration as to the status of the agreement on the date of the ruling.

Guidance letters may be provided by the Commission under the 2004 Notice on novel questions concerning Articles 81 and 82 of the Treaty: see Chapter 19. Like 'comfort letters' issued by the Commission under Regulation 17, guidance letters are not legally binding.

Under Regulation 1/2003, declarations that conduct is or is not forbidden under Article 81(3) may only be made by the Commission, an NCA or a national court under Article 1 and recital 4. NCAs may certify under Article 5 that there is no ground for action on their part. Fines or other penalties may be imposed by NCAs under national law. The Commission may also impose penalties, under Articles 23–24 of the Regulation and may make decisions on commitments offered by undertaking under Article 9.

INVESTIGATORY POWERS

Investigations

> **Key point**
>
> Article 18(1) of Regulation 1/2003 empowers the Commission by simple request or decision to obtain 'all necessary information' from undertakings and associations of undertakings. NCAs already have this power under national legislation. A copy of any request will be sent to the NCA: Article 18(5). At the request of the Commission, governments and NCAs must provide the Commission with all necessary information to carry out its duties under the Regulation: Article 18(6).

'Necessary information' was interpreted by the CFI in Case T-39/90 *SEP* v. *Commission*, a decision upheld by the ECJ in Case C-36/92P. The CFI found that the term must be interpreted by reference to the purposes for which the powers of investigation were conferred on the Commission. The Commission may demand information under Article 18 from the outset, whereas its predecessor, Article 11 under Regulation 17, required a two-stage approach. The Commission could begin proceedings on its own initiative or on application by a Member State or individual, as in Cases 48, 49, 51–57/69 *Imperial Chemical Industries* v. *Commission* ('*Dyestuffs*') in which complaints had been made by the printing industry.

If incorrect or misleading information is supplied or if information is not provided within the time limit, the Commission may take a formal decision, and impose a fine under Article 23(1)(b) or a periodical penalty under Article 24(d). The daily penalty under Article 24 has been increased to 5 per cent of average daily turnover of the undertaking. An undertaking should not be compelled to incriminate itself, as self-incrimination contravenes the right to a fair hearing: Case 374/87 *Orkem* v. *Commission* and Case 27/88 *Solvay & Co.* v. *Commission*. In Case C-60/92 *Otto BV* v. *Postbank NV* the ECJ held that information learned by the Commission and national authorities from proceedings before national courts may not be used in evidence in proceedings which may lead to the imposition of a penalty.

Inspections

The Commission has powers of inspection under Articles 19–21. It may enter the premises of an undertaking, or other premises, including the homes of directors, to examine and copy books and other records, and may ask for 'on the spot' oral explanations. It may also seal premises when it is unable to complete its inspection in one day. The introduction of the power to search the homes of directors under Article 21 was controversial. It is subject to a prior authorisation by a decision of the Commission and the national court.

NCAs must actively assist the Commission in its task, if requested to do so by the Commission: Article 20(5). If the inspection is opposed by the undertaking, the Member States must provide the assistance of the police or other enforcement authority: Article 20(6). The Commission may also interview members of staff or representatives about documents relating to the inspection: Article 20(2). NCAs may carry out inspections themselves under Article 22, either at their own instigation or at the request of the Commission. Any information obtained should only be used for the purpose of the enquiry: Article 28.

The Commission is permitted to take statements under Article 19. Regulation 773/2004 provides further detailed rules in relation to the procedure when taking a statement.

Under Article 14 of Regulation 17 the Commission was previously empowered to carry out inspections, although it did not have the right to enter the homes of directors.

Key case

A 'dawn raid' was carried out under Regulation 17 in *Hoechst* v. *Commission*. The Commission's investigation was challenged by Hoechst on the grounds that it breached the inviolability of the home and that the Commission's decision was insufficiently precise. The ECJ held that where the Commission intended to carry out an investigation without the co-operation of the undertakings concerned, it must observe procedural guarantees laid down by national law. The fundamental right to the inviolability of domicile applied to private residences and could not be extended to commercial premises. The Commission's statement of reasons was found to be drafted in general terms but containing sufficient detail about the products in which a cartel was suspected contrary to Article 81(1): Cases 46/87 and 227/88 *Hoechst* v. *Commission*.

This decision was upheld in Case 85/87 *Dow Benelux NV* v. *Commission* and Cases 97–99/87 *Dow Chemical Iberica SA* v. *Commission*. Under Regulation 17, investigations could be either 'voluntary' under Article 11(2) or 'compulsory' under Article 14(3). In Case 136/79 *National Panasonic* no prior notice of a 'dawn raid' was given to Panasonic. The ECJ rejected Panasonic's claim that prior notice should have been given to the undertaking and found that the Commission was entitled under Article

14(3) to carry out such undertakings as were necessary to reveal any breaches of Article 81 or 82. National Panasonic was found to have engaged in concerted practices contrary to Article 81.

Privilege may be claimed for correspondence between a client and independent lawyer in the EC or with an establishment in the EC, after proceedings have been initiated by the Commission. Correspondence with in-house lawyers, however, is not privileged: Case 155/79 *Australian Mining & Smelting Europe Ltd* v. *Commission*. It is the function of the CFI (or ECJ) to decide which documents are privileged.

Right to be heard

Article 27(1) of Regulation 1/2003 entitles the parties to present their views before any decision is taken on the merits. No fine or penalty may be imposed unless the parties have been given a chance to answer: Article 27(2). Where the Commission intends to adopt a decision under Article 9 (to take commitments) or Article 10 (to clear conduct as not an infringement), it must publish a concise summary of the case and of the commitments or main course of action: Article 27(4).

The case will be presided over by a Hearings Officer, whose task is to ensure that the procedures are correctly followed and the rights of the parties respected. Chapter V of Regulation 773/2004 makes detailed provision for the right to be heard. The parties are entitled to full access to all documents on the Commission's file except for business secrets, Commission internal documents and other confidential information: Case T-7/89 *Hercules*.

Previously, Article 19 of Regulation 17 provided for similar rights to be heard.

The decision

Decisions under Articles 7 to 10 (i.e. to clear, prohibit or accept commitments) must be published: Article 30. An appeal lies to the CFI under Article 230 EC: see Chapter 8. A further appeal on points of law may be made to the ECJ from a decision of the CFI. The CFI and ECJ may uphold or quash the decision of the Commission, and may increase or reduce any fine or periodic penalty: Article 31 of Regulation 1/2003 (previously Article 17 of Regulation 17).

Interim measures

The power to take interim measures for a specific period of time is provided by Article 8 of Regulation 1/2003, although it was not specified in Regulation 17 in cases of urgency where there is a risk of serious and irreparable damage to competition. Article 8 recongises the case law of the ECJ on interim measures, particularly the decision in *Camera Care*.

Key case

The ECJ annulled a Commission decision refusing to make an interim order requiring Hasselblad to supply its cameras to Camera Care. Holding that the power is implied in Article 3, the ECJ ruled that the Commission may take interim measures provided that:

- they are urgent and necessary to avoid serious or irreparable damage to the party seeking the remedy or in a situation intolerable to the public interest;
- there is a reasonably strong case of *prima facie* infringement of the competition rules;
- the principle of proportionality is observed;
- the decision is temporary and capable of review by the CFI: Case 792/79 R *Camera Care* v. *Commission*.

The ECJ ruled in Cases 228 and 229/82 *Ford of Europe* v. *Commission* that an interim order may only be granted if it falls within the framework of the final decision.

Key case

A Commission decision declaring the net book agreements in the UK void was temporarily suspended as there were clear *prima facie* arguments against the decision. An appeal to the CFI was unsuccessful, but this decision was also suspended pending hearing by the ECJ in Case 56/89. The ECJ set aside parts of the earlier decisions: Case T-66/89 *Publishers' Association* v. *Commission*: see Chapter 18.

CONFIDENTIAL INFORMATION

Professional secrecy and business secrets

Article 27(4) retains the requirement for the Commission to have regard for the 'legitimate interest of undertakings in the protection of their business secrets' previously in Article 19(2) of Regulation 17/62. In Case 53/85 *AKZO Chemie BV* v. *Commission* the ECJ held that it was for the Commission (subject to review by the ECJ) to decide whether a document contains business secrets. Once it is clear that a document contains business secrets (e.g. details of joint venture agreements, market shares or expansion plans), its contents must not be divulged. The degree of protection attaching to 'professional secrecy' is less clear: the Commission may be prepared to divulge information covered by professional secrecy where it considers that this is necessary.

Key case

Stanley Adams, formerly a senior executive at Hoffman-La Roche in Switzerland, succeeded in obtaining damages against the company in an action under Article 288 (ex 215). While employed by Hoffman-La Roche the applicant had secretly passed documents to the Commission which showed that the company was breaching Article 82. Although Adams requested confidentiality from the Commission, Hoffman-La Roche was able to identify Adams from the documents. As Adams had committed an offence by revealing the documents to the Commission he was charged with industrial espionage on re-entering Switzerland from Italy. While he was in custody his wife committed suicide. Adams was convicted and given a one-year suspended jail sentence. He sued the Commission for damages, claiming that his creditworthiness had been damaged by the conviction and that his business had been destroyed. Although damages were awarded they were reduced by half on account of his contributory negligence, namely his failure to warn the Commission that he could be identified from the documents, and his return to Switzerland despite the risk of prosecution: Case 145/83 *Adams* v. *Commission*.

FINES AND PENALTIES

Under Article 23(2) the Commission may impose fines for infringements of Articles 81 and 82 which are intentional or due to negligence, of up to 10 per cent of the undertaking's turnover in the preceding business year. Where the infringement of an association relates to the activities of its members, the fine shall not exceed 10 per cent of the sum of the total turnover of each Member State active on the market affected by the infringement of the association. Smaller fines of up to 1 per cent of an undertaking's turnover may be imposed under Article 23(1) for supplying incorrect or misleading information in response to a request under Article 17 or 18(3). In calculating turnover, fines are calculated by reference to the turnover of the *group*: Dec. 84/388 *Re Benelux Flat Glass cartel*. See also Cases 100–103/80 *Pioneer*, in which the ECJ imposed a fine of 10 per cent of the worldwide group turnover, a new and high level of fine.

Factors to be taken into account

Under a Notice[1] issued in 2006 (the most recent in a series of Notices) the Commission published guidelines for the imposition of fines on undertakings in breach of the competition rules, announcing that it would be imposing much higher fines on undertakings found to be in breach, where the statement of objections had been

---

[1] OJ 2006, C210/2.

issued after August 2006. Under the new method fines will be calculated from a basic amount which may be increased or decreased, depending on circumstances. The basic amount is the undertaking's turnover in the EEA, usually in the last business year (paras 13–18). The fine is a proportion, which is usually 30 per cent, of this figure (para. 19), depending on the gravity of the infringement. It is multiplied by the number of years the infringement has lasted (para. 24) and 15–25 per cent is added as a deterrent. Aggravating factors such as refusal to co-operate with the Commission may lead to the fine being doubled. It is too soon for cases to have reached the CFI based on appeals against the imposition of higher fines under the 2006 Notice.

Various factors have been accepted in mitigation by the Commission and the Courts. These include recession in the industry in question and the parties' willingness to terminate the offending behaviour: Dec. 85/202 *Wood Pulp*. (However, extensive parts of this decision were annulled on appeal to the ECJ in Cases 89/85 etc.) Providing an undertaking to establish a programme to ensure future compliance with the competition rules was a factor in Dec. 85/7a *John Deere*. Excessive duration of proceedings before the CFI (five and a half years) led the ECJ to reduce a fine by €50,000: Case C-185/95P *Baustahlgewabe* v. *Commission*.

Leniency programme

In the '*Cartonboard*' decision (1994) the Commission reduced the fine of one of the participants in a pricing cartel by two-thirds as a result of the information it provided on the other participants. In an attempt to improve the quality of the evidence on cartels presented in court, the Commission introduced a 'leniency' programme in its Notice in 1996.[2]

Key point

The most recent leniency Notice was published in 2006,[3] formalising its action in 2002 when it provided a powerful incentive to racing to 'blow the whistle' on a cartel. The Commission promised not to fine the first undertaking to give evidence of a secret cartel where it would not previously have had enough evidence to establish an infringement or authorise an inspection.

The undertaking which is blowing the whistle must co-operate fully with the Commission, must have ended its own involvement in the possible infringement and must not have coerced other undertakings to take part in the infringement. Total immunity from fines may be available to the first undertaking to blow the whistle in these circumstances, as the *Fine Art Auction Houses (Christie's and Sotheby's)* in

---

[2] OJ 1996 C207/4.
[3] OJ 2006 C298/17.

2006 demonstrates. Christie's informed the Commission of a price-fixing cartel and escaped a fine altogether. Sotheby's were fined €20.4 million (6 per cent of world-wide turnover).

Periodic penalties

Fines of up to 5 per cent of average daily turnover in the previous business year may be imposed under Article 24 on undertakings in order to compel them to:

- put an end to an infringement in accordance with a decision under Article 7;
- comply with an interim order under Article 8;
- comply with a commitment to a decision under Article 9;
- supply complete information pursuant to a request under Article 17 or 18(3).

Enforcement in the Member States

Although Regulation 1/2003 has led to the establishment of a network of national competition authorities, the Commission retains its central role in directing competition policy and in ensuring consistency of enforcement. Article 11 of the Regulation provides for the NCAs and the Commission to work in close co-operation. If the Commission decides to initiate proceedings under Article 11(6), or adopt a decision under Articles 7–10, the NCAs cease to be competent to apply Articles 81 and 82. In its 2004 Notice,[4] the Commission made it clear that it would only rarely initiate such proceedings. Article 12 provides for the exchange of information between the Commission and NCAs. As with Regulation 17, Regulation 1/2003 provides for the Commission to be assisted by an Advisory Committee on Restrictive Practices and Dominant Positions in certain circumstances. The Commission must consult the Committee under Article 14 in relation to decisions under Articles 7, 8, 9, 10, 23, 24(2) and 29(1).

Article 3 of the Regulation provides that where NCAs apply national law to concerted practices or abuses of a dominant position, they shall also apply Article 81 and 82, and should make decisions which are consistent with those Articles. Under Article 16, where a matter is already the subject of a Commission decision, NCAs cannot take decisions which are inconsistent with that decision.

Articles 81 and 92, as we have seen, are directly effective in the national courts: Case 127/73 *BRT* v. *SABAM*. Breach of Article 81 or 82 should lead to the application of the same remedies in the national courts as are available for similar breaches of national law: Case 33/76 *Rewe-Zentralfinanz*. In interlocutory proceedings an injunction or declaration may be obtained, but the national courts (particularly in the UK) are divided about whether or not damages are available: *Garden Cottage Foods* (HL, 1983).

[4] OJ 2004 C101/43.

> **Key case**
>
> The tenant of a public house was sued by the brewers, Courage, for various breaches of contract. The tenant argued that the beer tie to which he was subject infringed Article 81(1). If the agreement had been illegal, no damages would have been available under English law. The ECJ ruled under Article 234 that the national court must provide a remedy where someone is harmed by a breach of Article 81, and so the ban on recovery had to be set aside.

While accepting that EC law took priority over English law, the House of Lords held that a national court was not bound to accept the findings of the Commission that Article 81(1) had been infringed: Case C-453/99 *Courage* v. *Crehan*.

An interim order may be sought from the national court, in some cases by an individual claiming a legitimate interest who is not a party to the agreement.

> **Key case**
>
> The plaintiffs succeeded in obtaining an interim injunction to prevent the application of agreements to which they were not a party. The agreements in question were tenancy agreements between the defendants, brewers who had taken over a group of tied houses, and the tenants of those houses. Prior to the agreement the applicant had supplied pin-tables and other gaming equipment to the public houses in the group, but under the agreement the tenants were obliged to purchase such equipment only from named suppliers. The applicants were excluded from the list. The applicants complained to the Commission and succeeded in obtaining an interim injunction from the English High Court: *Cutsforth* v. *Mansfield Inns Ltd* (QBD, 1986).

Such applications, however, do not always succeed: see *Argyll Group plc* v. *Distillers Co. plc* (Court of Session, 1986), in which the Scottish Court refused to grant an interim interdict (injunction) to prevent a merger between Distillers and Guinness, stating that no *prima facie* case had been made out. Injunctions were also refused in *Plessey* v. *GEC* (QBD, 1990) and *Megaphone* v. *British Telecom* (QBD, 1989).

In Case T-114/92 *BENIM* v. *Commission* the CFI ruled that the Commission had acted properly in deciding not to pursue proceedings which were confined to a single state, France. However, in Case T-198/98 *Micro Leader Business* v. *Commission* the CFI held that the Commission was wrong to dismiss a complaint by the French software wholesaler Micro Leader Business when it was prevented from buying Microsoft software more cheaply in Canada for resale in France. The CFI considered that the Commission should have examined the documents for a possible breach of Article 82.

QUESTIONS

1 Why was it necessary to adopt Regulation 1/2003 in order to enforce EC competition rules in the Member States? How do the powers of the Commission and the NCAs inter-relate when carrying out an investigation?

2 What mechanisms exist to ensure that competition laws are applied consistently throughout the Member States?

Further reading

Blake, S. and Schnigels, D. (2004) 'Leniency Following Modernisation: Safeguarding Europe's Leniency Programmes' (2004) ECLR 765.

Chalmers, D., Hadjiemmanuil, C., Monti, G. and Tomkins, A. (2006) *European Union Law*, Cambridge University Press, Chapter 21.

Craig, P. and De Burca, G. (2007) *EU Law: Text, Cases and Materials*, 4th edition, Oxford University Press, pp.999–1003.

Drake, S. (2006) 'Scope of *Courage* and the Principle of Individual Liability for Damages: Further Development of the Principle of Effective Judicial Protection by the Court of Justice', (2006) 31 ELRev. 841.

Hunnings, N. M. (1987) 'The Stanley Adams Affair or the Biter Bit', (1987) 24 CMLRev. 65.

Jones, A. and Sufrin, B. (2008) *EC Competition Law: Text, Cases and Materials*, 3rd edition, Oxford University Press, Chapters 14 and 15.

Korah, V. (2007) *An Introductory Guide to EC Competition Law and Practice'*, 9th edition, Hart Publishing, Chapter 7.

Odudu, O. (2002) 'Article 81(3), Discretion and Direct Effect' (2002) 23 ECLR 17.

Perrin, B. (2006) 'Challenges Facing the EU Network of Competition Authorities: Insights from a comparative criminal perspective' (2006) 31 ELRev. 540.

Visit **http://www.mylawchamber.co.uk/kent** to access answer guidance to questions in the book to test yourself on this chapter.

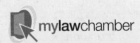

Use **Case Navigator** to read in full some of the key cases referenced in this chapter:

- C-46/49 and 48/93 **Brasserie du Pêcheur v. Federal Republic of Germany** and **R. v. Secretary of State for Transport, ex parte Factortame (Factortame III)** [1996] ECR I-1029

21 Intellectual property

INTRODUCTION

The term 'intellectual property' is used in this book to cover both industrial and artistic property, although the term used in Article 30 of the Treaty is 'industrial and commercial property'. 'Industrial property' covers valuable rights connected with the production and distribution of goods and services such as patents and trade marks. 'Artistic property' covers artistic and literary property such as copyright. Most intellectual property rights are established under national law, although there has been some harmonisation at EC level.

Key terms

- **Patent**: an exclusive right, usually held under national law, in relation to an invention. A patent enables the holder to prevent others from exploiting the invention, or from selling, using or importing any goods covered by the right. The holders of the right often grant licences to others to exercise the rights. A patent right protects creative activity and is of limited duration.
- **Trade mark**: a mark which can be represented graphically (e.g. by words or a logo) to distinguish the goods or services of one undertaking from another. The holder is entitled to exclusive use of the mark. Trade marks relate to the reputation of a particular product and last indefinitely
- **Copyright**: the exclusive right to reproduce works such as literary, dramatic or musical works. It may be transferred, for example, by assignment or licence. Like a patent, copyright protects creative activity and is of limited duration.

Scope of intellectual property rights

Intellectual property rights usually provide for the exclusive enjoyment of valuable property rights by the holder against the world in general. The granting of intellectual property rights has until the single market programme been left to the national authorities, supported by Article 295 (ex 222) which acknowledges national systems of property ownership: see below. However, the use and enjoyment of such rights on a national basis may disturb the free movement of goods and distort competition within the EC. It is therefore necessary to examine the use of intellectual property rights in the context of Articles 81 and 82, as well as Articles 28–30. While Article 30 recognises the protection of industrial and commercial property as a derogation from free movement rights, there must be no arbitrary discrimination or disguised restriction on trade between Member States. The decision in *Consten and Grundig* illustrates how the exercise of intellectual property rights may infringe Community law. This point is examined further below, in relation to the distinction between the existence and the exercise of the right.

Key case

Grundig had appointed Consten to be the exclusive distributor of Grundig products in France. The exclusive dealing agreement was reinforced by the sole use in France by Consten of Grundig's international trade mark, GINT. An action for annulment of the Commission decision refusing exemption was brought by the parties under Article 230 in the ECJ. The ECJ rejected the appeal and upheld the Commission decision: see Chapter 18. HELD: Articles 30 and 295 EC allow for the existence of national industrial property rights but their exercise is subject to Community control. The purpose of the GINT trade mark was not to protect the holder's legitimate rights but to partition the market, providing absolute territorial protection for Grundig products in France, in breach of Article 81(1): Cases 56 and 58/64 *Consten and Grundig* v. *Commission*.

There is a clear need for unification of intellectual property rights if market division on rigid national lines is to be avoided. Some progress towards the recognition of European rights has been made in trade marks and patents, but it is by no means complete. The Treaty of Lisbon will introduce an obligation to establish European intellectual property rights under Article 97A. The harmonisation of intellectual property rights is considered at the end of this chapter.

INTELLECTUAL PROPERTY RIGHTS AND THE FREE MOVEMENT OF GOODS

Treaty provision

While the competition rules may be invoked to prevent the division of the market on national lines by intellectual property rights, they do not provide a comprehensive answer to this problem. It is thus necessary to invoke the provisions in the free movement of goods in Articles 28–30 in the courts both at national level and in the ECJ (or CFI).

The key question arising in the context of intellectual property rights is: How far may the holders of national intellectual property rights rely on those rights to exclude imports from another Member State? Article 295 states that the Treaty shall 'in no way prejudice the rules in Member States governing the system of property ownership'. Article 295 must, however, be read subject to Article 30, which states that the prohibitions of Articles 28–30 'shall not preclude prohibitions or restrictions on imports, exports or goods in transit justified on grounds of . . . the protection of industrial and commercial property. Such prohibitions or restrictions shall not, however, constitute a means of arbitrary discrimination or a disguised restriction on trade between Member States'.

A compromise approach

In order to satisfy the requirements of Article 295, the ECJ has adopted a compromise approach, distinguishing between the existence and exercise of intellectual property rights. Restrictions are only permissible to protect the specific subject-matters of the rights: Case 119/75 *Terrapin* v. *Terranova*.

> **Key case**
>
> A German firm known by the trade name 'Terrapin' sought to prevent a UK firm from registering the name 'Terranova'. The German company claimed that consumers would be confused as both companies made building materials. The ECJ held under Article 234 that Article 30 could be invoked to prevent the importation of goods under the name which causes confusion where these rights are held by different proprietors under different national laws, provided they do not operate as a means of arbitrary discrimination, nor as a disguised restriction on trade between Member States.
>
> The Court again distinguished between the *existence* of intellectual property rights, recognised by national law, and the *exercise* of those rights, which may be restricted under the Treaty. However, the ECJ qualified this approach by stating that Article 30 only permits exceptions to the principle of the free movement of goods to the extent to which such exceptions are justified for the purpose of safeguarding the rights which constitute the specific subject-matter of that property: Case 119/75 *Terrapin* v. *Terranova*.

See also the earlier decision in Case 78/70 *Deutsche Grammophon Gesellschaft GmbH* v. *Metro-SB-Grossmärkte GmbH & Co. KG*, in which the ECJ drew a similar distinction between the existence and exercise of rights, this time in relation to copyright protection. While copyright protection under national law is legitimate, a prohibition on parallel imports resulting from the use of copyright to prevent goods moving from one Member State's territory to another would be an improper exercise of those rights and would be unjustifiable under Article 30.

Exhaustion of rights

Where the holder of an intellectual property right puts goods into circulation anywhere in the single market, he loses the right to prevent their importation from another Member State. His rights are said to be 'exhausted' as the right to exclude imports lawfully marketed in another Member State is not covered by the specific subject of the rights: see Case 15/74 *Centrafarm BV* v. *Sterling Drug Inc.* (patents) and Case 16/74 *Centrafarm BV* v. *Winthrop* (trade marks). Goods may be put into circulation either directly by the owner of the right or by the grant of a licence to a third party.

Examples are now considered in relation to the various different types of intellectual property rights.

Patents and trade marks

Case 35/87 *Thetford Corp.* v. *Fiamma Spa* illustrates how the exercise of a patent right can be relied on to prevent importation. In this case, the applicant sought to prevent the importation into the UK of portable lavatories made by the Italian company, on the basis that the products infringed a UK patent. The ECJ held that, as the patent was valid under national law, it was protected under Article 30, even though it would not have been granted elsewhere in the EC.

Many patent rights are held in conjunction with trade mark rights, particularly in the pharmaceutical industry. The Court's approach has evolved from one in which it emphasised the intention of the parties (Case 3/78 *Centrafarm BV* v. *American Home Products*) to one in which more emphasis is placed on the effects of the agreement (Cases C-427, 429 and 436/93 *Bristol-Myers Squibb* v. *Paranova*).

Key case

Centrafarm obtained drugs in the UK which the company repacked before selling in Germany. Hoffman-La Roche, the holder of the German trade mark for the drug, sued Centrafarm for trade mark infringement. HELD (ECJ): Enforcement of the trade mark would constitute a disguised restriction on trade between Member States contrary to Article 30 where the marketing system adopted by the trade mark holder involves an artificial partitioning of the market, provided repackaging cannot adversely affect the condition of the product and that the repackaging firm does not confuse users. The repackaging firm must state that the goods have been repackaged and must notify the trade mark holders of its intention to repackage: Case 102/77 *Hoffman-La Roche*.

In assessing whether or not a trade mark infringed Article 30, the Court in Case 3/78 *Centrafarm BV* v. *American Home Products Corporation* decided on the basis of the intention of the parties. In this case, Centrafarm bought drugs in the UK under the trade name 'Serenid D', reselling them in the Netherlands under the name 'Seresta'. American Home Products Corporation owned both trade marks, marketing an almost identical drug in the Netherlands under the name 'Seresta'. The ECJ held that the holder of a trade mark was entitled to prevent the unauthorised fixing of trade marks, unless the trade mark was intended to divide the market along national lines, as this would constitute a disguised restriction on trade between Member States, falling outside Article 30.

In *Bristol-Myers Squibb* v. *Paranova* the ECJ reconsidered its approach in *Centrafarm*, while affirming the principle in *Hoffman-La Roche*.

Key case

Paranova, a parallel importer, had purchased pharmaceutical products outside Denmark, repackaged them and resold them in Denmark, undercutting the trade mark holder. Although the ECJ accepted that repackaging may be opposed when there is a risk of damage to the contents, it was for the national court to assess this risk. The trade mark holder may oppose the marketing of the product where it was inappropriately packaged, as there may be damage to the reputation of the trade mark. (This was seen as particularly important in relation to pharmaceutical products, although the ECJ considered that a patient purchaser was more likely to be influenced by low-quality packaging than a healthcare professional.)

The ECJ further held that the trade mark must not contribute to the artificial partitioning of the market: Joined Cases C-427, 429 and 436/93 *Bristol-Myers Squibb and others* v. *Paranova*.

It should be noted that it is *not* the subjective intent of the trade mark holder which determines partitioning (unlike *American Home Products*). It is an objective test: the rights of the trade mark holder may be limited only to the extent that the repackaging undertaken by the importer was necessary in order to market the product in the Member State of import. Any further restriction would be an unreasonable restraint of parallel trade, and therefore illegal under Article 30.

In Case C-379/97 *Pharmacia & Upjohn* v. *Paranova* the ECJ again considered the importation of pharmaceutical products under trade mark. This time Paranova had purchased the products in France and Greece, where they were sold under the brand names 'Dalacine' and 'Dalacin C' respectively, substituting the name 'Dalacin' before importation into Denmark. The trade mark holder once more sought to prevent the sale of the imported products. The ECJ affirmed the approach in *Hoffman-La Roche* and *Bristol-Myers Squibb*. It held that, to determine whether a trade mark holder may prevent a parallel importer from substituting a trade mark from the State of export with a mark from the State of import, an assessment should be made as to whether it is objectively necessary to make the substitution in order that the product may be marketed by the parallel importer in that State.

In Case C-238/89 *Pall Corporation* v. *Dalhausen*, Dahlhausen distributed in the Federal Republic of Germany blood filters which it imported from Italy. The filters and packaging were marked 'Miropore', followed by the letter R in a circle (®). Pall sought to prevent Dahlhausen from using the ® symbol after the 'Miropore' trade mark on the ground that it constituted misleading publicity contrary to German law. The ECJ held that Article 28 prohibits the application of a national rule on unfair competition enabling a trader to seek, in the territory of a Member State, the prohibition of the distribution of a product bearing the letter R in a circle next to the trade mark, where that mark had been registered in another Member State, but not in the State in which the prohibition was sought: Case C-238/89 *Pall Corporation* v. *P.J. Dahlhausen & Co.*

Trade marks and luxury goods

A distinct line of case law has developed around the distribution of trade marked luxury goods, where the holder of the right has often invested in the brand which the trade mark represents.

Key case

In *Silhouette* the ECJ was concerned with the question of international exhaustion. Silhouette made high-quality spectacles under the trade mark 'Silhouette' registered in Austria (then a member of the EEA prior to accession to the EU). Hartlauer was a cut-price distributor of spectacles not permitted to distribute Silhouette's products. Hartlauer acquired a consignment of Silhouette's spectacles in Bulgaria and sought to sell them in Austria. Silhouette sought an injunction to stop Hartlauer from selling the spectacles under the Silhouette trade mark when they had not been put on sale in the EEA with the consent of the trade mark holder. The ECJ held (under Article 234) that national rules providing for the exhaustion of trade mark rights in respect of products put on the market outside the EEA under that mark by the proprietor or with his consent (international exhaustion) are contrary to Article 7(1) of the Trade Marks Directive: Case C-355/96 *Silhouette International* v. *Hartlauer.*

This approach was confirmed in Case C-173/98 *Sebago and Ancienne Maison Dubois* v. *GB-Unic*, but criticised by the UK High Court in *Davidoff* v. *A. & G. Imports* on the basis that the decision deprives parallel importers – and consumers – of access to cheap imports. The decision in *Silhouette* provoked discussion about the possible need for reform of the Trade Marks Directive.

Copyright

Differences between the level of copyright protection at national level do not permit a Member State to restrict the free movement of goods.

Key case

GEMA, the German copyright association, sought to rely on its German rights to prevent parallel imports of records from the UK which had been put on the market without GEMA's consent. The ECJ held that:

● Copyright in artistic works is within the term 'industrial and commercial property' in Article 30 and is therefore subject to the exhaustion principle. (GEMA was thus unable to use the German rights to keep out parallel imports.)
● It was irrelevant that the royalty rate in the UK was 2 per cent lower than in Germany, leading to a loss of profits by GEMA in Germany: Cases 55 and 57/80 *Musik Vetrieb Membran*.

In Case 341/87 *EMI* v. *Patricia* the copyright in the records of Cliff Richard had expired in Denmark but not in Germany. Patricia and other German recording companies sought to buy recordings in Denmark and import them for resale in Germany. The ECJ held that, although the recordings had been lawfully placed on the market, they had not been marketed by the holder of the copyright or with the holder's consent, but only because the copyright had expired. Thus, the copyright holder was able to rely on the mark, the disparity between the national laws amounting to an obstacle to the free movement of goods.

In Case 158/86 *Warner Brothers* v. *Cristiansen* local (Danish) law recognised a separate copyright in video rental rights from sale rights. The ECJ held that imports from one Member State to another could be blocked in relation to video rental rights (where the rights were not exhausted), but not in relation to sale (where the rights were exhausted).

In Case C-200/96 *Metronome Musik GmbH* v. *Musik Point Hokamp GmbH* the ECJ ruled on the validity of Article 1(1) of Directive 92/100 on rental and lending rights and on certain aspects of copyright. Emphasising the need for the holder of the right to obtain an adequate return on investment, the Court considered that the distinction between specific rental and lending right and distribution right was justified, It followed that the introduction of an exclusive rental right in German law did not infringe the principle of exhaustion of the distribution right, the purpose and scope of which are different.

● Registered designs

The ECJ has emphasised the importance of obtaining the consent of the holder of the right before exhaustion of rights may occur.

Key case

The proprietor in the Netherlands of a registered design for a handbag sought to prevent the importation into the Netherlands of an identical bag, made in France to a design registered to another owner. HELD (ECJ): The proprietor of the right was entitled under Article 30 to rely on the right to prevent importation from France where the bags had been manufactured without the consent of the owner of the right: Case 144/81 *Keukoop BV* v. *Nancy Keane Gifts BV*.

Renault was similarly found by the ECJ to be able to enforce its rights in Case 53/87 *Consorzio Italiano della Componentistica de Ricambio per Autoveicoli* v. *Régie Nationale des Usines Renault*. Renault sought to enforce its registered patent rights in designs for ornamental car body parts to prevent the copying of the designs, or marketing such parts in other Member States. The ECJ held that the holder of the right could rely on it to prevent the manufacture or marketing of copies of such parts in another Member State without the consent of the holder of the right. See also Case 238/87 *Volvo* v. *Eric Veng*, below.

Plant breeders' rights

The need to protect the investment of the holder of the right was also a factor in relation to plant breeders' rights in Case 27/87 *Erauw Jacquery* v. *La Hesbignonne*, a decision which may be relevant to other circumstances such as the licensing of computer software. In this case the holder of plant breeders' rights sought to enforce licensing agreements with various companies to propagate seeds for sale. The Court of Justice held that the plant breeder, having invested in the development of the basic product, should be able to protect himself against improper handling of the seed varieties and to control resale prices.

Common origin principle

The early position, now overruled in *Hag II*, was represented by the decision in Case 192/73 *Van Zuylen Frères* v. *Hag AG ('Hag I')*. Under *Hag I* it was considered unlawful, where different persons in different Member States held trade marks with a common origin, to prevent the sale in one Member State of goods subject to one of the national marks purely because the holder of the mark had national protection in that Member State. The common origin approach was restricted to trade marks, which were thought to pose a more serious threat to the free movement of goods than other property rights.

In *Hag II*, however, the Court reversed its earlier decision in *Hag I*. It recognised the role of trade marks in retaining customers' goodwill by permitting them to link the mark with a particular manufacturer's products or services.

Intellectual property

21

Key case

Hag GF AG was a German company which produced and distributed decaf-feinated coffee according to the process it had devised. It registered two trade marks under the name 'Kaffee Hag' in Belgium where it established a wholly owned subsidiary company, Café Hag SA. The subsidiary company held several trade marks, one of which bore the mark 'Café Hag'. Café Hag SA was seques-trated in 1944 as enemy property, being subsequently sold by the Belgian auth-orities to the Van Oevelen family. In 1971 Café Hag SA transferred the trade marks in Benelux to Van Zuylen Frères, a Belgian firm which was later transformed into a company known as SA CNL-Sucal NV. The German company, Hag GF AG, claimed that its product 'Kaffee Hag' was a famous brand in Germany, superior to the coffee produced by Sucal, and sought in the German courts to restrain Sucal from infringing its trade mark.

The ECJ held under Article 234 that Articles 28 and 30 EC do not prevent national legislation from allowing an undertaking which was the proprietor of a trade mark in one Member State from opposing the importation from another Member State of similar goods bearing an identical or confusingly similar trade mark to the protected mark. Reliance on a trade mark in these circumstances remained possible even when the mark under which the disputed product had been imported had initially belonged to a subsidiary of the undertaking which was opposing the importation and had been acquired by a third undertaking fol-lowing the sequestration (compulsory purchase) of that subsidiary: Case C-10/89 *SA CNL-Sucal NV v. Hag GF AG ('Hag II')*.

It should be noted that national laws on intellectual property may not be invoked, in the absence of unfair competition, merely because the public may be misled as to the origin of the goods: Case 177/83 *Theodor Kohl KG* v. *Ringelham and Rennett SA*.

Goods from third countries

Where undertakings within the EC seek to enforce their rights in intellectual property to prevent goods from third countries entering the EC, there is no contravention of Articles 28–30 on the free movement of goods: Case 51/75 *EMI* v. *CBS*. In this case trade mark disputes had arisen before the courts in the UK, Denmark and Germany over the importation of records manufactured by CBS in the USA with the trade mark 'Columbia'. EMI was therefore entitled to enforce the trade mark which it held throughout the EC against CBS, the holder (through a subsidiary) of the US trade mark.

INTELLECTUAL PROPERTY RIGHTS AND COMPETITION LAW

Intellectual property rights by their nature restrict competition. As we have seen, the ECJ has drawn a clear distinction between the *existence* of such rights and their *exercise*: Cases 56 and 58/64 *Consten and Grundig* v. *Commission*: see above. The existence of intellectual property rights does not necessarily infringe competition law: Case 40/70 *Sirena srl* v. *EDA srl*. The exercise of these rights may, however, restrict competition under Article 81 or constitute an abuse of a dominant position under Article 82.

Improper exploitation of intellectual property rights

Any exploitation of intellectual property rights which contravenes Article 81(1) is illegal: *Consten and Grundig*. Any agreement or concerted practice or abuse by a dominant undertaking such as the maintenance of artificial price levels or imposition of discriminatory conditions may contravene either Article 81 or Article 82, depending on the circumstances.

Key case

GEMA, a performing rights society in Germany, required copyright holders who wished to become members to assign all their rights, present and future, throughout the world until five years after leaving the society. Contractual rights were extended to cover non-copyright works. Only German residents could become ordinary members, foreign residents being excluded from valuable rights. HELD (Commission): The unfair conditions imposed as a result of the dominance of GEMA constituted an abuse under Article 82: *Re GEMA* (1971).

Non-discrimination and intellectual property rights

Discrimination against EC nationals on grounds of nationality in intellectual property rights contravenes Article 12 (ex 6 EC). Such a breach (then of Article 7 EC) was found by the ECJ in *Patricia* v. *EMI* (Case C-326/92). The case arose out of the failure of German law to allow Cliff Richard the same level of protection as German nationals in relation to unauthorised recordings of his music. A similar breach occurred in relation to Phil Collins. The ECJ held in a joint ruling with Case C-326/92 that denying the rock star the right to prevent unauthorised recordings made in Germany of concerts in the USA infringed Article 7: Case C-92/92 *Collins* v. *Imtrat Handelsegesellschaft*.

Licences

The ECJ confirmed in Case 24/67 *Parke, Davis & Co. Ltd* v. *Probe* that the distinction between the existence and exercise of rights in relation to trade marks applied equally to patent licences. The Commission followed the same line of reasoning in a series of patent licensing cases, culminating in *Windsurfing International Inc.* v. *Commission* (Case 193/83), a decision upheld by the ECJ.

Key case

The owners of patent licences in a special sail rig which comprised sail, mast, mast foot and curved booms for use with sailboards sought to impose on its licensees restrictions contrary to Article 81(1). These restrictions required the licensee: (a) to sell only complete sailboards rather than the patented rig on its own, with royalties charged on the complete sailboard, (b) to exploit the patents for the rigs, only to make sailboards using hulls approved by Windsurfing International, (c) to manufacture only at a specified plant and (d) not to challenge the licensed patents. HELD (ECJ, Article 230): Such provisions constituted an improper exercise of intellectual property rights contrary to Article 81(1): Case 193/83 *Windsurfing International Inc.* v. *Commission.*

In Case 238/87 *Volvo AB* v. *Eric Veng* the ECJ found that the refusal by the holder of an intellectual property right to grant a licence to another manufacturer was not an abuse of a dominant position, even though that manufacturer had offered to pay a reasonable royalty. The right in question was the design right owned by Volvo for the manufacture of spare parts, a similar issue to that in the Case 53/87 *Renault* case: see above. This decision should be contrasted with Case C-241/91P *Magill TV Guide*, where the CFI (and ECJ) took a very different line in relation to the supply of information about television listings: see below.

'No-challenge' clauses restraining the licensee from challenging the validity of an intellectual property right are usually found by the Court to be illegal. However, in Case 65/86 *Bayer & Hennecke* v. *Süllhöfer* the ECJ held that no-challenge clauses included as part of a settlement in a dispute over ownership or validity of intellectual property rights do not infringe Article 81(1).

In Case 320/87 *Ottung* v. *Klee* the ECJ held that an obligation on a licensee to continue paying royalties after the expiry of a patent does not necessarily restrict competition, unless the licensee may not terminate on giving reasonable notice or the licence restricts the licensee's freedom of action under termination.

● Specific subject-matter of the property

Both the Commission and the Court have ruled, in a number of decisions, that intellectual property rights may only be exercised to protect the specific subject-matter of the property concerned.

Patent rights

Patent rights require protection to reward the original effort of the inventor. Patent licensing agreements, however, infringe Article 81(1) unless exempted. The patent licensing block exemption in Regulation 2349/84 and the know-how licensing block exemption in Regulation 556/89 provided some protection until 1996, when both regulations were replaced by Regulation 240/96 on technology transfer agreements: see below.

Trade marks

The ECJ defined the specific subject-matter of a trade mark in Case 16/74 *Centrafarm BV* v. *Winthrop BV*: it is the protection of rights in the product, in order to protect the owner from competitors who sell goods improperly bearing the mark. Trade mark rights may not be invoked to prevent the parallel importation of goods bearing legitimate trade marks.

Copyright

There is no clear definition of the specific subject-matter of copyright. Conditions which are unnecessarily restrictive and discriminatory infringe the competition rules. A reciprocal copyright agreement between copyright management societies does not infringe Article 81 unless the terms of the agreement exceed what is necessary to protect the interests of members: Case 395/87 *Ministère Public* v. *Tournier*.

Key case

In the *Magill TV Guide Case*, Magill, a publisher complained to the Commission that the copyright in the listing of television programmes held by the *Radio Times, TV Times* and *RTE Guide* (for Ireland) contravened Articles 81 and 82. Under these copyright arrangements no publisher could publish a weekly programme schedule. The Commission decided that the refusal to allow third parties to publish a weekly schedule amounted to an abuse of a dominant position. The copyright owners were ordered to permit third parties to publish schedules by the grant of licences for which royalties would be paid.

The decision was upheld by the CFI, which accepted that the three television companies were dominant in the weekly listing of TV programmes, which constituted a separate market from the daily TV listings. While the existence of copyright did not necessarily amount to an abuse, the refusal to supply information to Magill was an abuse. The CFI considered that the essential function of copyright was 'to protect the moral rights in the work and to ensure a reward for the creative effort, while respecting the aims of, in particular, Article 86'. As the compilation of information on TV listings was not considered to involve creative effort, the companies were obliged to supply the information: Cases T-69/89, T-70/89 and T-76/89 *RTE* v. *Commission*, etc. The ECJ upheld the CFI decision in 1995 in Case C-241/91P.

The group exemption for technology transfer under Regulation 774/04

The fourth group exemption on technology transfer (the 'TTBER'), along with Guidelines, was adopted by the Commission in April 2004 as part of the modernisation programme. It came into force on 1 May 2004 and applies until 30 April 2014. The TTBER provides for a block exemption for technology transfer agreements. The Guidelines provide a framework of principles to administer Article 81 and intellectual property rights, as well as explaining the application of the TTBER and its relationship to Article 81(1) and 81(3).

As a result of the change, most licensing applications since May 2004 have been handled by the NCAs rather than the Commission. Liaison between the Commission and the NCAs takes place through the European Competition Network, as with other decision making under the devolved system. Considerations of space in this book do not permit detailed treatment of the TTBER. The main features of the Regulation are as follows:

- Article 1 defines the most important terms in the Regulation.

Key term

A **technology transfer agreement** is defined under Article 1(1)(b) to include a 'patent licensing agreement, a know-how licensing agreement, a software copyright licensing agreement' or a mixed agreement with elements from each type. There must be a transfer, so the term covers agreements such as a licence or sub-licence of the technology.

- Article 2 provides for the exemption of bilateral technology transfer agreements (i.e. agreements between two undertakings) within the Regulation.
- Article 3 sets out the thresholds for market share under the Regulation. Agreements will only benefit from the 'safe harbour' of the block exemption where their market shares do not exceed 20 per cent (if they are competitors) or 30 per cent (if they are not in competition).
- Article 4 provides a blacklist of 'hardcore' restrictions which will prevent the agreement from benefiting from the group exemption such as price fixing and allocations of market. There are separate lists for competitors under Article 4(1) and non-competitors under Article 4(2).
- Article 5 provides a list of excluded restrictions. These restrictions may be severed, so that the remainder of the agreement may be enforced.
- Article 6 enables the Commission and the NCAs to withdraw the benefit of the TTBER in certain circumstances.
- Article 7 enables the Commission to withdraw the exemption where parallel networks of similar transfer agreements cover more than 50 per cent of the relevant market.

Relationship between Articles 28–30 and Articles 81 and 82

The prohibitions in Articles 28–30 and Articles 81 and 82 apply cumulatively to intellectual property. As the provisions on the free movement of goods are fundamental to the EC, any conflict between the rules on free movement and the competition rules should be resolved in favour of Articles 28–30.

HARMONISATION OF INTELLECTUAL PROPERTY

Without further harmonisation of intellectual property rights, the exercise of intellectual property rights under national law continues to restrict the free movement of goods and to distort competition. Progress in relation to specific types of intellectual property rights, considered below, has been piecemeal. The position should change when the Treaty of Lisbon comes into force, as it provides, for the first time, an obligation in the Treaty to create Union-wide rights to protect intellectual property.

> **Key point**
>
> The Treaty of Lisbon will introduce an obligation under new Article 97A to establish measures under the ordinary legislative procedure to create European intellectual property rights. These rights will provide uniform protection of intellectual property rights throughout the Union and for the setting up of centralised Union-wide authorisation, co-ordination and supervision arrangements. The Article also provides for the Council to establish language arrangements for the European intellectual property rights under the special legislative procedure.

Patents

The wide differences in national approaches to intellectual property rights have led to a demand for integration at European level. There are two conventions in relation to patents.

1 The Community Patent Convention
The Community Patent Convention was signed in 1976 but has never been fully ratified. Under the Convention, which provides for the creation of a Community patent, recognised throughout the EC, litigation will take place in Community Patent Courts in each Member State, with a right of appeal to a Common Appeal Court. The Commission issued a Green Paper in 1997, concerned at the lack of progress on ratification. It proposed the adoption of a Regulation under Article 308 (ex 235).

2 The European Patent Convention
The European Patent Convention, in force since 1977, is not an EC measure but has been adopted by all the Member States and is effective in providing Europe-wide

protection for the States concerned. Under the Convention it is possible to obtain patent protection in some or all of the signatory States through a single application to the European Patent Office (EPO) in Munich. Patent rights, however, will have to be enforced separately in each country.

Decisions of the EPO have influenced developments on intellectual property rights in the EU, as the case of the 'Harvard mouse' demonstrates. In 1990, after prolonged review, the EPO considered the patentability of a mammal, with chromosomes modified by Harvard scientists to increase the chance of cancerous cell growth.[1] The Harvard scientists had sought patents for the mammal in a number of different jurisdictions, with mixed results. The EPO decided that animals which are the products of microbiological processes are patentable.

In 1988 the Council proposed a directive on the legal protection of biotechnical inventions, aiming to adapt existing patent law principles to establish a harmonised framework of standards to protect inventions. Directive 98/44 on the legal protection of biotechnical inventions was adopted by the Council and the EP in 1998. In response to ethical concerns, the Directive excludes from patentability the human body, processes for 'cloning' the human body, and plant and animal varieties. Products containing biological material are patentable under Article 3 if they are new, involve an intensive step and are susceptible to industrial application.

Trade marks

Directive 89/104, the first Trade Marks Directive, requires Member States to harmonise their trade mark laws in areas such as the rights conferred by a registered trade mark, although national trade marks continue to exist under the Directive. The Council adopted Regulation 40/94, under which a Community trade mark exists in parallel with national marks. A single application is made to the Community Trade Marks Office based in Alicante, Spain, with appeal to the CFI and ECJ. Rights may be enforced in Community Trade Mark Courts designated by the Member States.

Copyright

The Copyright Directive 93/98 harmonised the duration of copyright and related rights in the EC. It built on the Berne Copyright Convention to which all the Member States are signatories under international law and which provides a common level of copyright. Under Directive 93/98 copyright protection lasts for 70 years from the death of the author while the period of related rights (e.g. for performers) lasts for 50 years. The Directive also provides that distribution rights will not be exhausted except by sale in the EEA by the copyright holder or with his consent.

Directive 91/250 on computer programs was adopted in 1991, providing for protection of computer programs in the way that they are expressed but not of the underlying principles. Directive 96/9 provides for the legal protection of databases.

[1] http://www.newscientist.com/articlemg13217910.800-europe-rethinks-patent-on-the-Harvard-mouse

Directive 98/71 on the harmonisation of design rights was adopted in 1998, but there are gaps in its provision, with no coverage for spare parts for complex products. In 1999 the Commission presented an amended proposal for a single European registration procedure for industrial designs, administered by the Office for Harmonisation in the Internal Market, based in Alicante. However, it has proved impossible to adopt amending legislation.

Directive 92/100 was introduced to cover rental rights, lending rights and some aspects of copyright. The validity of the measure was unsuccessfully challenged in Case C-200/96 *Metronome Musik GmbH* v. *Music Point Hokamp GmbH*: see above. Harmonisation also occurred in relation to satellite broadcasting and cable transmission in Directive 93/83.

QUESTIONS

1 **When are rights in intellectual property said to be 'exhausted'? Consider this question in relation to patents, trade marks, copyright and registered designs.**

2 **In what ways may intellectual property rights infringe EC competition rules? Consider this question with particular reference to patent licences.**

Further reading

Aitman, D. and Jones, A. (2003) 'Competition and Copyright: Has the copyright owner lost control?', (2003) EIPR 137.

Anderman, S. D. and Kallaugher, J. (2006) *Techonology Transfer and the New EU Competition Rules: Intellectual Property after Modernisation*, Oxford University Press.

Cornish, W. R. (2007) *Intellectual Property: Patents, Copyright, Trade Marks and Allied Rights*, 6th edition, Sweet and Maxwell, Chapters 3 and 7.

Jones, A. and Sufrin, B. (2008) *EC Competition Law: Text, Cases and Materials*, 3rd edition, Oxford University Press, Chapter 11.

Korah, V. (2006) *Intellectual Property Rights and the EC Competition Rules*, Hart Publishing.

Korah, V. (2007) *An Introductory Guide to EC Competition Law and Practice'*, 9th edition, Hart Publishing, Chapters 10 and 11.

Shae, N. (1997) 'Parallel Importers' Use of Trade Marks', (1997) EIPR 103.

Visit **http://www.mylawchamber.co.uk/kent** to access answer guidance to questions in the book to test yourself on this chapter.

22 Competition law and state regulation

INTRODUCTION

This chapter covers the position of public undertakings under Article 86 (ex 90) and the restrictions on State aids (subsidies) in Articles 87–89 (ex 92–94) of the EC Treaty. The regime providing for a particular category of public undertakings, state monopolies of a commercial character, was examined in Chapter 11 in relation to the free movement of goods.

PUBLIC UNDERTAKINGS

The obligation under Article 86(1)

Article 86(1) provides that, in the case of public undertakings and undertakings to which Member States grant special or exclusive rights, Member States must neither enact nor maintain in force any measure contrary to the rules in Article 12 and Articles 81–89. Article 86 only began to be enforced in the mid 1980s.

In the early years of the Community, there was no real enforcement of Article 86, due to a belief that the state should be the main provider of public services. This view was challenged during the 1980s as Member States such as the UK embarked on extensive programmes of privatisation.[1] The Maastricht Treaty ensured that the change of emphasis was reflected in the EC Treaty which was amended to make explicit that the activities of Member States and the Community will include the adoption of economic policy based on the internal market and 'conducted in accordance with the principle of an open market economy with free competition': Article 4EC.

Categories of undertaking in Article 86(1)

The term 'undertaking' was considered in Chapter 18 in the context of Article 81. In relation to Article 86, the ECJ held in Case 155/73 Italy v. Sacchi, that even where the

---

[1] Chalmers et al. (2006: 1114–1115).

main objects of a company are non-economic, it will be considered an under-taking to the extent to which it engages in economic activity. If a local authority, for example, exercises its sovereign powers or acts as a consumer, it will not be con-sidered to be an undertaking for competition purposes, but if it engages in entre-preneurial activities such as carrying on a retail business, it will be considered a public undertaking subject to Articles 81 and 82.

To avoid inconsistencies arising from different national definitions of public under-takings the ECJ adopted the definition of public undertaking in Directive 80/723, the Transparency Directive, in Joined Cases 188–190/80 *France, Italy and the United Kingdom* v. *Commission*: see below. The Directive defines a public undertaking as 'any undertaking over which the public authorities may exercise directly or indirectly a dominant influence by virtue of their ownership of it, their financial participation therein, or the rules which govern it'.

Examples of public undertakings

Public undertakings include the following, when acting in a commercial context: cen-tral and local government, public services or authorities, as well as state-controlled undertakings acting under private law where the state exerts a dominant influence.

In Dec. 85/206 *Aluminium Products*, various producers of aluminium in Eastern Europe (before the collapse of Communism) claimed that Article 81(2) did not apply to them because under socialist law they were inseparable from the state and were thus entitled to sovereign immunity under international law. The Commission rejected their claim, holding that they were undertakings.

Scope of the obligation under Article 86(1)

It is not clear whether the duty of Member States is limited to a standstill provision, reinforced by the need to take positive measures to undo prohibitions, with account-ability for the behaviour of public undertakings, or whether Article 86 imposes a positive duty on States to act.

Key case

Under the green card system of motor insurance a measure gave a national insurance bureau sole responsibility for settling claims for damage caused by foreign vehicles. HELD (ECJ): The measure did not contravene under Article 86(1) (in conjunction with Articles 81 and 82): Case 90/76 *Van Ameyde* v. *UCI*.

Member States are responsible under Article 86(1) independently of any violation of EC law by the undertaking in question. In some cases the undertaking need not itself have acted, for example if it has received state aids contrary to Article 87. Where the undertaking has broken EC law (e.g. Article 81), the legal position of the

Member State is determined not under the same provision as the undertaking but under Article 86(1).

There is no ECJ ruling as to whether Article 86(1) is directly effective. In practice, it depends on whether it relates to a legal provision which is itself directly effective (e.g. Article 82).

Application of Article 86(1)

The practical effect of Article 86(1) is that a breach of EC competition law does not arise out of the mere existence of state-regulated activity. It depends how that power is exercised. In *Höfner* v. *Macrotron*, for example, a state measure which compelled an undertaking to infringe Article 82 was illegal under Article 86(1).

Key case

A German rule required persons looking for employment to contact potential employers through a state-licensed agency with exclusive powers in this area. HELD (ECJ): A breach of Article 86(1) had occurred where national rules restricted sources of supply without state ability to meet demand: Case C-41/90 *Höfner* v. *Macrotron*.

The developing case law of the ECJ demonstrates that an exclusive reservation of activities by the State raises a presumption that Article 86(1) has been infringed, giving rise to the possibility of a challenge in the national courts by a rival operator. In Case C-260/89 *ERT* v. *DEP* (the *Greek Broadcasting* case) it appeared that giving an exclusive right to an undertaking to retransmit foreign programmes to an undertaking already holding exclusive domestic broadcasting rights amounted to an abuse.

Key case

Italian law gave the port authority the exclusive rights to load and unload all ships at Genoa. Dominance was clearly established. Practices arising out of exclusive rights including excessive prices and the failure to use new technology were held to be an abuse: Case C-179/90 *Merci Convenzionali Porto di Genova* v. *Siderurgica*.

Exception for entrusted undertakings and fiscal monopolies: Article 86(2)

Under Article 86(2) undertakings entrusted with the operation of services of general economic interest or having the character of a revenue-producing monopoly are subject to the rules of Treaty except where the performance of particular tasks assigned to the undertakings is likely to be obstructed. A limitation is placed on the exception in that the development of trade must not be affected to such an extent that would be contrary to the interests of the Community: see Case C-393/92 *Municipality of Almelo*. Undertakings covered by Article 86(2) are likely to be State controlled. There are two categories: entrusted undertakings (the more important category) and undertakings with the character of a revenue-producing monopoly.

Entrusted undertakings

The category of 'entrusted undertakings' has been strictly defined by the ECJ. The key factor is that the State must have taken legal steps to secure the operation of services by the undertaking in question. This definition excludes an undertaking created by private initiative for the management of intellectual property rights: Case 127/73 *BRT v. SABAM*. 'Operation of services' appears to require the organisation of a regular performance (e.g. in relation to public utilities).

The phrase 'of general economic interest' indicates that there must be economic activity even if the aims are social. Examples include telecommunications undertakings and water supply companies, but not a bank transferring its customer's funds from one Member State to another: Case 172/80 *Züchner v. Bayerische Vereinsbank (Bank charges)*.

Examples of entrusted undertakings in the UK *before* privatisation included British Gas, British Rail, regional electricity boards, the BBC, British Airways *but not* British Coal (which produced a commodity rather than services).

Undertakings having the character of a revenue-producing monopoly

The main purpose of such undertakings is to raise revenue for the government through exploitation of an exclusive right (e.g. a state monopoly in the supply of alcohol). As such undertakings usually operate as commercial monopolies, they are also regulated by Article 31. The ensuing references to entrusted undertakings should be taken to include fiscal monopolies. The activities of such a monopoly may benefit from the exception in Article 86(2) (see below) but only to the extent that they relate to a revenue-producing function.

Exemption under Article 86(2)

An undertaking seeking to benefit from the exception must show that application of the rules under the Treaty would obstruct the performance of tasks assigned to it. In Case 41/83 *Italy v. Commission* Italy failed to establish that condemnation of British Telecom's activities as contrary to Article 82 would prejudice the specific tasks of BT. It follows that it is only possible to rely on the exception of Article 86(2) after the effects of applying the normal rule become clear. The exception does not, for example, permit the relaxation of any procedural rules. Usher has commented[2] that it appears that, after *Italy* v. *Commission*, Article 86 is relevant only to those activities of a public undertaking required or imposed by the State. The commercial activities of such an undertaking would be regulated by Articles 81 and 82.

Article 86(2) and the national courts

The main issue is the extent to which a claim that a matter is covered by the exception in Article 86(2) interferes with other provisions which normally create rights for individuals before their national courts.

In Case 101/71 *Ministère Public of Luxembourg* v. *Hein, née Muller* the defendants were prosecuted in Luxembourg for the unauthorised use of a wharf contrary to legislation giving special rights to the Société du Port de Mertout. They claimed that the legislation infringed EC competition law. The ECJ held under Article 234 that, as against entrusted undertakings, EC provision cannot be invoked by individuals in the national courts. In Case 155/73 *Sacchi* the ECJ reaffirmed that the general principles of the Treaty apply to entrusted undertakings, while creating a limited exception in their favour.

> **Key case**
>
> An Italian court referred to the ECJ the question of compatibility with the Treaty of a measure extending the national broadcasting monopoly, RAI. The ECJ held that the national court must ascertain the existence of abuse. It is the function of the Commission to remedy the abuse within the limits of its powers. Even within the framework of Article 86, Article 82 has direct effect and confers rights on individuals before the national courts: Case 155/73 *Italy* v. *Sacchi*.

Application of Article 86(2)

Despite its ruling in Case 172/82 *Inter-Huiles* (*Syndicat Nationale des Fabricants Raffineurs d'Huile de Graissage* v. *Inter-Huiles*) that Article 86(2) cannot create directly effective rights for individuals, the ECJ appears to have changed its position. As a result of the decisions in Case 66/86 *Ahmed Saeed, ERT* v. *DEP* (Case C-260/89) and Case 311/84 *Belgian Telemarketing* (*Centre Belge d'Etudes de Marché-Telemarketing* (*CCBEM*)) *SA* v. *Compagnie Luxembourgeoise de Télédiffusion SA et al.*, it is clear that national courts are entitled to investigate whether the application of Article 82 would obstruct the entrusted undertaking in the performance of its tasks. These later decisions confirm the ECJ's interpretation of Article 86(2) in *Sacchi* that the exception is a limited one. The exception to Article 86(2) was successfully invoked in *Corbeau*.

---

[2] Usher (1993: 434).

Key case

In this case a public agency held a monopoly over postal deliveries in Belgium. The ECJ held (under Article 234) that the exclusion of competitiveness was permissible under Article 86(2) to enable profits to subsidise loss-making aspects of the business: Case C-320/91 *Paul Corbeau*.

See also Case C-18/93 *Corsica Ferries France SA* v. *Gruppo Antichi Ormaggiatori del Porto di Genova Coop. arl* in which exclusive rights of a Member State to manage mooring services were found not to infringe Articles 81, 82 and 86(2).

Article 86(3): the powers of the Commission

The Commission is obliged under Article 86(3) to ensure that Article 86 is applied, to which purpose it is empowered to issue directives or decisions. It is also open to the Commission to use its other powers, for example, under Regulation 1/2003. The Commission does not have to wait for an infringement to act under Article 86(3), but may take preventive measures which are legally binding. The first directive adopted under Article 86(3) was Directive 80/723 on the transparency of financial relations between Member States and public undertakings: see above. Under the Directive, Member States must keep accounts of such relations for five years and make information available to the Commission on request.

Key case

The procedure under the Directive was invoked for the first time in 1983 requiring Member States to submit accounts for the previous three years in relation to certain aspects in industries involving public undertakings: motor vehicles, man-made fibres, textile machinery, shipbuilding and tobacco products. France, Italy and the UK claimed that Directive 80/723 was *ultra vires* and discriminated against public undertakings. Both claims were rejected by the ECJ: Joined Cases 188–190/80 *France, Italy and the United Kingdom* v. *Commission (the Transparency Directive case)*.

Decisions under Article 86(3)

The first decision of the ECJ following Commission action under Article 86(3) was Case 226/87 *Commission* v. *Greece (the Greek Insurance case)*. The Commission ordered Greece to alter its domestic legislation requiring all public property in Greece to be insured by Greek insurance companies in the public sector. When Greece failed to comply, the Commission issued proceedings under Article 226, resulting in a declaration that a decision under Article 86(3) is binding in its entirety on the person to whom it is addressed. As a result the addressee of a decision under Article 86(3) must comply with it until the ECJ suspends its decision or declares it void.

In Case C-141/02P *max mobile* the ECJ held that the Commission's decision not to act under Article 86(3) was not susceptible of judicial review. The Court has also made use of Article 86(3) in the context of the 'essential facilities' cases: see Chapter 19. In Cases T-374 etc/94 *European Night Services* the CFI held that a product or service could only be regarded as essential where there was no real or potential substitute. This essential facilities principle has been developed by the Commission in a series of cases involving access to ports.

Key point

The owner of an essential facility is obliged to supply a competitor by providing non-discriminatory access to its facilities: *Sealink/B&I Holyhead: Interim Measures*.

Key case

The port of Rødby in Denmark was owned by a publicly owned body (DSB) which controlled the ferry route between Rødby and Puttgarden in Germany, in conjunction with German national railways (DB). The Danish government refused to allow two rival undertakings to gain access to the port or to build a terminal nearby to two other undertakings, preventing them from offering alternative ferry services. The Commission decided that DSB was in a dominant position in relation to the Rødby–Puttgarden route (air travel was much more expensive and only open to people without cars); its refusal of access to the two ferry companies eliminated competition on the route.

The Commission followed the decisions of the ECJ in Cases C-271, 281 and 289/90 *Spain, Belgium and Italy* v. *Commission* in finding that DSB's refusal to allow other shipping operators access to the port it controlled was an abuse under Article 82. The further refusal to allow the companies to build a terminal nearby extended the dominance of DSB. As a result, it found that DSB had infringed both Article 86(1) and Article 82: *Port of Rødby, Denmark* (Commission).

Article 86(3) as the basis of directives

The Commission issued a number of directives from 1988 as part of the process to liberalise competition in telecommunications, such as Directive 94/46 on satellite communications, Directive 95/51 on cable television networks, Directive 96/2 on mobile and personal communications and Directive 96/19 to implement full competition in the telecommunications market. Similar directives were adopted in relation to electricity (Directive 2003/54) and gas (Directive 2003/55). The use of Article 86(3) as the legal basis of the directive was challenged by France in Case C-202/88 *France* v. *Commission*. However, the ECJ held that the Commission may proceed by way of directive under Article 86(3) where the conferral of exclusive rights cannot be justified. It is likely that Article 86 will be used increasingly to regulate anti-competitive state practices in areas such as energy supply.

STATE AIDS

The giving of State aids or subsidies to a particular undertaking or industry distorts competition and undermines the free movement of goods. Nevertheless, such assistance may be a vital element in national, regional or economic policy during a recession or period of high unemployment. The EC Treaty regulates State aids in Articles 87–89 (ex 92–94). Article 87(2) prohibits State aids which distort or threaten to distort competition by favouring certain undertakings or the production of certain goods, where inter-member trade is affected.

Derogations are permitted by Article 87(2) and (3), provided they are not disproportionate: see, for example, Case 249/81 *Commission* v. *Ireland*, in which the 'Buy Irish' campaign infringed Article 28: see Chapter 12. Reform of the approach to State aids is taking place under the Commission's Modernisation programme – see below – to ensure that State aids are fewer in number but better targeted.

Considerations of space do not permit detailed treatment of State aids in this book. The main provisions in the Treaty are outlined, and reference is made to some of the extensive case law on the subject.

Aid compatible with the common market: Article 87(2)

Key point

Aid which is permissible under Article 87 cannot infringe Article 28 or Article 31.

Article 87(2) lays down a number of categories reflecting legitimate goals in which State aid 'shall be compatible with the common market'. These are:

- aid having a social character granted to individual consumers, provided that the aid is granted without discrimination related to the origin of the products concerned;
- aid to make good the damage caused by natural disasters or exceptional circumstances;
- aid granted to the economy of certain areas of the Federal Republic of Germany affected by the division of Germany after the Second World War, in so far as the aid is required to compensate for the economic disadvantages caused by that division.

Aid which may be compatible with the common market: Article 87(3)

Article 87(3) lists categories of aid which may be compatible with the common market as follows:

- aid to promote the economic development of areas where the standard of living is abnormally low or where there is serious underemployment;
- aid to promote the execution of an important project of common European interest or to remedy a serious disturbance in the economy of a Member State;
- aid to facilitate the development of certain economic activities or of certain economic areas, where such aid does not adversely affect trading conditions to an extent contrary to the common interest (SGEIs), followed by specific restrictions in relation to State aids to shipbuilding.

SGEIs are referred to in Article 86(2) as being subject to the rules of the Treaty, particularly on competition, to the extent that such rules do not obstruct the performance of any tasks assigned to them. From 2000 the ECJ has been faced with deciding whether financial support to the providers of such public services to meet losses or charges was compensation or State aid. In Case C-53/00 *Ferring* v. *ACOSS* the ECJ considered the status of a French sales tax applicable to pharmaceutical laboratories that had an exemption for wholesalers supplying pharmacies directly. It found that, although the exemption appeared to give an advantage to the wholesalers, this was balanced by the obligation to stock a full range of products. Thus it could be regarded as compensation if there was equivalence between the exemption and the obligation. The *Ferring* decision was criticised by Advocates-General in subsequent judgments, but upheld by the ECJ in Case C-280/00 *Altmark*.

Key point

Compensation will *not* be classified as state aid if the following four conditions are satisfied:

1 The recipient undertaking must have public service obligations to discharge, and the obligations must be clearly defined.
2 The parameters on which the compensation is based must be established in an objective and transparent manner, to avoid giving the recipient undertaking an unfair advantage over its competitors.
3 Compensation cannot exceed what is necessary to cover all or part of the costs incurred in discharging the public service obligations.
4 Where an undertaking with a public service obligation is not chosen in a public procurement procedure, the level of compensation must be determined on the basis of the needs of a typical undertaking (i.e. well run and taking into account receipts and a reasonable profit): Case C-280/00 *Altmark*.

Although the ECJ did not clarify the relationship between the judgment in *Altmark* and Article 86(2), the Commission adopted a package of measures in 2005 including an amendment to the Transparancy Directive, a decision on compensation and a framework to measure compatibility with State aid for measures which go beyond compensation.

- Aid to promote cultural conservation, where it does not affect competition in a manner contrary to the common interest.
- Such other categories of aid as may be specified by decision of the Council acting by qualified majority on a proposal from the Commission.

Procedure

Articles 88 and 89 provide a procedure for the application of Article 87. Under Article 88(1) the Commission must, in co-operation with Member States, keep all systems of existing aid under review. Under Article 88(3) the Commission must be notified of any plans to grant or alter aids in sufficient time to enable it to make comments.

If the Commission finds that existing aid is incompatible with the common market or is being misused, it may require the Member State to abolish the aid within a specified time (normally two months if unspecified: Case 120/73 *Lorenz GmbH* v. *Germany*). Failure to comply with a decision may lead to action before the ECJ under Article 88(2). Decisions may be challenged in the ECJ under Article 230. It should be noted, however, that Article 87 is not directly effective: Case C-354/90 *Fédération Nationale* v. *France*.

New aids may not be implemented until the Commission has made a final decision under Article 88(3). Unlike Article 87, Article 88(3) was held to be directly effective in Case 120/73 *Lorenz GmbH* v. *Germany*. As a result an individual may challenge a state aid in a domestic court where this aid has been granted without notification under Article 88(3) or implemented before the decision of the Commission: see, for example, in the UK, *R.* v. *Attorney-General, ex parte ICI* (1987 Court of Appeal), and Case 74/76 *Ianelli & Volpi SpA* v. *Meroni*, see below. Exceptionally, a Member State may apply to the Commission for a decision that an existing or new aid to be granted is compatible with the common market. Any proceedings initiated by the Commission will be suspended until the Council has made its attitude known under Article 88(3).

Key point

The Treaty of Lisbon will add a new Article 88(4) which enables the Commission to adopt regulations relating to the categories of State aids that the Council has, under Article 89, decided may be exempt from the procedure in Article 88(3).

Under Article 89 the Council may make regulations concerning the application of Articles 87 and 88, acting by qualified majority on a proposal from the Commission.

Compliance

Key point

Member States must comply strictly with the requirements of Article 88, in particular the duty to inform the Commission of plans to grant or alter aid.

Failure to comply may result in the Commission directing defaulting States to recover the illegal payments, for example the payments made by Renault and Rover in 1989. Such repayment may be recovered despite the legitimate expectations of the party in question: Case C-5/89 *Commission* v. *Germany*. Firms which have received illegally paid aid have only rarely been allowed to keep it, for example when the Commission has delayed adopting a decision under Article 88: Case 223/85 *RSV Maschinenfabrieken and Scheepswerven NV* v. *Commission*, or where it is impossible to recover the money: Case 52/84 *Commission* v. *Belgium*. Impossibility does not arise where the obligation to repay conflicts with national principles of company law: Case C-142/87 *Belgium* v. *Commission (Re Tubemeuse)*.

In Case C-232/05 *Commission* v. *France* the ECJ ruled that a Member State was at fault for failing to execute a Commission recovery decision because of its national legal system, rather than its conduct. It held that a national law providing for the actions against recovery orders to be automatically suspended should be left unapplied by national judges.

Scope of state aids

Nearly all forms of government activity could be interpreted as a form of aid: infrastructural and environmental controls, for example, may reduce the direct expenditure of industry and lead to a reduction in the cost of a product. Such general benefits are outside the scope of Articles 87–89, although they are covered by Article 97, which provides for consultation with Member States and the issuing of directives to remedy distortions in competition caused by differences between the provision laid down by law, regulation or administrative action in the Member States.

Under Article 87 a State aid may be granted 'in any form whatsoever', with no distinction made between aid granted directly by the State or by public or private bodies: Case 78/76 *Steinike und Weinleg*.

Key point

A State aid will be judged by its effect, not by its name or policy purpose: Case 173/73 *Italy* v. *Commission (Re Aids to the Textile Industry)*.

There are many different types of state aid, including preferential interest rates, investment grants or subsidies, purchase of shares above market value and special prices for power: Cases 67, 68 and 70/85 *Kwekerij Gebroeders van der Kooy*. However, a system of minimum pricing was not a State aid, but was subject to Article 28: Case 82/77 *Van Tiggele*: see Chapter 12.

Commission policy on state aids

The Commission has placed great emphasis on the applications of the rules on State aids in the approach to completion of the internal market in its annual report. In its *First Report on State Aids in the European Community 1989* it reported a dramatic increase over the previous 10 years in the number of cases notified and investigated and the number of complaints made by aggrieved competitors. Aid is only permitted where it will contribute to sound economic structures, to make an industry competitive. Regional aids on a national basis have been progressively co-ordinated since 1971 when the first formal guidelines on regional aids were introduced. General aids usually fall outside Article 87 and may occasionally be permitted for short periods to counter a serious disturbance in the economy of a Member State under Article 87(3).

The legitimacy of a state aid will be determined in most cases by the Commission, apart from the exceptions under Article 87(3)(d) and Article 88(2) which are decided by the Council. Aid which falls within the scope of the mandatory provisions of Article 87(2) must be permitted, whereas aid which falls within the categories under Article 87(3)(a) to (c) is within the discretion of the Commission.

A number of 'soft law' instruments have been adopted in relation to particular industries and activities, such as the motor vehicle industry (1997), synthetic fibres (1996) and research and development (1996). The Commission was given the power to transform these soft law instruments into Regulations under Regulation 994/98. It may also adopt regulations providing for group exemptions.

Modernisation

The Commission launched its State Aid Action Plan (SAAP)[3] in 2005, in order to provide a comprehensive reform programme to transform State aid into an effective EU policy for growth and jobs. The SAAP is underpinned by four principles:

1 less and better targeted state aid;
2 more emphasis on economic analysis;
3 more effective procedure, including better enforcement and greater transparency;
4 shared responsibility between the Commission and Member States.

The Commission adopted a number of measures to simplify the application of the rules on state aids in 2006, including new Regional Aid Guidelines (RAG) for 2006–13. Under the RAG, a regional aid map identifies the disadvantaged regions eligible for aid. A block exemption regulation for regional investment aid was adopted under which Member States no longer need to notify the Commission if their aid is within the RAG and relates to one of the identified areas. A new framework was

---

[3] SEC(2005)795-COM(2005) 107 final.

adopted to support research, development and innovation. The *de minimis* thresholds were revised, so that there is no need to notify state aid under €200,000 received from all sources over a three-year period.

Exercise of discretion

The discretion exercised by the Commission covers both the decision on validity and also the extent of the exemption: Case 67/87 *Walloon Regional Executive & Glaverbell SA* v. *Commission* in which modernisation aid granted to Glaverbel, manufacturers of glass in Belgium, was held by the ECJ under Article 230 not to qualify as an important project of European interest under Article 87(3)(b), as it did not form part of a transactional European programme.

Key case

The French government challenged a Commission decision that a loan below market rate provided by a body, the Fonds Industriel de Modernisation (FIM), constituted a State aid. The loan had been illegally granted without notification and it was incompatible with the common market. FIM was itself financed by a savings scheme where the investors received a lower rate of interest in return for tax exemption. The ECJ held that the French government could not argue that the loan was not aid unless it raised issues not considered by the Commission. It also ruled that inter-member State trade could be affected even if the undertaking to benefit did not export, provided that its production competed with imports from other Member States: Case 102/87 *France* v. *Commission*.

In Case 730/79 *Philip Morris (Holland) BV* v. *Commission*, the ECJ under Article 230 upheld a Commission decision refusing to allow the Dutch government to grant aid to Philip Morris, a Dutch cigarette manufacturer, to increase production capacity in competition with a number of other producers of cigarettes within the EC.

Rights of individuals

Articles 87 and 89 are *not* directly effective, being dependent on the exercise of discretion by the EC institutions: Case 74/76 *Ianelli & Volpi SpA* v. *Meroni*. Article 88, on the other hand, is directly effective. It follows that an individual may challenge a grant of aid in breach of Article 88(3) but may not act when there has been no such decision on the legality of aid.

Any person to whom a decision on a State aid has been addressed may challenge the decision before the ECJ under Article 230. Where a decision affects a whole industry it may not be challenged by individual members unless they form an organisation which participated in the proceedings leading to the granting of the aid: Cases 67, 68 and 70/85 *Kwekerij Gebroeders van der Kooy*. An individual complaint may be lodged with the Commission if the individual suspects that an illegal State aid is being granted. Any action or inaction arising may be challenged under Articles 230 and 232: Case 166/86 *Irish Cement Ltd* v. *Commission*.

Individuals will also be able to sue Member States in the national courts where illegal State aids have been granted in circumstances where the conditions are met: Joined Cases 46 & 48/93 *Factortame III/Brasserie du Pêcheur*, see Chapter 6.

QUESTIONS

1 How and why has the Commission's approach to the regulation of public undertakings evolved in the past 25 years?

2 To what extent does Commission policy on State aids strike a balance between free competition and the need to protect deprived regions?

Further reading

Arnull, A., Dashwood, A., Dougan, M., Ross, M., Spaventa, E. and Wyatt, D. (2006) *Wyatt and Dashwood's European Union Law*, 5th edition, Thomson, Sweet and Maxwell, Chapter 26.

Boegar, N. (2007) 'Solidarity and EC Competition Law', ELRev. 319.

Chalmers, D., Hadjiemmanuil, C., Monti, G. and Tomkins, A. (2006) *European Union Law*, Cambridge University Press, Chapter 25.

Craig, P. and De Burca, G. (2007) *EU Law: Text, Cases and Materials*, 4th edition, Oxford University Press, Chapter 28.

Jones, A. and Sufrin, B. (2008) *EC Competition Law: Text, Cases and Materials*, 3rd edition, Oxford University Press, Chapter 8.

Korah, V. (2007) *An Introductory Guide to EC Competition Law and Practice*, 9th edition, Hart Publishing, Chapter 6.

Usher, J. (1993) *Plender and Usher's Cases and Materials on the Law of the European Communities*, 3rd edition, Butterworths.

Winter, J. (2004) 'Re(de)fining the Notion of State Aid in Article 87(1) of the EC Treaty', (2004) 41 CMLRev. 475.

Visit **http://www.mylawchamber.co.uk/kent** to access answer guidance to questions in the book to test yourself on this chapter.

Use **Case Navigator** to read in full some of the key cases referenced in this chapter:

- C-46/93 and C-48/93 **Brasserie du Pêcheur** v. **Germany** and **R.** v. **Secretary of State for Transport, ex parte Factortame (Factortame III)** [1996] ECR I-1029

Part 4

THE SOCIAL DIMENSION

23 Social policy

INTRODUCTION

The Treaty of Rome contained no direct reference to the 'social dimension' of the EC. Policies were originally conceived in economic terms. There were references in the Preamble to the purpose of the EC which was 'to ensure . . . social progress' and in Article 2 in which the objectives of the EC were stated to include an 'accelerated standard of living'. The European Social Fund was established under Article 146 (ex 123) to facilitate the employment of workers and to increase their geographical and occupational mobility within the EC.

The Paris Summit of 1972 provided the starting point for the development of social policy beyond the four freedoms and was followed by the first Social Action Programme in 1974. The Programme set out objectives for full and better employment and for improvement of living and working conditions, leading to a number of employment protection measures on collective redundancies and the transfers of undertakings, which guaranteed continuity of employment on the transfer of an undertaking. The Single European Act (SEA) 1986, the Preamble of which refers to the Council of Europe's Social Charter as a source of inspiration, gave further impetus to developing the social dimension. The Community Charter of Fundamental Social Rights for Workers was adopted by 11 of the 12 Member States in 1989, with the UK dissenting, as the basis for further employment protection measures: see below. A Social Chapter was originally contained in a Protocol to the TEU and incorporated into the EC Treaty by the Treaty of Amsterdam in 1997. More recently, the declaration of the Charter of Fundamental Rights at Nice, increasingly cited in the ECJ, shows the continuing commitment to the development of rights based on social rather than purely economic considerations.

Legal basis for social policy under the EC Treaty

Prior to amendment by the TEU and the TOA, action in the social sphere focused on the free movement provisions under Articles 39–42 (workers), Articles 43–48 (establishment) and Articles 49–55 (services): see Chapters 14 and 15. In addition, Article 94 provided for the approximation or harmonisation of measures to improve social relations, and Article 95 was added by the SEA, under which measures to complete the internal market may be adopted by qualified majority. Article 308, requiring unanimity, may also be invoked in harmonisation. It allows action to be taken by the EC if it proved necessary to attain, in the course of the operation of the common market, one of the objectives of the EC, and the Treaty has not provided the necessary powers.

After the TEU, the main obligations on social policy are contained in Title XI and comprise three chapters:

- Chapter 1 Social Provisions: Articles 136–145,
- Chapter 2 The European Social Fund: Articles 146–148,
- Chapter 3 Education, Vocational Training and Youth: Articles 149–150.

Social policy under Articles 136–150

Chapter 1 Social Provisions

Article 136 draws on earlier sources such as the European Social Charter 1961, but sets out the objectives in a modern context, namely the promotion of employment, improved living and working conditions, proper social protection, a dialogue between management and labour, the development of human resources with a view to lasting high employment and the combating of exclusion. Under Article 137(2) Member States are required to pay particular attention to encouraging improvements, especially in the working environment, in the health and safety of workers, and to set as their objective the harmonisation of conditions in this area. This Article (which replaced the Social Chapter: see below) provides legislative powers (by qualified majority) to achieve the objective. Article 140 obliges the Commission to promote close co-operation between Member States in matters such as employment, labour law and working conditions.

Key point

The social partners are entrusted with an important role under Articles 137–139. They represent employers' and employees' organisations in Europe, having been introduced into the decision-making process by the Social Policy Agreement (now repealed and replaced by Article 137) and are consulted on new agreements on social policy. Partners able to conclude formal agreements are restricted to organisations satisfying Commission criteria.

So far only three organisations (UNICE, CEEP and ETUC) have participated, although more have been recognised. An unsuccessful challenge to the parental leave Directive was brought by UAPME, an organisation representing small and medium-sized enterprises in Case T-135/96 *UAPME* v. *Council*. The position of the social partners is governed by:

- Article 137(4): empowers Member States, at their joint request, to entrust the social partners with implementation at national level of Directives adopted under Article 137.
- Article 138: requires the Council to promote dialogue between management and labour, and to consult the social partners before submitting legislation in the social field.
- Article 139: empowers the social partners to reach agreements at Community level for implementation in accordance with the procedures and practices specific to management and labour and to the Member States.

Article 137 empowers the Council to adopt Directives by qualified majority vote in the following areas: improvement of the working environment to protect health and safety, information and consultation of workers, integration of those excluded from the labour market, and equality of opportunity and treatment between men and women. Other measures may be adopted by unanimity, including social security and protection of workers, protection of workers whose employment contract is terminated, and financial contributions for promotion of employment and job creation. Member States are permitted under Article 137 to adopt more stringent measures compatible with the Treaty.

Article 141 provides the principle of equal pay for men and women for equal work: see Chapter 24. Article 142 requires Member States to maintain the existing equivalence in paid holiday schemes. Article 145 requires the Commission to make reports on particular problems of social conditions.

Chapter 2 The European Social Fund

The European Social Fund (ESF) was set up by the EC Treaty in 1958 under Articles 146–148. The aim of the Fund is 'to render the employment of workers easier and to increase their geographical and occupational mobility within the Community', as well as facilitating their adaptation to vocational training and retraining. The ESF, with the European Regional Development Fund, the European Investment Bank, and other financial instruments is responsible for administering the structural funds by which harmonious development is to be achieved within the EU.

Chapter 3 Education, Vocational Training and Youth

Article 149 provides that the Community will contribute to the development of quality education by encouraging cooperation between Member States and, if necessary, supporting and supplementing their action, while respecting the responsibility of the Member States to decide on the content of what is taught. The Commission has developed an active education policy, with successful programmes of staff and student exchange such as ERASMUS and SOCRATES.[1]

---

[1] ERASMUS is the EC Action Scheme for the Mobility of Students; SOCRATES is the EC Action Programme in the Field of Education.

The Social Charter and Supplementary Action Programme

The Social Charter was adopted in the form of a declaration by the heads of State and government apart from the UK in December 1989 at the European Council. The Charter sets out 12 main social themes, later implemented in a Social Action Programme (SAP) which provides initiatives relating mainly to social security, freedom of movement, employment and working conditions, vocational training and the improvement of the working environment.

The Social Charter and Social Action Programme

In 1974 the Commission had published the first SAP to implement the Paris Summit.[2] There were three main objectives:

1 the attainment of full and better employment;
2 the improvement of living and working conditions;
3 increased involvement of the 'social partners' in decision making (representation of employers and employees at EU level).

Progress under the first SAP was limited. The most successful measures related to equality in the workplace: see Chapter 24, as well as measures on health and safety. While the ECJ continued to reach decisions extending on equality at work, economic recession and lack of support in the Council effectively ended the SAP as a mechanism to develop social policy.[3]

The Social Chapter

The Social Chapter (more correctly known as the Agreement on Social Policy) provided a mechanism for the adoption of measures in relation to the workplace for participating States which could adopt directives to advance the objectives of the Agreement. The UK was opposed to the Agreement at the time of its adoption and remained outside until a change of government produced a commitment to the Agreement.

Key point

The Agreement on Social Policy was incorporated into Article 137 of the EC Treaty by the TOA, with effect from 1 May 1999. Its provisions now bind all the Member States.

---

[2] Bull.EC Supp.2/74.
[3] Shaw *et al.* (2007: 349).

Measures adopted under the Agreement (now regulated by Article 137) include:

(a) Directive 94/95 to establish a European Works Council to promote worker information and participation. It applies to undertakings with 1,000 or more employees of whom 150 work in two or more Member States.
(b) Directive 97/80 on the burden of proof in sex discrimination cases.
(c) Directive 97/81 on the framework agreement on part-time work (following an agreement between the 'social partners', a decision-making process involving management and labour, created by the Social Policy Agreement). It requires that part-time workers are treated no less favourably than full-timers.
(d) Directive 96/34 on the framework agreement on parental leave (following a similar process to (c)). It allows three months' unpaid leave for either parent after the birth or adoption of a child up to the child's eighth birthday.

POLICY AREAS INTRODUCED BY THE MAASTRICHT TREATY

A range of new policy areas was introduced by the TEU to provide a legal base for action in new areas. After the Treaty, the Union's competence was extended to the following: culture (Title XII), public health (Title XIII), consumer protection (Title XIV), trans-European networks in transport, telecommunications and infrastructure (Title XV), industry (Title XVI), research and technological development (Title XVIII) and the environment (Title XIX).

Key point

Further policy areas will be introduced by the Treaty of Lisbon. The Treaty will add the word 'Space' to Title XVIII, providing in Article 172a for the Union to draw up a European space policy, with measures, excluding any harmonisation, to be drawn up by the EP and the Council under the ordinary legislative procedure. There will be a new Title XX on Energy.

Other changes

The Maastricht Treaty also saw the introduction of the concept of Union citizenship, providing residence and political rights under Articles 17 and 18 EC which did not derive from economic status: see Chapter 13. Social policy has remained high on the EU's political agenda as a result of the Lisbon strategy in 2000.[4] The Charter of Fundamental Rights, declared at Nice, further affirms the Union's commitment to rights of a social nature, with six chapters covering dignity, freedoms, equality guarantees, solidarity rights, citizenship rights and justice: see pp.75–77. As we have seen,

[4] http://europa.eu/scadplus/leg/en/cha/c11325.htm provides a summary of the Lisbon stategy.

the Treaty of Lisbon will give legal effect to the Charter, which should set the commitment to equality on a stronger footing.

Non-discrimination

The TOA empowered the Council in Article 13 (ex 6a) to legislate against discrimination in areas not previously covered by the Treaty. These new areas are not economic in nature, and include controversial areas such as sexual orientation and religion.

Key point

Without prejudice to the other provisions of this Treaty, and within the limits of the powers conferred on it by the Community, the Council, acting unanimously on a proposal from the Commission, and after consulting the European Parliament, may take appropriate action to combat discrimination based on sex, racial or religious origin, religion or belief, disability, age or sexual orientation: Article 13 EC.

A package of three measures was adopted under Article 13:

1 Directive 2000/43 (the race directive) prohibiting discrimination in employment on grounds of racial or ethnic origin.
2 Directive 2000/78, the general framework directive, for combating discrimination on grounds of religion or belief, disability, age or sexual orientation as regards employment and occupation.
3 Decision 2000/75, setting up an action programme to support and complement the implementation of the directives, mostly through the exchange of information and experience.

Key point

The approach in the framework directive represents a departure from the more familiar approach such as that adopted in Directive 76/206 to implement the principle of equal treatment as regards access to employment and other areas relating to working conditions: see Chapter 24.

The package of measures represented a significant move away from a purely economic basis for discrimination. Directive 2000/43 prohibits both direct and indirect discrimination on racial grounds, defined by reference to the 'particular disadvantage' experienced by the individual. This makes complex statistical analysis unnecessary.[5]

---

[5] Shaw *et al.* (2007: 387).

Commentators have noted the potential of the race directive to affect EU life and policy, especially in relation to third-country nationals.[6]

Directive 2000/78 represents the EU's commitment to 'gender mainstreaming', defined by the Council of Europe as 'the reorganization, improvement, development and evaluation of policy processes, so that a gender equality perspective is incorporated in all policies at all levels, at all stages, by the actors normally involved in policy-making'.[7] The introduction of gender mainstreaming into the policy language of the EU has been attributed to the accession in 1995 of Austria, Sweden and Finland.[8] It requires the EU to consider gender at all stages of the decision-making process.

Directive 2004/113 was adopted four years after Directive 2000/78 under Article 13 to prohibit discrimination on grounds of gender in relation to the provision of goods and services.

Directive 2006/54 was adopted on the basis of Article 141 to recast existing legislation on equal pay, equal treatment, occupational social security and the burden of proof: see Chapter 24.

Soft laws

The EC has made increasing use of 'soft laws' in relation to social policy in recent years. These laws may take forms such as non-binding recommendations, memoranda and codes of practice. Examples include the Code of Practice on Sexual Harassment 1992, the Equitable Wage opinion 1993 and a Memorandum on Equal Pay for Work of Equal Value. Although such 'laws' are not binding under Article 249 EC they must not be disregarded by national courts: e.g. see *Insitu Cleaning Co.* v. *Heads* (1995) in which the Employment Appeals Tribunal (EAT) in the UK invoked the EC Code of Practice to identify the types of behaviour which constitute harassment.

The EC has adopted five action programmes (SAPs) to promote gender equality, the last one running from 2001–05. It has also pursued a 'framework strategy' on gender equality, with a 'Roadmap' for equality (2006–10), intended to provide an integrated approach.

QUESTIONS

1 **Why did the EC decide to develop a social policy which moved away from the mainly economic base of the original Treaty of Rome?**

2 **How have changes in the Treaty evolved so as to strengthen the legal basis for social policy?**

---

[6] Bell (2000).

[7] Council of Europe, EG-S-MS (98)2 (1998) at p.10 available on http://www.coe.int/t/e/humanrights/equality/02_gender_mainstreaming/092_EG-S-GB(2004)RAPFIN.asp#TopOfPage.

[8] Beveridge (2007: 195).

Social policy

23

Further reading

Bell, M. (2000) 'Equality and Diversity: Anti-Discrimination Law after Amsterdam' in J. Shaw (ed.), *Social Law and Policy in an Evolving European Union*, Hart Publishing.

Beveridge, F. C. (2007) 'Building against the past: the impact of mainstreaming on EU gender law and policy', (2007) 32 ELRev. 193.

Chalmers, D., Hadjiemmanuil, C., Monti, G. and Tomkins, A. (2006) *European Union Law*, Cambridge University Press, Chapter 20.

Craig, P. and De Burca, G. (2007) *EU Law: Text, Cases and Materials*, 4th edition, Oxford University Press, Chapter 24.

Shaw, J., Hunt, J. and Wallace, C. (2007) *Economic and Social Law of the European Union*, Macmillan, Chapter 14.

Shaw, J. (ed.) (2000) *Social Law and Policy in an Evolving European Union*, Hart Publishing.

Whittle, R. (2002) 'The Framework Directive for Equal Treatment in Employment and Occupation: an Analysis from a Disability Rights Perspective', (2002) 27 ELRev. 303.

Visit **http://www.mylawchamber.co.uk/kent** to access answer guidance to questions in the book to test yourself on this chapter.

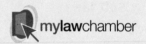

24 Equality of pay and treatment

INTRODUCTION

Under Article 141 (ex 119) EC Treaty each Member State is required to ensure and subsequently maintain the principle that men and women should receive equal pay for equal work. This obligation reflects both an economic objective (the avoidance of a competitive disadvantage in States implementing the principle) and a social objective (the improvement of living and working conditions of EC citizens): Case 43/75 *Defrenne*: see Chapter 6. In Joined Cases C-270 and 271/97 *Deutsche Post AG* v. *Sievers and Schrage* the ECJ held that the economic aim pursued by Article 141 is secondary to the social aim under the Article, which constitutes the expression of a fundamental human right. In addition to Article 141, Directives have been issued relating to equal pay for equal work, the equal value principle, equal treatment for men and women, equal treatment in social security, occupational pension schemes and self-employment, pregnancy, part-time work, and parental leave: see below.

Direct effect of Article 141

The direct effect of Article 141 enables claims for equal pay to be relied upon in the national courts both vertically and horizontally, in contrast with claims for equal treatment under the Equal Treatment Directives, which may only be enforced vertically against a Member State or public body: see below.

> **Key case**
>
> Ms Defrenne, an air hostess, sued her former employers, Sabena, in the Belgian courts. She relied on Article 141 (then Article 119), claiming equal pay on the same basis as male cabin stewards. The ECJ held in an Article 234 reference that Article 141 was directly effective from the date of the judgment both vertically and horizontally, entitling her claim for equal pay to succeed: Case 43/75 *Defrenne* v. *Sabena* (No. 2).

It follows from *Defrenne* that Article 141 applies equally in both the public and the private sectors. Employees and surviving spouses of deceased employees may invoke Article 141 directly against employers and trustees: Case C-200/91 *Coloroll Pension Trustees* v. *Russell*.

MEANING OF 'PAY'

Treaty definition

Article 141 provides that 'pay' means 'the ordinary basic or minimum wage or salary or any other consideration, whether in cash or in kind, which the worker receives directly or indirectly, in respect of his employment from his employer'. The ECJ has adopted a liberal interpretation to the question of what constitutes pay. The following have been held, in certain circumstances, to constitute pay.

(a) Non-pay benefits ('perks')
In Case 12/81 *Garland* v. *British Rail Engineering Ltd* the ECJ held that the grant of special travel facilities to former employees after employment constituted pay, even in the absence of contractual entitlement to such facilities.

(b) Supplementary payments
A supplementary payment by employers to male employees under 25 years of age, for the purpose of contribution to an employees' occupational pension scheme, was held to be pay under Article 141 in Case 69/80 *Worringham and Humphreys* v. *Lloyds Bank Ltd*.

In both *Garland* and *Worringham*, reliance on rights under Article 141 provided the basis for entitlement lacking under UK law, as s. 6(1)(a) of the Equal Pay Act 1970 excluded from its scope any provision made, in connection with death or retirement.

(c) Contributions under a contractual scheme
Contributions under an occupational pensions scheme are pay, unlike those under a statutory scheme: Case 170/84 *Bilka-Kaufhaus* v. *Weber von Hartz*.

Key case

The ECJ held that employer's contributions to an occupational pensions scheme under a *contractual* obligation were pay. In this case Ms Weber, a part-time worker, challenged her employer's occupational pension scheme. The scheme was non-contributory, being financed entirely by contributions from the employer. Part-time workers were excluded from benefits unless they had been employed by the firm for at least 15 out of 20 years. There was no such requirement for full-timers. As the majority of part-time employees were women, Ms Weber claimed that the scheme infringed Article 141. The ECJ held that a contractual (but not a statutory scheme) could fall within Article 141. Since the contributions were made by the employer to supplement existing social security schemes, they amounted to consideration paid by the employer to the employee within the meaning of Article 141: Case 170/84 *Bilka-Kaufhaus* v. *Weber von Hartz*.

The approach in *Bilka-Kaufhaus* is supported by the ECJ in *Barber* (see below) and Case C-7/93 *Bestuur* v. *Beaune*.

(d) Sick pay

In Case 171/88 *Rinner-Kuhn* v. *FWW Spezial Gebäudereinigung GmbH & Co. KG* a part-time office cleaner challenged German legislation permitting employers to exclude part-time workers (i.e. those working fewer than 10 hours a week, most of whom were female) from entitlement to sick pay. While such a claim might appear to be outside Article 141, the ECJ held that national legislation permitting employers to differentiate between two groups of workers, one of which was mainly female, infringed Article 141. This decision underlines the importance of the distinction between national legislation which *obliges* employers to differentiate between employees who are outside Article 141 and those where different treatment is *allowed* within Article 141.

(e) Retirement pensions

Retirement schemes within the state social security scheme are outside Article 141. However, the ECJ decided in Case 262/88 *Barber* v. *Guardian Royal Exchange Assurance Group*, a decision with important implications for pensions which is set out fully below, that a pension paid under a 'contracted-out' scheme was pay within the meaning of Article 141. Note that it is the prospective periodic payments rather than the employer's contributions which constitute pay: Case C-152/91 *Neath* v. *Hugh Steeper Ltd*: see below.

(f) Redundancy payments

Redundancy payments were held to be pay within Article 141 by the ECJ in *Barber*, irrespective of whether payment is made under a contract of employment, under statute or on a voluntary basis.

(g) Pensions paid to the spouses of deceased employees

The ECJ held in Case C-109/91 *Ten Oever* that pensions paid to the spouses of deceased employees were pay, but this was modified in Case C-200/91 *Coloroll Pension Trustees* to exclude single-sex pension schemes.

(h) Seasonal bonuses

These were held to be pay in Case C-333/97 *Lewen* v. *Lothar Denda*.

(i) Maternity pay

In Case C-342/93 *Gillespie* v. *Northern Ireland Health and Social Services Board* the ECJ held that the amount of maternity pay should not be so low as to undermine the protective purpose of leave. In addition, any pay increases awarded during a period of leave should be paid to the woman on maternity leave provided maternity pay is calculated by reference to pay received before taking leave.

Key point

It is clear from Case 80/70 *Defrenne* v. *Belgian State* (No. 1) that contributions paid into a *statutory* social security scheme used to calculate other forms of benefit are *not* pay within Article 141. The exclusion of statutory social security schemes from coverage by Article 141 was upheld by the ECJ in Case C-262/88 *Barber* v. *Guardian Royal Exchange Assurance Group*.

The *Barber* decision

The decision of the ECJ in Case C-262/88 *Barber* v. *Guardian Royal Exchange Assurance* is important, and illustrates a number of points on the nature of pay under Article 141.

Key case

Mr Barber was a member of a pension fund set up by Guardian Royal Exchange (GRE). The scheme was non-contributory and 'contracted-out' (i.e. a private, non-statutory scheme approved under UK legislation). Under the scheme, the normal pensionable age for women was 57 and for men, 62 years. The terms of Mr Barber's contract of employment provided that in the event of redundancy, members of the pension fund were entitled to an immediate pension on reaching 55 years (men) or 50 years (women). Mr Barber was made redundant in 1980, aged 52. He received from the GRE severance pay under the terms of his contract, statutory redundancy pay and an *ex gratia* payment. He was, however, refused payment of his pension until reaching pensionable age (62 years), although a woman made redundant in similar circumstances would have been entitled to an immediate pension. Mr Barber brought an action before an industrial tribunal, claiming unlawful discrimination contrary to the Sex Discrimination Act 1975 and EC law. The claim failed in the industrial tribunal and in the EAT. The Court of Appeal referred various questions to the ECJ for a preliminary ruling, the action having been taken over by the widow of Mr Barber after his death.

The ECJ held that:

● The benefits paid by an employer to a worker in connection with compulsory redundancy fell within the scope of Article 141, whether they were paid under a contract of employment, by virtue of legislative provisions or on a voluntary basis.

- A pension paid under a contracted-out private occupational scheme fell within the scope of Article 141.
- Article 141 was infringed where pension rights were deferred to the normal retirement age in a man made compulsorily redundant. Such a breach occurred in relation to a man when a woman made redundant would be entitled to an immediate pension, as a result of the application of an age condition varying according to sex (in the same way as the national statutory pension scheme). In deciding whether there is discrimination between the sexes, the court should consider each element of the remuneration separately, in accordance with the principle of 'transparency' in Case 109/88 *Danfoss*.
- Article 141 may be relied upon before the national courts, although its direct effect in pensions claims was limited to pension entitlement after the date of the judgment, except for cases pending before the national courts.

Impact of the *Barber* decision

Employers were required to harmonise pension ages for men and women in contracted-out schemes from the date of the judgment. (In practice, this usually meant at 65 years.) The ruling on temporal effect was incorporated into the TEU by a Protocol. The ECJ clarified the parameters of the *Barber* ruling in Case C-28/93 *Van den Akker* v. *Stichting Shell Pensioenfonds*. Between the date of the *Barber* judgment and the date of adoption of equality measures, equalisation had to be achieved without diminishing existing entitlements. After equalisation measures, the equality may be fixed at any level, including a less favourable level than applied previously. Directive 86/378 was amended to reflect Barber and later decisions, with Article 5 of the recast Directive 2006/54 consolidating the position: see below.

The position on equality of entitlement to pension may be contrasted with that on access to pension schemes. In Case C-57/93 *Vroege* the Court did not limit liability in relation to access to pension schemes in time as the position had been clear since Case 170/84 *Bilka-Kaufhaus*: see below.

In Case C-152/91 *Neath* v. *Hugh Steeper* the ECJ held that differentiation by the employer in contributions paid under a defined benefits scheme as a result of actuarial factors such as life expectancy are outside Article 141.

EQUAL WORK

Equal pay for work of equal value: Directive 75/117

Directive 75/117 was introduced to implement and define the scope of Article 141. Article 1 of the Directive introduced the principle of equal pay for work of equal value.

The case law under Article 75/117 will continue to be relevant, as an aid to interpreting the position under Article 14 of the recast Directive 2006/54.

Key point

Directive 75/117 will be repealed on 15 August 2009 by Directive 2006/54 which comes into effect on 15 August 2008. This is a recast directive on the implementation of the principle of equal opportunities and equal treatment of men and women in matters of employment and occupation. It consolidates the law, including Directive 75/117 (as well as the various equal treatment directives: see below) and the decisions of the ECJ.

Directive 2006/54 covers equal pay in a single chapter (Chapter 1), comprising a single Article (Article 4), in place of more detailed provision in Directive 75/117: see below.

Article 4(1) of Directive 2006/54 provides for the elimination of discrimination, either direct or indirect, on grounds of sex in relation to all aspects and conditions of remuneration.

Equal work

Under Article 1 of Directive 75/177 equal work means either the 'same work' or 'work to which an equal value has been attributed'. The 'same work' need not necessarily be identical work. It should include jobs displaying a high degree of similarity, following the submission of Advocate-General Capotorti in Case 129/79 *Macarthys* v. *Smith*. See also Case 69/80 *Worringham and Humphreys* v. *Lloyds Bank Ltd.*

Work of equal value

To determine whether a man and woman are engaged upon 'like work' a comparison should be made on the basis of an appraisal of work actually performed by employees of different sex within the same establishment or service; such comparisons, however, are not limited to men and women employed contemporaneously: Case 129/79 *Macarthys Ltd* v. *Smith*, nor to employment in the same State. A woman carrying out work of greater value is not entitled to be paid more than a male comparator: Case 157/86 *Murphy* v. *Bord Telecom Eireann*.

Direct and indirect discrimination

Discrimination in pay contravenes Article 141 where men and women are engaged in equal work or work of equal value and where it is based exclusively on the difference of sex of the worker. It may be either direct or indirect: Case 96/80 *Jenkins* v. *Kingsgate*

(Clothing Productions) Ltd. A clear example of direct discrimination may be seen in Case C-177/88 *Dekker* v. *Stichting Vormingscentrum Voor Jong Volwassenen* in which a pregnant woman was refused a teaching post. The ECJ held that since only a woman could be refused employment on the ground of pregnancy, such a refusal constituted direct discrimination based on sex, which could not be justified on the basis of financial loss suffered by the employer.

In several cases the question has arisen of whether a difference in pay between part-time and full-time workers constitutes a breach of Article 141.

> **Key case**
>
> Part-time workers (all but one of whom were female) were paid 10 per cent less than full-time workers. The ECJ held that a lower rate of pay for part-time workers did not necessarily infringe Article 141, provided the difference in pay was objectively justified and was in no way related to discrimination based on sex: Case 96/80 *Jenkins* v. *Kingsgate (Clothing Productions) Ltd.*

In Case C-127/92 *Enderby* v. *Frenchay Area Health Authority* the ECJ held that where statistics showed a real difference between pay for jobs of equal value where one is almost entirely carried out by women (in this case, speech therapists) and the other by men (pharmacists) the employer must show that the difference is objectively justified on grounds other than sex.

The ECJ ruled in another case involving discrepancies in pay between healthcare professionals in Case C-309/97 *Angestelltenbetriebsrat der Wiener Gebietskrankenkasse.* This case arose in Austria where social insurance institutions employed three different classes of psychotherapists: doctors who have completed GP or specialist training, graduate psychologists (qualified to practise) and others with a general education who had undergone specialised training in psychotherapy. The ECJ held that persons who perform seemingly identical tasks but who draw upon knowledge and skills acquired in different disciplines and who do not have the same qualifications to perform other tasks that may be assigned to them do *not* do the 'same work' for the purpose of EC law.

> **Key case**
>
> A part-time worker challenged her employer's occupational pension scheme, which discriminated against part-timers. This discrimination was suffered disproportionately by women since most of the part-timers were female. (Male part-timers constituted only 2.8 per cent of the total workforce.) The ECJ upheld its decision in *Jenkins* and held that, if a considerably smaller proportion of men than women worked part-time, and if the difference in treatment could only be based ➜

> on sex, the exclusion of part-time workers from an occupational pension scheme would infringe Article 141. Such difference in treatment would only be permissible if objectively justified by factors unrelated to discrimination based on sex: see below, Case 170/84 *Bilka-Kaufhaus GmbH* v. *Weber von Hartz*.

The Court in *Bilka* laid down guidelines as to what constitutes an objective justification for measures causing a difference in treatment, where there is indirect discrimination:

> If the national court finds that the measures . . . correspond to a real need on the part of the undertaking, are appropriate with a view to achieving the objectives pursued, and are necessary to that end, the fact that the measures affect a greater number of women than men is not sufficient to show that they constitute an infringement of Article 119 [now 141].

The guidelines were strictly applied by the ECJ in Case 171/88 *Rinner Kuhn* in the context of State legislation. The onus rests on the State to prove that the social policy objectives justify the means selected. In Case C-167/97 *R.* v. *Secretary of State for Employment, ex parte Seymour Smith* the ECJ held that the best way to determine whether a measure has a disproportionate effect on women is to compare the relevant statistics by considering the proportions of each sex able to satisfy the requirement (in this case, for two years' employment). The House of Lords considered the statistical differences to be marginal and the national measure objectively justified: *R.* v. *Secretary of State for Employment, ex parte Seymour Smith* (2000).

It is not necessary to justify the use of particular means, where they are considered appropriate as a general rule. In Case C-17/05 *Cadman* v. *Health and Safety Executive* the Court held that length of service could be used to determine pay as this was an appropriate criterion to attain the legitimate objective of rewarding experience without consideration in relation to a specific job unless the worker raised evidence of serious doubt in that respect.

In contrast, national legislation for a lower hourly rate for overtime for part-time workers (arising out of national legislation in relation to teachers) was found to discriminate indirectly against women and not to be objectively justified: Case C-300/06 *Ursula Voß* v. *Land Berlin*.

The Court found that the right to join an occupational pension scheme was covered by Article 141 in Cases C-57/93 *Vroege* and C-128/93 *Fisscher*. The exclusion of part-time workers from such schemes was held to be illegal, since it affected a disproportionate number of women. As a result, 60,000 part time workers in the UK brought claims in industrial tribunals. One such claim was Case C-78/98 *Preston and others* v. *Wolverhampton Healthcare NHS Trust,* a referral by the House of Lords. The case arose out of provisions under UK law which required workers to pursue a claim for retrospective membership of a pension scheme to within six months of ending their employment and which limited retrospective membership of the scheme to two years. While the six-month restriction was found not to contravene EC law, the limitation on membership infringed the principle of effectiveness, as it excluded from reckoning the period before the two-year point.

Assessment of equal value claims

Key point

Article 4(2) of Directive 2006/54 provides that job classification schemes, where these are used, shall be based on the same criteria for men and women, and drawn up so as to exclude discrimination on grounds of sex.

Article 4(2) repeats verbatim the provision in Article 1(2) of Directive 75/117.

Member States are required under Article 2 of the Directive to introduce into national legal systems the necessary measures to enable all employees who consider themselves wronged by the failure to apply the principle of equal pay to pursue their claims by judicial process after recourse to other competent authorities. Further, under Article 6, Member States must take the necessary measures to ensure that the principle of equal pay is applied and that effective means are available to take care that this principle is observed. This need not be by a job evaluation scheme.

In Case 61/81 *Commission* v. *United Kingdom (Re Equal Pay for Equal Work)* the UK was found to have infringed Articles 1 and 6 of Directive 75/117 by failing to provide a means of assessment of equal value claims in the absence of a job evaluation scheme. A similar ruling was made in Case 58/81 *Commission* v. *Luxembourg.*

Key case

The threshold conditions under the Employment Protection (Consolidation) Act 1978 excluded workers employed for fewer than eight hours a week, affecting women to a greater extent than men. The House of Lords held that parts of the Act contravened Article 141 and that this indirect discrimination was not objectively justified: *R.* v. *Secretary of State for Employment, ex parte Equal Opportunities Commission* (HL, 1994).

Criteria in job evaluation schemes

To avoid being discriminatory, the system for job evaluation must take account of the particular aspects of each sex. Criteria based entirely on the attributes of one sex may be discriminatory.

Key case

The Danish Employees' Union challenged criteria approved by the Danish Employees' Union and applied by the firm, Danfoss, including the criteria of flexibility and seniority. The ECJ held that where neutral criteria (e.g. flexibility) were applied, resulting in systematic discrimination against women workers, they must have been applied in an abusive manner. A system in which the criteria are not clear is described by the ECJ as lacking in 'transparency'. In such a case the proof of justification rests with the employer. Applying the principle of transparency, it would appear that each element of the remuneration package should be considered separately in an equal value claim. See also *Barber* in which the ECJ held that the application of the equal pay principle must be ensured in respect of each element of remuneration and not only on the basis of a comprehensive assessment of the consideration paid to workers: Case 109/88 *Danfoss (Handels-og Kontorfunktionaernes Forbund* v. *Dansk Arbejdsgiverforening for Danfoss).*

EQUAL TREATMENT IN EMPLOYMENT

The original wording of Article 141, prior to amendment by the TOA, was confined to pay and made no mention of equal treatment. This limitation was confirmed in Case 149/77 *Defrenne* v. *Sabena* (No.3), although the Court acknowledged that the elimination of sex discrimination was a fundamental human right.[1]

Directive 76/207 provided in Article 1(1) for the principle of equal treatment of men and women as regards access to employment, including promotion, and to vocational training and as regards working conditions, and to social security on the conditions referred to in Article 1(2). The Directive was based on Article 308 (ex 235), the general power of the institutions, as the harmonisation of living and working conditions was outside the scope of the equal pay principle. Exceptions to the principle were provided in relation to occupational qualification, pregnancy and maternity, and positive action: see below.

Key point

Directive 76/207, along with Directive 86/378, will be repealed and replaced on 15 August 2009 by recast Directive 2006/54. The implementation date for the recast Directive is one year earlier, 15 August 2008. Directive 79/7 on equal treatment in state social security schemes and Directive 2004/113 on goods and

---

[1] Craig and De Burca (2007: 908–909).

services continue to apply unaltered, as do the Directives on pregnancy and parental leave: see below.

The recast directive covers equal treatment in access to employment and promotion, vocational training, working conditions (including pay), and occupational social security. Title I covers the purpose and scope of the Directive, provides definitions and refers to positive action under Article 141(4) EC: see below. Title II provides the main substantive provisions, prohibiting discrimination on pay on grounds of sex in Chapter 1 Article 4: see above. Chapter 2 provides for equal treatment in occupational social security schemes. Chapter 3 covers equal treatment in access to employment, vocational training and promotion and working conditions. Article 14 prohibits direct or indirect discrimination on grounds of sex in public and private sectors: see below. Title III provides for remedies and enforcement in Chapter 1, the promotion of equal treatment through equality bodies and the social partners in Chapter 2, 'general horizontal provisions' in Chapter 3 on compliance, victimisation, penalties, minimum requirements, relationship to Community and national provisions, and gender mainstreaming (see Chapter 23 above), and dissemination of information.

The action provided for in Article 1(2) of Directive 76/207 was taken in Directive 79/7 on statutory schemes and Directive 86/378 on occupational schemes. Equal treatment is defined in Article 2 of Directive 76/207 as prohibiting all discrimination on grounds of sex either directly or indirectly by reference in particular to marital or family status. Derogation is permitted under Article 2(2): see below. The Directive has been invoked particularly in relation to the protection of pregnant women and mothers at work, to part-time employment and to retirement ages. The concept of discrimination under the Directive was extended to transsexuals: Case C-13/94 *P. v. S. and Cornwall County Council*: see below.

Key point

Article 14(1) of the recast Directive prohibits: direct and indirect discrimination on grounds of sex in the public or private sectors in relation to:

(a) Conditions for access to employment to self-employment or to occupation, including selection criteria and recruitment conditions, whatever the branch of activity and at all levels of the professional hierarchy, including promotion.

(b) Access to all types and all levels of vocational guidance, vocational training, advanced vocational training and retraining, including practical work experience.

(c) Employment and working conditions, including dismissals, as well as pay as provided for in Article 141 of the Treaty.

(d) Membership of, and involvement in, an organization or workers or employers, or any organization whose members carry on a particular profession, including the benefits provided for by such organizations.

Pregnancy and maternity

In Case C-177/88 *Dekker* v. *Stichting* the ECJ held that it was discriminatory to reject a woman as an instructor at a training centre on grounds of pregnancy. Such a rejection could only be made against one sex and thus amounted to direct discrimination. Refusal to appoint a pregnant woman for an indefinite period in order to comply with a national prohibition on employment infringes the Directive: Case C-207/98 *Mahlburg* v. *Land Meckleburg-Vorpommern*. However, the dismissal of a woman suffering from complications of pregnancy during maternity leave was held to be indirect sex discrimination and therefore capable of objective justification: *Hertz* (Case 179/88).

Key case

Ms Webb had been hired by EMO for an indefinite period while another employee was on maternity leave, though not specifically as a maternity leave replacement. She was dismissed when she herself was found to be pregnant. As she had not been employed for long enough to qualify for employment protection under UK law, Ms Webb sought to rely on Directive 76/207. The dismissal was found to be directly discriminatory contrary to the Directive: Case C-2/93 *Webb* v. *EMO*.

It could be argued that the decision in *Webb* did not cover women employed on short-term contracts as the ruling was specific to women hired for an unlimited period. This anomaly was rectified by Directive 92/85 which provides protection against dismissal for all pregnant employees, irrespective of the nature of contractual status. Article 10 of the Directive requires Member States to take the necessary measures to prohibit dismissal of pregnant workers other than in exceptional cases not connected with their pregnancy.

The Court found Article 10 to be directly effective in Case C-438/99 *Melgar* v. *Ayuntamiento de los Barrios*. It held that non-renewal of a fixed-term contract on grounds of pregnancy is direct discrimination contrary to Articles 2(1) and 3(1) of Directive 76/207. However, it also found that Article 10(1) of Directive 92/85 does not impose an obligation on a Member State to give its consent to the exceptional dismissal of a worker covered by the Directive. In Case C-109/00 *Tele Denmark*, the Court noted that the duration of a period of employment was usually uncertain, even where workers were taken on under a fixed-term contract and that the Equal Treatment and Pregnancy Directives did not distinguish between fixed-term and indefinite contracts.

The protection from dismissal under Article 10 not only prohibits notification of dismissal during the period of protection but also the taking of preparatory steps for such a decision. Thus a decision to notify dismissal after the period of protection is contrary to Articles 2(1) and 5(1) of Directive 76/207: Case C-460/06 *Paquay* v. *Société des Architectes*.

In Case C-506/06 *Mayr* v. *Bäckerei und Konditorei Gerhard Flöckner OHG* the dismissal of a woman at an advanced stage of *in vitro* fertilization (but before the transfer back into the ova of the fertilized eggs) was found to be outside the protection of Article 10 of Directive 92/85. The Court stated that the transfer might be postponed or may never happen. However, the dismissal of a worker in such circumstances amounted to direct discrimination contrary to Directive 76/207. The ECJ left it to the national court to decide whether the applicant had in fact been dismissed because she was undergoing *in vitro* fertilization treatment.

Directive 92/85 does not cover refusal to employ a pregnant woman. Neither does it nor Directive 76/207 cover dismissal after the expiry of maternity leave: Case 394/96 *Brown* v. *Rentokil*. Thus, if a woman is absent from work after maternity leave due to pregnancy or childbirth complications, she may be treated on a par with a sick man.

In Case 184/83 *Hofmann* v. *Barmer Ersatzkasse* the ECJ dismissed the claim of a father of a child in Germany for social security payment during a period of unpaid leave to look after a child when a mother would have been entitled to payment, holding that the Directive was not concerned with the sharing of family responsibilities but with the biological protection of the mother.

Parental leave

A Framework Agreement on Parental Leave was agreed by the social partners in 1996, leading to the adoption of Directive 96/34 under the Social Policy Agreement. This was extended to the UK by Directive 97/75. The Framework Agreement provides for a minimum level of parental leave of at least three months in the event of birth or adoption up to the age of eight years, to be specified by the Member States or social partners.

Retirement ages

The main provisions of Directive 76/207 which have been invoked in relation to retirement ages are Article 5 (conditions of work or dismisssal) and Article 6 (obligation to provide remedies).

In *Case C-207/04 Vergani* v. *Agenzia della Entrate, Ufficio di Arona* the Court held that a difference resulting from taxation (at a rate reduced by half) of sums paid on ceasing work (in this case, as a result of voluntary redundancy) for female workers reaching 50 years and male workers at 55 years constituted unequal treatment contrary to Article 5.

In Case 19/81 *Burton* v. *British Railways Board* the applicant failed to bring his application within the Directive because his voluntary redundancy at the same age as retirement was treated as covered by the Social Security Directive 79/7 which permits a derogation from the equal treatment principle. However, it is clear after the decision of the ECJ in *Barber*, that the calculation of pensionable age for the purpose of redundancy is now regarded as governed by Article 141: see above.

Determination of pensionable age 'for other purposes'

In Case 152/84 *Marshall* v. *Southampton and South West Area Health Authority* (No. 1) the ECJ distinguished *Burton* on the grounds that the benefits in *Marshall* were linked to a national social security scheme.

> **Key case**
>
> Mrs Marshall relied on Article 5(1) of Directive 76/207 to challenge the policy of the Area Health Authority which required women employees to retire at 60 whereas men could continue until 65. The ECJ held (on a reference from the EAT) that pensionable age was determined for the purpose of retirement, i.e. 'for other purposes' than those specified in Article 7 of Directive 79/7. Thus, it followed that the determination of pensionable age was not covered by the exclusion and Mrs Marshall could rely on Article 5(1): Case 152/84 *Marshall* v. *Southampton and South West Area Health Authority* (No. 1).

The ECJ has applied its approach in *Marshall* in Case 151/84 *Roberts* v. *Tate & Lyle Industries Ltd*, in which the applicant had challenged the compulsory early retirement scheme operated by her employers, with entitlement to an accelerated pension. The ECJ held that such a scheme fell within the scope of Directive 76/207, being a condition governing dismissal. To fix a different age for offering an early pension would be a breach of Article 5.

> **Key point**
>
> Article 9(1)(f) of the recast Directive provides that fixing different retirement ages for men and women contravenes the principle of equal treatment.

Derogation under Articles 2(2), 2(3) and 2(4) of Directive 76/207

Article 2(2)

Article 2(2) provides for exemption from the equal treatment principle for activities for which the sex of the worker constitutes a determining factor. In Case 165/82 *Commission* v. *United Kingdom (Re Equal Treatment for Men and Women)* the Commission brought an action against the UK government for failure to comply with Directive 76/207 in the Sex Discrimination Act 1975 which exempted from equal treatment employment in a private household and firms employing fewer than six staff. The ECJ held under Article 226:

- while individual exemptions might be appropriate in circumstances where the sex of a worker was a determining factor, blanket exemptions were not;
- Article 2(2) justified the UK in restricting male access to the profession of midwifery under s. 41 of the Sex Discrimination Act 1975.

Key point

The recast Directive 2006/54 provides for only one exception in Article 14(2): Member States may provide, as regards access to employment including training, that a difference of treatment based on a characteristic related to sex shall not constitute discrimination where, by nature of the particular occupational activities concerned or of the context in which they are carried out, such a characteristic constitutes a genuine and determining occupational requirement, provided that its objective is legitimate and the requirement is proportionate.

The areas of pregnancy and maternity, and positive action, are positively provided for in the recast Directive, rather than as exceptions.

There have been a number of decisions under Article 2(2) of the 1976 Directive in relation to the armed forces.

Key case

A female member of the Royal Ulster Constabulary (RUC) challenged an RUC decision to refuse to renew her contract of employment. The RUC had decided as a matter of policy not to employ any women as full-time members of the RUC Reserve as women were not trained in the use of firearms. HELD (ECJ, Article 234): Any claim for derogation from Directive 76/207 had to be decided in the light only of Directive 76/207, and not Article 48(3), as claimed by the RUC. There was no public safety exception to Directive 76/207. The national court was to decide how national legislation should be interpreted: Case 222/84 *Johnston* v. *Chief Constable of the RUC.*

In Case C-273/97 *Sirdar* v. *The Army Board and Secretary of State for Defence* the ECJ held that, normally, national decisions on the management of the armed forces must observe the principle of equal treatment between men and women. As special combat units pursuing activities for which sex is a determining factor, the Royal Marines are entitled to exclude women. However, in Case C-285/98 *Kreil* v. *Bundesrepublik*

Deutschland the Court held that a general exclusion of women from military posts including the use of arms allowing them only access to the medical and military-music services infringed the Directive.

The Court reached a very different conclusion in the third referral from a German court in relation to military service in Case C-186/01 *Dory* v. *Germany*. The case arose from a challenge by a German man that military service was only compulsory for men. Dory claimed that the requirement to complete military service delayed his entry into the labour market, putting him at a disadvantage relative to a woman. Unwilling to interfere with the very basis of military service in Germany, the Court held that Directive 76/207 did *not* apply to the rule limiting compulsory military service to men only. It found that the delay in entering the workforce for persons called up for military service was the inevitable result of the Member State's choice regarding military organisation and 'does not mean that that choice comes within the scope of Community law'. To rule otherwise, the Court found, would have forced Germany either to abolish compulsory military service or extend compulsory service to women.

Article 2(3)

Article 2(3) provides for the protection of women in relation to pregnancy. There are no equal benefits for men: Case 184/83 *Hofmann* v. *Barmer Ersatzkasse*, see above.

Article 2(4)

Article 2(4) permits measures giving 'a specific advantage to women with a view to improving their ability to compete on the labour market and to pursue a career on an equal footing with men': Case C-450/93 *Kalanke* v. *Frei Hausestadt Bremen*, but not affirmative action such as the use of quotas. Article 2(4) of the Directive states that it is 'without prejudice to measures to promote equal opportunity for men and women, in particular, by removing existing inequalities which affect women's opportunities in areas referred to in Article 1(1)'. This Article provided the basis for the decision in Case C-450/93 *Kalanke* v. *Frei Hausestadt Bremen*, the first case in the ECJ to raise the issue of positive action.

Key case

The case arose out of a reference from a German court faced with a challenge to a national measure which gave priority to women job applicants in areas where they were under-represented when both male and female candidates were equally qualified. The ECJ ruled that Article 2(4) permits measures 'giving a specific advantage to women with a view to improving their ability to compete on the labour market and to pursue careers on an equal footing with men'. A measure according clear priority to one sex was not covered: Case C-450/93 *Kalanke* v. *Frei Hausestadt Bremen*.

The decision in *Kalanke* was heaviliy criticised by academics, practising lawyers and women's groups.[2] The Commission issued a communication on the judgment[3] listing positive actions which would continue to be lawful after the ruling. A version of the ruling in *Kalanke* was included in the Social Protocol and then incorporated into Article 141 of the Treaty as follows:

> With a view to ensuring full equality in practice between men and women in working life, the principle of equal treatment shall not prevent any Member State from maintaining or adopting measures providing for specific advantages in order to make it easier for the under-represented sex to pursue a vocational activity or to prevent or compensate for disadvantage in professional careers.

Key point

Article 3 of the recast Directive continues to allow positive action. Member States are permitted to maintain or adopt measures within the meaning of Article 141(4) EC with a view to ensuring full equality in practice between men and women in working life.

The ECJ modified the position on positive action in another reference from a German court: Case C-409/95 *Marschall* v. *Land Nordhein Westfalen*. In this case the ECJ held that there was no infringement of the Directive arising out of a national rule requiring preference to be given to the promotion of women where there were fewer women than men at the level of the relevant post in a sector of the public service, unless reasons specific to an individual male candidate tilted the balance in his favour. The proviso in favour of the male candidate may only be invoked where an objective assessment of the candidature is made, taking account of the specific personal situations of all candidates.

A third ECJ ruling on a reference from a German court was made in March 2000 in Case C-158/97 *Georg Badek*. This arose out of a requirement in the *Land* of Hesse to contribute to equal treatment of men and women by means of advancement plans for women. Each plan had to provide that more than half of posts would be filled (by appointment or promotion) by women in a sector in which women are under-represented. As the rule was not absolute or unconditional, the ECJ found that there was no infringement of the Directive. It went on to state that it was for the national court to assess whether such a rule ensures that candidatures are objectively assessed, in line with the ruling in *Marschall*. Further aspects of the rule were also found to be compatible with the Directive:

---

[2] For example, Dagmar, S. (1996) 25 ILJ 239; Moore, S. (1996) 21 ELRev. 156; Szyszczak, E. (1996) 59 MLR 876.
[3] COM (96) 88.

- a special system of academic posts referring to the percentage of women in the sector;
- the reservation of half of training places for women;
- a recommendation for a target of half the membership of representative bodies at work to be women.

In Case C-407/98 *Abrahamsson* v. *Fogelqist*, a referral from the Swedish courts, the Court considered what level of positive action is permissible. Swedish law required preference to be given for a public post to the candidate from the under-represented sex where he or she was suitably qualified, subject to the proviso that the difference between the merits of the candidates of each sex was not so great as to result in a breach of the requirement of objectivity in making appointments. The Court held that such a requirement was disproportionate and was precluded by Article 141(4) and Article 2(4) of the Directive.

Remedies

Remedies are considered generally in Chapter 6 in the context of the direct effect of directives. Article 5 of Directive 76/207 was held to be directly effective but only against a public body: *Marshall*. In *Von Colson* the ECJ had held back from deciding that Article 6 of the Directive requires Member States to provide a mechanism for enforcement. Instead the Directive should be invoked as a means of statutory interpretation, i.e. the national courts should interpret national legislation so as to give effect to the Directive being implemented.

The Court has stressed the importance of the principle of effectiveness. National law must not deprive individuals of their rights under Community law. See, for example, Case C-208/90 *Emmott* (national limitation periods) and Case C-271/91 *Marshall* (No.2) (national limits on sum recoverable in an industrial tribunal). In both cases, national rules were set aside in order to ensure compliance with Community law. Later decisions were made in Case C-338/91 *Steenhorst Neerings* and Case C-410/92 *Johnson* v. *CAO*: see Chapter 6.

Obligations on Member States under Article 3(2) of Directive 76/207

Article 3(2) requires Member States to take the necessary steps to ensure that:

- Any laws, regulations and administrative provisions contrary to the principle of equal treatment are abolished.
- Any provisions contrary to the principle of equal treatment in collective agreements, individual contracts of employment, internal rules of undertakings or in rules governing the independent professions are annulled or amended: *see Commission* v. *United Kingdom (Re Equal Treatment for Men and Women)* (Case 165/82) in which the UK was held to be in breach of Article 3(2)(a) and (b).

Key point

The recast Directive 2006/54 provides for Remedies in Title III 'Horizontal Provisions'.

Chapter 1 Remedies and enforcement
Member States are required to:

- ensure that judicial procedures are available to all persons who consider themselves wronged by failure to apply the equal treatment principle, after recourse to other competent authorities including conciliation (where appropriate): Article 17 (defence of rights)
- introduce the necessary measures to ensure real and effective compensation: Article 18 (compensation or reparation)
- take the necessary measures to ensure that the burden of proof rests with the respondent to show that there has been no breach of the principle of equal treatment, except in relation to criminal procedures, unless otherwise provided by the Member States: Article 19 (burden of proof).

Chapter 2 Promotion of equal treatment – dialogue
Member States are required to:

- designate equality bodies to promote and monitor equal treatment: Article 20 (equality bodies)
- promote the social dialogue between the social partners in order to foster equal treatment: Article 21 (social dialogue)
- encourage dialogue with NGOs which have an interest in contributing to the fight against discrimination in order to promote equal treatment: Article 22 (dialogue with NGOs).

Chapter 3 General horizontal provisions
Member States are required to:

- abolish measures which conflict with the principle of equal treatment: Article 23 (compliance)
- introduce measures to protect employees against dismissal and other action following a complaint: Article 24 (victimisation)
- encourage employers and others to take action on grounds of sex, in particular harassment and sexual harassment in the workplace, in access to employment, vocational training and promotion: Article 25 (prevention of discrimination)
- introduce or maintain provisions on equal treatment which are more favourable than those laid down in the Directive: Article 26 (minimum requirements)
- take into account the objective of equality between men and women when formulating or implementing laws of policies: Article 28 (gender mainstreaming)
- ensure that measures under the Directive and those already in force are brought to the attention of persons concerned in the workplace: Article 29 (dissemination of information).

24

Equality of pay and treatment

Non-discrimination, sexual orientation and fundamental rights

In a bold decision prior to the introduction of Article 13 into the Treaty, the Court in *P. v. S.* recognised that discrimination based on sex infringes a fundamental right. It applied a liberal interpretation to discrimination on grounds of sex to include treatment of transsexuals.

Key case

P. v. S. arose out of the dismissal by Cornwall County Council of P following surgery for gender reassignment. Advocate-General Tesauro submitted that, as transsexuals do not constitute a third sex, they cannot be deprived of legal protection if they suffer discrimination. He reminded the Court that the elimination of discrimination based on sex is a fundamental right and that respect for fundamental rights is a general principle of EC law.

The ECJ followed his submissions and ruled that the Directive should be broadly interpreted and not limited to discrimination on grounds of gender: Case C-13/94 *P. v. S.*

The ECJ retreated from this stance in Case C-249/96 *Grant* v. *South West Trains Ltd.* This case arose out of a claim for travel concessions brought by a female employee in relation to her female partner, the concessions in question being available to different-sex partners. The ECJ ruled that the Directive did not cover discrimination based on sexual orientation.

A similar approach to *Grant* was taken by the CFI in Case T-264/97 *D.* v. *Council*, a decision on the Staff Regulations for Community Officials. The CFI confirmed a Council decision that an EC official living with a same-sex partner was not entitled to the household allowance. The Court refused to assimilate stable relationships between same-sex partners to married relationships.

As we have seen in Chapter 23, the legislative gap was filled by Article 13 EC, which established a new legal basis for action under which a package of two directives and an action programme was adopted. Directive 2000/43 provides a framework to combat discrimination on grounds of racial or ethnic origin. Directive 2000/78 provides a general framework to combat discrimination on grounds of religion or belief, disability, age or sexual orientation.

Equal treatment in relation to race or ethnic origin

Directive 2000/43 was adopted in 2000 to implement the principle of equal treatment between persons irrespective of racial or ethnic origin.

Key point

Article 2 of Directive 2000/43 prohibits discrimination, either direct or indirect, based on racial or ethnic origin.

Direct and indirect discrimination and harassment are defined under Article 2 on similar lines to Directive 2000/78: see below. Harassment is deemed to be discrimination when unwanted conduct related to racial or ethnic origin takes place with the purpose or effect of violating the dignity of a person and of creating an intimidating, hostile, degrading, humiliating or offensive environment. Harassment may be defined in accordance with national law.

The Directive applies to both the public and private sectors, including public bodies, in relation to a range of matters including conditions for access to employment: Article 3. Member States are permitted under Article 4 to provide that a difference in treatment based on a characteristic related to racial or ethnic origin shall not constitute discrimination, where it constitutes a genuine occupational requirement, provided that the objective is genuine and the requirement is legitimate. (This would enable a Chinese restaurant, for example, to employ Chinese chefs and waiters.) Article 5 provides for the possibility of positive action by permitting any Member State to maintain or adopt measures to prevent or compensate for disadvantages linked to racial or ethnic origin.

The Directive requires Member States to provide judicial or administrative procedures for enforcement and remedies in Chapters II to IV on similar lines to Directive 2006/54 (Title III).

The framework directive for equal treatment in employment and occupation

Directive 2000/78 was adopted in 2000 to implement the principle of equal treatment in employment and occupation.

Key point

The Directive lays down a general framework to combat discrimination on the grounds of religion or belief, disability, age or sexual orientation as regards employment or occupation, to give effect to the principle of equal treatment: Article 1. It prohibits direct and indirect discrimination in Article 2 on any of the grounds listed in Article 1.

Article 2 defines all the relevant terms, including direct and indirect discrimination, in similar terms to Directive 2000/43.

Key terms

- **Direct discrimination**: where one person is treated less favourably than another in a comparable situation on any of the grounds in Article 1: Article 2(1)(a).
- **Indirect discrimination**: where an apparently neutral provision, criterion or practice would put persons having a particular religion or belief, disability, age or sexual orientation at a particular disadvantage compared with other persons unless:
  - the provision, etc. is objectively justified by a legitimate aim and the means of achieving that aim are appropriate and necessary.
  - as regards persons with a particular disability, the employer or other person to whom the Directive applies, is obliged under national law to take appropriate measures in line with Article 5 to eliminate disadvantages: Article 2(1)(b).
- **Harassment**: where unwanted conduct relating to any of the grounds in Article 1 takes place with the effect of creating an intimidating, hostile, degrading, humiliating or offensive environment. Harassment may be defined in accordance with the national law and practice: Article 2(3).

Decisions of the Court on Article 1 of Directive 2000/78 are beginning to appear. In Case C-267/06 *Murako* v. *Versorgungsanstalt der deutschen Bühnen*, Court held that a survivor's occupational pension is pay and so covered by the Directive. It went on to find that Articles 1 and 2 of the Directive national legislation which does not recognise the benefit of a surviving life partner (i.e. a partner of the same sex under a registered partnership) as equivalent to that of a spouse. However, it left the national court to decide whether the situation of the surviving life partner was in a comparable situation to a spouse. The Directive applies to both the public and private sectors: Article 3. It recognises that a difference in treatment based on a genuine occupational requirement is not discriminatory, provided the objective is legitimate and the requirement proportionate: Article 4(1). National legislation may be retained or adopted to enable churches and other religious organisations to treat a person differently on the basis of religion or belief in occupation or employment. This would, for example, enable a church school to recruit teachers who are practising Christians.

Article 5 requires employers to make reasonable accommodation for persons with disabilities. In Case C-13/05 *Navas* v. *Eurest Colectivades SA* the Court found that dismissal on account of sickness was outside the Directive, as the term 'disability' did not cover sickness. It held the prohibition of dismissal on grounds of disability under Articles 2(1) and 3(1)(c), in view of the obligation to provide reasonable accommodation for people with disabilities, precludes dismissal which is not justified by the fact that the person concerned is not competent, capable and available to perform the functions of his or her post.

Article 6 enables Member States to provide that differences in treatment on grounds of age do not constitute discrimination if, within the context of national law, they are objectively and reasonably justified by a legitimate aim, including legitimate employment policy, labour market and vocational training objectives, and if the means of achieving that aim are appropriate and necessary.

Key case

A 56-year-old German lawyer, Mr Mangold, entered into a contract under which he was employed by Mr Helms for a fixed term, from July 2003 to February 2004. Such a contract was in accordance with German law, which authorised the conclusion of fixed-term contracts for workers over 52 years, with some exceptions. He brought proceedings in the German courts which referred questions to the ECJ under Article 234. The Court ruled that such a law did not infringe that Framework Agreement on fixed-term contracts 1999/70 (under the Social Agreement). However, it held that the national law infringed Article 6(1) of Directive 2000/78 unless there was a close connection with an earlier contract of employment of indefinite duration with the same employer. While the Court recognised that the purpose of the German law was to promote the integration of older workers into the workforce, the provision was unduly restrictive, as it excluded a significant body of workers from the benefits of stable employment and was not objectively justified: Case C-144/04 *Mangold* v. *Helm*.

Article 7 enables Member States to maintain or adopt positive action to promote equality for men and women. The Directive strengthens protection for employees complaining about discrimination, requiring Member States to establish bodies to enforce equal opportunities and to provide judicial remedies and sanctions. Article 9 provides for defence of rights and Article 10 for the burden of proof. Article 10 requires Member States to introduce measures against victimisation to protect employees who have complained. Articles 11 to 14 cover dissemination of information, the social dialogue and dialogue with NGOs, on similar lines to Directive 2000/43. Member States are required to take any necessary measures to abolish laws contrary to the principle of equal treatment under Article 16 and to lay down rules on sanctions, comprising payment of compensation to victims, under Article 17.

EQUAL TREATMENT IN MATTERS OF SOCIAL SECURITY

Equal treatment in matters of social security: Directive 79/7

Directive 79/7 implements in matters of social security the principle in Directive 76/207. It is directly effective: Case 71/85 *Netherlands* v. *FNV*.

Key point

Directive 79/7 remains in place as it has *not* been repealed by Directive 2006/54.

Personal scope

Article 2 states that the Directive applies to the working population, defined as 'self-employed persons, workers and self-employed persons whose activity is interrupted by illness, accident or involuntary unemployment and persons seeking employment' and to 'retired or invalided workers and self-employed persons'. The definition has been interpreted broadly by the ECJ.

Key case

Mrs Drake gave up paid work in order to care for her invalid mother. The ECJ held that Article 2 covers all benefits designed to maintain income where any of the risks specified in the Directive had been incurred. Mrs Drake was therefore considered to be within the scope of the Directive: Case 150/85 *Drake* v. *Chief Adjudication Officer.*

However, in order to be covered by the Directive, the claimant must have given up employment or been obliged to stop looking for work at the time the risk materialised: Case C-31/90 *Johnson* v. *Chief Adjudication Officer* (a woman who had given up work to care for her child was not covered by the Directive when claiming invalidity benefit for a serious back condition). The Directive does not cover persons who have not been employed and who are not seeking work, or whose work has not been interrupted by one of the risks in Article 3(1): see below. Thus a Dutchman who had given up work to care for a family was treated as voluntarily unemployed at the time of retirement and so not covered: Cases 48 etc./88 *Achterberg-te Riele and others* v. *Sociale Verzekeringsbank.*

Risks covered

Article 3(1) of Directive 79/7 provides that equal treatment principles apply to:

- statutory schemes which provide protection against sickness, invalidity, old age, accidents at work or occupational diseases and unemployment;
- social assistance, in so far as it is intended to supplement or replace those statutory schemes.

The Directive may be invoked in relation to benefits covered by the Directive but payable to third parties: *Drake* (invalidity allowance payable to Mrs Drake's mother). It also applies to schemes exempting persons of pensionable age from prescription charges: Case C-137/94 *R.* v. *Secretary of State for Health, ex parte Richardson* and to schemes for winter fuel payments for pensioners: Case C-382/98 *R.* v. *Secretary of State for Social Security, ex parte Taylor.*

To be covered by the Directive the benefit must be 'directly and effectively linked to the protection provided against one of the risks in Article 3(1)': Case C-243/90 *R.* v. *Secretary of State for Social Security, ex parte Smithson.* The ECJ held that housing benefit was not covered; its calculation was partly based on risks listed in Article 3(1). Similarly, in Case C-228/94 *Atkins* v. *Wrekin District Council* travel concessions granted by public authorities were not covered.

In Cases 63 and 64/91 *Jackson and Cresswell* v. *Chief Adjudication Officer* the ECJ held that a general benefit such as supplementary allowance intended as a replacement for a wage was not covered. Survivors' benefits and family benefits, except those granted by way of increases to benefits in statutory schemes covered by the Directive, are excluded: Article 3(2).

Meaning of the equal treatment principle

Key point

Article 4(1) provides that the principle of equal treatment means that there shall be no discrimination whatsoever on grounds of sex either directly or indirectly by reference to marital or family status, in particular concerning:

- the scope of schemes and the conditions of access thereto;
- the obligation to contribute and the calculation of contributions;
- the calculation of benefits including increases due in respect of a spouse and for dependants;
- the conditions governing the duration and retention of entitlement to benefits.

The principle of equal treatment is stated to be without prejudice to the provisions relating to the protection of women on grounds of maternity: Article 4(2). It has been interpreted similarly to Article 2(3) of Directive 76/207.

Examples

- Refusal to pay an invalidity allowance to a married woman where it was payable to a married man infringed Article 4(1): *Drake* (*but not* an invalidity benefit where the amount of the allowance was determined by the marital status and income of the spouse or existence of a dependent child: Case 30/85 *Teuling*).
- Refusal to pay invalidity benefits to part-time workers most of whom were female (under a Dutch minimum subsistence scheme) also infringed Article 4(1) unless it could be justified by factors unrelated to sex. In this case the amount payable under the scheme to part-timers was linked to the claimant's previous income whereas full-timers could receive a sum which corresponded to the Dutch minimum subsistence allowance: Case 102/88 *Ruzius-Wilbrink*.

- Refusal to pay a retirement pension to a person who had undergone male to female gender-reassignment surgery until the age of 65, when a woman would have been entitled to a pension at 60: Case C-423/04 *Richards* v. *Secretary of State for Work and Pensions.*

Exclusion from the equal treatment principle

Member States are permitted under Article 7 to exclude various matters from the principle of equal treatment, namely:

- the determination of pensionable age;
- pension benefits or other entitlements granted to persons who have brought up children;
- old-age or invalidity benefits deriving from a wife's entitlements;
- increases in benefits granted to a dependent wife.

> **Key point**
>
> As far as the determination of pensionable ages is concerned, the ECJ has ruled that Article 7(1)(a) of the Directive cannot justify early retirement at a pensionable age which is discriminatory: Case 152/84 *Marshall*; Case 262/84 *Beets-Proper.*

Where there is no such discrimination, retirement at pensionable age would be covered by the exception: Case 19/81 *Burton* v. *BRB*. However, in Case C-9/91 *R.* v. *Secretary of State for Social Security, ex parte EOC* the ECJ held that Article 7(1) may justify a difference in the number of contributions required for a full pension between men and women. Article 7(1) does not allow a Member State which had set the pensionable age for women at 60 and men at 65 to provide that women were exempt from prescription charges at 60 and men only at 65: Case C-137/94 *R.* v. *Secretary of State for Health, ex parte Richardson*. See also Case C-328/91 *R.* v. *Secretary of State for Social Security, ex parte Thomas*, involving a claim for severe disablement allowance and invalid care allowance. The women claimants argued that linking payment to pensionable age (60 for women, 65 for men) was discriminatory. The ECJ held that as the benefits were non-contributory, the principle of consistency meant that they should be available.

Thomas should be contrasted with Case C-92/94 *R.* v. *Secretary of State for Social Security, ex parte Graham* in which the ECJ held that differential treatment was necessarily and objectively linked to different retirement ages for men and women.

When a Member State adopts rules to allow persons previously discriminated against to become eligible on retirement to a pension scheme applicable to the other sex, a requirement for those brought into the scheme to pay adjustment contributions, as well as interest to take account of inflation, does not contravene the Directive: Joined Cases C-231 and 233/06 *National Pensions Office* v. *Jonkman and others.*

Remedies

Article 6 requires Member States to implement the Directive by providing adequate remedies. Case 286/85 *McDermott and Cotter* v. *Minister of State for Social Welfare* indicates that Directive 79/7 may be relied on to challenge national social security legislation by enabling a woman to claim that she should be treated in the same way as a man, even though this may result in payment of double benefit.

Where discrimination infringing Community law is found by the Court, the national court must set aside any discriminatory provision of national law, and must apply to the disadvantaged group the same arrangements as those enjoyed by those in the other category: *Jonkman.* It should not wait for a request to be made or a change in the law.

EQUAL TREATMENT IN OCCUPATIONAL SOCIAL SECURITY SCHEMES

Directive 86/378 was drawn up to implement the principle of equal treatment in relation to occupational social security schemes (i.e. occupational pension schemes) in similar terms to Directive 79/7. It was amended by Directive 96/97 to give effect to the *Barber* decision, after which it was clear that pensions paid under private occupational pension schemes are 'pay' and are therefore covered by Article 141.

Key point

Directives 86/378 and 96/97 were repealed by the recast Directive 2006/54, Title II Chapter 2 of which is headed 'Equal Treatment in Occupational Social Security Schemes'.

Article 5 of the recast Directive prohibits direct or indirect discrimination in occupational social security schemes in virtually identical terms to Directive 79/7, particularly in relation to:

- the scope of such schemes and conditions of access to them;
- the obligation to contribute and calculation of contributions;
- the calculation of benefits including supplementary benefits due in respect of a spouse or dependants; and
- the conditions governing the duration and retention of entitlement to benefits.

The recast Directive defines occupational social security in Article 2(f) as schemes other than those covered by Directive 79/7 where membership is voluntary or compulsory, the purpose of which is to provide workers or self-employed persons in an undertaking or sector with benefits to supplement or replace those under a statutory scheme. Article 8 provides a number of exceptions, including individual contracts for self-employed persons, insurance contracts to which the employer is not a party, and options to provide additional individual benefits.

Article 6 provides for the personal scope of the Directive: it covers members of the working population, including self-employed persons, persons whose activity is interrupted by illness, maternity, accident or involuntary unemployment and persons seeking employment and retired or disabled workers, and those claiming under them in accordance with national law and/or practice. Article 7 sets out the material scope of the Directive, again in similar terms to Directive 79/7.

Article 9 lists examples of provisions based on sex, either directly or indirectly which contravene the principle of equal treatment, including those which determine the persons who may participate in an occupational social security scheme, fix different retirement ages or set different levels of contribution. Article 10 provides for the implementation of the principle for self-employed persons and Article 11 specifies circumstances in which Member States may defer the compulsory application of the equal treatment principle.

EQUAL TREATMENT IN SELF-EMPLOYMENT

Directive 86/613 was adopted to complement Directives 76/207 and 79/7. It applies the principle of equal treatment to men and women engaged in an activity in a self-employed capacity or contributing to the pursuit of such an activity, in relation to those aspects not covered by other directives: Article 1. The Directive applies to all persons pursuing a gainful activity for their own account, including farmers and members of the liberal professions. It also covers their spouses (who are not already employees or partners) where they participate in the activities of the self-employed worker, performing the same or ancillary tasks: Article 2.

Key point

Directive 86/613 has *not* been recast by Directive 2006/54, so remains in force, unaffected.

Article 3 states that the equal treatment principle implies the absence of discrimination on the grounds of sex, either directly or indirectly, by reference in particular to marital or family status. However, this provision is without prejudice to the protection of women during pregnancy and motherhood: Preamble.

Member States must take all necessary measures to ensure the elimination of all provisions contrary to the principle of equal treatment under Directive 76/207, especially in respect of the establishment, equipment or extension of a business or the launching or extension of any other form of self-employed activity including financial facilities: Article 4.

Under Article 5 Member States must (without prejudice to the specific conditions for access to certain activities applying equally to both sexes) ensure that the conditions for the formation of a company between spouses are not more restrictive than the conditions for the formation of a company between unmarried persons.

Member States must ensure that the spouses who participate in the activities of the self-employed worker are enabled to join a contributory social security scheme voluntarily where they are not protected under the self-employed worker's social security scheme: Article 6.

Member States must introduce the necessary measures to enable all persons who consider themselves wronged to apply the principle of equal treatment in self-employed activities to pursue their claims through the judicial process, possibly after recourse to other competent authorities: Article 9.

The Directive is directly effective.

CONCLUSION

The EU has made significant progress since its inception, when equality was perceived simply in terms of pay. The law on equal treatment under Directive 76/207 has developed apace. Although the recast Directive 2006/54 does not consolidate *all* secondary legislation in relation to equal treatment, it represents a useful consolidation of certain areas. The insertion of Article 13 into the Treaty has led to important developments in prohibiting discrimination in relation to race and other areas covered by the general framework directive including religion, sexual orientation, disability and age. As a result, the EU has achieved a reasonably comprehensive and integrated package of measures to provide for the protection of equal treatment.

QUESTIONS

1 How has the Court of Justice developed the concept of equal pay under Article 141 EC and how have these developments been reflected in changes to the EC Treaty?

2 Why was it necessary to adopt the Equal Treatment Directive 76/207? How has the principle of equal treatment been developed in relation to age and race?

3 To what extent has the recast Directive 2006/54 identified common themes in relation to the protection of equal treatment? How far has the law been consolidated by the recast Directive?

Further reading

Barnard, C. (2006) *EC Employment Law*, 3rd edition, Oxford University Press.

Chalmers, D., Hadjiemmanuil, C., Monti, G. and Tomkins, A. (2006) *European Union Law*, Cambridge University Press, Chapter 20.

Costello, C. and Davies, G. (2006) 'The Case Law of the Court of Justice in the Field of Sex Equality since 2000' (2006) 43 CMLRev. 1567.

Craig, P. and De Burca, G. (2007) *EU Law: Text, Cases and Materials*, 4th edition, Oxford University Press, Chapter 24.

Hervey, C.T. (2005) 'Thirty Years of EU Sex Equality Law: Looking Backwards, Looking Forwards' (2005) 12 MJ 307.

Shaw, J., Hunt, J. and Wallace, C. (2007) *Economic and Social Law of the European Union*, Palgrave Macmillan, Chapter 15.

Sohrab, J. (1994) 'Women and Social Security Law: the Limits of EEC Equality Law' (1994) JSWFL 5.

Sohrab, J. (1996) *Sexing the Benefit*, Dartmouth.

Waddington, L. (2004) 'The Development of a New Generation of Sex Equality Directives' (2004) MJ 3.

Visit **http://www.mylawchamber.co.uk/kent** to access answer guidance to questions in the book to test yourself on this chapter.

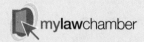

Appendix 1
Bibliography

MAIN SOURCES

Main sources of EC law

Official Journal ('L' and 'C' Series) (OJ): See Appendix 2.
European Court Reports (ECR): *Common Market Law Reports* (CMLR): See Appendix 2.
Encyclopaedia of European Community Law (Sweet & Maxwell, looseleaf): the constitutive treaties and secondary legislation (annotated).
Bulletin of the European Communities (Bull.EC): Reports on EC activities with supplements on specific areas.
Commission, *General Report on the Activities of the European Communities* (annual).
Commission, *Report on Competition Policy* (annual).

Periodicals

Cahiers de Droit Europeen (CDE)
Common Market Law Review (CMLRev.)
European Business Law Review (EBLR)
European Competition Journal (ECJ)
European Competition Law Review (ECLR)
European Intellectual Property Review (EIPR)
European Law Journal (ELJ)
European Law Review (ELRev.)
Industrial Law Journal (ILJ)
International and Comparative Law Quarterly (ICLP)
Journal of Common Market Studies (JCMS)
Journal of Social Welfare and Family Law (JSWFL)
Journal of World Trade Law (JWTL)
Law Quarterly Review (LQR)
Legal Issues of European Integration (LIFI)
Maastricht Journal of European and Comparative Law (MJ)
Modern Law Review (MLR)
Yearbook of European Law (YEL)

FURTHER READING

Statutes, case studies and materials

Craig, P. and De Burca, G. (2007) *EU Law: Text, Cases and Materials*, 4th edition, Oxford University Press.

Chalmers, D., Hadjiemmanuil, C., Monti, G., and Tomkins, A. (2006) *European Union Law: Text and Materials*, Cambridge University Press.

Foster, N. (2007–08) *EC Legislation*, 18th edition, Oxford University Press.

Oppenheimer, A. (1994) *The Relationship between European Community Law and National Law: the Cases*, Volume I and Volume II, Grotius.

Weatherill, S. (2007) *Cases and Materials on EC Law*, 8th edition, Oxford University Press.

General

Adenas, M. and Usher, J. (eds) (2003) *The Treaty of Nice: Enlargement and Constitutional Reform*, Hart Publishing.

Arnull, A. (2006) *The European Union and its Court of Justice*, 2nd edition, Oxford University Press.

Arnull, A., Dashwood, A., Dougan, M., Ross, M., Spaventa, E., and Wyatt, D. (2006) *Wyatt and Dashwood's European Community Law*, 5th edition, Sweet & Maxwell.

Barnard, C. (2004) *The Substantive Law of the EU: the Four Freedoms*, Oxford University Press.

Brown, L. and Kennedy, T. (2000) *The Court of Justice of the European Communities*, 5th edition, Sweet & Maxwell.

Craig, P. (2006) *EU Administrative Law*, Oxford University Press.

Craig, P. and De Burca, G. (eds) (1999) *The Evolution of EU Law*, Oxford University Press.

EC Commission, (1997) *Better Lawmaking*, COM (97) 626

Curtin, D. (2006) *The EU Constitution: the Best Way Forward?*, Cambridge University Press.

Hartley, T. (2003) *The Foundations of European Community Law*, 5th edition, Oxford, Clarendon Press.

Hervey, T. and Kenner, J. (2006) *Economic and Social Rights under the EU Charter of Fundamental Rights*, Hart Publishing.

Kennedy, T. (1998) *Learning European Law*, Sweet & Maxwell.

Lenaerts, K., and Van Nuffel, P. (2005) *Constitutional Law of the European Union*, 2nd edition, Thomson, Sweet & Maxwell.

Mathijsen, P. (2007) *A Guide to European Community Law*, 9th edition, Sweet & Maxwell.

O'Keefe, D. and Twomey, P. (1994) *Legal Issues of the Maastricht Treaty*, Chancery.

Peers, S. (2006) *EU Justice and Home Affairs Law*, 2nd edition, Longman.

Shaw, J. (2000) *Law of the European Union*, 3rd edition, Macmillan.

Shaw, J., Hunt, J., and Wallace, C. (2007) *Economic and Social Law of the European Union*, Palgrave Macmillan.

Slynn, G. (1999) *Introducing a European Legal Order*, Stevens.

Steiner, J., Woods, L., and Twigg-Flesner, C. (2006) *EC Law*, 9th edition, Oxford University Press.

Szyszczak, E. and Cygan, C. (2005) *Understanding EU Law*, Thomson.

Tridimas, T. (2006) *The European Court of Justice and the EU Constitutional Order: Essays in Judicial Protection*, Hart Publishing.

Tridimas, T. (2006) *The General Principles of EU Law*, 2nd edition, Oxford University Press.

Weatherill, S. and Beaumont, P. (1999) *EC Law*, 3rd edition, Penguin.

Appendix 2
Where to find the law

PUBLICATIONS

Primary and secondary legislation

EC legislation can be divided into primary legislation, in the form of treaties (e.g. the EC Treaty and the Single European Act) and secondary legislation in the form of regulations, directives and decisions of the EC institutions; see Chapter 3.

Official Journal of the European Union (OJ)

All legislation and important notices are published in the *Official Journal* of the European Union. Proposed legislation appears in the '*C*' section of the OJ and adopted secondary legislation in the '*L*' section.

Law reports

The official version of proceedings in the ECJ and CFI appears in the European Court Reports (ECR) and an unofficial version in the Common Market Law Reports (CMLR), also covering decisions in the national courts with an EC element. English cases with an EC element are also reprinted in the All England Reports (All ER (EC)).

ONLINE AND OTHER SOURCES

Databases

A number of databases in EC law exist, including CELEX, LEXIS and LAWTEL.

(a) **CELEX**. The official database in EC law is known as CELEX. It provides the full text of materials and is divided into sectors covering primary legislation, secondary legislation (as published in the OJ), reports of cases before the ECJ and CFI, Commission legislative proposals, questions in the EP and national legislation implementing EC directives, national decisions and publications on EC law. It may be accessed through 'Europa' the website of the EU: see below.

(b) **LEXIS**. EC law coverage includes law reports (European Court Reports and European Commercial Cases), unreported decisions and, where available, opinions of the advocates-general. LEXIS also covers Commission competition decisions.

Access to the CELEX database is now available through LEXIS, although some documents are not available in full-text form.

(c) **LAWTEL**. LAWTEL contains short summaries of cases and other developments on a subscription basis.

The internet

The *Europa* website on http://europa.eu.int. is the most readily accessible source of Community law. It is operated by the EU and provides open access to information about its activities, law and polices. The website is the main mechanism by which the EU gives effect to the principle of transparency introduced by the Treaty of Amsterdam.

The homepage on the main site lists headings including Activities, Institutions, Documents and Services. The 'Decisions' tab gives access to the **Eur-Lex** portal on http://eur-lex.europa.eu, with a link to EU legislation, both primary and secondary. All documents published in the *Official Journal* (OJ) since 1998 may be accessed through Eur-Lex.

The text of the Treaty of Lisbon may be found on http://www.consilium.europa.eu/igcpdf/en/07/cg00/cg00014.en07.pdf.

Under the 'Documents' tab it is also possible to purse the link to **Oeil**, the Legislative Observatory of the European Parliament, in order to track the progress of a legislative proposal before it becomes law, on http://www.europarl.europa.eu/oeil, or through the Commission's *Prelex* site on http://prelex.europa.eu.

Transcripts of decisions of the Court of Justice *and* Court of First Instance may be accessed through the Court's webpage on http://curia.europa.eu. They are published on the afternoon of the judgment.

European Documentation Centres (EDCs)

EDCs comprise major collections of EC documentation, including access to CELEX. The EDCs are based mainly in university libraries. While EDCs provide an academic service within their own institutions, they also serve the needs of the local community. For further information, see http://ec.europa.eu/europedirect/visit_us/edc/index_en.htm.

Appendix 3
Timeline

1950	Schumann Plan for economic recovery in France and Germany
1951	Treaty of Paris signed, creating the ECSC
1955	Messina Conference
1957	Treaties signed in Rome creating the EEC and Euratom
1959	EFTA founded
1961	UK applied unsuccessfully for membership of the EEC
1965	Merger Treaty
1965	UK reapplied for membership of the EEC, with Denmark, Norway and Ireland
1973	UK, Denmark and Ireland join the EEC
1981	Greece joins the EC
1986	Spain and Portugal join the EC
1985	White Paper on Completion of the Internal Market
1986	Single European Act signed
1989	Reunification of Germany
1990	Former East Germany absorbed into the EC
1990	IGCs convened to discuss EPU and EMU
1991	Treaty on European Union (TEU) signed at Maastricht
1992	Single Market Programme largely complete
1993	TEU ratified
1994	EEA Agreement in force
1995	Austria, Sweden and Finland join the EU
1996–97	IGCs convened to discuss TEU
1997	Treaty of Amsterdam signed
1999	Treaty of Amsterdam ratified
2000	IGC convened to discuss Treaty of Amsterdam
2000	Charter of Fundamental Rights signed
2001	Treaty of Nice signed
2001	Laeken Summit
2001	Convention on the Future of Europe established
2003	Treaty of Nice ratified

2003	Treaty establishing a Constitution for Europe (TEC) adopted by the Convention
2004	TEC agreed by IGC after amendment
2004	Cyprus, Czech Republic, Estonia, Hungary, Poland, Latvia, Lithuania, Malta, Slovenia and Slovakia join the EU
2005	France and the Netherlands vote against ratification of the TEC in separate referenda
2005	Entry negotiations begin for Croatia and Turkey
2007	Bulgaria and Romania join the EU
2007	Reform Treaty (Treaty of Lisbon) signed
2008	Irish people vote against ratification of the Treaty of Lisbon in referendum (June).

Index

abuse of a dominant position (Article 82) 294–316
anti-competitive agreements 301–2
assessing dominance 300–1
categories and examples of abuse 302–7
collective dominance 310–13
dominance 295, 310–13
enforcement and procedure 317–27
exemptions and negative clearances 295, 301–2
geographical market 299–300
import and export bans 307
intellectual property 337, 339
inter-member trade, effect on 307
market share 300–1
mergers and concentrations 307–15
oligopolies 294–5
prices 302–4
product market 296–9
reform 295
refusal to supply 303–5
relevant market, establishment of 295
rule of reason 306
substitution 296–8
temporal market 300
trading conditions 303
tying 305–6
'acquis communautaire' 7, 12, 16

acte clair and acte éclairé 153–5
actions for annulment 125–36
acts which may be challenged, list of 126–7
competence, lack of 134
consultation, lack of 26
decisions, measures must be equivalent to 128–9
direct and individual concern 129–33
EC Treaty or any rule relating to its application, breach of 135
essential procedural requirements, infringement of 134–5
grounds for challenge 133–6
misuse of powers 135–6
privileged and non-privileged applicants 128
right to challenge 127–33
time limits 126, 133
treaty reform 132–3
actions against member states see state liability in damages for breach of EC law
Acts of Accession, list of 54
acts of the institutions 55–9
Advocates-General 44, 45
age discrimination 391
animals, protection of 188–91

annulment see actions for annulment
anti-competitive agreements (Article 81) 274–93
abuse of a dominant position 301–2
associations of undertakings, decisions by 231, 277
block exemptions 286, 290–2
cartels 278
comfort letters 286
concerted practices 277–9, 282
de minimis principle 282–3
definition of agreement 275
distribution agreements 284–6
economic entity principle 277
effect on trade between member states 274, 279–82
effects doctrine 282
enforcement and procedure 317–27
exemptions and exceptions 274, 286, 287–92, 318
guidance and notices 286–7, 289–90, 318
infringement 275–87
intellectual property 337
likely to infringe, agreements 283–4
minor agreements 282–3
negative clearances 274, 318

anti-competitive agreements
(Article 81) (continued)
notification requirement,
abolition of 274–5, 318
prevention, restriction or
distortion of competition
274, 279–82
price-fixing 278–81
public authorities 276–7
reason, rule of 284
transport undertakings
276
undertakings, definition of
275–7
vertical agreements, block
exemptions and 291
Article 81 see
anti-competitive
agreements (Article 81)
Article 82 see abuse of a
dominant position
(Article 82)
artistic, historical or
archaeological value,
protection of national
treasures of 191
assent procedures 31
association agreements 61
associations of undertakings,
decisions by 231

barriers to trade 8–9
Belgium, supremacy of EC
law in 95–6
block exemptions 286,
290–2
border controls 14, 212–14
budget 24, 40, 48
business secrets 332–3

capital movements 253–6
direct effect 253
discrimination 255
economic and monetary
union 256, 259
internal market,
completion of 253–4
special or golden shares
256–7

tax 256
Treaty on European Union
254
cartels 268, 272, 278
charges having equivalent
effect 164, 165–6
Charter of Fundamental
Rights of the EU 16, 17,
59, 70, 75–7, 361, 365
Article 7 77
Article 8 77
Article 42 86
Articles 1–5 75
Articles 6–19 76
Articles 20–26 76
Articles 27–38 76
Articles 39–46 76
Articles 47–50 76
Articles 52, 53 76
binding nature 16
Citizens' Rights 76
citizenship 76
criminal proceedings 76
dignity 75
employment 76
equality 76
freedom 76
justice 76
list of fundamental rights
75–7
proportionality 76
social policy 361, 365–6
soft law, as 59, 77
solidarity 76
transparency 83
Treaty of Lisbon 16, 17,
77
Treaty on European Union
17, 73
Charter of Fundamental
Social Rights for Workers
1989 361
children 199, 225–6, 363
citizenship 195–214
assent procedure 31
Charter of Fundamental
Rights of the EU 76
children and parents,
rights of 199

direct effect 197–8
discrimination 195–7
exit and entry, rights of
205–13
families and spouses 199,
202–3
free movement of persons
194
fundamental status, as
197
integration, need for 198
job-seekers and
economically inactive
198–9
political rights 24,
199–200
residence rights 200–13
social advantages 228
Treaty on European Union
12–13
voting and elections
199–200
co-decision procedure 12,
14, 15–16, 22, 26–7,
29, 41, 55, 60
cohabitees and registered
partners, rights of 204
comfort letters 286
comitology 40–3
commercial agreements
61
Commission 37–43, 60–1
censure, motions of 25
co-decision procedure 41
comitology 40–3
Committee of Permanent
Representatives
(COREPER) 37
committees 42
competition 40, 270–1,
286, 289–90, 317–27,
350–1
composition 38, 54
Council of the European
Union 33–4, 39–42
Directorates General 39
European Parliament 21,
24–5, 29–33, 40–3
Executive 40

Commission (*continued*)
failure to fulfill obligations, actions for 117, 121
financial and representative function 40
Guardian of the Treaties 39–40
Legislation 39–43, 55–6, 68
non-legislative acts 60
President and Vice-President 39
state aids 356
Committee of Permanent Representatives (COREPER) 26, 37
Committee of the Regions 48–9
Committees of Inquiry 31
Common Agricultural Policy (CAP) 36–7, 56
common commercial policy 61
common foreign and security policy (CFSP) 11, 14, 16, 34, 53, 127
common market
creation of 5
definition of 4
state aid 352–3
competence 60–4
definition of 18
exclusive and non-exclusive competences 63, 64
express and implied powers (conferral, principle of) 60–2, 63–4
external competences 61–2
general powers 62
international agreements 64
legal proceedings 63
proportionality 63–4
subsidiarity 63–4
Treaty of Lisbon 18, 63–4

competition, 267–73 *see also* abuse of a dominant position (Article 82); anti-competitive agreements (Article 81); state regulation and competition law
appeals 321
associations of undertakings, decisions by 277
cartels 268, 272
Chicago school 269
Commission, role of the 40, 270–1, 286, 289–90, 317–27
Competition Appeal Tribunal 272
competition policy 270–2
confidential information 322–3
contestable competition, theory of 269–70
dawn raids 320–1
decentralization of enforcement 318
declarations 318–19, 325
economic entity principle 277
economic terms, list of 267–8
fines and penalties 319, 321, 325
heard, right to be 321
horizontal and vertical agreements 271
inspections 319–21
intellectual property 329, 336, 337–41
interim measures 321–2
investigatory powers 319–22
leniency programme 324–5
modernization 271–2, 286, 289–90
monopolies 169–70, 268, 347–8

national competition authorities, role of 271, 274–5, 317–19, 325–6
notification requirement, abolition of 271–2
Office of Fair Trading 272
oligopolies 268
perfect competition, theory of 268–9
periodic penalties 325
price-fixing 268
privilege 321
professional secrecy and business secrets 322–3
Regulation 1/2003 317–19
workable competition, theory of 269, 285
computer programs, copyright and 342
concerted practices 277–9, 282
Conciliation Committee 30–1
concurrent liability 146
conferral, principle of 63–4
confidential information 322–3
Constitutional Treaty (failed) 2004 16–17, 52, 54, 73, 88
Consultation 26, 49
contributory negligence 145
Copenhagen Criteria 7
copyright 328, 330, 333–4, 339–40, 342–3
Council of the European Union 33–7
access to documents 135
Commission 33–4, 39–42
composition and functions 33–4
European Parliament 21–2, 25–6, 29–31, 34
formations 33–4
legislation 33, 68
voting procedures 34–7
Court of Auditors 48

Court of First Instance (CFI)
43, 46–8, 157
Court of Justice *see* European
Court of Justice (ECJ)
criminal proceedings
Charter of Fundamental
Rights of the EU 76
criminal convictions,
rights of residence and
207–9
customs duties and union
164–6

damages *see also* state
liability in damages for
breach of EC law
failure to fulfill obligations,
actions for 122
non-contractual liability of
institutions 144, 145
dawn raids 320–1
de minimis principle 282–3
decisions 57–8, 107, 128–9
Declaration of Fundamental
Rights 2000 75
democratic deficit 22
designs 334–5, 343
development of EU law
3–19
direct and individual concern
129–33
direct enforcement actions
under Article 226
117–20
direct applicability and direct
effect 101–11
capital movements 253
citizenship 197–8
competition, state
regulation and 347
directives and decisions
104–11
equal pay 105–6, 360–70
general principles of law
107
international treaties 107
regulations 56, 103
requirements 67
Treaty articles 102, 106

vertical and horizontal
direct effect 102–3,
104–5, 108–11
direct effect *see* direct
applicability and direct
effect
directives
competition, state
regulation and 351–2
direct effect 104–8
failure to fulfill obligations,
actions for 119
horizontal effects 109–11
implementation 57,
104–6, 109–15, 119
public bodies 105–6
Social Chapter 57
state liability 104–15
Directorates-General (DGs)
39
disability discrimination,
reasonable
accommodation and
390
discrimination *see* equal
treatment and
discrimination
distribution agreements
284–6
divorce and judicial
separation, residence
rights and 203–4
dominant position *see* abuse
of a dominant position
(Article 82)
dualism 89, 95
due process, right to 83

EC law and EU law 13
economic entity principle
277
economic and monetary
union (EMU) 7,
258–62
capital movements 256,
259
definition 10
economic policies of
member states 261–2

European Central Bank 49,
259–61
management 261–2
opting out 10, 259, 262
single currency 258–62
Stability Pact 261–2
Treaty on European Union
9–10, 12, 54
economic and political union
(EPU) 10, 54
Economic and Social
Committee (ESC) 48
education 225–6, 247,
249–51, 363
effects doctrine 282
elections 13, 24, 199–200
employment *see also* equal
pay; free movement of
workers
Charter of Fundamental
Rights of the EU 76
citizenship 198–9
equal treatment and
discrimination 378–91
equality 79
job-seekers 198–9, 205–6,
216–18, 222, 229, 392
public service employment
219–20
self-employment 396–7
Social Chapter 10
social policy 362–4
social security 392
solidarity 76
unemployed 216–18, 222,
229
EMU *see* economic and
monetary union (EMU)
enforcement actions 117–24
enlargement of EU 6–8, 15,
16, 23, 35–6, 38
environment 15
equal pay 363, 367, 369–78
bonuses 371
comparators 374
direct effect 105–6,
360–70
equal work of equal value
373–8

equal pay (*continued*)
job evaluation schemes
377–8
maternity pay 372
non-pay benefits 370
pensions 370–3, 375–7
sick pay 371
supplementary payments
370
equal treatment and
discrimination 18,
79–80, 378–97
age discrimination 391
capital movements 255
Charter of Fundamental
Rights of the EU 76, 77
citizenship 195–7
customs duties 166
derogations 382–6
disability discrimination,
reasonable
accommodation and
390
employment 79, 221–6,
378–91
free movement of workers
215–16, 221–6
freedom to provide
services and freedom of
establishment 237–9
freedom to receive services
247–8
fundamental rights 388
gender mainstreaming
367
harassment 389, 390
imports, taxation of
168–9
intellectual property 329,
337, 339
marital status 379
occupational pension
schemes 395–6
parental leave 381
pensions 390, 394–6
positive action and
promotion of equal
treatment 384–7, 389,
391

pregnancy and maternity
372, 379, 380–1, 384
prices 302–4
public authorities 389,
390
quantitative restrictions
and measures having
equivalent effect 176,
178, 181, 186, 188,
190
race or ethnic origin 79,
388–9
religion 80, 390
remedies 386, 387, 395
residence rights and rights
of exit and entry 205
retirement age 381–2
self-employment 396–7
sex discrimination 79–80,
363, 378–88, 396
sexual orientation 80, 388
social policy 366–7
social security 228, 391–5
state monopolies 169–71
taxation 167–71
transsexuals 379, 388
Treaty of Amsterdam 14
victimization 391
essential procedural
requirements 26, 49,
134–5, 351
establishment, freedom of
see freedom to provide
services and freedom of
establishment
Euratom 3–4, 11
Europe Agreements 6–7
European Central Bank (ECB)
49–50, 259–61
European Coal and Steel
Community (ECSC)
3–4, 11, 52
European Communities Act
(1972) 92–5
European Community 11,
13, 17
European Convention on
Human Rights (ECHR)
16, 18, 62, 68, 71–5

accession of EU 72–3
European Court of Justice
73–5
European Parliament 13
supremacy of EC law 89
values of the EU 72
European Council 12, 19,
32–3, 34, 37
European Court of Justice
(ECJ) 19, 43–8, 53, 63,
68 *see also* preliminary
rulings
Advocates-General 44, 45
composition and functions
44
European Convention on
Human Rights (ECHR)
73–5
failure to fulfill obligations,
actions for 121–2
full court, Grand Chamber
and Chamber 45
fundamental rights 70–1
interpretation 62, 89–90,
108–10
judges 44, 45
new legal order 90
precedent 46
role 21–2, 45–6
subsidiarity 85
supremacy of EC law
89–92
European Economic Area
(EEA) 7, 63, 211
European Economic
Community 3–4, 11,
13
European Free Trade
Association (EFTA) 6
European Monetary System
(EMS) 257–8
European Ombudsman 77
European Parliament 22–33
assent procedure 31
budget 24
co-decision procedure 22,
26–7, 29, 60
Commission 21, 24–5,
29–33, 40–3

European Parliament
(*continued*)
Committee of Permanent
Representatives
(COREPER) 26
common positions 30
composition 23
Conciliation Committee
30–1
consultation procedure 26
Council of European Union
21, 22, 25–6, 29–31, 34
elections 13, 24
European Convention on
Human Rights 13
European Council 32–3
legislative role 22, 25–31,
56
maladministration 31
Members of the European
Parliament 22, 23
national parliaments, role
of 32–3
ordinary decision-making
procedure 22, 28–9, 60
political groups 23–4
revision procedure 33
special decision-making
procedure 22–3, 60
European Social Fund 361,
363
European System of Central
Banks 259, 260
European Union
change of name 13
EC law and EU law 13
legal personality 18, 73
three pillars 17
exchange rate mechanism
257–60
exit and entry, rights of *see*
residence rights and
rights of exit and entry
exports *see* imports and
exports
expulsions 209, 210

failure to act, actions for
136–8

failure to fulfill obligations,
actions for
administration and judicial
stages of procedure
118–19
Commission 117, 121
damages 122
defences 119–20
direct actions under Article
226 117–20
directives, implementation
of 119
European Court of Justice
121–2
free movement of workers
220–1
internal disturbances,
failure to prevent 123
parallel proceedings with
national courts 120
sanctions against member
states 122
state aid, change or
abolition of 122–3
voluntary procedure 121
families
children 199, 225–6, 363
citizenship 199, 202–3
free movement of workers
220–1
freedom to provide
services and freedom of
establishment 239
residence rights and rights
of exit and entry 201,
202–4, 210–11
spouses 199, 202–4,
210–11
financial services,
harmonization of rules
of 242
fines and penalties 319,
321
flexibility principle 15
framework decisions 58
France, supremacy of EC law
in 96–7
free movement of capital *see*
capital movements

free movement of goods 9,
163, 169–73, 176, 186,
329–36, 341, 352
free movement of persons 9,
194 *see also* free
movement of workers
free movement of workers
56, 215–30
accession states, workers
from 218–19
definition of workers
216–17
economic activities 217,
218
educational training,
children's access to
225–6
equality of treatment
215–16, 221–6
families, rights of 220–1
job-seekers and
unemployed 216–18,
222, 229
nationality discrimination
215–16, 221–6
part-time workers
216–17
public health, public
policy and public
security 216
public service,
employment in the
219–20
residence, right of 201–2,
210, 216, 217
self-employed 217
social security 227–9
tax and social advantages
223–4, 228
trade union activities, sport
and housing, rights
relative to 225
freedom of establishment *see*
freedom to provide
services and freedom of
establishment
freedom, security and justice,
area of 14, 18, 19, 32,
156, 212

freedom to provide services
and freedom of
establishment 9,
231–45
branches, subsidiaries and
agencies 232–3
discrimination 237–9
family life, right to respect
for 239
financial services,
harmonization of rules
on 242
General Programme 232,
235
industrial property rights
246
insurance cases 241
mutual recognition and
harmonization of
professional
qualifications 235–7,
239–40, 242–4
professions 235–7,
239–40, 242–4
public policy, public
security and public
health 235, 245
rules and standards of
member states, respect
for 240–1
self-employed 231, 236–7,
242
Services Directive 245–6
single market 242–4
taxation 233
freedom to receive services
246–51
discrimination 247–8
medical treatment
248–9
vocational training and
education 247, 249–51
fundamental rights 15, 68,
70–7, 91 see also
Charter of Fundamental
Rights of the EU;
European Convention
on Human Rights
equal treatment 388

European Court of Justice
70–1

General Agreement on Tariffs
and Trade (GATT) 55
General Court, renaming of
Court of First Instance
as 43
general principles of law
68–87, 107
Germany, supremacy of EC
law in 97

harmonization or
approximation of laws
5, 8, 242, 337, 361–2
harassment 389, 390
health, protection of 188–91
see also public health,
public policy and public
security
heard, right to be 82–3, 321
High Representative 19, 34
horizontal agreements 271
housing rights 225
human rights 15 see also
Charter of Fundamental
Rights of the EU;
European Convention
on Human Rights
(ECHR); fundamental
rights

illegality, plea of 138–9
immigration policy 14
imports and exports
abuse of a dominant
position 307
quantitative restrictions
174–85, 188–9
taxation, discriminatory
168–9
improper use of powers,
states making 123
indirect effect and indirect
applicability 92, 93,
107–11
indirect review under Article
241 138–9

institutions 21–51 see also
particular institutions
(for example,
Commission)
acts 55–9
changes 15, 21
failure to act, actions for
136–8
inter-institutional
agreement 24
liability 141–7
insurance cases 241
intellectual property
328–44
abuse of a dominant
position 337, 339
anti-competitive
agreements 337
biotechnological
inventions 342
common origin principle
335–6
competition law 329, 336,
337–41
computer programs,
copyright and 342
copyright 328, 330,
333–4, 339–40, 342–3
designs 334–5, 343
discrimination 329, 337,
339
exemptions 340
exhaustion of rights 331,
334–5
free movement of goods
329–36, 341
freedom to provide
services and freedom of
establishment 246
harmonization 329, 341–3
improper exploitation of
rights 337
licences 337–8, 340
luxury goods, trade marks
and 333
parallel imports 331–3
patents 328, 329, 331–3,
337–8, 339–42
plant breeders' rights 335

411

intellectual property
(*continued*)
quantitative restrictions
and measures having
equivalent effect 192
registered designs 334–5
specific subject-matter of
property 338–9
technology transfer 340
third countries, goods
from 336
trade marks 328, 329,
331–3, 335–9, 342
intergovernmental
conferences 10
internal market 9, 18, 78,
163, 192 *see also* Single
European Act
international agreements 54,
64, 107
Italy, supremacy of EC law in
98

job evaluation schemes
377–8
job-seekers 198–9, 205–6,
216–18, 222, 229, 392
joint ventures 308
judges
European Court of Justice
44, 45
police and judicial co-
operation in security
matters 11, 13, 53, 54,
127, 156–7

languages 46
lawyers 236, 240
legal certainty 80–2
legal personality of EU 18,
73
legislation *see also*
directives
Better Lawmaking 85
Commission 39–43, 55–6,
68
Council of the European
Union 33, 68
delegated acts 60

European Parliament 22,
25–31, 56
Implementation 60
legislative and non-
legislative acts 59–60
regulations 56
subsidiarity 84–5
Treaty of Lisbon 59–60
legitimate expectations
81–2, 142–3, 145
leniency programmes in
competition cases
324–5
life, protection of 188–91
Luxembourg Accords 1996
36–7
Maastricht Treaty *see* Treaty
on European Union
Maladministration 31
marital status, discrimination
and 379
maternity and pregnancy
372, 379, 380–1,
384
measures having equivalent
effect *see* quantitative
restrictions and
measures having
equivalent effect,
mergers and concentrations
abuse of a dominant
position 307–15
collective dominance
310–13
co-operative joint ventures
308
legitimate interests,
protection of 314
one-stop shopping
313–15
regulations 307–15
minor agreements 282–3
misuse of powers 135–6
monism 89, 95
monopolies 169–71, 268,
347–8
mutual recognition 8, 176,
180, 235–7, 239–40,
242–4

national security 192–3, 212
national treasures 191
natural justice 82–3, 135
negative clearance 274, 318
non-contractual liability of
institutions 68, 141–6
causation 145
concurrent liability 146
contributory negligence
145
damage 145–5
damages 144, 145
discretion, exercise of 141,
143–5
failures of administration
and negligent acts 142
lawful acts, liability arising
from 144–5
legitimate expectations
142–3, 145
national courts, role of the
146
Schöppenstedt formula
142–3
standing and limitation
141
sufficiently serious breach
142–3
superior rules of law
142–3

Official Journal 46
oligopolies 268, 294–5
opinions 58–9

parallel imports 331–3
parallel proceedings 120
parental leave 381
part-time employment
216–17
patents 328, 329, 331–3,
337–8, 339–42
pay *see* equal pay
pensions 370–3, 375–7,
390, 393–6
plant breeders' rights 335
plants, protection of 188–91
Poland, supremacy of EC law
in 98–9

police and judicial
co-operation in security
matters 11, 13, 53, 54,
127, 156–7
political groups in European
Parliament 23–4
political rights 24, 199–200
positive action 384–7, 389,
391
precautionary principle 191
pregnancy and maternity
372, 379, 380–1, 384
preliminary rulings 15, 45–6,
58, 89–90, 149–59
acte clair and *acte éclairé*
153–5
Court of First Instance 157
courts or tribunals,
definition of 150
discretion to refer, court's
with 151
freedom, security and
justice, area of 156
genuine issues of EC law
152
guidance 152–3
interpretation and validity
of EC law 149–52,
155–7
mandatory, where
reference is 153–5
police and judicial
co-operation in criminal
matters 156–7
reform 157
simplified procedure 157
when reference is
necessary 151–3
President of European
Council 19
Prices 268, 278–81,
302–4
privatization 345, 348
privilege 321
procedural rights 82–4
due process 83
hearing, right to a 82–3
natural justice 82–3
reasons, duty to give 83

professions
conduct, rules on
professional 235,
239–40
confidentiality 322–3
freedom to provide
services and freedom of
establishment 235–7,
239–40, 242–4
lawyers 236, 240
mutual recognition of
qualifications 235–7,
239–40, 242–4
qualifications 8, 235–7,
239–40, 242–4
regulated professions,
definition of 243
proportionality 69, 77–9
access to documents 135
Charter of Fundamental
Rights of the EU 76
commercial activity,
freedom of 78–9
competence 63–4
internal market 78
misuse of powers 136
quantitative restrictions
and measures having
equivalent effect 177,
180–1, 186, 190–2
residence rights and rights
of exit and entry 201,
206
Treaty of Lisbon 85
public authorities
annulment actions 276–7
competition, state
regulation and 344–52
directives 105–6
equal treatment 389, 390
free movement of workers
219–20
public health, public policy
and public security
free movement of workers
216
freedom to provide
services and freedom of
establishment 235, 245

quantitative restrictions
and measures having
equivalent effect 185–8
residence rights and rights
of exit and entry 201,
205, 206–12
public service employment
219–20

qualifications 8, 235–7,
242–4
qualified majority voting 9,
19, 34–5, 54
qualitative restrictions 285
quantitative restrictions and
measures having
equivalent effect 163,
172–93
artistic, historical or
archaeological value,
protection of national
treasures of 191
consumers, justification in
interests of 179–80
Dassonville formula 174–6
Derogations 186–93
distinctly and indistinctly
applicable measures
174, 176, 177, 183–5
dual burden and equal
burden rules 177–8,
182–3
exports 184–5
free movement of goods
172–3, 176, 186
health, life of humans,
animals and plants,
protection of 188–91
imports 174–85, 188–9
industrial and commercial
property, protection of
192
mandatory requirements
176–8, 180
member states, measures
taken by 173
mutual recognition,
principle of 176, 180
national security 192–3

quantitative restrictions
and measures having
equivalent effect
(*continued*)
nationality discrimination
176, 178, 181, 186,
188, 190
necessity, establishment of
179
non-tariff barriers 172
precautionary principle in
respect to health 191
product requirements
182–4
proportionality 177,
180–1, 186, 190–2
public policy, morality and
security 185–8
reason, rule of 177
selling arrangements
181–4
tariff barriers 172

race discrimination 79,
388–9
reason, rule of 177, 284,
306
reasons, duty to give 83
recommendations 58–9
refusal to supply 303–5
registered designs 334–5
regulations 56
religion 80, 390
residence rights and rights
of exit and entry
201–13
border controls 212–14
categories 200–2
citizenship 200–13
cohabitees and registered
partners 204
common immigration
policy 213
convictions 207–9
divorce and separation,
effect of 203–4
EEA Agreement 211
equal treatment 205
expulsion 209, 210

families 201, 202–4,
210–11
free movement of workers
216, 217
freedom, security and
justice, area of 212
infectious or contagious
diseases 210
information, supply of 209
job-seekers 205–6
marriages of convenience
203
national security 212
notification of decisions
209
permanent residence
rights 201–5
personal conduct 207
procedural safeguards 209
proportionality 201, 206
public policy, public
security or public health
201, 205, 206–12
resources 201
Schengen Agreement 211
self-employed 201–2
spouses 202–4, 210–11
students 201
third country nationals
210–11, 213
workers 201–2, 210, 216,
217
retirement ages 381–2
retroactivity 80–1
rule of reason 177, 284,
306

Schengen Agreement 14,
211
self-employment 201–2,
217, 231, 236–7, 242,
396–7
selling arrangements 181–4
services 246–51 *see* freedom
to provide services and
freedom of
establishment,
sex discrimination 79–80,
363, 378–88, 396

sexual orientation
discrimination 80, 388
sick pay 371
single currency 258–62
Single European Act 8–9,
57
barriers to trade 8–9
co-operation procedure
54
free movement of goods,
persons and services 9,
242–4
qualified majority voting
(QMV) 9
social policy 361
social advantages 223–4,
228
Social Chapter (Agreement
on Social Policy)
directives 57
employment protection
10
opting out 10, 12, 57
social policy 361, 364–5
social policy 361–8
Charter of Fundamental
Rights of the EU 361,
365–6
Discrimination 366–7
education, vocational
training and youth 363
employment 362–4
equal pay 363, 367
European Social Charter
1961 362
European Social Fund 361,
363
gender mainstreaming
367
harmonization 361–2
legal basis 361–2, 365
Single European Act 361
Social Action Programme
364
Social Chapter (Agreement
on Social Policy) 10, 12,
57, 361, 364–5
Social Charter 364
soft laws 367

social policy (*continued*)
  Supplementary Action
    Programme 364
  Treaty on European Union
    12
social security 227–9
  employed persons 392
  equal treatment and
    discrimination 228,
    391–5
  free movement of workers
    227–9
  job-seekers 392
  pensions 393–4
soft laws 58–9, 77, 367
sources of EU law 52–69
sovereignty 4–6 *see also*
    supremacy of EC law
sport 225
spouses 199, 202–4,
    210–11
Stability Pact 261–2
state aids 122–3, 352–8
  Commission 356
  compatible with common
    market, aid which is
    352–4
  compensation 353–4
  compliance 354–5
  failure to fulfill obligations,
    actions for 122–3
  free movement of goods
    352
  individual rights 357–8
  modernization 356–7
  notification 354
  procedure 354–5
  regional aids 356–7
  reviews 354
state liability in damages for
    breach of EC law 94–5,
    111–15
  directives, implementation
    of 104–15
  discretion, exercise of
    113–14
  national courts, liability
    and approach of
    114–15

sufficiently serious breach
    95, 112–15
supremacy of EC law 92
state monopolies 169–71
state regulation and
    competition law 345–58
  see also state aid
  categories of undertakings
    345–6
  Commission 350–1
  direct effect 347
  directives 351–2
  entrusted undertakings
    and fiscal monopolies,
    exceptions for 347–8
  essential facilities 351
  national courts 349
  privatization 345, 348
  public undertakings
    345–52
  revenue-producing
    monopolies 348
  special or exclusive rights
    345, 347, 352
students, residence rights of
    201
study of EU law 52–3
subsidiarity 12, 32, 63–4,
    84–5
Sunday trading 180–1
supranationalism 4–5
supremacy of EC law 4–5,
    18–19, 88–100
  Belgium 95–6
  conflicting national law 91
  constitutions of member
    states 89
  direct effect 88, 89, 93–4
  European Communities
    Act 1972 92–5
  European Convention on
    Human Rights 89
  European Court of Justice,
    role of 89–92
  France 96–7
  Germany 97
  incorporation of treaties
    89
  indirect applicability 93

indirect effect 92, 93
Italy 98
member states, EC law in
    other 95–8
monist or dualist approach
    89, 95
national law, setting aside
    91–2
Poland 98–9
state liability 92
three pillars 92
Treaty of Lisbon 88

taxation
  capital movements 256
  discriminatory taxation
    167–71
  free movement of workers
    223–4, 228
  freedom to provide
    services and freedom of
    establishment 233
  imports 168–9
  internal discriminatory tax
    167–71
  state monopolies 169–71
terrorism 127
TEU *see* Treaty on European
    Union
third states
  common foreign and
    security policy 11
  intellectual property
    336
  residence rights and rights
    of exit and entry
    210–11, 213
three pillars 11–13, 14,
    16–17, 52–3, 58, 92
tortious liability *see*
    non–contractual liability
    of institutions
trade unions 225
trade marks 328, 329,
    331–3, 335–9, 342
transparency principle 15,
    86
transport 276
transsexuals 379, 388

treaties 53–5 *see also*
  individual treaties (for
  example, Treaty of
  Lisbon)
  annulment actions 135
  consolidation 16
  direct applicability and
  direct effect 103
  direct effect 102, 106
  EC Treaty 53–4
  incorporation 89
  international treaties 89
  list of treaties 54
  protocols 10
  ratification 52
  reform 132–3
  sources of EU law 52
  subsidiary treaties 55
  supremacy of EC law 89
  Treaty on the Functioning
  of the Union (TFU) 17,
  19, 52, 53, 54, 73
Treaty of Amsterdam 10, 11,
  26, 54
  Discrimination 14
  effects of 113–14, 193
  environment 15
  subsidiarity 84
Treaty of Lisbon
  aims of the EU 18
  budget 24
  Charter of Fundamental
  Rights of the EU 16, 17,
  77

competence, distribution
  of 18, 63–4
conferral, principle of
  63–4
consultation and co-
  operation provisions 26
decision-making procedure
  22–3
legal personality 18
legislative and non-
  legislative acts 59–60
national parliaments, role
  of 32–3
proportionality 85
supremacy of EC law 88
transparency 86
Treaty on European Union
  18–19, 54
Treaty on the Functioning
  of the Union (TFU)
  17–19, 53, 54
Treaty of Nice 15–16, 35–6,
  38, 53, 54
Treaty on European Union
  9–14, 17, 19
capital movements 254
Charter of Fundamental
  Rights of the EU 17, 73
Citizenship 12–13
co-decision procedure 12,
  22, 26
economic and monetary
  union 9–10, 12, 54
human rights 15

international treaty, as 89
ratification 13–14
social policy 12
subsidiarity 12
three-pillar structure
  11–12, 52–3, 54, 58, 92
titles and terminology 13
Treaty of Lisbon 18–19, 54
trialogues 29–30
Turkey 8
tying 305–6

unanimity 35, 36–7, 49
unemployed 216–18, 222,
  229

values of the EU 72
vertical agreements 271,
  291
victimization 79–80
vocational training 225–6,
  247, 249–51, 363
voting
  citizenship 199–200
  Council of the European
  Union 34–7
  qualified majority voting
  9, 19, 34–5, 54

workers *see* employment;
  free movement of
  workers
World Trade Organization
  (WTO) 55

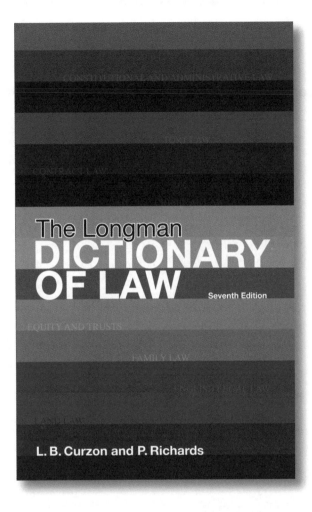